Cisco Exam Objectives
Exam 640-506: Support

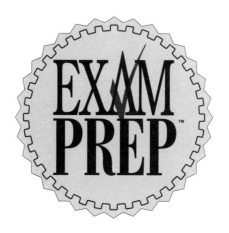

CCNP™ Support

Sean Odom
Gina Galbraith

CCNP™ Support Exam Prep

Limits of Liability and Disclaimer of Warranty

The author and publisher of this book have used their best efforts in preparing the book and the programs contained in it. These efforts include the development, research, and testing of the theories and programs to determine their effectiveness. The author and publisher make no warranty of any kind, expressed or implied, with regard to these programs or the documentation contained in this book.

The author and publisher shall not be liable in the event of incidental or consequential damages in connection with, or arising out of, the furnishing, performance, or use of the programs, associated instructions, and/or claims of productivity gains.

Trademarks

Trademarked names appear throughout this book. Rather than list the names and entities that own the trademarks or insert a trademark symbol with each mention of the trademarked name, the publisher states that it is using the names for editorial purposes only and to the benefit of the trademark owner, with no intention of infringing upon that trademark.

The Coriolis Group, LLC
14455 N. Hayden Road, Suite 220
Scottsdale, Arizona 85260

(480)483-0192
FAX (480)483-0193
www.coriolis.com

Library of Congress Cataloging-in-Publication Data
Odom, Sean
    CCNP support / by Sean Odom and Gina Galbraith.
        p.   cm. -- (Exam prep)
    Includes index.
    ISBN 1-57610-779-5
    1. Electronic data processing personnel--Certification.   2. Computer networks--Examinations--Study guides.   3. Telecommunication--Switching systems--Examinations--Study guides.   I. Galbraith, Gina.   II. Title.
III. Series.
QA76.3 .O34   2000
004.6--dc21
                                                        00-047542
                                                        CIP

President and CEO
Keith Weiskamp

Publisher
Steve Sayre

Acquisitions Editor
Shari Jo Hehr

Product Marketing Manager
Brett Woolley

Project Editor
Dan Young

Technical Reviewer
Paul Rodriguez

Production Coordinator
Todd Halvorsen

Cover Designer
Jesse Dunn

Layout Designer
April Nielsen

CD-ROM Developer
Chris Nusbaum

Printed in the United States of America
10 9 8 7 6 5 4 3 2 1

The Coriolis Group, LLC • 14455 North Hayden Road, Suite 220 • Scottsdale, Arizona 85260

ExamCram.com Connects You to the Ultimate Study Center!

Our goal has always been to provide you with the best study tools on the planet to help you achieve your certification in record time. Time is so valuable these days that none of us can afford to waste a second of it, especially when it comes to exam preparation.

Over the past few years, we've created an extensive line of *Exam Cram* and *Exam Prep* study guides, practice exams, and interactive training. To help you study even better, we have now created an e-learning and certification destination called **ExamCram.com**. (You can access the site at **www.examcram.com**.) Now, with every study product you purchase from us, you'll be connected to a large community of people like yourself who are actively studying for their certifications, developing their careers, seeking advice, and sharing their insights and stories.

I believe that the future is all about collaborative learning. Our **ExamCram.com** destination is our approach to creating a highly interactive, easily accessible collaborative environment, where you can take practice exams and discuss your experiences with others, sign up for features like "Questions of the Day," plan your certifications using our interactive planners, create your own personal study pages, and keep up with all of the latest study tips and techniques.

I hope that whatever study products you purchase from us—*Exam Cram* or *Exam Prep* study guides, *Personal Trainers*, *Personal Test Centers*, or one of our interactive Web courses—will make your studying fun and productive. Our commitment is to build the kind of learning tools that will allow you to study the way you want to, whenever you want to.

Help us continue to provide the very best certification study materials possible. Write us or email us at **learn@examcram.com** and let us know how our study products have helped you study. Tell us about new features that you'd like us to add. Send us a story about how we've helped you. We're listening!

Visit ExamCram.com now to enhance your study program.

Good luck with your certification exam and your career. Thank you for allowing us to help you achieve your goals.

Keith Weiskamp
President and CEO

Look for these other products from The Coriolis Group:

CCNP Switching Exam Prep
By Sean Odom and Douglas Hammond

CCNP Routing Exam Prep
By Robert Larson, Corwin S. Low, Paulden Rodriguez

CCNP Remote Access Exam Prep
By Richard A. Deal and Barry Meinster

This book is dedicated to my father, Ronald F. Odom.
There is no man I look up to more in this world.
—Sean Odom

૨‍

This book is dedicated to my mother, Susan D. Helbing.
—Gina Galbraith

૨‍

About the Authors

Sean Odom has been in the computer networking field for approximately 12 years and is currently a senior instructor teaching Cisco CCNA and CCNP courses for Globalnet (**www.globalnettraining.com**). In addition, Sean has been a private consultant for many companies such as CH2M Hill, Advanced Computer Systems, American Licorice Company, NCR, Wells Fargo Bank, The Money Store, and Intel. Along with working as a Cisco instructor and consultant, Sean has authored and co-authored many Cisco related white papers, labs, and books. You can email Sean at **sodom@rcsis.com** or you can visit his Web site at **www. thequestforcertification.com**.

Gina Galbraith is currently a CCNA network analyst for UC Davis Medical Center in Sacramento, which supports over 6,000 LAN/WAN users. Gina has been employed by the medical center for nine years, and has helped design and support the infrastructure at UC Davis Medical Center. Gina is currently on the board of the Sacramento Placer County Cisco Users Group (SPCCUG). Gina has also contributed to Sean Odom's *Switching Exam Prep* book released in 2000.

Acknowledgments

Writing a book of this size takes many individuals and I always feel bad if I miss someone. First I would like to thank Gina Galbraith for being so reliable and dependable. Next, fellow instructor Jon Turner, Hanson Nottingham, and Albert Ip for all the time they worked with me behind the scenes doing research, technical editing, writing and lab construction. Rayomond Doucette for helping me with galley reviews. Chas Coffman for always pushing me to do more, Dan Young for putting up with such a guy like me, Bill McManus for editing and finding all my typos, the technical editor Paul Rodriguez for all his great suggestions for the book, Shari Jo Hehr my acquisitions editor, Todd Halvorsen for doing the layout, and Jesse Dunn for designing the cover.

I would also like to thank my father for believing in a son that in the beginning must have looked to him as the lost soul of the litter. I always hope to make my dad the proudest of all dads. To my mom who couldn't be a better and more under-standing person. Through all the trials and tribulation, you not only raised one child right, you did it four more times! I also want to thank the rest of my family for all the hours they lived without me during the writing process. It takes day and night for many months to write just even one book, then after that, do copy edits, and the galley reviews.

—*Sean Odom*

Thanks to all my friends and family for their understanding and support while writing this book. Thanks to Akwai Hinman, Ginger King, Dad, Jesse, David, Ashley, Susan, and my step-dad Gene. To my co-workers and friends Sheila Green and Sylvia Baldwin for always being there. Most of all I would like to say to my mother, "This one's for you" for all your sacrifices over the years to make sure I had the best of everything and most of all, teaching me to be a good person. You are the best example! I love you Mom. Thanks to Carlos Tillmanshofer, Esther Almazan, Gary Jellis, Lee Smith, and Becky Stratman who gave me an opportunity early on in my career. Thanks to all my co-workers for putting up with me in the mornings after a long night. A thank you to the special person in my life who really helped me through all the long hours of sitting in front of a computer (you know who you are).

Thank you Adele Galus and Carmen McGrath for your fine technical writing. At The Coriolis Group, thank you Deb Doorley for helping me refine my writing

skills, (it was a tough job I'm sure) and to Dan Young for your humor and under-standing that I am a "die-hard" Raider fan. Thanks to Steve Clevenger who has always provided me with knowledge and guidance. Dan Keister for sharing his expertise with me. Ray Santana for his precise technical skills and Rich Reiser. Last but surely not least, Sean Odom for giving me, "the chance of a lifetime."
—*Gina Galbraith*

Contents at a Glance

Table of Contents

Chapter 6

Exam Insights

Welcome to *Support Exam Prep*! This book aims to help you get ready to take—and pass—Cisco certification Exam 640-506, titled "Support." This Exam Insights section discusses exam preparation resources, the testing situation, Cisco's certification programs in general, and how this book can help you prepare for Cisco's certification exams.

Exam Prep books help you understand and appreciate the subjects and materials you need to pass Cisco certification exams. Our aim is to make sure all key topics are clearly explained and to bring together as much information as possible about Cisco certification exams.

Nevertheless, to completely prepare yourself for any Cisco test, we recommend that you begin by taking the Self-Assessment included in this book immediately following this Exam Insights section. This tool will help you evaluate your knowledge base against the requirements for a CCNP under both ideal and real circumstances.

Based on what you learn from that exercise, you might decide to begin your studies with some classroom training or some background reading. You might decide to read The Coriolis Group's *Exam Prep* book that you have in hand first, or you might decide to start with another study approach. You may also want to refer to one of a number of study guides available from Cisco or third-party vendors.

We also strongly recommend that you install, configure, and fool around with the network equipment that you'll be tested on, because nothing beats hands-on experience and familiarity when it comes to understanding the questions you're likely to encounter on a certification test. Book learning is essential, but hands-on experience is the best teacher of all!

How to Prepare for an Exam

Preparing for any Cisco career certification test (including CCNP) requires that you obtain and study materials designed to provide comprehensive information about Cisco troubleshooting and the specific exam for which you are preparing. The following list of materials will help you study and prepare:

➤ *Instructor-led training*—There's no substitute for expert instruction and hands-on practice under professional supervision. Cisco Training Partners, such as GeoTrain Corporation, offer instructor-led training courses for all of the Cisco career certification requirements. These companies aim to help prepare net work administrators to run Cisco Troubleshooting skills to isolate and fix network problems and pass the Cisco tests. Although such training runs upwards of $350 per day in class, most of the individuals lucky enough to partake find them to be quite worthwhile.

➤ *Cisco Connection Online*—This is the name of Cisco's Web site (**www.cisco.com**), the most current and up-to-date source of Cisco information.

➤ *The CCPrep Web site*—This is the most well-known Cisco certification Web site in the world. You can find it at **www.ccprep.com** (formerly known as **www.CCIEprep.com**). Here, you can find exam preparation materials, practice tests, self-assessment exams, and numerous certification questions and scenarios. In addition, professional staff members are available to answer questions that you can post on the answer board.

➤ *Cisco training kits*—These are available only if you attend a Cisco class at a certified training facility or if a Cisco Training Partner in good standing gives you one.

➤ *Study guides*—Several publishers—including Certification Insider Press—offer study guides. The Certification Insider Press series includes:

  ➤ *The Exam Cram series*—These books give you information about the material you need to know to pass the tests.

  ➤ *The Exam Prep series*—These books provide a greater level of detail than the *Exam Cram* books and are designed to teach you everything you need to know from an exam perspective.

  Together, the two series make a perfect pair.

➤ *Multimedia*—These Coriolis Group materials are designed to support learners of all types—whether you learn best by listening, reading, or doing:

  ➤ *The Practice Tests Exam Cram series*—Provides the most valuable test preparation material: practice exams. Each exam is followed by a complete set of answers, as well as explanations of why the right answers are right and the wrong answers are wrong. Each book comes with a CD-ROM that contains one or more interactive practice exams.

  ➤ *The Exam Cram Flash Card series*—Offers practice questions on handy cards you can use anywhere. The question and its possible answers appear on the front of the card, and the answer, explanation, and a valuable reference appear on the back of the card. The set also includes a CD with an electronic practice exam to give you the feel of the actual test—and more practice!

➤ *The Exam Cram Audio Review series*—Offers a concise review of key topics covered on the exam, as well as practice questions.

By far, this set of required and recommended materials represents an unparalleled collection of sources and resources for preparing for the CCNP exam. We anticipate that you'll find that this book belongs in this company. In the next section, we explain how this book works and give you some good reasons why this book counts as a member of the required and recommended materials list.

Taking a Certification Exam

Alas, testing is not free. Each computer-based exam costs between $100 and $200, and the CCIE laboratory exam costs $1,000. If you do not pass, you must pay the testing fee each time you retake the test. In the United States and Canada, computerized tests are administered by Sylvan Prometric. Sylvan Prometric can be reached at (800) 755-3926 or (800) 204-EXAM, any time from 7:00 A.M. to 6:00 P.M., Central Time, Monday through Friday. You can also try (612) 896-7000 or (612) 820-5707. CCIE laboratory exams are administered by Cisco Systems and can be scheduled by calling the CCIE lab exam administrator for the appropriate location.

To schedule a computer-based exam, call at least one day in advance. To cancel or reschedule an exam, you must call at least 24 hours before the scheduled test time (or you may be charged regardless). When calling Sylvan Prometric, have the following information ready for the telesales staffer who handles your call:

➤ Your name, organization, and mailing address.

➤ Your Cisco Test ID. (For most U.S. citizens, this is your Social Security number. Citizens of other nations can use their taxpayer IDs or make other arrangements with the order taker.)

➤ The name and number of the exam you wish to take. For this book, the exam name is "Support" and the exam number is 640-506.

➤ A method of payment. The most convenient approach is to supply a valid credit card number with sufficient available credit. Otherwise, Sylvan Prometric must receive check, money order, or purchase order payment before you can schedule a test. (If you're not paying by credit card, ask your order taker for more details.)

When you show up to take a test, try to arrive at least 15 minutes before the scheduled time slot.

The Exam Situation

When you arrive at the testing center where you scheduled your exam, you'll need to sign in with an exam coordinator. He or she will ask you to show two forms of identification, one of which must be a photo ID. After you've signed in and your time slot arrives, you'll asked to deposit any books, bags, or other items you brought with you. Then, you'll be escorted into a closed room.

All exams are completely closed book. In fact, you will not be permitted to take anything with you into the testing area. However, you are furnished with a blank sheet of paper and a pen. We suggest that you immediately write down on that sheet of paper all the information you've memorized for the test. Although the amount of time you have to actually take the exam is limited, the time period does not start until you're ready, so you can spend as much time as necessary writing notes on the provided paper. If you think you will need more paper than what is provided, ask the test center administrator before entering the exam room. You must return all pages prior to exiting the testing center.

You will have some time to compose yourself, to record this information, and even to take a sample orientation exam before you begin the real thing. We suggest you take the orientation test before taking your first exam, but because they're all more or less identical in layout, behavior, and controls, you probably won't need to do this more than once.

Typically, the room will be furnished with anywhere from one to half a dozen computers, and each workstation will be separated from the others by dividers designed to keep you from seeing what's happening on someone else's computer. Most test rooms feature a wall with a large picture window. This permits the exam coordinator to monitor the room, to prevent exam-takers from talking to one another, and to observe anything out of the ordinary that might go on. The exam coordinator will have preloaded the appropriate Cisco certification exam—for this book, that's Exam 640-506—and you'll be permitted to start as soon as you're seated in front of the computer.

All Cisco certification exams allow a certain maximum amount of time in which to complete your work (this time is indicated on the exam by an on-screen counter/clock, so you can check the time remaining whenever you like). All Cisco certification exams are computer generated and most use a multiple-choice format. Although this may sound quite simple, the questions are constructed not only to check your mastery of basic facts and figures, but they also require you to evaluate one or more sets of circumstances or requirements. Often, you'll be asked to give more than one answer to a question. Likewise, you might be asked to select the best or most effective solution to a problem from a range of choices, all of which technically are correct. Taking the exam is quite an adventure, and it involves real thinking. This book shows you what to expect and how to deal with the potential problems, puzzles, and predicaments.

When you complete a Cisco certification exam, the software will tell you whether you've passed or failed. All tests are scored on a basis of 100 percent, and results are broken into several topic areas. Even if you fail, we suggest you ask for—and keep—the detailed report that the test administrator should print for you. You can use this report to help you prepare for another go-round, if needed. Once you see your score, you have the option of printing additional copies of the score report. It's a good idea to print it twice.

If you need to retake an exam, you'll have to call Sylvan Prometric, schedule a new test date, and pay another testing fee.

Note: The first time you fail a test, you can retake the test the next day. However, if you fail a second time, you must wait 14 days before retaking that test. The 14-day waiting period remains in effect for all retakes after the second failure.

In the next section, you'll learn more about how Cisco test questions look and how they must be answered.

Exam Layout and Design

Whichever type of test you take, questions generally belong to one of four basic types:

➤ Multiple-choice with a single answer

➤ Multiple-choice with one or more answers

➤ Multipart with a single answer

➤ Multipart with one or more answers

A few of the questions may be in a different format, such as fill in the blank, ordering, matching, or command output. We've included a few such questions in the sample test in Chapter 16 to familiarize you with these question types as well.

Always take the time to read a question at least twice before selecting an answer, and always look for an Exhibit button as you examine each question. Exhibits include graphics information related to a question. An exhibit is usually a screen capture of program output or GUI information that you must examine to analyze the question's contents and formulate an answer. The Exhibit button brings up graphics and charts used to help explain a question, provide additional data, or illustrate page layout or program behavior.

Not every question has only one answer; many questions require multiple answers. Therefore, it's important to read each question carefully, to determine how many answers are necessary or possible, and to look for additional hints or instructions when selecting answers. Such instructions often occur in brackets immediately following the question itself (as they do for all multiple-choice questions in which one or more answers are possible).

The following multiple-choice question requires you to select a single correct answer. Following the question is a brief summary of each potential answer and why it is either right or wrong.

Question 1

Which command determines a step-by-step routing path to a destination?

○ a. **ping**

○ b. **trace**

○ c. **telnet**

○ d. **show**

○ e. **debug**

Answer b is correct. The **trace** commands are used to "trace" a route; in other words, they are used to report a path to its destination by using ICMP. Answer a is incorrect because **ping** tests for connectivity. Answer c is incorrect because **telnet** is used in connecting to a device and acting as a dumb terminal. Answer d is incorrect because the **show** commands provide a snapshot. Answer e is incorrect because **debug** commands are used for aiding in troubleshooting an interface.

This sample question format corresponds closely to the Cisco certification exam format—the only difference on the exam is that questions are not followed by answer keys. To select an answer, you would position the cursor over the radio button next to the answer. Then, click the mouse button to select the answer.

Let's examine a question where one or more answers are possible. This type of question provides checkboxes rather than radio buttons for marking all appropriate selections.

Question 2

A network management system (NMS) uses what two protocols to communicate with devices? [Choose the two best answers]

❑ a. Simple Network Management Protocol (SNMP)

❑ b. Routing Information Protocol (RIP)

❑ c. Cisco Discovery Protocol (CDP)

❑ d. Open Shortest Path First (OSPF)

Answers a and c are correct. SNMP and CDP are used by an NMS to communicate with devices. Answers b, d, and e are incorrect because they are protocols; they are mainly used for routing. For this particular question, two answers are required. As far as the authors can tell (and Cisco won't comment), such questions are scored as wrong unless all the required selections are chosen. In other words, a partially correct answer does not result in partial credit when the test is scored. For Question 2, you have to check the boxes next to items a and c to obtain credit for a correct answer. Notice that picking the right answers also means knowing why the other answers are wrong!

Question-Handling Strategies

Based on exams we have taken, some interesting trends have become apparent. For those questions that take only a single answer, usually two or three of the answers will be obviously incorrect, and two of the answers will be plausible—of course, only one can be correct. Unless the answer leaps out at you (if it does, reread the question to look for a trick; sometimes those are the ones you're most likely to get wrong), begin the process of answering by eliminating those answers that are most obviously wrong.

Almost always, at least one answer out of the possible choices for a question can be eliminated immediately because it matches one of these conditions:

➤ The answer does not apply to the situation.

➤ The answer describes a nonexistent issue, an invalid option, or an imaginary state.

After you eliminate all answers that are obviously wrong, you can apply your retained knowledge to eliminate further answers. Look for items that sound correct but refer to actions, commands, or features that are not present or not available in the situation that the question describes.

If you're still faced with a blind guess among two or more potentially correct answers, reread the question. Try to picture how each of the possible remaining answers would alter the situation. Be especially sensitive to terminology; sometimes the choice of words ("remove" instead of "disable") can make the difference between a right answer and a wrong one.

Only when you've exhausted your ability to eliminate answers, but remain unclear about which of the remaining possibilities is correct, should you guess at an answer. An unanswered question offers you no points, but guessing gives you at least some chance of getting a question right; just don't be too hasty when making a blind guess.

Numerous questions assume that the default behavior of a particular utility is in effect. If you know the defaults and understand what they mean, this knowledge will help you cut through many Gordian knots.

Mastering the Inner Game

In the final analysis, knowledge breeds confidence, and confidence breeds success. If you study the materials in this book carefully and review all the practice questions at the end of each chapter, you should become aware of those areas where additional learning and study are required.

After you've worked your way through the book, take the practice exam in the back of the book and test yourself with some of the varying exam formats on the CD-ROM. This will provide a reality check and help you identify areas to study further. Make sure you follow up and review materials related to the questions you miss on the practice exams before scheduling a real exam. Only when you've covered that ground and feel comfortable with the whole scope of the practice exams should you set an exam appointment. Only if you score 75 percent or better should you proceed to the real thing (otherwise, obtain some additional practice tests so you can keep trying until you hit this magic number).

Armed with the information in this book and with the determination to augment your knowledge, you should be able to pass the certification exam. However, you need to work at it, or you'll spend the exam fee more than once before you finally pass. If you prepare seriously, you should do well. Good luck!

The next section covers the exam requirements for the various Cisco certifications.

The Cisco Career Certification Program

The Cisco Career Certification program is relatively new on the internetworking scene. The best place to keep tabs on it is the Cisco Training Web site, at **www.cisco.com/certifications/**. Before Cisco developed this program, Cisco Certified Internetwork Expert (CCIE) certification was the only available Cisco certification. Although CCIE certification is still the most coveted and prestigious certification that Cisco offers (possibly the most prestigious in the internetworking industry), lower-level certifications are now available as stepping stones on the road to the CCIE. The Cisco Career Certification program includes several certifications in addition to the CCIE, each with its own acronym (see Table 1). If you're a fan of alphabet soup after your name, you'll like this program:

Note: *Within the certification program, there are specific specializations. For the purposes of this book, we will focus only on the Routing and Switching track. Visit **www.cisco. com/warp/public/10/wwtraining/certprog/index.html** for information on the other specializations.*

➤ *Cisco Certified Design Associate (CCDA)*—The CCDA is a basic certification aimed at designers of high-level internetworks. The CCDA consists of a single exam (640-441) that covers information from the Designing Cisco Networks (DCN) course. You must obtain CCDA and CCNA certifications before you can move up to the CCDP certification.

➤ *Cisco Certified Network Associate (CCNA)*—The CCNA is the first career certification. It consists of a single exam (640-507) that covers information from the basic-level class, primarily Interconnecting Cisco Network Devices (ICND). You must obtain CCNA certification before you can get your CCNP and CCDP certifications.

➤ *Cisco Certified Network Professional (CCNP)*—The CCNP is a more advanced certification that is not easy to obtain. To earn CCNP status, you must be a CCNA in good standing. There are two routes you can take to obtain your CCNP. For the first route, you must take four exams: Routing (640-503), Switching (640-504), Remote Access (640-505), and Support (640-506). For the second route, you must take the Foundation (640-509) and Support (640-506) exams.

Although it may seem more appealing on the surface, the second route is more difficult. The Foundation exam contains more than 130 questions and lasts almost 3 hours. In addition, it covers all the topics covered in the Routing, Switching, and Remote Access exams.

➤ Whichever route you choose, there are four courses Cisco recommends that you take:

➤ *Building Scalable Cisco Networks (BSCN)*—This course corresponds to the Routing exam.

➤ *Building Cisco Multilayer Switched Networks (BCMSN)*—This course corresponds to the Switching exam.

Table 1 Cisco Routing and Switching CCNA, CCNP, and CCIE Requirements

CCNA

Only 1 exam required	
Exam 640-507	Cisco Certified Network Associate 2.0

CCNP*

All 4 of these are required	
Exam 640-503	Routing 2.0
Exam 640-504	Switching 2.0
Exam 640-505	Remote Access 2.0
Exam 640-506	Support 2.0

* You need to have your CCNA before you become a CCNP.

CCIE

1 written exam and 1 lab exam required	
Exam 350-001	CCIE Routing and Switching Qualification
Lab Exam	CCIE Routing and Switching Laboratory

➤ *Building Cisco Remote Access Networks (BCRAN)*—This course corresponds to the Remote Access exam.

➤ *Cisco Internetworking Troubleshooting (CIT)*—This course corresponds to the Support exam.

Once you have completed the CCNP certification, you can further your career (not to mention beef up your resume) by branching out and passing one of the CCNP specialization exams. These include:

➤ *Security*—Requires you to pass the Managing Cisco Network Security exam (640-422).

➤ *LAN ATM*—Requires you to pass the Cisco Campus ATM Solutions exam (640-446).

➤ *Voice Access*—Requires you to pass the Cisco Voice over Frame Relay, ATM, and IP exam (640-447).

➤ *SNA/IP Integration*—Requires you to pass the SNA Configuration for Multiprotocol Administrators (640-445) and the SNA Foundation (640-456) exams.

➤ *Network Management*—Requires you to pass either the Managing Cisco Routed Internetworks—MCRI (640-443)—or the Managing Cisco Switched Internetworks—MCSI (640-444) exam.

➤ *Cisco Certified Design Professional (CCDP)*—The CCDP is another advanced certification. It's aimed at high-level internetwork designers who must understand the intricate facets of putting together a well-laid-out network. The first step in the certification process is to obtain the CCDA and CCNA certifications (yes, both). As with the CCNP, you must pass the Foundation exam or pass the Routing, Switching, and Remote Access exams individually. Once you meet those objectives, you must pass the Cisco Internetwork Design exam (640-025) to complete the certification.

➤ *Cisco Certified Internetwork Expert (CCIE)*—The CCIE is possibly the most influential certification in the internetworking industry today. It is famous (or infamous) for its difficulty and for how easily it holds its seekers at bay. The certification requires only one written exam (350-001); passing that exam qualifies you to schedule time at a Cisco campus to demonstrate your knowledge in a two-day practical laboratory setting. You must pass the lab with a score of at least 80 percent to become a CCIE. Recent statistics have put the passing rates at roughly 20 percent for first attempts and 35 through 50 percent overall. Once you achieve CCIE certification, you must recertify every two years by passing a written exam administered by Cisco.

➤ *Certified Cisco Systems Instructor (CCSI)*—To obtain status as a CCSI, you must be employed (either permanently or by contract) by a Cisco Training Partner in good standing, such as GeoTrain Corporation. That training partner must sponsor you through Cisco's Instructor Certification Program, and you must pass the two-day program that Cisco administers at a Cisco campus. You can build on CCSI certification on a class-by-class basis. Instructors must demonstrate competency with each class they are to teach by completing the written exam that goes with each class. Cisco also requires that instructors maintain a high customer satisfaction rating, or they will face decertification.

Tracking Cisco Certification Status

As soon as you pass any Cisco exam (congratulations!), you must complete a certification agreement. You can do so online at the Certification Tracking Web site (**www.galton.com/~cisco/**), or you can mail a hard copy of the agreement to Cisco's certification authority. You will not be certified until you complete a certification agreement and Cisco receives it in one of these forms.

The Certification Tracking Web site also allows you to view your certification information. Cisco will contact you via email and explain it and its use. Once you are registered into one of the career certification tracks, you will be given a login on this site, which is administered by Galton, a third-party company that has no in-depth affiliation with Cisco or its products. Galton's information comes directly from Sylvan Prometric, the exam-administration company for much of the computing industry.

Once you pass the necessary exam(s) for a particular certification and complete the certification agreement, you'll be certified. Official certification normally takes anywhere from four to six weeks, so don't expect to get your credentials overnight. When the package arrives, it will include a Welcome Kit that contains a number of elements, including:

➤ A Cisco certificate, suitable for framing, stating that you have completed the certification requirements, along with a laminated Cisco Career Certification identification card with your certification number on it

➤ Promotional items, which vary based on the certification.

Many people believe that the benefits of the Cisco career certifications go well beyond the perks that Cisco provides to newly anointed members of this elite group. There seem to be more and more job listings that request or require applicants to have a CCNA, CCDA, CCNP, CCDP, and so on, and many individuals who complete the program can qualify for increases in pay or responsibility. In fact, Cisco has started to implement requirements for its Value Added Resellers: To attain and keep silver, gold, or higher status, they must maintain a certain number of CCNA, CCDA, CCNP, CCDP, and CCIE employees on staff. There's a very high demand and low supply of Cisco talent in the industry overall. As an official recognition of hard work and broad knowledge, a Cisco career certification credential is a badge of honor in many IT organizations.

About the Book

To aid you in fully understanding the internetworking concepts required for CCNP certification, there are many features in this book designed to improve its value:

➤ *Chapter objectives*—Each chapter in this book begins with a detailed list of the topics to be mastered within that chapter. This list provides you with a quick reference to the contents of that chapter, as well as a useful study aid.

➤ *Illustrations and tables*—Numerous illustrations of screenshots and components aid you in the visualization of common setup steps, theories, and concepts. In addition, many tables provide details and comparisons of both practical and theoretical information.

➤ *Notes, tips, and warnings*—Notes present additional helpful material related to the subject being described. Tips from the author's experience provide extra information about how to attack a problem, or what to do in certain real-world situations. Warnings are included to help you anticipate potential mistakes or problems so you can prevent them from happening.

➤ *Real-world projects*—Although it is important to understand the theory behind Cisco internetworking technology, nothing can improve upon real-world experience. To this end, along with theoretical explanations, many chapters provide numerous projects aimed at providing you with real-world implementation experience.

➤ *Chapter summaries*—Each chapter's text is followed by a summary of the concepts it has introduced. These summaries provide a helpful way to recap and revisit the ideas covered in each chapter.

➤ *Review questions*—End-of-chapter assessment begins with a set of review questions that reinforce the ideas introduced in each chapter. These questions not only ensure that you have mastered the concepts, but are written to help prepare you for the Cisco certification examination. Answers to these questions are found in Appendix A.

➤ *Sample tests*—Use the sample test and answer key in Chapters 16 and 17 to test yourself. Then, move on to the interactive practice exams found on the CD-ROM. The testing engine offers a variety of testing formats to choose from.

Where Should You Start?

This book is intended to be read in sequence, from beginning to end. Each chapter builds upon those that precede it, to provide a solid understanding of CCNP topics. After completing the chapters, you may find it useful to go back through the book and use the review questions and projects to prepare for the CCNP test (Exam 640-506). Readers are also encouraged to investigate the many pointers to online and printed sources of additional information that are cited throughout this book.

Please share your feedback on the book with us, especially if you have ideas about how we can improve it for future readers. We'll consider everything you say carefully, and we'll respond to all suggestions. Send your questions or comments to us at **learn@examcram.com**. Please remember to include the title of the book in your message; otherwise, we'll be forced to guess which book you're writing about. And we don't like to guess—we want to *know*! Also, be sure to check out the Web pages at **www.examcram.com**, where you'll find information updates, commentary, and certification information. Thanks, and enjoy the book!

Self-Assessment

The reason we included a Self-Assessment in this *Exam Cram* is to help you evaluate your readiness to tackle CCNP certification. It should also help you understand what you need to master the topic of this book—namely, Exam 640-506, "Support." But before you tackle this Self-Assessment, let's talk about concerns you may face when pursuing a CCNP, and what an ideal CCNP candidate might look like.

CCNPs in the Real World

In the next section, we describe an ideal CCNP candidate, knowing full well that only a few real candidates will meet this ideal. In fact, the description of that ideal candidate might seem downright scary. But take heart: Although the requirements to obtain a CCNP may seem pretty formidable, they are by no means impossible to meet. However, you should be keenly aware that it does take time and requires some expense and substantial effort to get through the process.

The first thing to understand is that the CCNP is an attainable goal. You can get all the real-world motivation you need from knowing that many others have gone before, so you will be able to follow in their footsteps. If you're willing to tackle the process seriously and do what it takes to obtain the necessary experience and knowledge, you can take—and pass—all the certification tests involved in obtaining a CCNP. In fact, we've designed these *Exam Crams*, and the companion Exam Preps, to make it as easy on you as possible to prepare for these exams. But prepare you must!

The same, of course, is true for other Cisco career certifications, including:

➤ CCNA, which is the first step on the road to the CCNP certification. It is a single exam that covers information from Cisco's Introduction to Cisco Router Configuration (ICRC) class and the Cisco LAN Switch Configuration (CLSC) class. Cisco also has developed a class that is geared to CCNA certification, known as Cisco Routing and LAN Switching (CRLS).

➤ CCDA, which is the first step on the road to the CCDP certification. It is a single exam that covers the basics of design theory. To prepare for it, you should attend the Designing Cisco Networks (DCN) class and/or the Cisco Internetwork Design (CID) class.

➤ CCDP, which is an advanced certification regarding internetwork design. It consists of multiple exams. There are two ways to go about attaining the CCDP. You could pass the individual exams for ACRC, CLSC, CMTD, and CIT. However, if you're not one for taking a lot of exams, you can take the Foundation Routing/Switching exam and the CIT exam. Either combination will complete the requirements.

➤ CCIE, which is commonly referred to as the "black belt" of internetworking. It is considered the single most difficult certification to attain in the internetworking industry. First you must take a qualification exam. Once you pass the exam, the real fun begins. You will need to schedule a two-day practical lab exam to be held at a Cisco campus, where you will undergo a "trial by fire" of sorts. Your ability to configure, document, and troubleshoot Cisco equipment will be tested to its limits. Do not underestimate this lab exam.

The Ideal CCNP Candidate

Just to give you some idea of what an ideal CCNP candidate is like, here are some relevant statistics about the background and experience such an individual might have. Don't worry if you don't meet these qualifications, or don't come that close— this is a far from ideal world, and where you fall short is simply where you'll have more work to do.

➤ Academic or professional training in network theory, concepts, and operations. This includes everything from networking media and transmission techniques through network operating systems, services, and applications.

➤ Three-plus years of professional networking experience, including experience with Ethernet, token ring, modems, and other networking media. This must include installation, configuration, upgrade, and troubleshooting experience.

➤ Two-plus years in a networked environment that includes hands-on experience with Cisco routers, switches, and other related equipment. A solid understanding of each system's architecture, installation, configuration, maintenance, and troubleshooting is also essential.

➤ A thorough understanding of key networking protocols, addressing, and name resolution, including TCP/IP, IPX/SPX, and AppleTalk.

➤ Familiarity with key TCP/IP-based services, including ARP, BOOTP, DNS, FTP, SNMP, SMTP, Telnet, TFTP, and other relevant services for your internetwork deployment.

Fundamentally, this boils down to a bachelor's degree in computer science, plus three years of work experience in a technical position involving network design, installation, configuration, and maintenance. We believe that well under half of all certification candidates meet these requirements; in fact, most meet less than half of these requirements—at least, when they begin the certification process. But because thousands of people have survived this ordeal, you can survive it too—especially if you heed what our Self-Assessment can tell you about what you already know and what you need to learn.

Put Yourself to the Test

The following series of questions and observations is designed to help you figure out how much work you must do to pursue Cisco career certification and what kinds of resources you should consult on your quest. Be absolutely honest in your answers, or you'll end up wasting money on exams you're not yet ready to take. There are no right or wrong answers, only steps along the path to certification. Only you can decide where you really belong in the broad spectrum of aspiring candidates.

Two things should be clear from the outset, however:

➤ Even a modest background in computer science will be helpful.

➤ Extensive hands-on experience with Cisco products and technologies is an essential ingredient to certification success.

Educational Background

1. Have you ever taken any computer-related classes? [Yes or No]

   If Yes, proceed to Question 2; if No, proceed to Question 4.

2. Have you taken any classes included in Cisco's curriculum? [Yes or No]

   If Yes, you will probably be able to handle Cisco's architecture and system component discussions. If you're rusty, brush up on **show** and **debug** commands and know the impact on the router when these commands are used. You'll want to brush up on serial links, Frame Relay, and protocols including TCP/IP and how they function.

   If No, consider some extensive reading in this area. We strongly recommend instructor-led training offered by a Cisco Training Partner. However, you may want to check out a good general advanced routing technology book, such as *Cisco Internetwork Troubleshooting* by Laura Chappell, Dan Farkas.(Cisco Press, 1999 ISBN: 1-57870-092-2). If this title doesn't appeal to you, check out reviews for other, similar titles at your favorite online bookstore.

3. Have you taken any networking concepts or technologies classes? [Yes or No]

If Yes, you will probably be able to handle Cisco's internetworking terminology, concepts, and technologies. If you're rusty, brush up on basic internetworking concepts and terminology, network models, technologies such as Ethernet, token ring, FDDI, Frame Relay, ISDN and serial links.

If No, you might want to read one or two books in this topic area. Check out Appendix B for some suggestions, as well as online resources.

4. Have you done any reading on routing protocols and/or routed protocols (IP, IPX, AppleTalk, and so on)? [Yes or No]

If Yes, review the requirements stated in the first paragraphs after Questions 2 and 3. If you meet those requirements, move on to the next question.

If No, consult the recommended reading for both topics. A strong background will help you prepare for the Cisco exams better than just about anything else.

Hands-on Experience

The most important key to success on all of the Cisco tests is hands-on experience with Cisco routers and related equipment. If we leave you with only one realization after taking this Self-Assessment, it should be that there's no substitute for time spent installing, configuring, and using the various Cisco products upon which you'll be tested repeatedly and in depth. It cannot be stressed enough that quality instructor-led training will benefit you greatly and give you additional hands-on configuration experience with the technologies upon which you are to be tested.

5. Have you installed, configured, and worked with Cisco routers? [Yes or No]

If Yes, make sure you understand basic concepts as covered in the classes Introduction to Cisco Router Configuration (ICRC), Advanced Cisco Router Configuration (ACRC), Cisco LAN Switch Configuration (CLSC), and Configuring, Maintaining, and Troubleshooting Dial-up Services (CMTD), before progressing into the materials covered here, because this book expands on the basic topics taught there.

Tip: You can download objectives and other information about Cisco exams from the company's Training and Certification page on the Web at **www.cisco.com/training**.

If No, you will need to find a way to get a good amount of instruction on the intricacies of configuring Cisco equipment. You need a broad background to get through any of Cisco's career certification. You will also need to have hands-on experience with the equipment and technologies on which you'll be tested.

Tip: If you have the funds, or your employer will pay your way, consider taking a class at a Cisco Training Partner (preferably one with "distinguished" status for the highest quality possible). In addition to classroom exposure to the topic of your choice, you get a good view of the technologies being widely deployed and will be able to take part in hands-on lab scenarios with those technologies.

Before you even think about taking any Cisco exam, make sure you've spent enough time with the related software to understand how it may be installed and configured, how to maintain such an installation, and how to troubleshoot that software when things go wrong. This will help you in the exam, and in real life!

Testing Your Exam-Readiness

Whether you attend a formal class on a specific topic to get ready for an exam or use written materials to study on your own, some preparation for the Cisco career certification exams is essential. At $100 to $200 (depending on the exam) a try, pass or fail, you want to do everything you can to pass on your first try. That's where studying comes in.

6. Have you taken a practice exam on your chosen test subject? [Yes or No]

If Yes, and you scored 70 percent or better, you're probably ready to tackle the real thing. If your score isn't above that crucial threshold, keep at it until you break that barrier.

If No, obtain all the free and low-budget practice tests you can find and get to work. Keep at it until you can break the passing threshold comfortably.

We have included a practice exam in this book, so you can test yourself on the information and techniques you've learned. If you don't hit a score of at least 70 percent after this test, you'll want to investigate the other practice test resources we mention in this section.

For any given subject, consider taking a class if you've tackled self-study materials, taken the test, and failed anyway. The opportunity to interact with an instructor and fellow students can make all the difference in the world, if you can afford that privilege. For information about Cisco classes, visit the Training and Certification page at **www.cisco.com/training** or **www.geotrain.com** (use the "Locate a Course" link).

If you can't afford to take a class, visit the Training and Certification page anyway, because it also includes pointers to additional resources and self-study tools. And even if you can't afford to spend much at all, you should still invest in some low-cost practice exams from commercial vendors, because they can help you assess your readiness to pass a test better than any other tool. The following Web sites offer some practice exams online:

➤ CCPrep.com at **www.ccprep.com** (requires membership)

➤ Network Study Guides at **www.networkstudyguides.com** (pay as you go)

Tip: When it comes to assessing your test readiness, there is no better way than to take a good-quality practice exam and pass with a score of 70 percent or better. When we're preparing ourselves, we shoot for 80-plus percent, just to leave room for the "weirdness factor" that sometimes shows up on Cisco exams.

Assessing Readiness for Exam 640-506

In addition to the general exam-readiness information in the previous section, there are several things you can do to prepare for the Support exam. You will find a great source of questions and related information at the CCprep Web site at **www.ccprep.com**. This is a good place to ask questions and get good answers, or simply to watch the questions that others ask (along with the answers, of course).

You should also cruise the Web looking for "braindumps" (recollections of test topics and experiences recorded by others) to help you anticipate topics you're likely to encounter on the test.

Tip: When using any braindump, it's OK to pay attention to information about questions. But you can't always be sure that a braindump's author will also be able to provide correct answers. Thus, use the questions to guide your studies, but don't rely on the answers in a braindump to lead you to the truth. Double-check everything you find in any braindump.

For Support preparation in particular, we'd also like to recommend that you check out one or more of these resources as you prepare to take Exam 640-506:

➤ Cisco Connection Online (CCO) Documentation (**www.cisco.com/ univercd/home/home.htm**). From the CCO Documentation home page you can select a variety of topics, including but not limited to Troubleshooting Internetwork Systems and Internetwork Troubleshooting guides, as well as Internetwork Technologies Overviews and Design Guides.

➤ Laura A. Chappell. *Novell's Guide to LAN/WAN Analysis: IPX/SPX*. IDG Books Worldwide, Foster City, CA, 1998. ISBN: 0764545086.

➤ Douglas Comer. *Internetworking with TCP/IP, Volume 1: Principles, Protocols, and Architecture*, Prentice Hall, Englewood Cliffs, NJ, 1995. ISBN: 0-13-216987-8.

➤ Radia Perlman. *Interconnections: Bridges and Routers*. Addison Wesley Publishing Company, Inc. Reading, MA, 1992. ISBN: 0-201-56332-0.

➤ Gursharan S. Sidhu, Richard F. Andrews, and Alan B. Oppenheimer. *Inside AppleTalk, 2nd Edition*. Addison-Wesley. Reading, MA, 1990. ISBN: 0-201-55021-0.

Stop by the Cisco home page, your favorite bookstore, or an online bookseller to check out one or more of these resources. We believe CCO Documentation provides a wealth of great material, the first two books are the best general all-around references on IPX/SPX and TCP/IP, and the final two books cover general routing and bridging conventions, as well as providing a broad coverage of the AppleTalk protocol.

One last note: Hopefully, it makes sense to stress the importance of hands-on experience in the context of the Support exam. As you review the material for that exam, you'll realize that hands-on experience with the Cisco IOS with various technologies and configurations is invaluable.

Onward, through the Fog!

Once you've assessed your readiness, undertaken the right background studies, obtained the hands-on experience that will help you understand the products and technologies at work, and reviewed the many sources of information to help you prepare for a test, you'll be ready to take a round of practice tests. When your scores come back positive enough to get you through the exam, you're ready to go after the real thing. If you follow our assessment regime, you'll not only know what you need to study, but when you're ready to make a test date at Sylvan Prometric. Good luck!

CHAPTER ONE

The Network Models

After completing this chapter, you will be able to:

✓ Identify responsibilities of each layer of the OSI Reference Model

✓ Identify responsibilities of each layer of the Hierarchical Internetworking Model

✓ Use the steps of the Internetwork Troubleshooting Model

✓ Identify a peer-to-peer network

✓ Identify a client/server network model

✓ Identify responsibilities of the TCP/IP Internetworking Model

✓ Identify the differences between connection-oriented and connectionless protocols

In the networks of today, Cisco Systems uses a layered-model approach to the network and troubleshooting. In terms of networking, a reversal has occurred to the old 80/20 rule that implies that 80 percent of traffic on a given network is local and not more than 20 percent of the traffic requires internetworking. In a world with mergers and acquisitions occurring daily, addressing all the needs of the networking backbone is very complicated. As the administrator, you may be the one responsible for planning, deploying, and troubleshooting your network, and implementing its resources.

Network Models

The following sections look at the current networking models. Network models divide problems, such as moving information between nodes over a network medium or troubleshooting, into smaller, more manageable services. By giving each layer a requirement to fulfill, when a component needs to be implemented or troubleshooting needs to be performed, you can associate a problem component, protocol problem, or a missing function with a layer in the particular model.

When vendors want to implement new components—hardware or software—they can design their components to fit within certain layers of a standardized model. By doing this, the vendor can achieve a degree of compatibility with other vendors' components.

The following sections discuss the most common hierarchical models and how protocols, routers, switches, servers, and other network nodes on the network fit into the different models. Although numerous models exist, we will concentrate on the models that are the focus for the CCNP 2.0 Support Exam. The following sections look at these models:

➤ OSI Reference Model

➤ Cisco Hierarchical Internetworking Model

➤ Internetworking Troubleshooting Model

➤ Peer-To-Peer Networking Model

➤ Client/Server Networking Model

➤ TCP/IP Internetworking Model

OSI Reference Model

In almost any networking class, whether it is a Cisco class, a Microsoft class, or almost any other networking vendor's class, the most well-known hierarchical model is the Open Systems Interconnection (OSI) Reference Model (or simply *OSI model*). Thus, because this is a networking and troubleshooting book, coverage of the OSI Reference Model is essential.

The OSI Reference Model is not a network implementation. This model describes the functions that each layer should perform. For many years, I was a systems administrator for CH2M HILL, one of the largest engineering firms in the United States. When engineers design a bridge, they create the plans for the bridge and a step-by-step process for the construction companies to follow to build the bridge. Any number of construction companies may be involved in the building process. Because of building standards, any one of the builders that bids on the construction phase of the project can build a single portion of the bridge independently, based on the plans. The standards used in the plans enable a builder to bring its precon-structed pieces of the bridge to the construction site with confidence that each piece will connect together with another builder's pieces. This means that the builder who builds the pilings and the upper deck of the bridge will be able to connect the railings that are built by another company.

After the plans (standards) are created, any number of builders may do the actual work. The same premise applies to the networking model. Multiple network vendors can build a product with an implementation from a protocol specification, and their results will differ from each other only in relatively minor ways, remain-ing similar enough that they can communicate with products from other vendors, including those providing the same function on the network.

The OSI Reference Model describes how information makes its way from applica-tions (such as an FTP application), flows through all the layers, and is eventually translated to a medium that can flow through the physical network cabling to another PC, up the same model, and to the application program in another com-puter. As the information to be sent descends through the layers of a given system, it looks less and less like the data you entered and ends up as ones and zeros before it hits the physical network cabling.

The seven layers of the OSI Reference Model, which are depicted in Figure 1.1, can be divided into upper and lower layers. The *upper layers* relate to application issues and generally are implemented only in software. The lower layers handle both data transport issues and physically placing the data on the network wire to one or more devices.

Network devices and protocols typically are implemented in all seven layers of the OSI Reference Model. Some implementations try to streamline operations by skipping one or more of the OSI layers. The following sections describe each of the seven layers individually and its functions.

Application Layer (Layer 7)

The Application layer provides communication between the application services and is the layer that's closest to the user. This layer defines the common services to a specific application program and provides the user with the applications needed to

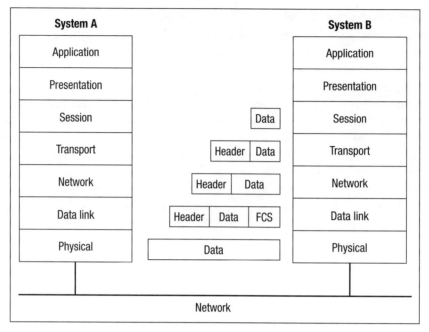

Figure 1.1 The division of The OSI Reference Model into upper and lower layers.

communicate through the network. This layer does not provide services to any other OSI layer. It provides services only to other applications not included in the OSI Reference Model.

The Application layer identifies and establishes the availability of nodes to communicate on the network, application synchronization, error recovery, and the control of data integrity. The following are some applications that can be found at this layer:

➤ File Transfer Protocol (FTP)

➤ Hypertext Transfer Protocol (HTTP)

➤ Network File System (NFS)

➤ Network Time Protocol (NTP)

➤ Server Message Block (SMB)

➤ Simple Mail Transfer Protocol (SMTP)

➤ Simple Network Management Protocol (SNMP)

➤ Telnet

➤ Trivial File Transfer Protocol (TFTP)

➤ Web browsers

Presentation Layer (Layer 6)

The Presentation layer is used to ensure that information sent by an application from the Application layer of one system will be readable by the Application layer of the receiving system. The Presentation layer is concerned with the data format, including encryption and decryption, representation of the user data, and the data structure itself.

This layer's main purpose is to define data formats. The following are some of the protocols that are represented at this layer:

➤ Abstract Syntax Notation 1 (ASN.1)

➤ American Standard Code for Information Interchange (ASCII)

➤ Extended Binary Coded Decimal Interchange Code (EBCDIC)

➤ External Data Representation (XDR)

➤ Graphics Interchange Format (GIF)

➤ Joint Photographic Experts Group (JPEG)

➤ Motion Picture Experts Group (MPEG)

➤ Moving Pictures Experts Group (MPEG)

➤ QuickTime

➤ Tag Image File Format (TIFF)

Session Layer (Layer 5)

The Session layer starts, controls, and terminates sessions between applications. Sessions can consist of data exchanges between two or more presentation entities. This may include the control and management of more than one bidirectional message, enabling an application to be notified when some of a series of messages are completed. This layer also creates formal conversations with two nodes, with an agreement of exchange formatting to exchange data. This takes place in one of three modes:

➤ Simplex

➤ Half duplex

➤ Full duplex

The Session layer synchronizes dialogue between other Presentation layer entities and manages the data exchange. The following are some of the protocols that can be found at this layer:

➤ AppleTalk Session Protocol (ASP)

➤ DECnet

➤ NetBIOS

➤ Network File System

➤ OSI Session Protocol

➤ Remote Procedure Call (RPC)

➤ Structured Query Language (SQL)

The Session layer enables nodes to communicate in an organized manner. Each session has three phases:

➤ Connection establishment

➤ Data transfer

➤ Connection release

In addition to regulating conversations between nodes, the Session layer offers provisions for data expedition, class of service, and reporting of Session layer, Presentation layer, and Application layer problems.

Transport Layer (Layer 4)

The Transport layer is the layer between the upper-layer protocols and lower-layer protocols. The upper layers, such as the Application, Presentation, and Session layers, address application issues. The lower layers relate to the physical transportation of data.

The Transport layer provides data transport services that aid in shielding the upper layers from learning the implementation details of the lower layers. This layer is concerned with issues such as how reliable the transportation of data is over the network. This layer provides reliable transportation of data by providing reliable service mechanisms for the establishment, maintenance, and discontinuation of virtual circuits, fault detection, data recovery, and flow control to prevent a node from overwhelming another node with data.

Another function of the Transport layer is to divide messages into fragments that fit within the size limitations established by the physical network. For example, Ethernet limits the size of the data field to 1,500 bytes. So, if a 1MB file is being sent, the Transport layer must break that 1MB into 1,500-byte segments that already include header information in the data payload.

The following are some examples of protocols that can be found at this layer:

➤ Transmission Control Protocol (TCP)

➤ User Datagram Protocol (UDP)

➤ Sequenced Packet Exchange (SPX)

Network Layer (Layer 3)

The Network layer provides connectivity and path determination between two end systems that may be located on geographically different networks or subnets. A *subnet* is essentially a single network cable sharing a common network identification number and individual host address.

The distance between networks may be one of great geographic distance, and many subnets or networks may separate the two end systems that are trying to communicate. The Network layer is the layer in which routing is performed using a network or logical address, such as an IP address. Routing protocols are used to determine the most optimal paths through the series of interconnected subnets or networks to route data from one node to another. The Network layer protocols then move the data through these paths.

The Network layer's main function is to define end-to-end delivery of packets. To accomplish this goal, the Network layer defines logical addressing so that any endpoint in the network can be identified. This layer also defines how routing works and how routes are learned with routing protocols so that the packets can be delivered efficiently. The Network layer also defines how to separate, or *fragment*, packets into smaller packets to accommodate the physical media with smaller maximum transmission packets.

The Network layer defines most of what a Cisco router considers when routing a packet, including examining the destination address of a packet, comparing the address to a routing table, fragmenting the packet if necessary, and queuing the packet to be sent out to the outbound interface.

The following are some examples of the routed protocols found at the Network layer:

➤ AppleTalk

➤ Connectionless Network Layer Protocol (CLNP)

➤ Connection-mode Network Service (CMNS)

➤ Datagram Delivery Protocol (DDP)

➤ Internet Protocol (IP)

➤ Internetwork Packet Exchange (IPX)

➤ X.25 Packet-Layer Protocol (PLP)

➤ Border Gateway Protocol (BGP)

➤ Enhanced Interior Gateway Routing Protocol (EIGRP)

➤ Integrated Intermediate System to Intermediate System (IS-IS)

➤ Interior Gateway Routing Protocol (IGRP)

➤ Internetwork Packet Exchange (IPX) Routing Information Protocol (RIP)

➤ Open Shortest Path First (OSPF)

➤ Routing Information Protocol (RIP)

➤ Routing Table Maintenance Protocol (RTMP)

Data Link Layer (Layer 2)

The Data Link layer is concerned with physical addressing, such as the Media Access Control (MAC) address assigned to a network interface card (NIC), the network topology, how end systems will use the network link, error notification, the delivery order of frames, and flow control of data being sent.

The Data Link layer is responsible for providing node-to-node communication on a single, local network. To provide this service, the Data Link layer must perform two functions:

➤ Provide an address mechanism for correct delivery

➤ Translate upper-layer data into bits

The Data Link layer specifications are concerned with getting data to transit reliably across one particular link or medium to another. The protocols at this layer are concerned with defining how the WAN and LAN Physical layer protocols work. The OSI Reference Model often does not create any original specification for the Data Link layer, but instead relies on other standards bodies such as the Institute of Electrical and Electronics Engineers (IEEE) to create new standards for the Data Link layer and the Physical layer.

The following are some examples of protocols found at the Data Link layer:

➤ Asynchronous Transfer Mode (ATM)

➤ Binary Synchronous Communication (BSC)

➤ Fiber Distributed Data Interface (FDDI) MAC

➤ Frame Relay

➤ Ethernet II

➤ High-Level Data Link Control (HDLC)

➤ IEEE 802.2

➤ IEEE 802.3

➤ IEEE 802.5

➤ Integrated Services Digital Network (ISDN)

➤ Point-To-Point Protocol (PPP)

The Data Link layer is commonly associated with two sublayers:

➤ Media Access Control (MAC)

➤ Logical Link Control (LLC)

The MAC sublayer assigns a unique address to a device on the network, called the *MAC address*. This address contains six octets. Three octets are used to identify the manufacturer of the NIC, also known as the *Organizationally Unique Identifier (OUI)*. The last three octets form a unique number that identifies the individual NIC. Sort of like a serial number, no other NIC on the network has the same embedded MAC address. The MAC address is critical to the operation of bridges, switches, and routers, because this is the physical address by which interfaces are identified on the network.

The MAC and LLC sublayers are agreed-upon standards by IEEE. This layer is used to add additional functionality to the Data Link layer itself. The LLC is defined in the IEEE 802.2 specification. Some of the most popular 802 specifications are listed in Table 1.1.

Physical Layer (Layer 1)

The Physical layer is used to define the physical electrical, mechanical, and procedural functions for activating, maintaining, and deactivating the physical link between end connections. This later defines characteristics such as voltage levels, timing, data rates, maximum transmission distances, physical connectors, and light modulation.

The specifications for the Physical layer are typically standards from other organizations that reference the OSI Reference Model to deal with the physical characteristics of the many transmission mediums. Sometimes, more than one specification is

Table 1.1   IEEE 802 specification numbers and a description of each.

Specification	Description
IEEE 802.1	802 specification overview
IEEE 802.2	Logical Link Control
IEEE 802.3	CSMA/CD and Ethernet
IEEE 802.4	Token bus
IEEE 802.5	Token Ring
IEEE 802.6	Metropolitan area network (MAN)
IEEE 802.7	Broadband technology
IEEE 802.8	Fiber-optic technology
IEEE 802.9	Voice/data
IEEE 802.10	LAN security
IEEE 802.11	Wireless networks
IEEE 802.12	100BaseVG-AnyLAN

used to complete all the needs of the Physical layer. As an example, RJ-45 is used to define the shape of the connector and the number of wires and pins in the cable or connector. Then, IEEE 802.3, the Ethernet standard, defines the use of the pins and the category of cable to use.

The following are some of the specifications that can be found at the Physical layer:

➤ EIA/TIA-232

➤ EIA/TIA-449

➤ Ethernet

➤ Fiber Distributed Data Interface (FDDI)

➤ IEEE 802.3 Ethernet

➤ IEEE 802.5 Token Ring

➤ V.24

➤ V.35

➤ RJ-45

Communication between the Layers

Each layer of the OSI Reference Model is not permitted to speak directly to another peer layer. Instead, each layer communicates with its own layer on the system for which a data session is open for communication. Each layer in one system must rely on services provided by another system's peer layers to communicate. Each layer of the OSI Reference Model communicates with its peers by using the services provided by a layer service called *service access point (SAP)*. The relationship between adjacent layers in a single system is shown in Figure 1.1.

When System A has data from a software application to send to System B, the data is passed to the Application layer. The Application layer in System A adds a header to the data and then passes the data to the Presentation layer. The Presentation layer then adds its own header that contains information intended for the Presentation layer in System B. Each successive layer in the source system adds its own control information to the data, and each layer in the destination system analyzes and removes the control information from that data. The information unit grows in size as each layer adds its own header (and in some cases a trailer) that contains control information to be used by its peer layer in System B. The Physical layer is where the entire information unit is placed onto the network medium.

The Physical layer in System B receives the information and passes it up its Data Link layer. The Data Link layer in System B then reads the control information contained in the header added by the Data Link layer in System A. The header is removed, and the remainder of the information unit is passed to the Network layer, with each successive layer performing the same actions until reaching the Application layer.

The OSI Reference Model provides the conceptual framework for communication between computers, but the model itself is not a method of communication. Actual communication is made possible only by using communication protocols. A *protocol* is a set of rules that controls how computers exchange information. A protocol uses the functions of one or more of the OSI layers. The most common types of communication protocols are the following:

➤ *Routed protocols (network)*—Define upper-layer functions, for protocols such as TCP/IP or IPX.

➤ *Routing protocols*—Define Network layer functions such as path determination and network topology discovery.

➤ *WAN protocols*—Define communication over a WAN functioning at the Physical, Data Link, and Network layers.

Protocol data units (PDUs) are used to define the network data units used by the protocols. Each PDU is associated with one and only one protocol. Different data units are used at each layer of the OSI Reference Model, as described in Table 1.2.

The Cisco Hierarchical Internetworking Model

Cisco uses hierarchical models to break down complex networks in an organization's campuses into more manageable segments. A great example is the Cisco Hierarchical Internetworking Model. Phone companies were the first to use this type of model, which Cisco adopted early in the networking era. This model is designed to provide the maximum bandwidth to the nodes on the network while allowing policy routing (filtering) and switching of data traffic in an efficient manner.

Note: *Cisco defines a* campus *as a group of buildings connected into an enterprise network of more than one LAN. A campus has a fixed geographical location and is owned and controlled by the same organization.*

The motivation for developing an internetworking model is the recognition that most network failures are caused by poor network design. Poor network design

Table 1.2   The protocol data unit types and the layer at which each type is located.

Protocol Data Unit Type	Layer
Messages	Application
Segments	Transport
Datagrams (or packets)	Network
Frames	Data Link
Bits	Physical

creates unstable network links and routing loops, which inevitably lead to a failure in the network, particularly when redundancy devices fail to converge in time to prevent a major problem.

Designing your network using a hierarchical model helps to prevent a network failure, by providing logical points to aggregate, route, block, and summarize network traffic. This configuration prevents a failure in one part of the network from affecting the entire network, and provides for policy decisions to be made on equipment that can handle making the policy decisions with the least amount of *latency*. Latency is the amount of time data takes to get from the port of entry of a device, travel the circuitry, and exit the device. The Cisco Hierarchical Model and the Cisco Switched Hierarchical Model divides the network into the following three layers, each of which has its own individual goal or goals:

➤ *Core layer*—This layer's goal is to forward traffic as quickly as possible.

➤ *Distribution layer*—The goals of this layer are to summarize traffic, combine routes, and make policy decisions.

➤ *Access layer*—The goal of this layer is to pass traffic to the network. This is the user's point of entry into the network.

Figure 1.2 shows the Cisco Switched Hierarchical Model, which is an example of the three-tiered model. The following sections take a more in-depth look at each layer of this model.

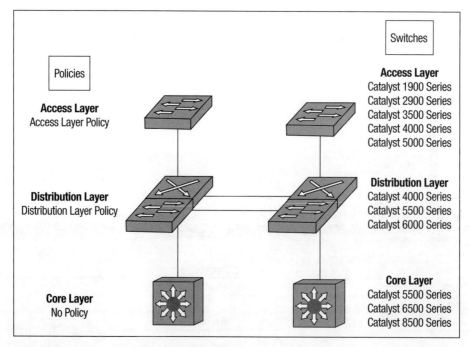

Figure 1.2   The Cisco switched-campus model.

Access Layer

The access layer is the user point of access into the network. This layer passes data traffic to from the network to the end-user nodes and vice-versa. This layer also provides some security and filtering capabilities for the Layer 2 traffic that enters. The network device at this layer then passes traffic either to another port on the device itself, if it can, or to a distribution layer device. The Access layer is the point at which network nodes, whether they are local or remote, are connected to the physical network. This is also the logical termination point for Virtual Private Networks (VPNs).

In most networks, routers are located at this level—usually the Cisco 1600, 2500, and 2600 family of routers. Most often, hubs and switches also are located at this layer, such as the Catalyst 1900 or 2820 series for small or medium-size networks, the Catalyst 2900 or 3500 series for medium-size networks with fewer than 50 users, and the Catalyst 4000 series for high-performance networks with up to 96 users. In a larger network, you may find a Catalyst 5000 family switch.

Distribution Layer

The Distribution layer is the demarcation point in the network between the Access layer and the Core layer. This is the layer that should provide most of your security, routing of VLANs, policy-based decisions, foreign media translations, summarization of traffic, and processing of broadcast traffic that originates from the Access layer before passing data to the Core layer.

The Distribution layer is also the layer where interdomain traffic is redistributed and is the point at which static and dynamic route redistribution occurs. This layer is commonly used as the demarcation point for remote sites to connect into the network.

The devices commonly found at this layer are switches such as the 2926G, 2948G, and 2980G and the Catalyst 4000, 5500, and 6000 family. The 5500 and the 6000 are configurable with a route processor. The Catalyst 5000 can be configured with an internal route processor that can provide Layer 3 functionality. The switches at this layer usually can work with an external router to provide Layer 3 routing functions.

Core Layer

The Core layer is designed to switch and route packets at the fastest possible speed. This should be the final aggregation point for data in the campus network. The devices at this layer must be fast and reliable. You will find that the connections at this level must be of the highest possible bandwidth—not only with the backbone links, but also with the devices connecting with trunk links. This is also the layer where, if applicable, the campus network connects to a WAN link to other company sites or to the Internet. Some of the attributes of the Core layer are as follows:

➤ *No decision making*—At the Core layer, no decisions about packet filtering or policy routing should take place. Any filtering or policy decisions at this layer will add latency delays in forwarding packets, and mistakes at this level will severely impact the rest of the network, resulting in bottlenecks.

➤ *Reachability*—At the Core layer, the placement of devices should be such that the devices in this layer can reach any device in the network. This doesn't mean a physical link to each device is required; it simply means that they need to be reachable in the routing table.

Switch devices that are commonly found at this level are the Cisco Catalyst 5500, 6500 and 8500. The routers typically found at this layer are high-end routers such as the Cisco 7000 family of routers. These devices have wire-speed capabilities and provide strong routing features that make them a good fit for the Core layer of the network.

The Internetworking Troubleshooting Model

Among the many Cisco hierarchical models is the *Internetworking Troubleshooting Model*, which is a major focus of this study guide. This model is a layered approach to the network troubleshooting for network administrators who are managing existing networks.

As you will read many times in this book, today's networks are complex, hetero-geneous environments, which sometimes will make your job of resolving net-work problems difficult. As your network grows, so does your challenge to deliver quality network service with the many different types of media and devices in the network.

If your network is like most company networks, it has to be complex and sophisticated for your company to survive. The network users cannot tollerate degraded or nonexistent network performance, because they rely on the network for their livelihood.

In today's networks, administrators have so many projects and responsibilites that the very network on which the business depends usually are ignored until a noticable problem occurs. At that point, an administrator faces a crisis situation, with upset users and lost company revenue.

If you're the network administrator, this is the point at which you want to go hide under a desk, because you're the one suddenly getting calls from the help desk and sometimes even users. Everyone in the company is looking at you for answers, and everyone wants to know when the network will be up again, including the manag-ers, who need to make decisions regarding how best to save the company money during the outage.

In looking at the root cause of the problem, models are available on which you can rely to identify the problem component or components. Knowing such models as the OSI Reference Model and the functions of each layer will help you to match the missing functions of the network with a particular layer. The Internetworking Troubleshooting Model will help you identify and resolve the problem.

Many problems can be overcome quickly by experience and by knowing which component is having problems and whether fixing the configuration or replacing the component will solve the problem. However, you may be new to the networking world or may experience a network problem you are unfamiliar with.

Unfortunately, unlike a child, your network can't tell you when its sick. Even worse, when your network is "sick," it can't call in sick and rest up to get better. If you are the network administrator, you have to give the network medication to fix its ills immediately. When a network issue or problem does arise, you need a systematic method of troubleshooting the network, or you may waste time and the company's valuable dollars. This systematic method to troubleshooting complex networks is spelled out in the Internetworking Troubleshooting Model, shown in Figure 1.3.

Troubleshooting Steps

Remember, just because a user complains that a problem exists in the network does not mean that one really does exist. The problem could be related to the user's local

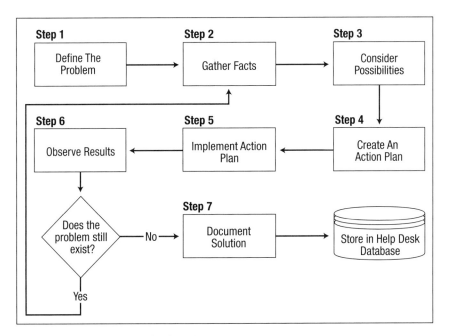

Figure 1.3   The troubleshooting flow chart.

machine, or there may not be a problem at all. The problem may just be the user's perception based on a function the user was performing on his PC.

You need to use the following steps (shown in Figure 1.3) to determine whether a network problem exists and, if one does, to resolve it:

1. *Define the problem in the network.* If you have a help-desk ticket, always assume that the user placing the trouble ticket has misinformed the help-desk consult-ant. Often, the ticket will under- or overestimate the problem. As the system administrator, you need to evaluate the problem firsthand and form your own opinion regarding how complex the problem really is. During this first step, gather a list of symptoms and possible causes.

2. *Gather the facts.* Gather the available facts and historical data, such as baseline information, on the problem. Gather facts by using the **debug** or **show** command on the routers or switches. Try to determine whether this problem has happened before and, if so, whether a documented solution to the problem exists already. If this issue affects more than one person, ask as many people as possible about their view of the problem. Asking more than one person about what problems they're having may point you in a different direction or give you a clearer picture of the severity of the problem. For example, suppose that you talk to one person and he states that he can't access his SQL server to run a query. This would lead you to believe a problem exists with the SQL server or a connection to the server. However, suppose you then talk to another person who doesn't use the SQL server, and she states that she can't get any-thing to print and can't access her email. This information points you in a different direction. You now know it is not a server problem, and most likely is a network problem. Ask some of the following questions:

   ➤ *What are the common symptoms?*

   ➤ *What devices are affected?*

   ➤ *What services in the network are affected?*

3. *Review and evaluate the possibilities.* Now that you have evalutated the problem, gathered statistical information, interveiwed many people, and reveiwed the past network problems and solutions, you are ready to consider possible causes. Create a list of possible causes by brainstorming and bouncing possibilities off other system administrators. Don't discard an idea just because at first glance it doesn't seem realistic. After you go through this exercise, narrow the list down to the most probable causes.

4. *Design a plan of action.* Narrowing down the possibilites is one of the features of using this model to troubleshoot the network. In this step, you want to use the data that you have gathered and your Cisco networking knowledge to determine the OSI layer and physical component that is having a problem; then, slowly isolate

Baseline Information

Network *baselines* are the result of recording and documenting of the devices and typical activity levels of a particular device or interface in the network. Baselining your network is critical for determining later the health of your network. The following is the typical information you want to gather:

➤ *Bandwidth utilization*—The typical bandwidth during both normal periods and peak-usage periods. You also want to collect the number of frames passing through at these times.

➤ *CPU utilization*—Information on the CPU usage on network servers, routers, and switches.

➤ *Error statistics*—Information on frame collisions, runts, and other frame-related error statistics.

➤ *Network infrastructure*—Information regarding the protocols in the network running on servers, routers, and switches. You should also document the places devices reside in the network, and the configuration on each networking device.

Devices that can be used to collect LAN information for short periods of times are as follows:

➤ LAN tester

➤ Protocol analyzer

➤ Small cable meters

➤ LAN testers

Note: The devices are discussed in Chapter 3.

The following are some devices that can be used to collect LAN information for long periods of time for large-scale and complex networks. These protocol analyzers, which usually are PC-equipped, sample network utilization over a long period of time and store the data for analysis. This data can be used to find intermittent network problems.

➤ Fluke's LANMeter

➤ Microtest's Compas

➤ WireScope's FrameScope

➤ Simple Network Management Protocol

➤ Remote Monitor (RMON)

who is not having the problem or problems, to determine where the problem ends or begins. For example, if a group of people on the same subnet can't access the Internet, but users on the same subnet on the other side of the building can, that tells you that the WAN link and router are still functional. At this point, you can narrow down the problem to a switch or hub, to a trunk link, and then all the way to the particular patch panel the affected users are connected to. By doing this, you slowly close the window of possibilities that the problem resides in.

5. *Implement the action plan.* With all of the information you have gathered thus far, you have a pretty good idea about where the problem lies and have developed a course of action to take. Take this plan and carefully implement the solution

step by step, watching for changes or resolutions with each step taken. Make sure you document everything so that you can return the network back to its original configuration if this is not the solution. If you do not thoroughly document your steps, you can actually make matters worse by making it harder to determine whether you have compounded the issue with another problem.

6. *Evaluate and observe the solution.* Observe the results and make sure that your plan has created an error-free solution that does not cause other problems or disabilities in the network. If you have resolved the problem and tested to make sure all correlated issues have been resolved, use the information you have gathered to determine what caused the problem, and to make sure the problem will not reoccur. If the problem has not been resolved, you need to return to step 2 to reevaluate the problem. Make sure that you have documented everything you have tried, in case this problem needs to be escalated to a third party, manufacturer, or other entity to resolve.

7. *Document the solution.* Document the solution, cause, and symptoms so that if the problem happens again, you can quickly retrieve the solution. Also, keep a record of any problem component that had to be replaced. If you have a help desk, it should use help-ticket tracking software that maintains an easily accessible database regarding the problems and solutions in the network, for quick reference. You may have a perfect memory, but what happens if another network administrator must deal with an identical issue in your absence? The more detailed and descriptive your documentation is, the easier it will be for you or someone else to resolve the issue the next time the error occurs. Documenting your network should be an ongoing process. Keep your documentation up to date and modify it whenever an addition or change occurs in the network device configurations or the network topology. Gathering these statistical facts creates a network baseline that you can use for future troubleshooting or to identify a problem in the network before the problem escalates to a severe problem. Information that is collected can be converted into a spreadsheet or chart for future analysis.

Peer-To-Peer Networking Model

This is the network model used in early networks, but it is still common in small network environments. Typically, you will find this type of network used when two PCs are used to play video games with one another in a private network. In this topology, every network node sees the conversations of every other network node.

This type of network is identified by the lack of centralization. No servers or centralized database exist for purposes of authentication. The nodes on the network share files, printers, and other network resources. Assigning a password individually to each network asset provides security in this type of network. Peer-to-peer networks share data with one another in a noncentralized fashion. This type of network can span only a very limited area, such as a room or building.

Client/Server Networking Model

Unlike Peer-To-Peer model networks, client/server model networks use servers to share applications and data storage with the clients, forming a somewhat more centralized network. This setup includes a little more security by providing a centralized database for authentication and login privileges. This is the preferred model of today's networks and provides an easier method of administration for the multiple users trying to access data.

WANs were developed to overcome the limitations of LANs. Early WANs were used to connect LANs across normal telephone lines using protocols such as X.25. WANs of today continue to use the X.25 protocol suite, but use digital lines such as ISDN and Frame Relay. WANs allow networks to ignore geographical limitations in distributing network resources to network clients.

TCP/IP Internetworking Model

The OSI Reference Model maps to the TCP/IP Internetworking Model. The TCP/IP model identifies four layers, each of which has a specific function. Only the model is covered in this section, because TCP/IP is covered in great detail in Chapter 4. Table 1.3 lists and describes each layer and its basic responsibilities.

The following sections look deeper at each layer of the TCP/IP Internetworking Model and how each layer matches to the OSI Reference Model. These sections also explore which TCP/IP applications are found at each layer of both models, as depicted in Figure 1.4.

OSI Reference Model	DOD Model	TCP/IP Applications at Each Layer
Application	Application	FTP, Telnet, SMTP, HTTP
Presentation		
Session		
Transport	Host-to-Host	TCP, UDP
Network	Internetwork	IP, ICMP
Data Link	Network Access	Ethernet, Token-Ring, and so on
Physical		

Figure 1.4 How the TCP/IP Internetworking Model matches to the OSI Reference Model, and the TCP/IP applications found at each layer of both models.

Table 1.3 The TCP/IP Internetworking Model layers and each layer's designated function.

TCP/IP Layer	Layer Function
Application	Responsible for applications, messages, or data streams
Host-to-host	Responsible for the transportation of data packets and end-to-end data integrity
Internetwork	Responsible for providing TCP/IP packet-delivery services
Network access	Responsible for getting data across the physical network

Application Layer

The Application layer of the TCP/IP Internetworking Model is responsible for providing the managed sessions, functionality for users and applications. One of the main responsibilities is to provide the services accessed by users to communicate over the network. The Application layer is the layer at which users access network processes, including all the processes with which users directly interact.

The following are some of the applications and protocols defined in the Application layer:

➤ File Transfer Protocol (FTP)

➤ Web browsers (HTTP)

➤ Telnet

➤ Simple Network Management Protocol

Host-to-Host Layer

The Host-to-Host layer maps to the OSI Reference Model's Transport layer. This layer is used to ensure end-to-end data integrity and provides reliable communication services for network elements that want to perform two-way communication. This layer handles the following functions and protocols:

➤ Data management mechanisms

➤ Flow control

➤ Retransmission

➤ Transmission Control Protocol (TCP)

➤ User Datagram Protocol (UDP)

Internetwork Layer

The Internetwork layer provides the basic packet-delivery service for all TCP/IP networks. This layer is where IP is defined. IP is an unreliable and connectionless protocol that does not guarantee packet delivery. If by chance packets are sent and an IP packet is dropped or lost due to a collision, the sender and receiver are not notified.

The Internetwork layer uses a logical scheme for host addresses. This addressing scheme is known as IP addresses. These addresses are used to identify devices connected to the network. Other networks in the world can use these addresses to communicate on the Internet. The Internetwork layer and higher layers use these IP addresses for routing functionality. IP addresses use a 32-bit addressing scheme with a dotted-decimal notation, such as 130.77.20.123. This 32-bit address comprises two parts: a network portion and a host portion. The network

Connection-Oriented vs. Connectionless Protocols

Using a *connection-oriented* protocol is comparable to sending a letter that requires a return receipt. The receiving node sends an acknowledgement of each frame or packet of data received. Conversely, using a *connectionless* protocol is comparable to sending a letter by standard, regular mail. No guarantee exists that the letter will be delivered on time, thus providing only best-effort delivery.

Both connection-oriented and connectionless protocols have their own characteristics. A connection-oriented protocol has the following characteristics:

➤ Provides for virtual circuits

➤ Sends an acknowledgement of packet delivery to the sending device

➤ Provides sequential delivery of packets and frames

➤ Has a single path through the network for all packets and frames

A connectionless protocol has the following characteristics:

➤ Provides dynamic flow through the network

➤ Provides for multiple paths

➤ Includes a potential for nonsequential delivery of packets and frames

➤ Sends packets with best-effort delivery

➤ Does not send acknowledgements of data delivery

portion identifies the network, and the host portion identifies the network node in that network.

Network Access Layer

The Network Access layer, sometimes referred to as the *Network Interface layer*, maps to both the Data Link layer and the Physical layer of the OSI Reference Model. This layer is responsible for getting data across the physical network using physical media such as Ethernet, FDDI, or token ring. IP datagrams are encapsulated at this layer into frames mapping the frame from an IP address to a physical address called a *Media Access Control (MAC) address*. After information is received from the Internetwork layer, the Network Access layer routes the data and adds the necessary routing information to each frame header.

Chapter Summary

This chapter covered some of the different networking models that are addressed in this book. Networking models enable you to simplify complexities of networks into simple solutions with steps, processes, and solutions.

The OSI Reference Model is the most commonly used networking model. When vendors design a network device, application, or protocol, they try to design it around the OSI Reference Model to maintain a standard that can be used by other networking products. The OSI model describes how information makes its way from application programs, flows through all the layers of the model, and is translated to a medium that can flow through the physical network cabling.

The Cisco Hierarchical Internetworking Model defines three layers that have become the building blocks of networking. This model is used to aid in the determination of what type of networking equipment should be placed at each layer of the model, and the types of functions each layer should perform for the most optimum routing and switching performance.

The Internetworking Troubleshooting Model is used to aid in troubleshooting network problems. It is a proven step-by-step method to aid network administrators overcome a fault in the network in one of the most efficient and time-saving ways.

The Peer-To-Peer Networking Model is used in networks without any centralized authentication, data storage, or network services. This model was used in early networks and is still used in basic networks for such things as data sharing and most often in the video gaming industry for private gaming networks.

The Client/Server Networking Model was developed to overcome the limitations of the Peer-To-Peer Networking Model. It provides for centralized security, data storage, application servers, and network device sharing.

The TCP/IP Internetworking Model illustrates how this model maps to the OSI Reference Model and the different layered functions of each layer. This model contains four layers, with each layer providing specific functions in the network. TCP/IP provides both connection-oriented and connectionless protocols.

A connection-oriented protocol requires a return receipt. The receiving node sends an acknowledgement of each frame or packet of data received. A connectionless protocol uses a best-effort delivery, in which no guarantee exists that the packet will be delivered, and no notification is provided if the delivery fails.

Review Questions

1. The Data Link layer of the OSI Reference Model defines which of the following?

   a. Frame Relay

   b. ISDN

   c. MAC addresses

   d. All of the above

1

2. Fragmenting data into usable sizes, such as Ethernet's 1,500-byte datagrams, is the responsibility of which OSI Reference Model layer?

   a. Transport layer

   b. Network layer

   c. Physical layer

   d. Data Link layer

3. The Network Access layer is part of which of the following network models?

   a. OSI Reference Model

   b. Peer-To-Peer Networking Model

   c. TCP/IP Internetworking Model

   d. Internetworking Troubleshooting Model

   e. All of the above

4. File Transfer Protocol and Telnet are examples of applications found at what layer of the TCP/IP Internetworking Model?

   a. Network layer

   b. Transport layer

   c. Data Link layer

   d. Internetwork layer

   e. Session layer

   f. Application layer

   g. All of the above

5. Which of the following are connection-oriented protocols?

   a. TCP

   b. IP

   c. UDP

   d. Ethernet

6. Which step of the Internetworking Troubleshooting Model is used to collect user information?

   a. Gather facts

   b. Define the problem in the network

   c. Review and evaluate possibilities

   d. All of the above

7. To which of the following Hierarchical Internetworking Model layers should policy networking not be applied?

   a. Application layer

   b. Access layer

   c. Distribution layer

   d. Core layer

8. Which of the following best describes the benefits of network baselining?

   a. Enables you to generate usage reports

   b. Provides a history of network usage

   c. Enables you to find networking bottlenecks

   d. Enables you to identify expansion needs

   e. All of the above

9. How many layers make up the TCP/IP Internetworking Model?

   a. 7

   b. 3

   c. 4

   d. 5

10. The Network Access layer of the TCP/IP Internetworking Model maps to which two layers of the OSI Reference Model? [Choose the two best answers]

    a. Network layer

    b. Physical layer

    c. Data Link layer

    d. Transport layer

11. Which of the following is the last step in the Internetworking Troubleshooting Model?

    a. Implement an action plan

    b. Document the solution

    c. Evaluate and observe the solution

    d. Complete the plan of action

12. Which best represents a peer-to-peer network?

    a. A server providing authentication to network nodes

    b. A small network with each node sharing services

    c. A centralized network

    d. All of the above

13. X.25 PLP, IP, and IPX are all examples of protocols defined at which layer of the OSI Reference Model?

    a. Transport layer

    b. Network layer

    c. Physical layer

    d. Data Link layer

14. Which IEEE specification defines the standards for Ethernet and Collision Sense Multiple Access/Collision Detection (CSMA/CD)?

    a. IEEE 802.1

    b. IEEE 802.2

    c. IEEE 802.3

    d. IEEE 802.5

15. Which of the following services enables peer layers of the OSI model to communicate?

    a. SAP

    b. IP

    c. MAC

    d. None of the above

16. To which of the following Hierarchical Internetworking Model layers should most policy networking functions be applied?

    a. Application layer

    b. Access layer

    c. Distribution layer

    d. Core layer

17. Hierarchical networking models provide which of the following?

    a. Compatibility between vendors

    b. Simplification of the complexities of the network

    c. A way to identify placement of devices in the network

    d. All of the above

18. Which of the following Hierarchical Internetworking Model layers is the access point for network nodes into the network?

    a. Internetwork layer

    b. Access layer

    c. Distribution layer

    d. Core layer

19. Which of the following should be gathered for a complete network baseline?

    a. CPU utilization statistics

    b. Bandwidth utilization statistics

    c. Error statistics

    d. Network infrastructure information

    e. All of the above

20. Data formatting, including encryption and decryption, is defined in which layer of the OSI Reference Model?

    a. Network layer

    b. Transport layer

    c. Data Link layer

    d. Presentation layer

    e. Session layer

    f. Application layer

CHAPTER TWO

LAN Technologies

After completing this chapter, you will be able to:

✓ Identify different LAN topologies

✓ Understand different LAN devices in a network

✓ Recognize the different cabling used in LANs

✓ Understand Ethernet technology and its speed capabilities

✓ Understand Token Ring and the ring topology

✓ Identify FDDI and its dual-ring topology

✓ Understand the capabilities of ATM and its advantages

✓ Understand the advantages of segmenting

✓ Segment a LAN

Knowing the wide varieties of options that are available for today's networks helps you in maintaining and implementing new technology. As a system administrator, you will deal with the day-to-day problems that every network experiences. Most of these problems are invariably blamed on "the network," and everyone starts clamoring to buy something to fix the problem (workstations, servers, routers, operating systems, and so on)—everyone, that is, except the people who must pay for it. They, of course, want you to fix it and make it better, and, in most cases, you can do just that. However, you must know the different devices to use so that you can make definite improvements to your network. This chapter discusses the different topologies that are used in LANs such as bus, ring, star, and tree—as well as the different technologies such as Ethernet, FDDI, Token Ring, ATM, and wireless networks—and how those, too, can be used in LANs. It also covers the cabling used in LANs and how to segment LANs.

LAN Topologies

LAN topologies describe the way in which network devices are organized to utilize resources using cabling. To fully understand a network, you must understand its physical structure. Most networks will have been designed and implemented before your arrival, so understanding how they are formed helps in implementing the technology you'll propose in the future. The four common LAN topologies are bus, ring, star, and tree. (Each of these topologies is described in more detail in the following sections.) Although these topologies are organized in a logical manner, they do not necessarily need to be physically organized in these manners. For example, topologies that are logically buses and rings are commonly physically organized as stars.

Bus Topology

A bus topology resembles a row of devices that are arrayed side-by-side and attached to a single cable or link. When a device sends a transmission, the signal propagates the length of the medium and is received by all of the attached devices. The bus topology is one of the most widely used LAN implementations used by Ethernet (IEEE 802.3) standards. Figure 2.1 helps describe a bus topology. In the figure, you notice the following:

➤ The stations are attached to a linear multiport medium.

➤ Half-duplex operations exist between a station and a bus.

➤ Frames that are submitted to the bus provide the address of its destination.

➤ Frames get lost when they reach the end of the bus.

➤ This topology has no security, because every station can "hear" the other.

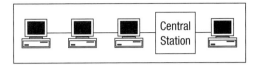

Figure 2.1 A bus topology in a LAN.

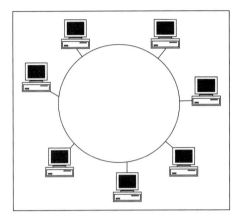

Figure 2.2 A ring topology in a LAN.

Ring Topology

A ring topology consists of devices that are connected to one another in the shape of a ring or circle. Both Token Ring/IEEE 802.5 and FDDI networks implement this topology. Figure 2.2 illustrates a ring topology and its following characteristics:

➤ A break in the ring affects all stations.

➤ A ring has a limit to the number of repeaters that are allowed, due to timing distortions within signals.

➤ Centralized access makes it easy to detect and isolate faults.

➤ Multiple rings can be connected to allow for increased reliability.

Star Topology

A star topology is a series of devices connected together in such a way that the endpoints are connected to a common central hub, or *switch*, by dedicated links. Logical bus and ring topologies are often physically implemented in a star topology. The following list summarizes the workings of the star topology, and Figure 2.3 illustrates how it is laid out for a network:

➤ The central node resubmits to all stations, and the addressed station retrieves the frame. The central node acts as a frame-switching device.

➤ Easy installation and wiring.

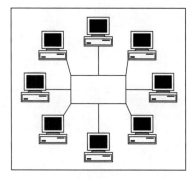

Figure 2.3   A star topology in a LAN.

➤ Installation and removal of devices will not disrupt the network.

➤ Easily detected faults.

Tree Topology

A tree topology is identical to the bus topology, except that it has the physical appearance of branches or a sharing of devices on a link. It is this branching effect (as shown in Figure 2.4) that gives the tree topology its name.

Ethernet LAN Structure

The two main LAN technologies are Ethernet and Token Ring. Although we'll describe each of these in more detail in the following sections, note for now that they share similar qualities, such as defining techniques that adapters use, the LAN wiring, the media access control (MAC) protocols, and the type of signals that they

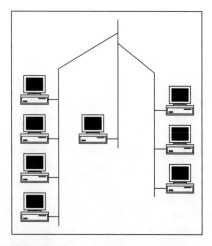

Figure 2.4   A tree topology in a LAN.

transmit over the wiring. The adapters that you choose determine which MAC and signaling parameters you'll be using.

In the sections below, we'll describe the various Ethernet standards and protocols and discuss the significance of each. We'll also address full-duplex Ethernet and gigabit Ethernet technologies and describe some of their most common uses.

About Ethernet

The Ethernet LAN standard is the oldest and most widely used in the industry today. It has survived so long for two simple reasons: Ethernet provides high-speed transmission at an affordable price, and it offers a variety of support for a LAN. The Ethernet system consists of three basic elements:

➤ *Physical medium*—Used to carry Ethernet signals between computing.

➤ *Set of medium access control rules*—Allow multiple computers to share the Ethernet channel.

➤ *Ethernet frame*—Consists of a set of bits that are used to carry data over the system.

Ethernet frames data and traverses the network by taking packets from upper-layer protocols and building frames to send across the network in a process that is commonly referred to as *data encapsulation* or *framing*. Ethernet frames travel at the Data Link layer of the OSI model and must be a minimum of 64 bytes and a maximum of 1518 bytes. Figure 2.5 illustrates an Ethernet frame and an IEEE 802.3 frame.

Here is a brief explanation of each field in an IEEE 802.3 frame:

➤ *Preamble*—an alternating pattern of ones and zeros pattern that is used by the receiver to establish bit synchronization. Both Ethernet and IEEE 802.3 frames begin with a preamble.

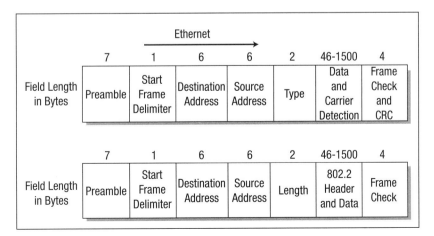

Figure 2.5   An Ethernet frame and a IEEE 802.3 frame.

➤ *Start frame delimiter*—indicates where the frame starts and is the byte before the destination address in both the Ethernet and IEEE 802.3 frame.

➤ *Destination Address and Source Address*—are each six bytes long in both Ethernet and IEEE 802.3 frames and are contained in hardware on the Ethernet and IEEE 802.3 interface cards. The IEEE standards committee specifies the first three bytes of the address to a specific vendor. The source address is always a unicast (single-node) address, whereas the destination address may be unicast, multicast (group), or broadcast (all nodes).

➤ *Type Field In Ethernet frames*—is the two-byte field after the source address. After Ethernet processing, the type field specifies the upper-layer protocol to receive the data.

➤ *Length Field In IEEE 802.3 frames*—is also a two-byte field following the source address. The length field indicated the number of bytes of data that follow this field and precede the frame check sequence field.

➤ *Data Field*—is the actual data contained in the frame and follows the type and length fields. After Physical-layer and Link-layer processes are complete, this data is sent to an upper-layer protocol. With Ethernet, the upper-layer protocol is identified in the type field. With IEEE 802.3, the upper-layer protocol must be defined within the data portion of the frame. If the data of the frame is not large enough to fill the frame to its minimum size of 64 bytes, padding bytes are inserted to ensure at least a 64-byte frame.

➤ *FCS (frame check sequence) and CRC (cyclic redundancy check) fields*—are at the end of the frame. The frame check sequence recalculates the number of frames to make sure that none are missing or damaged. The CRC applies to all fields except the first, second, and last.

CSMA/CD Protocol

The CSMA/CD protocol (IEEE 802.3) was first published in 1985, with the formal title of *"IEEE Standard 802.3, Carrier Sense Multiple Access with Collision Detection (CSMA/CD) Access Method."* All Ethernet equipment since 1985 is built according to the IEEE 802.3 standard, and Ethernet networks employ the CSMA/CD protocol. CSMA/CD was created to overcome the collisions that occur when packets are sent simultaneously from different nodes. This protocol listens before talking: in an Ethernet environment, only one node on the segment is allowed to transmit at any given time.

Ethernet uses a communication concept called *datagrams* to get messages across the network. The CSMA/CD makes sure that two datagrams aren't sent out at the same time, and, if they are, it acts as a mediator to retransmit. A good analogy to CSMA/CD is that of a police radio system. If you are on the correct channel, you can hear everything, but, if you want to speak and be heard, you must wait for a clear moment. If you try to talk when another person is speaking, one or both of you won't be heard clearly. You must wait for a break in communication to speak and be heard. It's obvious how this slows the communication process, just as it does in a network environment. If a channel is busy on the network, other stations cannot transmit.

The IEEE committee finalized a specification for running Ethernet-type signaling over unshielded twisted-pair (UTP) wiring. The IEEE calls the 10-Mbps UTP standard *10Base-T*, which indicates a signaling speed of ten megabits per second, a baseband signaling scheme, and twisted-pair wiring. Although many smaller companies still use 10Base-T technology because they don't have the need to change, I am sure that they notice that their newer applications are more demanding of resources. In fact, 10Base-T isn't always fast enough: transmission speeds of 100Base-T and Gigabit are needed for today's demands.

100Base-T Fast Ethernet

In 1995, the IEEE released the 100Base-T Ethernet standard, formally entitled *"IEEE Std 802.3u for Carrier Sense Multiple Access with Collision Detection (CSMA/ CD) Access Method and Physical Layer Specifications: MAC Parameters, Physical Layer, Medium Attachment Units and Repeater for 100 Mb/s Operation"*. This standard— which defines the physical and Data Link layers of the OSI model—was definitely needed as larger applications began to demand more from a network. The standard also served as a welcomed introduction to existing Ethernet LANs as technology was calling for faster speeds. Fast Ethernet uses the CSMA/CD protocol and has ten times the performance of 10Base-T. Because 100Base-T uses the same protocol as 10Base-T (CSMA/CD), you can integrate 100Base-T in existing 10Base-T networks. It uses the same network wiring and equipment as the 10Base-T networks, provided the wiring and equipment is not too old. However, the biggest issue that a network administrator will face is at the workstation. To allow the workstation to transmit and receive at either 10Mbps or 100Mbps, the PCs need an NIC (network interface card) that is 10/100 capable, and older NICs allow only 10Mbps. Replacing these could get quite costly when dealing with a large network of several hundred—or several thousand—workstations.

Other than the idea of replacing NICs in every workstation, something else to consider is the actual implementation of 100Base-T in your network. 10Base-T uses a larger collision domain diameter than 100Base-T and thus has a different signaling system. The diameter of 100Base-T is 205 meters, which is approximately ten times smaller than that of 10Base-T. What does this mean, though? Because 100Base-T uses the same collision-detection mechanism as 10Base-T, the network diameter has to be reduced for 100Base-T. Think of it in terms of time slots. Time slots require a station to transmit all of its bits before another station can transmit its packets. For 100Base-T networks to transmit in the same time slots as 10Base-T, the distance must be reduced (because 100Base-T travels at a faster rate). This also means 100Base-T networks cannot use the standard 5-4-3 rule (five network segments, four repeaters, only three segments) rule. With 100Base-T, repeaters can extend a network.

100Base-T Repeaters

As with standard Ethernet, repeaters are used in Fast Ethernet networks in the same manner that they are used in 10Base-T networks. The 100Base-T specification defines two kinds of repeaters—Class I and Class II—and these are differentiated by their propagation delay (latency). A Class I repeater has a repeater delay value of 140 bit times and is known as a *translator repeater*. Class I can support both kinds of physical signaling (100 BaseX *and* 100BaseT4). The delay value of a Class II repeater is 92 bit times, which is shorter than the Class I's value. A Class II repeater can support only one physical signaling at a time (100BaseX *or* 100BaseT4). With the Class II repeater's lower bit times, it can support only one signal to maintain the bit times. Because of the delay characteristics, you can use only one Class I repeater in a collision domain, but you can use two Class II repeaters.

The use of repeaters is limited by maximum distances. In looking at Table 2.1, you can see the different distances that can be achieved with a repeater.

Autonegotiation

A 100Base-T network also supports an optional feature called *autonegotiation*, which allows a hub and a device to communicate their compatibilities and to agree upon an optimal communication. Autonegotiation can detect speed matching for 10 and 100Mbps, full-duplex, and automatic signaling configuration for 100Base-T4 and 100Base-TX stations. Autonegotiation can be enabled or disabled on hubs or switches.

Devices usually have autonegotiation on by default to automatically negotiate a mutual speed for both devices for communication. Such autonegotiation is a nice feature now that most networks run at speeds of 100Mbps and many NICs are 10/100. Autonegotiation saves much time in configuring devices, rather than having to configure a device each time it's added to the network.

Table 2.1   Maximum distances using repeaters.

Type and Number of Repeaters	Using UTP	Using Fiber
One Class I repeater	200 meters	261 meters
One Class II repeater	200 meters	308 meters
Two Class II repeaters	205 meters	216 meters

Full Duplex

Full-duplex Ethernet was another advancing technology for Ethernet. Full duplex allows data to be sent and received simultaneously over a link. You may find full-duplex capabilities in autonegotiation hubs and interfaces. In a half-duplex link, data can either be sent or received, but not both at the same time. In theory, with full duplex, you can have twice the bandwidth of normal (half-duplex) Ethernet. The full-duplex mode requires that each end of the link connect to only a single device, such as a workstation, server, or a switched hub port. The devices also have to be running at the same speed, such as both at 10Mbps or both at 100Mbps.

The full-duplex mode doesn't need to adhere to the Ethernet MAC system, because the link is not attempting to create a shared Ethernet channel with multiple devices and so doesn't have to listen for other transmissions or collisions when sending data. The 10Base-T, 100Base-T, and 100Base-FX can support full-duplex operations because they have transmitting and receiving paths that can be simultaneously active.

Gigabit Ethernet

Gigabit Ethernet was a welcomed technology for many companies pushing large applications. Hospitals especially welcomed the speed of gigabit (it's ten times faster than 100Base-T, with speeds up to 1000Mbps or 1Gbps (gigabit per second)), because pushing large files, such as those resulting from CAT scans, across a network was nearly impossible with standard Ethernet. Gigabit Ethernet—which is another addition to the 802.3 Ethernet standards family—allowed for more resources to be shared throughout a network. It can run in half-duplex or full-duplex mode. Most products that use gigabit technology use fiber-optic cable. Category 5 UTP can be used for distances of approximately 25 meters, but fiber optics greatly extend this distance. Implementing Gigabit Ethernet in your network increase its bandwidth and capacity, improves Layer 2 performance, and can eliminate Layer 2 bottlenecks.

Gigabit Ethernet looks identical to Ethernet from the Data Link layer upward. To increase the speed from 100Mbps to 1000Mbps (1Gbps), the physical interface needed to be changed. This change was accomplished by merging two technologies—IEEE 802.3 Ethernet, which we previously described, and the ANSI X3T11 Fibre Channel. The purpose of the ANSI Fibre Channel—a general name for the integrated set of standards developed by ANSI—is to provide a means for the high-speed transfer of data in a serial link between supercomputers, mainframes, workstations, desktop computers, storage devices, displays, and other peripherals. The Fibre Channel protocol manages the data transfer between nodes and thus interoperates with existing upper-level protocols. Figure 2.6 shows how the two technologies are combined. The resulting merge takes advantage of the existing high-speed physical interface technology of Fibre Channel while maintaining the

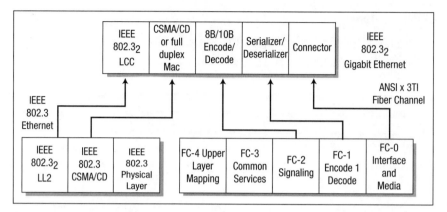

Figure 2.6 Gigabit Ethernet.

IEEE 802.3 Ethernet frame format, compatibility for installed media, and use of duplexing (via CSMA/CD). Also shown in Figure 2.6 is how the Gigabit Ethernet protocol stack was developed by merging two existing technologies.

The three types of media for Gigabit Ethernet are longwave, shortwave, and copper medium, as described below:

➤ Longwave (LW) laser using single-mode and multimode fiber. This is referred to as *1000BaseLX*.

➤ Shortwave (SW) laser using multimode fiber. This is generally referred to as *1000BaseSX*.

➤ Copper cabling (CX) using shielded 150-ohm copper. This is referred to as *1000BaseCX*.

Gigabit Ethernet is most commonly used as a backbone between switches. In fact, switch vendors offer gigabit interface connectors (GBICs) to support this new technology. With the GBICs, the 1000BaseSX (short haul) gives the option for multimode fiber-optic cable connections up 850 feet to 1,800 feet. The 1000BaseLX (long haul) GBICs can pass data up to 1.8 miles (three kilometers), which allows a good deal of flexibility in LANs with distance and bandwidth issues.

Half-Duplex Gigabit

Because the CSMA/CD protocol is delay sensitive, Gigabit speeds for half-duplex Ethernet has created some challenges. Implementation of CSMA/CD is the same with standard Ethernet and Fast Ethernet and allows shared gigabit Ethernet via hubs or switches. At gigabit speeds, smaller packets are smaller than the length of the slot time in bits. The slot time needs to be a minimum amount of time to allow for the Ethernet to handle collisions. Because gigabit speeds are sending packets too fast for the protocol, a carrier extension has been added to the Ethernet specification. This extension adds frames to make up the difference to meet the minimum requirements for slot time.

In reality, half duplex is not recommended for gigabit Ethernet, because the frame sizes are insufficient and because frames need to be added to allow for proper transmission. You achieve faster speeds with half-duplex gigabit than you do with Fast Ethernet, but you won't be utilizing the full capabilities of Gigabit Ethernet technology by running at half duplex.

2

LAN Transmission Methods

Sometimes different types of broadcasts can bring your network to its knees. As a network administrator, you must understand these different types of broadcasts so that you can identify what they are and where they are coming from. Sometimes rushing to the network while the network is slow can be very helpful, because doing so allows you to connect a device to monitor the broadcasts and who is sending them. This monitoring can be helpful in diagnosing the problem. The three types of LAN data transmissions are unicast, multicast, and broadcast. In all three transmissions, a single packet is sent to one or more nodes, but in different manners:

➤ *Unicast transmission*—a single packet is sent from the source node to the destination node on a network. The source node sends a packet by sending it to the address of the destination node, and the packet is then sent on the network to find the address of the destination node.

➤ *Multicast transmission*—a single data packet is copied and sent to a specific set of nodes on the network. The source node uses a multicast address to send a packet addressed to several nodes. The packet is then sent on to the network where it's copied and sent to each destination node that is part of the multicast address.

➤ *Broadcast transmission*—a single data packet is copied and sent to all nodes on the network. In this transmission, the source node sends a packet addressed to all destination nodes on the network. The packet is then sent on the network where it's copied and sent to every destination node on that network. If broadcasts are sent all the time, this type of transmission can be very taxing on the network. This is why you may want to segment your network into smaller sections to reduce the broadcast domain.

Cables Used in LANs

The type of adapters that you buy dictates the types of cables that will work in the network, the physical and electrical form of the network, the type of signaling, and the shared access of network PCs. The most widely used cable in a LAN is Category 5 unshielded twisted pair (UTP) and fiber optic. Both are described in the following paragraphs, along with the various other available types of cable.

Most networks use UTP cable, and it can handle the fastest network connections that you'll run to the desktops. Twisted-pair cables are made of copper wiring, and the twists of the wire provide a degree of shielding from electromagnetic currents. The more twists that the cable has, the more efficient it is in passing data. Not only does UTP meet all of your networking needs, it's not that expensive for either Ethernet or Token Ring.

Shielded twisted pair (STP) has a construction that is very different from UTP. It also costs more than UTP and is difficult to work with as it requires longer installation time for connectors, larger connectors than UTP, and most of all, problems with *ground loops.* Ground loops happen in cases where the ground voltage at each end of the cable run is different, causing current to flow in the cable's shield. This in turn causes a magnetic field, which creates noise and disturbs the transmission. In addition, STP requires custom installation that adds to the cost. IBM uses STP for Token Ring installations.

Coaxial cable consists of a cord of copper wire, either solid or stranded, that is surrounded by an exterior shield of woven copper braid or metallic foil. Coax (as it is commonly referred to) is one of the older networking cables, and it is used to supply the signal to your cable television. To connect devices to a LAN using coax, special T connectors must be crimped to the cable ends.

Fiber-optic cables are made of glass fibers instead of wire. The cables are lightweight and can eliminate hundreds of pounds of wiring in fairly routine installations. Because fiber-optic cabling is made of a hair-thin strand of glass surrounded by a strengthening material, it carries signals as bursts of light or small lasers that represent the zeros and ones of a digital message.

Fiber-optic cables have many advantages over copper wire, such as their insusceptibility to electrical interference, their smaller size (thus allowing smaller-diameter conduits), and their ability to carry large amounts of data at high speeds over a long distance. However, the main disadvantage is that fiber-optic cabling is expensive, costing up to $200 per network node. Of course, this cost estimate can fluctuate depending upon factors such as the region, costs of labor, and any special requirements that are unique to the installation.

Many LAN technologies use two strands of fiber, with each strand carrying data in opposite directions. Fiber-optic links can run without a repeater to distances of more than 3.5 kilometers, which is more than 11 times the maximum distance for coax, and 15 times the distance for twisted pair.

Listed below are a few examples of how you might see cables referred to in LANs:

➤ *10Base2/Thinnet*—Segments up to 185 meters using RG58 coax at 50 ohms.

➤ *10Base5/Thicknet*—Segments up to 500 meters using RG8 or 11 at 50 ohms.

➤ *10BaseT/UTP*—Hosts connect to a hub or a switch using unshielded twisted-pair cables. Category 3 UTP is specified at 10Mbps, Category 5 to 100Mbps, Category 6 to 155Mbps, and Category 7 to 1Gbps.

➤ *100BaseFX*—Ethernet over fiber-optic cable at 100Mbps. It uses a two-strand, multimode, fiber-optic cable.

➤ *100BaseT4*—Carries 100Mbps over Category 3, 4, or 5 UTP cabling with a standard RJ-45 connector.

➤ *100BaseTX*—Fast Ethernet over Category 5 UTP.

➤ *100BaseX*—Either 100BaseTX (over Cat 5) or 100BaseFX media (over fiber optic).

➤ *100VG AnyLan*—Used by Fast Ethernet and Token Ring, but is not compatible with the 802.3 standards. Cisco does not support it, and it is not heavily used.

Token Ring

After Ethernet, Token Ring is the second most widely used LAN technology, and its second rank is due mostly to its cost factor. Ethernet technology is simply cheaper to implement than is Token Ring. Judging by the name, we know it's a ring topology. Created by IBM in the 1970s, Token Ring was popular with customers who needed to migrate from a mainframe environment. The IEEE 802.5 subcommittee—with help from IBM representatives—developed a set of standards that described a token-passing network in a ring topology.

Token-passing networks move a stream of data, called a *token*, around the network, and this token circulates like a freight train through the network stations when they are idle. A station with a message or data to transmit waits until it receives a free token. It then changes the free token to a busy token and transmits a block of data called a *frame*, which contains the data that needs to be sent to the rest of the network. The token circulates around the ring, passing through as many as three stations at a time until it finds the receiving station.

The receiving station copies the data from the frame, and the frame continues around the ring, making a complete round trip back to the original transmitting station. The transmitting station now knows the frame has been received, and the station then purges the busy token and inserts on the ring a new free token for others to use. A relay race serves as a good way to conceptualize this token passing. The first person in the race must possess the baton and run full circle around the track. The next person cannot run without having been given the baton, and so on. The use of a token-passing MAC system prevents messages from interfering with one another by guaranteeing that only one station at a time is transmitting. Therefore, collisions cannot occur on the network. Unlike Ethernet, token passing ensures the delivery of the frame.

The Token Ring topology runs at the physical and Data Link layer of the OSI model, and it is modeled as a star topology using STP wiring. Each station is connected to a central hub called a *multistation access unit* (*MSAU*) that houses electromechanical relays to make the physical star into a logical ring. The logical ring is where each station receives signals from its nearest active upstream neighbor (NAUN) and repeats these signals to its downstream neighbors. Figure 2.7 shows how the MSAUs can be wired together to form one large ring in a Token Ring network.

Frame Format of Token Ring

Token Ring is similar to FDDI frames, in that they both support token formats as well as data. Figure 2.8 illustrates this frame format in a Token Ring network.

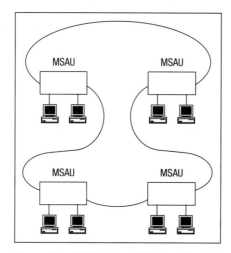

Figure 2.7   MSAUs in an IBM Token Ring Network.

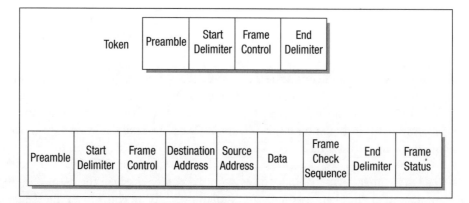

Figure 2.8   The frame format in a Token Ring network.

Here is a brief explanation of each field in a frame.

➤ *Start Delimiter*—alerts each station of a token and uses a unique coding for the frame.

➤ *Access-Control Byte*—contains the following bits that circulate throughout the ring and are used by the active monitor to ensure delivery: Priority bit to indicate the priority of the frame or token. A Reservation bit to indicate the priority required for the next token to gain access to the ring. A Token bit to differentiate a token from a data or command frame and a Monitor bit to determine whether a frame is circling the ring endlessly.

➤ *Frame Control*—indicates the frame type and contains the Frame type bit, the Reserved bit, and the Control bits.

➤ *Destination Address*—indicates the address of the receiver.

➤ *Source Address*—identifies the address of the sender.

➤ *Data*—indicates the actual data being sent from the upper layers.

➤ *Frame Control Sequence*—ensures that all the frames are delivered without damage.

➤ *End Delimiter*—defines the end of the token or frame and contains bits to indicate if a frame is damaged.

➤ *Frame Status*—terminates the frame and ensures that the frame has been copied to the destination address.

Priority System of Token Ring

Token Ring networks use a priority system that permits certain user-designated, high-priority stations to use the network more frequently. Priority levels are configured by the network administrator, and a Token Ring network has two fields that control priority: the priority field and the reservation field. When a priority token is transmitted, it can be seized by only those stations with a priority that is equal to or higher than the priority value contained in that token. The token is then seized and changed to an information frame, and only stations with a priority value higher than that of the transmitting station can reserve the token for the next pass around the network. When the next token is generated, it includes the higher priority of the reserving station. Stations that raise a token's priority level must reinstate the previous priority after the transmission is complete.

Active Monitor

Token Ring networks employ a mechanism for detecting network faults and compensating for them. Any station on a Token Ring network can be selected to be the active monitor. This active monitor station acts as a centralized source of timing information for the Token Ring stations and makes sure that there isn't more than one token on the ring at any given time. Also, when a sending device fails, its frame may continue to circle the ring. This can prevent other stations from transmitting their frames, which may lock up the network. The active monitor can detect such frames, remove them from the ring, and generate a new token. The active monitor also has several standby monitors that act as backups in case the active monitor goes offline.

Ring Speed

The original IBM Token Ring product ran at speeds of 4Mbps. In 1989, IBM released a faster version of Token Ring, which ran at 16Mbps. Over time, a high-speed Token Ring (HSTR) was released that operated at 100Mbps and lead to 1Gbps Token Ring in the future. The speed has maintained with the evolving technology and is a serious contender with Ethernet.

In summary, you must know that Token Ring is a reliable, efficient LAN. It is secondary to Ethernet only because it is pricey by comparison. However, Token Ring is much more resilient than Ethernet is, and it is better suited for heavy workloads. Its future evolution will be a gigabit Token Ring over fiber-optic cable for backbone connections.

FDDI

Another type of common LAN technology is based upon the FDDI (Fiber Distributed Data Interface) standard. One of the main reasons that FDDI is appealing to network administrators is the redundancy that FDDI offers at a high speed. FDDI is an American National Standards Institute (ANSI) standard that defines a dual Token Ring LAN operating at 100Mbps over a fiber-optic medium. The FDDI standard defines two physical rings that simultaneously send data in different directions. FDDI uses a token-passing protocol that operates on dual counter-rotating rings. Some stations—such as servers or other high-profile systems—may be attached to both rings for redundancy reasons. Under normal operation, data flows on the primary ring, and the secondary ring is idle. If something happens to the primary ring, the secondary ring takes over, thus providing redundancy to the network. Figure 2.9 shows the dual rings of a FDDI network.

The four specifications of FDDI are Physical layer protocol (PHY), physical medium dependent (PMD), media access control (MAC), and station management (SMT):

➤ *PHY specifications*—Define encoding/decoding procedures, clocking requirements, and framing.

➤ *PMD specifications*—Define the characteristics of the transmission medium, including fiber-optic links, power levels, bit error rates, optical components, and connectors.

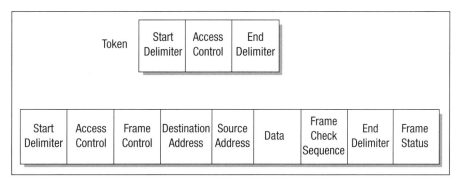

Figure 2.9 The dual rings of a FDDI network, which maintain network reliability.

➤ *MAC specifications*—Define how the medium is accessed, including frame format, token handling, addressing, algorithms for calculating cyclic redundancy rate (CRC) value, and error-recovery mechanisms.

➤ *SMT specifications*—Define FDDI station configuration, ring configuration, and ring control features, including station insertions and removals, initialization, fault isolation and recovery, and statistics.

FDDI standards reside on the Physical layer and the MAC sublayer. Because FDDI specifies communication over fiber-optic cable, it's best used in environments in which nodes are separated by large distances, or in which networks must operate in an environment with lots of different electromagnetic devices that can cause interference. However, FDDI has certain limitations:

➤ 500 nodes per FDDI LAN

➤ 100-kilometer maximum ring circumference

➤ Two-kilometer distance between FDDI nodes using multimode fiber

FDDI uses fiber-optic as the primary transmission medium, but it can be run using copper wiring. FDDI defines two types of optical fiber: single mode and multi-mode. (A *mode* is described as a ray of light entering the fiber at a particular angle.) Multimode fiber uses a light-emitting diode (LED) as the light-generating device, and single mode uses laser.

Attachments for FDDI

FDDI has multiple attachments that provide the devices with different options regarding placement on the rings. The three types of devices that are used as attachments are single-attachment station (SAS), dual-attachment station (DAS), and a concentrator. The SAS attachment is designed for PCs and other devices that are regularly powered on and off. The SAS attaches to the primary ring through a concentrator, and the primary purpose of this attachment is to prevent any detrimental effect to the ring when devices are powered down. Normally, when a device drops off in a ring environment, it causes the ring to go down. Each FDDI DAS has two ports allowing for designated A and B ports. The A and B DAS ports attach to the primary and secondary rings, providing connections for both rings.

Finally, FDDI uses a concentrator as the building block of the FDDI network. The concentrator is attached to the primary and secondary rings and ensures that the failure or powering down of any SAS does not also bring down the ring. The concentrator acts as a shield for the FDDI so that SAS attachments/detachments do not affect the ring.

FDDI is designed for reliability, flexibility, and high throughput. Thus, FDDI is currently popular in high-speed backbone technologies because of its support for high bandwidth and greater distances than copper. Recently, a copper specification called *Copper Distributed Data Interface* (*CDDI*) has emerged that provides 100Mbps using copper wiring. FDDI is also used in campus networks or mainframe environments because of its speed and redundancy.

FDDI Frame Format

FDDI frame formats are larger than that of an 802.3 frame and are very similar to a Token Ring frame. FDDI supports two frame types: one data and the other token. Figure 2.10 illustrates the format of a FDDI frame.

Here is a brief explanation of the each field in a frame.

➤ *Preamble*—Shares a unique sequence for the following frame.

➤ *Start Delimiter*—Is the beginning of the frame and has a different signaling pattern than the rest of the frame.

➤ *Frame Control*—Shows the size of the address fields and the type of data (asynchronous or synchronous data).

➤ *Destination Address*—Contains a unicast, multicast, or broadcast address and is six bytes long.

➤ *Source Address*—Identifies the single station that sent the frame. It also is six bytes long.

➤ *Data*—Contains upper-level protocol information.

➤ *Frame Check Sequence*—Checks to see if the frame that was sent was received in the same condition. It is dependent on the frame contents, and the destination device checks to see if the frame was damaged by calculating the value that was sent by the source station. If the values do not match, the frame will be discarded.

➤ *End Delimiter*—Contains symbols that indicate the end of the frame.

➤ *Frame Status*—Tells the source address if the frame was received by the destination address.

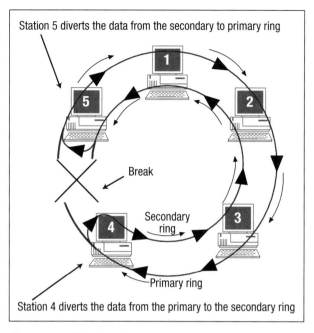

Station 5 diverts the data from the secondary to primary ring

Break

Secondary ring

Primary ring

Station 4 diverts the data from the primary to the secondary ring

Figure 2.10   The frame format of a data frame and a token frame.

ATM

Asynchronous Transfer Mode (ATM) is an adaptable technology that can be used in LANs and WANs (wide-area networks). (You'll read more about the WAN capabilities later in this book.) ATM is based on the efforts of the ITU-T Broadcast Integrated Services Digital Network (BISDN) standard. ATM can provide a very high bandwidth with few delays that uses both switching and multiplexing. It was originally conceived as a high-speed transfer technology for voice, video, and data over public networks, and ATM's chief advantage is its capability to create a seamless and fast network reaching from the desktop out across a wide area. Ultimately, ATM could do away with routers, allocate bandwidth, and be able to run high-end applications. Although this certainly sounds like a dream for networks, it's almost too good to be true. Because most organizations are only pushing data through their network with a few higher-end applications, the need for millisecond synchronization is not a necessity. ATM has a large overhead, and most companies—only pushing data and very little video—may not even notice the difference for the large overhead and its attendant expense.

ATM appeals mainly to companies that need to deliver synchronized video and sound. The companies that would benefit are movie and entertainment players such as Time-Warner, which wants to deliver on-demand video and sound to your home. Instead of using frames like Ethernet uses, ATM uses 53-byte, fixed-size cells. The first five bytes contain cell-header information, and the remaining 48 bytes contain the "payload" (user information). Small fixed-length cells are best suited for transferring voice and video traffic because they are intolerant of delays that result from having to wait for a large data packet to download (among other network activities). Although ATM is not dependent on a Physical-layer implementation, it does require a medium such as fiber optics to support the amount of bandwidth that's needed to run ATM. At this point, ATM is overkill for most companies passing data, but it has continued to gain popularity over the years and may continue to do so in the future.

Wireless LANs

Wireless LANs are an evolving technology that many companies find worth watching. Although such networks aren't totally wireless, they do primarily use radio or infrared technology to connect subnets to the main body of a network. Although wireless networks are extensions of cabled networks, they cannot replace them. Technically, a few laptops joined together could constitute a wireless network, but, for our purposes, we will consider wireless networks that are connected to wired networks.

Without a doubt, wireless networks have more constrictions and far fewer capabilities than do cabled LANs. But the convenience factor sometimes outweighs the hassle of cabling in a difficult area, and mobility is usually the major benefit.

802.11 B

The IEEE standards committee has identified the 802.11 as the standard for wireless LAN radio systems. This standard specifies signaling at 11Mbps across the radio link. Wireless LANs use specific radio-frequency bands and transmissions to allow the data to be transferred through the air. Although it sounds faster than a wired Ethernet, the practicality is that wireless LANs have much more interference and overhead. The 11Mbps speed is the maximum, and most have tested below that in normal working conditions. Towards the end of 2000, consumers should see wireless speeds of up to 22Mbps.

With most wireless LANs, you have an access point that is connected to a wired network via a coax cable or Ethernet connection. Because most wireless LANs are extensions of a wired LAN, this access point is usually placed up high or in a similar location without many objects around it. The devices you want to connect to the wireless LAN must have a device to communicate with the access point. For laptops, this device is usually just a card to fit in the PCM/CIA slot; for PCs, the card fits like a standard NIC. Short-distance WANs will probably start incorporating wireless LAN technology. If so, expect wireless to replace the high-cost T-1 connections through your phone company.

Bandwidth

One measurement of a network's capabilities is its *bandwidth*, which measures how much information can flow on it at a given time. When speaking about bandwidth, we speak of two types of signals—digital and analog—but, for our purposes, we'll be referring to digital. A basic measurement of bandwidth is *bits per second (bps)*, and a *bit* is described as a cycle of digital information that passes from one location to another.

An easy way to conceptualize the concept of bandwidth is to think of your experiences of gridlock in morning traffic. As the traffic is moving along, more commuters want to get on the freeway, which causes a trigger reaction to slow down and allow more users to join the fun. This phenomenon also happens as a network grows. As networks grow and more users are on it, performance begins to slow. As a network administrator, you might even notice that it is slower at different times of the day. Usually, when you arrive at 8:00 in the morning, the network is much slower than it is at noon. Of course, this is because, in the morning, everyone hops on the computer at the same time, and, around noon, everybody is usually at lunch. Just as freeways are only so big and can handle only so much traffic at any given time, the same applies to bandwidth. The limitations of bandwidth depend upon the cabling used and the applications that are running on the network. You must understand, however, the bandwidth limit of certain cables. Table 2.2 displays different cables and their bandwidth capabilities.

Segmentation of a LAN

Fixing a network's congestion is not always as simple as increasing bandwidth. One thing to look into is the source of all the traffic. Sometimes bad NICs can send out tons of broadcasts onto your network and you would never know. Servers also send broadcasts, and examining these can yield important insight into the problem of network congestion. In general, to avoid jumping to any conclusions about the network, it's best to use a network sniffer so you can know what's really going on. Once you have isolated the issue of network congestion, you can implement devices that are designed to alleviate unnecessary traffic.

Table 2.2   Bandwidth and cables.

Media Type	Bandwidth
50-ohm coax	10Mbps to 1000Mbps
75-ohm coax	10Mbps to 100Mbps
Cat 5	100 Mbps
Multimode fiber	100Mbps
Single-mode fiber	1000Mbps

One way of solving congestion problems and increasing performance on a LAN is to divide a single Ethernet segment into multiple network segments. Doing so reduces the size of the collision domain and maximizes available bandwidth by reducing the number of users on a collision domain. Fortunately, you have at your disposal a few tried-and-true devices to segment a LAN and help relieve Ethernet congestion: bridges, routers, and LAN switches.

Segmenting with a Bridge

Segmenting a LAN with a bridge provides more bandwidth per user because it reduces the number of users on a segment. A bridge can also connect several LANs to relieve collisions. Bridges operate on the Data Link layer or Layer 2, and they dynamically build a forwarding table of information that comprises MAC addresses and their corresponding segments based on the source address. Based on the destination address, the bridge makes a forwarding decision. As we discussed earlier, bridges read the destination MAC or hardware address in each frame; if the frame is not destined for that segment, the bridge forwards it on. By using a bridge to segment the network into smaller pieces, you ensure reliability, manageability, and smaller collision domains.

However, bridges are rarely used in production networks because they do have a few drawbacks—chiefly the amount of latency that they require for overhead processing. The longer distance of the network and the number of devices that some frames must traverse can add latency and potentially cause a serious delay in any large network for the time it takes for the rest of the network to look at the frame. The bridge also lacks the ability to filter broadcast storms: You may have just implemented a bridge to decrease the collision domain, but the bridge is forwarding broadcast storms that can lock up the network. Although it solves one problem of congestion, isn't doesn't do enough to help the useless traffic by broadcast storms.

Segmenting with a LAN Switch

LAN switches use packet switching to enable high-speed data exchanges. The functions of switches are similar to bridges (learning the topology, and forwarding and filtering frames). However, switches support dedicated communication be-tween devices, which increases file-transfer throughput and enables a dedicated collision-free conversation. Switches read the destination MAC address and often forward it before the entire packet is received. This ability results in lower latency and very fast packet forwarding. Switches also give you a higher port density than bridges do, and they cost less than a bridge. In looking at switches, you'll find a switch is really a multiport bridge. Because switches can filter to the port via MAC addresses, the network has fewer collisions, especially compared to a shared environment or hub.

The advantages to a LAN switch include full-duplex communication, media rate adaptation, and easy migration. Also, implementing LAN switches usually doesn't require many changes to the network: you can still use the existing wiring, and you don't have to remove existing hubs. In fact, you can slowly migrate to a switched environment instead of replacing everything all at once. Many companies have been migrating to switched environments as the budget allows.

Segmenting with a Router

A router creates a smaller network—not just a smaller segment—and thus creates a broadcast domain of its own. Routers can connect networks that use different media, and they are generally more useful for segmenting than bridges. As you know, bridges operate at the Data Link layer and filter by MAC addresses, and routers operate at the Network layer and filter by logical address. (A hardware address is found in a frame, and a logical address is found in a packet.) Routers are used to route packets using a logical address, which is usually assigned by a protocol such as IP or IPX. Like bridges, routers also keep a table of where devices are located on the network. The difference, however, is that a bridge keeps track of the hosts or addresses on the network, and the router keeps track of networks, not hosts. Using the routing tables, the router can make an informed routing decision.

By default, routers won't forward broadcasts to the rest of the network, which alleviates unnecessary traffic on the network caused by broadcasts. To make a more informed routing decision, routers use the destination service access point (DSAPs) and service access point (SSAPs) and metric paths. With router segmentation, you'll get more-informed routing decisions, with increased functionality of addressing, flow, error, and congestion control.

Advantages of LAN Segmentation

Some of the advantages of LAN segmentation are achieved by separating the network using various devices. You can create smaller broadcast domains by using routers throughout the network. Also, using switching in the network can drastically reduce the number of collisions and create smaller collision domains, which can allow for high-end devices or demanding applications to be placed on the network with dedicated circuits and less congestion. You can see that it's important to know which devices help you best utilize a network's bandwidth.

Chapter Summary

A variety of LAN topologies are available to fit any network. Knowing the different devices to use to capitalize on your existing network ultimately saves time and money. No one wants to pay for a new infrastructure every time there is a problem. Ethernet technology is most widely used because of its efficiency and its cost.

Ethernet technology is constantly evolving to maintain its status and to stay ahead of the network demands. Ethernet is fairly easy to install because of the wide variety of equipment on the market and the standards that accompany it. Ethernet speed ranges from 10Mbps to 1000Mbps, for a wide variety of networks.

Second to Ethernet's popularity is Token Ring. Although it's a bit pricey in comparison to Ethernet, Token Ring offers greater reliability and more resiliency than Ethernet. Token Ring is great for heavy workloads such as a mainframe environment on a large campus. As with Ethernet, Token Ring has standards and protocols in place to make it a sound LAN, and it has the speed capabilities to compete with other LANs.

FDDI is a dual-ring LAN that can maintain redundancy for your network. FDDI operates at speeds of 100Mbps using fiber optics. Like Token Ring, it uses the token technology. FDDI is best used in campus environments to utilize the capabilities of redundancy at a high speed.

ATM is great for high-speed technologies such as video and voice. Companies such as Time-Warner can appreciate this technology because of its speed over long distances and its flawless transmissions. Most companies, however, do not pass large amounts of video or sound; they send mainly straight data. ATM has such a large overhead, these companies don't need to pay the extra money for ATM simply because they won't fully utilize its capabilities.

Wireless LANs are very convenient and will likely be highly considered for short-distance WANs. Wireless LANs will almost always be connected to a wired network. Although wireless technology boast speeds as high as 11Mbps, they are probably running at a speed of 5Mbps to 7Mbps in reality. However, new wireless capabilities will have speeds up to 22Mbps.

Bandwidth is always the buzz word in most networks. Realizing the amount of bandwidth has limitations, making full use of the current bandwidth is usually sufficient for most network problems.

Segmenting a LAN helps relieve network congestion. First, you have to identify the source of the traffic, and then you can find a solution. Knowing how to segment a LAN is a necessity. Bridges can link several LANs together to reduce the size of the segments. Implementing switches can reduce the size of the collision domains. Routers can also reduce the size of broadcast domains.

Review Questions

2

1. What are the two main LAN technologies in use today? [Choose the two best answers]

   a. Token Ring

   b. FDDI

   c. Ethernet

   d. CSMA/CD

   e. Wireless

   f. ATM

2. Ethernet LAN technology employs which protocol?

   a. FDDI

   b. CSMA/CD

   c. CSMA

   d. RIP

   e. BGP

3. Autonegotiation is used with what type of device?

   a. Hub

   b. Switch

   c. LAN extender

   d. FDDI

   e. Token Ring

4. What is another way to write Gigabit Ethernet?

   a. 10Mbps

   b. 100Mbps

   c. 1000Mbps

   d. 1Mbps

5. What does *UTP* stand for?

   a. Unknown twisted pair

   b. Unusual twisted pair

   c. Unshielded twisted pair

   d. Usual token protocol

6. Token Ring uses a _____ to pass a stream of data in a network.

   a. Full duplex

   b. Broadcast

   c. Baton

   d. Token

   e. Terabit

   f. CSMA/CD

7. How many rings are used in a FDDI network?

   a. 4

   b. 3

   c. 5

   d. 2

   e. 7

   f. 1

8. ATM is used best for networks using lots of _____? [Choose the two best answers]

   a. Data

   b. Video

   c. Sound

   d. Ethernet

   e. Interference

   f. Tokens

9. Which device uses the DSAPs and SSAPs protocols and metric paths to make a more-informed routing decision?

   a. Hub

   b. Repeater

   c. Switch

   d. Router

   e. LAN Extender

   f. FDDI

10. A _____ copies and sends this type of transmission to every destination node on that network?

    a. Unicast

    b. Broadcast

    c. Full duplex

    d. FDDI

    e. Multicast

11. Token Ring employs this mechanism for detecting and compensating for network faults and multiple tokens in a Token Ring network.

    a. Multicast

    b. FDDI

    c. Active monitor

    d. Ethernet

    e. MAU

    f. Token

12. What is the maximum frame size (in bytes) for an Ethernet frame?

    a. 1518

    b. 64

    c. 15

    d. 1510

    e. 1516

    f. 1500

13. The IEEE 802 defines Ethernet as which IEEE standard?

    a. 802.3

    b. 802.5

    c. 802.1

    d. 802.9

    e. 802.11

    f. 803.1

14. What is the minimum frame size for an Ethernet Frame?

    a. 45

    b. 60

    c. 25

    d. 64

    e. 12

    f. 1518

15. What does the acronym *ATM* stand for?

    a. After Time Message

    b. Asynchronous Transfer Mode

    c. Asynchronous Time Management

    d. Associate Team Manager

16. If used to segment the LAN, what device decreases the size of segments and can connect several LANs?

    a. Switch

    b. Hub

    c. Bridge

    d. Router

    e. FDDI

    f. Token Ring

17. When segmenting a LAN, what device reduces the size of a broadcast domain?

    a. Hub

    b. Switch

    c. Router

    d. LAN Extender

    e. Bridge

18. When segmenting a LAN, what device cannot be used to reduce the collision domain?

    a. Bridge

    b. Switch

    c. Hub

    d. Router

19. A Wireless LAN is capable of what speed?

    a. 8Mbps

    b. 16Mbps

    c. 3Mbps

    d. 11Mbps

    e. 100Mbps

    f. 1000Mbps

20. What is the IEEE standard for Wireless LANs with high-rate speeds?

    a. 802.3

    b. 7.03

    c. 802.5

    d. 802.11B

    e. 802.1q

    f. 802.4

2

CHAPTER THREE

Basic Troubleshooting Tools

After completing this chapter, you will be able to:

✓ Recognize various troubleshooting devices

✓ Know how to use basic tools such as Telnet, Ping, and Traceroute

✓ Using commands such as **show** and **debug** to look at router activity

✓ Isolate network problems using **debug** and **traceroute**

✓ Understand the need for Network Monitoring Systems

✓ Know what SNMP is and how it works with Network Monitoring Systems

✓ Use workstation tools to aid in troubleshooting

In this chapter, you will learn how to utilize tools that can help identify the possible causes of TCP/IP network problems. This chapter will teach you the basics of troubleshooting, such as using the **show** and **debug** commands. This chapter shows you general tools to use with routers and desktops to aid in troubleshooting network problems. It provides an overview of network devices, such as packet analyzers and network monitors, without focusing on the details of each. More advanced troubleshooting skills will be discussed throughout this book.

One small, but very critical piece of troubleshooting is documentation. If your network is documented, troubleshooting is much easier. Documentation includes labeling, using descriptions on the router interfaces, and having a router topology with the networks defined.

It is very tedious, but putting labels on fiber and ports will ease the pain in finding where the cabling is connected when a problem arises. If you are in a large campus environment, the network operations center (NOC) may have 30 to 40 pieces of fiber strung across the racks. When you need to find a particular fiber belonging to a network you believe to be down, you will be thankful that you put labels on the port of the device and on the fiber.

Placing a description of the network on the router interfaces will ensure less time being spent scrolling for the correct interface. If an interface only shows an IP address, you will have to correlate it with the correct network and, sometimes, that can be stressful and time-consuming. Taking the time to provide a description will alleviate a lot of headaches in the end, especially when you are in a panic.

Most people are visual creatures and thus like to see a visual overview of the network in order to understand it better. Having a visual router topology identifying the backbone of a network and devices that stem from routers provides easy access to information regarding the network. If your network is a large campus environment, the topology can identify which networks are stemming from different routers, thereby easing the search for a particular subnet or network.

Physical Test Equipment

In troubleshooting, you will find a lot of Layer 1 (Physical) problems. These can be some of the simplest problems to solve, and some of the hardest. So many factors can contribute to errors and loss of connectivity that isolating the exact problem may be hard at times. Noise levels, heat, or humidity can all make subtle changes that affect cabling or devices. Luckily, tools are available that can help in testing physical infrastructure, such as volt-ohm and digital meters (devices that measure parameters such as AC and DC voltage, currents, resistance, and cable continuity) and time domain reflectors (TDRs), which can isolate a break in the cabling. Knowing the different types of equipment and how and when to use them can alleviate a lot of headaches for troubleshooting.

Cable Testers

A cable tester is a must for anyone who works with the infrastructure in the network. Because so many Layer 1 problems are possible, you need to be able to isolate such problems and fix them quickly. Cable testers can be used to test for physical connectivity on the existing wiring. Different types of cable testers exist, and some can be for general use while others may focus on a specific type of cabling.

One of the most common types of cable testers focuses on 10BaseT or 100BaseT UTP for Ethernet networks. Specific testers are made for fiber-optic cabling, but they are used mainly by companies that install fiber because of the expense. By using a cable tester for Ethernet, you can find problems with physical connectivity, test the wire mapping, and report cable conditions, including near-end crosstalk (NEXT), attenuation, and noise. Figure 3.1 shows an example of a cable tester.

If you are using an advanced cable tester, you can configure the tester with an IP address to test for LAN connectivity, as well as display MAC addresses, provide information about LAN traffic, and provide a generic look at network utilization. You also can perform tests such as **ping** and **arp** to test the LAN connectivity, which report the time a packet takes to reach a destination. In a large campus environment, cable tester devices are helpful in testing the basic equipment, such as data jacks and connectivity. Cable testers are usually compact in size, and because of their capabilities (if you are using an advanced tester), you can do a lot of testing with one device. This will alleviate carrying a combination of devices, such as a laptop, cable tester, and analyzer.

Time Domain Reflectors

Time domain reflectors (TDRs) are sophisticated and complex cable testers. They not only will report a problem with a cable but also can isolate where the problem is on the cable. Some of the problems TDRs look for are open circuits, short circuits, crimped wires, and anything that may inhibit the connectivity on the wire. Figure 3.2 shows a TDR.

Figure 3.1   Cable testers are a necessity in a large network.

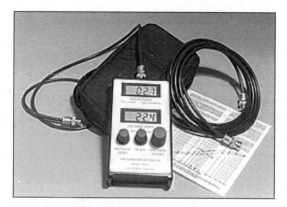

Figure 3.2 Using TDRs will save a lot of time in cable testing.

TDRs work with a principle similar to **ping**. A TDR sends an electronic signal down the wire, and the TDR waits until the same signal returns to the device, reporting the time intervals from sending and receiving. When the TDR receives the signal back, it looks at the signal for any abnormalities, such as with the signal strength and amplitude, and determines whether a problem exists. If the TDR detects a problem, it helps determine where the problem could be located. Depending on the signal, the TDR reports whether the problem is a short, a crimp, open cabling, or any other abnormality. The TDR determines where on the cable the signal may be failing by looking at the time factor of receiving the signal. TDRs usually can determine where on the cable the problem exists within a foot or two of the actual cause. This type of equipment is imperative to have when you are looking at thousands of wires that may be 100 to 200 feet each.

Optical time domain reflectors (OTDRs) are another type of TDR. OTDRs test exclusively for fiber-optic cabling using optical pulses rather than electronic signals. OTDRs and TDRs test using the same principle of sending and receiving a signal. After receiving the signal, the testers analyze the signal for abnormalities.

Router Troubleshooting Commands

Because your network is not failure-proof, you need to know how to use basic troubleshooting tools to isolate and fix any problems that might arise. If it were a criminal investigation, the devices would be the interviewees. The Cisco IOS has a few basic troubleshooting tools that help isolate any network problems. The four most basic command types for the Cisco IOS are as follows:

➤ *Show commands*—Report the status of a router, monitor network performance and congestion, and help in detecting and isolating network problems, including router interfaces, nodes, media, servers, and applications.

➤ *Debug commands*—Check the traffic flow on an interface (including protocol-specific traffic), report error messages generated by nodes, and provide information about overall traffic. Debug commands are helpful in isolating problems rather than monitoring problems.

➤ *Ping commands*—Enable you to see the connectivity of the network by sending ICMP messages and receiving a response from the destination.

➤ *Trace commands*—Enable you to monitor the path from the source address to the destination address, recording the path in hops.

As a network administrator, you likely will be notified at some point that a user can't reach a device, and will be asked whether something is wrong with the network. A good rule in troubleshooting is to use various tools, such as those just described, to isolate your problem area. The best way to do this is to use a source address and a destination address. Use the **show** commands to help you navigate the interfaces. You may use **ping** to verify whether the two hosts are communicating. If **ping** reports a "time out," the next step is to use a traceroute to identify a possible point of failure. After you use traceroute to identify a possible point of failure, use the **debug** commands to isolate the problem. Using the troubleshooting tools in conjunction with one another is very helpful, but each also can be used alone.

show Commands

If you have ever reviewed a book of Cisco IOS commands, you are aware that literally hundreds of **show** commands are available. The reason they are so numerous is that they are so helpful in giving insight of what is happening on the router or interface. After you apply a **show** command, the IOS will "take a picture" of the current traffic on the interface, including packets, events, configurations, and processes—just to name a few.

The various **show** commands are based on the IOS that your router is running and the router's purpose. To see your **show** commands, type "show ?" at the User and Exec mode. The following is an example of a few **show** commands that you may use in troubleshooting your network; so many options exist for the **show** command that the list has been scaled down to the most commonly used commands:

```
Support#show ?
  access-lists     List access lists
  accounting       Accounting data for active sessions
  arp              ARP table
  async            Information on terminal lines used as router interfaces
  buffers          Buffer pool statistics
  cdp              CDP information
  context          Show context information about recent crash(s)
```

```
controllers          Interface controller status
debugging            State of each debugging option
frame-relay          Frame-rRelay information
interfaces           Interface status and configuration
ip                   IP information
logging              Show the contents of logging buffers
ppp                  PPP parameters and statistics
processes            Active process statistics
protocols            Active network routing protocols
queue                Show queue contents
rmon                 rmon statistics
route-map            route-map information
running-config       Current operating configuration
sessions             Information about Telnet connections
snapshot             Snapshot parameters and statistics
snmp                 snmp statistics
startup-config       Contents of startup configuration
tacacs               Shows tacacs+ server statistics
tarp                 TARP information
tcp                  Status of TCP connections
terminal             Display terminal configuration parameters
translate            Protocol translation information
ttycap               Terminal capability tables
users                Display information about terminal lines
version              System hardware and software status
vlans                Virtual LANs Information
x25                  X.25 information
xns                  XNS information
xremote              XRemote statistics
```

One of the most common **show** commands that you will use is **show interfaces**, which enables you to see what is happening on all the interfaces on the router. It gives you a quick glance at an interface by indicating whether it is up or down, by providing a bit of information on its configuration, and by providing a look at the packets on it. The following is example output from **show interfaces**:

Note: The following code is designed to give you only the basic principle, and thus has been truncated.

```
Support#show interfaces
Async1 is down, line protocol is down
  Hardware is Async Serial
  MTU 1500 bytes, BW 9 Kbit, DLY 100000 usec,
     reliability 255/255, txload 1/255, rxload 1/255
  Encapsulation SLIP, loopback not set
```

```
Ethernet2/1 is up, line protocol is up
  Hardware is cxBus Ethernet, address is 1203.ef12.1d41 (bia
1203.ef12.1d41)
  Description: Subnet 211 for Pismo Beach Site
  Internet address is 198.132.211.254/24
  MTU 1500 bytes, BW 10000 Kbit, DLY 1000 usec,
     reliability 255/255, txload 4/255, rxload 1/255
  Encapsulation ARPA, loopback not set
  Keepalive set (10 sec)
  ARP type: ARPA, ARP Timeout 04:00:00
  Last input 00:00:00, output 00:00:05, output hang never
  Last clearing of "show interface" counters never
  Queueing strategy: fifo
  Output queue 0/40, 22591 drops; input queue 0/75, 929 drops
  5 minute input rate 44000 bits/sec, 25 packets/sec
  5 minute output rate 174000 bits/sec, 23 packets/sec
     293110943 packets input, 4194038437 bytes, 0 no buffer
     Received 42837453 broadcasts, 0 runts, 0 giants, 71 throttles
     0 input errors, 0 CRC, 0 frame, 0 overrun, 25 ignored
     0 input packets with dribble condition detected
     264542130 packets output, 1810892381 bytes, 0 underruns
     0 output errors, 31586499 collisions, 2 interface resets
     0 babbles, 0 late collision, 0 deferred
     0 lost carrier, 0 no carrier
     0 output buffer failures, 0 output buffers swapped out
Ethernet2/2 is administratively down, line protocol is down
  Hardware is cxBus Ethernet, address is 1203.ef12.1d42 (bia
1203.ef12.1d42)
  Description: Subnet 212 Monterey Site
  Internet address is 198.132.212.254/24
  MTU 1500 bytes, BW 10000 Kbit, DLY 1000 usec,
     reliability 255/255, txload 1/255, rxload 1/255
  Encapsulation ARPA, loopback not set
  Keepalive set (10 sec)
  ARP type: ARPA, ARP Timeout 04:00:00
  Last input never, output never, output hang never
  Last clearing of "show interface" counters never
  Queueing strategy: fifo
  Output queue 0/40, 0 drops; input queue 0/75, 0 drops
  5 minute input rate 0 bits/sec, 0 packets/sec
  5 minute output rate 0 bits/sec, 0 packets/sec
Support#
```

The preceding code shows you the status of each interface along with a description and packet status the interface is currently operating. Also notice that the purpose of each interface is described under its name. This is an example of using the description field in the IOS help identify interfaces, especially when troubleshooting. Too often, administrators spend too much time searching for the correct interface to troubleshoot, or troubleshooting the wrong interface.

Another **show** command that may be useful is the **show arp** command, which is very helpful when you're trying to locate a particular device on your network. The ARP cache records all the devices that have traversed the router. The ARP cache lasts only for a short time after the device is no longer on the network, so this command is time-sensitive. By using this command, you can find the MAC address and associate it to an IP address on the network, enabling you to see how long the device was on the network. The **arp** command also identifies which interface the devices are using. The following is example output from **show arp**:

```
Support#show arp
Protocol   Address            Age (min)   Hardware Addr    Type    Interface
Internet   198.132.210.254                0083.12eb.1dd5   ARPA    Ethernet2/1
Internet   198.132.51.224            3    00a0.b8be.9512   ARPA    Ethernet2/4
Internet   198.132.201.65           63    0080.5abc.55b4   ARPA    Ethernet2/5
Internet   198.132.211.135         221    0010.c11d.55f5   ARPA    Ethernet2/2
Internet   198.132.211.134           3    0080.bbbe.002a   ARPA    Ethernet2/2
Internet   198.132.210.203          63    00a0.123a.15d6   ARPA    Ethernet2/1
Internet   198.132.210.104          89    0080.aebb.4011   ARPA    Ethernet2/1
Internet   198.132.210.122         146    0060.bas0.128e   ARPA    Ethernet2/1
Internet   198.132.210.220           3    0800.000c.d112   ARPA    Ethernet2/1
Internet   198.132.51.204           88    0080.54bb.610f   ARPA    Ethernet2/4
Internet   198.132.51.106            3    0800.021e.5b97   ARPA    Ethernet2/4
Internet   198.132.210.199           4    08a7.2c12.54f9   ARPA    Ethernet2/1
Internet   198.132.210.214          92    08a6.0912.10e4   ARPA    Ethernet2/1
Internet   198.132.211.191           3    08a5.9854.5b86   ARPA    Ethernet2/2
Internet   198.132.211.197          63    0000.dddd.9170   ARPA    Ethernet2/2
Supoort#
```

You can gather a vast amount of information about a specific subject by using the **show** commands. Once again, using the **show ?** command in the Exec and privileged modes is the best way to see the **show** commands available on your routers. The privileged mode has a lot more command options for using the **show** command to aid in troubleshooting.

debug Commands

When you suspect that a problem exists on an interface or a router, use the **debug** command. Although the **debug** command is a great tool for isolating network problems, it is not very useful for monitoring the network because of its impact on the router when it is applied. When the **debug** command is used in EXEC mode, it provides information such as traffic seen or not seen, error messages, protocol-specific diagnostic packets, and other types of information.

This sounds like a wonderful monitoring tool, but before you rush out and apply it to every router you have, you need to realize the overhead this command generates. Using the **debug** command forces the router to process every packet entering the router, causing a hardship on the route processor. When the router is "debugging," the route processor has to run, manage, and analyze every packet that enters the router. This amount of overhead on a router might cause it to fail, or run entirely too slow for the amount of traffic trying to be routed. For this reason, the **debug** command should be used sparingly and only when you know a problem exists.

Implementing the **debug** Command

Before you apply a **debug** command, you need to check a few things. First, you should make sure that a time/date stamp is being applied to all messages that are reported. Using this tool enables you to see when events are happening and correlate this information to any other problems your network may be experiencing. If you are not directly connected to the console port of the router, you must apply a **terminal monitor** command to see the debugging. By default, debugging is sent to the console port of the router. Most of the time, you are telneting to the router and are not able to connect to the console port. The **terminal monitor** command enables you to see the dubugging while you are connected via Telnet. The following code shows how to implement the **debug** commands on a router:

```
Support#
Support#terminal monitor
Support#
Support#config t
Support(config)#service timestamps debug datetime msec localtime
Support(config)#service timestamps log datetime msec localtime
Support(config)#^Z
Support#
```

The preceding commands provide terminal monitoring and the application of time/date stamps to the logging results. The following is a partial listing of the possible **debug** commands that can be used on the router:

```
Support#
Support#debug ?
  aaa              AAA Authentication, Authorization and Accounting
  all              Enable all debugging
  arp              IP ARP and HP Probe transactions
  async            Async interface information
  cdp              CDP information
  custom-queue     Custom output queueing
  domain           Domain Name System
  eigrp            EIGRP Protocol information
```

```
ethernet-interface   Ethernet network interface events
ip                    IP information
isdn                  ISDN information
lapb                  LAPB protocol transactions
list                  Set interface or/and access list for the next debug
                      command
nvram                 Debug NVRAM behavior
packet                Log unknown packets
ppp                   PPP (Point-to-Point Protocol) information
priority              Priority output queueing
serial                Serial interface information
snmp                  SNMP information
tacacs                TACACS authentication and authorization
tbridge               Transparent Bridging
telnet                Incoming telnet connections
tftp                  TFTP packets
tunnel                Generic Tunnel Interface
x25                   X.25 information
Support#
```

Just like the **show** commands, the **debug** commands enable you to isolate a particular type of information that your troubleshooting leads you to. You can debug ISDN events if you are working with an ISDN problem, and the router will report all the events that are happening on the ISDN. Applying the command is a simple task, as demonstrated in the following code and output of the ISDN debugging:

```
Supoort#
Support#debug isdn events
ISDN events debugging is on
Support#show logging
ISDN BR0: Outgoing call id = 0x800B
ISDN BR0: Event: Call to 2518971 at 64 Kb/s
ISDN BR0: Event: incoming ces value = 2
ISDN BR0: received HOST_PROCEEDING pa
ISDN BR0: Event: incoming ces value = 2
ISDN BR0: received HOST_CONNECT
%LINK-3-UPDOWN: Interface BRIO:2, changed state to up
BRI 0 B2: Set bandwidth to 64Kb

ISDN BR0: Event: Connected to 2518971 on B2 at 64 Kb/sck
%LINEPROTO-5-UPDOWN: Line protocol on Interface BRIO:2, changed state to up
%ISDN-6-CONNECT: Interface BRIO:2 is now connected to 2518971 Support
Support#
```

When you use the **debug** command, the router spits out tons of information all at once, probably more information than you ever wanted to know. After you look at the information that you need to help diagnose the problem, you should turn off debugging and the terminal monitoring. This alleviates the stress the router may be experiencing while debugging. It may look like the router is not responding because it is overwhelmed, but it will eventually process your request. One of the easiest ways to stop debugging is to use the **undebug all** command. This will stop all debugging.

Warning! When using the **debug** commands, take into consideration the overhead placed on the router. Be careful when using the command **debug all**, because it will generate so much output that it may bring the router down.

Knowing how to use the **debug** command properly will alleviate a lot of headaches for troubleshooting a router as it spits out so much information about every process the router is operating, it will take you far more time to find the small piece of information you are looking for. One of the main things to remember about the **debug** command is that you should use it only when you know a problem exists with the router, not as a constant monitor of the router.

PING

The ping (Packet Internet Groper) tool is probably the most widely used tool in network troubleshooting. It is an easy tool to use to test the reachability of a network destination and to prove/disprove network connectivity. Ping provides the quickest test of connectivity between routers and other devices. By using the **ping** command, you send an Internet Control Message Protocol (ICMP) message (or echo request) to a particular host and wait to see whether the host you are trying to reach is working. Every device (that is using IP) will respond to an ICMP echo request with an ICMP echo reply if the device is working. While the ICMP request is being sent, ping starts to time the delivery of the reply and reports back how long it took to receive the reply request.

Although using the ping tool is very helpful, you have to keep in mind that the amount of information you receive from it can be limited. For example, if you want to test network paths between networks, echo requests and echo replies may use different paths in large, redundant networks. This might give the impression that all devices within the network path are working, when in actuality many paths may be broken. Similarly, ICMP echo request packets may be dropped due to congestion, so ping may give the false impression that the target host is not working.

Exec Mode Ping

The **ping** command can be used in the exec and privilege mode of a Cisco router and will work with various protocols, including IP, IPX, AppleTalk, DECnet, and more. When using the **ping** command in exec mode, the router sends five ICMP messages at a time and waits two seconds for each request to return with a reply. If the device you are trying to ping is working properly, code similar to the following example is displayed:

```
Support>
Support>ping 198.132.210.25
Type escape sequence to abort.
Sending 5, 100-byte ICMP Echos to 198.132.210.25, timeout is 2 seconds:
!!!!!
Success rate is 100 percent (5/5), round-trip min/avg/max = 1/1/4 ms
Support>
```

The ! symbol is indicating that the device at 198.132.210.25 sent back a reply and the device is responding properly. The following is an example of an unsuccessful ping:

```
Support>
Support>ping 198.132.210.26

Type escape sequence to abort.
Sending 5, 100-byte ICMP Echos to 198.132.210.26, timeout is 2 seconds:
.....
Success rate is 0 percent (0/5)
Support>
```

The "." symbol in the preceding block indicates that the request has "timed out" and the request is not being returned from 198.132.210.26. Also notice that the timeout is set at two seconds for the message to time out.

Privileged Mode Ping

In the privilege mode of the router, you can do an extended ping, which enables you to monitor a large number of packets traversing the network. With standard ping, the **ping** command sends out only a small number of packets. Most networks will return successful pings not allowing you to see whether the network is running very slow or losing packets because the small amounts of packets being passed over the network. Sending small amounts of data usually are not a great test for network slowness. Using the extended ping will get a better test of how the network is operating. When you send an extended ping, you are allowed to see any possible slowness or packet loss. Be careful when sending numerous packets onto a network that is already congested, because doing so may make the network even slower or possibly make it go down, trying to respond to enormous ICMP requests and replys. The following is an example of sending a successful extended ping:

```
Support#
Support#ping
Protocol [ip]:
Target IP address: 198.132.210.25
Repeat count [5]: 10
Datagram size [100]: 150
Timeout in seconds [2]:
Extended commands [n]: y
Source address or interface: 119.52.41.1
Type of service [0]:
Set DF bit in IP header? [no]:
Validate reply data? [no]:
Data pattern [0xABCD]:
Loose, Strict, Record, Timestamp, Verbose[none]:
Sweep range of sizes [n]:
Type escape sequence to abort.
Sending 10, 150-byte ICMP Echos to 198.132.210.25, timeout is 2 seconds:
!!!!!!!!!!
Success rate is 100 percent (10/10), round-trip min/avg/max = 1/2/4 ms
Support#
```

Of course, not all ping requests will be 100 percent successful. Sending extended pings enables you to see dropped packets even if the standard ping is successful. When sending an extended ping with large datagrams, the ping tool may hang and report the problem as a "." symbol in between "!!!!" successful replies. This "." symbol implies a dropped packet and will probably look similar to "!!!!!!!.!!!!!". An occasional dropped packet isn't unusual if you are sending large ping counts with a large datagram size. The following is an example of an unsuccessful extended ping request:

```
Support#
Support#ping
Protocol [ip]:
Target IP address: 198.132.210.26
Repeat count [5]: 10
Datagram size [100]: 150
Timeout in seconds [2]:
Extended commands [n]: y
Source address or interface:
Type of service [0]:
Set DF bit in IP header? [no]:
Validate reply data? [no]:
Data pattern [0xABCD]:
Loose, Strict, Record, Timestamp, Verbose[none]:
Sweep range of sizes [n]:
Type escape sequence to abort.
```

```
Sending 10, 150-byte ICMP Echos to 198.132.210.26, timeout is 2 seconds:
.......
Success rate is 0 percent (0/10)
Support#
```

The "." symbol indicates that no reply was received from the device and that the device is not responding properly. If this is a mission-critical device that is supposed to be up and running, the "." symbol is not a good sign, because it means the device is not responding properly.

Traceroute

When troubleshooting a path on a network, it is a good idea to start with the source and the destination to isolate the problem. In using the **ping** command, you can establish whether a given destination is reachable. But, if **ping** fails, it doesn't tell you whether the device is unreachable or the network needed to reach the device is not working. Traceroute enables you to trace your steps to reach the destination device, and if it does not reach the destination, it tells you where it failed on the network. For example, traceroute will map each intermediate router on the way from host A to host F, reporting routers as hops in the network. After finding the point of failure, you can start from the opposite direction and work your way back. Traceroute has a maximum value of 30 hops before it will stop tracing the route.

Traceroute works by causing each router along the path to send back an ICMP error message that is generated by expired TTL values in the IP packet header. The IP packets contain a time-to-live (TTL) value, which the router decrements until it reaches 0, at which point the router discards the packet and sends an ICMP TTL Exceeded message back to the source address, allowing traceroute to send its first packet with a TTL value of 1. When the first router decrements this value and sends back the ICMP error message, traceroute discovers the first router. It then sends a packet with a TTL value of 2, which the first router decrements and routes. The second router decrements it to 0, which causes it to send an ICMP error message, allowing traceroute to learn the second hop. Traceroute continues until it causes each router along the path to send an ICMP error message and identify itself. When the TTL reaches the destination host, it is complete.

Traceroute is a great troubleshooting tool but there are a few things you should know about traceroute before using it. Traceroute will not report a device if the device hasn't been configured correctly, does not conform to the IP standards, or because it is blocked by a firewall. A firewall can be configured to block out certain ports and will not allow for a traceroute and the traceroute will not report back a route. The following is example code of a traceroute in the privilege mode:

```
Supoort#
Support#trace
Protocol [ip]:
Target IP address: 198.132.210.25
Source address:
Numeric display [n]:
Timeout in seconds [3]: 2
Probe count [3]:
Minimum Time to Live [1]:
Maximum Time to Live [30]:
Port Number [33434]:
Loose, Strict, Record, Timestamp, Verbose[none]:
Type escape sequence to abort.
Tracing the route to 198.132.210.25
  1 172.79.2.11 4 msec 0 msec 4 msec
  2 128.120.239.1 0 msec 4 msec 0 msec
  3 198.32.249.29 4 msec 4 msec 4 msec
  4 198.32.249.70 4 msec 4 msec 4 msec
  5 206.24.211.133 4 msec 4 msec 4 msec
  6 204.70.9.131 8 msec 8 msec 8 msec
  7 204.70.4.81 12 msec 8 msec 8 msec
  8 206.157.77.66 12 msec 8 msec 12 msec
  9 144.232.4.33 8 msec 8 msec 12 msec
 10 144.232.4.78 12 msec 8 msec 12 msec
 11 192.31.7.9 20 msec 24 msec 20 msec
 12 198.132.210.25 20 msec 24msec 20msec
Support#
```

Notice that traceroute shows every hop on the left side of the traceroute. The traceroute also reports the IP address of each hop the packet takes along the way, reporting the time before the packet reaches its destination. The preceding sample code shows a successful traceroute reaching its destination. Usually, you use traceroute because the path was unsuccessful, and you want to know where the problem may lie. The following code shows an example of a traceroute that does not reach its destination and indicates where the trace stops:

```
Support#
Support#trace
Protocol [ip]:
Target IP address: 198.132.210.25
Source address:
Numeric display [n]:
Timeout in seconds [3]: 2
Probe count [3]:
Minimum Time to Live [1]:
```

```
Maximum Time to Live [30]:
Port Number [33434]:
Loose, Strict, Record, Timestamp, Verbose[none]:
Type escape sequence to abort.
Tracing the route to 198.132.210.25
  1 172.79.2.11 4 msec 0 msec 4 msec
  2 128.120.239.1 0 msec 4 msec 0 msec
  3 198.32.249.29 4 msec 4 msec 4 msec
  4 198.32.249.70 4 msec 4 msec 4 msec
  5 206.24.211.133 4 msec 4 msec 4 msec
  6 204.70.9.131 8 msec 8 msec 8 msec
  7 204.70.4.81 12 msec 8 msec 8 msec
  8 206.157.77.66 12 msec 8 msec 12 msec
  9 144.232.4.33 8 msec 8 msec 12 msec
 10 144.232.4.78 12 msec 8 msec 12 msec
 11 *  *  *
 12 144.232.4.78 !H  *  *
Support#
```

The point of failure is at the hop beyond 144.232.4.78. You have now isolated the problem from 144.232.4.78 to 198.132.210.25, and can start troubleshooting the path in between these devices. The best solution is to start from your target of 198.132.210.25 and work your way back to the point of failure.

Telnet

Telnet is the TCP/IP standard network virtual terminal protocol used for remote terminal emulation. Using Telnet as a troubleshooting tool sometimes is more efficient than using ping or traceroute, because Telnet runs on top of the TCP protocol. Even if a device is not working properly, it may send an echo reply to an ICMP message, giving the impression that the device is working properly. By running on top of the TCP protocol, Telnet establishes a more reliable indicator of connectivity than do ICMP echo requests, because Telnet is operating at a higher level. Telnet enables you to log in to a device and check for connectivity, rather than receiving a reply from the device.

Telnet acts as a dummy terminal for the device you are connecting to. Telnet is widely used in connecting to routers because most companies have routers offsite, and Telnet enables you to communicate from your desk. Why walk around with a router console cable when you can Telnet from your office? You can use Telnet from virtually any OS and from routers.

After you are logged in to a router, the IOS enables you to telnet to another router while you are still logged in to the first one. The following code shows an example of Telnet in the IOS:

```
Support#
Support#telnet 198.132.211.197
Trying 198.132.211.197... Open


User Access Verification

Username: ggalbraith
Password:

CCNP#sh version Cisco Internetwork Operating System Software
IOS (tm) 7200 Software (C7200-IS56-M), Version 11.3(5), RELEASE SOFTWARE
(fc1)
Copyright (c) 1986-1998 by cisco Systems, Inc.
Compiled Tue 11-Aug-98 06:39 by phanguye
Image text-base: 0x600088E0, data-base: 0x60976000

ROM: System Bootstrap, Version 11.1(10) [dschwart 10], RELEASE SOFTWARE
(fc1)
BOOTFLASH: 7200 Software (C7200-BOOT-M), Version 11.1(16)CA, EARLY DEPLOY-
MENT RE
LEASE SOFTWARE (fc1)

CCNP uptime is 20 weeks, 4 days, 16 hours, 11 minutes
CCNP#exit

[Connection to 198.132.211.197 closed by foreign host]
Support#
```

Desktop Support

Most large networks require a help desk group for users to call when they are experiencing network or computer problems. A help desk can use the basic tools included with the operating system to aid in solving many user problems. The Windows 95/98/2000, Windows NT, and Unix operating systems include many tools that enable administrators to perform basic troubleshooting of a desktop computer and aid in troubleshooting network problems. The tools are simple to use, and they tell you a lot about network activity right from your desk.

Windows Support

Windows 95/98, Windows 2000 Professional, and Windows NT Workstation contain several tools for performing network tests. One of the first things that most people in the networking world learn is the ability to use ping from the DOS prompt. It is very simple and lets you know about network connectivity from your desktop as well as the health of the network. The golden rule is "If you can ping, you have network connectivity." Pinging from your desktop enables you to look at connectivity of other machines as well as the desktop you are using. The output looks a little different from the output of a router IOS, but it performs the same function, as the following example output demonstrates:

```
C:\WINDOWS\Desktop>ping 198.132.211.197
Pinging 198.132.211.197 with 32 bytes of data:

Reply from 198.132.211.197: bytes=32 time=30ms TTL=125
Reply from 198.132.211.197: bytes=32 time=29ms TTL=125
Reply from 198.132.211.197: bytes=32 time=29ms TTL=125
Reply from 198.132.211.197: bytes=32 time=29ms TTL=125

Ping statistics for 198.132.211.197:
    Packets: Sent = 4, Received = 4, Lost = 0 (0% loss)
Approximate round trip times in milli-seconds:
    Minimum = 29ms, Maximum =  30ms, Average =  29ms
```

A few other commands that are helpful in troubleshooting connectivity problems are **winipcfg** and **ipconfig**. Windows 95/98/2000 uses **winipcfg**, and Windows NT uses **ipconfig**, but these commands do the same thing. If you want to run **winipcfg** from Windows 95/98, click Start, click Run, and then type "winipcfg". A window appears displaying the MAC address of the device, the IP address, default gateway, and subnet mask. This enables you to check your configurations for the machine to join the network if you are experiencing problems getting the device to communicate on the network. For Windows NT, you can use the DOS prompt and type "ipconfig" to receive information concerning the same IP settings as Windows 95/98/2000.

Another commonly used command in Windows is **netstat**, which enables you to look at various protocol statistics and connections. The following is a list of possible commands to use with the **netstat** command:

```
NETSTAT [-a] [-e] [-n] [-s] [-p proto] [-r] [interval]

   -a           Displays all connections and listening ports.
   -e           Displays Ethernet statistics. This may be combined with the
   -s           option.
   -n           Displays addresses and port numbers in numerical form.
   -p proto     Shows connections for the protocol specified by proto;
                proto may be TCP or UDP. If used with the -s option to
                display per-protocol statistics, proto may be TCP, UDP,
                or IP.
   -r           Displays the routing table.
```

```
      -s          Displays per-protocol statistics. By default, statistics
                  are shown for TCP, UDP and IP; the -p option may be used
                  to specify a subset of the default.
   interval       Redisplays selected statistics, pausing interval seconds
                  between each display. Press CTRL+C to stop redisplaying
                  statistics. If omitted, netstat will print the current
                  configuration information once.
```

Unix

On Unix machines, a few commands are available that can be used to help in troubleshooting a network or a machine. One of the commands used in Unix is **netstat**. By using various combinations of **netstat** (similar to Windows IOS), you can see the connections of Unix sockets, TCP, UDP, RAW, addresses, statistics, and routing tables on the machine.

Another commonly used command in Unix is **ifconfig**. This is very similar to the Windows version of **winipcfg**. The **ifconfig** command is actually a utility that enables you to configure your machine for the network and verify your configurations. Because the machine is being configured to run on a TCP/IP network, the configurations of the IP address, subnet mask, and default gateway are very similar to those for Windows. For a machine to run on a TCP/IP network, these are basic configurations for the protocol.

Network Management Systems

As networks have grown larger over the years, so has the need for a better monitoring system. As the number of devices you have on your network increases, the complexity, monitoring, and possible number of network failures also increase. Network management has been defined by the International Organization for Standardization (ISO) as having five key areas: accounting management, configuration and name management, fault management, performance management, and security management. Fault management and configuration management are the two areas of network management that deal with troubleshooting.

Configuration management relies on the initial configuration of devices with agents to be able to be seen and communicate on the network, and report to a central monitoring system. The network will be configured centrally to interact with the devices and respond to network upgrades the administrator may implement. The centrally monitored network will also be able to respond to failures and be able to recover quickly. This is where fault management comes into play. Fault management is described as an abnormal network event, which is usually defined as failing components or an excessive amount of errors. With early intervention of any network faults, the network downtime is minimal to none.

Network management systems (NMSs) use different methods to discover the network. The NMS begins by utilizing a central device to slowly discover anything that is configured for the central device to see. For the discovering device to be able to identify the network devices, those devices must contain information of the type the discovering device is searching for. Along with the discovery of the network, an NMS uses monitoring to be able to keep track of the network.

Network Monitors

When you think of a network monitor, you might think of it as a particular device or piece of equipment. However, a network monitor consists mainly of software that oversees the network monitoring. Network monitors continuously monitor the packets that are traversing the network, and track the information to provide a current snapshot of the network activity. Even though a network monitor looks at the packets, it does not analyze the packets.

A network monitor's main function is to keep track of all the statistical information about the network to provide a *baseline*, an average sample (using statistical data) of the activity on the network. After a baseline has been established, it can be configured to report any network activity that is considered abnormal. The most common protocol used in network monitoring is the Simple Network Management Protocol (SNMP), discussed later in this chapter. Network monitors alleviate the headache of trying to manually monitor the network all day, every day. Network monitors collect several pieces of information that enable you to see an accurate picture of the network. Some information a network monitoring system may gather includes the following:

➤ The number of packets being received or transmitted

➤ The size of the packets being sent and received

➤ Any errors in the packets

➤ Network utilization statistics

➤ Identities of hosts and their MAC addresses

➤ Connectivity with other devices

➤ Baseline statistics

➤ Average performance

Simple Network Management Protocol

A large network environment has hundreds and possibly thousands of devices promising a flawless network, especially in a large campus environment that is maintained 24 hours a day, 7 days a week. A network administrator or a group of network administrators can't possibly monitor all the devices without a monitoring system in place. An online system needs to be in place to control and report any network faults, as well as any performance, security, and accounting issues. Online systems that use SNMP have proven to be dependable. SNMP is a reporting and signaling protocol that enables network devices to exchange detailed device information about monitored devices.

SNMP enables you to monitor network utilization, performance, uptime, and even traffic on ports for up to thousands of devices. Because most current network devices communicate with SNMP, an NMS can scan a network in about an hour, whereas it would take days for someone to physically walk around to all the devices and monitor each LAN or WAN segment. An SNMP online system enables system administrators to monitor the whole network from a central point, which can be anywhere from a network operations center to the desktop of the system administrator. To have your network managed by SNMP, you have to implement the following types of devices:

➤ *Managed devices*—Any node (including routers, servers, switches, computers, or printers) on your network running an SNMP agent that is being monitored. The agent collects management information and sends it back to the NMSs using SNMP.

➤ *Agent*—The actual software module that runs on the managed devices and enables SNMP to communicate with the devices. The major requirement of the agent is to gather statistical information and store it in a *management information base (MIB)*, a directory of the information and resources collected from the network that pertain to network management. The agent can also send traps or alarms, depending on the events happening on the network and how the agent is configured.

➤ *Network management system*—An application that provides control and management of the devices connected to it. The information is gathered by the managed devices, and is sent back to the NMSs to monitor the network.

For the SNMP manager and the agent to communicate, the SNMP *community string* must be set. The community string can be thought of as a string of passwords that need to be set to permit access to the agent on the router. Strings or community names can be created with the characteristics of access control lists, read-only rights, read-write rights, and MIB views. The string can be made up of characteristics that associate the access with the string name. For example, you can set a string name of **Cisco** that allows access to a specific MIB, or you can assign a string name of **Router** that associates read-only or read and write permissions for specified MIB objects. To configure a community string, use the following commands in Global Configuration Mode:

```
Support(config)#
Support(config)#snmp-server community router ?
  <1-99>  Std IP accesslist allowing access with this community string
ro      Read-only access with this community string
rw      Read-write access with this community string
view    Restrict this community to a named MIB view
Support(config)#snmp-server community router ro
Support(config)#snmp-server community Cisco rw
Support(config)#snmp-server community Support view ?
  WORD  MIB view to which this community has access
Support#
```

TRAPS

A *trap* is an SNMP notification of an event that the router transmits to an NMS at the time of a severe network change. The event for which a trap should be sent can be defined by the network administrator. Configuring traps in your network will make life a lot easier for you as a network administrator, because you will be notified of any network problems when they happen. The trap is sent to the central location, thus triggering an alarm. Most systems are configured to alert a pager, for a faster response time, and usually enable you to be one step ahead of users' calls. Hopefully, with the few moments of advanced notice from the network monitoring system, you can fix the problem before it has a large impact on users.

A trap is sent only once and is discarded as soon as it is sent so that it does not cause any congestion on the network, especially in cases in which the network may be suffering from congestion already. You can configure the router to send a trap to the central location when a network problem occurs, thereby sending an alarm. The following is an example of how to configure a router to send traps:

```
Support#
Support(config) #snmp-server enable traps ?
  appn          Enable SNMP appn traps
  bgp           Enable BGP state change traps
  config        Enable SNMP config traps
  dlsw          Enable SNMP dlsw traps
  entity        Enable SNMP entity traps
  frame-relay   Enable SNMP frame-relay traps
  isdn          Enable SNMP isdn traps
  rtr           Enable SNMP Response Time Reporter traps
  snmp          Enable SNMP traps
  syslog        Enable SNMP syslog traps
  <cr>
Support#
```

The next example shows how to designate a trap to be sent to a specific source for logging:

```
Support(config)#
Support(config)#snmp-server trap-source ?
  BRI       ISDN Basic Rate Interface
  Ethernet  IEEE 802.3
  Null      Null interface
  Serial    Serial

Support(config)#snmp-server trap-source ethernet ?
  <0-0>   Ethernet interface number

Support(config)#snmp-server trap-source ethernet0
Support(config)#
```

RMON

One of the most common MIBs is the Remote Monitoring, or RMON MIB. The RMON MIB is used in most devices to allow monitoring of different LAN segments in a network. RMON was defined by the user community (with the help of the Internet Engineering Task Force) to provide a mechanism for device communications; it became a standard as RFC 1757. RMON enables agents and network management systems to communicate with each other and exchange data. RMON also provides for comprehensive network-fault diagnosis, planning, and performance-tuning information using the MIB.

Several RMON groups apply to the standard, such as statistics for RMON (group 1) and history for RMON (group 2). Cisco devices are embedded with various RMON groups, depending on the device.

Management Software

As stated previously, a monitoring system mainly consists of software. Cisco offers several software packages to maintain an NMS. The software is often referred to as Cisco Network Management Solutions. The software enables you to update the IOS, change configurations, provide baselines of your network, aid in troubleshooting, and instantly send an alarm in case of failure. These types of software include the following:

➤ *CiscoWorks and CiscoView*—The CiscoWorks software allows for monitoring, configuration, fault management, troubleshooting, and performance tuning using CiscoView to graphically display a physical view of the network. CiscoView software can be integrated with Sun Microsystems, HP OpenView, and IBM NetView.

➤ *Traffic Director*—Analyzes network traffic patterns and reports the network trends in a switched internetwork. It can also be used for troubleshooting protocol problems and setting alarms to notify a system administrator in case of failure. Traffic Director utilizes the embedded RMON agents in catalyst switches to compile the data.

➤ *CiscoWorks for Switched Internetworks (CWSI)*—A software suite that includes Traffic Director, CiscoView, and VlanDirector. CWSI works with SNMP, Cisco Discovery Protocol (CDP), Virtual Trunk Protocol (VTP), automated VLAN arrangement, and RMON for traffic monitoring. CWSI auto-discovers and creates a topology to allow system administrators to view the relationships and display VLANs.

➤ *Cisco Netsys*—A simulation tool that enables the system administrator to see and test network performance of a new design before implementing it in the production network. Netsys uses object-oriented code that enables existing infrastructure code to be imported into Netsys, thereby allowing Netsys to simulate the performance of the new design before it is implemented.

Protocol Analyzers

The main function of a protocol analyzer is to capture, display, and analyze how a communications protocol is operating on the given network on a per-packet basis. The analyzer captures packets that are on the network at the given time, thus reporting in real time. To provide an accurate reading, the protocol analyzer must be physically attached to the specific network or broadcast domain you are trying to monitor. The protocol analyzer decodes the various layers and reports them in reference to each layer of the OSI model. A few examples of packet analyzers are Etherpeek, Network Associates "Sniffer" (very popular), Agilent's Internet Advisor (formerly WP), and several others.

When monitoring traffic, the protocol analyzer copies packets into its memory so that the packets can be analyzed without affecting the traffic. Using analyzers enables you to isolate a particular type of traffic or specify that you want to see only source and destination traffic. For example, if you are having an Ethernet problem, you don't need to look at all the routing traffic. This enables you to troubleshoot and analyze a particular area without spending a lot of time. Because many protocols are used in large campus environments, it is necessary to have a protocol analyzer that can discern different protocols.

Chapter Summary

A lot of troubleshooting time may be spent in search of Layer 1 (Physical layer) problems. Many little things can cause loss of connectivity, such as a wire break or a noise that is affecting the wire. If you have tools such as cable testers that enable you to test wiring and find problems with connectivity, the time you spend looking for the problem will be reduced. Time domain reflectors enable you to isolate a problem with wiring within a few feet from the cause.

A few troubleshooting commands are available that will make your life easier: **show**, **debug**, **ping**, and **traceroute**. The **show** commands enable you to monitor the status of network performance, and aid in detecting any network problems. The **debug** commands enable you to focus on a particular problem, to isolate the problem area. Using the **debug** command adds some overhead to the router, so you have to use it only when necessary. The **ping** command tests for connectivity using an ICMP message. The **trace** command enables you to monitor the path from a source to a destination using ICMP messages, and reports the path in hops.

Window 95/98, Windows NT, and Unix workstations offer a variety of desktop troubleshooting support. These tools are inherit to the operating systems and enable you to test for connectivity of the network and the workstation you are using. The tools include **ping**, **winipcfg** (enables you to see IP configurations with Windows 95/98), and **netstat** (enables you to look at protocol statistics), to name a few.

NMSs enable you to monitor your network 24 hours a day from a central location, and alerts you in case of failure or configured alarms by the administrator. An NMS enables you to gather information about a network, such as details about packets, errors, hosts, connectivity, and performance. NMSs use the SNMP protocol to communicate with devices on the network. For your network to be managed by SNMP, you must have managed devices, such as routers and switches, running an SNMP software agent, and a central point that acts as the monitoring system. SNMP uses MIBs to aid in monitoring the network. The device uses a MIB to store information about network management. The RMON MIB is one of the most widely used MIBs for remote access.

The main function of a protocol analyzer is to capture, display, and analyze how a communications protocol is operating on the given network on a per-packet basis. The protocol analyzer decodes the various layers of a packet and reports them in reference to the OSI model. To monitor a certain network, the device must be attached to the specific link.

Review Questions

1. A cable tester that sends electric signals and waits for the signals to return is a _____.

    a. Volt-ohm meter

    b. Digital meter

    c. Time domain reflector (TDR)

    d. Circuit tester

    e. Ping tester

2. The best command to use in a router to monitor network performance or congestion is the _____ command.

    a. **ping**

    b. **trace**

    c. **debug**

    d. **show**

    e. **netstat**

3. The best command to use in a router to isolate (not monitor) network problems is the _____ command.

    a. **show**

    b. **ping**

    c. **debug**

    d. **netstat**

    e. **trace**

4. A _____ command sends an ICMP message and waits for a reply.

    a. **show**

    b. **ping**

    c. **debug**

    d. **winipcfg**

    e. **netstat**

3

5. You can monitor a path from a source address to a destination address by using the _____ command.

    a. **trace**

    b. **ping**

    c. **debug**

    d. **show**

    e. **netstat**

6. Which **show** command enables you to look at all the interfaces on a router?

    a. **show debug**

    b. **show trace**

    c. **show interfaces**

    d. **show IPX**

    e. **show arp**

7. A _____ command causes extreme overhead on the router and should be used only when you know a problem exists.

    a. **show running**

    b. **show interfaces**

    c. **debug**

    d. **show logging**

    e. **traceroute**

8. When using the **debug** command, the router sends the debugging log to the _____ port by default.

    a. Aux

    b. Ethernet

    c. Serial

    d. Router

    e. Console

9. What is the maximum number of hops **traceroute** will report?

    a. 21

    b. 15

    c. 20

    d. 30

    e. 60

10. What command is used in Windows 95/98 to find out the IP address on the device?

   a. **ipconfig**

   b. **ipcfg**

   c. **winconfig**

   d. **winip**

   e. **winipcfg**

11. On a Windows-based machine using DOS, what command is used to find out protocol statistics and connections?

   a. **statprotocol**

   b. **netprotocol**

   c. **netstat**

   d. **statnet**

   e. **protocol**

12. Network _____ continuously monitor(s) packets and provide(s) a current snapshot of the network activity.

   a. Systems

   b. Logging

   c. Monitors

   d. Statistics

   e. Protocols

13. The most common protocol used in network monitoring is _____.

   a. SNMP

   b. TCP/IP

   c. RIP

   d. OSPF

   e. Monitor

14. A(n) _____ is a directory of information and resources collected from the network that pertains to network management.

   a. Monitoring base

   b. Base

   c. Information base

   d. Database

   e. Management information base

15. For the SNMP manager and agent to communicate, SNMP _____ _____ must be configured.

    a. Community strings

    b. Management names

    c. Management properties

    d. Community MIBs

    e. Information bases

16. One of the most common MIBs used for remote monitoring is _____.

    a. MIB 3

    b. RMON

    c. ROMN

    d. ROMAN

    e. MIB4

17. The NMS software suite that contains Traffic Director, CiscoView, and VlanDirector is _____.

    a. Traffic Director

    b. CiscoWorks

    c. CiscoWorks for Switched Internetworks (CWSI)

    d. Cisco Basics

    e. Cisco Suite

18. The main function of a _____ is to capture, display, and analyze (on a per-packet basis) how a communication protocol is operating on the network.

    a. protocol packet

    b. analyzer pro

    c. analyzer protocol

    d. protocol analyzer

    e. packet ro

19. Which router mode enables you to perform an extended ping?

    a. Command

    b. Exec

    c. Privilege

    d. Passive

    e. Enable

20. Which **debug** command may produce so much output that it brings the router to a halt?

   a. **debug all**

   b. **debug ISDN**

   c. **debug IP**

   d. **debug PPP**

   e. **debug SNMP**

CHAPTER FOUR

LAN Protocols

After completing this chapter, you will be able to:

✓ Identify routed protocols within a LAN environment

✓ Understand the functions of TCP/IP, IPX/SPX, and AppleTalk

✓ Describe the TCP/IP protocol and commonly used protocols within the suite

✓ Describe the IPX/SPX protocol and commonly used protocols within the suite

✓ Describe the AppleTalk Protocol and commonly used protocols within the suite

✓ Configure IP, IPX, and AppleTalk on an Ethernet interface

✓ Configure IP, IPX, and AppleTalk on a serial interface

This chapter begins by describing the various LAN protocols, including their applications and protocol suites, and follows with troubleshooting issues regarding those protocols at the end of the chapter. The LAN protocols covered in the Support Exam include TCP/IP, Novell IPX, and AppleTalk. The following sections take an in-depth look at each of the protocols, including how to configure each on a router's interface.

TCP/IP

The name TCP/IP represents a suite of protocols designed for wide area networks (WANs). The U.S. Department of Defense Advanced Research Projects Agency, for a resource-sharing experiment called ARPANET, developed TCP/IP in 1969. The primary purpose behind the project was to provide high-speed communication to various government agencies. TCP/IP provides communication in heterogeneous environment. Figures 4.1 and 4.2 map the various data communication protocols within the suite. The suite gets its name from two of the protocols belonging to the suite: Transmission Control Protocol (TCP) and Internet Protocol (IP).

The TCP/IP protocol suite has been implemented on almost all of today's major operating systems, routers, switches, and workstations. The specification for each protocol within the TCP/IP suite is defined within one or more Requests for Comments (RFCs).

The following section provides the function of Transmission Control Protocol (TCP).

Upper Protocol Layer			
			TCP/IP Suite
Application Layer 7	Presentation Layer 6	Session Layer 5	Transport Layer 4
E-mail	POP/SMTP	Pop/25 SMTP110	
Newsgroup	Usenet	532	Transmission Control Protocol (TCP)
Web Applications	HTTP	80	
File Transfer	FTP	20 21	
Host Sessions	Telnet	23	
Directory Services	DNS	53	
Network Management	SNMP	161 162	User Datagram Protocol (UDP)
Files Services	NFS	RPC Portmapper	

Figure 4.1   How TCP/IP maps to the upper layers of the OSI Reference Model.

Lower Protocol Layer		
Network **Layer 3**	**Data Link** **Layer 2**	**Physical** **Layer 1**
		RS-X CAT 1
Internet Protocol Version 6	SLIP PPP	ISDN
		ADSL
		ATM
		FDDI
	802.2 SNAP	
Internet Protocol Version 4	802.3 CSMA/CD	CAT 1-5
	802.5 Token Ring	
	ISL-ISL	
	Ethernet II	Coaxial Cables

Figure 4.2 How TCP/IP maps to the lower layers of the OSI Reference Model.

Transmission Control Protocol

TCP is a reliable, connection-oriented transfer protocol residing at the Transport layer of the OSI model. Before it starts transmitting information, it contacts the TCP protocol of the receiving host and establishes a connection. After this virtual circuit is established, both parties start negotiating the reliability factors, such as the amount of data that will be sent before receiving an acknowledgement from the destination host's TCP protocol. After sending the agreed-upon number of segments, TCP waits for the acknowledgement that states the segments have arrived and are intact. Missing segments (by number) will be re-sent.

Because TCP breaks down large blocks of data into segments, it numbers and sequences them so that they can be reassembled by TCP running at the receiving end. All of this error-checking and resending (if necessary) causes this full-duplex transport protocol to have a large overhead; therefore, TCP should not be used for transmissions that don't require an acknowledgement, such as broadcasts. If every broadcast received were acknowledged back to the sender, the network would be clogged very quickly. Today's networks are much more reliable than networks used to be, which means the use of acknowledgements is not as important.

TCP is the protocol that ensures reliability in the TCP/IP protocol suite. TCP operates at the Transport layer of the OSI Reference Model and uses the following mechanisms:

➤ *Acknowledgments*—Used to inform the source host that data has been received. Acknowledgments are made to sequence numbers to identify the exact data that was received. If the source host does not receive an acknowledgment for sent data in a specified amount of time, the source host assumes that the data has been lost or that a collision of the data has occurred. The sender then retransmits the data.

➤ *Exclusive TCP connections*—When TCP sessions are established, the connection is exclusive to the two hosts. This negotiation of the session between the two hosts allows data traffic to be exchanged between the two hosts.

➤ *TCP sequence numbers*—Provide chronology numbering to the TCP data that is sent and received. Data sent and received is assigned a TCP sequence number to uniquely identify the data being sent. This numbering ensures that data packets arriving in a different order than the order in which they were sent are reassembled in the correct order.

Format of a TCP Segment

TCP uses port numbers, just as UDP distinguishes different user requests. And, as previously mentioned, TCP adds a unique header at the Transport layer and breaks data received from the upper layers into segments. These segments, as shown in Figure 4.3, are as follows:

➤ *Source port*—Specifies the port from which data was sent

➤ *Destination port*—Specifies the port to which data was sent

➤ *Sequence number*—Used when reassembling data into the correct order

➤ *Acknowledgement number*—Specifies the next octet to be received

➤ *HLEN (header length)*—Specifies the number of 32-bit words in the header

➤ *Reserved*—Set to zero at all times

➤ *Code bits*—Used to set and terminate sessions

➤ *Window*—Used to specify the window size of the sender

➤ *Checksum*—Counts the number of bits in a transmission unit

➤ *Urgent pointer*—Used to specify the end of urgent data

➤ *Option*—Used to set the maximum segment size

➤ *Data*—Used to specify the data itself

Remote Host Access with TCP/IP

Remote host access is the ability to access a network from a remote location. The need for remote access, also known as *telecommuting*, is steadily increasing. Many

Establishing a TCP Connection

Establishing a TCP connection is a multipart process involving what is commonly known as a *three-way handshake*. Before any data can be passed between any two hosts, the process must be completed. The client or source host initiating a connection to the server or destination host must request some kind of service from another host. The following steps outline the three-way handshake process from a host to a server:

1. The host sends a SYN packet, which is a request for a TCP connection to the server.

2. If the server is available, has services to offer, and can accept the incoming connection, it sends a connection request of its own, signaled by a new SYN to the host, and acknowledges the host's connection request with an ACK packet.

3. When the host receives the SYN and ACK, it replies with a final ACK to the server, acknowledging that it has received the server's request for a connection.

After the three-way handshake has been executed, the connection has been established and data can be exchanged between the two hosts. TCP uses port numbers to identify connections between hosts. In the past, well-known TCP ports fell into the range of 1 through 1023. TCP services use these well-known ports and never use any others. This means that if FTP uses ports 20 and 21 today, it should use the same ports tomorrow.

Many well-known port numbers are assigned to services in the range of 1 through 1023, such as Telnet on port 23 and SNMP on port 25. Some of the newer services, such as Lotus Notes, use TCP port 1352 (and thus don't fall into the well-known port numbers), because more services now exist than well-known port numbers.

Ephemeral port numbers are known as host ports and are selected for a particular connection on a temporary basis and are reused after the connection is freed. These ports typically are numbered higher than the well-known port numbers, but not always. When the host in the three-way handshake tries to initiate the connection to the server, the host uses an ephemeral port. The host and the server will continue to exchange data on these two ports for the entirety of their session. If you are using TCP/IP for your connection to the Internet, your host connection will use this combination of source IP address and source port to connect to the destination IP address and destination port.

You may find many other connections originating from other source IP addresses to this same destination IP and destination port, but that host will have a different source IP address and probably a different source port. When you open two different Internet windows on the same host connecting to the same Web server, the ephemeral source ports involved keep the communications separated.

When the session needs to be terminated, two methods are available: the general method, or an abrupt stop method. The general method is similar to saying "goodbye" and hanging up in a phone conversation. When the TCP session termination is conducted, one of the hosts (either the host or the server) signals with a FIN to the other that it wants to terminate the session. The receiving host signals back with an ACK to acknowledge the request. This terminates only one half of the connection, however, because the other host must initiate a FIN as well, which the receiving host must then acknowledge. Then both sides will initiate a FIN and acknowledge the other side's FIN, because TCP is reliable connection oriented protocol.

The second method of termination is to halt the connection abruptly by informing the other end of the connection that the conversation is completed and thus it should hang up. This method is achieved by one host sending the other a RESET to communicate its desire to abruptly terminate the connection.

Format of a TCP Segment					
16 Bits	16 Bits	32 Bits	32 Bits	4 Bits	6 Bits
Source Port	Destination Port	Sequence Number	Ack Number	HLEN	Reserved
6 Bits	16 Bits	16 Bits	16 Bits	0/32 Bits	Varies
Code Bits	Window	Checksum	Urgent Pointer	Option	Data

Figure 4.3 Format of a TCP segment.

people work from home, work additional hours after they get home, or are involved in business travel. The concept is to provide access from remote locations to one or more hosts on a network.

Remote access is often essential to the operation of an enterprise network. Remote users can be provided with the same level of privileges and services that they would have if they were sitting at the PC at their office desk. Applications used in this process are most often associated with email, file transfer, scheduling, database tasks, and, occasionally, printer access.

A network can take on many different forms, depending on availability, cost, and bandwidth. Conventional data networks include Public Switched Telephone Network (PSTN), X.25, Integrated Services Digital Network (ISDN), Switched 56, and Frame Relay. Also available are cellular radio and packet radio networks to support true mobile, remote network access. The equipment used for remote access depends on what network is in place.

Technology improvements have made cost-effective LAN-to-LAN access possible using TCP/IP through WANs. Equipment to do this may include the following, depending on the type of network:

➤ X.25 networks require packet assemblers/disassemblers (PADs)

➤ ISDN needs terminal adapters (TAs)

➤ Frame Relay requires the use of Frame Relay Access Devices (FRADs)

To access a cellular network, a wireless modem is necessary. The LAN side of this scenario requires the installation of modem pools, routers, switches, and various other devices in support of the remote user. Other ways to access a host remotely include the use of certain protocols, such as FTP, TFTP, and Telnet, which provide a way for file transfer and manipulation, or the use of remote-control software. However, using remote control software can create some problems, from finding someone to physically reboot the machine after a crash, to having logged-in machines with no local user on the network (which, of course, creates a huge security risk).

TCP/IP-Multihomed

A computer with two or more network interface cards (NICs) installed is called a *multihomed* computer. Each NIC has an individual IP address and subnet mask assigned to it. This feature enables traffic to be routed between different subnets over TCP/IP or IPX. The fact that a multihomed computer has multiple NICs installed does not necessarily mean that it is functioning as a router. The benefit of having separate physical networks is that traffic can be separated, so that certain traffic can be kept away from users by placing them on a different subnet, with the multihomed computer acting as the separator.

A multihomed computer may also be described as a Web server with connections to the Internet through multiple ISPs, thus providing redundancy. Multihomed computers also support multiple domains, which is useful when Web clients are unable to make a connection to one of the domains.

A multihomed Windows NT 4 server or Windows 2000 server can be used as a router, allowing for interconnection of several networks. Such a server uses a service called a Multiprotocol Router (MPR), which utilizes the Routing Information Protocol (RIP) for TCP/IP at Layer 3. MPR also supports IPX routing and Dynamic Host Configuration Protocol (DHCP) relay agents. Unfortunately, no support for Macintosh exists as part of the MPR service suite.

User Datagram Protocol

UDP is an unreliable, connectionless transport protocol running on top of IP. It does not make a connection with the destination host before it delivers a datagram, nor does it require an acknowledgement that the message has been received at the other end (message may get lost). UDP receives blocks of data from the upper layers and breaks them down into segments, numbering them for reassembly. However, UDP itself is not responsible for putting the segments back into sequence. UDP simply leaves this task to the upper layers.

The upper-layer protocols, such as NFS, already provide reliability. UDP has low overhead, which makes it an efficient communications method. Network applications save a great deal of processing time by using UDP for the exchange of small data units, where the cost for establishing, and later breaking down, a connection would be a waste of time and money.

UDP provides two features that are not provided by the IP layer:

➤ *Port numbers*—Used to distinguish different user requests. A list of well-known ports is used for special purposes, such as FTP, Telnet, and email.

➤ *Checksum capability*—Allows verification to be made that data arrived intact, by using a calculated number associated with the data packet.

Format of a UDP Segment

Each UDP segment is called a *user datagram* and consists of a UDP header and UDP data. The header is comprised of four 16-bit fields specifying the following (as shown in Figure 4.4):

➤ *Source port*—Specifies the port from which the message was sent.

➤ *Destination port*—Specifies the port to which the message is sent.

➤ *Length*—Specifies the message length with the header included.

➤ *Checksum*—Used to verify that the message arrived intact.

Internet Control Message Protocol

ICMP is a management protocol and delivery service for error messages in the form of IP datagrams. ICMP is even simpler than UDP, because it doesn't contain any port numbers in its header. Port numbers are not needed when directing an ICMP message.

The following are some situations in which ICMP is called upon to deliver what's often considered bad news:

➤ If a datagram reaches the maximum amount of hops assigned to it before reaching its destination, it will be deleted by the router on its last hop. This router then uses ICMP to send a time-exceeded message informing the sender of the deleted datagram.

➤ When a router receives a datagram with a destination network that is unknown to it—meaning that it is not listed in its routing table—the router will send a message to the sender via ICMP stating "Destination unreachable."

➤ A router's memory buffer can hold only a certain amount of data, and when this limit is reached, the router uses ICMP to send a source quench message.

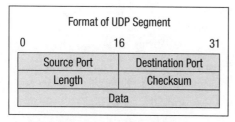

Figure 4.4 Format of a UDP segment.

ICMP Redirect

The ICMP router discovery message only enables a host to discover neighboring routers—it will not specify which router to use for a specific destination (that's the job of a routing protocol). A host may make a poor decision and choose a first-hop router even though a much better route is available. In this case, the first-hop router should send an *ICMP Redirect*, informing the host of the better route. After it's redirected to a specific destination, the route will be put into cache so that this "mistake" doesn't happen again.

A router advertisement includes a preference level for each address. If a host has not been configured to use a default router address, it is expected to choose the router with the highest preference level. Preference levels of a router address can be manually configured to encourage, or discourage, the use of specific routers as default gateways.

4

➤ Ping uses ICMP echo messages when testing connections to another machine. In this case, it may even deliver good news in the form of a reply from the destination.

Routers advertise addresses of their interfaces periodically with *router advertisements*. An ICMP router discovery message is independent of a specific routing protocol. Hosts become aware of their neighboring routers simply by listening to these advertisements. A host that just started up may also send a *router solicitation*, which forces immediate router advertisements. Routers that are not being advertised because a link is down temporarily eventually will be discovered when the link is back up and periodic advertisements (unsolicited) are being sent.

Address Resolution Protocol

ARP is used by the Cisco IOS software to provide dynamic mapping of 32-bit IP addresses and 48-bit MAC (hardware) addresses. The ARP cache is a table of these listings and is checked every time communication is initiated between machines. If the required hardware address cannot be found in the cache, a broadcast is sent out to resolve it. The broadcast address (FFFFFFFF) is already stored, although not visible in the table. After the previously unknown address is found, it is entered in the cache and is readily available the next time around. No broadcast will be necessary, which saves bandwidth. Every listing in the cache has a timestamp and a time-to-live (TTL). When this time expires, the entry is deleted from the table to make room for new address resolutions. If the cache becomes full and no TTLs have expired yet, then the oldest entry (or entries) must be deleted.

Proxy ARP is enabled by default and is used for address resolution of hosts residing on other networks or subnets. When a router receives an ARP request for a host that's not on the same interface as the ARP request sender, the router will generate a proxy ARP reply packet giving out its own local data link address. The packet then will be sent to the router, which in turn will forward it to the destination host.

ARP Caching

When defining a static ARP cache, you are making permanent entries to the table of listings. You can do so globally by using the **arp *ip-address hardware-address type*** command. The router will then use this entry to resolve the IP address to the associated hardware address.

You can also set the length of time an entry will stay in the cache by using the **arp timeout** *seconds* command. Depending on your network, the encapsulation can be set to one of three different types, to control the interface-specific handling of address resolution. The standard Ethernet-style encapsulation *arp* is enabled by default (shows as *arpa*), but you can change it to *SNAP* by using the **snap** syntax or to *HP Probe* by using the **probe** syntax if your network requires it. Here are a few common commands to get specific information on the ARP cache:

➤ *arp (arpa | snap | probe)*—Specifies the encapsulation type

➤ *show interfaces*—Displays the encapsulation and the timeout value

➤ *show arp*—Displays the contents of the ARP cache

➤ *show ip arp*—Displays all IP to MAC address entries

➤ *clear arp-cache*—Removes all nonstatic entries from the ARP cache

Domain Name System

DNS is a name resolution protocol that converts hostnames to IP addresses, and vice versa. Its structure is that of a hierarchical database, much like the directory structure of a file system. DNS is the reason you don't have to remember the IP address of every Web site. The DNS database consists of the *root domain* ("."") residing at the top of the hierarchy, and *top-level domains* directly underneath it (such as .com and .edu). Subdomains follow (*example.com*), which in turn can have other subdomains (*specifics.example.com*). Hostnames are based on this system, where each level is separated by a dot.

DNS servers provide the service for name resolution. It happens that a server receives a request for name resolution for a host outside of its domain. In this case, the server simply needs to know the address of the root name server, to which it will forward the request. The root server then filters the request through the appropriate domain beneath it, and so on until the correct name server is reached and the information about the host is available.

A router can use the services of DNS, as well. Configuring the router with DNS servers is easier than having to set up a table of hostnames. By default, the **ip domain-lookup** command is enabled. When the router can't resolve a hostname, it generates a broadcast to look for a DNS server. This can cost you valuable time when you're in a hurry. To terminate this process rather than wait for the broadcast timeout, you can press Ctrl+Shift+6. Setting up the router to use specific DNS servers for name resolution, use the **ip name-server *ip-address*** command.

If you decide to use a hostname table, you have to disable the **ip domain-lookup** command by using the **no ip domain-lookup** command. You must then use the **ip host *hostname ip-address*** command to build your hostname table. You can have up to eight IP addresses for a hostname. Depending on the size of your network, making all of these entries may take a fair amount of time. To view the hostnames in the table and their corresponding IP addresses, use the **show hosts** command.

DNS Caching

The concept of caching DNS entries is of great value. DNS caching saves time and bandwidth. After a DNS server has resolved a name, it stores this mapping in its cache, making it available the next time the server receives a query for one of the already stored mappings. This means that if a query is for a host address that has already been resolved, the mapping is already stored and thus a query does not need to be made across the network a second time.

The expiration of an entry is set by the time-to-live (TTL) value, which is entered in the domain Start of Authority (SOA) record. This ensures room for new map-pings and updates. Information about a particular name can change, if the old mapping stayed in the cache too long. This would cause the DNS server to provide the wrong information when queries are made.

Default Gateways

Part of a router's job is to send packets to remote networks. The default gateway is utilized when a host needs to send a packet to a host on a network other than its own, for which the router does not have a specific route in its routing table. This is also known as the *gateway of last resort*. A router sends the packet to the remote network. From there, the next router can direct the packet to other gateways, and so on, until it reaches its final destination. The default gateway parameter is an IP address specifying the router interface, on which the gateway is configured.

Dynamic Host Configuration Protocol

For hosts to communicate with each other on a TCP/IP network, they have to be configured with several IP addresses, one IP address and subnet mask representing the host itself, a default gateway, DNS servers, and occasionally WINS servers. On small networks, having static addresses assigned manually at each workstation or server is no big deal, and coping with those changes on the network that will affect every single machine, such as the default gateway, is relatively easy.

On a large network, keeping up with network changes and the necessary manual configurations creates a lot of work for the administrator. These changes are time-consuming and potentially prone to errors. If the network changes frequently and has limited address space, assigning a static address to a machine that accesses the network infrequently, such as a remote user's laptop or workstation that is used only a few hours a day, is a waste.

This is where a DHCP server works well in the network. DHCP is a protocol developed from BOOTP (Boot Protocol), with a few modifications, such as the BOOTP relay agent. BOOTP was used (or may still be used) to allow diskless workstations to be configured with the necessary TCP/IP parameters to communicate on the network. DHCP dynamically assigns the IP address, subnet mask, DNS server, and WINS information. All information is only valid until the lease time assigned by an administrator expires or the host is manually released before the expiration period. You can set up your DHCP server to assign all necessary information that a host needs to function properly. This process consists of various messages being sent between the host and the server.

DHCP Message Types

DHCP uses the following message types to send messages between the host and server:

➤ *DHCPDISCOVER*—A client message sent to locate servers.

➤ *DHCPOFFER*—A server message sent in response to DHCPDISCOVER, offering configuration information.

➤ *DHCPREQUEST*—A client message requesting the offered configuration, or requesting to extend the lease of the current address. This message is also sent if the host had to reboot and needs to verify the correctness of the previously assigned address.

➤ *DHCPACK*—A server message with configuration parameters.

➤ *DHCPNAK*—A server message indicating that the address the client is requesting is incorrect (for example, the client may now be on a different subnet).

➤ *DHCPDECLINE*—A client message informing the server that the address is already in use.

➤ *DHCPRELEASE*—A client message releasing an address by canceling the remaining lease.

➤ *DHCPINFORM*—A client message requesting only local configuration parameters.

It is not necessary to have a DHCP server on each subnet, because DHCP can work across routers, or function with the help of BOOTP relay agents which listen to the DHCP messages and then forward them. Certain addresses have to remain the same with every reboot of a host and thus need to be configured as *address reservations* on the DHCP server. This ensures the correct address assignment for default gateways, DNS servers, and so forth.

File Transfer Protocol

FTP is an application used to transfer files between hosts and is found at the Application layer of the OSI model. FTP enables any two machines running this application to transfer files using ports 20 and 21. Most administrators set up specific usernames and passwords for specific directories and files to be accessed. This is done for security reasons and depends on the nature of the activities required. However, the network administrator can make the option to log in as "anonymous" available, but this login method usually comes with severe restrictions in terms of the user's ability to manipulate files.

4

IP Helper Addresses

In a network environment, routers are commonly placed between two segments, to prevent broadcasts from being forwarded between them. This design keeps local traffic local on the network segment and forwards only unicast traffic. When a DHCP server and DHCP client are implemented into a network, all requests are broadcast within that segment. But what happens if you have a client in a different segment of the network that needs access to its resources? How do you allow DHCP to send broadcasts across the router and still keep other broadcasts local on the segment? A feature called an *IP Helper Address* is used in this situation.

The IP Helper Address is a specialized address-translation command that converts broadcast messages into directed broadcast or unicast messages. The **ip helper-address** command is used on a router to instruct the router to convert the messages accordingly.

If the IP Helper Address is specified and UDP forwarding is enabled, broadcast packets destined for the following eight protocols and their associated port numbers are forwarded by default:

➤ TFTP (port 69)

➤ DNS (port 53)

➤ Time (port 37)

➤ TACACS (Terminal Access Controller Access Control System) (port 49)

➤ BOOTP client (port 68)

➤ BOOTP server (port 67)

➤ NetBIOS name server (port 137)

➤ NetBIOS datagram service (port 138)

If only one server is located on a remote segment, the IP Helper Address is configured with the address of that server. Any broadcast traffic of the type just listed is forwarded to that server. If several servers are located on a remote segment, the IP

Helper Address is configured with the broadcast address for that segment. Broadcast traffic of the type in the preceding list is sent in the form of a directed broadcast to all the servers on the segment.

Before you use this setting, make sure you consider all the other broadcast issues you might unleash on your network. Just imagine what the impact would be if you were to have 40 subnets' worth of broadcast traffic hitting this segment.

Configuring an IP Address on a Router

On a router, the IP address and subnet mask are required on each interface. The default gateway is not necessary on a router, but it is configured on a Cisco switch. Routing is handled by configuring a default route or a routing protocol configured in global configuration mode. The following is an example of configuring an IP address on an Ethernet0, and Serial0 interface:

```
Router>enable
Router#config terminal
2514(config)#interface ethernet0
2514(config-if)#ip address 192.1.1.1 255.255.255.0
2514(config-if)#no shut

Router>enable
Router#config terminal
2514(config-if)#interface serial0
2514(config-if)#ip address 172.16.20.2 255.255.255.0
2514(config-if)#clock rate 64000
2514(config-if)#no shut
```

Novell IPX/SPX

Internetwork Packet Exchange/Sequenced Packet Exchange(IPX/SPX) was developed by Novell for use with the NetWare operating system (version 4 and earlier). However, with NetWare 5, IPX no longer is required, but rather is an option. TCP/IP is now the default communications protocol. Like TCP/IP, IPX/SPX is a suite of protocols used for network interactions, such as transport, routing, and so forth. Figure 4.5 shows how the Novel IPX/SPX suite of protocols maps to the OSI Reference Model.

Protocol Overview

Even though the IPX/SPX suite cannot be perfectly mapped to the OSI model, it provides layered functions. The following protocols are used with Novell:

➤ *Internetwork Packet Exchange (IPX)*—Provides functions at Layers 3 and 4 of the OSI model and is a connectionless protocol much like UDP. IPX does not require an acknowledgement from the destination host. It is also responsible for

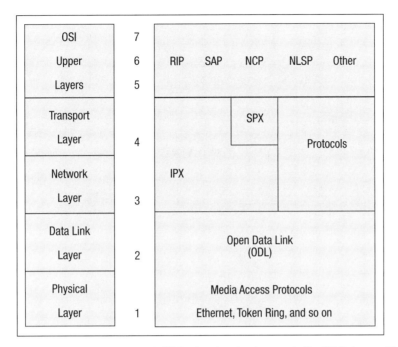

Figure 4.5   How the Novell IPX/SPX suite of protocols maps to the OSI Reference Model.

assigning software addresses (IPX addresses) to hosts on a network, controlling packet delivery, and making routing decisions with information provided by RIP or NLSP. Sockets are used for communication with upper-layer protocols and ensure addressing of applications running on the same host.

➤ *Sequenced Packet Exchange (SPX)*—A connection-oriented protocol that establishes virtual circuits between hosts before transporting data. Each virtual circuit has its own ID, which is part of the SPX header. SPX assures the upper layers that data was transferred from point A to point B—in other words, that the data sent actually arrived at its destination.

➤ *Routing Information Protocol (RIP)*—A routing protocol that uses both hops and ticks at 1/8 of a second for metrics. Although this is a different RIP than TCP/IP's Routing Information Protocol, it is also a distance-vector routing protocol used to discover IPX routing paths in an internetwork. NetWare servers build RIP tables, which they broadcast every 60 seconds.

➤ *Service Advertisement Protocol (SAP)*—Advertises IPX resources on a network.

➤ *NetWare Link Services Protocol (NLSP)*—An advanced link-state routing protocol developed by Novell.

➤ *NetWare Core Protocol (NCP)*—Allows the network operating system (NOS) to send and receive messages; is also a series of server routines that enable clients to access requested resources.

IPX Addresses

IPX addresses are not separated into different classes, as are IP addresses. Instead, they are 80 bits (10 bytes) in length, of which the first 4 bytes (or 8 hex digits) represent the network address (leading zeros may be dropped) and the remaining 6 bytes represent the node address. The last 6 bytes translate into 12 hex digits which represent the MAC address assigned to the NIC card connected to the network, 8 hex digits are used for the node address and 4 hex digits make up the socket. The following is an example of how an IPX address is broken down:

IPX Address: 0000.7C80.0000.8609.33E9, this address breaks down as follows:

Network Address: 0000.7C80 or 7C80

Node Address: 0000.8609

Socket Address: 33E9

This process provides the advantage that the administrator does not have to configure each individual machine with an IPX address. If you were to run both IPX and TCP/IP on a network, you could convert the IP address to hexadecimal and use that portion as the network address for the given segment. However, when configuring machines for proper communication on an IPX network, you also need to consider the encapsulation method.

Encapsulation Method

The *encapsulation method* is the process of taking a Layer 3 packet and converting it to Layer 2 frames before transmission over the physical media. Specifying the encapsulation method in a Cisco router interface configuration is done by typing "**ipx network** *network numb*er **encapsulation** *encapsulation type*", as shown in Figure 4.6. Always use the Cisco keyword, which, when in doubt, can be found on

Interface Type	Frame Type	Cisco Keyword	Comments
Ethernet	Ethernet_802.3 Ethernet_802.2 Ethernet_II Ethernet_snap	novell-ether (default) sap arpa snap	Default up to Netware 3.11 Default since NetWare 3.12 Supports TCP/IP and IPX Supports TCP/IP, IPX, and AppleTalk
Token Ring	Token_Ring Token_Ring_snap	snap (default) snap	
FDDI	Fddi_snap Fddi_802.2 Fddi_raw	snap (default) sap novel-fddi	

Figure 4.6 Encapsulation types.

the help screen. These frame types are incompatible; therefore, it is important to use the same frame type throughout the network.

You can use different frame types simultaneously on an interface by configuring separate virtual IPX networks using subinterfaces on a router's interface. A secondary option is to add the **sec** syntax to the end of the **ipx network** command. This option will not be supported in future IOSs. To create a subinterface on an Ethernet 0 interface (subinterface of 100), use the following example syntax:

```
2514#config t
2514(config)#ipx routing
2514(config)#interface e0.100
2514(config-sub-if)# ipx network 10 encap sap
```

Warning! Only machines with the same frame type across all virtual IPX networks can communicate with each other.

Service Advertisement Protocol

SAP is an important part of a Novell Network, because it has only two types of machines: clients and servers. Servers build SAP tables, listing all known services and their locations across the network. When a client requires access to a specific service, it sends out a GNS (Get Nearest Server Request) broadcast to locate a server offering this resource.

The servers receiving this broadcast will check their SAP table and respond with a GNS (Get Nearest Server Response) to the client, pointing it to the NetWare server providing the requested service. If the client does not receive a response, then the servers receiving the client's broadcast neither provide the requested service nor know of a server that does. This leaves the client unable to locate and access the needed resource. Only local servers will see a GNS broadcast. If there isn't a local server, a router will answer the GNS request with a GNS Response.

For cases in which no local NetWare server exists, the client's broadcast cannot cross a WAN link in search of a responding server. This is where Cisco routers come into action. Cisco routers build SAP tables, too, and list all resource locations across the whole network. Therefore, the router that connects to the client's segment is able to send a GNS response to the client, informing it of where the specific server can be found and giving the impression that the resources are local.

Servers advertise their SAP tables (SAP broadcasts) every 60 seconds, which enables other servers to add newly learned services and their locations to their own SAP tables. This way, every server eventually knows about every resource on the network. A Cisco router listens to all SAP broadcasts heard on any of its IPX-enabled interfaces and builds a SAP table of its own. It then broadcasts this table from each of those interfaces, just like a NetWare server, in a 60-second interval. This default setting can be changed. SAP is not needed to locate different services on networks running NetWare 4 or later.

Note: With the introduction of NetWare Directory Service (NDS), the server can be consulted by clients to locate services. The client utilizes SAP only when booting up and trying to locate the NDS server.

SAP Filters

Using SAP filters in large Novell networks in which hundreds of SAP services exist makes a lot of sense. Filtering SAP advertisements on a router's interface ensures that no unnecessary SAPs use up bandwidth. So, if a particular service is not required on a specific network, you are recommended to implement a SAP filter for it. A SAP output filter at the central site, or a SAP input filter that uses the SAP identifier for a particular service at the remote site, prevents the router from including this service in SAP updates.

NetWare Core Protocol

NCP enables the NOS to send and receive messages, and it is also a series of server routines that enable clients to access requested resources. These resources, or services, include file and printer sharing, file synchronization, security, name management, and accounting.

NCP provides for its own session control and error checking and therefore does not have to rely on other protocols for these tasks. Delivery is guaranteed based on acknowledgements of receipt from the destination. NCP request packets have a sequence number assigned by the client, where the first request carries the number 1, the second request number 2, and so on, with the numbers increasing with each subsequent request. The server handling the request places its sequence number into the response packet. This way, the client can be assured that it has received the correct response to a certain request.

Packet Burst (Protocol)

PBP can provide two functions for IPX. One function allows large packet support, also called Large Internet Packet (LIP), meaning the maximum size of a normal IPX packet can be exceeded to almost three times its size, but it is not supported by default. It requires loading NetWare Loadable Module (NLM) on the server, and a packet burst shell on the client. Packet Burst must be enabled on both the client and the server side, or it won't work properly. In addition, the name net.cfg file must be correctly configured with a line reading **PB BUFFERS =** (*0 - 10*, zero means that packet burst is disabled), or packet burst will not be enabled. Different numbers of buffers offer different performance.

The other function that PBP can provide allows multiple packets to be sent before the sender receives an acknowledgement. This works very much like *windowing* or *sliding windows* in TCP/IP. The Packet Burst provides for NCP's read/write requests and is a connection-oriented protocol that has been optimized to avoid the overhead of acknowledging every single packet. Burst mode uses multipacket units (called *bursts*) to communicate, and these units include the IPX header, the burst headers for each packet, and the request or reply itself.

A *burst transaction* lasts from the beginning of the burst request to the end of the reply, which carries an *End of Burst* flag. Unless fragments are missing and the client has to send a *missing fragment list* to the server for retransmission, the burst transaction is complete. It may take more than one burst transaction for a complete file read or write. Completion of the entire request is called a *service transaction*. Keep in mind that an End of Burst flag exists for every burst transaction, not for every service transaction.

IPX NetBIOS

NetBIOS is responsible for providing an interface to network applications to communicate with other compatible applications. It also establishes logical names on the network, opens a connection (session) between two machines (using the logical names), and transmits data between those two machines.

The Novell specification uses it's own driver to emulate the NetBIOS protocol. This emulator does not transmit NetBIOS packets; instead, they are encapsulated in an IPX packet, and the IPX packets are transmitted. Like SPX, NetBIOS provides Transport-layer services, such as guaranteed packet delivery and packet sequencing. Novell NetBIOS emulation still works most effectively with small-scale networks.

NetWare Link Services Protocol

NLSP is a link-state protocol designed to make up for some of the limitations that RIP and SAP present. NLSP is based on the OSI IS-IS (Intermediate System-to-Intermediate System) protocol and provides improved routing, better efficiency, and better scalability compared to RIP and SAP, which were developed when networks were relatively small.

NLSP routers are backward-compatible with RIP routers and guarantee delivery by employing a reliable transport protocol. Because NLSP is a link-state protocol, it stores the entire map of the network, which is used for routing decisions. This protocol is very efficient, especially across WAN links, because it not only supports IPX header compression, making it possible to reduce the packet size, but also supports multicast addressing and sends its routing information only to other NLSP routers.

In addition, NLSP can balance loads across parallel paths and support up to 127 hops. By permitting hierarchical addressing, NLSP is used for three levels of hierarchical routing:

➤ *Level 1*—Connects network segments within a given routing area. An *area* is a collection of connected networks, all sharing the same area address. This router is required to store information only about its own areas. To exchange information with other areas, it simply has to find a Level 2 router.

➤ *Level 2*—Connects areas, creating a *domain*, and also acts as a Level 1 router within its own area. Between areas, these routers advertise only the information pertaining to their respective areas.

➤ *Level 3*—Connects domains and also acts as a Level 2 router within its own domain. These routers behave similarly to Level 2 routers with respect to information between domains.

Router Adjacency

An *Adjacency* is a record kept by the router to indicate the connectivity and state of its neighboring router. These Adjacencies are established with the exchange of Hello Packets, but vary in procedure over a WAN or LAN. Adjacency establishment over a WAN starts with the data-link connection; then, the routers exchange identities by utilizing the IPX WAN Version 2 protocol to determine operational characteristics of the link. The next step is to exchange Hello Packets, which let the routers update their databases.

Link-State Packets (LSPs) are sent next, describing the state of the routers' links. Maintaining a WAN link depends on the router's state variable, which indicates whether the link is up, down, or initializing. If the router doesn't hear from its neighbor within the time specified in the holddown timer, it generates a message indicating that the link is down and deletes the Adjacency.

Hello Packets enable the routers to discover each other's identity, whether they are in the same routing area, and whether the other routers and links are operational. Routers send these packets when the link is first established, when the contents of the Hello Packet to be sent are different from the contents in the previously sent Hello Packet, or when a timer expires. WAN adjacency and LAN adjacency have different ways of establishing themselves.

Link-State Packet

An LSP contains certain information that the router extracts from the adjacency database, as well as local information added by the NLSP router. This LSP describes the router's immediate neighbors, and the collections of all LSPs from all routers make up the link-state database for the area. All routers must maintain a copy of the link-state database and keep these copies synchronized with each other. Database

WAN and LAN Adjacency

WAN adjacency is established in the following manner: The typical startup between two routers (Router 1 and Router 2) begins with the link in the down state. Router 1 sends a Hello Packet to Router 2, indicating that the link is down. Router 2 changes the state for the link to initializing and sends a Hello Packet to Router 1. Router 1 takes this information, also changes its state for the link to initializing, and sends another Hello Packet to Router 2. Now that Router 2 knows that Router 1 is initializing the link, it changes its link state to up and informs Router 1 with yet another Hello Packet. Router 1 receives this information and changes its link state to up, too.

LAN adjacency works a little differently than WAN adjacency: A router starts sending and accepting Hello Packets from other routers on the LAN and starts the process for the Designated Router election. The Designated Router maintains a link-state database, representing the LAN as a whole, and is able to make routing decisions on behalf of the complete LAN. It originates LSPs on behalf of the LAN, which ensures that the link-state databases of the individual routers stay within a reasonable size. Every router on the LAN sends a Hello Packet periodically. The router with the highest priority becomes the Level 1 Designated Router. In case of a tie, the router with the higher MAC address is chosen. Hello Packets sent on a LAN let the router do the same thing as on a LAN; namely, discover the identity of other Level 1 routers in the same area. Routers start sending these "Hellos" as soon as the broadcast circuit is enabled. These packets then are sent to a special multicast destination address on that circuit. Routers listen on this address for Hello Packets.

4

synchronization happens through the use of LSPs propagating through the area, when a router notices a change in the topology. The following two ways exist to ensure that accurate topology-change information is propagated:

➤ *Flooding*—When a topology change is detected, the router transmits an LSP to each of its neighbors. On a WAN, such packets are directed packets, and on a LAN, they are multicast packets. The router uses the sequence number in the packet to find out whether the packet is newer than the current information in its database. If it turns out to be a newer LSP, the router then retransmits it to all of its neighbors, except on the circuit on which the packet was received.

➤ *Receipt Confirmation*—On a WAN, the router receiving the LSP replies with an acknowledgement, but on a LAN, no explicit acknowledgement occurs. Instead, a special packet called a *Complete Sequence Number Packet (CSNP)* is periodically multicasted by the Designated Router. This specific packet contains all the LSP's identifiers and sequence numbers for the entire area. The router takes this information out of its database when constructing the CSNP. This way, other routers find out whether they are synchronized with the Designated Router.

NLSP employs a hierarchical addressing scheme, where each routing area is identified by two 32-bit quantities, which make up the *network address* and the *mask*. This address is expressed in hexadecimal, where the first 24 bits make up the network address (routing area) and the remaining 8 bits are used to identify individual network numbers within the routing area. Utilizing more than one area address allows the area to be reorganized without interrupting operations. A routing area can have up to three different area addresses (each with a different mask), and any combination of area addresses can be used within a domain.

Bindery Mode

In NetWare 2.x and 3.x, resources regarding server names and object names are stored in a flat database, called the *bindery*. In Novell NetWare 4.x, bindery emulation is an NDS service that makes the Directory database emulate a flat database. A *flat* database is one in which all objects in the database exist as entries. An object cannot contain another object. In NetWare 4.x, network objects and their related information are contained in a hierarchical database, called the *Directory*. A *hierarchical* database can contain several levels of objects, which means that objects can contain other objects.

Bindery emulation enables programs written (application processing interface) to run under NetWare bindery to find the network object information they need in NetWare 4.x's Directory, by making the information in the Directory appear as a flat structure. Such bindery emulation is provided by the *bindery services utility*, which makes the bindery's contents look appropriate for whatever server is querying it.

NDS Mode

NDS is an object-oriented implementation of directory services that enables you to build sophisticated naming schemes and databases across network-wide resources. The NDS architecture provides global access to all network resources regardless of where the resources are physically located—thereby forming a single information system.

NDS was developed as a hierarchical design with multiple levels of organizational units, users, groups, and network resources. This structure is referred to as the *Directory Tree*. NDS functions within the network. The management of the NDS architecture includes the creation and management of objects and the distribution of the Directory partitions and replicas. Management utilities are provided as part of the NOS to help maintain the NDS database within the network. The following is a list of utilities that are available for maintaining the database:

➤ DSMERGE

➤ DESREPAIR

➤ DSTRACE

➤ INSTALL

> ➤ NETADMIN

> ➤ NETWARE ADMINISTRATOR

> ➤ PARTMGR

> ➤ SET (NDS PARAMETERS)

> ➤ TIMESYNC

> ➤ UIMPORT

4

NDS uses the X.500 specification developed by the Institute of Electrical and Electronic Engineers (IEEE) to provide a standard method for organizing information that is accessed transparently on a global basis. Users can log into a multiserver network and view the entire network as a single information system. This system is the basis for increased productivity and reduces administrative costs. NDS features and functionality provide for implementation on small, medium, and large networks.

Configuring IPX

To enable IPX routing on an interface, first enter the **ipx routing** command in global configuration mode, and then enter the interface configuration mode and assign an IPX network and an encapsulation type, as follows:

```
2514#config t
2514(config)#ipx routing
2514(config)#int e0
2514(config-if)#ipx network 10 encapsulation snap
```

AppleTalk

AppleTalk comprises a stack of protocols. Figure 4.7 shows how each protocol maps to the OSI Reference Model. The protocols include the following:

> ➤ *AppleTalk Address Resolution Protocol (AARP)*—Used to dynamically assign addresses to individual machines and to map Layer 3 addresses to Layer 2 addresses, therefore making it similar to TCP/IP's ARP.

> ➤ *Datagram Delivery Protocol (DDP)*—Provides connectionless transport of data, meaning that it does not require an acknowledgement from the destination node that all packets have been received or are in the right order. DDP ensures unique addressing of all machines on an AppleTalk internetwork.

> ➤ *Name Binding Protocol (NBP)*—Used by applications and processes using AppleTalk to make their services known and available throughout the internetwork. It also maps hostnames to Layer 3 addresses.

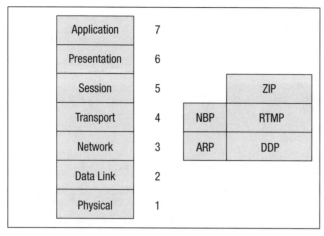

Figure 4.7 The AppleTalk protocols and how they map to the OSI Reference Model.

➤ *Routing Table Maintenance Protocol (RTMP)*—A distance-vector routing protocol that shares its updates with other routers every 10 seconds. RTMP employs split horizon (described in the accompanying sidebar) to prevent routing loops. The AppleTalk protocol running on a workstation contains a small part of RTMP as well, which is called the *RTMP stub*. DDP uses this stub to determine the network address of the workstation, as well as the network address and node ID of a router on that segment.

➤ *Zone Information Protocol (ZIP)*—Responsible for mapping zone names to network addresses and for providing applications and processes with access to zone names. This can include their own node's zone name, the names of all zones on the local network, or the names of all the zones throughout the internetwork. The next section discusses zones in more detail.

Split Horizon, Route Poisoning, Poison Reverse, and Holddowns

Many solutions are available for routing loop problems. S*plit horizon* reduces incorrect routing information and routing overhead used in a distance-vector network by enforcing the rule that information cannot be sent back in the same direction from which it was received. Split horizon prevents a router from sending updated network information it just received from one router back to that router.

Route poisoning is another way to avoid problems caused by inconsistent updates. If a network link fails, a router initiates route poisoning by entering a table entry for the failed network and lists the failed network as unreachable. This is sometimes referred to as an *infinite number*. When a router receives a route poisoning from one router and sends an update back, it is called a *poison reverse*.

Route poisoning uses *holddowns*, which speed up convergence time, because neighboring routers don't make neighboring routers wait 30 seconds to converge. Holddowns are timers that are used to prevent routes from changing too rapidly, by allowing time for either the downed route to come back or the network to find the next best route for data to take if redundancy exists in the network.

AppleTalk Routing and Access

Zones are logical network segments that you can create to overcome limitations of your physical network. These logical segments are based on users and enable you to group together departments which may be located on different floors of a building but have the same need for certain resources.

Normally, communication between floors occurs with the use of routers, and every floor's physical network represents the broadcast domain used by the users of that particular floor only. AppleTalk utilizes broadcasts to locate resources, and zones enable you to let users who are part of the same department but located on different floors share the same broadcast domain. So, by creating departmental zones, you have the ability to group together users and needed resources. For example, suppose your building houses three Engineering departments: one on the first floor, one on the third floor, and another on the sixth floor.

When creating the zone for the Engineering department, the router interfaces on the first, third, and sixth floor have to be configured to be part of the Engineering department. The routers build tables of zones, enabling them to forward broadcast requests to network segments within the zone and forward the replies back to the source workstation's network segment. *Chooser* is an application used by Mac users to locate resources on the network. When Chooser is launched, the user selects a zone and the type of resource needed, such as a printer or file server. Chooser then builds a list of workstations providing the requested service within that zone, and lets the user select one. After that, the user can continue with the task.

This scenario makes it pretty clear that proper broadcast forwarding is important, because the users employ Chooser only to find out about the resources on the network, from which they pick the one they want. A new peripheral (such as a printer) on the network simply needs to be told what zone it belongs to, and Chooser will find and represent it to the requesting user.

As on any network, nothing works without addressing. AppleTalk addresses are 24 bits long, where 16 bits are used for the network address and the other 8 bits make up the node address. No subnetting exists, but AppleTalk comes in two different versions, Phase 1 and Phase 2, the feature differences of which are shown in Table 4.1.

Table 4.1   The feature differences of AppleTalk Phase 1 and Phase 2.

Feature	Phase 1	Phase 2
Number of network addresses per segment	1	Unlimited
Number of host addresses per network	127	Unlimited
Number of server addresses per network	127	Unlimited
Number of zones per network	1	255

As this table shows, quite a few limitations are placed on Phase 1. You can have only 127 hosts, because only 8 bits are used for the node. Because only one network address exists per segment, no room is left to go beyond the 127 hosts. No option of creating logical networks is available because of the limitation to one zone. Phase 2, on the other hand, provides a way to implement AppleTalk in a larger network.

Of course, you can't really have unlimited network addresses, because even with Phase 2 you are required to use 16 bits for the network address—no more and no less. However, even this limitation would give you 65,000 different network addresses. Also, you now have the option of creating up to 255 zones, or logical networks.

The ability to assign multiple network addresses on a single network in Phase 2 is called *extended addressing* and is done by assigning a range of addresses to one segment. For example, configuring the range of 100-110 would provide 11 network addresses, whereas configuring the range of 100-1000 would provide 901 network addresses and, therefore, many more node addresses. The question still remains of how a workstation receives its address. It would seem simple, because node addressing is dynamic and no administration is involved.

When the node starts up, AppleTalk first sends out a ZIP to find the network address, or to find out whether extended addressing applies the network range. Then it selects a random node address and uses AARP to find out whether another node on the network is already using this particular address. If no response is received, it's a keeper.

When a node starts up for the very first time, it sets up a provisional address by randomly selecting a network number between 65,280 and 65,534. This is called the *startup range*. After that, it randomly selects the node address. If this is not the first time the node starts up, it can use the previous address as a *hint* and again use AARP to check whether it's really available. If the node finds that another node on that network is already using this newly assigned address, it assigns another random number. If AppleTalk can't find an available address on the network, it simply chooses a new network address from the startup range, selects a new node number, checks it with AARP, and uses this provisional address (if it's available).

At this point, the network node can send a ZIP GetNetInfo request to a router and find out what the actual segment's cable range is. If the provisional address does not fall into the segment's cable range, the node will select one that does fit in that range. After the node finds an unused address, it uses it as a future *hint*. Just like IP, though, AppleTalk has a few reserved addresses. The network number 0 cannot be used, because nodes that haven't learned their segment's address use it. Node addresses 254 and 255 are reserved, as well.

AppleTalk Discovery

Even though the *discovery mode* cannot be used on serial interfaces, it eases the configuration of Ethernet interfaces and also prevents configuration errors on large networks. On a single Ethernet segment with three routers attached, you could configure the Ethernet interfaces manually or use AppleTalk discovery.

In the latter case, you would only configure the first router's Ethernet interface, cable range, and zone information. This router will become the *seed router*, which means it will provide the cable-range and zone information to the other routers.

Only the seed router has to be modified; if the segment needs reconfiguration, the other routers will learn about the new information when they're rebooted or if AppleTalk is restarted on the interface. Any router can function as a seed router, after it has its node address.

Enabling AppleTalk

AppleTalk routing requires you first to enable the AppleTalk Protocol in global configuration mode and then configure the individual interfaces on the router with the network and zone information. It is not uncommon to assign all serial interfaces to a single AppleTalk zone.

Here is an example of enabling AppleTalk routing:

```
2514#config terminal
Enter configuration commands, one per line.  End with CTRL/Z.
2514(config)#appletalk routing
2514(config)#^Z
2514#
```

The following is an example of configuring the Ethernet0 and Serial0 interfaces with network, cable range, and zone information:

```
Router1#config terminal
Enter configuration commands, one per line.  End with CNTRL/Z.
Router1(config)#interface ethernet0
Router1(config-if)#appletalk cable-range 100-150
Router1(config-if)#appletalk zone Coriolis
Router1(config-if)#interface serial0
Router1(config-if)#appletalk cable-range 1000-1000
Router1(config-if)#appletalk zone Coriolis2
Router1(config-if)#^Z
```

Note: The cable range of 1000-1000 in the preceding command specifies a single network. When using nonextended addressing, the syntax is **appletalk address address**.

Chapter Summary

This chapter has discussed the TCP/IP, IPX/SPX, and AppleTalk suites of protocols. The subject of this book is on the Support Exam and troubleshooting. Before you can troubleshoot your network, you must understand how the network functions and how to properly configure the protocols that you need to troubleshoot.

You learned in this chapter how to determine which transport protocols are being used. The key differences between the transport protocols discussed in this chapter are how the protocols allow you to remotely access servers, files, send broadcasts and how error messages are sent.

Each protocol has its own address resolution and name resolution protocols. This chapter covered all of these protocols and the way in which this information is buffered for reuse the next time around. It also covered in detail how services are advertised on a Novell network, and where Cisco routers fit into that picture. You also discovered that NetWare enables you to change the packet size, or the amount of data being transferred simultaneously.

You also learned about a few protocols used by AppleTalk in internetworks for tasks, such as routing, name lookup, and resource discovery. This chapter covered AppleTalk addressing (Phase 1 and Phase 2), what zones are, how zones are utilized in the internetwork, and what role routers play in these situations. Thereafter, you found out that routers receive their configuration information either manually or through discovery mode. Finally, some common problems and their resolutions were listed, as a guideline for AppleTalk troubleshooting.

Review Questions

1. At what layer of the OSI model does IP belong?

    a. Transport

    b. Network

    c. Presentation

    d. Session

2. What device may be necessary for ISDN communication to occur?

    a. Packet Assembly Disassemblers

    b. Terminal Adapter

    c. Frame Relay Access Device

    d. File Transport Protocol

3. Which protocol would be used on a server if you were to multihome the server with two NICs?

   a. RIP

   b. DHCP

   c. IPX

   d. MPR

4. Which fields are present in a TCP segment that is sent across the network? [Choose the best answers]

   a. Two-byte frame

   b. Destination Port

   c. Preamble

   d. Checksum

5. The Time-Exceeded message indicating that a hop count limit has exceeded is sent by which of the following components?

   a. ARP

   b. ICMP

   c. UDP

   d. IP

6. Which of the following is a broadcast sent by ARP when it is unable to locate a host on the network?

   a. 224.255.255.255

   b. FFFFFFFF

   c. 11111111

   d. 00000000

7. Which of the following will resolve a hostname to an IP address?

   a. DHCP

   b. Windows

   c. DNS

   d. NetBIOS

8. When configuring a workstation to access the Internet from a LAN, you need an IP address, subnet mask, and gateway.

   a. True

   b. False

9. What well-known TCP ports does FTP use?

   a. 121

   b. 23

   c. 21

   d. 20

10. Which of the following is a concern you would have when using an IP Helper Address on your router?

    a. Getting a response would take a long time

    b. Eight protocols would broadcast on the segment at one time

    c. It wouldn't be easy to configure

    d. It would present a difficult DHCP concept

11. Which of the following is used to control routing loops in the network?

    a. Split Horizon

    b. Route Poisoning

    c. Poison Reverse

    d. Holddowns

    e. All of the above

12. Using Novell routing protocols, which protocol uses ticks and hop counts as part of its metrics?

    a. IPX

    b. SAP

    c. RIP

    d. SPX

13. How often does SAP advertise on a Novell network?

    a. Every 30 seconds

    b. Every 90 seconds

    c. Every 60 seconds

    d. Every 120 seconds

14. What are some of the benefits of using a Packet Burst (Protocol)? [Choose the two best answers]

    a. The server or workstation can send a whole set (burst) of packets before it requires an acknowledgement

    b. Too much administration

    c. Great for sending video

    d. Reduces network traffic

15. NDS benefits a large network environment with many branch offices within the United States and overseas?

    a. True

    b. False

16. What protocols within the AppleTalk suite provide addressing? [Choose the two best answers]

    a. ZIP

    b. RTMP

    c. NBP

    d. DDP

    e. AARP

17. Why would you use a zone in a large organization that has several floors and departments? [Choose the two best answers]

    a. To organize end users into groups

    b. It is managed by DHCP server

    c. To overcome limitations of your physical network

    d. Because you are using AppleTalk

18. Which of the following best describes Route Poisoning?

    a. Bad cable

    b. Protocol not enabled

    c. Prevents route loopbacks

    d. Congestion

19. In which Cisco router configuration mode would you use the **appletalk routing** command?

    a. Global configuration mode

    b. Interface configuration mode

    c. Router configuration mode

    d. Privileged EXEC mode

20. Which of the following protocols are routed protocols? [Choose the two best answers]

    a. IP

    b. IGRP

    c. NLSP

    d. IPX

CHAPTER FIVE

Basic Configurations

After completing this chapter, you will be able to:

✓ Understand the several different Cisco router series

✓ Configure router interfaces and subinterfaces

✓ Use several CLI commands

✓ Use descriptions to help identify interfaces

✓ Download and upload router IOS

✓ Assign router passwords using CLI commands

✓ Create banners for your router

✓ Troubleshoot an interface

✓ Administratively bring down an interface

✓ Configure clock rate and bandwidth

✓ Determine DCE or DTE connections on an interface

This chapter presents an overview of routers and their architectures. Knowing different routers will help you in troubleshooting. This chapter does not discuss in depth the architecture of each router, but instead introduces basic commands for configuring interfaces. More-complex commands are discussed later in this book. This chapter introduces basic skills for troubleshooting an interface, whereas more-advanced troubleshooting skills are presented in Chapter 12. This chapter covers basic router configurations, saving configurations, and how to load an IOS to a router by using the command-line interface (CLI).

Router Overview

Most Cisco routers are modular in design and offer a wide range of modules for every technology. Cisco's product line of routers begins with the 600 series and goes up through the 12000 series. Usually, the smaller the number, the smaller the router load; for example, the 600 series is for SOHO (small office-home office) use, and the 12000 series is a core router for large-volume businesses.

SOHO Routers

Cisco's 600, 700, 800, 1000, 1400, and 1600 series routers are mainly for the small office or home use for telecommuters. Like any Cisco routers, these are not exclusively for SOHO use; they can be combined with other routers in a large network environment.

The 600 series routers are mainly for Digital Subscriber Line (DSL) and Asymmetric Digital Subscriber Line (ADSL) use. They can be used with ATM and can provide data service unit (DSU) connectivity to business-class routers. The 700 series routers are mainly used for ISDN, and are great for consolidating multiple modems and reducing costs of multiple phone lines. The 800 and 1000 series routers offer more flexibility with value-added services such as class of services, Virtual Private Networks (VPNs), and security. The 800 series routers can connect to a LAN via ISDN, Frame Relay, X.25, asynchronous dial-up, IDSL, and ADSL. The 800 series routers are optimal for corporate telecommuters. The 1400 and 1600 series routers are optimal for a small corporate LAN office or VPN because they offer firewall capabilities, ATM IP Quality of Service (QoS), and multimedia capabilities. The 1600 series also connects LANs to WANs via ISDN as well as asynchronous and synchronous serial connections. As with all series of these routers, Cisco offers many cards or slots to meet the SOHO requirements of today.

Small/Medium Routers

Cisco offers a wide variety of middle-sized routers for use in small to medium-sized businesses, as well as for combining with a large corporation using various sizes of routers. Cisco's 2500/2600, 3600, and 4000 series routers are modular in design and are able to maintain a small to medium-sized business environment.

The 2500 series router can support the most widely used protocols, including IP, IPX, and Apple Talk, as well as offer an integrated hub. The 2600 model is very similar to the 2500, except the 2600 model has slots, including one module slot for features such as voice and fax, and two WAN slots for options such as built-in CSU/DSU, ISDN, serial ports, asynchronous ports, and so forth.

The 3600 series is a more powerful router that is able to support a medium- to large-sized business and that is able to support various solutions such as data, voice, video, hybrid dial access, VPNs, multiprotocol data routing, voice over Frame Relay (VoFR), voice over IP (VoIP), and enhanced queuing functionality.

The 4000 series routers are capable of supporting medium-sized LANs with WANs connected to it. The 4500 series offers powerful CPUs for greater processing performance, to grow with your network's needs. The 4000 series routers are able to maintain most bandwidth needs, and allow for power redundancy in the network with a 600-watt AC power system. Because of the large volume of these routers on the market, Cisco is constantly updating the IOSs for these routers to support the newer technologies, such as VoIP and custom queuing.

Core Routers

The core routers are found in large corporations and campus environments to support the massive amounts of data and other routing needs that are needed to support a large business's. Core routers mainly consist of the 7000, 7500, 10000, and the 12000 series routers. These high-end routers are also modular in design and offer a full range of customizing to fit your network needs. The Cisco 7000 series has stopped being sold as of July 31, 1997 due to the increased popularity of the 7500 series. You may still need to know a bit about the 7000 series, though, because they are still used in some networks and you may need to know the architecture for troubleshooting.

The 7000 series uses a silicon switch process (SSP) to store the switched cache and autonomous switched cache that allows for faster performance. The 7000 series also provides a Cisco Extended Bus (CxBus) for transmitting data to and from processor modules. The distributed processing is accomplished by the Route Processor (RP), Switch Processor (SP), and the Silicon Switch Processor (SSP). The 7100 and 7200 series are still being sold because they offer specialized features. The 7100 series router is a high-end VPN router offering VPN tunneling, data encryption, security, a firewall, and advanced bandwidth management. It also supports cost-effective remote offices. The 7200 series provides high density and broad media support at a lower port cost than some other routers, thus making it a good all around general routing platform capable of supporting large bandwidth.

The Cisco 7500 series is used for high-speed backbone aggregation for high-speed enterprise interconnectivity. This series uses an integrated route switch processor (RSP) to increase frame transmission rates, along with a Cisco Extended Bus

(CyBus), the data bus used for processor modules. The Cisco 7500 series router provides high packet-forwarding performance by distributing the switching operation to the Versatile Interface Processors (VIPs). The multiprotocol/multimedia network router enables integration of multiple WAN technologies and provides the necessary bandwidth and service requirements for most networks.

The Cisco 7500 integrates Layer 3 services including QoS, security, encryption, and traffic management. The multichannel technology in the 7500 offers a scalable and cost-effective WAN solution where high-density, leased-line services are needed. The 10000 series is an Edge Service Router (ESR) that is solely designed for ISPs requiring advanced IP services such as QoS and VPN for a large, customer-based business. This router offers the new forwarding technology called Parallel eXpress Forwarding (PXF) and is designed to support thousands of T1 ports per chassis. The 12000 series offers Gigabit Switch Routers (GSRs) that provide high-performance solutions ranging from 5 to 60 Gbps for Internet and large-scale WAN intranet backbone applications.

The IOS

The Cisco Internetworking Operating System (IOS) was designed by Cisco to deliver network services and enable networked applications. The Cisco IOS is the kernel of Cisco routers and most switches. This is very helpful in working with Cisco equipment, because the switches and routers are configured and maintained using the same IOS, but different versions. As Cisco has emerged as a huge corporation, it has acquired many companies and devices. With the new devices coming on board as Cisco products, Cisco is in the process of implementing the Cisco IOS on all of its products.

The Cisco IOS software is used to enable the following services on Cisco devices:

➤ Many different network protocols and commands of the IOS

➤ Interoperability with Cisco equipment (while still supporting high-speed traffic delivery)

➤ Scalability, for network growth and redundancy and for new services on existing equipment

➤ Network security to stop unauthorized access, using policy-based networking (discussed in Chapter 11)

Connecting to a Cisco Router

You can connect to a Cisco router in any of several ways. Typically, you would use the console port to connect to a desktop or laptop running terminal-emulation software, such as HyperTerminal, found in Windows 95, 98, NT, and 2000. This software can also be downloaded from **www.hilgraeve.com**.

A second way of connecting to a Cisco router is through an auxiliary port. This is very similar to using a console port, but it enables you to configure modem commands and supports a modem connection to the router. This enables you to dial in to a remote router and attach to the Aux port if the router is down and you need to configure it. This is very important if you have routers that are not on-site.

A third way to connect to a Cisco router is through Telnet, an emulation program that enables your computer to act like a dumb terminal for the router. You can use Telnet to connect to any active interface of a router.

The 2520 router is the router that will be configured in this chapter. This router has two low-speed serial (asynchronous/synchronous) interfaces, two high-speed serial interfaces, one ISDN interface, and either one Ethernet port with AUI or one Ethernet 10BaseT interface. This model is mainly used as a single LAN router.

5

Turning on a Router

When first turning on a router, it will run a power-on self test (POST). If it passes this test, it will load the IOS from flash memory. *Flash memory* is erasable and programmable read-only memory that holds the IOS software retained while the router is powered off. After the IOS loads, the router looks for a configuration called the startup configuration, which is stored in nonvolatile RAM (NVRAM).

If the router does not find a configuration in NVRAM, the router will bring up Setup mode. A router straight from the box will not have a configuration file. Setup mode will guide you through a step-by-step process to configure the router. Setup is a very basic configuration that allows only global commands, but it's helpful for configuring certain protocols that are not widely used, such as DECnet.

Note: *You can enter Setup mode any time by typing "setup" from the global configuration mode.*

Router Modes

IOS software uses a command-line interpreter called EXEC that interprets the commands you type at the prompts. The EXEC has two levels of access to commands:

➤ *User EXEC Mode*—When logging into a router, you are automatically at this level. This mode in indicated by the > symbol as the router prompt. This mode is a lower-level mode that enables you to connect to remote devices, perform basic tests, give visibility of configurations, and contains basic commands that do not allow for configuration changes to the router. This mode allows you to view the current picture of the router. Access to this mode is especially helpful in a help-desk situation for lower-level troubleshooting without allowing for destructive changes to be made to the router.

➤ *Privilege EXEC Mode*—To enter this mode, you type "enable", and if the router prompts for a password, you then type the password. This mode is indicated by the pound sign (#) as the router prompt. This mode has all the capabilities of the user mode plus access to change configurations of the router. This mode includes high-level troubleshooting and configuration commands. This mode should always be password-protected because of the capabilities Privilege EXEC Mode offers. If the commands are not implemented correctly, you can take down your network.

Setup Mode

Setup mode gives you two options:

➤ *Basic Management*—This mode prompts for very few options and has just enough configuration commands to allow you to connect to the router.

➤ *Extended Setup*—Provides more commands that will allow more configurations for the router and each interface.

Extended Setup guides you through the step-by-step process, and appears as follows:

```
- System Configuration Dialog -

Continue with configuration dialog? [yes/no]: y
At any point you may enter a question mark '?' for help.
Use ctrl-c to abort configuration dialog at any prompt.
Default settings are in square brackets '[]'.
First, would you like to see the current interface summary? [yes]: y

Configuring global parameters:
Enter host name [router1]: Support
The enable secret is a password used to protect access to privileged EXEC
and configuration modes. This password, after entered, becomes encrypted in
the configuration. Enter enable secret: prep

The enable password is used when you do not specify an enable secret pass-
word, with some older software versions, and some boot images.
Enter enable password: prep
% Please choose a password that is different from the enable secret
Enter enable password: security
```

*Note: The IOS provides a reminder to have different passwords for **enable secret password** and **enable password**.*

```
The virtual terminal password is used to protect
access to the router over a network interface.
Enter virtual terminal password: security
Configure SNMP Network Management? [no]: n
```

```
Configure LAT? [yes]: n
Configure AppleTalk? [no]: n
Configure DECnet? [no]: n
Configure IP? [yes]: y
Configure IGRP routing? [yes]: n
Configure RIP routing? [no]: n
Configure CLNS? [no]:
Configure IPX? [no]:
Configure Vines? [no]:
Configure XNS? [no]:
Configure Apollo? [no]:
```

5

Note: *Any dialog in square brackets is the default settings. You simply press Enter to accept the default settings.*

```
BRI interface needs isdn switch-type to be configured
Valid switch types are :
[0]  none.........Only if you don't want to configure BRI.
[1]  basic-1tr6....1TR6 switch type for Germany
[2]  basic-5ess....AT&T 5ESS switch type for the US/Canada      [3]
   basic-dms100..Northern DMS-100 switch type for       US/Canada[4]
   basic-net3....NET3 switch type for UK and Europe[5]  basic-ni......
   National ISDN switch type
[6]  basic-ts013...TS013 switch type for Australia
[7]  ntt..........NTT switch type for Japan
[8]  vn3..........VN3 and VN4 switch types for France
Choose ISDN BRI Switch Type [2]: 2
Configuring interface parameters:
Do you want to configure BRI0 (BRI d-channel) interface? [no]: n

Do you want to configure Ethernet0  interface? [no]: n

Do you want to configure Serial0  interface? [no]: n

Do you want to configure Serial1  interface? [no]: n

Do you want to configure Serial2  interface? [no]: n

Do you want to configure Serial3  interface? [no]: n

The following configuration command script was created:

hostname Support
enable secret 5 $1$yYRK$cKu7UVrFMP6jlfCmv9hP4.
enable password security
```

```
line vty 0 4
password security
no snmp-server
!
[0] Go to the IOS command prompt without saving this config.
[1] Return back to the setup without saving this config.
[2] Save this configuration to nvram and exit.
```

Setup mode can help you configure a router, but using the CLI instead of Setup gives you much more flexibility and is faster to use for well-versed router users. (CLI is discussed in more detail later in this chapter.) First, you need to learn how to save your configurations.

Saving Configurations

At the end of Setup mode, the IOS gives you a few options about your created configuration. After the configuration is created, the router will offer two options: not saving the configuration, or saving the configuration to NVRAM. If you choose to save the configuration, the IOS will save it in DRAM (the running configuration) and then to NVRAM or startup configuration. Using the saving command in Setup does all the work for you. To manually save the command from DRAM to NVRAM, you can use the command **copy running-config startup-config** (all one command). A shortcut for this command is **copy run start**. When you're doing a lot of configurations on a router, you should use this command often in the process. After you have saved your configurations, use the **show running** command periodically to check what you have configured.

Command-Line Interface

Using the CLI to configure a router is much easier, and allows for more flexibility than using the Setup mode. The CLI supports a set of commands telling the router what you want it to do. To use the CLI, you have to respond "no" in the initial configuration dialog box prompt when you first turn on the router. When you respond "no" to Setup mode, you see messages stating the status of all the router interfaces.

To configure a router using the CLI, you can use the **configure terminal or (config t)** command to enter global configuration mode. The global configuration commands, shown next, are commands that affect the system as a whole, rather than just one interface or protocol:

```
Router# config
Configuring from terminal, memory, or network? [terminal]: returnEnter
configuration commands, one per line. End with CNTL/Z.
```

```
Router(config)#
Router#config t
Enter configuration commands, one per line.  End with CNTL/Z.
```

When you reach this point in the configuration, you are ready to make changes in the router in global configuration mode. All changes made here will affect the entire router, not just one interface. The first thing you can do is name your router. This is very helpful when connecting to the router from a remote site. The following is an example of naming your router:

```
Router(config)#hostname Support
Support(config)#
```

Setting the Passwords

Router security is mostly dependent on setting and maintaining passwords on your routers. It is a good idea to change them often and have a password set on all accesses to the router. Five passwords can be used in securing the router. The first two are usually set when first initializing the router. They are the enable password and the secret password. The other three access ports that need passwords to be set are the console port, the auxiliary port, and Telnet accesses or VTY ports.

You always set the enable passwords from global configuration mode. The following are a few examples of setting passwords on your router:

```
Support# config t
Enter configuration commands, one per line.  End with CNTL/Z.
Support(config)#enable password prep
Support(config)#enable secret book
```

Note: The IOS does not recommend having the enable secret and the enable password the same. If you try to assign the same password for both, it will prompt you to choose an enable password that is different from the enable secret password.

User mode passwords are assigned by using the **line** command in global configuration mode. The following is an example of configuring a console port:

```
Support(config)#line ?
<0-9>    First Line number
aux      Auxiliary line
console  Primary terminal line
tty      Terminal controller
vty      Virtual terminalvty 0
Support(config)#line console 0
Support(config-line)#login
Support(config-line)#password prepbook
```

While setting the console password, you may also want to set a timeout for the console port. The **line console** command will enable you to specify how long the session is allowed to remain open. The following is an example of setting a timeout session for a console port:

```
Support(config)#line console 0
Support(config-line)#exec-timeout ?
<0-35791> Timeout in minutes
Support(config-line)#exec-timeout 0 ?
<0-2147483> Timeout in seconds
Support(config-line)#exec-timeout 0 0
```

The first amount of time can be configured in minutes, and the second amount for seconds. Usually, the timeout is set at 0 minutes and 0 seconds, so that it never times out. Having a short timeout could get frustrating if you routinely log on to the router for a long period of time for troubleshooting.

The following is an example of setting the password for the auxiliary port:

```
Support(config-line)#line aux 0
Support(config-line)#login
Support(config-line)#password supportprep
```

When setting the Telnet password, it is always a good idea to see how many VTY lines exist on the router. Typically, five VTY lines exist, lines 0–4. However, there may be more, depending on the IOS on the router. The following is an example of setting Telnet passwords on all VTY lines:

```
Support(config-line)#line vty 0 ?
<1-5> Last Line Number
Support(config-line)#line vty 0 4
Support(config-line)#login
Support(config-line)#password supportprepbook
```

Note: The passwords used in the preceding code are just examples. The importance of using different passwords and passwords longer than seven digits, using numbers and letters, cannot be stressed enough.

It is recommended in a large network to use a TACACS server to log in to your routers. This provides added security and also allows for password changes to occur on all the routers, as opposed to changing them individually.

Command-Line Help

Many ways exist to manipulate the command lines when using the CLI. In fact, you probably won't use all the possible commands to maneuver in the command line. However, you will become accustomed to using certain commands. If you type anything like I do, you will utilize the up arrow or Ctrl+P to the fullest. The up arrow recalls the last command; for example, if you misspell a word and the command is returned with an error, you can simply press the up arrow key and correct your mistake. Table 5.1 shows some commonly used commands.

Context-Sensitive Help

5

When you use the CLI, Cisco offers you help when you're configuring a router. You can always type a question mark at any prompt to obtain a list of all the commands available at the prompt you are at. You can implement **?** at any time in the command line.

When using context-sensitive help, the space (or lack of a space) before the question mark is significant. To obtain a list of commands that begin with a particular character sequence, type those commands followed by the question mark. Do *not* include a space. To obtain a list of keywords or arguments, enter a question mark in place of a key word or argument, and include a space before the question mark. The following is an example of using **?** without a space:

```
Support#co?
```

The router will list these options:

```
configure  connect  copy
Support# configure
Support(config)#
```

Table 5.1   Commonly used commands.

Command	Purpose
Ctrl+P or the up arrow	Recalls commands in the buffer, starting with the most recent
Show history	Recalls several commands while in EXEC mode
Ctrl+A	Moves the cursor to the beginning of the line
Ctrl+L	Redisplays the current command line if the screen is interrupted
Ctrl+E	Moves the cursor to the end of the line
Ctrl+W	Deletes the word to the left of the cursor
Ctrl+Z	Ends configuration mode and returns you to EXEC mode
Ctrl+U	Erases a line

Here is an example of using *?* with a space:

```
Support#configure ?
```

The router will list these options:

```
Memory    configure from NV memory
Network    configure from a TFTP network host
Terminal   configure from the terminal
Support# terminal
Support(config)#
```

Another helpful context-sensitive help command is the Tab key, which will complete a partial command. The following is an example:

```
Support#conf<tab>
Support#configure
```

When using the Tab key, the IOS looks for a command that starts with "conf" and then completes the command. If you simply type "con," the IOS will not know which command you are trying to enter. The Tab key is very helpful, but you need to make sure that you type enough of the command so that the IOS knows what you want.

Loading the IOS

The Cisco IOS software contains system images. When you receive a router out of the box, it already has a system image on it, but you may want to load a different image on it. Cisco constantly has software upgrades, and loading different images enables you to keep the same version of software throughout your network. It is a good idea to frequently check the Cisco Web site, **www.cisco.com**, for new versions of code for your router. Two main types of images exist for your router:

➤ *System image*—The image you receive when receiving your router; it has the complete IOS software. This image is usually located in flash memory. The **show file systems** command will help you find which file systems your router supports.

➤ *Boot image*—Used mainly to perform network booting or to load IOS images onto the router. This image can also be used if the router cannot find a valid system image. It is a subset of the complete IOS software and may be referred to as *xboot image, rxboot image, bootstrap image,* or *bootloader/helper image*. Most boot images are contained in ROM, whereas others may be in flash memory. You can specify which image should be used as the boot image by using the command **boot bootldr**.

The IOS on the router affects the entire router, not just the interfaces. Thus, you must be in global configuration mode. After logging in to your router, the best way to see what version of IOS is running is to use the command **show version**. The italic text in the following code indicates the version of code running on this router:

```
Support#sh version
Cisco Internetwork Operating System Software
IOS (tm) 2500 Software (C2500-AJS40-L), Version 11.3(5)T,  RELEASE
   SOFTWARE (fc1)
Copyright (c) 1986-1998 by cisco Systems, Inc.
Compiled Wed 12-Aug-98 05:53 by ccai
Image text-base: 0x0305770C, data-base: 0x00001000

ROM: System Bootstrap, Version 11.0(10c), SOFTWARE
BOOTFLASH: 3000 Bootstrap Software (IGS-BOOT-R), Version 11.0(10c),
   RELEASE SOFTWARE (fc1)
```

Copying Images

Whether you're copying images to a server or another flash memory card on your router, saving your configurations should be commonplace for your everyday network documentation. This is a good rule regardless of whether a business has two routers or 400 routers. At any given time, your router may lose its configuration file or have other problems. Uploading or downloading a configuration file is much easier than re-creating the configuration, especially in a network that is expected to be running 24 hours a day.

Making changes to a copy of a configuration and downloading the changes to a router is much more handy than making changes to the router while experiencing downtime.

Copy from Flash Memory to a TFTP Server

It is a good idea to always have your router configurations stored on a Trivial File Transfer Protocol (TFTP) server, in case something perilous happens to a router. In a large network, this is very helpful when you need to use hot-standby routers. These are usually spare routers that can be incorporated into your production network at any time simply by uploading an image from the TFTP server to the router. Then, you simply attach the router to the network network, enabling you to fix the problem router without much downtime. The following is an example of uploading flash memory to a TFTP server:

```
Support#copy flash tftp
IP address of remote host [255.255.255.255]?152.61.10.10
Filename to write on tftp host?S25AHL-12.0.5T

Writing S25AHL-12.0.5T  !!!!!!!!
```

Copy an Image from Flash Memory to an FTP Server

When sending an image to an FTP server, the image must have a username and password associated with the FTP server. The FTP server must be properly configured to accept the FTP request from the user on the router. The client must send a remote username and password on each FTP request to send any configurations to the FTP server. When copying a configuration file to the FTP server, the IOS sends a valid username and then a valid password. The router then forms a password *username@routername.domain*. The username is associated as the username with the current session, the router name is the configured host name, and the domain of the router is the domain. After completing this process, sending a configuration to an FTP server is not any different than sending a configuration to a TFTP server, as shown in the following example:

```
Support#copy flash ftp
IP address of remote host [255.255.255.255]?152.61.10.10
Filename to write on tftp host?S25AHL-12.0.5T

Writing S25AHL-12.0.5T  !!!!!!!!
```

Copy from a TFTP Server to Flash Memory

One of the first things to remember when copying to flash memory is to check to see how much memory the router has. If not enough flash memory exists for the IOS image, your router will usually give you an error of "buffer overflow." But, you may not always get that nice reminder before the router locks up. Rebooting the router without an image in flash memory is not recommended, but sometimes the router will not respond, and you will try anything to get it to respond.

Note: The router will ask you "Erase flash before writing?" Commonly, you will not have enough flash memory to support two images, so before you answer yes, be sure you have enough flash memory.

Here is an example of the commands used for copying an image to flash:

```
Support#copy tftp flash
Destination filename[S25AHL-12.0.5T]?enter
Accessing tftp: S25AHL-12.0.5T…Translating….domain server (152.61.10.1)
   [OK]
```

Copy Images Between Flash Memory Devices

Routers with multiple flash memory file systems can copy an image from one flash file to another. A good example is to copy an image from an internal flash memory card in a PCMCIA slot to another flash memory file PC card in another slot on the router. This creates a backup image of the IOS for the router. Here is an example of the commands used to copy images locally on a router:

```
Support# copy flash:1:cisco/ios/new-ios slot0:cisco/ios/new-ios
Verifying checksum for 'cisco/ios/new-ios' (file # 1)…OK
Erase falsh device before writing?[confirm]
Flash contains files. Are you sure you want to erase? [confirm]
Copy 'cisco/ios/new-ios' from flash: device as 'cisco/ios/new-ios' into
    slot0: device with erase? [yes/no] yes
Erasing Device……eeeeeeeeeeeeeeeeeeeeeeeeeeeee…erased
!!!!!!!!!!!!!!!!!!!!!!!!!!!!!!!!!!!!!!!!!!!!!!!!!!!!!!!!!!!!!!!!!!!!!!!!
!!!!!!!!!!!!!!!!!!!!!!!!!!!!!!!!!!!!!!!!!!!!!!!!!!!!!!!!!!!!!!!!!!!!!!!!
[OK- 2142413/2142413 bytes]
```

Banners

A banner is a message displayed on the router screen when logging in to a router. Placing a banner on your router accomplishes a few things. It enables you to know what router you are logging on to, and it can help you in court. The latter of these accomplishments is the most important. Hackers sometimes like to hack into routers to see what havoc they can create. Previously, when prosecuting hackers was fairly new, a company could not prosecute an intruder because they didn't have a banner placed on the router that stated the router is private property. Until banners were placed on routers, a hacker's defense was simply, "I didn't know I was entering private property." Now, you can display a banner that states that the router is private property and that illegal entry will be prosecuted. Including a banner is such a small thing to remember, but it may help you tremendously in case a breach occurs.

The *message-of-the-day (MOTD)* banner is displayed to all terminals connected and is very useful in notifying staff of impending problems or scheduled outages. Configuring your router with a banner is very simple, as the following example shows:

```
Support#config t
Enter configuration commands, one per line.  End with CNTL/Z.
router2(config)#banner motd ?
LINE  c banner-text c, where 'c' is a delimiting character
Support(config)#banner motd #
Enter TEXT message.  End with the character '#'.
Welcome to Support Prep, if you are an unauthorized user, please log out
    immediately#
Support(config)#^Z
04:20:49: %SYS-5-CONFIG_I: Configured from console by console
Support#exit

Support con0 is now available

Press RETURN to get started.
```

```
Welcome to Support Prep, if you are an unauthorized user, please log out
    immediately
Support>
```

When someone logs on to the router, the MOTD is displayed before the router prompt. After logging in to the router, another message, called an *EXEC banner*, can be displayed. The EXEC banner will be displayed in all connections except in the case of a reverse Telnet login. The EXEC banner can display any messages that you would like the staff to read, and is a good way of conveying important messages. The command to activate this banner is **banner exec**. If you want to remove the banner, use the command **no exec-banner**.

Another type of banner used is the *incoming banner*, which can be used for reverse Telnet sessions. These sessions are initiated from the network side of the router and can display MOTD banners and incoming banners, but can't display EXEC banners. To configure this banner on your router, type the command **banner incoming**; to disable it, use **no banner incoming**.

Like the MOTD banner, the *login banner* can be displayed before the username and password. To activate the login banner, use the command **banner login**. To disable it, use the command **no banner login**.

If you are configuring a banner and don't specify which type, the IOS defaults to the MOTD banner. When configuring a new banner, the new banner automatically overwrites any previous banner that was configured.

Configuring Interfaces

Interfaces are the network connections through which packets enter and exit the router at the Network layer. Several interfaces can be configured, and the exact configuration of each interface depends on a working interface. Some of the configurable interfaces are Ethernet, Token Ring, serial interface, BRI, ATM, FDDI, and HSSI, just to name a few.

Configuring an interface is very simple. You have to be in interface configuration mode to configure an interface. The following is an example configuring a serial interface:

```
Support(config)#interface serial 0
Support(config-if)#
```

Subinterface

A single physical interface has multiple interfaces, called subinterfaces. These interfaces are seen by the router as one physical interface and are commonly referred to as *virtual interfaces*. Subinterfaces are commonly used with Frame Relay, which can use several point-to-point links or private virtual connections (PVCs). When configuring these PVCs on a router interface, you can configure the interface with several subinterfaces. The router sees each subinterface as a separate bridge port and can route incoming frames of a subinterface out another subinterface, all within one physical interface.

Subinterfaces are very useful for allowing a protocol with multiple encapsulations to exist on one physical interface. A router can receive an ARPA-framed IPX packet on a subinterface and forward the packet as a SNAP-framed packet using the same subinterface. The following is an example of configuring a subinterface:

Note: *Remove any Network layer address on the physical interface. If the physical interface has an address, frames will not be received by the local physical interfaces.*

```
Support(config)#interface serial 1
Support(config-if)#no ip address
Support(config-if)#encapsulation frame-relay
```

Note: *Cisco is the default encapsulation; if you are connecting to a non-Cisco router, use **ietf**.*

```
!
Support(config-if)#interface serial 1.1 point-to-point
Support(config-subif)#
```

Descriptions

An easy way to identify your interface is to include a description of the interface when you are configuring it. This is a good habit to get into and may save you time in the long run. Nothing is worse than having five people standing over you claiming part of the network is down while watching you search for the interface. The following is an example of adding a description to an interface:

```
Support#config t
Enter configuration commands, one per line.  End with CNTL/Z.
Support(config)#int e0
Support(config-if)#description Main Building
Support(config-if)#int s0
Support(config-if)#description E Street Building
Support(config-if)#^Z
Support#sh running
04:30:47: %SYS-5-CONFIG_I: Configured from console by consolesh runn
Building configuration...
```

```
Current configuration:

hostname Support
!
interface Ethernet0
description Main Building
ip address 152.25.25.10 255.255.255.0 secondary
ip address 152.25.15.10 255.255.255.0
no ip route-cache
no ip mroute-cache
interface Serial0
description E Street Building
ip address 152.25.10.10 255.255.255.0
no ip route-cache
no ip mroute-cache
no fair-queue
```

Clock Rate

If you are configuring an interface that will act as data circuit-terminating equipment (DCE), you must specify a clock rate for it. In an environment in which a modem or a channel service unit/data service unit (CSU/DSU) is not being used, a clock rate must be specified. As an easy way to remember which side needs a clock rate, think of the "C" in DCE as standing for clock rate. The clock rate is set in bits per second, as follows:

```
router2(config)#int s0
router2(config-if)#clock rate ?
Speed (bits per second)
1200
2400
4800
9600
19200
38400
5600064000
72000
125000
148000
250000
500000
8000001000000
1300000
2000000
4000000
```

```
<300-8000000>    Choose clockrate from list above

router2(config-if)#clock rate 64000
router2(config-if)#^Z
```

Note: If you try and put a clock rate on a DTE connection, the router will give you an error.

To remove the clock rate from the interface, use the **no clock rate** command.

Determining DCE and DTE

In determining on which side to place the clock rate, it is easier to determine first which side is DTE and which side is DCE. It has to be one or the other, but you first have to find out one of them to determine the other. By default, Cisco routers are DTE devices, but you need to be able to make them DCE devices if you are connecting routers without a modem or CSU/DSU between them. As you know, the clock rate is configured on the DCE side. You can find out which side is DTE and which is DCE by using the **show controllers serial** command:

```
Support#sh controllers serial 1
HD unit 1, idb = 0x16AD0C, driver structure at 0x170058
buffer size 1524  HD unit 1, V.35 DCE cable
cpb = 0x63, eda = 0x2940, cda = 0x2800
RX ring with 16 entries at 0x632800
00 bd_ptr=0x2800 pak=0x172FD8 ds=0x63CD28 status=00 pak_size=0
```

The third line of this output tells you that it is a DCE cable. From this, you know you have to configure a clock rate on this interface.

Bandwidth

The next step in configuring serial interfaces is the bandwidth. The default bandwidth for a Cisco router is 1.544 Mbps, or a T1. The bandwidth of a serial link is used by routing protocols such as IGRP, EIGRP, and OSPF, and these protocols are used to determine the least-cost path to a remote network. The bandwidth does not calculate RIP routing, so the bandwidth of a serial link with this protocol is not utilized. The following is an example of setting a bandwidth on an interface:

```
Support#(config-if)#bandwidth ?
<1-10000000>  Bandwidth in kilobitsSupport(config-if)#bandwidth 64
```

Setting the bandwidth on the serial interface overwrites the default bandwidth.

Configuring an IP address on an Interface

To configure an IP address on your router, you first have to be in global configuration mode and identify which interface you are going to configure. The following example configures the Ethernet 0 interface:

```
Support# config t
Support(config)#int e0
Support(config-if)# ip address 152.61.25.10 255.255.255.0
Support(config-if)#no shutdown
Support(config-if)#^Z
```

*Note: The **no shutdown** command tells the interface not to shut down. Without this command, the interface will be shutdown.*

You can also configure a secondary IP address on the same interface. You have to state that the address is secondary or the interface will not accept the IP address as an addition to the existing IP, as shown in the following example:

```
Support(config-if)#ip address 152.61.15.10 255.255.255.0 secondary
Support(config-if)#^Z

Support#show running
02:29:49: %SYS-5-CONFIG_I: Configured from console by console runn
Building configuration...

Current configuration:
hostname Support
!
interface Ethernet0
ip address 152.61.15.10 255.255.255.0 secondary
ip address 152.61.25.10 255.255.255.0
no ip route-cache
no ip mroute-cache

02:29:18: %LINEPROTO-5-UPDOWN: Line protocol on Interface Ethernet0,
   changed state to up
02:29:19: %LINK-3-UPDOWN: Interface Ethernet0, changed state to up
```

Shutting Down an Interface

After all of your hard work to bring up an interface, the thought of shutting down an interface likely is anathema to you. However, know that shutting down an interface is a necessity if you are going to be working on the interface for hardware maintenance or upgrade. Turning off the interface is also helpful in troubleshooting a network. You can turn off the segment by shutting down the interface to isolate the problem, or turn off the interface until the problem is fixed. To shut down an interface, use the command **shutdown**:

```
Support#config t
Support(config)#int s0
Support(config-if)#shutdown
```

To bring the interface back up, use the **no shutdown** command at the interface.

Interface Status and Troubleshooting

Use the command **show interface serial** to view the output of the line and data-link protocol status:

```
Support#show interface serial 1
Serial1 is administratively down, line protocol is down
Hardware is HD64570
MTU 1500 bytes, BW 1544 Kbit, DLY 20000 usec, rely 255/255, load 1/255
Encapsulation HDLC, loopback not set, keepalive set (10 sec)
```

Notice in this status, serial 1 is administratively down and the line protocol is down. This indicates an interface problem. In using this command, you can tell what is happening with the interface. When looking at the status, a few ways exist to determine where the problem may be. Table 5.2 shows different messages received when looking at the interface and possible problems/reasons for the interface status.

The first part of the message of the router output indicates serial 1 is down. This refers to the hardware of the interface. If this is down, the interface is not receiving the Carrier Detect signal from the other end. The second part of the message of the router output indicates that the line protocol is down, which indicates that the Data Link layer protocol keepalives are not being received. This could mean the connector is loose or that some other hardware problem exists.

If the router output states that serial 1 is administratively down, this indicates someone has shut down the interface.

If the router states that serial 1 is up and the line protocol is down, this could indicate any of several possible problems: no keepalives, no clock rate, a wrong connector, an encapsulation mismatch, or the other end is down.

Ideally, you want to see all the time that serial 1 is up and the line protocol is up, except for during scheduled downtimes. This means the interface is up and operational. It is always a good idea to **ping** another interface to be sure the interface is working fine. So when people come rushing into your office screaming part of the network is down, looking at the interface in the up and up mode will make it easy to say the interface is good working condition.

Table 5.2   Interface status messages.

Status of the Interface	Message Received from the Interface
Interface problem	Serial 1 is down, line protocol is down
Disabled	Serial 1 is administratively down, line protocol is down
Connection Problem	Serial 1 is up, line protocol is down
Operational	Serial 1 is up, line protocol is up

Chapter Summary

Knowing the various types of routers will help in troubleshooting problems in your network. SOHO routers usually are the lower-end routers, such as Cisco's 600, 700, 800, 1000, 1400, and 1600 series routers. These are mainly for the small office or home use for telecommuters. Cisco's 2500/2600, 3600, and 4000 series routers are modular in design (modules can be added to perform different tasks, enabling you to design a router to fit your needs) and are able to maintain small or medium business environments. The core routers, such as the 7000, 7500, 10000, and the 12000 series, are mainly used as a high-speed backbone aggregation for large campuses or corporations. As with any of these routers, they are usually combined in networks to offer the most appropriate router for all needs. Most of these routers offer new technologies, such as QoS and queuing.

This chapter has introduced the Cisco IOS and various ways to use a few of the CLI commands. The EXEC mode should be password-protected and supports all other troubleshooting that can be done from the router. Setup mode is a step-by-step process that makes configuring a router easier.

Configuring a router can be made very easy by using the command line help in the CLI. One of the first things you should do when configuring a production router is to set passwords, for security purposes. Usually, five passwords are set on a router for various types of access to the router: enable, secret, console, telnet, and auxiliary. Setting a different password for the enable and secret passwords is highly recommended; in fact, the router will remind you of this if you try to use the same password for both.

Uploading and downloading the IOS software for your router can be done in several different ways. You can copy your current configurations to a TFTP server for a backup copy or to make changes to your current configuration without experiencing downtime. At your convenience, you may download the "new" configuration from the TFTP server. If your router needs a new version of IOS, you can easily download the version to your TFTP server and, at your convenience, download the new version to the flash memory of your router without much interruption. Understanding that several ways exist to save and load IOS is very helpful in a production network.

Placing a MOTD banner on your routers can be done with very little effort (one command), and enables you to provide an introduction to your router while also warning trespassers that the router is private property. Utilizing other banners, such as the EXEC banner, can inform staff of any important messages and updates when they log into a router.

When configuring an interface that will act as a DCE, you must set a clock rate on the interface or it will not communicate. If you are unsure about whether you are configuring a DTE or a DCE, use the **show controllers {serial}** command and you will see the interface you are configuring.

Looking at the status of an interface is one of the first steps in troubleshooting the interface. The status of the interface enables you to know what problems may be present. If the hardware of the interface is down, the status would indicate no Carrier Detect signal being received. A hardware problem may be anything from a loose cable, to a power outage at the other end, to a phone company problem. If the interface is administratively down, someone (probably a coworker) has taken the interface down for maintenance or troubleshooting reasons. The status of the serial interface being up and up (meaning both the hardware and line protocol are up) indicates an operational interface. It is a good idea, once seeing this, to **ping** another interface and make sure the connectivity is good.

5

Review Questions

1. Which router is mainly used as a high-speed backbone router for large campuses, and virtually replaced the 7000 because of its popularity?

   a. 1000

   b. 5000

   c. 7500

   d. 1004

   e. 600

2. Which router is best for a telecommuter with low bandwidth needs?

   a. 1000

   b. 5000

   c. 7500

   d. 12000

   e. 10000

3. Which router is a gigabit switch router (GSR) that provides high-performance solutions ranging from 5 to 60 Gbps for Internet and large-scale WAN intranet backbone applications?

   a. 1000

   b. 1700

   c. 12000

   d. 600

   e. 7010

4. Which router is the best core router for the sole purpose of ISPs and supports several thousand T1 ports?

    a. 7000

    b. 7500

    c. 10000

    d. 12000

    e. 1000

5. Which core router provides high packet-forwarding performance by distributing the switching operation to the Versatile Interface Processors (VIPs)?

    a. 1000

    b. 600

    c. 7000

    d. 7500

    e. 12000

6. Which command shows you which version of IOS is currently running on the router?

    a. **show flash**

    b. **show version**

    c. **show ip route**

    d. **show controllers**

    e. **show all**

7. Which command enables you to see the contents of the flash memory?

    a. **show version**

    b. **show flash**

    c. **show ip route**

    d. **show all**

    e. **show history**

8. Which command shows you whether the interface is connected to a DTE or DCE cable?

    a. **config t**

    b. **sh controllers**

    c. **show controllers s1**

    d. **sh controllers s 1**

    e. **show interface**

9. Which command enables you to *not* set a password on the VTY sessions?

   a. **login**

   b. **no login**

   c. **no password**

   d. **password no login**

   e. **password none**

10. What command enables you to set the AUX port password in global configuration mode?

   a. **line aux**

   b. **configure line aux**

   c. **line aux 0**

   d. **command line aux**

   e. **line aux 4**

11. If the interface gives you the output "serial 1 is up, line protocol is down," what is the most likely reason?

   a. The keepalives are set wrong

   b. The cable is not connected or is very loose

   c. A coworker has shut down the interface because it was having problems

   d. The interface is working fine

   e. The interface has been hacked into

12. Which cable needs a clock rate set if the routers do not have a modem or CSU/DSU between them?

   a. DTE

   b. DCE

13. What is the command to prevent an interface from shutting down?

   a. **shutdown interface**

   b. **shutdown**

   c. **no shutdown interface**

   d. **no shut**

   e. **interface shutdown**

5

14. What does "MOTD" stand for?

    a. Mode of transportation day

    b. Method of timing day

    c. More of the day

    d. Message of the day

    e. Message of the dark

15. When configuring an IP address on an interface, what are the two things that are defined after the IP address (in the same command line)?

    a. Subnet mask

    b. Subnet

    c. Serial interface

    d. IP address

    e. configure

16. What is the command for naming a description for an interface?

    a. **name**

    b. **description**

    c. **building**

    d. **command description**

    e. **subnet**

17. What is the command to set the timeout for a console port to no timeout?

    a. **exec-timout**

    b. **exec timeout 1 1**

    c. **exec-timeout 0**

    d. **exec-timeout 0 0**

    e. **Exec timeout 0**

18. Which protocol does not need the bandwidth configured?

    a. IGRP

    b. OSPF

    c. EIGRP

    d. RIP

    e. Novell

19. If you want to copy an image from flash memory to a TFTP server, which command would you use?

    a. **copy flash tftp**

    b. **copy tftp flash**

    c. **copy memory tftp**

    d. **copy tftp memory**

    e. **copy flash flash**

20. If you want to copy an image from a TFTP server to flash memory, which command would you use?

    a. **copy flash tftp**

    b. **copy tftp flash**

    c. **copy memory flash**

    d. **copy memory tftp**

    e. **copy tftp memory**

21. Subinterfaces are commonly used with which type of interface?

    a. Frame Relay

    b. Ethernet

    c. HSSI

    d. Console

    e. Telnet

22. The IOS is loaded from which type of memory?

    a. Flash

    b. POST

    c. NVRAM

    d. RAM

    e. Setup

23. To manually save a configuration from DRAM to NVRAM, you can use which commands? [Choose the two best answers]

    a. **copy run start**

    b. **copy running-config startup-config**

    c. **copy startup-config running config**

    d. **copy startup-config tftp**

    e. **copy running-config**

24. What is the command to use to name your router?

    a. **name**

    b. **name router**

    c. **hostname**

    d. **host name**

    e. **router hostname**

25. What does the command Ctrl+P do?

    a. Moves the cursor to the beginning of the line

    b. Deletes the word to the left of the cursor

    c. Ends configuration mode

    d. Moves the cursor to the beginning of the line

    e. Recalls commands in the buffer, starting with the most recent

Real-World Projects

Note: This exercise assumes the router is on a network and does not need to be configured to be on a network. It also assumes that the passwords have been configured on all accesses to the router, and the RIP protocol is being used in the network.

Joe Snow is very excited about his new job. He has little router experience, but is looking to gain more in his new position. On his first day on the job, his boss informs him of his first assignment: configure a router that will be used in the production network for an outlying area across town. Joe, trying not to show his anxiety, agrees to the task. Joe knows he doesn't have much experience configuring routers, but knows he has to learn fast if he wants to keep his job.

The first thing Joe does is download a current version of the code to the router, using the steps described next.

Project 5.1

To load a current version of IOS, perform the following steps:

1. Go to **www.cisco.com** and find your router type and the latest version of code for your router.

2. Check the router you are configuring to see what the current version is, using the command **show version**.

3. Download the newest version from the Cisco site to a TFTP server.

4. Using the console port of the router, type the passwords to allow you in Privilege EXEC Mode.

5. From Privilege EXEC Mode, use the command **copy tftp flash** and then fill in the IP of the TFTP server and the file name.

6. After the IOS load is complete, use the **show version** command to see the current version.

After the new version of IOS is loaded on the router, Joe configures the interface using CLI commands and a lot of the command-line help.

Project 5.2

To configure a serial interface, perform the following steps:

1. At the EXEC mode, type the enable secret password, if one exists.

2. Type the command **config t** to enter global configuration mode.

3. In global configuration mode, type **interface serial {#}** to configure the particular interface.

4. Use the **description** command to briefly describe the interface for the remote site.

5. Assign the protocol being used (such as RIP, for this example) by typing the command **router rip**.

6. Assign an IP address and a subnet mask to the interface.

7. Use the **no shut** command to make sure the interface will not shut down.

8. Press **Ctrl+Z** to return to the exec mode.

9. Use the **copy running start** command to save your configurations from running configurations to startup configurations.

After Joe has the interface configured, he checks to make sure the interface is working.

Project 5.3

To check the interface status, perform the following steps:

1. At the EXEC mode or the Privilege EXEC mode, type **show interface {#}** to see the interface status.

2. The interface status should read: "Serial {#} is up, line protocol is up."

Joe tests the interface by pinging another router across the network, by typing **ping 131.32.x.x**, and making sure all packets are a success.

CHAPTER SIX

Frame Relay, Serial Links, and X.25 Troubleshooting

After completing this chapter, you will be able to:

✓ Troubleshoot Frame Relay problems

✓ Troubleshoot X.25 problems

✓ Troubleshoot serial link problems

✓ Determine whether the problem is a hardware or software issue

✓ Perform a local or remote loopback test

✓ Troubleshoot IOS serial link configuration issues

✓ Use IOS commands that will aid in isolating problems

The reason this chapter combines troubleshooting issues regarding Frame Relay, serial links, and X.25 is that many of the commands and techniques to troubleshoot these components are the same. This chapter first looks at serial links, including X.25 links, and then covers troubleshooting.

An in-depth discussion of configuring Frame Relay and X.25 is quite lengthy and beyond the scope of this book. If you would like to learn more about configuring Frame Relay and X.25, I recommend reading the following books from The Coriolis Group:

➤ *Remote Access Exam Cram*, by Craig Dennis and Eric Quinn (ISBN: 1-57610-437-0), 2000

➤ *Remote Access Exam Prep*, by Barry Meinster (ISBN: 1-57610-692-6), 2001

Troubleshooting Serial Links

Because a variety of different types of encapsulations and protocols can run over serial links, many configuration problems can occur. Most serial link problems unrelated to hardware are caused by a mismatched configuration on either side of the serial link.

Trying to diagnose and resolve a serial link problem can be difficult if you don't know what to look for or don't have experience using them.

This section provides step-by-step lists to help you troubleshoot various serial link problems. A lot of information can be gathered by using the **show interface** command. The output of the **show interface** command gives you a variety of information about each interface's status. Knowledge of how to resolve these status issues will aid you in troubleshooting each specific problem.

The following are the serial interface symptoms diagnosed in this chapter:

➤ Interface is administratively down; line protocol is down

➤ Interface is down; line protocol is down

➤ Keep alive sequencing not incrementing

➤ Interface is up; line protocol is down

➤ Interface is up; line protocol is up (looped)

➤ Incrementing carrier transition counter

➤ Incrementing interface resets

➤ Input drops, errors, CRC, and framing errors

Interface Is Administratively Down; Line Protocol Is Down

To troubleshoot this problem, use the following steps:

1. Check that the interface has not been placed in shutdown state.

2. Check that a duplicate IP address has been used.

Interface Is Down; Line Protocol Is Down

To troubleshoot this problem, use the following steps:

1. Check the cabling.

2. Check that a carrier signal from a local provider exists.

3. Consider a hardware failure on the interface or CSU/DSU.

Interface Is Up; Line Protocol Is Down

To troubleshoot this problem, use the following steps:

1. Check the interface configurations.

2. Check with the local provider to verify that it is not having line issues.

Keepalive Sequencing Not Incrementing

To troubleshoot this problem, use the following steps:

1. Check for a local hardware failure.

2. Check for a remote hardware failure.

3. Check whether the line is noisy.

4. Check for a timing mismatch.

Interface Is Up; Line Protocol Is Up (Looped)

To troubleshoot this problem, use the following step:

1. Verify whether the circuit is in loopback.

Incrementing Carrier Transition Counter

To troubleshoot this problem, use the following steps:

1. Check for cable faults.

2. Check for line issues with the local provider.

3. Consider a hardware failure on the interface or CSU/DSU.

Incrementing Interface Resets

To troubleshoot this problem, use the following steps:

1. Check for cable faults causing the loss of the Carrier Detect.

2. Consider a hardware failure on the interface or CSU/DSU.

3. Check for congestion of the line.

Input Drops, CRC, and Framing Errors

To troubleshoot this problem, use the following steps:

1. Check for mismatched line speeds.

2. Check with the local provider for issues.

3. Check whether the line is noisy.

4. Check for faulty cabling.

5. Consider a hardware failure on the interface or CSU/DSU.

6. Check that the line speed does not overload the router's capacity.

Now that you have reviewed the list of symptoms and the checklist associated with each symptom, walk step by step through the directions for how to handle each item on the checklist. The following is a step-by-step checklist of how to troubleshoot each of the items in the preceding checklists:

➤ Check for cable faults causing the loss of the Carrier Detect (CD)

➤ Check for faulty cabling

➤ Check the interface configurations

➤ Check keepalive problems

➤ Verify whether the circuit is in loopback mode

➤ Check that the interface has not been placed in shutdown state

➤ Check that the line speed does not overload the router's capacity

➤ Check if the interface speed is higher than the line speed can support

Check for Cable Faults Causing Loss of the Carrier Detect

To troubleshoot this problem, use the following steps:

1. Check the CD, RX, and TX on the CSU/DSU to verify the circuit is transmitting and receiving data.

Signaling Lights on the CSU/DSU

Serial connections send their data one bit at a time over their transmission path or circuit. This is unidirectional traffic. Parallel transmissions are bidirectional, traveling in both directions, enabling the connection to transmit and receive simultaneously.

Certain display signaling lights are located on the front of a CSU/DSU. The following is a list of these lights and a description of what each means when lit:

➤ TX—Transmitting data.

➤ RX—Receiving data.

➤ RTS—A request to send. This is sent on one of the two hardware flow control wires to signal the DTE side of a link that it can receive data from the DCE side.

➤ CTS—A clear to send. The DCE is sending a clear to send on the second hardware flow control wire.

➤ DTR—Data terminal ready. This is sent on the modem control signaling wire that the DTE interface can accept a call from a DCE interface.

➤ CD—A carrier detect. The DCE interface has detected the signal from the local service provider.

6

2. Contact the local service provider to check for problems and for help in troubleshooting the problem.

Check for Faulty Cabling

To troubleshoot this problem, use the following steps:

1. Make sure that you are using the proper cable for the equipment being used.

2. Use a breakout box to verify throughput on the cables.

3. Replace the faulty cables.

Check the Interface Configurations

To troubleshoot this problem, use the following steps:

1. Use the **show running-config** command to verify the proper configuration.

2. Verify the proper configuration for the interfaces, both on the problem device and on the device at the opposite end of the link.

3. Use the **show interface** command to verify the proper configuration of the interface, including the encapsulation type being used.

Check Keepalive Problems

To troubleshoot this problem, use the following steps:

1. Use the **show interface** command to verify that keepalives are being sent.

2. Use the **debug serial interface** command to view the keepalive sending process.

3. Verify that sequence numbers are incrementing properly.

4. If the sequence numbers are not incrementing, you can run loopback tests at the local or the remote ends of the circuit.

Note: If you still cannot get the sequence numbers to increment, even when the CSU/DSU is in loopback, you most likely have a hardware problem where the faulty hardware resides on either the router or the CSU/DSU.

Verify Whether the Circuit Is in Loopback Mode

To troubleshoot this problem, use the following steps:

1. Use the **show interface** command to check the interface configuration.

2. Use the **no** command to disable any loopback entries in the interface configuration.

3. Check the CSU/DSU to make sure that it is not in loopback mode.

4. Check with the local service provider for possible problems and to make sure that the circuit is not in loopback mode.

Check That the Interface Hasn't Been Placed in Shutdown State

To troubleshoot this problem, use the following steps:

1. Use the **show interface** command to verify the interface has not been manually shut.

2. Check to make sure that the IP address is not being used on another interface.

3. In interface configuration mode for the interface having problems, use the **no shut** command.

Check That the Line Speed Doesn't Overload the Router's Capacity

To troubleshoot this problem, use the following steps:

1. Use the **hold-queue** command to reduce input queue size.

2. Increase the output queue's size on the other interfaces.

LMI Types

The following three LMI types can be used. Routers with version 11.2 or later can autosense the LMI type used on the CO switch. You must configure the LMI type manually on all Cisco routers prior to that release.

➤ *Cisco*—The LMI type developed by what is known as the "The Gang Of Four"—Cisco, StrataCom, Northern Telecom, and Digital Equipment Corporation.

➤ *Ansi*—The ANSI standard T1.617.

➤ *Q933a*—The standard developed by ITU-T.

Check That the Interface Speed Is Higher Than the Line Speed

6

To troubleshoot this problem, use the following steps:

1. Implement Quality of Service (queuing) to control traffic.

2. Increase the output queue size.

3. Reduce the broadcast traffic that utilizes the link, if possible.

CSU/DSU Loopback Testing

By using loopback testing, you can isolate serial line problems. Four different loopback tests can be performed on a circuit to aid in troubleshooting it. The administrator of the local equipment can perform two of these tests, and the local service provider can perform the other two tests.

The *Local Management Interface (LMI)* is the signaling standard between the local router connecting to the CSU/DSU and the CO switch, and provides support for keepalive devices to verify data flow. *Keepalives* are packets that each device in the virtual circuit generates and sends to notify the other devices of connectivity. Just as their name suggests, keepalives "keep alive" a connection.

Figure 6.1 depicts the different loopback tests listed here:

➤ Local CSU/DSU loopback to the local router

➤ Remote CSU/DSU loopback to the local router

➤ Loopback from the local CO switch to the remote CSU/DSU

➤ Loopback from the remote CO switch to the local CSU/DSU

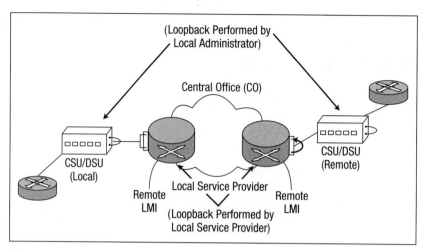

Figure 6.1 The local and remote loopback tests.

When using loopback tests for troubleshooting, you should follow these steps:

1. Perform the local loopback test from the local router to the CSU/DSU, by placing the CSU/DSU in loopback mode.

2. Check the LMI status when using Frame Relay on the interface.

3. Perform a local loopback test with the remote CSU/DSU if the local router passes its loopback.

Note: If the LMIs are showing 1023 for the Cisco type's LMI, and you cannot get the non-LMI DLCI to the remote side of the circuit to loop back, you need to contact your CSU/DSU for testing.

If you see the local router's interface to the interface on the CSU/DSU working properly during a loopback test, the local protocol and link is functioning properly. This confirms only that the local equipment is functioning properly, not that the remote equipment is functioning properly.

When putting the CSU/DSU into loopback mode, the signal is sent from the local router interface to the CSU/DSU and is immediately sent back by the CSU/DSU as though it were a remote signal coming back. When using the **show interface** command, the line protocol shows up when the connection is functioning normally.

When configuring end-to-end connectivity to a remote site, both side's LMI (routers) status should say that the interface and protocol are up, and the LMI DLCI should state 1023, as shown in the following output:

```
Sean2514#sh int s0

Serial0 is up, line protocol is up
  Hardware is HD64570
  Internet address is 63.78.39.174/24
  MTU 1500 bytes, BW 64 Kbit, DLY 20000 usec, rely 255/255, load 1/255
  Encapsulation FRAME-RELAY IETF, loopback not set, keepalive set (10 sec)
  LMI enq sent  7307, LMI stat recvd 7164, LMI upd recvd 0, DTE LMI up
  LMI enq recvd 119, LMI stat sent  0, LMI upd sent  0
  LMI DLCI 1023  LMI type is CISCO  frame relay DTE
  Broadcast queue 0/64, broadcasts sent/dropped 1195/0, interface broadcasts 0
  Last input 00:00:01, output 00:00:01, output hang never
  Last clearing of "show interface" counters 22:23:54
  Input queue: 0/75/0 (size/max/drops); Total output drops: 0
  Queueing strategy: weighted fair
  Output queue: 0/1000/64/0 (size/max total/threshold/drops)
     Conversations  0/1/256 (active/max active/max total)
     Reserved Conversations 0/0 (allocated/max allocated)
  5 minute input rate 0 bits/sec, 0 packets/sec
  5 minute output rate 0 bits/sec, 0 packets/sec
     11501 packets input, 586321 bytes, 0 no buffer
     Received 888 broadcasts, 0 runts, 0 giants, 0 throttles
     0 input errors, 0 CRC, 0 frame, 0 overrun, 0 ignored, 0 abort
     9455 packets output, 184195 bytes, 0 underruns
     0 output errors, 0 collisions, 51 interface resets
     0 output buffer failures, 0 output buffers swapped out
     124 carrier transitions
     DCD=up  DSR=up  DTR=up  RTS=up  CTS=up

Sean2514#
```

All the *carrier operation switches* (also known as the *central office,* or *CO,* switches) that participate in the permanent virtual circuit (PVC) or switched virtual circuit (SVC) provided by the local service provider must be working properly as well. The local service provider can perform loopback tests on its equipment to confirm the functionality of the circuit.

Serial Link Troubleshooting Commands

Many different protocols can use a serial link. Serial links send data bit by bit over their link or circuits. Several **clear**, **show**, and **debug** commands can be used to troubleshoot serial links. This section covers the following commands:

➤ **clear counters serial**

➤ **debug serial interface**

➤ **debug serial packet**

➤ **show buffers**

➤ **show controllers serial**

➤ **show interface serial**

The clear counters serial Command

The **clear counters serial** command clears the counters that are displayed using the **show interfaces serial** command. The following is the output from using this command:

```
Sean2514#clear counters serial 0

Clear "show interface" counters on this interface [confirm]
03:54:37: %CLEAR-5-COUNTERS: Clear counter on interface Serial0 by console

Sean2514#
```

By using the command you will see the counters reset after using the command. Let's take a look:

```
Sean2514#show interfaces serial 0
1d03h: %CLEAR-5-COUNTERS: Clear counter on interface Serial0 by console
Serial0 is up, line protocol is up
  Hardware is HD64570
  Internet address is 63.78.39.174/24
  MTU 1500 bytes, BW 64 Kbit, DLY 20000 usec, rely 255/255, load 1/255
  Encapsulation FRAME-RELAY IETF, loopback not set, keepalive set (10 sec)
  LMI enq sent  1, LMI stat recvd 1, LMI upd recvd 0, DTE LMI up
  LMI enq recvd 0, LMI stat sent  0, LMI upd sent  0
  LMI DLCI 1023  LMI type is CISCO  frame relay DTE
  Broadcast queue 0/64, broadcasts sent/dropped 0/0, interface broadcasts 0
  Last input 00:00:01, output 00:00:02, output hang never
  Last clearing of "show interface" counters 00:00:02
  Input queue: 0/75/0 (size/max/drops); Total output drops: 0
  Queueing strategy: weighted fair
  Output queue: 0/1000/64/0 (size/max total/threshold/drops)
     Conversations  0/1/256 (active/max active/max total)
     Reserved Conversations 0/0 (allocated/max allocated)
  5 minute input rate 0 bits/sec, 0 packets/sec
  5 minute output rate 0 bits/sec, 0 packets/sec
     0 packets input, 0 bytes, 0 no buffer
     Received 0 broadcasts, 0 runts, 0 giants, 0 throttles
     0 input errors, 0 CRC, 0 frame, 0 overrun, 0 ignored, 0 abort
     0 packets output, 0 bytes, 0 underruns
     0 output errors, 0 collisions, 0 interface resets
```

```
0 output buffer failures, 0 output buffers swapped out
0 carrier transitions
DCD=up  DSR=up  DTR=up  RTS=up  CTS=up
```

Sean2514#

The **debug serial interface** Command

This **debug** command is used to check the line status, DTE status, and sequencing information. Debugging of the serial interface displays information on the HDLC and Frame Relay communication messages. Here is an example of output for HDLC messages:

```
Sean2514#debug serial interface
Serial network interface debugging is on

1d03h: Serial0(out): StEnq, myseq 80, yourseen 79, DTE up
1d03h: Serial0(in):  Status, myseq 80
1d03h: Serial0(out): StEnq, myseq 81, yourseen 80, DTE up
1d03h: Serial0(in):  Status, myseq 81
1d03h: Serial0(out): StEnq, myseq 82, yourseen 81, DTE up
1d03h: Serial0(in):  Status, myseq 82
1d03h: Serial0(out): StEnq, myseq 83, yourseen 82, DTE up
```

Table 6.1 defines the acronyms from the preceding output.

When the sequence numbers for an interface don't increment, the cause may be a timing or line issue. If two out of six consecutive keepalive packets fail to increment their sequence numbers, the line resets. In this situation, the Layer 3 protocol considers the line protocol to be down, but the protocol operating at Layer 2 continues to send keepalive messages. As soon as the Layer 2 protocol receives three consecutive sequenced keepalive packets, the line protocol will be brought back up.

The next section takes a look at the debugging output using HDLC.

Table 6.1   The output fields from the debug serial interface command.

Field	Description
StEnq	The LMI status enquiry sent from the LMI (router) to the local service provider's Frame Relay switch.
Status	The reply sent to the LMI from the Frame Relay switch.
mysec	The local keepalive number, also known as the sequence identifier.
yourseen	The keepalive sent by the opposite side of the serial connection.
DTE	The data-termination equipment status.
in/out	Specifies the direction the packets were sent through the interface. Outbound packets are keepalives sent by the local interface. Inbound packets are the keepalives sent from the opposite side of the serial link.

HDLC Debugging Output

Using the **debug serial interface** command, look at the debugging output for HDLC:

```
Sean2514#debug serial interface
Serial network interface debugging is on

03:52:22: Serial0: HDLC myseq 1390, mineseen 1390*, yourseen 1404, line up
03:52:32: Serial0: HDLC myseq 1391, mineseen 1391*, yourseen 1405, line up
03:52:42: Serial0: HDLC myseq 1392, mineseen 1392*, yourseen 1406, line up
03:52:52: Serial0: HDLC myseq 1393, mineseen 1393*, yourseen 1407, line up
```

Fields in the output are defined in Table 6.2.

The **debug serial packet** Command

You can use the **debug serial packet** command to receive information about why packets are not sent or received correctly. This command is used when troubleshooting the Switched Multimegabit Data Service (SMDS) protocol.

The **show buffers** Command

The **show buffers** command is used to show the router buffer pool statistics. The following is its output:

```
Sean2514#show buffers

Buffer elements:
     500 in free list (500 max allowed)
     3156 hits, 0 misses, 0 created
```

SMDS

SMDS is a connectionless protocol that local service providers use in their switches to connect LANs and WANs together. This protocol is similar to Frame Relay and the Asynchronous Transfer Mode (ATM) protocol. SMDS uses 53-byte cells formatted to the IEEE 802.6 standard and access-control features such as line screening, verification, and blocking.

An advantage to SMDS is that it is scalable and makes it relatively easy to connect additional LANs together. SMDS is connectionless and supports WAN speeds comparable to the speeds found on the LAN. The speeds can range from 56K to 45 Mbps.

One additional feature of SMDS is that it is compatible with ATM.

Table 6.2   The output fields from the debug serial interface command.

Field	Description
mysec	The local keepalive number or the sequence identifier.
yourseen	The keepalive that is sent by the opposite side of the serial connection.
mineseen	The keepalive that is sent by the local interface seen on the remote side interface.

HDLC

The High-Level Data Link Control (HDLC) protocol is an enhancement over SDLC, which was created by IBM for its Systems Network Architecture (SNA). HDLC operates in three different transfer modes: normal, asynchronous response, and asynchronous balanced.

The HDLC protocol allows secondary nodes to talk to other nodes in the network, which is an improvement over SDLC. SDLC allows secondary nodes to talk only to the primary node in the network. The asynchronous response mode enables the secondary node to communicate with the primary node without first having to obtain any permissions from a primary node. Asynchronous balanced mode, known as a *combination node*, combines the roles of a primary and secondary node.

HDLC provides a 32-bit checksum and is used by default on Cisco serial interfaces. You should always check that the same encapsulation type is used on both sides of a serial link. The following is output for an HDLC-encapsulated link configured correctly:

```
Sean2514#show interface s0
Serial0 is up, line protocol is up
  Hardware is HD64570
  Internet address is 63.78.39.174/24
  MTU 1500 bytes, BW 64 Kbit, DLY 20000 usec, rely 255/255, load 1/255
  Encapsulation HDLC, loopback not set, keepalive set (10 sec)
  Last input 00:00:00, output 00:00:04, output hang never
  Last clearing of "show interface" counters 00:02:29
  Input queue: 0/75/0 (size/max/drops); Total output drops: 0
  Queueing strategy: weighted fair
  Output queue: 0/1000/64/0 (size/max total/threshold/drops)
     Conversations  0/1/256 (active/max active/max total)
     Reserved Conversations 0/0 (allocated/max allocated)
  5 minute input rate 0 bits/sec, 0 packets/sec
  5 minute output rate 0 bits/sec, 0 packets/sec
     17 packets input, 886 bytes, 0 no buffer
     Received 17 broadcasts, 0 runts, 0 giants, 0 throttles
     0 input errors, 0 CRC, 0 frame, 0 overrun, 0 ignored, 0 abort
     18 packets output, 1182 bytes, 0 underruns
     0 output errors, 0 collisions, 0 interface resets
     0 output buffer failures, 0 output buffers swapped out
     0 carrier transitions
     DCD=up  DSR=up  DTR=up  RTS=up  CTS=up
Sean2514#
```

6

```
Public buffer pools:
Small buffers, 104 bytes (total 50, permanent 50):
     49 in free list (20 min, 150 max allowed)
     1366 hits, 0 misses, 0 trims, 0 created
     0 failures (0 no memory)
Middle buffers, 600 bytes (total 25, permanent 25):
     25 in free list (10 min, 150 max allowed)
     20 hits, 0 misses, 0 trims, 0 created
     0 failures (0 no memory)
Big buffers, 1524 bytes (total 50, permanent 50):
     50 in free list (5 min, 150 max allowed)
     232 hits, 0 misses, 0 trims, 0 created
     0 failures (0 no memory)
VeryBig buffers, 4520 bytes (total 10, permanent 10):
     10 in free list (0 min, 100 max allowed)
     0 hits, 0 misses, 0 trims, 0 created
     0 failures (0 no memory)
Large buffers, 5024 bytes (total 0, permanent 0):
     0 in free list (0 min, 10 max allowed)
     0 hits, 0 misses, 0 trims, 0 created
     0 failures (0 no memory)
Huge buffers, 18024 bytes (total 0, permanent 0):
     0 in free list (0 min, 4 max allowed)
     0 hits, 0 misses, 0 trims, 0 created
     0 failures (0 no memory)


Interface buffer pools:
Ethernet0 buffers, 1524 bytes (total 32, permanent 32):
     8 in free list (0 min, 32 max allowed)
     24 hits, 0 fallbacks
     8 max cache size, 8 in cache
Ethernet1 buffers, 1524 bytes (total 32, permanent 32):
     8 in free list (0 min, 32 max allowed)
     24 hits, 0 fallbacks
     8 max cache size, 8 in cache
Serial0 buffers, 1524 bytes (total 32, permanent 32):
     7 in free list (0 min, 32 max allowed)
     25 hits, 0 fallbacks
     8 max cache size, 8 in cache
Serial1 buffers, 1524 bytes (total 32, permanent 32):
     7 in free list (0 min, 32 max allowed)
     25 hits, 0 fallbacks
     8 max cache size, 8 in cache


Sean2514#
```

The small buffers show all the frames received under 104 bytes. Buffer hits are good; when the number of misses increases, you should concern yourself with the number of buffer misses. The failures indicate the number of frames that were discarded due to unavailable memory in the buffers.

The **show controllers serial** Command

Using the **show controllers serial** command, you can display the interface status and whether a data terminal equipment (DTE) cable or a data communication equipment (DCE) cable is connected to an interface or is reversed. Rising hardware and data link errors may indicate a problem with the cable or a misconfigured interface.

The **show controllers serial** command provides information on the interface status, cable types, missed datagrams, overruns, bad encapsulated frames, memory errors, underruns, clock rate, and bit errors. In addition, it indicates the interface clock rate, as well as the cable type that is connected to the interface.

6

Tip: This is a particularly good command if you have a router in a rack and can't physically see that the serial cables are connected properly to the interface.

The following is the output you should see from the **show controllers serial** command (this output is the DCE end of the cable; the DTE end is connected to the serial port on a Cisco 1005):

```
Sean2514#show controller serial 0

HD unit 0, idb = 0xF7A98, driver structure at 0xFCF18
buffer size 1524  HD unit 0, V.35 DCE cable, clockrate 64000
cpb = 0x62, eda = 0x2918, cda = 0x292C
RX ring with 16 entries at 0x622800
00 bd_ptr=0x2800 pak=0x0FE350 ds=0x6267C4 status=80 pak_size=22
01 bd_ptr=0x2814 pak=0x0FE150 ds=0x626108 status=80 pak_size=22
02 bd_ptr=0x2828 pak=0x0FDF50 ds=0x625A4C status=80 pak_size=22
03 bd_ptr=0x283C pak=0x0FFF50 ds=0x62C60C status=80 pak_size=22
04 bd_ptr=0x2850 pak=0x100150 ds=0x62CCC8 status=80 pak_size=22
05 bd_ptr=0x2864 pak=0x0FFD50 ds=0x62BF50 status=80 pak_size=22
06 bd_ptr=0x2878 pak=0x0FFB50 ds=0x62B894 status=80 pak_size=278
07 bd_ptr=0x288C pak=0x0FF950 ds=0x62B1D8 status=80 pak_size=22
08 bd_ptr=0x28A0 pak=0x0FF750 ds=0x62AB1C status=80 pak_size=22
09 bd_ptr=0x28B4 pak=0x0FF550 ds=0x62A460 status=80 pak_size=22
10 bd_ptr=0x28C8 pak=0x0FF350 ds=0x629DA4 status=80 pak_size=22
11 bd_ptr=0x28DC pak=0x0FF150 ds=0x6296E8 status=80 pak_size=22
12 bd_ptr=0x28F0 pak=0x0FEF50 ds=0x62902C status=80 pak_size=22
13 bd_ptr=0x2904 pak=0x0FED50 ds=0x628970 status=80 pak_size=278
```

```
14 bd_ptr=0x2918 pak=0x0FEB50 ds=0x6282B4 status=80 pak_size=22
15 bd_ptr=0x292C pak=0x0FE750 ds=0x62753C status=80 pak_size=22
16 bd_ptr=0x2940 pak=0x0FE550 ds=0x626E80 status=80 pak_size=278
cpb = 0x62, eda = 0x3014, cda = 0x3014
TX ring with 1 entries at 0x623000
00 bd_ptr=0x3000 pak=0x000000 ds=0x653E04 status=80 pak_size=284
01 bd_ptr=0x3014 pak=0x000000 ds=0x622EA4 status=80 pak_size=22
0 missed datagrams, 0 overruns
0 bad datagram encapsulations, 0 memory errors
0 transmitter underruns
0 residual bit errors

Sean2514#
```

The next code block is the output from the DTE end of the interface, connected to a Cisco 1005 router:

```
Seans1005#show controllers serial 0

QUICC Serial unit 0, idb at 0x22C2C20, driver data structure at 0x22C495C
SCC Registers:
General [GSMR]=0x2:0x00000030, Protocol-specific [PSMR]=0x0
Events [SCCE]=0x0000, Mask [SCCM]=0x001F, Status [SCCS]=0x0006
Transmit on Demand [TODR]=0x0, Data Sync [DSR]=0x7E7E
Interrupt Registers:
Config [CICR]=0x00368460, Pending [CIPR]=0x04004804
Mask   [CIMR]=0x48000012, In-srv  [CISR]=0x00000000
Command register [CR]=0x6C0
Port A [PADIR]=0x0008, [PAPAR]=0x5AC3
       [PAODR]=0x0000, [PADAT]=0xD06A
Port B [PBDIR]=0x020F1F, [PBPAR]=0x0000C0
       [PBODR]=0x000000, [PBDAT]=0x000EC0
Port C [PCDIR]=0x038C, [PCPAR]=0x0001
       [PCSO]=0x0C30, [PCDAT]=0x0300, [PCINT]=0x0000
DTE V.35 serial cable attached. TX and RX clocks detected.

SCC GENERAL PARAMETER RAM (at 0xFF00F00)
Rx BD Base [RBASE]=0x560, Fn Code [RFCR]=0x18
Tx BD Base [TBASE]=0x5E0, Fn Code [TFCR]=0x18
Max Rx Buff Len [MRBLR]=1524
Rx State [RSTATE]=0x18008240, BD Ptr [RBPTR]=0x598
Tx State [TSTATE]=0x18000348, BD Ptr [TBPTR]=0x5E8

SCC HDLC PARAMETER RAM (at 0xFF00F38)
CRC Preset [C_PRES]=0xFFFF, Mask [C_MASK]=0xF0B8
Errors: CRC [CRCEC]=0, Aborts [ABTSC]=0, Discards [DISFC]=0
```

```
Nonmatch Addr Cntr [NMARC]=0
Retry Count [RETRC]=0
Max Frame Length [MFLR]=1524
Rx Int Threshold [RFTHR]=0, Frame Cnt [RFCNT]=55929
User-defined Address 0000/0000/0000/0000
User-defined Address Mask 0x0000

buffer size 1524
RX ring with 16 entries at 0xFF00560, Buffer size 1524
Rxhead = 0xFF00598 (7), Rxp = 0x22C4994 (7)
00 pak=0x22C7B3C buf=0x2395FE0 status=9000 pak_size=0
01 pak=0x22C798C buf=0x2395928 status=9000 pak_size=0
02 pak=0x22C77DC buf=0x2395270 status=9000 pak_size=0
03 pak=0x22C762C buf=0x23A1548 status=9000 pak_size=0
04 pak=0x22C747C buf=0x23A0E90 status=9000 pak_size=0
05 pak=0x2309D88 buf=0x23B942C status=9000 pak_size=0
06 pak=0x230A7A8 buf=0x23BBC7C status=9000 pak_size=0
07 pak=0x230A0E8 buf=0x23BA19C status=9000 pak_size=0
08 pak=0x230A958 buf=0x23BC334 status=9000 pak_size=0
09 pak=0x230A448 buf=0x23BAF0C status=9000 pak_size=0
10 pak=0x230A5F8 buf=0x23BB5C4 status=9000 pak_size=0
11 pak=0x2309BD8 buf=0x23B8D74 status=9000 pak_size=0
12 pak=0x2309A28 buf=0x23B86BC status=9000 pak_size=0
13 pak=0x2309F38 buf=0x23B9AE4 status=9000 pak_size=0
14 pak=0x22C7E9C buf=0x2396D50 status=9000 pak_size=0
15 pak=0x22C7CEC buf=0x2396698 status=B000 pak_size=0

TX ring with 2 entries at 0xFF005E0, tx_count = 0
tx_head = 0xFF005E8 (1), head_txp = 0x22C49D8 (1)
tx_tail = 0xFF005E8 (1), tail_txp = 0x22C49D8 (1)
00 pak=0x0000000 buf=0x0000000 status=0000 pak_size=0
01 pak=0x0000000 buf=0x0000000 status=2000 pak_size=0
QUICC SCC specific errors:
0 input aborts on receiving flag sequence
0 throttles, 0 enables
0 overruns
0 transmitter underruns
0 transmitter CTS losts

Seans1005#
```

The **show interface serial** Command

The **show interface serial** command provides a wealth of information to help you troubleshoot serial line- and serial interface-related problems. It is recommended that you use the **clear counters serial** command before using this command.

The output from this command is shown here:

```
Sean2514#show interface serial 0

Serial0 is up, line protocol is up
  Hardware is HD64570
  Internet address is 63.78.39.174/24
  MTU 1500 bytes, BW 64 Kbit, DLY 20000 usec, rely 255/255, load 1/255
  Encapsulation HDLC, loopback not set, keepalive set (10 sec)
  Last input 00:00:08, output 00:00:06, output hang never
  Last clearing of "show interface" counters never
  Input queue: 0/75/0 (size/max/drops); Total output drops: 0
  Queueing strategy: weighted fair
  Output queue: 0/1000/64/0 (size/max total/threshold/drops)
     Conversations  0/1/256 (active/max active/max total)
     Reserved Conversations 0/0 (allocated/max allocated)
  5 minute input rate 0 bits/sec, 0 packets/sec
  5 minute output rate 0 bits/sec, 0 packets/sec
     1609 packets input, 94022 bytes, 0 no buffer
     Received 1609 broadcasts, 0 runts, 0 giants, 0 throttles
     0 input errors, 0 CRC, 0 frame, 0 overrun, 0 ignored, 0 abort
     1600 packets output, 97280 bytes, 0 underruns
     0 output errors, 0 collisions, 1 interface resets
     0 output buffer failures, 0 output buffers swapped out
     2 carrier transitions
     DCD=up  DSR=up  DTR=up  RTS=up  CTS=up

Sean2514#
```

Table 6.3 shows the description of the variables found in the preceding output.

Troubleshooting Frame Relay

Using Frame Relay is a common solution for connecting one or more LANs through a WAN. It uses PVCs. These virtual circuits are built by using a Data-Link Connection Identifier (DLCI), which is used to identify the virtual circuits in a Frame Relay cloud.

These DLCI numbers are only significant locally. The packets sent through the Frame Relay cloud are actually encapsulated with an identifier to enable each packet to traverse the local service provider's switched network. This encapsulation is added by the CSU/DSU and is stripped off by the remote end's CSU/DSU when the packet reaches its destination.

Table 6.3   Variables listed in the show interface serial 0 command output.

Variable	Description
Serial0	Shows the port or VLAN number of the displayed interface, and the status Indicates whether the interface is active or disabled. A status of "disabled" indicates that the router has received more than 5,000 errors in 10 seconds, which is the default keepalive interval.
Line protocol	An indicator of whether the line protocol believes the interface is usable based on the keepalives it has received or the interface has been manually shut down.
Internet address	The IP address of the interface.
MTU	Displays the maximum transmission unit (MTU) size for the interface.
BW	Displays the bandwidth the interface is configured to use. You can modify this parameter by using the **bandwidth** command in Interface Configuration mode.
DLY	Displays the interface delay in microseconds.
Rely	Displays the interface in a fraction of 255. This means that if the interface is running at 100 percent, the displayed value would be 255 out of 255.
Load	Displays the interface load in a fraction of 255. This means that if the interface is running a 100 percent load, the displayed value would be 255 out of 255.
Encapsulation	Displays the encapsulation method used by the interface.
ARP Type	Displays the frames encapsulation type—ARPA, SNAP, Novell-Ether, or SAP.
Loopback	Indicates whether the interface is in loopback mode.
Keepalives	Indicates whether keepalives are being sent.
Last Input/Output	Indicates how much time has occurred since the last packet was received by the interface.
Last Clearing	Indicates the amount of time since the counters have been reset.
Input/Output Queues	Displays the maximum size of the queue as well as the number of packets dropped due to a full queue.
Input/Output Rates	Displays the average number of bits and packets transmitted in the last 300 seconds.(5 minutes)
Packets Input	Displays the number of successfully received packets to the interface since the last interface counter reset.
No Buffer	Displays the number of received packets discarded by a full buffer.
Broadcasts	Displays the number of multicast and broadcast packets received.
Runts	Displays the number of packets discarded because they were smaller than the MTU size allowed on the physical media.
Giants	Displays the number of packets discarded because they exceeded the maximum MTU size of the physical media.
CRC	Displays the number of CRC errors received on an interface.
Frame	Displays the number of packets received with CRC errors.
Overrun	Displays the number of times the receiver was unable to receive data into its buffers because the data input rate exceeded the rate which the receiving buffers and interface could handle.
Underruns	Displays the number of instances in which the transmitter has run faster than the router.
Output Errors	Displays the total number of transmitted errors on the interface.
Collisions	Displays the number of collisions that took place with transmitted media on an Ethernet interface.
Interface Resets	Displays a count of the number of times an interface has been recycled.

6

(continued)

Table 6.3 Variables listed in the **show interface serial 0** output. *(continued)*

Variable	Description
Ignored	Displays the number of packets ignored by the interface due to exceeded buffer demands.
Packets Output	Displays the total number of packets transmitted on the interface.
Input Errors	Displays the total number of errors, which includes the runts, giants, CRC's, discarded frames, overruns, and ignored errors.

The frame does not make a straight connection to its destination. In fact, many other companies will use the same link that your packet is traveling on. The local service provider shares the bandwidth with multiple customers, giving each customer a guarantee of bandwidth called the *committed information rate (CIR)*.

To troubleshoot this problem, use the following steps:

1. Check the Physical layer cabling.

2. Check the interface encapsulation and LMI type.

3. Check the DLCI-to-IP address mapping.

4. Check the broadcast mapping.

5. Check the Frame Relay PVCs.

6. Check the Frame Relay LMI.

7. Check the Frame Relay mappings.

8. Use loopback mode and test the local and remote CSU/DSU's.

Frame Relay Troubleshooting Steps

This section provides the troubleshooting steps to take to resolve each of the individual troubleshooting step from the previous section.

Frame Relay Link Is Down

To troubleshoot this problem, use the following steps:

1. Check the cabling.

2. Check for faulty hardware.

3. Check with the local service provider for problems.

4. Check for an LMI type mismatch.

5. Check whether keepalives are being sent.

6. Check the encapsulation type.

7. Check for a DLCI mismatch.

Can't Ping a Remote Host Across a Frame Relay Network

To troubleshoot this problem, use the following steps:

1. Check whether the DLCI is assigned to the wrong subinterface.

2. Check the encapsulation types on both ends.

3. Check access list entries.

4. Check the interface configuration.

Faulty Cabling

To troubleshoot this problem, use the following steps:

1. Check the cabling for physical breaks and to make sure they are secure.

2. Use a breakout box to test the leads.

3. Replace faulty cables.

Faulty Hardware

To troubleshoot this problem, use the following steps:

1. Use loopback tests to isolate the faulty hardware components.

2. Move the cable to a different interface on the router and configure that interface to see whether the link comes up; if it does, you know that you have a configuration or hardware issue on the other interface. If it doesn't come up there is most likely another hardware or software issue you need to look for.

3. Replace the hardware component that has failed.

Local Service Provider Issue

To troubleshoot this problem, use the following steps:

1. One of the best indications that a local service provider issue exists is if you perform a loopback test and the LMI state changes to "up."

2. Check for a DLCI mismatch or an encapsulation mismatch. If this is not the issue go to Step 3.

3. Contact the local service provider to help resolve the issue.

LMI Type Mismatch

To troubleshoot this problem, use the following steps:

1. Check that the LMI type on the router matches the LMI used by the CO switches on the DCE end of the circuit.

2. If you do not know the LMI type the local service provider uses, you need to contact them, or set the LMI type to dynamically detect the LMI type (if you are using IOS version 11.2 or later).

Keepalive Issues

To troubleshoot a keepalive issue, follow these steps:

1. Use the **show interface** command to verify that keepalives are not disabled or misconfigured.

2 Verify that the keepalive interval is correct on the interface.

Encapsulation Type Issues

To troubleshoot this issue, follow these steps:

1. Check that the same encapsulation types are used on both sides of the router.

2. Use the **show frame-relay map** command if you are using non–Cisco equipment. Also verify that the encapsulation types on both interface in the PVC are set to IETF. Use the **encapsulation frame-relay ietf** command to change the encapsulation type from Cisco to IETF.

DLCI Mismatch

To troubleshoot this issue, follow these steps:

1. Use the **show running-config** command to display the DLCI number to verify the DLCI number is assigned to the proper interface. The **show frame-relay pvc** command can also display the DLCI assigned to the interface.

2. If the correct DLCI number is configured on the proper interface, contact the local carrier to verify that it has the same DLCI configured on the Frame Relay switch.

Access List Issues

To troubleshoot this issue, follow these steps:

1. Use the **show ip interface** command to display all the access lists applied to the routers interfaces.

2. Check each access list, keeping in mind that an invisible, implied "deny all" is at the end of the list.

3. Remove the access list to see whether the problem is resolved.

4. Make modifications to the access list and then reapply the access list.

You can use the following **show** and **debug** commands, discussed in the following sections, to troubleshoot Frame Relay:

➤ **debug frame-relay events**

➤ **debug frame-relay lmi**

➤ **show frame-relay lmi**

➤ **show frame-relay map**

➤ **show frame-relay pvc**

➤ **show interface**

The **debug frame-relay events** Command

The **debug frame-relay events** command enables you to analyze packets and events occurring on a Frame Relay network. Data provided by this command is useful because it gives details about protocols and applications using the DLCI. This includes the interface of arrival, the datagram size, and the type of frame received.

```
Sean2514#debug frame-relay events

Frame Relay events debugging is on
Sean2514#
07:05:20: Serial0: FR ARP input
07:05:20: datagramstart = 0x628970, datagramsize = 30
07:05:20: FR encap = 0x18E10300
07:05:20: 80 00 00 00 08 06 00 0F 08 00 02 04 00 09 00 00
07:05:20: 3F 4E 26 AE 18 E1 3F 4E 27 AE
07:05:20:


Sean2514#
```

This output shows that the Serial0 interface received an ARP reply, and also displays the datagram size. The numbers **08 06** means 0x0806, which indicates an Ethernet type code. The packet type also indicates the types of applications on the circuit. Use this command to troubleshoot connectivity problems during the installation of a new Frame Relay network.

The **debug frame-relay lmi** Command

The **debug frame-relay lmi** command enables you to obtain information with the router and the local service provider's switched network. The following is example output:

```
Sean2514#debug frame-relay lmi

Frame Relay LMI debugging is on
Displaying all Frame Relay LMI data

06:53:30: Serial0(out): StEnq, myseq 174, yourseen 173, DTE up
06:53:30: datagramstart = 0x622EA4, datagramsize = 13
06:53:30: FR encap = 0xFCF10309
06:53:30: 00 75 01 01 01 03 02 AE AD
06:53:30:
06:53:30: Serial0(in): Status, myseq 174
06:53:30: RT IE 1, length 1, type 1
06:53:30: KA IE 3, length 2, yourseq 174, myseq 174
```

Table 6.4 lists the definitions of the preceding output.

The **show frame-relay lmi** Command

Using the **show frame-relay lmi** command, you can obtain LMI statistical information. The LMI provides communication and synchronization between the network and the local demarcation point devices.

The following is an example of the output produced by using the **show frame-relay lmi** command:

```
Sean2514#show frame-relay lmi

LMI Statistics for interface Serial0 (Frame Relay DTE) LMI TYPE = CISCO
    Invalid Unnumbered info 0        Invalid Prot Disc 0
    Invalid dummy Call Ref 0         Invalid Msg Type 0
    Invalid Status Message 0         Invalid Lock Shift 0
    Invalid Information ID 0         Invalid Report IE Len 0
    Invalid Report Request 0         Invalid Keep IE Len 0
    Num Status Enq. Sent 288         Num Status msgs Rcvd 288
    Num Update Status Rcvd 17        Num Status Timeouts 0

Sean2514#
```

The highlighted line indicates the interface and its role in the network. In this case, it acts as the DTE side of the interface. If the number of sent messages does not match the number received, a problem may exist with the sending and receiving keepalive messages. This type of problem can indicate a potential problem with the network equipment.

Table 6.4   The fields and descriptions in the debug frame-relay lmi ouput.

Field	Description
StEnq	The LMI status enquiry sent from the LMI (router) to the local service provider's frame relay switch
Status	The reply sent to the LMI from the Frame Relay switch
mysec	The local keepalive number, also known as the sequence identifier
yourseen	The keepalive sent by the opposite side of the serial connection
RT IE	Report Type Information Element
KA IE	Keepalive Information Element

The show frame-relay map Command

Using the **show frame-relay map** command, you can obtain information about the DLCI numbers, encapsulation type, and status of all the Frame Relay interfaces. The status of the interface is indicated with the up or down state. This command also indicates whether this is a static or dynamic interface and whether the interface type is point-to-point or multipoint.

The following is an example of the output produced by using the **show frame-relay map** command:

```
Serial0 (up): ip 62.78.38.174 dlci 120(0x78,0x1C80), static,
            broadcast,
            IETF, status deleted
Serial0 (up): ip 62.78.38.175 dlci 102(0x66,0x1860), dynamic,
            broadcast,
            IETF, status defined, active
Serial0 (up): ip 63.78.38.174 dlci 120(0x78,0x1C80), static,
            broadcast,
            IETF, status deleted
Serial0.2 (down): point-to-point dlci, dlci 202(0xCA,0x30A0), broadcast
                status deleted
```

The show frame-relay pvc Command

The **show frame-relay pvc** command provides statistics about the PVCs and the LMI status of every DLCI on the router.

Two types of DLCI numbers exist: those used on the local DTE and those used on the CO switched network. This command gives statistics regarding the number of dropped frames, congestion notification messages, and discard-eligible packets.

An example of the output from produced by this command follows:

```
Sean2514#show frame-relay pvc
```

```
PVC Statistics for interface Serial0 (Frame Relay DTE)
DLCI = 120, DLCI USAGE = LOCAL, PVC STATUS = DELETED, INTERFACE = Serial0

  input pkts 0             output pkts 0            in bytes 0
  out bytes 0              dropped pkts 0           in FECN pkts 0
  in BECN pkts 0           out FECN pkts 0          out BECN pkts 0
  in DE pkts 0             out DE pkts 0
  out bcast pkts 0         out bcast bytes 0
  pvc create time 00:33:13, last time pvc status changed 00:24:49

DLCI = 202, DLCI USAGE = LOCAL, PVC STATUS = DELETED, INTERFACE = Serial0.2

  input pkts 0             output pkts 0            in bytes 0
  out bytes 0              dropped pkts 0           in FECN pkts 0
  in BECN pkts 0           out FECN pkts 0          out BECN pkts 0
  in DE pkts 0             out DE pkts 0
  out bcast pkts 0         out bcast bytes 0
  pvc create time 00:37:35, last time pvc status changed 00:24:20

Sean2514#
```

You should monitor the number of Forward Explicit Congestion Notifications (FECNs) and Backward Explicit Congestion Notifications (BECNs), which are packets created when the transmitted rate is above the CIR. Each packet sent is given a *discard eligible bit*, which means that if the CO switches get congested, they will drop those packets with the discard eligible bit. When the packets are discarded, the FECN packets are sent to the receiving DTE participating devices to notify them to implement flow control. BECN messages notify the sending station that congestion was experienced and to reduce the transmission rate.

The **show interfaces** Command

The **show interfaces** command, previously discussed with regard to troubleshooting serial links, can also be used to troubleshoot Frame Relay problems. Line-by-line detail has already been given for a normal serial interface earlier in the chapter.

The following is an example of the command's output:

```
Sean2514#show interface s0

Serial0 is up, line protocol is up
  Hardware is HD64570
  Internet address is 63.78.39.174/24
  MTU 1500 bytes, BW 64 Kbit, DLY 20000 usec, rely 255/255, load 1/255
  Encapsulation FRAME-RELAY IETF, loopback not set, keepalive set (10 sec)
  LMI enq sent  270, LMI stat recvd 127, LMI upd recvd 0, DTE LMI up
  LMI enq recvd 119, LMI stat sent  0, LMI upd sent  0
```

```
LMI DLCI 1023  LMI type is CISCO  frame relay DTE
Broadcast queue 0/64, broadcasts sent/dropped 22/0, interface broadcasts 0
Last input 00:00:06, output 00:00:06, output hang never
Last clearing of "show interface" counters 02:51:08
Input queue: 0/75/0 (size/max/drops); Total output drops: 0
Queueing strategy: weighted fair
Output queue: 0/1000/64/0 (size/max total/threshold/drops)
   Conversations  0/1/256 (active/max active/max total)
   Reserved Conversations 0/0 (allocated/max allocated)
5 minute input rate 0 bits/sec, 0 packets/sec
5 minute output rate 0 bits/sec, 0 packets/sec
   1238 packets input, 66402 bytes, 0 no buffer
   Received 888 broadcasts, 0 runts, 0 giants, 0 throttles
   0 input errors, 0 CRC, 0 frame, 0 overrun, 0 ignored, 0 abort
   1245 packets output, 57524 bytes, 0 underruns
   0 output errors, 0 collisions, 51 interface resets
   0 output buffer failures, 0 output buffers swapped out
   124 carrier transitions
   DCD=up  DSR=up  DTR=up  RTS=up  CTS=up
```

Sean2514#

Table 6.5 lists and describes the troubleshooting fields contained in the preceding output.

Note: When the router is working properly, the Cisco LMI type should state 1023 for the LMI DLCI, and the ANSI type should state 0. The three types are Cisco, ANSI, and ITU-T. The default is Cisco. The LMI type configured on the router must be the same LMI type used by the CO switches.

Table 6.5   The troubleshooting fields in the show interface command output.

Field	Description
Encapsulation	One of two encapsulation methods supported by Cisco switches for Frame Relay, which are Cisco and IETF
LMI enq sent	The number of LMI enquiries sent
LMI stat recvd	The number of LMI status packets received
LMI upd recvd	The number of LMI updates received
DTE LMI	The DTE LMI status
LMI enq recvd	The number of LMI enquiries received
LMI stat sent	The number of LMI status updates sent
LMI upd sent	The number of LMI updates sent
LMI DLCI	The DLCI number used for LMI
LMI type	The LMI type used by the interface

Troubleshooting X.25

Troubleshooting X.25 is similar to the way in which you would troubleshoot a serial line or a Frame Relay line. This section first looks at some of the steps you can use to resolve X.25 circuit issues, and then looks at some of the **show** and **debug** commands that can be useful to resolving and identifying the issues.

X.25 Basics

X.25 has been around for quite some time and is actually a suite of protocols. The first of these protocols originated some time in the 1970s, shortly after the successful introduction of Telnet and TYMNET packet-switching networks (PSNs). The creators of the X.25 protocol suite had a goal of enabling data to be transmitted and received between two alphanumeric terminals through analog, plain old telephone system (POTS) phone lines. Early versions of X.25 enabled alphanumeric terminals to communicate remotely and access applications on servers and mainframes located on both ends of the analog telephone line.

One drawback existed, however—modern desktop applications needed to connect two, sometimes dissimilar, LANs with a WAN. This meant that LAN-to-WAN-to-LAN data communications were necessary. Again, the designers went back and created newer forms of wide-area networking technology, such as Integrated Services Digital Network (ISDN) and Frame Relay. These newer WAN protocols complement or extend the features of the X.25 protocol suite in the network without replacing the need for the protocol.

Many different Layer 3 protocols can be transmitted across X.25 VCs. The X.25 protocol is only the tunnel that enables Layer 3 protocol packets within the X.25 Layer 3 packets to find their way from one end of a VC to the other. X.25 is the protocol that keeps the addressing valid for each Layer 3 protocol while the X.25 VC transports the packet through a circuit.

PVCs vs. SVCs

A *virtual circuit (VC)* is a logical connection between two devices in foreign networks. VCs are used to create a reliable communication session between the two network devices with a logical, bidirectional path from one DTE device to another across an X.25 network. Two types of X.25 virtual circuits exist:

➤ *Switched virtual circuits (SVCs)*—Temporary connections used for convenient data transfers. They require that two DTE devices establish, maintain, and terminate a session each time the devices need to communicate.

➤ *Permanent virtual circuits (PVCs)*—Permanently established connections used for consistent data transfers. PVCs do not require that sessions be established or terminated. PVCs allow DTE devices to begin transferring data whenever necessary, because the session is always active.

The Packet-Layer Protocol (PLP) is used by the X.25 protocol to manage packet exchanges within a VC. PLP can be used over Logical-Link Control 2 (LLC2) or Integrated Services Digital Network (ISDN) operating on interfaces running Link Access Procedure on D channel (LAPD). PLP operates in five different modes:

➤ *Call Setup Mode*—Used to create an SVC between two DTE devices, using the X.121 addressing scheme (discussed in the following section) to create a VC.

➤ *Data-transfer Mode*—Used to transfer the physical data between two DTE devices through an already established VC. This mode assists PLP with packet segmentation, packet reassembly, and error and flow control.

➤ *Idle Mode*—Used when a VC is established and data transfer is not occurring. This mode is executed on a per-VC basis on SVCs.

➤ *Call-clearing Mode*—Used by an SVC to end communication sessions between two DTE devices.

➤ *Restarting Mode*—Used to restart a transmission between a DTE device and a DCE device located within the PSN.

Note: *Call setup and Call-clearing are used on SVCs only. PVCs are constant connections.*

X.25 PLP packet headers are made up of three fields, as shown in Figure 6.2:

➤ *GFI*—A 4-bit field used to indicate the general formatting of the packet header.

➤ *LCI*—A 12-bit field used to identify the VC information, and whether the packet is for a DTE or DCE interface.

➤ *PTI*—An 8-bit field used to identify individual packet types.

X.121 Address Format

The standard format defined for an X.25 VC is called X.121 and is an ITU-T standard. In a private X.25 network, each network is assigned a base address in decimal digits. These decimal digits, which are 1 to 15 digits, are defined for X.121 addresses to enable network protocols to connect across an X.25 link. The X.121

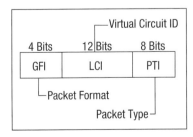

Figure 6.2 The X.25 PLP Packet header.

address enables the DTE end router to map the next-hop Layer 3 address to an X.121 address. These statements are logically equivalent to the Media Access Control (MAC) address. Maps are required for each protocol, because ARP is not supported in an X.25 network.

The first four digits of the X.121 address define the Data Network Identification Code (DNIC). The first three digits specify the country code. The fourth digit is the provider number assigned by the ITU-T. Countries that require more than 10 provider numbers are assigned multiple country codes. For example, the United States is assigned country codes 310 through 316. To view the complete listing of ITU-T country code assignments, visit ITU-T's Web site (**www.itu.org**) and refer to the ITU-T Recommendation X.121.

The remaining 8 to 11 digits specify the network terminal number (NTN) assigned by the PSN provider. You must contact your local service provider to get your individual DNIC code. Figure 6.3 shows an example of the X.121 used across a PVC.

Now that you have a basic overview, you are ready to look at some troubleshooting techniques.

X.25 Troubleshooting Steps

This section provides a step-by-step troubleshooting list for each of the following issues:

➤ Faulty hardware or cabling

➤ LABP connect state failure

➤ Misconfigured interfaces or protocol

➤ X.25 connection failures

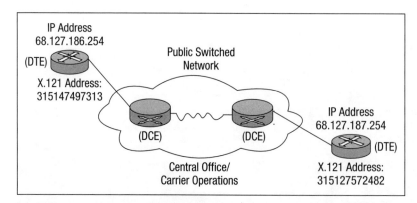

Figure 6.3 An X.121 address used over an X.25 PVC.

X.25 Connection Failure

To troubleshoot this issue, follow these steps:

1. Check whether the link is down.

2. Check for faulty-hardware issues.

3. Check whether the cables are seeded correctly.

4. Consider whether a cable may be faulty.

5. Check whether the interface is configured properly.

Unwarranted Errors

To troubleshoot this issue, follow these steps:

1. Check for faulty hardware.

2. Check for incorrect cabling.

3. Consider faulty cabling.

LABP CONNECT State Failure

To troubleshoot this issue, follow these steps:

1. Check the interface to verify that the LAPB is in a CONNECT state.

2. Use the **debug lapb** command to determine why the interface is failing to go into the CONNECT state.

3. Replace the faulty equipment.

Misconfigured Interfaces or Protocol

To troubleshoot this issue, follow these steps:

1. Use the **show running-config** command to verify the configuration.

2. Use the **debug labp** command to see whether Set Asynchronous Balance Mode (SABMs) requests are being sent.

3. If no SABMs are being sent, use the **debug x25 events** command to learn more about why they are not being sent.

4. Observe the output of the debugging commands for RESTART messages.

5. Check the LAPB parameters on the interface.

X.25 Troubleshooting Commands

As discussed earlier in the chapter with respect to troubleshooting Frame Relay and serial links, certain **debug** and **show** commands can be used to obtain more information about the troubleshooting issues you are facing. This section looks at the following X.25 troubleshooting commands:

➤ **debug x25 events**

➤ **debug lapb**

➤ **show interface serial**

The **debug x25 events** Command

The **debug x25 events** command can be used to detect events and obtain diagnostics information on X.25-configured interfaces. Note that when using this command, due to the large amount of output generated by calls and other data such as Receive Ready (RR) flow control packets, these events are not displayed by the router.

The **debug lapb** Command

The **debug lapb** command debugs the events at Layer 2 of the x.25 circuits. This command should be used when an X.25 interface experiences frequent restarts. Because x.25 relies on LAPB to maintain stability, if problems arise with the LAPB configuration, it effects the X.25 protocol and the participating x.25 interfaces.

The **show interface serial** Command

When a serial interface is configured to use X.25, the **show interface serial** command provides information specific to the X.25 protocol. Table 6.6 provides a description of the fields found in the output below. Here is a sample of the **show interface serial** command's output when X.25 is configured on the interface:

```
Sean2514#show interfaces serial 0
1d03h: %CLEAR-5-COUNTERS: Clear counter on interface Serial0 by console

Serial0 is up, line protocol is up
  Hardware is HD64570
  Internet address is 63.78.39.174/24
    Hardware is HD64570
  Internet address is 172.16.30.5/30
  MTU 1500 bytes, BW 1544 Kbit, DLY 20000 usec, rely 255/  255, load 51/255
  Encapsulation X25, loopback not set
LAPB DTE, state CONNECT, modulo 8, k 7, N1 12043, N2 10
T1 3000, interface outage (partial T3) 0, T4 0
```

Table 6.6   The fields of the show interface serial command on an interface configured for X.25.

Field	Description
RNRs	Displays the number of Receiver Not Ready events
REJs	Displays the number of rejects
SABMs	Displays the number of Set Asynchronous Balance Mode requests
FRMRs	Displays the number of protocol frame errors
DISCs	Displays the number of disconnects
RESTARTs	Displays the number of restarts

```
 VS 1, VR 1, Remote VR 1, Retransmissions 0
    IFRAMEs 1/1 RNRs 0/0 REJs 0/0 SABM/Es 1/0 FRMRs 0/0 DISCs 0/0
X25 DTE, address 190118, state R1, modulo 8, timer 0
Defaults: cisco encapsulation, idle 0, nvc 1
Input/output window sizes 2/2, packet sizes 128/128
Timers: T20 180, T21 200, T22 180, T23 180, TH 0
Channels: Incoming-only none, Two-way 5-1024, Outgoing-only none
RESTARTs 1/1 CALLs 0+0/0+0/0+0 DIAGs 0/0
  Last input 00:00:00, output 00:00:00, output hang never
  Last clearing of "show interface" counters 00:48:96
  Input queue: 1/75/0 (size/max/drops); Total output drops: 0
  Queueing strategy: weighted fair
  Output queue: 0/1000/64/0 (size/max total/threshold/drops)
     Conversations  0/2/256 (active/max active/max total)
     Reserved Conversations 0/0 (allocated/max allocated)
  5 minute input rate 0 bits/sec, 0 packets/sec
  5 minute output rate 0 bits/sec, 0 packets/sec
     0 packets input, 0 bytes, 0 no buffer
     Received 0 broadcasts, 0 runts, 0 giants, 0 throttles
     0 input errors, 0 CRC, 0 frame, 0 overrun, 0 ignored, 0 abort
     0 packets output, 0 bytes, 0 underruns
     0 output errors, 0 collisions, 0 interface resets
     0 output buffer failures, 0 output buffers swapped out
     0 carrier transitions
     DCD=up  DSR=up  DTR=up  RTS=up  CTS=up

Sean2514#
```

Chapter Summary

This chapter presented many troubleshooting techniques for dealing with problems related to serial links, HDLC, LMI types, X.25, and Frame Relay. Step-by-step checklists can be used to troubleshoot each issue, whether it is related to hardware, cabling, IOS configuration, or connectivity.

The CSU/DSU loopback test is an important tool in making sure that no hardware issues exist. You can perform this test all the way to the remote CSU/DSU to help isolate a PVC or SVC problem.

Debug commands are another useful tool in troubleshooting. You do need to make sure that your debugging doesn't overwhelm the processing power of the router. The **debug serial packet** command is one of the most processor-intensive tools, because it looks at every packet in depth. Some debug commands are complicated, and you may need to contact the Cisco Technical Assistance Center to decipher the output.

Don't be afraid to contact the local service provider to help troubleshoot your problem. As the administrator, you may deal with this problem infrequently. The local service provider most likely deals with this on a daily basic. Even if the problem isn't with the provider's link or equipment, its employees may be able to give you pointers on your failed links.

One of the most important steps in troubleshooting is documenting what you have done and making sure you can relay that information to someone on the other end of the link.

Review Questions

1. Which encapsulation is used by default on Cisco serial interfaces?
   a. HDLC
   b. Frame Relay
   c. SDLC
   d. X.25

2. Which of the following commands will display the DLCI numbers associated with a serial interface? [Choose the two best answers]
   a. **show frame-relay lmi**
   b. **show running-config**
   c. **show frame-relay map**
   d. **show serial all**
   e. **show x25**

3. Which of the following is true of the DLCI number?
   a. The DLCI number has local significance.
   b. The DLCI number must be matched to the other end of a SVC.
   c. The DLCI number must be a number between 1 and 65.
   d. The DLCI number can be used only to pass IPX data, and not IP data.

4. Which of the following elements are displayed by using the **show controller serial** command? [Choose the two best answers]

   a. Clock rate

   b. Cable type

   c. LMI type

   d. Error information

5. Using the **debug serial interface** command displays which of the following information fields?

   a. mineseen

   b. myseq

   c. yourseen

   d. None of the above

   e. All of the above

6. Which of the following should you do if the interface is administratively down? [Choose the two best answers]

   a. Check the cabling

   b. Check whether the interface is manually shut down

   c. Check for duplicate IP addresses

   d. Check with the local service provider

7. If the keepalives are not sequencing on a serial interface, which of the following is not a troubleshooting step?

   a. Check the local hardware

   b. Check for noise on the line

   c. Check for a timing mismatch

   d. Check the local router's hostname

8. Which of the following are displayed when using the **show interface serial** command? [Choose the two best answers]

   a. Error information

   b. Encapsulation type

   c. AUI interface configuration

   d. Switch model information

9. Which of the following commands displays the FECN and BECN statistics?

   a. **show x25 events**

   b. **show frame-relay pvc**

   c. **show interface serial**

   d. **show running-config**

10. Which of the following are valid LMI types? [Choose the two best answers]

    a. DLCI

    b. Cisco

    c. ANSI

    d. IEEE

11. Which of the following are LABP-related fields found in the output from the **show interface serial** command? [Choose the three best answers]

    a. BECNs

    b. RNRs

    c. REJs

    d. FECNs

    e. SABMs

12. To test end-to-end connectivity on a serial link, which of the following would be used?

    a. Route trace test

    b. SNMP test

    c. Loopback test

    d. Connectivity test

    e. Ping 127.0.0.1

13. Which of the following are not valid LMI types? [Choose the two best answers]

    a. ANSI

    b. DLCI

    c. IETF

    d. ITU-T

    e. Cisco

14. The following output is displayed using which of the following commands?

```
Serial0 (up): ip 62.78.38.174 dlci 120(0x78,0x1C80), static,
              broadcast,
              IETF, status deleted
Serial0 (up): ip 62.78.38.175 dlci 102(0x66,0x1860), dynamic,
              broadcast,
              IETF, status defined, active
```

   a. **show frame-relay map**

   b. **debug frame-relay**

   c. **show frame-relay pvc**

   d. **show frame relay lmi**

15. Which of the following are valid Frame Relay encapsulation types? [Choose the two best answers]

   a. Cisco

   b. ANSI

   c. DLCI

   d. IETF

   e. ITU-T

16. The following output is displayed using which of the following commands?

```
Serial0 is up, line protocol is up
  Hardware is HD64570
  Internet address is 63.78.39.174/24
  MTU 1500 bytes, BW 64 Kbit, DLY 20000 usec, rely 255/255, load 1/255
  Encapsulation FRAME-RELAY IETF, loopback not set, keepalive set (10 sec)
  LMI enq sent  270, LMI stat recvd 127, LMI upd recvd 0, DTE LMI up
  LMI enq recvd 119, LMI stat sent  0, LMI upd sent  0
  LMI DLCI 1023  LMI type is CISCO  frame relay DTE
  Broadcast queue 0/64, broadcasts sent/dropped 22/0, interface
  broadcasts 0
  Last input 00:00:06, output 00:00:06, output hang never
  Last clearing of "show interface" counters 02:51:08
  Input queue: 0/75/0 (size/max/drops); Total output drops: 0
  Queueing strategy: weighted fair
  Output queue: 0/1000/64/0 (size/max total/threshold/drops)
```

   a. **show frame-relay map**

   b. **show interface**

   c. **show frame-relay pvc**

   d. **show frame relay lmi**

6

17. If you need to connect a Cisco router to a non-Cisco device, which encapsulation type would you use.

    a. DLCI

    b. X.25

    c. ANSI

    d. Cisco

    e. IETF

18. The following output is displayed using which of the following commands?

```
LMI Statistics for interface Serial0 (Frame Relay DTE) LMI TYPE = CISCO
   Invalid Unnumbered info 0          Invalid Prot Disc 0
   Invalid dummy Call Ref 0           Invalid Msg Type 0
   Invalid Status Message 0           Invalid Lock Shift 0
   Invalid Information ID 0           Invalid Report IE Len 0
   Invalid Report Request 0           Invalid Keep IE Len 0
   Num Status Enq. Sent 288           Num Status msgs Rcvd 288
   Num Update Status Rcvd 17          Num Status Timeouts 0
```

    a. **show frame-relay map**

    b. **show interface**

    c. **show frame-relay pvc**

    d. **show frame relay lmi**

19. Which of the following fields is not a Frame Relay or LMI-related field displayed with the **show interface serial** command?

    a. LMI stat sent

    b. LMI enq recvd

    c. DTE LMI

    d. PVC Status

    e. LMI upd recvd

20. Which of the following is the default LMI type on a Cisco router?

    a. IETF

    b. ANSI

    c. Cisco

    d. X.25

Real-World Project

The Coriolis Group ("Coriolis") has a Frame Relay PVC from its office building containing its sales, marketing, acquisitions, and editorial staff to its shipping warehouse. This is a very important link because of the volume of shipments coming in and out of the warehouse.

The main server farm is located in the office building that houses all the sales and shipping transactions, which provide the work for the staff of approximately 250. The link between the two buildings has been lost. This means that the 250 employees are basically taking a long, paid breakfast and lunch.

As Joe Snow answers his cellular phone, a very upset manager, Jay Heckman, explains that the $1,200 per month PVC between the office building and the warehouse is costing him $15,000 per hour in lost wages and lowered productivity. Jay explains that his internal desktop IT staff has contacted the local service provider who has run a test on the link and determined that a local hardware issue exists.

Begging for leniency on the four-hour response time agreed upon in the service contract, Joe assures Jay that he will be on his way to Coriolis, which is about a 20-minute drive from his location.

On Joe's way out, he grabs a spare router, WIC card, cables, and CSU/DSU. This will ensure that any piece of equipment he may need will be readily accessible, because this is a situation that can't wait for a parts shipment.

As Joe arrives, he finds Jay waiting at the door and is immediately hurried upstairs. The following are the steps that Joe uses to resolve this issue:

1. Joe first looks at the router interface to see what errors are displayed and the current interface states. The cable to the CSU/DSU is on the serial 0 interface, and Joe uses the **show interface serial 0** command to look at the interface. The output is as follows:

```
CoriolisRouter#show interface serial 0

Serial0 is down, line protocol is down
  Hardware is HD64570
  Internet address is 63.78.39.174/24
  MTU 1500 bytes, BW 64 Kbit, DLY 20000 usec, rely 255/255, load 1/255
  Encapsulation FRAME-RELAY IETF, loopback not set, keepalive set (10 sec)
  LMI enq sent  270, LMI stat recvd 127, LMI upd recvd 0, DTE LMI up
  LMI enq recvd 119, LMI stat sent  0, LMI upd sent  0
  LMI DLCI 1023  LMI type is CISCO  frame relay DTE
  Broadcast queue 0/64, broadcasts sent/dropped 22/0, interface
```

```
broadcasts 0
Last input 00:00:06, output 00:00:06, output hang never
Last clearing of "show interface" counters 02:51:08
Input queue: 0/75/0 (size/max/drops); Total output drops: 0
Queueing strategy: weighted fair
Output queue: 0/1000/64/0 (size/max total/threshold/drops)
   Conversations  0/1/256 (active/max active/max total)
   Reserved Conversations 0/0 (allocated/max allocated)
5 minute input rate 0 bits/sec, 0 packets/sec
5 minute output rate 0 bits/sec, 0 packets/sec
   0 packets input, 0bytes, 0 no buffer
   Received 0 broadcasts, 0 runts, 0 giants, 0 throttles
   0 input errors, 0 CRC, 0 frame, 0 overrun, 0 ignored, 0 abort
   0 packets output, 0 bytes, 0 underruns
   0 output errors, 0 collisions, 51 interface resets
   0 output buffer failures, 0 output buffers swapped out
   124 carrier transitions
   DCD=up  DSR=up  DTR=up  RTS=up  CTS=up

CorolisRouter#
```

2. Immediately, Joe notices that the line and protocol are down. Joe also notices that the router must have been rebooted, because no statistics are given. He checks the cables and they appear to be seated correctly, but he replaces them with his good cables anyway.

3. Because replacing the cables does not resolve the issue, he immediately opens the cabinet containing the CSU/DSU. The lights on the CSU/DSU are indicating that there is no CD (Carrier Detect).

4. He places the CSU/DSU in loopback mode to see whether the interface can send data packets back and forth. This in a sense checks the CSU/DSU hardware to see whether it is functioning correctly.

5. Joe realizes that there is still no activity. He pulls a new CSU/DSU out of the box, compares the dip switches, and moves the cables from the old CSU/DSU to the new one.

Immediately after powering on the CSU/DSU, Joe is a networking hero.

CHAPTER SEVEN

Troubleshooting Novell NetWare Environments

After completing this chapter, you will be able to:

✓ Recognize problem symptoms that relate to IPX

✓ Resolve IPX problems utilizing a troubleshooting method

✓ Identify the inner workings of Novell IPX

✓ Understand and troubleshoot SAP

✓ Identify how GNS messages work

✓ Configure and troubleshoot IPX access lists

✓ Identify the advantages and disadvantages of RIP and NLSP

✓ Use IPX troubleshooting tools and commands

For some time, Novell NetWare has been one of the more popular network operating systems. NetWare's network protocols, Internetwork Packet Exchange (IPX) and Sequenced Packet Exchange (SPX), removed many of the client-configuration issues that were inherent with other protocols. Because of this, the release of version 3.11 quickly earned market share and a great reputation for stability, quick installation, and low maintenance.

In today's version of NetWare, version 5.0, NetWare stopped relying on the IPX and SPX protocols and started supporting TCP/IP. Although version 5.0 centers around TCP/IP, many legacy applications and networks exist that still use the IPX protocol, so legacy-protocol support is still included. Some of the features that simplify the functions of IPX for network administrators are the same functions that IP uses with Dynamic Host Configuration Protocol (DHCP), Address Resolution Protocol (ARP), Domain Name Service (DNS), and Windows Internet Name Service (WINS), all of which are included in the installation of NetWare.

This chapter focuses more on troubleshooting commands than on configuration commands. It also looks at the connection sequences and the diagnostic tools that relate to troubleshooting in an IPX environment. For those who do not frequently use the IPX protocol, this chapter includes a quick overview of IPX networks and the IPX addressing scheme.

IPX Addressing

IPX operates at Layer 3 of the OSI Reference Model and can share addressing schemes with the IP protocol, which makes it is easy to configure as well as administrate in the network. Just like an IP address, an IPX address is divided into a network identifier, which is 4 octets, and a node (host) address. The node address is combined with the physical MAC address of the network interface card (NIC) located inside the node, which creates a 10-octet address. The IPX addressing scheme is independent of the IP addressing scheme, which uses a subnet mask. This also allows IPX to have any number of nodes belonging to the IPX network, as long as the physical media or bandwidth can support the data and broadcast traffic.

IPX addresses can be found in several formats. Hexadecimal is the most common format, however. A hexadecimal address of 0000018A.0000.834A.3D51, for example, can be broken down into two parts. The first part consists of the 8 hexadecimal digits, 0000018A, and indicates the network the node resides in. The other 12 hexadecimal digits, 0000.834A.3D51, indicate the node address. Most of the time, when you see the network portion of the address, the 0s preceding the network number are dropped. Therefore, the full IPX network address, including the network and node, would appear as 18A.0000.834A.3D51.

Although both IP and IPX are Layer 3 protocols, they can be used simultaneously in the same network. Commonly, in a network utilizing both protocols, you will find that a different addressing scheme is used. This type of scheme uses the IP decimal values or the hexadecimal values to make up the IPX network number. So, if your network is 63.78.39.0, for example, the network address becomes 63d78d39 if it uses the decimal version, or becomes 3fd4ed27 if it uses the hexadecimal version. The *d* represents the dot separator.

Many other networking schemes are used, including the area code, office identifier, and even a frame type code, and many ways of creating your network addresses exist.

IPX Components

Understanding how IPX encapsulations work, as well as the Get Nearest Server and Service Advertising protocols, are critical to your understanding of IPX components. Both of these protocols must be functioning in the IPX network after connectivity is established for service broadcasts to begin. The following sections take a look at these three components.

Encapsulation Process

NetWare uses encapsulation as well as a framing method to take an IPX datagram at Layer 3 and add it to an appropriate Layer 2 frame. An important piece of knowledge in troubleshooting Novel is the framing process and how it relates to Ethernet, token ring, and Fiber Distributed Data Interface (FDDI) physical topologies.

When an IPX frame type mismatch exists in the network, the IPX networked components cannot communicate, because this situation is somewhat similar to two people trying to communicate in two different languages without a translator. The following are the five Ethernet IPX frame types (the Cisco identifier name that is used to set the frame type is in parentheses):

➤ *Ethernet_802.3 (novell-ether)*—The default IPX frame type up to NetWare version 3.11. This version supports only IPX and the Ethernet physical media.

➤ *Ethernet_802.2 (sap or iso1)*—The default IPX frame type beginning in NetWare version 3.12. This frame type is supported on multiple physical media types, including Ethernet, FDDI, and token ring, and is recommended for networks with multiple media types.

➤ *Ethernet_II (arpa)*—This frame type supports TCP/IP and IPX. An ether type value is placed after the source MAC address to identify the protocol. The ether value for IPX is 8137 and 0800 for IP.

> ➤ *Ethernet_SNAP (snap)*—This frame type supports AppleTalk, IPX, and TCP/IP on multiple physical media types, which are token ring, Ethernet, and FDDI, using a SNAP header.

> ➤ *Token Ring (token)*—This frame type supports only token ring traffic for IP, IPX, or Novell Layer 3 traffic.

NetWare 5.0 uses IP as a default. When IPX is used with version 5.0, the default is Ethernet 802.2 and only supports IPX. You must assign an IPX network number for each segment, and each number must be unique for each frame type used, even if two frame types are bound to the same physical network interface.

Get Nearest Server

To connect to a Novell server, a client must be able locate the server. The Get Nearest Server (GNS) protocol handles this task with the Service Advertising Protocol (SAP). GNS uses broadcasts that are answered by all IPX servers on the network accepting the first broadcast for the initialization process. The first server that responds is not always the preferred server identified in the client's configuration file.

Novell differs from AppleTalk and Microsoft networking in that a Novell client can't also be a server. In Novell, a server is a server, and a client uses resources from the server. IPX assigns a GNS listener to each IPX network. The router contains an SAP table that can respond to a GNS request. Both routers and servers can reply to a GNS request. Cisco routers do not respond to a GNS request if a NetWare server is on the segment.

Note: *GNS requests are broadcasts that are not forwarded by a router.*

If the router must respond to a GNS request because a server is on another segment, a client will request routing information from the router. The router will provide this information and the client will establish a direct connection to the server.

The following are the steps used to resolve a GNS request when the server resides on another segment and a router must handle the request:

1. The Novell client sends a GNS request.

2. No server reside on the segment, so the router responds with a GNS reply.

3. The client responds with an IPX RIP request to get the routing information to the server.

4. The client sends a *NetWare Control Protocol (NCP)* request, which is a connection-oriented protocol used for primary Novell functions. After the client and server establish an NCP session, the client proceeds to the login phase after an IPX NCP reply.

Service Advertising Protocol

Every 60 seconds, by default, NetWare servers use SAP to advertise their services to other servers and routers. It's through these advertisements that Novell clients find the servers that they need. The nearest server needs to have an entry in its SAP table for that resource. Unless the router has a security policy using access lists, all the servers and routers are aware of all the resources in the internetwork, which enables any client to obtain the information from any server or router if one isn't available on the client's segment.

All the services that are learned from SAP are entered into either the servers or routers table. This table is a summarized list of where resources reside in the network. This information is then re-sent out each interface on the router or server to help inform all the other routers and servers in the network of the existence of other resources. If a problem arises when forwarding or storing the SAP table on any server or router, it can cause services to become unavailable. If a new service is introduced, it is automatically broadcast and added to local SAP tables and added to new SAP advertisements to populate the other servers' and routers' SAP tables.

This service has a drawback, though. In terms of scalability, the more servers and clients you have, the more GNS and SAP broadcasts and responses you have. Broadcasts can be both good and bad in a network. They're good because they help you to find resources, but they are bad because they eat up the available bandwidth on the network. This is a significant issue with WAN links, because bandwidth may be limited. If these broadcasts are listed as interesting traffic on an ISDN connection, the connection will never terminate. You can read more about ISDN in Chapter 13.

Note: When troubleshooting SAP advertisements, keep in mind that an access list may be configured on a router to filter them.

Troubleshooting Novell

You should approach a Novell problem just as you would approach any other problem, by following these steps:

1. Identify and define the problem.

2. Gather as many facts as possible.

3. Consider possible problems and solutions.

4. Create an action plan.

5. Implement the plan.

6. Gather information on the problem based on the results of step 5 and assess the new information.

7. After the problem has been resolved, document the resolution for future use.

You can narrow down the source of the problem by doing the following:

➤ Check the frame types and the client configuration. This includes checking the frame type and hardware settings (including the IRQ and DMA settings) and making sure the client has the proper drivers for the NIC and has physical connectivity to the network.

➤ Check the local Cisco router configuration. This includes checking the configured network numbers, access lists, frame types, and SAP table sizes.

➤ Check for non-IPX protocol–related problems. This include overloaded segments, down links, processor overloads on the routers, IP configuration, and AppleTalk issues.

The following sections look at how to troubleshoot some of these common issues, particularly the following:

➤ SAP advertisement issues

➤ Configuration issues

➤ Remote server issues

➤ IPX RIP

➤ IPX EIGRP

➤ NLSP

SAP Advertisement Issues

Novell has some common issues that arise, such as the router not propagating SAP updates. The SAP updates are important to Novell because they are the component that tells the clients where to get resources. When SAP advertisements are not being propagated, check the following on the router:

➤ Configured access lists

➤ Duplicated network numbers on interfaces

➤ Mismatched frame type configurations

➤ Incorrectly set timers

Tip: An administrator in a Novell network should have a thorough knowledge of how to use the **debug** and **show** commands on a Cisco router. The administrator should also be proficient at using a protocol analyzer, and know the server and client applications running in the network, to provide quick troubleshooting resolutions.

Configuration Issues

Novell networks and their clients can use any of the four frame types discussed earlier in the chapter. The client, server, and router must understand and use the same frame type to communicate. Depending on the Cisco IOS you are using, you can view the configuration and frame types configured on the router by using the following commands:

➤ **write terminal** (IOS version 11.1 or later)

➤ **show running-config** (IOS version 11.2 or later)

In the following example, the 11.1 IOS has been installed on a Cisco 2514 to show how the configuration looks. The router is using the Cisco default frame type of NOVELL-ETHER-, or Ethernet 802.3, on all interfaces. If it does not show the frame type, this is the frame type that is being used.

```
Seans2514# write terminal
Building configuration...
Current configuration:
!
version 11.1
service timestamps debug datetime localtime show-timezone
service timestamps log datetime localtime show-timezone
!
service password-encryption
service udp-small-servers
service tcp-small-servers
!
hostname Seans2621
!
ipx routing 0100.0d28.6710
ipx maximum-paths 3
!
interface Ethernet0
 mtu 1500
 ip address 172.16.1.1 255.255.255.0
 ipx network 100
!
interface Ethernet1
 ip address 172.16.2.1 255.255.255.0
 no keepalive
 ipx network 200
!
end
```

7

Warning! A good indicator of a misconfigured network number is an error that is similar to "00:60:80:2A:23:AA claims network 300 should be 100". All the network servers and routers need to have their external IPX network numbers set to the same value.

Remote Server Issues

IPX networks can be designed without a locally attachable server. The file server and other network resources can be located on another segment of the network. You can also configure the routers to dial a server remotely over a switched virtual connection (SVC) or a permanent virtual connection (PVC) connecting across a WAN link.

When setting up an SVC connection to dial only when traffic is present, remember to turn off IPX RIP (discussed in the next section) routing or the connection will not terminate. On a PVC, as an IPX network begins to grow, the sheer volume of IPX RIP traffic and SAP traffic also grows. Eventually, a WAN connection will be overwhelmed with RIP and SAP updates where data cannot be sent successfully over the links without high latency. In some medium to large networks, a T1 line can easily be saturated, causing difficulty sending RIP messages, SAP messages, and data. That's without including any other protocols, such as IP and AppleTalk, that may be running in the network. Always remember that very few networks in existence today have only Novell NetWare's IPX protocol running on them.

In an SVC where the router must dial when interesting traffic exists to send, the router must respond when a server is not present. The time it takes a router to dial and make a connection may cause GNS queries to fail due to timeouts or other unforeseen issues. Debugging commands can be used in this situation to find the problem, but use them with caution and don't rely on them. The debugging commands can actually cause a timeout issue, because the commands are given a high priority on the processor and are processor-intensive.

The **ipx gns-round-robin** command can help on the router if the servers are overloaded. This command can be used if multiple servers are an equal distance from the router. This command provides a form of load balancing between the servers. If a problem occurs in the network whereby the router responds to a client more quickly than the client can handle a return request, although rare, you can set a delay. The default delay is 0 milliseconds (ms), but this can be changed by using the **ipx gns-response-delay** command.

IPX RIP

If your network consists of just a few locations connected by three routers using T1 WAN lines, and not too many servers, RIP and SAP can probably run successfully in your network. The reason is that SAP and RIP broadcast everything that they know every 60 seconds throughout the network. In a small network, SAP and RIP tables are pretty small and don't use up a lot of bandwidth. Imagine having 100 servers and 50 locations. This may sound far-fetched to some, but chances are good that if you're administering a Novell network, it is going to be at least this size.

Note: Because Novell is a very stable network operating system, it is implemented in the networks of many financial and emergency service providers.

Now, imagine that SAP updates advertising all of those servers are crossing your WAN connections every 60 seconds. You probably realize that you might need to implement some flow control or buffering, or perhaps a lot more than that. You have to leave some bandwidth for data traffic, too. You might not want to add multimedia to this type of environment. Your network likely will be spending all of its time and bandwidth keeping itself up to date. You might want to tell your users to start data transfers and print jobs just before they go home at night, so they will have them conveniently ready in the morning. If this is acceptable in your network, you might not need to know about IPX EIGRP or NLSP. The *convergence time* is the amount of time required to update IPX network addresses and services from its SAP tables if a link or server problem exists in the network. If you are using IPX RIP, the convergence time is longer. IPX RIP doesn't notify other servers and routers until it is time for their regularly scheduled 60 second spaced broadcast. If you have more than one hop (you can have up to 15 with RIP), you can add up to an extra minute to that convergence time per hop. Any idea of how long a minute is in network time? An eternity.

Note: IPX RIP doesn't like redundant paths, either.

The bottom line is that IPX RIP and SAP just don't scale well in networks, so you need to consider a better routing protocol. Of course, if you have lots of cash and patience, you can buy bandwidth. A better way may exist, though. Even if nothing else but the convergence time or redundancy is important to you, you should consider IPX EIGRP and NLSP.

Configuring IPX RIP

Configuring IPX RIP is rather simple. Use the **ipx router rip** command at the global configuration prompt and identify the network numbers running in the network. The following is an example of configuring IPX RIP:

```
Seans2514(config)#ipx router rip
Seans2514(config-ipx-router)#network 100
Seans2514(config-ipx-router)#network 200
Seans2514(config-ipx-router)#network 300
Seans2514(config-ipx-router)#^Z
Seans2514#
```

IPX EIGRP

In a total Cisco routed environment, a better choice over IPX RIP is Cisco's Enhanced Interior Gateway Routing Protocol (EIGRP). This is a routing protocol for a growing network. Table 7.1 compares the main differences between IPX RIP and IPX EIGRP.

The **show ipx eigrp** command is used to help troubleshoot problems with EIGRP. The following are the available syntaxes for the command:

```
Sean2514#show ipx eigrp ?
 interfaces IPX EIGRP Interfaces
 neighbors  IPX EIGRP Neighbors
 topology   IPX EIGRP Topology Table
 traffic    IPX EIGRP Traffic Statistics
```

If you have IPX EIGRP configured, you can use the **show ipx eigrp neighbors**, **show ipx eigrp topology**, and **show ipx route** commands to see whether the routing tables are updating correctly and to see the known routes through the network. These three commands are discussed next.

The **show ipx eigrp neighbors** Command

Seans2514 is running IPX EIGRP process 10 and is connected to IPX network 100 on its Ethernet 1 interface and to IPX network 300 via its Ethernet 0 interface. The following is the output from the **show ipx eigrp neighbors** command:

```
Seans2514# show ipx eigrp neighbors
IPX EIGRP Neighbors for process 10
H  Address             Interface  Hold  Uptime    Q  Seq  SRTT  RTO
1  100.0000.604a.3d7d Ethernet1  12    06:12:43  0  2614 15    30
0  300.0000.604a.5a4b Ethernet0  12    06:12:46  0  2617 15    30
```

This shows the first EIGRP neighbor the router learned about a little over 22 hours ago on the Ethernet1 interface, which is the second AUI port on the Cisco 2514 router. Since the learned route, 2,614 updates have been received on that interface. The Smooth Round Trip Time (SRTT) is set to 15 seconds and the Retransmission TimeOut (RTO) is set to 30 seconds. This information can be used

Table 7.1   IPX RIP and IPX EIGRP compared.

Component	IPX RIP	IPX EIGRP
Maximum hop count	15	224
Convergence	Slow	Fast
Bandwidth used	High	Low
Updates	60 seconds	Only when needed

to find the directly connected neighbors or to identify routes that are coming up and down, which can be identified by an increase of sequence numbers on a certain interface.

The **show ipx eigrp topology** Command

The following output from the **show ipx eigrp topology** shows that for IPX EIGRP process 10, networks 100, 200, and 300 are available out the Ethernet 0 interface on the router:

```
Seans2514# show ipx eigrp topology

Topology Table for process 10
Codes: P-Passive, A-Active, U-Update, Q-Query, R-Reply, r-Reply status

P 100, 1 successors, FD is 225488
     via 300.0000.604a.5a4b (225488/274200), Ethernet0
P 200, 1 successors, FD is 265486
     via 300.0000.604a.5a4b (265486/302430), Ethernet0
P 300, 1 successors, FD is 211852
     via Connected, Ethernet0
```

The **show ipx route** Command

The following output from the **show ipx route** command provides information on static and IPX routing protocols, including RIP, EIGRP, and NLSP discovered routes:

```
Seans2514# show ipx routes
Codes: C - Connected primary network, c - Connected secondary network, S -
Static, F - Floating static, L - Local (internal), W - IPXWAN, R - RIP, E -
EIGRP, N - NLSP, X - External, A - Aggregate, s - seconds,  u - uses
4 Total IPX routes. Up to 1 parallel paths and 16 hops allowed.
No default route known.
L 400 is the internal network
C 300 (NOVELL-ETHER), Ethernet0
C 200 (NOVELL-ETHER), Ethernet1
E 100 [284228/0] via 300.0000.604a.5a4b, age 2w5d, 1u, E0
```

*Note: The default behavior of Cisco routers is to consider only one IPX route. This means that no redundant paths are considered. The **ipx maximum-paths** command can be used to change this default to up to six routes to a destination network.*

This output shows that network 400 is the internal network, Ethernet0 is directly attached to network 300, Ethernet1 is attached to network 200, and network 100 can be reached through a network 300 interface out Ethernet0.

Configuring EIGRP

Configuring IPX EIGRP is about as simple as configuring IPX RIP. You need to use the **ipx router rip** command and identify both an autonomous system number and the network numbers in the network. You must have IPX routing enabled, and all the interfaces must be configured with an IPX network number and encapsulation type. The following shows an example of configuring IPX EIGRP:

```
Seans2514#config terminal
Seans2514(config)#ipx router eigrp 10
Seans2514(config-ipx-router)#network 100
Seans2514(config-ipx-router)#network 200
Seans2514(config-ipx-router)#network 300
```

NLSP

The NetWare Link Services Protocol (NLSP) has several advantages over IPX RIP. The routing protocol enables you to remove IPX SAP advertisements from an identified network segment. NLSP then handles network updates. The protocol reduces both IPX RIP and SAP advertisements by sending updates on changes to a database, rather than by sending the complete table every 60 seconds. This is another routing protocol that sends an update only if a change in the network topology has occurred, unless no activity takes place for two hours, after which time the NLSP-enabled interface will send an update to all of its neighbors.

To enable NLSP, use the **ipx nlsp enable** command on each interface connecting to segments that need to have NLSP enabled. You must then identify the NLSP area address. The **area-address** command is used to define which IPX addresses are part of a particular area. The syntax is as follows:

```
area-address area mask
```

You can use zero for this address and zero for the mask. Using zeros indicates that all area addresses are to be included in this area.

*Note: NLSP requires use of the **ipx internal-network** command to identify the IPX internal network.*

When configuring NLSP, we must first enable IPX routing by using the **ipx internal-network** command to identify the IPX internal network for the router. Next, configure both active the default encapsulation (HDLC on Serial 0, novell-ether on Ethernet 0) on the interface, and identify the networks connected to each interface. The following shows an example:

```
Seans2514#conf t
Seans2514(config)# ipx routing
```

```
Seans2514(config)# ipx internal-network d
Seans2514(config)# ipx router nlsp
Seans2514(config-ipx-router)# area-address 0 0
Seans2514(config)# int s0
Seans2514 (config-if)# ipx network 100
Seans2514(config-if)# ipx nlsp enable
Seans2514 (config-if)# int e0
Seans2514 (config-if)# ipx network 300
Seans2514(config-if)# exit
Seans2514(config)#
```

You can use the following **show** commands to verify the configuration and functioning of NLSP:

➤ **show ipx route**

➤ **show ipx servers**

➤ **show ipx nlsp neighbors**

➤ **show ipx nlsp database**

The following sections describe each of these commands.

The **show ipx route** Command

When you configure NLSP, the routing table output produced by using the **show ipx route** command shows a serial route, as in this example:

```
Seans2514# show ipx route
Codes: C - Connected primary network,
       c - Connected secondary network
       S - Static, F - Floating static, L - Local
       (internal), W - IPXWAN
       R - RIP, E - EIGRP, N - NLSP, X - External,
       A - Aggregate
       s - seconds, u - uses
3 Total IPX routes. Up to 1 parallel paths and 16 hops allowed.
No default route known.
L 400 is the internal network
C 500 (HDLC), Serial0
C 200 (NOVELL-ETHER), Ethernet0
```

The **show ipx servers** Command

You can use the **show ipx servers** command to view all the known routes to the servers learned by the router. The following is an example of using the **show ipx servers** command:

```
Seans2514# show ipx servers
Codes: S - Static, P - Periodic, E - EIGRP, N - NLSP,
       H -Holddown, + = detail
2 Total IPX Servers
Table ordering is based on routing and server info
    Type  Name      Net Address           Port Route  Hops Itf
N   4     File&Print1 100.0000.0000.0001:0000 12/02  2    Se0
N   4     CAD1        100.0000.0000.0002:0000 12/02  2    Se0
```

The show ipx nlsp neighbors Command

The **show ipx nlsp neighbors** command can be used to display all the known NLSP neighbors, which are NLSP resources that are directly connected to the router's interfaces. The following is an example of using the **show ipx nlsp neighbors** command as well as the output.

Note: NLSP are not forwarded by the router. They are forwarded on local segments only.

```
Ginas2621# show ipx nlsp neighbors
NLSP Level-1 Neighbors: Tag Identifier = notag
System Id Interface State Holdtime Priority  Circuit Id
Seans2514  Se0        Up    55      0          04
Ginas2621 has one NLSP neighbor, Seans2514. By adding the detail command,
the output includes the IPX internal network number and the uptime.

Ginas2621# show ipx nlsp neighbors detail
NLSP Level-1 Neighbors: Tag Identifier = notag
System Id Interface State Holdtime Priority Circuit Id
Seans2514 Se0        Up    43      0          04
IPX Address: 100.0000.0000.0001
IPX Areas: 00000000/00000000
Uptime: 01:13:09
```

The show ipx nlsp database Command

The **show ipx nlsp database** command provides information on the NLSP processes, as in the following example:

```
Seans2514#show ipx nlsp database
NLSP Level-1 Link State Database
LSPID              LSP Seq       Num LSP      Checksum LSP Holdtime ATT/P/OL
Seans2501.00-00 * 0x0000043B    0x2C77       203          0/0/0
Seans2514.04-00 * 0x000001D2    0x1A2D       440          0/0/0
Seans2514.00-00   0x00000023    0x1CAA       2311         0/0/0
Ginas2621.03-00   0x00000A22    0x9DE9       892          0/0/0
Ginas2621.00-00   0x00000342    0xCD9B       821          0/0/0
RSM1.00-00        0x00000221    0x2C99       16           0/0/0
RSM.02-00         0x00000361    0x235B       16           0/0/0
```

ipx ipxwan

The interface-specific **ipx ipxwan** command allows the interface to send an announcement of the entire known topology of the network. After the initial announcement, the router will only send SAP state change messages. This command is primarily used to reduce SAP traffic on a very limited bandwidth WAN link.

The **debug ipx ipxwan** command produces troubleshooting information during state changes and the startup of serial interfaces configured for **ipxwan**. During the NLSP routing process, a router is elected as the master. Although it is seldom used in Cisco networks, ipxwan is defined in RFC 1634, and may be required for connecting IPX resources on WAN links, especially when connecting to non-Cisco devices.

This command shows each entry in an NLSP database using a link state protocol identifier (LSPID). This column contains a value including a system identifier, a pseudonode circuit identifier, and a fragment number. The link state protocol (LSP) is the foundation of NLSP, and the **show ipx nlsp database** command reports significant information, including the last sequence number, the checksum, and the LSP holdtime. The holdtime indicates when the information will be flushed from the database, if a Hello packet or update is not received. The ATT/P/OL field is used by the Cisco Technical Assistance Center (TAC) for troubleshooting. This field is used to describe the Layer 2 attachments and the overload bits. The P bit (partition) indicates whether or not a partition is used.

IPX Access Lists

Cisco routers provide access lists to enable security and control the types of traffic passed between interfaces. One of the options of access lists is the ability to control SAP advertisements coming into or leaving the router's interfaces. In addition to management of SAP advertisement traffic, an administrator may use access lists to filter certain IPX packets for network security.

Another common situation where access lists are used is referred to as the *backdoor bridge*, in which a bridge connects two IPX networks and then leaks routing information. The **show ipx traffic** command can be used to determine whether the bad hop counter is incrementing or not incrementing. A protocol analyzer can also be used in this situation to find a source address that matches the remote node and not that of the router.

IPX access lists are similar to an IP access list, which also uses both standard and extended access lists in configurations. In IPX, the standard IPX access lists are numbered from 800 to 899, and extended lists are numbered from 900 to 999. Access lists are then applied to an interface using the **access-group** command followed by the access list number and whether the access list should filter data going in or out of an interface. The following shows the access list command and the available syntaxes for the command:

```
access-list access-list-number [deny | permit]
source-network[.source-node [source-node-mask]]
[destination-network[.destination-node [destination-node-mask]]
```

With IPX standard access lists, a packet can be filtered based only on the source and destination address information contained in a packet header. To add filtering capabilities for IPX traffic based on socket numbers, protocol, or other IPX identifiers, an extended access lists must be used. The following are the syntaxes for the **access-list** command using an extended access list:

```
access-list access-list-number [deny|permit] protocol
[source-network][[[.source-node] source-node-mask] |
[.source-node source-network-mask.source-node-mask]]
[source-socket][destination.network][[[.destination-node] destination-
node-mask] | [.destination-node destination-network-mask.destination-
nodemask]] [destination-socket]
```

Warning! Just as with an IP access list, there is an implied "deny" any at the end of each access list. You can't see it, but it is there.

Understanding all the syntaxes is somewhat easier by using an example. The following output shows an example of a simple extended access list. It lists the syntax fields and then the output.

```
access-list [number] [permit|deny] [protocol] [source]
[socket][destination] [socket number].

Seans2514#config terminal
Enter configuration commands, one per line. End with CNTL/Z.
Seans2514(config)#access-list 900 deny -1 100 0 200 0
Seans2514(config)#int ethernet0
Seans2514(config-if)#ipx access-group 900 in
Seans2514(config-if)#exit
```

You can substitute the **any** syntax for **–1**, which is the wildcard **all** syntax (if your IOS supports this syntax). The extended access list 910 is configured to deny all IPX protocols from network 100 that are sent to network 200 through the Ethernet0 interface.

The service advertisements generated by SAP can send a significant amount of traffic in medium-scale networks. In larger networks, SAP can cause high processor utilization and overall degradation of the network because of the amount of bandwidth being used from the large number of sent advertisements.

Standard and extended IPX access lists are used to control traffic between IPX network interfaces. You use SAP access lists to control SAP traffic between network interfaces on a router using access list numbers in the range of 1000 to 1099. The following lists the syntaxes used to configure IPX SAP access lists:

```
access-list [number] [permit/deny] [source] [service type]
```

This is a relatively simple type of access list to use. The following output lists an example of denying SAP traffic from any server from network 100 on Ethernet0. The service type 0 represents all service types. You can use service type 4 to identify file servers, and type 7 to identify only print servers. Instead of using the **access-group** command to apply this to an interface, you must use the **ipx input-sap-filter** command on an inbound interface, or the **output-sap-filter** command to filter on an outbound interface. The command must be followed by the configured access list number. The following example shows how this is accomplished:

```
Seans2514# config terminal
Enter configuration commands, one per line. End with CNTL/Z.
Seans2514(config)# access-list 1000 deny 100.0000.0000.0001 0
Seans2514(config)# int eEthernet0
Seans2514(config-if)#ipx input-sap-filter 1000
Seans2514(config-if)# exit
```

To disable IPX access lists for troubleshooting purposes, use the following commands:

```
no ipx access-group access-group number
no ipx input-sap-filter access-list number
no ipx output-sap-filter access-list number
```

IPX Troubleshooting Commands

A wide variety of commands can be used to aid in troubleshooting Novell protocols, including the configuration, statistics, IPX, and SAP protocols. The Cisco router's **show** commands provide a wealth of information regarding IPX. Table 7.2 lists the **show ipx** command and the available syntaxes that can be used to acquire information about the IPX servers, configuration, and routing protocols.

Tip: Some commands are not available on certain IOS versions, and some versions support additional syntaxes. You should always use the **show ipx ?** command to see the available syntaxes.

Table 7.2   The show ipx command syntaxes and a description of what each displays.

show ipx Command Syntax	Displays
accounting	The active IPX accounting database
cache	The IPX fast-switching cache
compression	The IPX compression information
eigrp	The IPX EIGRP syntaxes
interface	The IPX interface configuration and status
nasi	The NetWare Asynchronous Services Interface status
nhrp	NHRP information
nlsp	NLSP information
route	The IPX routing table
servers	The known SAP servers
spx-protocol	The Sequenced Packet Exchange protocol status
spx-spoof	The SPX Spoofing table
traffic	IPX protocol statistics

The remainder of this chapter reviews the output only from the most commonly used IPX troubleshooting commands, which include the following:

➤ **debug ipx routing**

➤ **debug ipx packet**

➤ **debug ipx sap activity**

➤ **debug ipx sap events**

➤ **ping: px**

➤ **show ipx interface**

➤ **show ipx route**

➤ **show ipx servers**

➤ **show ipx traffic**

The **debug ipx routing** Command

The **debug ipx routing** command displays the IPX routing protocol processes running on the router. These include the IPX routing protocols IPX RIP, IPX-EIGRP, and NLSP. An example of the output follows:

```
*Sep 30 01:14:47.301 UTC: IPXRIP: Deleting network 100
*Sep 30 01:14:47.303 UTC: IPX: cache flush
*Sep 30 01:14:47.304 UTC: IPX: Setting state of E0:300 to [up]:[up]
*Sep 30 01:14:47.304 UTC: IPX: cache flush
*Sep 30 00:38:47.304 UTC: IPXRIP: Marking network 100 for Flash Update
```

The **debug ipx packet** Command

The **debug ipx packet** command is used to display all the IPX traffic either entering or exiting the router. This command should be used with caution because the **debug** command is assigned a high priority on the router's processor and can actually shut down your router. One thing to note about this command is that it doesn't display IPX packets that are fast-switched. If you need to view all packets, including those that are fast-switched, use the **no ipx route-cache** command to each interface that you wish to include in the debug capture. This may be good to remember, because if the problem you are experiencing is related to fast switching, the **debug ipx packet** command may not show you the answer to your problem. The following is an example of the output. It shows the entry of a packet destined for a server on the 200 network, with the response sent to the gateway on network 200:

```
IPX: src=253.0000.604c.12bf, dst=200.0000.0000.0001, packet received
IPX: src=253.0000.604c.12bf, dst=200.0000.0000.0001,gw=200.0000.80a5.abd1,
sending packet
```

The **debug ipx sap activity** Command

Using the **debug ip sap activity** command, you can view the SAP traffic, which provides information regarding whether or not the SAP processes are functioning correctly. If SAP is not functioning properly, you can prevent access to services and cause other connectivity issues in your network. An example of the output follows:

```
Seans2514# debug ipx sap activity
IPX service debugging is on
Oct 30 10:06:31.424:  type 0x30C, "PTR_1",800.0006.0d86.5380(401C), 4 hops
Oct 30 10:06:31.424:  type 0x30C, "PTR_2",800.0006.0d6e.1a65(400C), 4 hops
Oct 30 10:06:31.618:  type 0x44C, "AR3",  300.0000.0000.0001(8600), 3 hops
Oct 30 10:06:31.618:  type 0x23F, "SRL03",300.0000.0000.0001(907B), 3 hops
Oct 30 10:06:31.704: IPXSAP: at 690465B4:
I SAP Response type 0x2 len 480 src:800.0060.837b.4a19
   dest:200.ffff.ffff.ffff(452)
```

The **debug ipx sap events** Command

The **debug ipx sap events** command, at first glance, appears to include the same information as the **debug ipx sap activity** command. The following is an example of using this command:

```
Seans2514# debug ipx sap event
IPX service events debugging is on
Oct 30 10:05:59.401: IPXSAP: at 608FD48C:
O SAP Update type 0x2 len 480 src:300.0d6e.ab2a.1b1a
dest:200.ffff.ffff.ffff(452)
```

```
Oct 30 10:06:31.424:   type 0x30C, "PTR_1",800.0006.0d86.5380(401C), 4 hops
Oct 30 10:06:31.424:   type 0x30C, "PTR_2",800.0006.0d6e.1a65(400C), 4 hops
Oct 30 10:06:31.618:   type 0x44C, "AR3",  300.0000.0000.0001(8600), 3 hops
Oct 30 10:06:31.618:   type 0x23F, "SRL03",300.0000.0000.0001(907B), 3 hops
Oct 30 10:06:31.704: IPXSAP: at 690465B4:
dest:200.ffff.ffff.ffff(452)
```

The **ping ipx** Command

Just like in IP where the **ping** command uses the ICMP protocol and an IP
address, you can use the **ping ipx** command and an IPX address to verify connectivity with another device. By using this utility for troubleshooting IPX connectivity problems, you can verify that the routing tables are being updated correctly and
verify that connectivity to other networks and devices is taking place. The following shows an example of using the **ping ipx** command to ping a Cisco router's
network 18a interface:

```
Seans2621# ping ipx 18a.0000.834a.3d51
Type escape sequence to abort.
Sending 5, 100-byte IPX cisco Echoes to 18a.0000.834a.3d51, timeout is 2
seconds
:
!!!!!
Success rate is 100 percent (5/5), round-trip min/avg/max =  16/19/31 ms
```

*Note: Novell IPX resources need to be configured to respond to pings. You do this by using
the **ipx ping-default novell** command or the Novell Standard Echo.*

The following is an example of using the Novell Standard Echoreply:

```
Seans2621#ping
Protocol [ip]: ipx
Target IPX address: 18a.0000.834a.3d51
Repeat count [5]: 5
Datagram size [100]: 100
Timeout in seconds [2]: 2
Verbose [n]: y
Novell Standard Echo [n]: y
Type escape sequence to abort.
Sending 5, 100-byte IPX Novell Echoes to 18a.0000.834a.3d51, timeout is 2
seconds:
0 in 20 ms
1 in 20 ms
2 in 31 ms
3 in 16 ms
4 in 20 ms
Success rate is 100 percent (5/5), round-trip min/avg/max = 16/22/31 ms
```

The **show ipx interface** Command

The **show ipx interface** command is used to provide information on IPX interfaces. Often, out-of-date access lists are a cause of network problems. Using this command, you can view the access lists, view NetBIOS over IPX packet types, manage network security, and look at lost, misunderstood, and forgotten access lists. The following is an example of using this command:

```
Seans2514# show ipx interface

Hssi3/0 is up, line protocol is up
IPX address is 200.001d.ab1c.6755 [up] line-up, RIPPQ: 0, SAPPQ: 0
Delay of this IPX network, in ticks is 1 throughput 0 link delay 0
 IPXWAN processing not enabled on this interface.
 IPX SAP update interval is 1 minute(s)
 IPX type 20 propagation packet forwarding is disabled
 Incoming access list is not set
 Outgoing access list is not set
 IPX helper access list is not set
 SAP GNS processing enabled, delay 0 ms, output filter list  is not set
 SAP Input filter list is not set
 SAP Output filter list is not set
 SAP Router filter list is not set
 Input filter list is not set
 Output filter list is not set
 Router filter list is not set
 Netbios Input host access list is not set
 Netbios Input bytes access list is not set
 Netbios Output host access list is not set
 Netbios Output bytes access list is not set
 Updates each 60 seconds, aging multiples RIP: 3 SAP: 3
 SAP interpacket delay is 55 ms, maximum size is 480 bytes
 RIP interpacket delay is 55 ms, maximum size is 432 bytes
 Watchdog spoofing is disabled, SPX spoofing is disabled,  idle time 60
 IPX accounting is disabled
 IPX fast switching is configured (enabled)
 RIP packets received 19923, RIP packets sent 67323
 SAP packets received 458932, SAP packets sent 372677
```

The **show ipx route** Command

The **show ipx route** command can be useful when you need to know the state of a NetWare network. You can use this command to verify that certain paths exist through the network. Using this command, you can view the routes learned, path decisions made by IPX RIP, NLSP and IPX-EIGRP, IPXWAN, and the static routes that are configured on the interface. The following shows an example of using this command:

```
Seans2514# show ipx route

Codes: C - Connected primary network
c - Connected secondary network, S - Static, F - Floating static, L - Local
(internal), W - IPXWANR - RIP, E - EIGRP, N - NLSP, X - External,
A - Aggregate
  s - seconds, u - uses
1 Total IPX routes. Up to 3 parallel paths and 16 hops allowed.
No default route known.
R    1  [03/02] via    300.0060.602a.1d4c,  8s, Hs3/0
```

The **show ipx servers** Command

The **show ipx servers** command displays all servers known to the router that have
been learned from SAP advertisements. If servers are missing, there may be an
access list misconfiguration, duplicate network numbers, a downed link or interface,
network congestion, or misconfigured frame types. The following is the output
from the command, followed by an explanation of the fields that are listed:

```
Seans2514#show ipx servers
Codes: S - Static, P - Periodic, E - EIGRP, N - NLSP,
 H - Holddown, + = detail
2 Total IPX Servers
Table ordering is based on routing and server info
Type Name        Net Address         Port   Route   Hop  Itf
N  4 File&Print1  100.0000.0000.0001:0451  727/03  2    E1
N+ 4 EmailSAC     200.0000.0000.0001:0451  729/03  2    E1
```

The Net Address field shows the MAC addresses as 0000.0000.0001. This is the
internal IPX network address indicator. The output shows the SAP type, number of
known servers, how the information was learned, the number of hops to the server,
and the server name.

The **show ipx traffic** Command

The **show ipx traffic** command displays information regarding IPX packets that
have been transmitted or received. An example of the output from this command
follows:

```
Seans 2514# show ipx traffic

System Traffic for 300.0000.0000.0001 System-Name: Seans2514

Rcvd:    3298322 total, 158 format errors, 0 checksum errors,
         0 bad hop count, 6 packets pitched
         65955970 local destination, 0 multicast
```

```
Bcast:    3287985 received, 139078 sent
Sent:     1324204 generated, 4 forwarded
          0 encapsulation failed, 0 no route
SAP:      0 SAP requests, 0 SAP replies, 2 servers
          0 SAP advertisements received, 8 sent
          5 SAP flash updates sent, 0 SAP format errors
RIP:      0 RIP requests, 0 RIP replies, 6 routes
          0 RIP advertisements received, 0 sent
          0 RIP flash updates sent, 0 RIP format errors
Echo:     Rcvd 0 requests, 0 replies
          Sent 0 requests, 0 replies
          0 unknown: 0 no socket, 0 filtered, 0 no helper
          0 SAPs throttled, freed NDB len 0
Watchdog:
          0 packets received, 0 replies spoofed
Queue lengths:
    IPX input: 0, SAP 0, RIP 0, GNS 0
    SAP throttling length: 0/(no limit), 0 nets pending lost route reply
    Delayed process creation: 0
EIGRP: Total received 4413, sent 1784
    Updates received 58, sent 128
    Queries received 32, sent 17
    Replies received 17, sent 32
    SAPs received 0, sent 0
NLSP:  Level-1 Hellos received 0, sent 0
    PTP Hello received 0, sent 0
    Level-1 LSPs received 0, sent 0
    LSP Retransmissions: 0
    LSP checksum errors received: 0
    LSP HT=0 checksum errors received: 0
    Level-1 CSNPs received 0, sent 0
    Level-1 PSNPs received 0, sent 0
    Level-1 DR Elections: 0
    Level-1 SPF Calculations: 0
    Level-1 Partial Route Calculations: 0
```

Chapter Summary

The latest NetWare version, 5.0, no longer relies on the IPX and SPX protocols. It now supports TCP/IP. Even though the new version centers around TCP/IP, many legacy applications and networks still use the IPX protocol, so legacy-protocol support is still included in version 5.0. This chapter focused on the configuration and troubleshooting commands associated with NetWare. It also looked at the connection sequences and the diagnostic tools that can be reliably used to troubleshoot problems in an IPX environment.

This chapter also included common NetWare network problems and a list of troubleshooting commands that can be used to resolve those issues. The most important IPX configuration and IPX routing protocol troubleshooting commands were covered, including the **show**, **debug**, and **ping ipx** commands.

You should remember the troubleshooting steps involved in resolving a NetWare problem:

1. Identify and define the problem.

2. Gather as many facts as possible.

3. Consider possible problems and solutions.

4. Create an action plan.

5. Implement the plan.

6. Gather information on the problem, based on the results of step 5, and assess the new information.

7. After the problem has been resolved, document the resolution for future use.

Remember that you can also narrow down the problem by checking the following:

➤ The frame types and client configuration

➤ The local Cisco router configuration

➤ Non-IPX protocol–related problems

If you use NetWare in a working environment, this is a great chapter to keep handy in case you ever need to troubleshoot an issue.

Review Questions

1. Which of the following commands should an administrator use to get detailed information about SAP packets, such as timestamps?

    a. **debug ipx sap activity**

    b. **show ipx sap detail**

    c. **debug ipx sap detail**

    d. **show ipx timestamps**

2. Which of the following commands was used to display this output?

```
S/0 is up, line protocol is up
IPX address is 20.0060.1a30.289a [up] line-up, RIPPQ: 0, SAPPQ: 0
Delay of this IPX network, in ticks is 1 throughput 0 link delay 0
 IPXWAN processing not enabled on this interface.
 IPX SAP update interval is 1 minute(s)
 IPX type 20 propagation packet forwarding is disabled
 Incoming access list is not set
 Outgoing access list is not set
 IPX helper access list is not set
 SAP GNS processing enabled, delay 0 ms, output filter list  is not set
 SAP Input filter list is not set
 SAP Output filter list is not set
 SAP Router filter list is not set
 Input filter list is not set
 Output filter list is not set
 Router filter list is not set
 Netbios Input host access list is not set
 Netbios Input bytes access list is not set
 Netbios Output host access list is not set
 Netbios Output bytes access list is not set
 Updates each 60 seconds, aging multiples RIP: 3 SAP: 3
 SAP interpacket delay is 55 ms, maximum size is 480 bytes
 RIP interpacket delay is 55 ms, maximum size is 432 bytes
 Watchdog spoofing is disabled, SPX spoofing is disabled,  idle time 60
 IPX accounting is disabled
 IPX fast switching is configured (enabled)
 RIP packets received 32146, RIP packets sent 3525
 SAP packets received 23633, SAP packets sent 23154
```

a. **show interface s0**

b. **show ipx protocol interface s0**

c. **show ipx interface s0**

d. **debug ipx interface s0**

7

3. Which of the following commands was used to produce this output?

```
Codes: S - Static, P - Periodic, E - EIGRP, N - NLSP,
 H - Holddown, + = detail
3 Total IPX Servers
Table ordering is based on routing and server info
Type Name      Net Address        Port  Route Hops Itf
P+ 4 SRV-00001  10.0000.0000.0001:0451  4/03 3     s0
P+ 4 SRV-00002  20.0000.0000.0001:0451  4/03 3     s1
```

   a. **debug ipx server**

   b. **show ip route**

   c. **show ipx route**

   d. **show ipx server**

4. Which of the following commands would provide an administrator with a list of known Novell servers on the network?

   a. **debug ipx ipxwan**

   b. **show ipx servers**

   c. **show ipx traffic**

   d. **show ipx all**

5. When will a Cisco router respond to a GNS request?

   a. GNS unicast request.

   b. GNS request addressed to FFFFFFFF.

   c. Only when no local server exists on the network segment.

   d. A Cisco router will not respond to GNS requests.

6. Which of the following number ranges can be used to number an IPX standard access list?

   a. 1–99

   b. 800–899

   c. 900–999

   d. 1000–1099

7. Which of the following routing protocols cannot be used with IPX?

   a. IGRP

   b. EIGRP

   c. RIP

   d. NLSP

8. Which of the following number ranges can be used to number an IPX extended access list?

   a. 1–99

   b. 800–899

   c. 900–999

   d. 1000–1099

9. By default, SAP packets are sent how often?

   a. 120 seconds

   b. 30 seconds

   c. 60 seconds

   d. You must manually specify the default

10. What is the maximum number of hops supported by IPX RIP?

   a. 7

   b. 15

   c. 64

   d. Unlimited

11. Which of the following commands was used to produce this output?

```
IPX EIGRP Topology Table for process 20
Codes: P - Passive, A - Active, U - Update, Q - Query, R - Reply,
r - Reply status
P A, 1 successors, FD is 342217
      via 20.0060.3a7b.ab21 (342217/307200), s0
P D, 1 successors, FD is 152221
      via Connected, s1
```

   a. **show ipx eigrp topology**

   b. **show ipx eigrp events**

   c. **show ipx eigrp detail**

   d. **show ipx eigrp neighbors**

12. Which of the following is the default encapsulation type for Novell NetWare 5.0 clients and servers?

   a. ARPA

   b. Ethernet_II

   c. NOVELL-ETHER

   d. Ethernet_802.3

   e. IP

7

13. Which of the following devices can respond to a GNS request?

    a. Layer 2 switches

    b. A Cisco router

    c. Novell servers

    d. All Novell clients

14. When an IPX client is powered up and attempts to locate a server, which of the following protocols is used?

    a. SAP

    b. GNS

    c. NLSP

    d. IPX RIP

15. A Novell client is using Ethernet II. Which of the following frame types can be used? [Choose the two best answers]

    a. Ethernet II

    b. 802.3

    c. ARPA

    d. 802.5

16. An IPX extended access list can filter based on which of the following?

    a. IPX socket number

    b. IPX protocol

    c. Source network/node

    d. Destination network/node

    e. All of the above

17. Which of the following is a valid IPX network address?

    a. 20.0000.0000.0001

    b. FileServer.0000.0000.0001

    c. 132.16.4.0

    d. 6.0000.0a24.1211

18. The SAP interpacket delay is available from which of the following commands?

    a. **debug ipx sap**

    b. **show ipx sap**

    c. **show all**

    d. **show ipx interface**

19. Which of the following commands can be used to view the available options for IPX debugging?

    a. **ipx debug commands ?**

    b. **debug ipx ?**

    c. **debug all**

    d. **show ipx debug**

20. Which command should be used when trying to obtain information regarding SAP, watchdog, EIGRP, and NLSP packets?

    a. **show ipx traffic**

    b. **debug ipx**

    c. **show ipx protocols**

    d. **show ipx route**

7

CHAPTER EIGHT

VLAN

After completing this chapter, you will be able to:

✓ Understand the benefits of implementing VLANs

✓ Understand the differences between trunk links and access links

✓ Understand how to use VTP and VTP pruning

✓ Explain the differences between dynamic and static VLAN ports

✓ Understand the differences between internal and external route processing

✓ Configure VLANs, trunking, VTP, and VTP pruning on a Catalyst 5000

✓ Configure VLANs, trunking, VTP, and VTP pruning on a Catalyst 1900

✓ Configure a route processor to route VLANs

Although the target of this book is troubleshooting, you can't troubleshoot something that you don't understand. As an administrator, the installation that you are troubleshooting may not be one that you implemented, especially in light of the relatively high turnover rate for most networking positions. Systems administrators often are enticed to switch to another company that is willing to pay more. Often, the main reason a company hires me as a consultant is that one of their more knowledgeable administrators has left the company.

Typically, when considering the topic of virtual local area networks (VLANs), most administrators who support an already existing network first think of switches, because switches are the access point for the workstations and the point where the VLANs are created.

After a VLAN is created, though, how do nodes in the network talk to one another if they are in different VLANs? Better yet, because you can assign only one VLAN to a switch port, how do you get the traffic from more than one VLAN to float down a single link to your router to route the data between VLANs?

Troubleshooting VLANs is covered in Chapter 14; for now, this chapter explains what VLANs are, why they are needed, the components of VLANs, and how to configure them.

Why Do We Need VLANs?

Recall from earlier in the book the discussion on flat topology LANs, which are LANs that are connected by hubs. The primary drawback of this type of network is that every node in the network sees the data being passed by every other node on the network. Every node tries to process each frame to make sure that it doesn't miss any frames that are destined for itself. This eats up an incredible amount of processing power on each machine and limits the available bandwidth on the physical wire, even without the number of collisions forcing data to be re-sent on the physical wire.

As the number of nodes grows on a flat topology network, the network begins to slow down due to traffic, collisions, and other bottlenecks. This can also include faulty equipment and other unnecessary protocols running on the network. As these problems grow, network administrators usually begin to encounter speed problems even with state-of-the-art Pentiums. The processor in each node handles the task of processing every frame on the network, which depletes the processing power needed for other tasks and for applications.

Switches and VLANs solve the problems related to a flat topology network without the need for upgrading the cabling or segmenting the network with a bunch of routers. Switches are Layer 2 devices that replace the hubs at Layer 1, which send data they receive out every single port, thereby forcing every node attached to them to process the data whether the node is meant to receive the data or not with switches. Switches take care of the collisions on the network by reading the MAC address on incoming frames and learning what nodes are attached to each port. The switch then routes the data from the source port to the destination port. Unlike a hub, the switch does not send the data out every port.

In the early 1980's, when LANs were introduced as revolutionary technology, the transmission speeds were considered more than adequate for the largest networks of the time. At that time, most computers used no more than 640K of RAM.

Soon, the computers on the networks got faster, they offered higher storage capacities, larger databases, and multiple types of data traffic that need to use the network. These huge collision and broadcast domains needed to be made smaller so the physical wire attached to each node was less utilized.

Two methods are available for segmenting networks into smaller broadcast domains to improve performance: bridging and routing.

Bridges

Like switches, bridges are Layer 2 devices that are designed to connect two network segments. A bridge is a relatively simple device that receives a packet on one interface, stores it in a buffer, and immediately queues it for transmission by the other interface. The following are the four different types of bridges:

➤ *Source-route bridges*—Used in token ring networks. The name refers to the fact that these bridges assume the complete source-to-destination route is placed in frames sent by the source node.

➤ *Source-route transparent bridges*—Combine transparent bridging and source-route bridging for communication in a network environment that contains Ethernet and token ring.

➤ *Translational bridges*—Also used to translate between different physical media types such as Ethernet and token ring.

➤ *Transparent bridges*—Primarily used in Ethernet environments. The name refers to the fact that the existence of these bridges is transparent to all the nodes in the network.

Bridges learn the location of the network stations without any manual intervention from a network administrator or any manual configuration of the bridges' internal software. This is commonly referred to as *self-learning*. When a bridge is turned on and begins to operate, it examines the MAC addresses of the traffic that passes through it to build a table of known destinations. If a frame arrives at the bridge and the bridge knows that the destination is on the same segment as the source, it drops the frame because it doesn't need to be transmitted to the other segment. If

The Problem with Broadcasts

Switches and bridges are similar to one another: both help to reduce network traffic by segmenting the network in to smaller broadcast domains, filtering frames, and forwarding frames to the destination port. Hubs on the other hand flood broadcasts. As a result, when networks grow, so does the amount of flooded broadcast traffic. This situation, in turn, causes bandwidth problems called *network broadcast storms*. Broadcast storms occur when broadcasts throughout the LAN use up all the available bandwidth on a LAN. Guess what happens when this occurs? Nothing! No one gets their data, and traffic stops.

There are a number of protocols that use broadcasts by default. When this is built-in to the protocol traffic we call the protocols "chatty." A chatty network protocol can be either of two types. One type broadcasts on the network to locate another particular device; for example, "Hey, where's this device named Mike?" The other type of protocol broadcasts continuously to announce its location; for example, a device running a network protocol, such as IPX Service Advertising Protocol (SAP), constantly broadcasts to other devices on the network "Hey, I'm Mike and I'm right here!" These broadcasts are built into the network protocols and are essential to the operation of the network operating systems, but they tend to eat up bandwidth.

the bridge knows that the destination is on another segment, the bridge transmits the packet on that segment only. If the bridge does not know the destination segment, the bridge transmits copies of the frame to all the attached network segments except the source segment. This is known as *flooding*.

Switches

The earliest LAN switches functioned like multiport intelligent bridges. They offered very little in the way of segmentation and typically didn't address routing issues. Each node connected to the switch was in the same broadcast domain. To get another broadcast domain, you simply had to purchase another switch.

Note: The primary reason to segment your network is to relieve network congestion and increase the available bandwidth. Segmentation is often necessary to satisfy the bandwidth requirements of a new application or types of data the network needs to be able to support, such as multimedia or graphical design applications.

Virtual LANs were created by the different switch manufacturers to provide individual broadcast domains. By assigning each port to an individual VLAN, each VLAN is referred to as a *color*, each VLAN becomes its own individual broadcast domain. Only those ports that are members of the same VLAN will receive broadcasts from any other member of their assigned VLAN. VLAN *trunks* are used to provide a way for data frames belonging to more than one VLAN to travel a single physical link between network devices. The following section looks at the different types of trunk links.

Note: The coloring of data traffic across a backbone is done by inserting a header between the source MAC address and the Link Service Access Point (LSAP) of frames leaving a switch. The 4-byte header is called the VLAN ID, or color.

VLAN Trunk Links

Trunk links enable multiple VLANs to travel from one switch port to another switch port, from one switch port to a router, from router to router, or, in some cases, a server using a NIC card that supports a trunking protocol. Trunk links are point-to-point high-speed links, from 100Mbps to 1,000Mbps, configured to carry multiple VLANs, as shown in Figure 8.1.

Warning! The trunk protocols, frame tagging, and additional headers must be stripped from the frames before they are sent out the Access layer switch to the end user. This process must remain transparent to the end users' interface, because they do not understand the trunking process.

Four different methods or protocols enable you to track VLAN frames as they traverse a trunk link:

➤ IEEE 802.10

➤ IEEE 802.1Q

➤ Inter-Switch Link (ISL)

➤ LAN Emulation (LANE)

IEEE 802.10

The IEEE 802.10 standard is used to send multiple VLAN traffic over a Fiber Distributed Data Interface (FDDI) physical link. This standard uses a *clear header*, which is added to VLAN frames traversing an FDDI trunk. A clear header contains three fields: a Security Association Identifier (SAID), a Link Service Access Point (LSAP), and the Management Defined Field (MDF).

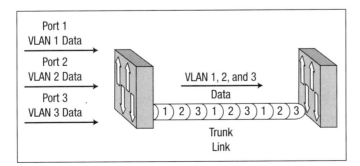

Figure 8.1 A trunk link carrying traffic of multiple VLANs.

VLAN Standards

A *standard* is a basis that participating vendors use to maintain compatibility between different vendors' products. Cisco chose to submit its standardization to the body of the IEEE Internetworking Subcommittee. Other standards have been created for VLANs by the Internet Engineering Task Force (IETF), the ATM forum, and many other entities creating and distributing standards.

Most organizations implement high-speed switched networks in order to create a network that can efficiently handle the growing demands of their organization.

The SAID field in the frame header is the field used to identify which VLAN the port that the data was sent through is a member of. This protocol is proprietary to Cisco devices and is used primarily to transport VLAN information over FDDI backbones between Cisco routers and switches.

IEEE 802.1Q

The IEEE 802.1Q standard is referred to as the "Standard for Virtual Bridged Local Area Networks." This standard was agreed upon by members of the IEEE as a method of *frame tagging*, the process of inserting into a frame a field that is used to identify the frame's VLAN membership over a trunk link.

This process works as follows:

1. As a frame enters the switch fabric through a VLAN port, the data is tagged with information regarding the VLAN information belonging to the port the frame arrived on. Just as in ISL, the tag remains in the frame as it is forwarded from switch to switch, and is removed prior to exiting the access link to the destination interface. Unlike ISL, however, which uses an external tagging process, 802.1Q uses an internal tagging process, by modifying the existing Ethernet frame itself.

2. IEEE 802.1Q changes the frame header with a standard VLAN format, which allows multiple-vendor VLAN implementations. This enables a Bay Networks device or a 3Com device to pass VLAN traffic to a Cisco device and vice versa.

3. When the frame is passed to an Access layer device to be sent directly to the destination interface, the frame is stripped of the tagging information, making the whole process transparent to the destination and sending device.

Inter-Switch Link Protocol

Cisco created the ISL protocol and chose to keep ISL proprietary in nature to Cisco devices. ISL is a way of explicitly tagging VLAN information onto an Ethernet frame traversing the network through trunk links. This tagging information enables VLANs to be multiplexed over a trunk link through an external encapsulation method. By running ISL, you can interconnect multiple switches and still maintain VLAN information as traffic travels between switches on trunk links. The ISL process works like this:

1. Each frame is tagged as it enters a trunk link on the switch. The original frame is not altered; it is encapsulated within a new 26-byte ISL header and a 4-byte frame check sequence (FCS) at the end of the frame.

2. After the frame is tagged with the appropriate VLAN information, the frame can go through all Cisco devices in the network without being reencapsulated.

3. The ISL encapsulation is removed from the frame if the frame is set to exit out of a nontrunked link.

Note: ISL is an external tagging process.

The ISL header, shown in Figure 8.2, is entered into the frame. The ISL header contains the following:

➤ *Destination address (DA)*—A 40-bit multicast address set to 01-00-0c-00-00. This address signals to the receiver that this packet is in ISL format.

➤ *Type*—Indicates the media type the frame is supporting. The possible options are 0000 for Ethernet, 0001 for token ring, 0010 for FDDI, and 0011 for Asynchronous Transfer Mode (ATM).

➤ *User field*—A 4-bit field used to identify one of four possible priorities of the frame: XX00 for normal, XX01 for priority 1, XX02 for priority 2, and XX11 for the highest priority.

➤ *Source MAC address (SA)*—Shows the sending switch port's IEEE 802.3 MAC address. Some receiving devices ignore the SA field.

➤ *LEN field*—This 16-bit field shows the length of the packet, in bytes, minus the excluded fields. The excluded fields are the CRC, DA, Type, User, and SA fields, as well as the LEN field itself. The total of the excluded fields is 18 bytes. Therefore, the LEN field contains the total packet size minus 18 bytes from the excluded fields.

ISL Header	Encapsulated Frame	Frame Check							
DA	Media Type	Frame Priority	SA	Frame Length	AAAA03	HSA	VLAN	BPDU	Index	Reserve

Figure 8.2 The ISL header inserted into an ISL encapsulated packet.

➤ *AAAA03*—Indicates an 802.2 Logical Link Control (LLC) header.

➤ *High bit of source address (HSA)*—The 3-byte manufacturer's portion of the SA field or vendor field of the source port's MAC address.

➤ *15-bit descriptor*—Used to distinguish the frame from other VLANs or colors; 10 bits are used to indicate the source port.

➤ *Bridge Protocol Data Units (BPDU) bit*—Used to indicate Spanning Tree Protocol (STP) or Cisco Discovery Protocol (CDP) topology information.

➤ *Index*—Used to indicate the port address as the frame exits the switch. This 16-bit index value can be set to any value and can be used for diagnostic purposes only.

➤ *Reserve*—Used by FDDI and token ring. In token ring, the Frame Control (FC) and token ring AC bits (AC) fields are placed in the header. For FDDI, the FC is placed in the field. For Ethernet, the field contains all zeros.

LAN Emulation

LANE is an IEEE standard for transporting VLANs over ATM networks. This process uses no encapsulation or frame tagging. ATM and LANE are beyond the scope of this book and thus are not covered in great detail.

The VLAN Trunking Protocol is used to provide administrators an easy way of managing VLANs across Cisco network. The following section looks at how this protocol works.

VLAN Trunk Protocol

The VLAN Trunk Protocol (VTP) was created to provide administrators an easy way to manage and distribute VLAN configuration information across a switched network. VTP enables you to configure a VLAN on one switch and have the information propagate to all of your switches in a VTP domain. This enables an administrator to fairly easily add, delete, and rename VLANs.

One of the best features of VTP is its ability to maintain consistent VLAN configurations throughout the network by keeping all the switches assigned to a VTP to keep an identical VLAN configuration by propagating the VLAN mapping scheme of the VTP domain across the network regardless of the different physical media type being used in the network. VTP provides for a plug-and-play type of connection. When you add additional VLANs, VTP provides tracking, monitoring, and reporting of VLANs in the network.

Note: A Cisco switch can be a member of only one VTP domain.

Two versions of VTP exist, described next, and each has significant differences.

VTP Modes

To allow VTP to manage your VLANs across the switched internetwork, you must first designate one or more of your Cisco switches as a VTP server. All the VTP servers that need to share VLAN information must use the same domain name and password. A switch configured as a server can share VTP configuration information only with switches configured as members of the same VTP domain.

The following three individual VTP modes can be configured on a switch that will be used to participate in a VTP domain:

➤ Client Mode

➤ Server Mode

➤ Transparent Mode.

Client Mode allows the switch to have the same functions as Server Mode, with the exception that it cannot change any VLAN information for other switches participating in a VTP domain. A switch in Client Mode cannot create, modify, or delete VLANs on any VTP client or switch except when it receives an advertisement from a switch operating in Server Mode. A Client Mode switch can, however, advertise its own VLAN configuration, synchronize the VLAN information with other switches on the network, specify VTP configuration information such as the VTP version, and participate in VTP pruning. Switches operating in this mode lose their global VLAN information when the switch power is cycled.

Server Mode is configured by default on Cisco switches. This mode enables you to create, modify, and delete VLANs for the configured VTP management domain. Configuration changes are then sent to all other participating members of the VTP domain. At least one VTP server should exist in the VTP management domain. You can configure more than one switch participating in a VTP domain, for redundancy purposes. When a server's power is cycled, the switch configured as a server maintains its global VLAN information.

Transparent Mode enables VTP switches to be configured to not accept VTP information. A switch operating in this mode merely forwards advertisements the switch receives for a VTP domain to other switches participating in the VTP domain. In this mode, the switch does not participate in any VTP functions, such as sending VTP advertisements or synchronizing VLAN information.

VLAN Trunk Protocol Versions

In IOS version 3.1(1) of the Catalyst software, a second version of VTP was introduced, thereby making two versions: version 1 and version 2. The primary differences between the two version are significant enough to render them incompatible. They will not work together in the same network. Version 1 is the default on Cisco Catalyst switches. If all the switches in the network support VTP version 2, then only one switch needs to have version 2 enabled to enable version 2 on all the switches participating in a VTP domain.

Version 2 provides the following additional features beyond support for Ethernet:

➤ *Consistency checks*—Performed when new information is entered by an administrator through the command-line interface (CLI) or through the Simple Network Management Protocol (SNMP).

➤ *Token ring support*—Includes token ring LAN switching and VLANs.

➤ *Transparent Mode change support*—Allows switches to only forward messages and advertisements. A switch using this mode will not add to its own database any new information received.

Note: Version 1 allows the switch to check the domain name and version before forwarding. Version 2 allows the switches to forward VTP messages and advertisements without checking the version number.

➤ *Unrecognized type-length value support*—If a VTP advertisement is received and has an unrecognized type-length value, the VTP server or client will continue to propagate its configuration changes to the configured trunk links, even for TLVs that it is unable to parse. The unrecognized Type Length Value(TLV) is then saved in non-volatile random access memory (NVRAM).

VLAN Trunk Protocol Advertisements

Switches in a VTP management domain share VLAN information through the use of VTP advertisement messages. Three types of advertisement messages exist:

➤ *Advertisement (Client) request*—Clients use this type of advertisement to request VLAN information for the current network. A VTP client sends this type of advertisement in response to requests with the appropriate summary and subset advertisements. The advertisement frame includes a version field, code field, reserved field, management domain name field (up to 32 bytes), and start value field.

➤ *Summary advertisement*—This type of advertisement is sent automatically every five minutes (300 seconds) to all the switches on the network. A summary advertisement can also be sent when a topology change to the network occurs, such as a switch drop or addition. The summary advertisement frame contains the version field, the code field, a follower's field, a management domain name field, a configuration revision number field, the updater's identity, the updater's timestamp, and the MD5 digest field.

➤ *Subset advertisement*—This type of advertisement contains very detailed information about the network. It contains the version, code, sequence number, management domain name, configuration revision number, and VLAN information fields.

Warning! VTP will work only if at least one trunk port is configured to carry at least one valid VLAN. A trunk link using ISL encapsulation can carry up to 1024 VLANs.

How Do You Secure VTP?

On Cisco Catalyst switches, the default configuration places VTP in a nonsecure mode that allows any switch configured for the domain name to join the VTP domain and make changes to the VLAN configuration on each switch. To ensure that other switches do not join your domain without your knowledge, and to avoid security violations that can occur when inconsistent VLAN configurations reside on the network, when VLANs cross-connect using duplicate names on the network, configure a secure-mode password for your VTP management domain.

The management domain name can be up to 32 characters long. The password you provide to place the switches in secure mode can be from 8 to 64 characters long. Every member of the VTP domain must be configured to use this password.

VTP advertisement frames are sent to a multicast address so that all the VTP devices in the same management domain are able receive the frames. All VTP management domain clients and servers update their databases regarding all deletions and additions to the network based on information contained in the VTP advertisements and the revision number contained in the advertisements the switch receives.

VLAN Trunk Protocol Advertisement Revision Numbers

Each advertisement contains a revision number, which is one of the most important parts of the VTP advertisement. When a new VTP revision number is sent throughout the VTP domain, the switches believe the highest revision number has the most up-to-date information about all the VLANs. If a switch participating in a VTP domain receives an advertisement with different VLAN configuration information than it currently has, it updates its information only if the revision number in the received advertisement is higher than the one that allowed the last change.

VLAN Trunk Protocol Pruning

VLAN Trunk Protocol pruning increases network bandwidth by reducing network traffic across switch trunk links. VTP pruning filters network traffic such as broadcasts, multicasts, and unicasts on trunk links that connect to switches that contain no VLAN member ports for the VLAN that data is broadcasted to. This means that if a member of VLAN 2 sends a broadcast to all the other members of VLAN 2, switches that contain no members in VLAN 2 will not receive the broadcast unless they are the gateway to another switch that contains a VLAN 2 member.

When VTP pruning is enabled on a VTP server, the information is propagated to all the other Client and Server Mode switches in the VTP management domain. This step automatically enables VTP pruning on these switches. By default, VLANs 2 through 1,000 are eligible for VTP pruning, and VLAN 1 is always ineligible. VTP pruning usually takes several seconds to propagate to the other VTP management domain clients.

As a VTP server's database is modified, the VTP server increments the revision number by 1. The VTP server then advertises this information from the database with the new configure revision number.

VTP aids in propagating VLAN information, and trunk links allow for the traffic of more than one VLAN to traverse a link. How do switches use these trunk links to allow VLANs to communicate with one another? Through a process called inter-VLAN routing, which is explained in the next section.

Inter-VLAN Routing

Trunking protocols are designed to allow VLANs to flow from one networking device to another. These trunking protocols either tag the VLAN frames or add a header that uniquely identifies the source and destinations of the data as well as the VLAN the data is a member of. If data from one VLAN needs to be forwarded to another VLAN, it requires some type of Layer 3 device to do the routing. This process is shown in Figure 8.3, in which switch A is sending data from VLANs 1 through 3 to VLAN 6, which is configured on switch B.

To route VLAN frames between VLANs requires a Layer 3 device, which can be an external router or any number of modules known as *internal route processors* that are located inside a switch.

When a node needs to communicate with a member of another VLAN on the same network, the node sends a packet to the other node, assuming that it resides on the same network. The packet destined for another VLAN, which can even be another port on the same switch, must find a path on which to send the frame.

Because switches operate at Layer 2 and are designed to isolate traffic to broadcast domains or subnets, they cannot, by default, forward data from one VLAN to another VLAN without some other Layer 3 device, such as an internal or external route processor. The Layer 3 device is known as a "router on a stick." This device is used to route the data and create routing tables of other networks and devices. This also adds a layer of security, because now access lists can be added to permit and deny certain traffic.

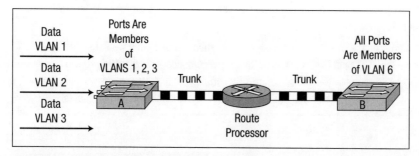

Figure 8.3   The inter-VLAN routing process.

Route processors can be used to route data between foreign VLANs and other logically segmented parts of the network, such as subnets. They also route data to remote WAN segments, networks, or the Internet.

An internal route processor uses internal modules or cards located inside the switch chassis that are similar to routers to route data between VLANs. The following are the available types of internal route processors for Catalyst switches:

➤ NetFlow Feature Card and NetFlow Feature Card II

➤ Route Switch Module

➤ Multilayer Switch Module

➤ Multilayer Switch Feature Card

➤ Route Switch Feature Card

Note: *The Catalyst 6000 series also uses a FlexWAN module, a description of which is beyond the scope of this book.*

The following series of routers are external route processor with 100BaseT interfaces that support ISL:

➤ Cisco 2600 series routers

➤ Cisco 3600 series routers

➤ Cisco 4500 series routers

➤ Cisco 7000 series routers

➤ Cisco 7500 series routers

By configuring VLANs, you control the size of your broadcast domains and keep local traffic local. A problem is created, however, when an end station in one VLAN needs to communicate with an end station in another VLAN. To fix the problem inter-VLAN routing needs to take place to resolve the address even if the ports belonging to different VLANs are side by side in the same switch. This type of communication is called using inter-VLAN routing where a Layer 3 device resolves the address just as it would if they were nodes residing on two different network segments. You configure one or more routers to route traffic to the appropriate destination VLAN.

Configuring VLANs on a Catalyst 5000

All ports on the switch are configured as static access ports to VLAN 1 by default. VLAN 1 is also assigned as the default management VLAN. You can change the VLAN port information using the console, Cisco Visual Switch Manager (CVSM), or SNMP. This section covers the basics of VLAN configuration as well as how to assign multi-VLAN memberships and how to view the configuration on each type of switch. It also covers configuring VLANs on a Set/Clear command–based switch as well as on a CLI-based switch.

The following are the available options for the **set vlan** command:

```
set vlan <vlan_num> [name <name>] [type <type>] [state <state>][said
<said>] [mtu <mtu>] [ring <hex_ring_number>][decring
<decimal_ring_number>][bridge <bridge_number>] [parent <vlan_num>][mode
<bridge_mode>] [stp <stp_type>] [translation <vlan_num>] [backupcrf
    <off|on>][aremaxhop <hopcount>] [stemaxhop <hopcount>]
```

To begin configuring the VLANs, you need to be in Privileged Mode on your switch and identify an interface on the switch. If you have a 12-port 10/100 module in slot 7 of a Catalyst 5500 series switch which has 13 available slots, the ports are referred to as "7/1–12". Most of the commands on this series of switches use this method to identify the interface. Cisco routers begin with slot and port numbers that start at 0. On the Cisco Catalyst 5000 and 6000 family of switches, the slot and port numbers start at 1. The first port on a Cisco router would be 0/0, but on a Catalyst 5500, it would be 1/1.

To configure the four ports on VLAN 3 for ports 3 through 6 on the module residing in slot 7, use these commands:

```
set vlan <vlan_num> <mod/ports>
```

```
set vlan 3 7/3
set vlan 3 7/4
set vlan 3 7/5
set vlan 3 7/6
```

You could also use a shortcut and configure all the ports at once by using this command:

```
set vlan 3 7/3-6
```

Warning! Using a space between the numbers creates an error. The switch views the number following the space as a new command argument.

You can assign a VLAN a name that is up to 32 characters to help identify it when doing troubleshooting. To assign VLAN 3 and identify it as the VLAN that engineers use, use the following command:

```
set vlan <vlan_num> name <name>
```

```
set vlan 3 name Engineering
```

You can set the type of VLAN using one of the valid type, which are **ethernet**, **fddi**, **fddinet**, **trcrf**, and **trbrf**. The default is Ethernet if a type is not specified. Use the following command to map VLAN 3 to Ethernet:

```
set vlan <vlan_num> type <type>

set vlan 3 type ethernet
```

Active is the default state for a configured VLAN, but you can configure it for **active** or **suspend**. Use the following command to suspend VLAN 3:

```
set vlan <vlan_num> state <state>

set vlan state suspend
```

SAIDs are used as a VLAN identifier when trunking across 802.10 FDDI or CDDI networks. The default SAID value is 100000 plus the VLAN number. For example, VLAN 3's SAID would be a value of 100003. You should be able to leave the SAID at the configured default. However, if a conflicting SAID exists in the network, you can use the following command to change the SAID to 100103:

```
set vlan <vlan_num> said <said>

set vlan 3 said 100103
```

Different media types have different maximum transmission unit (MTU) sizes, which are shown in Table 8.1. Ethernet, for example, is 1,500 bytes. If you need to change the MTU, use the following command:

```
set vlan <vlan_num> mtu <mtu>

set vlan 3 mtu 1500
```

Table 8.1   The MTU and media types available for VLANs.

VLAN Type	MTU Size (Bytes)
Ethernet	1500
FDD/FDDI-Net	4352
Token ring	2048
TR-Net	2048

If a node on the network is attached to a port on the switch and does not have the ability to negotiate the port speed, you can set the speed. To set the port speed manually, use the following command:

```
set port speed <mod_num/port_num> <4|10|16|100|auto>
```

```
set port speed 7/1 100
```

To set the port duplex on an Ethernet module, use the following command:

```
set port duplex <mod_num/port_num> <full|half>
```

```
set port duplex 7/1 full
```

Warning! You cannot set the duplex if the duplex is manually configured to auto, or the port speed has been set manually.

Enabling security on a Catalyst switch means that the switch will accept frames only from a particular MAC address on Ethernet modules. You can identify a specific MAC address. If the MAC address is not identified, the first interface to use the port will be the only interface allowed to use that port. If an unauthorized MAC address attempts to use the port, the port will become disabled and the light on the switch corresponding with that port will change from the color green to orange. To configure port security, use the following command:

```
set port security  <mod_num/port_num> <enable|disable> [mac_addr]
```

```
set port security 3/1 enable
```

To verify the configured VLAN information, at the Privilege EXEC Mode prompt, you can use the **show vlan** command, which is used for all Catalyst switches:

```
show vlan
```

To remove a VLAN configured on a port, at the Privilege EXEC Mode prompt, you can use the following command (the VLAN being removed is VLAN 3, affecting all ports that have VLAN 3 configured):

```
clear vlan 3
```

Note: When you clear a VLAN that has ports assigned to it, by default, those ports revert to VLAN 1. Every port must be assigned to a VLAN.

Configuring Trunks and VTP on a Catalyst 5000

VLAN trunks can be configured between two switches, between two routers, or between a switch and a router. In some special circumstances, a file server has an ISL- or 802.1Q-aware NIC card that understands VLAN tagging.

One thing to be aware of when configuring a trunk is that your device needs to be able to handle the load so that the introduction of latency doesn't affect your network devices. This latency will not be noticeable on small data files, but it will be very noticeable when you're using voice or video if your equipment cannot handle the load placed upon it.

Before you create a trunk, you must understand some of the main pieces of the trunk subvariables. You must know whether the trunking method to be used is 802.1Q, 802.10, ISL, LANE, or negotiate.

Note: VLANs can be configured as local VLANs, which means that they are local to one specific geographical area. Trunk links allow VLANs to be created end to end, meaning they can span more than one geographical area.

For Fast Ethernet or Gigabit Ethernet, you set the trunking mode for each port as well as the protocol to use. Table 8.2 explains each variable for the different trunking modes. Table 8.3 explains each possible variable for each protocol.

To configure the domain name and set the password on the switch, use the following command in Privileged Mode (the name *coriolis* refers to the switch domain name, and the password is set to 1234):

```
set vtp domain coriolis passwd 1234
```

Table 8.2 Fast Ethernet and Gigabit Ethernet subvariables for configuring VLAN trunks.

Variable	Description
auto	Used if the port uses Dynamic Inter-Switch Link (DISL) which is the default trunking method used on the 1900 series switch to initiate trunking. This is the default mode for Fast Ethernet and mimics Plug and Play. You cannot configure a trunk when both ends' switch ports are configured for Auto mode. One switch must be set to On or Desirable mode.
desirable	If using DISL, this mode actively tries to configure itself as a trunk link. The other end of the trunk link must be configured to Auto, Nonegotiate, On, or Desirable to complete the trunk initiation.
off	Disables the port from becoming a trunk. Typically used when the device on the other end does not support ISL or IEEE 802.1Q. The port on the other end might be a 10Mbps Ether port or FDDI interface.
on	Basically makes the port a trunk port, regardless of whether the other end is configured to be or cannot become a trunk. Use this option when the port on the other end does not understand DTP, such as a third-party adapter. Set this to **on** when the other end supports DISL.
nonegotiate	Used when DISL negotiation that takes place on ISL trunks is not supported. When using **dot1q** as the final parameter, this tells the switch that ISL will not be used for trunking the ports. This mode makes the port a trunk port without sending DISL frames.

Table 8.3 The different protocol variable choices that can be used when configuring VLAN trunks.

Variable	Description
isl	Applies the Inter-Switch Link protocol encapsulation to an Ethernet trunk.
dot1q	Used for Ethernet trunks using the IEEE 802.1Q standard.
dot10	Used when assigning an FDDI trunk link to the port.
lane	Used when applying ATM to a trunk link port.
negotiate	Puts the port into permanent trunking mode. It disallows the port from generating DTP frames. Typically, this command is used with *switch-to-router* trunks.

Note: The domain can be 1 to 32 characters long, and the password can be 8 to 64 characters long.

To see the VTP domain information, use the following **show** command from the Privileged Mode prompt:

```
show vtp domain
```

The output will look similar to this:

```
Domain Name Domain Index VTP Version Local Mode  Password
----------- ------------ ----------- ----------  --------
Coriolis    1            2           server      -
Vlan-count Max-vlan-storage  Config Revision  Notifications
---------- ----------------  ---------------  -------------
12         1023              8                disabled
Last Updater  V2 Mode   Pruning   PruneEligible on Vlans
------------  -------   -------   ----------------------
172.1.1.1     disabled  disabled  2-1000
```

To set the VTP mode to Server, Client, or Transparent Mode, use the following Privileged Mode command (*coriolis* refers to the domain that the switch will join):

```
set vtp domain <domain name> mode [client|server|transparent]

set vtp domain coriolis mode server
```

Use the following command to configure a trunk port. The port being configured is on module 3, port 1, and the VLAN range is VLANs 2 through 12:

```
set trunk <mod_num/port_num> [on|off|desirable|auto|nonegotiate] <vlan_
    range> [isl|dot1q|dot10|lane|negotiate]

set trunk 3/1 desirable 2-12 isl
```

To remove a VLAN from a trunk, use the following Privileged Mode command (in this demonstration, the module number is 3 and the port number is 1; the VLAN being removed is 13):

```
Clear trunk <mod_num/port_num> <vlan_range>

Clear trunk 3/1 13
```

For more than one VLAN, such as VLANs 13 through 200, issue the following Privileged Mode command:

```
Clear trunk 3/1 13-200
```

To display all the trunks configured on the switch, use the following command in Privileged Mode:

```
Switch> (enable) show trunk
```

The output should look similar to this:

```
Port   Mode           Encapsulation  Status      Native vlan
----   ----           -------------  ------      -----------
1/1    desirable      isl            trunking    1
2/1    desirable      isl            trunking    1
2/2    desirable      isl            trunking    1
2/3    desirable      isl            trunking    1
3/1    desirable      isl            trunking    1
Port           Vlans allowed on trunk
----           ----------------------
1/1            1-100,1003-1005
2/1            1-100,1003-1005
2/2            1-100,1003-1005
2/3            1-100,1003-1005
3/1            1-100,1003-1005
Port           Vlans allowed and active in management domain
----           --------------------------------------------
1/1            1,6-9,1003-1005
2/1            1,6-9,1003-1005
2/2            1,6-9,1003-1005
2/3            1,6-9,1003-1005
3/1            1,6-9,1003-1005
```

8

```
Port            Vlans in spanning tree forwarding state and not pruned
----            --------------------------------------------------------
1/1             1,1003-1005
2/1             1,1003-1005
2/2             1,1003-1005
2/3             1,1003-1005
3/1             1,1003-1005
```

To get a statistical view of the VTP traffic, use the following command:

```
show vtp statistics
```

Configuring VTP Pruning on the Catalyst 5000

VTP pruning requires all switches to be set to Server Mode and the establishment
of the same common VTP domain between all the switches. To enable pruning on
a Set/Clear-based switch, use this command in Privileged Mode:

```
set vtp pruning <enable|disable>
```

```
set vtp pruning enable
```

When you enable VTP pruning, it affects all the VLANs on the switch. If you want
to enable VTP pruning only on certain VLANs, first clear the VLAN prune-eligible
list using the following command for all VLANs:

```
clear vtp pruneeligible <vlan_range>
```

```
clear vtp pruneeligible 2-1000
```

Next, set the VLANs for which you wish to enable pruning:

```
set vtp pruneeligible <vlan_range>
```

```
set vtp pruneeligible 2-30
```

*Note: VTP pruning cannot be enabled on VLAN1, and every switch participating in VTP
pruning must be configured as a VTP server. Enabling VTP pruning on one server enables
VTP pruning on all the servers in the management domain. By default, VLANs 2
through 1,000 are eligible for pruning. VTP pruning will not take place on VLANs that
are pruning-ineligible.*

Configuring VLANs on a Catalyst 1900

On the 1900 series switch, you must choose "k" from the initial user interface menu to get into command-line interface for the switch IOS, as shown here:

```
1 user(s) now active on Management Console.

        User Interface Menu

    [M] Menus
    [K] Command Line
    [I] IP Configuration

Enter Selection:  k

    CLI session with the switch is open.
    To end the CLI session, enter [Exit].
```

To configure the 1900 series switch ports with VLANs, you must enter global configuration mode, as shown next; to help identify the switch, we will give it the hostname **1912EN**:

```
>enable
#config terminal
Enter configuration commands, one per line.  End with CNTL/Z
(config)#hostname 1912EN
```

To configure VLANs on an IOS-based switch, use the following command:

```
vlan <vlan> name <vlan name>

1912EN(config)#vlan 3 name engineering
```

You can configure each interface (port) on a switch to be in a VLAN by using the **vlan-membership** command. Unfortunately you must configure VLANs one by one for each port, because no command exists to assign more than one port to a VLAN. The following is the **vlan-membership** command and its options:

```
1912EN(config-if)#vlan-membership ?
  dynamic  Set VLAN membership type as dynamic
  static   Set VLAN membership type as static
1912EN(config-if)#vlan-membership static ?
  <1-1005>  ISL VLAN index
```

8

Static and Dynamic VLANs

A static VLAN is the most common and easiest VLAN—in terms of administration—of the two ways of creating VLANs. The switch port always remains in the VLAN that is assigned by an administrator until an administrator changes the port assignment. Static VLAN configurations allow for VLAN configurations that are easy to configure, monitor, and work well in a network in which the movement of users within the network remains controlled. You can also use network management software, such as CiscoWorks for Switched Internetworks (CWSI), to configure the ports on the switch. This software is available from any Cisco Value Added Reseller(VAR). If you are work for a VAR you can get this software online from the Cisco CO login and choose **software**.

A dynamic VLAN determines a node's VLAN assignment automatically using a server called a *VLAN Management Policy Server (VMPS)* to set up a database of MAC addresses that can be used for dynamic addressing of VLANs. VMPS is a MAC-address-to-VLAN mapping database that contains a database of allowable MAC or physical addresses that are mapped to a particular VLAN. When the user boots up, the switch learns the MAC address and checks the database for the appropriate VLAN assigned to that MAC address. This enables a user to remain in the same VLAN throughout the network regardless of the location in which the user resides.

A lot of network management is required to maintain the databases of MAC addresses. Therefore, these types of VLANs are not very effective in larger networks. Using intelligent network management software enables you to match a VLAN number to a hardware (MAC) address, protocol, or even an application address to create static VLANs.

Now, enter the interface configuration mode for ports 1 and 2 and assign those two ports to VLAN 3 by using the following commands:

```
1912EN(config-if)#interface e0/1
1912EN(config-if)#vlan-membership static 3
1912EN(config-if)#interface e0/2
1912EN(config-if)#vlan-membership static 3
```

Configuring Trunks and VTP on a Catlayst 1900

The Catalyst 1900 switch has the same options as the 5000 and 6000 series do for ISL. The 1900 switch does, however, run the Dynamic Inter-Switch Link (DISL) encapsulation method to create trunks. The Cisco Catalyst 1912EN switch has two trunkable ports that are Fast Ethernet ports: Interface 26 (Port A) and Interface 27 (Port B). The following lists the available options of the **trunk** command and sets the trunk to **on** for Port B:

```
1912EN(config)#interface f0/27
1912EN(config-if)#trunk ?
   auto         Set DISL state to AUTO
   desirable    Set DISL state to DESIRABLE
   nonegotiate  Set DISL state to NONEGOTIATE
```

```
off         Set DISL state to OFF
on          Set DISL state to ON
```

```
1912EN(config-if)#trunk on
```

To remove a VLAN from a trunk port on a 1900EN series switch, use the interface configuration mode command **no trunk–vlan** command. The following takes a look at the syntaxes available and then removes VLAN 3 from its ability to send VLAN traffic across the trunk:

```
1912EN(config-if)#no trunk-vlan ?
  <1-1005>  ISL VLAN index

1912EN(config-if)#no trunk-vlan 3
```

Note: Again, no command exists to clear more than one VLAN simultaneously.

To view the trunks on a Cisco Catalyst 1900EN, use the **show trunk** command just as you would on a 5000 series switch. A difference does exist, however: this command can be used only on Fast Ethernet ports 26 (Port A) and 27 (Port B). The following are the **show trunk** command options:

```
1912EN#show trunk ?
  A  Trunk A
  B  Trunk B

1912EN#show trunk a ?
  allowed-vlans   Display allowed vlans
  joined-vlans    Display joined vlans
  joining-vlans   Display joining vlans
  prune-eligible  Display pruning eligible vlans
```

As an example of the **show trunk** command, look at the allowed VLANs on Port B:

```
1900EN#show trunk b allowed-vlans
1-3, 6-8
```

The following lists the options when enabling VTP in global configuration mode on the 1900 series switch:

```
1912EN(config)#vtp ?
  client    VTP client
  domain    Set VTP domain name
  password  Set VTP password
```

```
pruning      VTP pruning
server       VTP server
transparent  VTP transparent
trap         VTP trap
```

Let's go ahead and configure this switch as a VTP server for the Coriolis domain, and set the password using the commands in the preceding list:

```
1912EN(config)#vtp server
1912EN(config)#vtp domain coriolis
1912EN(config)#vtp password 1234
```

Internal Route Processors

When a switch receives a packet from a port on one VLAN destined for the port of another VLAN, the switch must find a path on which to send the frame. Switches work at Layer 2 and are designed to isolate traffic to collision domains or subnets; they cannot, by default, forward data from one VLAN to another VLAN or network without some other Layer 3 devices. The Layer 3 device known as a *router on a stick* is used to route the data and create routing tables of other networks and devices.

Route processors can be used to route data between foreign VLANs and other logically segmented parts of the network, such as subnets. They also route data to remote WAN segments, networks, or the Internet.

Quite a few types of route processors are available for Catalyst switches, including the following:

➤ Route Switch Module (RSM)

➤ Route Switch Feature Card (RSFC)

➤ Multilayer Switch Module (MSM)

➤ Multilayer Switch Feature Card (MSFC)

Note: Inter-VLAN routing using RSM, RSFC, MSM, and MSFC will be covered in Chapter 6.

How Inter-VLAN Routing Works

Layer 3 routing takes place between VLANs. This can become a challenging problem for an administrator to overcome. Two types of route processors exist: external and internal. As you learned in the previous section, an external route processor uses an external router (such as the Cisco devices you are familiar with) to route data from one VLAN to another VLAN. An internal route processor uses internal modules and cards located inside the switch route data between VLANs.

Each type of Layer 3 routable protocol that does not have to be IP can have its own mapping for a VLAN. In an IP network, each subnetwork is mapped to an individual VLAN. In an IPX network, each VLAN is mapped to the IPX network number. With AppleTalk, a cable range and AppleTalk zone name are associated with each VLAN.

By configuring VLANs, you control the size of your broadcast domains and keep local traffic local. However, when an end station in one VLAN needs to communicate with an end station in another VLAN, this communication is supported by inter-VLAN routing. You configure one or more routers to route traffic to the appropriate destination VLAN.

Figure 8.4 shows Switch 1 handling traffic for a PC in VLAN 1, and Switch 2 handing traffic for VLAN 2. The router has an ISL-configured interface connecting both switches.

Configuring IP Inter-VLAN Routing on an External Cisco Router

8

To understand this section, you need to become familiar with Cisco IOS software running on Cisco routers. This demonstration is going to configure a Cisco 7505, with the goal of making the process as clear as possible:

1. To enable IP routing on the router, enter the global configuration mode and use the **ip routing** command:

```
7505#configure terminal
Enter configuration commands, one per line.  End with CNTL/Z.
7505 (config)#ip routing
```

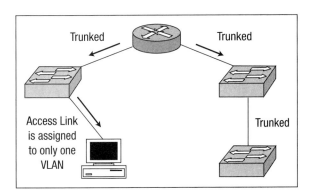

Figure 8.4   An example of an external router routing inter-VLAN traffic.

2. Specify an IP routing protocol, such as OSPF, RIP, IGRP, or EIGRP, and identify the network:

```
Cisco7505(config)#router rip
Cisco7505(config-router)#network 192.1.0.0
```

3. Create a subinterface on a physical interface in interface configuration mode for the port connected to the switch:

```
7505(config-router)#interface fastethernet2/0.100
```

4. Specify the encapsulation type and VLAN number to use on the subinterface:

```
7505 (config-subif)#encapsulation isl 100
```

5. Assign an IP address and subnet mask to the subinterface:

```
7505 (config-subif)#ip address 192.1.1.1 255.255.255.0
```

6. To configure any other interfaces, repeat Steps 3 through 5 for each VLAN you need to become a member of the trunk link or would like to route traffic between:

```
7505 (config-router)#interface fastethernet2/0.200
7505 (config-subif)#encapsulation isl 200
7505 (config-subif)#ip address 192.1.2.3 255.255.255.0
```

Configuring IPX Inter-VLAN Routing on an External Router

To configure inter-VLAN routing for IPX, perform this task beginning in global configuration mode:

1. To enable IP routing on the router, enter the global configuration mode and use the **ipx routing** command:

```
7505#configure terminal
Enter configuration commands, one per line.  End with CNTL/Z.
7505 (config)#ipx routing
```

2. Specify an IPX routing protocol, such as IPX RIP, and identify all the networks:

```
Cisco7505(config)#ipx router rip
Cisco7505(config-router)#network all
```

3. Create a subinterface on a physical interface in interface configuration mode for the port connected to the switch:

```
7505(config-router)#interface fastethernet2/0.1
```

4. Specify the encapsulation type and VLAN number to use on the subinterface:

```
7505 (config-subif)#ipx encapsulation isl 1
```

5. Assign a network number to the subinterface and identify an encapsulation type for IPX, such as **snap**, **novell-ether**, **arpa**, or **sap**:

```
7505 (config-subif)# ipx network 1 encapsulation sap
```

6. To configure any other interfaces, repeat Steps 3 through 5 for each VLAN you need to become a member of the trunk link or would like to route traffic between.

```
7505(config-subif)#interface fastethernet2/0.2
7505(config-subif)#encapsulation isl 2
7505(config-subif)#ipx network 2 encapsulation sap
```

8

Chapter Summary

Any administrator who has the task of using and maintaining switches will tell you the value of this chapter.

Typically, when thinking of VLANs, most administrators who merely support an already configured network think of switches, because the switch is both the access point for the workstations and the location where the VLANs are created.

After a VLAN is created, inter-VLAN routing enables nodes in one VLAN to talk to a node in another VLAN. An access port leading to the end user can be assigned only to one VLAN, sometimes referred to as a color. You learned that trunking using certain protocols, listed next, enables you to send the traffic of more than one VLAN down a single pipe between wiring closet devices such as switches or routers:

➤ *IEEE 802.10*—A Cisco proprietary protocol used primarily to transport VLAN information over FDDI.

➤ *IEEE 802.1Q*—The standard protocol used for inserting a frame tag VLAN identifier in the frame header. As a frame enters the switch fabric, it is tagged with additional information regarding the VLAN properties. The tag remains in the frame as it is forwarded between switches, and is removed prior to exiting the access link to the destination interface. This process is completely transparent to the end user.

➤ *Inter-Switch Link (ISL)*—A special Cisco proprietary Ethernet protocol that assigns a 26-byte header and a 4-byte checksum, sometimes referred to as the FCS or the CRC, to an encapsulated frame header.

➤ *LAN Emulation (LANE)*—An IEEE standard for transporting VLANs over ATM networks. This process uses no encapsulation or frame tagging. ATM and LANE are beyond the scope of this book and thus will not be covered in great detail.

This chapter also covered the VLAN Trunking Protocol (VTP), which is used to enable a single server operating in a VTP domain to configure all the switches in the domain with VLAN information to keep them consistent in the network. VTP enables you to configure one device and have the same configuration propagated to all the devices in the switch block. The different VTP modes, Server, Client, and Transparent, were also discussed.

Finally, this chapter covered ways to configure basic VTP trunks, maintain VLAN configuration consistency using VTP domains, and configure VTP pruning trunk links.

Review Questions

1. What are the two basic methods for implementing VLAN boundaries? [Choose the two best answers]

    a. WAN topology

    b. End-to-end VLANs

    c. Local VLANs

    d. LAN wire speeds

2. Which of the following are benefits of implementing switches and virtual LANs?

    a. Efficient bandwidth utilization

    b. Load balancing among multiple paths

    c. Isolation between problem components

    d. All of the above

3. Which of the following is not a valid VTP management mode?

   a. Server Mode

   b. Help Mode

   c. Client Mode

   d. Transparent Mode

4. Which VTP management mode would you configure your switch for if you did not want to participate in a VTP management domain but still pass VTP management information to other VTP domain members?

   a. Server Mode

   b. Change Mode

   c. Client Mode

   d. Transparent Mode

5. How many slots can be found on a Cisco Catalyst 5500 series switch?

   a. 5

   b. 9

   c. 13

   d. 2

6. Which type of device is used to communicate between VLANs?

   a. Layer 2 switch

   b. Route processor

   c. Hub

   d. Token ring MAU

7. Which of the following best describes a trunk link?

   a. A link that enables access to the Internet

   b. A link that enables FTP and HTTP to flow together

   c. A link that can carry traffic for multiple VLANs

   d. A link that is used only in token ring environments

8. To verify your VLAN configuration on your Set/Clear-based command switch, in which command mode would you use the **show vlan** command?

   a. Global Configuration Mode

   b. Privilege EXEC Mode

   c. User EXEC Mode

   d. Interface Configuration Mode

8

9. On the Catalyst 5000 series switch, all ports are set to which VLAN by default?

    a. Ports are set to VLAN 1000

    b. Ports are set to VLAN 10

    c. Ports are set to VLAN 1

    d. Ports do not belong to a VLAN

10. Which of the following devices enables you to route between VLANs?

    a. An external route processor

    b. A Route Switch Module (RSM)

    c. A Route Switch Feature Card (RSFC)

    d. All of the above

11. Which of the following is not a feature of VTP?

    a. A switch can belong to multiple management domains

    b. VTP is a grouping of switches that share VLAN information

    c. Each management domain must use a unique name

    d. VTP requires a management domain

12. Which best describes a static VLAN?

    a. A VLAN that is assigned by pruning

    b. VLANs that can be configured by CiscoWorks software

    c. Ports change VLANs based on MAC address

    d. A port is assigned to a VLAN

13. Ports on a Cisco 1900 series switch are identified by which module slot number?

    a. 0

    b. 1

    c. 2

    d. 3

14. Which is a true definition of a native VLAN?

    a. The VLAN a port would be assigned to if it were not participating in a trunk

    b. Assigned to an access switch port

    c. A VLAN to two servers

    d. A VLAN assigned to token ring only

15. Which command enables you to assign port 2 on module 3 to VLAN 10 on a 5500 series switch?

    a. **set vlan to 10 port 2**

    b. **set vlan 3/10 2**

    c. **set vlan 10 2-3**

    d. **set vlan 10 3/2**

16. Which command enables you to set the switch VTP domain name to **coriolis**?

    a. **set domain coriolis**

    b. **set vtp host coriolis**

    c. **set coriolis to domain VTP**

    d. **set vtp domain coriolis**

17. Which of the following answers are not true of Inter-Switch Link Protocol? [Choose the two best answers]

    a. Runs only on a single VLAN access link

    b. Uses a two-level tagging scheme with a 26-byte header and a 4-byte checksum

    c. Implemented in the hardware ASICs to provide wire-speed performance

    d. Cannot be used with Spanning Tree Protocol

18. Which of the following issues have VLANs been introduced to address? [Choose the two best answers]

    a. Making WAN communication possible

    b. Segmenting networks

    c. Resolving scalability problems of a flat network

    d. Issuing IP addresses

19. What reason best describes why access link ports should not be configured as VLAN trunks?

    a. Trunk ports send packets faster than the end-user interface can receive them

    b. Trunk ports send VLAN information only for VLANs other than the VLAN assigned to the port

    c. VLAN tags are not removed when tagged frames are sent out trunk ports

    d. End-user interfaces do not understand VLAN tagging and encapsulation methods

8

20. What is the purpose for VTP?

    a. To map access ports together

    b. To add trunking information to VLAN headers

    c. To perform cut-through switching

    d. To keep VLAN information in a VTP domain synchronized between switches

Real-World Projects

Joe Snow has arrived from his weekend out of town to find a new Catalyst 5500 sitting in his cubicle at work. He has been waiting for this to arrive for quite some time for one of his customers, The Coriolis Group. Because he rarely gets a chance to work on such a powerful Cisco product immediately, he checks the VLAN configuration from The Coriolis Group's older switches and decides that The Coriolis Group is growing so large that it needs to implement VTP to save time in implementing new switches. Another Cisco Catalyst 5500 series switch should be arriving for The Coriolis Group soon. By configuring VTP on the switches, only this switch needs to be configured with VLAN information.

The following is a list of things that need to be configured on the switch:

➤ Set port 3/1 to VLAN 10

➤ Set ports 3/6 and 3/7 to VLAN 50

➤ Keep ports 3/2-5 and 3/8-12 in VLAN 1

➤ Set trunk ports 5/1-3, 3/2-5, and 3/8-12 to autonegotiate with ISL

➤ Set trunks 4/1-2, 3/1, and 5/6-7 to On with ISL

➤ Assign the VTP domain name as Coriolis

➤ Set VTP to Server Mode

Project 8.1

First we need to configure the basic configuration which includes these items from our "to do" list:

➤ Set port 3/1 to VLAN 10

➤ Set ports 3/6 and 3/7 to VLAN 50

➤ Keep ports 3/2-5 and 3/8-12 in VLAN 1

To configure these items, perform the following steps:

1. Configure the VTP domain for the switch using the following command:

```
set vtp domain Coriolis
```

2. Configure the VTP mode for the switch using the following command:

```
set vtp mode server
```

3. Configure the VLANs using the following commands:

```
set vlan 10 3/1
set vlan 50 3/6-7
```

Note: By default, all VLANs are in VLAN 1.

Project 8.2

Looking at the list, several trunk links need to be added to the configuration.

The following is a list of things that still need to be configured on the switch:

➤ Set trunk ports 5/1-3, 3/2-5, and 3/8-12 to autonegotiate with ISL

➤ Set trunks 4/1-2, 3/1, and 5/6-7 to On with ISL

➤ Secure the VTP domain with a password

Perform the following steps:

1. To set the ports to the configuration specified in the preceding list, use the following commands:

```
set trunk 5/1-3 auto
set trunk 4/1-2 on isl
set trunk 3/1 on isl
set trunk 3/2-5 auto isl
set trunk 5/6-7 on isl
set trunk 3/8-12 auto isl
```

2. To secure the VTP domain, give it the password 4321 with the following command:

```
set vtp domain coriolis passwd 4321
```

CHAPTER NINE

Spanning Tree Protocol

After completing this chapter, you will be able to:

✓ List the qualities of a transparent bridge

✓ Identify Bridge Protocol Data Unit (BPDU) data fields

✓ Identify how a root bridge is selected

✓ Modify spanning tree timers

✓ Understand switch diameters

✓ Understand convergence time calculations

✓ List the five switch port states

✓ Understand Common Spanning Tree (CST)

✓ Understand Per-VLAN Spanning Tree (PVST)

✓ Understand Per-VLAN Spanning Tree Plus (PVST+)

✓ Configure Spanning Tree Protocol (STP)

✓ View the Spanning Tree Protocol settings

In today's networks, it is typical to create a network with redundant links. Virtually every network provides a backbone not only for the users data but also for the welfare of the company. Upper management in medium to large companies almost demand redundancy the first time any network outage occurs that effects their day-to-day operations. Most administrators provide this redundancy after they learn the difference in the cost of providing this redundant link versus the cost of keeping a huge number of employees idle for a long period of time. Redundant links provide consistent network availability when a network outage occurs on a link.

Routers use routing protocols to map the network for Layer 3 traffic. The routing protocols use these mappings to create a routing table, to make sure routing loops do not occur in the network. For Layer 2 traffic, this job is left to the Spanning Tree Protocol (STP).

Redundancy is defined as the ability to provide an immediate backup solution to a fault in the network. This chapter focuses on link redundancy using STP and the IEEE 802.1D algorithm used to support this protocol.

In this chapter, you will also learn the properties of a transparent frame and the processes used in configuring STP through multiple switches, BackboneFast, UplinkFast, and many other solutions to solve STP problems. It also focuses on the Layer 2 network data loops, associated with providing a redundant link in the network, that are the reason behind the creation of STP as an IEEE standard.

Spanning Tree Protocol

Earlier in the book, you learned how routing protocols operating at Layer 3 in the network aid Layer 3 devices, such as routers, in handling load balancing and path determination to route data and change known routes if a link's service is interrupted. STP is a protocol designed to perform the same functions—but faster and at Layer 2.

STP uses the Spanning Tree Algorithm (STA), which was originally submitted to the IEEE by Digital Equipment Corporation (DEC). This protocol was intended to prevent the occurrence of Layer 2 data loops. After the IEEE 802 committee revised the submission into what is now known as the IEEE 802.1D standard, it was different enough from DEC's version to render the two incompatible with each other.

A data loop is created when multiple links to a destination exist in the network, as shown in Figure 9.1. Data flowing from one interface on the network returns to a second interface on the same network because of the second path creating a loop. The data will move in a continuous circle unless some protocol or algorithm is used to stop the data or a maximum time-to-live (TTL) is assigned to the data frame.

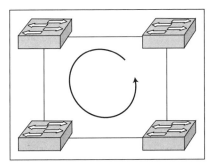

Figure 9.1   An example of more than one path residing in the network. Any data sent on this path will form a data loop.

The data loop can actually become a disastrous problem, and could grow much worse than the original loop itself. The properties of transparent bridging cause it to retransmit a broadcast and never mark the frame. This results in bridges actually creating broadcasts in an expanding fashion when a data loop occurs. This process of creating new broadcasts will eventually bring down the entire network when the number of broadcasts frames eats up all the available bandwidth on the network. This is referred to as a *broadcast storm*.

STP forces certain redundant data paths into a standby mode or a blocked state. By blocking the paths to destinations other than the given root path, this creates only one path through the network. If any of the forwarding paths through one of the network segments in the spanning tree becomes unreachable, the STA will then reconfigure the spanning tree topology and reestablish communication with the destination interface by activating the standby path.

Common Spanning Tree Protocol

Common Spanning Tree (CST), also known as Mono Spanning Tree (MST), uses the IEEE 802.1Q standard. This standard allows STP to run only on VLAN 1, by default. All the switches in the network elect a single root bridge and form an association with that switch. In this situation, the single root bridge is optimized for a single VLAN; but, in networks with multiple VLANs, data may take a less-than-optimal path to get to file servers and other interfaces on the network.

CST has some major disadvantages in larger-scale networks, such as the inability of all switches in the network to send data through the most optimum path for all devices in the network. Another disadvantage is in the spanning tree topology. When the topology increases in size to encompass all ports in the switch fabric, greater convergence times and more frequent reconfiguration may result.

CST has some advantages over Per-VLAN Spanning Tree (PVST), (discussed later in this chapter). It has fewer BPDUs (also discussed later) consuming bandwidth, and each switch requires less processing overhead. Although CST has some advantages, a single spanning tree is not an optimal solution for scalability or stability in larger networks.

Note: STP executes STA and is actually two separate entities. To find the redundant links in the network, the STA chooses a reference point in the network and calculates the redundant paths to that reference point. If the STA finds a redundant path, it will choose one path to forward and use the redundant paths to block. This process effectively severs all the redundant links within the network.

STA uses a graph theory, developed by Edsger Dijkstra, to construct a loop-free subset of the network topology. This theory is discussed next.

Graph Theory

The STA uses solutions obtained by a graph theory known as the *Shortest Path Algorithm* to construct a loop-free subset of the network's topology. This protocol is also used in other link-state protocols, such as Open Shortest Path First (OSPF), to calculate routing solutions.

This theory uses a connected graph consisting of straight-through points and weighted edges. The calculation between each of these points and edges from one point in the network to the other creates a graph which the STA can use to decide the best paths through the network. It can then disable links which are not optimal paths to create a single path through the network which contains no loops.

The algorithm provides a *directed graph*, in which vertices and weighted edges represent each link, as shown in Figure 9.2. Each link represents a cost. The weighted edges, which usually have more hops from one point in the network to another part of the network than the straight-through points, are assigned higher values. Each link in the path has a value, and the total of the values to a given point or destination is the total weighted value of the path. The lowest total weighted value represents the most efficient path from one point to another point.

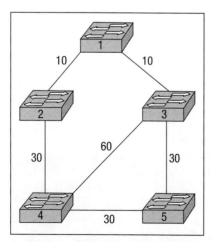

Figure 9.2 An example of a directed graph.

Using STA, each switch in the network is assigned a unique identifier. This identifier is one of the switch's Media Access Control (MAC) addresses, as well as an assigned priority, which is explained in more detail later in the chapter. After STA assigns each switch this unique identifier, STA then assigns each port in every switch a unique identifier. This identifier is typically the port's own individual interface's MAC address. Each bridge port is then associated with a *path cost,* which represents the cost of transmitting a frame onto the network through the port. Path costs are assigned by default, but can be assigned manually by a network administrator.

Root Bridge Assignment

One of the first actions of the STA computation is to select a root bridge and root port. The *root bridge* is the bridge with the lowest-value bridge identifier. Switches or bridges using STP exchange using multicast frames called *Bridge Protocol Data Units (BPDUs).* Other switches then send their bridge IDs to other devices by using BPDUs. After the root bridge is selected, the root ports on all other bridges are determined.

Tip: BPDUs are used to send configuration messages using multicast frames; they are discussed in depth later in the chapter.

Figure 9.3 shows the switch acting as the root bridge calculating the least-cost path to switch D. Notice the numbers associated with the root bridge's path to each individual destination. The path with the lowest number has the highest priority. The higher the number between each individual segment, the higher the cost of transmitting a frame between those two segments. The port through which the root bridge can be reached with the least amount of hops or cost determines a bridge's root port; this is referred to as the least path cost.

Broadcasts, Unknown Unicasts, and Multicast Frames

One of the unique features of a broadcast and multicast frame is that neither has a specified destination hardware address and the source address is always the hardware address of the device that sent the frame. In the case of broadcasts, the destination address shown in the header is all 1s, which indicates that it goes to all nodes in a network. A multicast specifies a network but changes all the host addresses bits to all 1s. For example, a broadcast and multicast in binary would be as shown in Table 9.1.

When switches receive a broadcast or a multicast, the frame is then sent out all the ports of the switch, with the exception of the port the frame arrived on. VLANs can be used to break down the broadcasts into smaller broadcast domains. In the case of a VLAN, if a broadcast arrives on a port assigned to VLAN 5, only ports assigned to VLAN 5 will receive the broadcast. An unknown unicast is similar to a broadcast. This type of unicast is sent to a specific address but when the switch has not learned the destination the switch forwards the frame just like a broadcast and it is sent out all ports except the port on which it arrived.

Table 9.1 A broadcast and multicast destination address.

Frame Type	Binary Value	Broadcast Address
Broadcast	11111111.11111111.11111111.11111111	255.255.255.255
Multicast	00001010.00000001.11111111.11111111	10.1.255.255

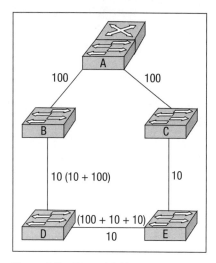

Figure 9.3 The root bridge calculating the path cost to switch D.

In some instances, the lowest calculated path is not the most ideal path. For example, if multiple high-speed links to a destination exist, the links may total more than the cost of a very slow link, such as a modem. Even though the straight path has the fewest hops, it is much slower than using a high-speed, longer path. To overcome this problem, you can manually change a lower-speed links port cost to reflect a higher path cost, forcing a change in the root port selection. The goal is to make changes to the network so that the fastest, most efficient route to the root port on the designated bridge is used. The fastest links should always have the lowest port costs.

The *designated bridge* is the bridge on each LAN that provides the shortest route with the least path cost. The designated bridge is the only bridge that is allowed to forward frames to and from the other bridges. A *designated port* on the switch is the port that connects the switch to the physical interface of the designated bridge.

We have learned through experience that the STA is sometimes incorrect in its calculation of the most efficient path. How does this algorithm choose a path when two equal cost paths exist? Let's take a look.

Equal Cost Path Problems

When two or more links have the same root path cost, such as the two running between the two switches depicted in Figure 9.4, STA has a problem choosing the designated port or a root path through the network using the lowest path cost.

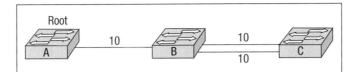

Figure 9.4   Two ports with equal cost paths through the network from switch A to switch C.

You have two options in this situation. You can manually assign the path cost, or the switch or bridge can use the lowest port ID. You can assign lower path costs to the faster physical media, and you can assign slower media a higher path cost. The range of numbers that can be assigned to the port costs is 1 through 65,535. Typically, the path cost is determined by dividing 1,000 by the physical wire speed in megabits per second (Mbps), as shown in Table 9.2.

If configured correctly, this process should eliminate all but one of the ports directly connected to each switch, thereby removing all the loops in the network.

All of this takes place in a network using transparent bridging. The following section looks at STP and how it functions in a transparent network.

Transparent Bridging

To help you understand STP, this section first looks at the behavior of a transparent bridge without STP. Transparent bridging, by definition, has to be transparent to the devices on the network. The developers of transparent bridging wanted to make sure that end-user interface configurations did not have to be modified or that sent and received frames needed to be modified through the sending and receiving process.

Bridges learn of other interfaces connected to them by looking at the frames they receive through each port for the source address of a device. This process is sometimes referred to as *listening*. When a frame with a source address comes from a specific port, the bridge automatically assumes that the source address can be found on the port of arrival.

The next step in the transparent bridging process for the switch is to build a table of the source addresses it has received through the port from which the frame arrived.

Table 9.2   Examples of path cost calculations.

Physical Wire Speed	Path Cost
10Mbps	100
100Mbps	10
155Mbps	6
1,000Mbps (1Gbps)	1
10,000Mbps (10Gbps)	1

This process is referred to as *learning*. A bridge is always listening and learning by examining the frames received on each port.

Transparent bridging works very well, as long as it remains simple and the network contains no redundant links. Transparent bridging begins to have problems when a redundant path is added to the bridged network. STP was created to overcome the problems of transparent bridging in redundant multilink networks. STP enables transparent bridging to eliminate loops in the network and thereby provide a loop-free path through the network.

STP determines where loops exist in the network and shuts down links that are redundant. It ensures that only one path exists to each destination and that a bridging loop can never occur. In case of a link failure, the bridge knows which redundant links exist and will activate a link that was previously blocked.

After STA has leaned and calculated the costs of using each link, STA performs a recalculation. This occurs whenever a bridge joins the network or when a topology change is detected in the network. This calculation requires communication between the spanning tree bridges, which is accomplished through the passing of BPDU messages between switches.

The next section takes an in-depth look at BPDUs and the information they contain.

Bridge Protocol Data Units

A BPDU message contains information that identifies the bridge presumed to be the root bridge by using a root identifier contained in the message. The message also contains the distance from the sending bridge to the root bridge with the calculated root path cost. And, each configuration message contains the bridge and port identifiers of the sending bridge, as well as the age of the information contained in the message.

Bridges exchange BPDU messages at configurable intervals, which are usually every one to four seconds. By default, BPDUs are sent out every two seconds on every port that is not disabled or blocked, to ensure a stable topology without data loops. A topology change is caused if one or more bridges fail or another switch enters the network. The neighboring bridges will detect the lack of configuration messages and initiate an immediate STA recalculation.

Each transparent bridge topology decision is made locally on each switch, and the configuration messages are then exchanged between each neighboring switch. No central authority or administration exists in the network topology.

The following are the fields of the transparent bridge configuration message or BPDU, as shown in Figure 9.5:

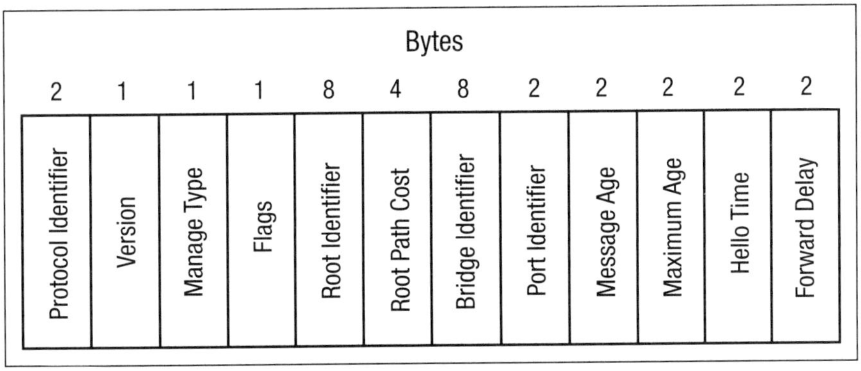

Figure 9.5 The 12 fields of the IEEE 802.1D BPDU.

➤ *Protocol Identifier*—Contains 2 bytes and the value of 0.

➤ *Version*—Contains 1 byte and the value of 0.

➤ *Message Type*—Contains 1 byte and the value of 0.

➤ *Flag*—Contains 1 byte; only the first 2 bits are used. The topology change (TC) bit signals that a topology change has occurred. The topology change acknowledgment (TCA) bit is then set to acknowledge receipt of a configuration message with the TC signal bit set.

➤ *Root ID*—Contains 8 bytes that identify the root bridge by listing a 2-byte priority followed by a 6-byte ID.

➤ *Root Path Cost*—Contains 4 bytes containing the cost of the path from the bridge sending the configuration message to the root bridge.

➤ *Bridge ID*—Contains 8 bytes identifying the priority and ID of the bridge sending the message.

➤ *Port ID*—Contains 2 bytes identifying the port from which the configuration message was sent. This field enables STP to immediately detect loops created by multiple attached bridges.

➤ *Message Age*—Contains 2 bytes specifying the amount of time since the root sent the configuration message on which the current configuration message is based.

➤ *MaximumAge*—Contains 2 bytes indicating when the current configuration message should be discarded.

➤ *Hello Time*—Contains 2 bytes providing the time period between root bridge configuration messages.

➤ *FwdDelay*—Contains 2 bytes providing the length of time that the bridge should wait before transitioning to a new state following a topology change in the network. If a bridge transitions too soon, all network links might not be ready to change their state, and loops can result.

The next section looks at how the BPDUs are used in the process of selecting a root bridge.

Selecting the Root Bridge

The process of selecting a root bridge begins when the switch is first powered on. The root bridge is the reference point that all switches must use to determine whether loops exist in the network and what the path costs are through the network. The switch immediately assumes at startup that it gets to be the root bridge and thus configures its bridge ID equal to the root ID in the BPDU. The bridge ID field of a BPDU message is actually made up of two parts, as follows:

➤ *Two-byte priority set by the switch*—This number is the same for all Cisco switches and is set to a priority 0x8000 or 32,768 by default.

➤ *Six-byte MAC address*—The MAC address of the switch or bridge.

By using these two parts of the bridge ID field, the switch can determine a value that is compared with other switches' BPDU bridge ID fields, to determine which switch will become the root bridge. The lower the bridge ID field value, the higher the chance of a root-bridge assignment. If one or more switches have the same lowest bridge priority value, the bridge with the lowest MAC address then becomes the root bridge.

Every switch participating in STP will form an association with the root bridge shortly after the root bridge has been elected. Each switch examines each BPDU as it arrives on each port. If a switch receives BPDUs on more than one port, it is an indication that the switch has more than one path to the root bridge. The switch will determine which port will be forwarding data and which ports will be blocked from sending data if redundant links exist through the network. This is done by analyzing the path cost and port ID fields of the BPDUs.

STP switches or bridges look at the path cost first to determine which port owns the lowest-cost path to the root switch. If the port has the lowest port cost, the port is placed in forwarding mode. All the other ports that are receiving BPDUs are placed in blocking mode. In *blocking mode*, the port will still forward BPDU and system information to the switch processor. BPDU timers are discussed next.

STP Timers

STP timers are used to prevent bridging loops and to determine how long STP will take to converge after a failure or loss of a link. When BPDUs travel through

Switch Diameter

A switch's diameter is a unit of measurement between the root switch and child switches. The root bridge counts as the first switch. Each subsequent child switch out from the root bridge is added to come up with the diameter number. A parent switch brings you closer to the root bridge, and a child switch takes you farther away from the root bridge.

Each root bridge can be configured with a diameter from a minimum of two switches to a maximum of seven switches. By modifying the diameter, you will subsequently change the timer values that are advertised by the root to reflect a more accurate network diameter. For example, a diameter of 2 yields a MaxAge of 10 seconds and a FwdDelay of 7 seconds. Cisco recommends that you change the diameter to correctly reflect your network, instead of manually changing the timers.

the switched network, switches face propagation delays. Propagation delays occur due to such things as bandwidth utilization, packet length, switch processing, or any other port-to-port delay encountered as a frame traverses the network.

One possible result of propagation delays is a change in the network topology that can take place at different times and at different locations within the network. When a switch port converts from a blocked state to a forwarding state, the port can inadvertently create temporary data loops, because the port may not have completed the learning process to obtain the entire network topology.

STP members use timers to force the ports to wait for the correct topology information. The timers are set by default on the switch. Table 9.3 shows the three different STP timers and the default timer settings based on a default setting of 2 for the Hello Time and 7 for the switch diameter. The diameter is the limit in the number of hops away from the root bridge that will be calculated. Based on these assumptions, the network should always form a stable topology.

Convergence Time Calculation for STP

Convergence is the time that STP members take to begin transmitting data on a redundant link after a link in forwarding mode has failed. It is also the initial

Table 9.3 The default STP timers and their default settings.

STP Timer Variable	Description
Hello Time (default 2 seconds)	Determines how often the switch will broadcast hello messages to other switches
Maximum Time/MaxAge (default 20 seconds)	Determines how long protocol information received on a port is stored by the switch
FwdDelay (default 15 seconds)	Determines how long listening and learning will last before the port begins forwarding

period between the time an STP member powers up and all the active links are placed in forwarding mode. In both cases, during the convergence time, no data is forwarded.

Note: Convergence is important to make sure that all devices have the same topology information when there is a change in the nework topology.

By default, MaxAge is 20 seconds and FwdDelay is 30 seconds, because FwdDelay is used by both the listening and learning states. The values have meaning only at a root bridge. You can adjust FwdDelay and MaxAge; however, doing so may cause a data loop temporarily in more complex networks. Using the following example, the downtime could be as high as 50 seconds using the following calculations:

```
2 * FwdDelay + MaxAge = Down Time

For example, using the defaults:

2 * 15 + 20 = 50 seconds
```

The next section takes a closer look at the different STP port states.

STP Port States

STP transitions each port through four port states in a designated order before the port can forward frames. These states are blocking, listening, learning, and forwarding. The disabled state is a fifth state that can be manually configured by the switch.

The following are the different port states, along with a description of when each is used, as shown in Figure 9.6:

➤ *Blocking*—The port is not forwarding frames or learning new addresses. All ports start in blocking mode to prevent the bridge from creating a bridging loop. The port stays in a blocked state if STP determines that a lower-cost path to the root bridge exists.

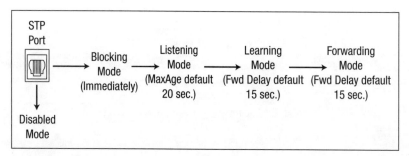

Figure 9.6　The convergence process of the port states in STP.

➤ *Listening*—The port is not forwarding frames or learning new addresses. It is progressing to a forwarding state and listening to traffic coming in on the switch ports. Ports transition from a blocked state to the listening state. Ports use this time to attempt to learn whether any other paths exist to the root bridge. During the listening state, the port can listen to frames but cannot send or receive data. The port does not put any of the information it hears into the address table.

➤ *Learning*—The port is not forwarding frames but is learning addresses and putting them in the address table. The learning state is similar to the listening state, except the port can now add information it has learned to the address table. The port is still not allowed to send or receive frames.

➤ *Forwarding*—The port is forwarding frames, learning addresses, and adding addresses to the routing table. This state means that the port is capable of sending and receiving frames. A port is not placed in a forwarding state until no redundant links exist or the port determines the lowest-cost path to the root bridge or switch.

➤ *Disabled*—The port has been removed from all STP functions. Disabled is a special state indicating that the port has been manually shut down by the network administrator or by the system due to a hardware problem.

The following describes what happens to a port when the switch is powered up:

1. After the switch's initialization or startup, all the ports immediately go to a blocking state.

2. After the configured MaxAge has been reached, the switch transitions from the blocking state to the learning state.

3. After the configured FwdDelay time has been reached, the port enters the learning state.

4. After the configured FwdDelay has been reached in the learning state, the port either transitions into the forwarding mode or back to the blocking mode. If STP has decided the port will be a forwarding port, it is placed in forwarding mode; if the port is a higher-cost redundant link, the port is placed in the blocking mode again.

Each port state can be manually modified by using management software. If properly configured, the ports should create a stable network and transition the ports of each switch to either a forwarding or blocking state.

Network Topology Changes

If a change occurs to the structure of the network with one or more links in a network running STP, certain steps occur using STA:

1. When a bridge or switch notices that a change has occurred to a link in the network, the bridge or switch sends a topology change BPDU out the root port to the root bridge. The topology change BPDU indicates a change within the flag field of the topology change BPDU.

2. The originating bridge or switch continues to send out topology change BPDUs to the designated destination bridge, which may be a parent bridge if the bridge is not attached directly to the root bridge.

3. The designated bridge responds with a topology change acknowledgement, which is also contained in the 1-byte flag field of a BPDU.

4. The designated bridge or switch sends a topology change BPDU out its root port destined for either another designated parent or the root bridge.

5. After the root bridge receives the topology change message, it changes its configuration BPDUs to indicate that a topology change has occurred. The root bridge sets the topology change in the configuration parameters for a period of time equal to the sum of the FwdDelay and MaxAge parameters.

6. All child bridges or switches receiving the topology change configuration message from the root bridge use the FwdDelay timer to age out entries located in their address table. By doing this, the device can age out entries more quickly than the default of 300 seconds (5 minutes) assigned to each entry as its TTL in the Content Addressable Memory (CAM) table.

7. Each child bridge and switch continues this process until it no longer receives topology change configuration messages from the root bridge.

Configuring Spanning Tree Protocol

Two types of command-line switches are found in enterprise networks. One type mimics the Cisco IOS-based interface that is found on all Cisco routers. The other type is based on the Set/Clear command set found on switches such as the Catalyst 5000 series. So, you really have to learn the commands for STP twice. Although all the Catalyst 1900 series switches are included with the Enterprise Network (EN) edition of the IOS standard, the old standard IOSs may still include some switches that use a single-letter-command interface type. This type of IOS is beyond the scope of this book, but if you still have it around and would like more information on it, see Chapter 7 of The Coriolis Group's *Switching Exam Prep* by Sean Odom and Doug Hammond, 2000 (ISBN 1-57610-689-6).

The IOS command-line interface is similar to the interface found on a standard or enterprise Cisco router. The second version in this book is referred to as the Set/Clear-based IOS. Its name derives from the fact that most of the configuration and monitoring commands start with either **set**, **clear**, or **show**. Some of the commands do not start with those three commands, but these constitute a very low percentage overall.

Although the commands are similar in some ways, the similarity doesn't make learning them easier. In fact, in my opinion, the similarity makes learning them more confusing. However, previous experience with Cisco routers and the Cisco IOS can make this process a little easier.

This section shows you how to enable STP on both types of switch IOSs, as well as how to disable STP. Pay close attention to the mode that you are in on each individual switch when configuring STP, because this will help you to understand the different modes you should be in to configure the different IOSs.

To help you understand how to configure the switch, this section also shows you some of the basic commands for viewing and verifying the current STP configuration. Because some of the configuration information you will see on your screen is confusing, this section covers the definition of each field displayed when viewing the configuration on an IOS-based switch.

Before you begin to configure the Set/Clear-based switch, take a look at the options available for the **set spantree** command, which is the basic command:

```
Seans5002> (enable) set spantree ?

Set spantree commands:
--------------------------------
set spantree backbonefast      Enable or disable fast convergence
set spantree disable           Disable spanning tree
set spantree enable            Enable spanning tree
set spantree fwddelay          Set spantree forward delay
set spantree hello             Set spantree hello interval
set spantree help              Show this message
set spantree maxage            Set spantree max aging time
set spantree multicast-address Set multicast address type for trbrf's
set spantree portcost          Set spantree port cost
set spantree portfast          Set spantree port fast start
set spantree portpri           Set spantree port priority
set spantree portstate         Set spantree logical port state
set spantree portvlancost      Set spantree port cost per vlan
set spantree portvlanpri       Set spantree port vlan priority
set spantree priority          Set spantree priority
```

9

```
set spantree root                Set switch as primary or secondary root
set spantree uplinkfast          Enable or disable uplinkfast groups

Seans5002> (enable)
```

Set/Clear-Based Switch Configuration

You can use the Set/Clear-based switch to enable and disable STP on a per-port basis. Every port on the switch is enabled for STP by default. If STP has been disabled on the switch, you can reenable it from the privileged mode prompt.

Note: Cisco recommends that STP remain enabled on the switch, especially on any trunk port where the possibility exists of a bridging loop in the network.

To enable STP on a Set/Clear-based switch, use the following privileged mode command:

```
set spantree enable
```

Disabling STP on a Set/Clear-Based Switch

To disable STP on a Set/Clear-based switch, use the following privileged mode command:

```
set spantree disable
```

Enabling STP by Port on a Set/Clear-Based Switch

To selectively enable specific ports on the switch, use the following privileged mode command (3/1 represents module 3 on port 1):

```
set spantree enable 3/1
```

Disabling STP by Port on a Set/Clear-Based Switch

To selectively disable specific ports on the switch, use this Privileged Mode command (4/1 represents module 4 on port 1):

```
set spantree disable 4/1
```

Enabling STP on a Set/Clear-Based Switch for All VLANs

To enable STP on all VLANs, use the following command in Privileged Mode:

```
set spantree enable all
```

Show Spantree Command Fields

Some of the description fields may mislead you into believing they provide certain information. Here is a brief description of the fields:

➤ *Spanning tree enabled*—Shows that STP is in use.

➤ *Spanning tree type*—Typically, IEEE standard.

➤ *Designated Root*—The 6-byte MAC address for the designated root bridge.

➤ *Designated Root Priority*—A 2-byte priority setting for the root bridge. By default, the priority for a secondary root bridge or switch should be 32,768; the priority for the root bridge or switch should be 8,192.

➤ *Designated Root Cost*—Total cost to get to the root bridge from this switch. If the root cost equals 0, this switch is the root bridge or switch.

➤ *Designated Root Port*—The port used to get to the root bridge.

➤ *Root timers*—Timer values of the root bridge or switch.

➤ *Bridge ID MAC ADDR*—A 6-byte address that the switch uses for its bridge ID.

➤ *Bridge ID Priority*—The 2-byte priority of this bridge. This number is formed from a combination of the bridge ID priority and bridge ID MAC address. If the Bridge ID Priority value is identical to the Designated Root value, this bridge is the root bridge.

➤ *Bridge Max Age*—The maximum values from the root bridge.

The list at the bottom of the preceding listing shows the ports in use in the spanning tree. It states the port, port-state, and priority, as well as whether Fast-Start (PortFast) is enabled.

9

Viewing the STP Configuration on a Set/Clear-Based Switch

To view the current configuration of STP on your switch, use this Privileged Mode command (11 refers to the VLAN number):

```
show spantree 11
```

The output should look similar to this:

```
Spanning tree enabled
Spanning tree type        ieee
Designated Root           00-ad-13-18-d5-34
Designated Root Priority  8192
Designated Root Cost      0
Designated Root Port      1/0
Root Max Age 10 Sec       Hello Time 2 sec    Forward Delay 7 sec
Bridge ID MAC ADDR        00-ad-13-18-d5-34
Bridge ID Priority        8192
Bridge Max Age 20 Sec   Hello Time 2 sec     Forward Delay 15 sec
```

```
Port  vlan  Port-State   Cost  Priority  Fast-start  Group-Method
----  ----  ----------   ----  --------  ----------  ------------
4/1   4     forwarding   19    32        disabled
4/2   5     forwarding   19    32        disabled
4/3   5     blocking     19    32        disabled
4/4   4     blocking     19    32        disabled
```

STP Configuration on an IOS-Based Switch

Unlike the Set/Clear-based switch, enabling STP on a Cisco IOS-based switch is performed in global configuration mode. To enableSTP on a Cisco IOS based switch, enter the following command (5 is the VLAN number and is considered a VLAN-list field; you can list up to 10 VLANs in the list):

```
spantree 5
```

Tip: The Cisco Catalyst 1900 and Catalyst 2820 series switches support a maximum of 1,005 VLANs. On the 1900 and 2820, you can enable STP on only 64 of the 1,005 VLANs at any given time. By default, STP is enabled on VLANs 1 through 64. Although the two switches support more than 64 VLANs, any number of VLANs over 64 must have STP disabled.

Disabling STP on an IOS-Based Switch

To disable STP on a VLAN, in global configuration mode, use this command (5 is the VLAN number and is considered a VLAN-list field):

```
no spantree 5
```

Viewing the STP Configuration on an IOS-Based Command-Line Switch

To view the configuration, you use the same command that you would use in the Set/Clear-based switches:

```
show spantree
```

However, you will receive a much different output, which should look similar to this on your console:

```
VLAN1 is executing the IEEE compatible Spanning Tree Protocol
Bridge Identifier has priority 8192, address 002C.800A.AD51
Configured hello time 2, max age 20, forward delay 15
Current root has priority 8192, address 002C.800A.AD51
Root port is FastEthernet 1/1, cost of root path is 0
```

```
Topology change flag not set, detected flag not set
Topology changes 21, last topology change occurred 1d3h19m59s ago
Times: hold 1, topology change 9211
hello 2, max age 20, forward delay 15
Timers: hello 2, topology change 35, notification 2
Port Ethernet 0/5 of VLAN1 is Forwarding
Port path cost 0, Port priority 100
Designated root has priority 8192, address 002C.800A.AD51
Designated bridge has priority 8192, address 002C.800A.AD51
Designated port is Ethernet 0/5, path cost 10
```

Timers: Message Age 20, Forward Delay 15, Hold 1 Root Bridge Selection

When defining the location of the root bridge, certain commands can help you determine which device will become the root bridge. The proper placement of the root bridge(s) optimizes the paths that are chosen by STP to allow data traffic to flow through the network. It also provides deterministic paths for data to take.

Occasionally, to get the most optimal paths for data through the network, you must manually configure the bridge that should be the root bridge. It may also be necessary to configure the secondary root bridge, whose function is to become the root bridge if the original root bridge fails.

The Cisco switch software is used to configure the STP configuration parameters. Before you decide to change the default parameters of STP, you need to give careful consideration to switching paths. This is particularly important before changing the root bridge configuration.

The placement of the root bridge in the spanning tree should be as close to the center of the network as possible. Typically, most root bridges are Distribution layer switches, not Access layer switches. The root bridge should never be a Core layer switch, because the Core layer's responsibility is to move traffic as quickly as possible.

Configuring the STP Root Switch

This sections take a look at the commands needed to configure the spanning tree to allow a switch to become the root switch on a Set/Clear-based switch. Table 9.4 shows the root and secondary bridge configuration command parameters.

To configure the switch to become the root bridge, enter the following command in Privileged Mode:

```
set spantree root 5 dia 3 hello 2
```

Table 9.4   Root and secondary bridge configuration command parameters.

Command Parameter	Definition
root	Designates the root switch. The default priority of the root bridge is 8,192.
secondary (optional)	Used to designate the switch as a secondary root switch if the root bridge fails. The default priority of the secondary bridge is 16,384.
n (optional)	Specifies the VLAN. If you do not specify the VLAN, VLAN 1 is used. The valid value range is 1 through 1,005.
dia *n* (optional)	Specifies the diameter value, discussed earlier in the chapter. It is essentially the number of bridges between any two points. The diameter should be measured starting from the root bridge. Valid values are 2 through 7.
hello *n* (optional)	Specifies in seconds how often configuration messages should be generated by the root switch. Valid values are 1 through 10.

Configuring the STP Secondary Root Switch

To configure the switch to become the secondary root bridge, enter the following Privileged Mode command:

```
set spantree secondary 5 dia 3 hello 2
```

Setting the Root Bridge for More Than One VLAN on the Set/Clear-Based IOS

To set the primary root switch for more than one VLAN on a Set/Clear-based switch, use the Privileged Mode command to change configuration to a root bridge. The default priority automatically changes to 8,192, which is the default when the command is used to configure the switch as the root bridge. The default STP port settings are shown in Table 9.5. The following command specifies the root bridge for VLANs 1 through 3:

```
set spantree root 1-3 dia 2
```

When the root bridge is configured correctly, the output on the console should be similar to this:

```
VLANs 1-3 bridge priority set to 8192
VLANs 1-3 bridge max aging time set to 10 seconds.
VLANS 1-3 bridge bello time set to 2 seconds.
VLANS 1-3 bridge forward delay set to 7 seconds.
Switch is now the root switch for active VLANs 1-3.
```

Table 9.5 The default port settings for STP.

Variable	Default
Port priority	32
Port cost	62
Bridge priority	32,768
Secondary root bridge priority	16,384
Root bridge priority	8,192

Assigning Port Costs

After the root bridge has been elected, all the switches determine the best loop-free path to the root switch. STP uses several different costs, with the port priority as the tiebreaker. The sum of all the port costs to a destination through all the ports the frames must travel makes up the path cost.

When the BPDU is sent to the other bridges, it carries the port cost. The sum of all the port costs is the path cost. The spanning tree looks first at the path cost and decides which ports should forward and which ports should be blocked. If the path costs are equal for more than one port, then the spanning tree looks at the port ID. The bridge with the lower Bridge ID has priority, making that port the forwarding port. If the path cost and the Bridge ID are the same, then the STP will use the port ID then the port priority as the tiebreaker.

Assigning a Port Cost to a Port Using the Set/Clear-Based IOS

To manually change the port cost on a Set/Clear-based switch, use the following privileged mode command: (4 is the module number, 2 is the port number, and 10 is the configured port cost):

```
set spantree portcost 4/2 10
```

Assigning a Port Cost to a Port Using a CLI-Based Switch

To manually change the port cost on a Cisco IOS-based switch, use this Interface Configuration Mode command (10 is the port cost):

```
spantree cost 10
```

Tip: For both the CLI-based and Set/Clear-based switches, you should assign lower numbers to ports attached to faster media, such as FDDI, and higher numbers to ports attached to slower media, such as UTP. The possible value range is 1 to 65,535. The default differs for different media. The path cost is typically 1,000 divided by the physical wire speed in Mbps.

9

Verifying the Port Cost Configuration on Both a Set/Clear- and CLI-Based Interface

To verify the port cost on the port configured previously, use the following Privileged Mode command:

```
show spantree 4/3
```

The output on the console should look similar to this:

Port	Vlan	Port-State	Cost	Priority	Fast-StartGroup-method
4/3	2	forwarding	10	32	disabled
4/3	5	forwarding	10	32	disabled
4/3	2	forwarding	10	32	disabled
4/3	5	blocked	10	32	disabled

Assigning a Port Priority

The Spanning Tree Protocol port priority parameter can be modified to influence the links that are forwarding or blocking. The port with the lowest priority value forwards frames for all VLANs. In the event that all ports have the same priority value, the port with the lowest port number will forward the frames. The possible port priority value range is from 0 to 63. The default port priority value is 32. To change a port's priority, enter the following Privileged Mode command (4 is the module number, 3 is the port number, and 10 is the port priority):

```
set spantree portpri 4/3 10
```

Verifying the STP Port Priority on a Set/Clear- and CLI-Based Switch

To verify the proper port priority setting, use this command (only the module and port numbers are required):

```
show spantree 4/3
```

The output should look similar to this:

Port	Vlan	Port-State	Cost	Priority	Fast-StartGroup-method
4/3	3	forwarding	10	10	disabled
4/3	3	forwarding	10	10	disabled

```
4/3     6     forwarding     10    10     disabled
4/3     6     blocked        10    10     disabled
```

Setting the Port Priority on a Cisco CLI-Based IOS Switch

On a Cisco IOS-based switch, the priority value is a numerical value from 0 to 255. To set the port priority on a Cisco IOS-based switch, enter the following Interface Configuration Mode command (100 is the priority value):

```
spantree priority 100
```

Assigning VLAN Port Priority

Instead of setting the priority by port, you can set the priority on a per-VLAN basis. Configuring each port with a VLAN priority allows load sharing on links by allowing VLANs to individually determine which links to forward and which links to block.

Just as with the port priority setting, the lowest priority value gets to forward the frames. However, in this case, STP goes one step further and decides the value for each specific VLAN. If more than one or all the ports have the same priority value for a particular VLAN, the port with the lowest port number gets to forward the frames for that VLAN.

Configuring the port priority by VLAN is useful for distributing data across parallel paths. If a parallel connection exists between two devices, STP will block one of the links. Traffic from all VLANs will travel on one link, and one link will be used only as a backup. However, by changing the port priority for a specific group of VLANs, VLAN frames can be distributed across both of the links.

Adjusting the VLAN Priority on a Set/Clear-Based Switch

To change the port VLAN priority for a port on a Set/Clear-based switch, use the following privileged mode command (3 represents the module, 5 represents the port, 10 represents the priority, and 1-3 represents the range of VLANs):

```
set spantree portvlanpri 3/5 10 1-3
```

Verifying the VLAN Priority Settings

To verify the port's VLAN priority settings, enter the following command in privileged mode (only the module and port number are required):

```
show spantree 3/5
```

PVST and PVST+

To create a fault-tolerant large internetwork, continuous loop-free paths must exist between all interfaces in the network. STA calculates the least-cost, loop-free path throughout the switched network. Per-VLAN Spanning Tree (PVST) is a Cisco proprietary solution to the scaling and stability problems associated with CST in large-scale spanning tree networks. PVST creates a separate instance of PVST on each VLAN in the switch block. This setup gives each VLAN a unique STP topology containing its own port cost, path cost, priority, and root switch.

Using separate instances of PVST on each VLAN reduces the convergence time for STP recalculation and increases reliability of the network. By implementing PVST, the overall size of the spanning tree topology is reduced significantly. PVST also improves scalability and decreases the convergence time, providing faster recovery in the event of network faults. It also allows control of forwarding paths on a per-subnet basis while providing a simple technique for Layer 2 redundancy.

PVST does have some disadvantages in the spanning tree. PVST uses more processing power and consumes more bandwidth to support spanning tree maintenance and BPDUs for each VLAN. Inter-Switch Link (ISL) uses one spanning tree per VLAN, using PVST over ISL trunks. PVST implementation requires the use of Cisco ISL encapsulation in order to function.

Per-VLAN Spanning Tree Plus (PVST+) is not well documented by Cisco. IEEE 802.1Q can use PVST+ to map multiple spanning trees to the spanning tree of authentic IEEE 802.1Q switches.

You will find PVST+ available in Catalyst software versions 4.1 or newer. Cisco Catalyst switches configured with version 4.1 or later are considered Cisco PVST+ switches. A really great feature of PVST+ is its compatibility and interoperability with legacy-type Mono Spanning Tree (MST) and PVST switches without any user intervention of any kind. This gives PVST+ a type of plug-and-play functionality.

To provide support for the IEEE 802.1Q standard, Cisco's existing PVST has been modified with additional features, enabling it to support a link across the IEEE 802.1Q CST region.

PVST+ performs many useful functions, such as the following:

➤ Blocks ports that receive inconsistent BPDUs, to prevent forwarding loops. PVST+ also notifies users about all inconsistencies via syslog messages.

➤ Tunnels PVST BPDUs through the 802.1Q VLAN region as multicast data.

➤ Adds mechanisms to ensure that no unknown configuration exists.

➤ Eliminates inconsistencies related to port trunking or VLAN identification across the switches.

➤ Provides compatibility with IEEE 802.1Q's CST and Cisco's PVST protocols.

➤ Interoperates with 802.IQ-compliant switches using CST through 802.1Q trunking. A CST BPDU is transmitted or received with an IEEE standard bridge group MAC address.

➤ Transmits or receives a BPDU with Cisco's Shared STP (SSTP) address for each VLAN on a trunk. For VLANs equal to the PVID (native port VLAN), the BPDU is not tagged; however, for all other VLANs, BPDUs are tagged.

➤ Checks for port and VLAN inconsistencies.

Adjusting the Default Timers

You should modify the Hello, MaxAge, and FwdDelay timers during spanning tree network instability to influence the convergence times for different port states. The timers are included in STP to prevent bridging loops from occurring in the network. Having timers in place gives the network enough time to get all the correct information about the topology and to determine whether any unknown redundant links exist.

Using the default timers could take up to 50 seconds after a link failure for the link's redundant backup to take over. The length of time that the spanning tree takes to converge when a link fails can be too much for most protocols and applications, resulting in lost connections, session timeouts, and lost data.

You can configure three different timing parameters related to the timers on port states: MaxAge, Hello Time, and FwdDelay. Refer to Table 9.3 for a definition of each timer and the defaults for each.

Adjusting the FwdDelay Timer on a Set/Clear-Based IOS

To change the FwdDelay default setting, use the following Privileged Mode command (4 indicates a four-second delay and 3 indicates the VLAN):

```
set spantree fwddelay 4 3
```

Adjusting the Hello Time on a Set/Clear-Based IOS

To change the default Hello Time on the bridge, use this privileged mode command (4 indicates a four-second interval):

```
set spantree hello 4
```

Adjusting the MaxAge Timer on a Set/Clear-Based IOS

To change the default MaxAge timer for a particular VLAN, use this privileged mode command (5 refers to the MaxAge time and 1 refers to the VLAN):

```
set spantree maxage 5 1
```

EtherChannel

Fast EtherChannel and Gigabit EtherChannel both allow high-speed redundant links in a STP environment. These two protocols do this by allowing dual parallel links to be treated as though they were only one link. Cisco's Fast EtherChannel technology uses standards based on the IEEE 802.3 full-duplex Fast Ethernet standard that provide a high-speed solution for the campus network backbone.

Fast EtherChannel can provide scaled bandwidth within the campus using full-duplex bandwidth at wire for up to eight bundled links. A *bundle* is a series of links simulating a single link between two points in the network. This means that eight wires can be used to simulate one link and load balancing data across those links, as shown in Figure 9.7.

The following sections focus on several qualities provided by EtherChannel, after which you will prepare to configure, and then configure, EtherChannel.

Load Balancing

EtherChannel uses load distribution to share a group of links called a bundle. This load balancing enables the link to appear and carry data as though the bundle is one single physical link. Broadcast traffic, as well as unicast and multicast traffic, is distributed equally across all the links in the channel or bundle.

Link Failure

Fast EtherChannel also provides redundancy in the event of a link failure. The EtherChannel bundle is managed by the Fast EtherChannel process and the Ethernet Bundle Controller (EBC). If one link in the bundle fails, the EBC informs the Enhanced Address Recognition Logic (EARL) ASIC of the failure. The EARL ASIC then immediately ages out all addresses learned on that link. The EBC

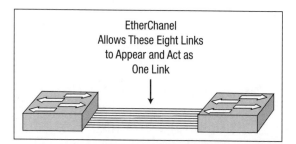

Figure 9.7   Eight equal cost links between two switches creating a bundle of eight channels acting as a single link.

Failover Time

The convergence time is sometimes referred to as the *failover time*. It is the time it takes for the new address to be relearned. Assuming that one packet to the destination results in an instant response, convergence takes place as quickly as 10 microseconds. This process may take longer, however, due to the windowing used by a particular application. In this situation, relearning should not take more than a few milliseconds, so no timeout occurs, and the user is never aware of the link failure.

and the EARL then recalculate in the hardware, sending queries to the other switches and learning the destination link based on the responses. The data traffic is then immediately rerouted on one of the other links in just a few milliseconds, making the convergence transparent to the user.

Port Aggregation Protocol

The Port Aggregation Protocol (PAgP) manages the Fast EtherChannel bundles and aids in the automatic creation of Fast EtherChannel links. PAgP packets are sent between Fast EtherChannel–capable ports. PAgP learns of the neighbors and their group capabilities dynamically and then informs its neighbors of the local group capabilities. After the protocol determines all the paired, point-to-point, or bidirectional links, the protocol groups into a single channel those ports that have the same neighbor device ID and neighbor group capability. Then, the channel is added to spanning tree as a bridge port.

Warning! Dynamic VLAN ports can force a VLAN change; therefore, PAgP cannot be used to form a bundle on ports that are configured for dynamic VLANs. The VLANs must be Static VLANs, meaning that the port on the switch must be assigned to a VLAN. PAgP also requires that all ports in the channel belong to the same VLAN or are configured as trunk ports.

If there is an already configured EtherChannel bundle and a VLAN of a port contained in the bundle is modified, all ports in the bundle are modified to match the VLAN configuration. PAgP will not group ports running at different speeds or duplex. You must configure PAgP by manually changing the port speed and duplex for all ports in the bundle.

All ports in a Fast EtherChannel bundle should be assigned to the same VLAN or configured as trunked ports. You must also configure both ends of the link with the same trunking mode.

Tip: You can configure the broadcast limits by percentage limit or by packets-per-second. Packets-per-second allows unicast packets to be dropped when the broadcast limit is exceeded.

Now that you have looked at EtherChannel and its components, you are ready to take a look at how to configure EtherChannel.

Getting Ready to Configure EtherChannel

When preparing to configure EtherChannel, you should check the following four items before configuring an EtherChannel bundle:

1. If a bundle uses trunked ports, each port must be configured with the same allowed VLAN range. If the VLAN ranges are not configured identically for both ends of all the trunked links in the bundle, the data traffic for the particular missing VLAN traffic is not allowed and the frames for that VLAN are dropped.

2. Trunked ports will form a channel when set to any two compatible modes using the **set port channel** command. Trunked ports on which VLANs are allowed will, however, continue to transmit data traffic across their trunk links.

3. You must verify that port security is disabled on all channeled ports. By enabling port security, the port shuts down when it receives packets containing a source address that doesn't match the secure address of the port.

4. All ports in a channel must be enabled. If any disabled ports are present, they are considered by the switch as link failures, and traffic for those ports is automatically transferred to any remaining ports in the bundle.

If these criteria are not met, you will receive an error for each item that is not configured correctly when you try to configure EtherChannel. To demonstrate these errors, I have configured a Cisco Catalyst 5002 switch with all the problems in the preceding list. At this point, ignore the configuration command, because it will be discussed shortly. However, look at the errors I receive when I try to enable EtherChannel on the switch:

```
Catalyst5002> (enable) set port channel 3/1-4 on

Mismatch in trunk mode.
Mismatch in port duplex.
Mismatch in STP port priority.
Failed to set port(s) 3/1-4 channel mode to on.

Catalyst5002> (enable)
```

Configuring EtherChannel on a Set/Clear-Based Switch

To configure EtherChannel on a Set/Clear-based switch, use the following command in privileged mode to verify that a line card is capable of being channeled on a Set/Clear command-based switch; then, compare the settings to make sure they match the other ports waiting to be configured as a bundle (3 is the module number and 1 is the port number):

```
show port capabilities 3/1
```

The output, which should look similar to the following, shows that the port is already configured to participate in a bundle:

```
Catlayst5002> (enable) show port capabilities 3/1

Model                    WS-X5509
Port                     3/1
Type                     100BaseTX
```

```
Speed                   100
Duplex                  full
Trunk encap type        ISL
Trunk mode              on
Channel                 3/1-4
Broadcast suppression   percentage(0-100)
Flow control            no
Security                no
Membership              static
Fast start              yes
Rewrite                 no

Catalyst5002> (enable)
```

You must create a bundle on two or more ports. On a Set/Clear-based switch, use the following privileged mode command to enable EtherChannel (3 is the module number and 1-4 are the port numbers):

```
set port channel 3/1-4 mode auto
```

Table 9.6 explains the syntax available for the mode option. The mode on each port can be set to either **on**, **off**, **auto**, or **desirable**.

To verify the EtherChannel configuration on a Set/Clear-based switch, use this command:

```
show port channel
```

Using the auto and desirable modes enables the configured ports to automatically negotiate whether or not to form a channel. The channel ports can be in different modes, as long as the modes are compatible. For example, if a port is in desirable mode, the port can form a bundle with another port that is in desirable or auto mode. If a link in a channel fails, the traffic that would have been carried over the failed link is automatically carried by the remaining link.

Table 9.6   The four mode options for configuring an EtherChannel bundle on a switch.

EtherChannel Mode Option	Mode Description
on	Enables the port to channel or bundle without any negotiation.
off	Disables the port from channeling or creating a bundle.
auto	Enables a port to negotiate the state in which the port will respond to PAgP packets it receives. The syntax does not, however, initiate PAgP packet negotiation. This is the default setting.
desirable	Enables a port to actively negotiate creation of a bundle with the port on the opposite side of the link by continuously sending PAgP packets.

Now that you have seen how to configure and troubleshoot the Set/Clear-based switch, you're ready to look at how to configure the IOS-based switch for EtherChannel.

Configuring EtherChannel on an IOS-Based Switch

To configure EtherChannel on an IOS-based switch such as the 1900 and 2800 series switches, use the global configuration **port-channel** command followed by the mode, which can be either **on**, **desirable**, or **auto**:

```
port-channel mode <on|desirable|auto>

Catalyst1900(config)# port-channel mode auto
```

With the IOS-based switches, you must identify the template port for the port channel parameters. To do this, use the following command in global configuration mode (Fast Ethernet 0/26 is port A on the 1900 series switch):

```
port-channel template-port <template port>

Catalyst1900(config)# port-channel template-port fastethernet 0/26
```

To verify the configuration on an IOS-based switch, use the privileged mode command:

```
show interface

Catalyst1900(config)# show interface


PortChannel is Enabled
802.1d STP State: ForwardingForward Transitions: 1
Port-channel mode: auto, preserve-order: Disabled
Port parameters template port: A
Active port: A
PortMemberPriorityCap.PartnerPartnerPartnerPartner
Device-idPort-idPriorityCap.
--------------------------
AYes128100-00-00-00-00-0000
BYes128100-00-00-00-00-0000
```

PortFast

When a switch using STP is powered up, the ports running STP go through four states before forwarding frames through each port. To get to the forwarding state, the STA makes each port wait up to 50 seconds before data is allowed to be forwarded on a port. This delay may cause problems with certain protocols and applications.

PortFast can be used on ports where a single server or workstation is connected, to allow a port to enter the forwarding mode almost immediately. This keeps the port from entering the listening and learning states and immediately transition into the forwarding state.

Enabling PortFast on a Set/Clear-Based Switch

To enable PortFast on a Set/Clear-based switch port, use the following privileged mode command (3 is the module number and 8 is the port number):

```
set spantree portfast 3/8 enable
```

Disabling PortFast on a Set/Clear-Based Switch

To disable PortFast on a Set/Clear-based switch port, use the following privileged mode command (3 is the module number and 8 is the port number):

```
set spantree portfast 3/8 disable
```

Enabling PortFast on an IOS-Based Switch

To enable PortFast on a Cisco IOS-based switch, use this interface configuration mode command:

```
spantree start-forwarding
```

Disabling PortFast on an IOS-Based Switch

To disable PortFast on a Cisco IOS-based switch, use this interface configuration mode command:

```
No spantree start-forwarding
```

9

Verifying the PortFast Configuration

To verify the PortFast configuration on a Set/Clear-based switch, enter the following Privileged Mode command (3 is the module number and 8 is the port number):

```
show spantree 3/8
```

UplinkFast

Convergence time is an important factor in a redundant link network. If network outages are still waiting for the links to converge after a failure, the redundant links are useless. The convergence time does a failover, and the time to reach a loop-free topology should not be lengthy. By implementing UplinkFast, you can reduce this time by optimizing convergence times, and ensure that a loop-free topology is maintained even during link faults or topology changes.

Because of the convergence time of STP, some end stations become inaccessible, depending on the current state of each switch port. By decreasing convergence time you reduce the length of the disruption. UplinkFast enables a port in a blocked state on a switch to almost immediately begin forwarding when the switch detects a link failure or a topology change. However, UplinkFast must have direct knowledge of the link failure in order to move a blocked port into a forwarding state.

An Uplink Group is a root port that is in a forwarding state and a set of blocked ports that does not include self-looping ports. The Uplink Group is the alternate path when the currently forwarding link fails.

UplinkFast should be placed only on Access-layer switches. UplinkFast is not designed for use within network Core-layer switches, such as the Catalyst 5000 and 6000 family of switches. Because it is a Core-layer feature, some people wonder why Cisco has not included this function on the Cisco Catalyst 8500 series switches.

To utilize UplinkFast, several criteria must be met. First, UplinkFast must be enabled on the switch and the switch must have at least one blocked port and the failure must be on the root port. When the failure occurs on the primary root link, UplinkFast transitions the blocked port to a forwarding state. UplinkFast changes the port status to forwarding, by ignoring the listening and learning modes. This occurs in about three to four seconds, allowing convergence to begin immediately without waiting for the MaxAge timer to expire.

Note: UplinkFast becomes a global setting on the switch. It affects all the VLANs on the switch and cannot be applied on just one individual VLAN. When you enable UplinkFast, it automatically increases the path cost, making it unlikely that the switch will become the root switch. If UplinkFast is not being used, you should use the Catalyst default settings.

Enabling UplinkFast on a Set/Clear-Based Switch

To enable UplinkFast on a Set/Cleat-based switch, use the following privileged mode command:

```
set spantree uplinkfast enable
```

Tip: Some other options to the **set spantree uplinkfast** command are available, such as adding a rate station update rate or adding the **on** or **off** syntax for all protocols. The station update rate value is the number of multicast packets transmitted per 100 milliseconds (by default, it is set to 15 packets per millisecond). For more information on how to execute a change in the rate station update rate, use the Help command on the console.

Disabling UplinkFast on a Set/Clear-Based Switch

To disable UplinkFast on a Set/Clear-based switch, use the following privileged mode command:

```
set spantree uplinkfast disable
```

Verifying the UplinkFast Configuration

To verify the UplinkFast configuration on a Set/Clear-based switch, you can use the following Privileged Mode command:

```
show spantree uplinkfast
```

You should get output similar to the following—notice that the VLANs followed by a comma, module number, and port number are forwarding to 3/1:

```
station update rate set to 15 paxkets/100ms.
uplinkfast all-protocol field set to off.
VLAN        port list
----        ---------
1           3/1(fwd)
2           3/2(fwd),3/1
2           3/3(fwd),3/1
5           3/4(fwd),3/1
```

Enabling UplinkFast on a Cisco IOS-Based Switch

To enable UplinkFast on a Cisco IOS-based switch, in global configuration mode, use this command:

```
uplink-fast
```

Disabling UplinkFast on a Cisco IOS-Based Switch

To disable UplinkFast on a Cisco IOS-based switch, in global configuration mode, use this command:

```
no uplink-fast
```

Viewing UplinkFast Configuration on an IOS-Based Switch

To view the UplinkFast configuration on an IOS-based switch, enter the following Privileged Mode command:

```
show uplink-fast
```

Viewing UplinkFast Statistics on an IOS-Based Switch

To view UplinkFast statistics, use this Privileged Mode command:

```
show uplink-fast statistics
```

BackboneFast

When the root port or a blocked port on a switch receives an inferior BPDU from its designated bridge, this event in turn triggers a root Link Query with the use of BackboneFast. Inferior BPDUs are sent when a root port link from the designated switch has been lost to the root bridge. The designated switch transmits these BPDUs with new information that it is now the root bridge as well as the designated bridge, and the BPDUs begin arriving on a port that is blocked on the switch. The switch receiving inferior BPDUs will ignore the message until the configured MaxAge Time timer has expired unless BackboneFast has been configured. If BackboneFast has been configured the MaxAge Time is expired as soon as the first inferior BPDU is received.

If inferior BPDUs continue to arrive after the MaxAge Time timer has been used, the root port and other blocked ports on the switch become alternate paths to the root bridge. The switch will send another kind of BPDU, called the root Link Query PDU, if more than one line exists to the root bridge. The switch will send a root Link Query PDU out all the available alternate paths to the root bridge to determine which one will forward.

If no other blocked ports exist, the switch automatically assumes that it has lost connectivity to the root bridge, causes the maximum aging time on the root to expire, and becomes the root switch. BackboneFast must be enabled on all switches in the network for this to function properly.

Note: *BackboneFast cannot be used in a token ring network.*

Enabling BackboneFast on a Set/Clear-Based Switch

To enable BackboneFast on a Set/Clear-based switch, enter the following privileged mode command:

```
set spantree backbonefast enable
```

Disabling BackboneFast on a Set/Clear-Based Switch

To disable BackboneFast on a Set/Clear-based switch, enter the following privileged mode command:

```
set spantree backbonefast disable
```

Viewing the BackboneFast Configuration

To view the configuration on a Set/Clear-based switch, use the following privileged mode command:

```
show spantree backbonefast
```

The output of this command is fairly simple:

```
Catalyst5002> (enable) show spantree backbonefast
Backbonefast is enabled.
Catalyst5002> (enable)
```

Chapter Summary

This chapter discussed Layer 2 switching and how redundant links are used to provide redundancy in a network. Redundant links are great in the event of a link failure, but they also cause problems in a network.

By using STP, you can stop network loops and prevent them from becoming broadcast storms, which can cripple your network. This chapter covered STP in detail, including the information you need to know to be successful in enabling and disabling STP in your Layer 2 switched network.

The following are some of the key points and features that you should review:

➤ The Spanning Tree Algorithm (STA) and the Spanning Tree Protocol (STP) are bridge-to-bridge link-management protocols that provide path redundancy while preventing loops in the network.

➤ BPDUs are never forwarded to another switch, but receipt of a topology change BPDU will cause a switch to generate a new BPDU and forward a topology change BPDU to another switch.

➤ STA is responsible for performing STP topology recalculations when a switch is powered up and when a topology change occurs.

➤ STP communicates topology changes from switch to switch with the use of Bridge Protocol Data Units (BPDUs).

➤ Common Spanning Tree (CST) is the IEEE 802.1Q solution to VLANs and spanning tree. CST defines a single instance of spanning tree for all the VLANs in a LAN, sending the BPDU information on VLAN 1 by default.

➤ Per-VLAN Spanning Tree (PVST) is a Cisco proprietary implementation on VLANs. PVST runs a separate instance of STP for every VLAN.

➤ Per-VLAN Spanning Tree Plus (PVST+) is a Cisco proprietary implementation that allows CST information to be transferred to PVST.

➤ CST allows for only one instance of STP for all VLANs on the switch. BPDUs are forwarded on VLAN 1.

➤ The *diameter* is a unit of measurement between the root switch and child switches. The measurement is calculated from the root bridge, with the root bridge counting as the first switch. Each subsequent child switch out from the root bridge is added to come up with the diameter number.

The end of the chapter reviewed the more advanced components of STP: EtherChannel, which enables you to bundle more than one physical link into a single channel; UplinkFast, which enables you to place a port in the forwarding state almost immediately; and BackboneFast, which allows for faster convergence during a link failure.

Review Questions

1. Which of the following enables you to bundle multiple physical links into a single logical link?

   a. EtherChannel

   b. BackboneFast

   c. UplinkFast

   d. DownlinkFast

2. STP was created to overcome the problems associated with what type of bridging?

    a. Transparent bridging

    b. Source route bridging

    c. Internet bridging

    d. Channel bridging

3. EtherChannel can be used only on which of the following types of links? [Choose the two best answers]

    a. Token ring

    b. Ethernet

    c. Fast Ethernet

    d. Gigabit Ethernet

4. Common Spanning Tree (CST) defines a single spanning tree for all the VLANs on a network. Which VLAN are Bridge Protocol Data Units sent on by default?

    a. VLAN 64

    b. VLAN 1005

    c. VLAN 1

    d. VLAN 10

5. Which Cisco Systems proprietary protocol provides for a separate instance of STP for every VLAN?

    a. Common Spanning Tree (CST)

    b. Spanning Tree Algorithm (STA)

    c. Port Aggregation Protocol (PAgP)

    d. Per-VLAN Spanning Tree (PVST)

6. To configure a switch as the STP backup root bridge for a Set/Clear-based switch, what command would be used?

    a. **set spanning tree backup**

    b. **set spantree backup**

    c. **set spantree secondary**

    d. **spanning tree 2**

9

7. The Catalyst 1900 and 2820 switches support 1,005 VLANs, of which how many can be configured to support STP?

   a. 1005

   b. 10

   c. 512

   d. 64

8. What is the command to use to change the VLAN port priority on an IOS-based switch to a value of 20?

   a. **set spantree priority 20**

   b. **spantree priority 20**

   c. **config spantree priority 20**

   d. **change spantree priority 20**

9. What is the maximum number of physical links that can be used in a single logical EtherChannel bundle?

   a. 4

   b. 8

   c. 16

   d. 64

10. Bridge Protocol Data Units (BPDUs) are responsible for providing information for which services in a spanning tree? [Choose the two best answers]

    a. Determining the locations of data loops

    b. Assigning a VLAN to a link

    c. Sending Trap messages

    d. Deciding the manufacturer's MAC address on a physical interface

    e. Notifying other switches of network changes

11. The VLAN port priority is a numerical value between what two numbers?

    a. 1 and 64

    b. 1 and 1005

    c. 0 and 63

    d. 1 and 10

12. PAgP is used to aid which protocol establish and maintain links?

    a. BackboneFast

    b. UplinkFast

    c. EtherChannel

    d. All of the above

13. If the port costs are equal on a switch using STP, STP refers to which value to make its forwarding decision?

   a. Bridge ID

   b. MAC address

   c. Bridge name

   d. Hello Timer

14. What is the default bridge priority value of a bridge designated as the secondary root bridge?

   a. 8,192

   b. 16,384

   c. 32,768

   d. 1

15. If two paths, such as a primary path and a secondary path, exist between two points in the network, the second path is referred to as which of the following?

   a. A cheaper path

   b. A redundant path

   c. A forced path

   d. A helper path

16. You can use dynamic VLANs with Fast EtherChannel.

   a. True

   b. False

17. Which of the following is not a timer used to influence the convergence time of STP?

   a. Hello Time

   b. MaxAge Time

   c. Link State Time

   d. FwdDelay

18. How many active root bridges are allowed in each instance of STP?

   a. 1

   b. 32

   c. 64

   d. 1,005

19. Without loop avoidance schemes in place, which of the following is a worst-case scenario?

    a. Slow convergence times

    b. A broadcast storm

    c. Links won't be able to send a multicast

    d. Serial link failure

20. Which of the following is the default priority of STP?

    a. 16,384

    b. 8,192

    c. 100

    d. 10

    e. 32,768

Real-World Projects

Joe Snow has just arrived at work to find out that he needs to train a new employee who has never used switches. He has mastered VLANs and has set up STP on a switch, but he now needs to know the advanced features of STP, including how to configure PortFast, UplinkFast, and EtherChannel.

To train the new employee, Joe has configured a quick lab consisting of a Cisco Catalyst 1912EN and a Cisco 5002 with a Supervisor Engine II card in slot 1 and a 10/100 card in slot 2, as shown in Figure 9.8.

This lab assumes that the configuration is a fresh startup configuration with only the hostname, interface descriptions, passwords, VTP domain information, IP address, IP default gateway, VLANs, and trunk links configured. (Make sure that the **no shut** command is used on interfaces fa0/26 and fa0/27.)

Project 9.1

To configure a 1900 Switch and a 5000 Switch, perform the following steps:

1. On interface e0/1, type **spantree start-forwarding**, which turns on PortFast for that port:

```
EN1912(config) interface e0/1
EN1912(config-if) spantree start-forward
```

2. Type **show spantree 1** to see which port is blocking and whether e0/1 or e0/2 is forwarding.

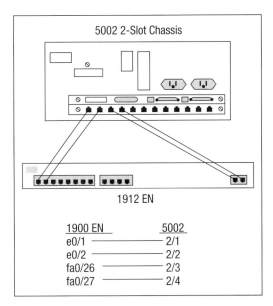

Figure 9.8 The Cisco 1912EN and 5002 lab port configuration.

3. Assuming that e0/1 is the forwarding port, use the **uplink-fast command** from global configuration mode to start uplink:

```
EN1912(config) uplink-fast
```

4. Move over and configure the 5002 series switch as the STP root switch by typing **set spantree root 1-10 dia 2** from the enable mode of the switch. The diameter of the network is determined by counting the switches connected to the root, including the root, which in this case is two. Remember that 1-10 identifies the VLANs to be configured.

5. If you use the command **show spantree 1**, you should notice that the switch is now the root bridge.

6. Verify that your ports 2/1 to 2/4 are trunked, by using the **show trunk** command on the 5002 series switch. If they are not trunked, refer to Chapter 8 and use the VLAN **set trunk** command.

7. Just for fun, change the port cost on the 1900EN's port 0/1. Remember in Step 2 that it was forwarding. Changing the port cost to 100 should make the blocked port now the forwarding port. To do this, use the **spantree cost 100** command from interface configuration mode for port e0/1:

```
EN1912(config) interface e0/1
EN1912(config-if) spantree cost 100
EN1912(config-if)
```

8. Use the **show spantree** command. You should now notice that the blocked port, which was e0/2, is now the forwarding port, and that the port costs have changed.

9. Next, change the port priority on port e0/2, which currently is forwarding. This will ensure that STP always uses this port to forward. Use the command **spantree priority 32** which is well below the default interface priority of 128.

```
EN1912(config) interface e0/2
EN1912(config-if) spantree priority 32
EN1912(config-if)
```

Project 9.2

To configure EtherChannel between the two switches, perform the following steps:

1. Recall that you shut down fa0/26(port A) and fa/27(port B), which are the 10/100 ports. You need to use the **no shut** command on each of those interfaces. You also need to go into interface configuration mode for ports e0/1 and e0/2 and shut down those ports so that they do not interfere with the EtherChannel you are creating.

2. Use the **show interface** command on both the 1912EN and the 5002 to verify that the duplex of the links to full duplex of both the 1912EN Fast Ethernet ports and the 5002 ports 2/3-4 are set to 100Mbps and full duplex.

3. Enable Fast EtherChannel bundle on the 1912EN switch by using the **port-channel mode on** command from global configuration mode.

4. On the 5002 switch, turn on EtherChannel by using the command **set port channel 2/3-4 on**.

5. At this point, you should be able to verify that the EtherChannel bundle is working by using the **show port channel** command.

CHAPTER TEN

Catalyst 5000 Troubleshooting

After completing this chapter, you will be able to:

✓ Troubleshoot switched connections

✓ Identify switch troubleshooting commands

✓ Troubleshoot switch hardware and software

✓ Troubleshoot VTP, ISL, and Spanning Tree Protocol configurations

✓ Identify switch troubleshooting and configuration software

✓ Recover a lost password

✓ Learn the diagnostic tools to apply to Catalyst 5000 problems

✓ Learning which diagnostic tools to apply to VLAN configuration problems

✓ Troubleshoot inter-VLAN routing configurations

✓ Troubleshoot trunk links and switches and routers

One of the latest innovations making its way into many networks is switches. In fact, Cisco is introducing so many new switching innovations and protocols that it seems natural that implementing different switches will cause implementation problems. Switches seem to be becoming the golden jewel of the century for manufacturers and customers alike.

Switches have provided so many advantages over hubs and bridges that Cisco has implemented components as well as software to support data traffic not only at Layer 2, but also at Layers 3 and 4.

This chapter covers the commands and techniques used to troubleshoot switches, the switch Internetwork Operating System (IOS), and switching components. The following are a few recommendations to help you refine your skills at troubleshooting switches:

➤ Learn the similarities between troubleshooting commands used on a Cisco router IOS and the Set/Clear command–based IOS used on the Catalyst 5000 family of switches.

➤ Regularly practice and perform labs that aid your knowledge in troubleshooting switching hardware and software. If you can't afford the equipment to practice on, many places are available on the Web that enable you to attach to a configurable network virtually through Telnet over the Internet.

➤ Find a mentor. When I entered this industry, I had a coworker who liked to play jokes on me by changing the configuration of my Cisco routers and switches. This turned out to be great training, because I then had to figure out what he did to the configuration. A manager even realized that this joking around was honing our troubleshooting skills, and thus recommended it as a common practice.

Most of the commands in this chapter are similar to the Cisco Command Line Interface IOS found on the Access and Core layer switches. However, the focus of this chapter will remain on the Set/Clear–command based IOS troubleshooting commands.

Troubleshooting Basics

This section defines the following switch basics:

➤ Broadcast and unicast forwarding

➤ Aggregate bandwidth

➤ Full-duplex and half-duplex

➤ Media types supported by hubs and switches

➤ Bridge and switch differences

Broadcast and Unicast Forwarding

When troubleshooting switches, knowing how switches and hubs treat broadcasts and unicasts can be an asset. A general rule to remember about unicasts is that on a switch, unicasts are sent only to the destination port unless the switch has not learned the port the destination resides on. In this situation, the switch forwards the unicast out all the ports that are members of the same virtual LAN (VLAN) of the source, with the exception of the port of arrival. A hub forwards unicasts and all data traffic out of its ports.

Broadcasts are sent to all the ports with the same VLAN membership as the receiving port, because everyone is the destination. A hub could care less about VLANs, and will send broadcasts to all of its ports.

Aggregate Bandwidth

Sometimes bottlenecks can develop in your network because the total number of ports that can bring data in equals more than the speed the trunk links can handle. For instance, a switch with 24 ports at 10 Mbps each is capable of providing a total aggregate bandwidth of 240 Mbps. If you have a 100 Mbps trunk link between switches, the total amount of data coming from the ports can overwhelm the trunk link and cause a bottleneck. On a hub, the speed of the entire network is always equal to the speed of the physical media. For example, if you have a 10BaseT hub, the hub provides a total of 10 Mbps of throughput.

10

Full-Duplex vs. Half-Duplex

Switches support half-duplex or full-duplex communications. *Full-duplex* refers to two-way communication that can take place simultaneously. A telephone call is an example of two-way communications. Both parties can speak and hear each other simultaneously.

Hubs support only half-duplex, which is communication that takes place on a single line. This can be similar to communication that takes place with a CB radio. The person holding down the button gets to speak while the other must listen. If both try to communicate simultaneously, a "collision" occurs.

Supported Media Types

The Catalyst 5000 family of switches can support multiple mixed physical media types, such as Token Ring, Ethernet, Gigabit Ethernet, and FDDI depending on the switch and the modules you have installed. The different modules in the Cisco Catalyst 5000 family provide the translations necessary between the physical media. Some differences exist between bridges and switches and the types of physical media supported.

Differences between Bridges and Switches

Bridges and switches can provide support for mixed physical media environments, depending on the configuration and components installed on them. Switches process frames using *application-specific integrated circuits (ASICs)*, which are chips that provide one or two tasks faster than a processor can. Bridges use software or generic hardware to provide processor tasks.

Another difference is the number of ports. Switches can provide ports that number in the hundreds. Bridges are typically 2- to 16-port devices.

Catalyst Switch Troubleshooting Software

Cisco Catalyst switches have quite a few network designs, diagnostics, and administrative tools available to administer Cisco switches. These tools are located in several pieces of software that are available from Cisco or third parties. For the exam, you need to know how to troubleshoot the switch issues with the Cisco Set/Clear IOS troubleshooting commands, Remote Monitor (RMON), and the components of CiscoWorks for Switched Internetworks (CWSI), which is software that's available from Cisco to manage a switched internetwork.

The next section looks at some of the components of CWSI and then looks at the troubleshooting commands that can be used on the Cisco IOS found on Cisco's line of enterprise switches.

CWSI

CiscoWorks for Switched Internetworks, also known as *Campus Manager,* can run as a standalone application on Windows NT or Unix operating systems. This includes Solaris, HP-Unix, and AIX. This application includes numerous components that aid not only in troubleshooting, but also in installing, designing switched networks, and monitoring. The following list describes these components, all of which are GUI applications:

➤ *CiscoView*—Provides a virtual look at the chassis, configuration, and performance monitoring (see Figure 10.1). This component provides very little in the way of troubleshooting functionality.

➤ *User Tracking*—Used in the creation and management of dynamic VLANs. Cisco switches permit VLAN assignments based on dynamic VLAN assignments. This means that the MAC address is used to assign the port to a specific VLAN. User Tracking defines these dynamic VLANs and maintains the whereabouts of workstations throughout the network.

➤ *VlanDirector*—A very powerful tool to aid in the creation of multiple VLANs on a switch. This tool helps the administrator add users and assign ports, and makes managing VLANs easy.

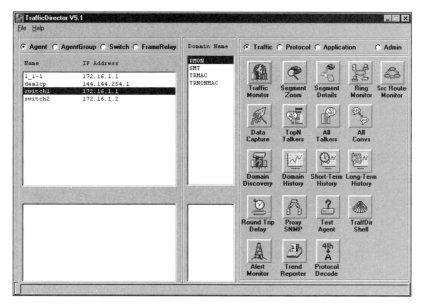

Figure 10.1   The CiscoView interface.

➤ *TrafficDirector*—A great tool to create usage baselines and troubleshoot switched environments. This tool, shown in Figure 10.2, enables you to view both the switched network and trunked and switched ports. TrafficDirector requires a VTP server to be configured in the network.

➤ *ATMDirector*—In Asynchronous Transfer Mode (ATM) networks, this tool can be used to configure, administer, and troubleshoot ATM switched networks.

RMON

Remote Monitoring is an industry-standard method used to provide statistics on a network using Simple Network Management Protocol (SNMP) as the medium to report its findings. A switch configured for RMON enables a network administrator to obtain information about a switch's Layer 1 and Layer 2 environment.

RMON collects a lot of information regarding the switch's physical connections, performance, configuration, and other pertinent statistics. After RMON is configured on the switch, it runs continuously even when no clients are checking statistics. In fact, communication with an SNMP management station is not necessary. RMON can be configured to send Trap messages to notify a management station when an error condition occurs that exceeds a currently configured maximum threshold.

Nine different groups are available that can provide RMON information, four of which can be configured to provide information on a Cisco Catalyst switch without an external device such as a Switched Port Analyzer (SPAN).

Figure 10.2 An example of the TrafficDirector GUI interface.

Cisco Catalyst switches support RMON information for Ethernet traffic for the following four groups:

➤ *Statistics*—This group's basic function is to maintain utilization and error statistics. It monitors collisions, oversized packets, undersized packets, network jabber, packet fragmentation, and multicast and unicast bandwidth utilization.

➤ *History*—This group provides periodical statistical information, such as bandwidth utilization, frame counts, and error counts that can be stored for later use.

➤ *Alarm*—This group enables you to configure thresholds for alarms and the intervals to check statistics. Any monitored event can be set to alarm the management station with a Trap message regarding an absolute or relative value or threshold.

➤ *Event*—This group's responsibility is to monitor log events on the switches. It also sends Trap messages to the management station with the time and date of the logged event. This enables the management station to be able to create customized reports based on the Alarm group's thresholds. Reports can be printed or logged for future use.

On Token Ring switches, RMON provides support for the following groups of the Token Ring extensions:

➤ *MAC-layer statistics*—A collection of statistics from the MAC sublayer of the Data Link layer, kept for each Token Ring interface. This group collects information such as the total number of MAC layer packets received and the number of times the port entered an error state.

➤ *Promiscuous statistics*—A collection of promiscuous statistics kept for non-MAC packets on each Token Ring interface. This group collects information such as the total number of good non-MAC frames received that were directed to a Logical-Link Control (LLC) broadcast address.

➤ *Ring station*—A collection of statistics and status information associated with each Token Ring station on the local ring. This group also provides status information for each ring being monitored.

➤ *Ring station order*—A listing order of stations on the monitored Token Ring network's rings.

Virtual LAN Troubleshooting

VLAN configurations were covered in great detail in Chapter 8. Encountering Cisco switches in small-, medium-, or large-sized networks with multiple VLANs configured to segment the network into smaller broadcast domains is not uncommon. As with any network electronic device, understanding the configuration and the ports assigned to each VLAN, and what nodes are attached to each port, can be crucial in troubleshooting. This may require you to have a well-documented network—not just the device locations, but also the locations where the jacks on the walls terminate in the wiring closet.

Another common occurrence is to encounter an unknowledgeable workforce who has placed switches in the wiring closet and has not configured any VLANs to segment the broadcast domain, thereby leaving all the devices in one VLAN, VLAN 1 (the default VLAN).

Next, you need to know what the IP configuration is for each component, and ensure that the switch is configured with the correct default gateway for each VLAN. The **show port** command is used to find and resolve these types of issues.

Inter-Switch Link

Because switches operate at Layer 2, a switch cannot forward data from one VLAN to another VLAN without a Layer 3 device, such as a router or internal route processor, to perform a Layer 3 resolution function. An Access layer port can carry the traffic of only one VLAN; a port that is trunked using ISL can carry more than one or all of the VLANs configured on the switches.

As discussed in Chapter 8, *Inter-Switch Link (ISL)* is a Cisco proprietary protocol used to interconnect two devices with a trunk link to carry multiple VLANs. ISL must be configured on a 10/100BaseTX port between two Cisco devices that support ISL. ISL operates in a point-to-point VLAN environment supporting up to 1000 VLANs. You can define VLANs as you would logical networks.

Chapter 8 covered switch-to-switch ISL-configured links in depth already, so this section covers router-to-switch troubleshooting. ISL is available on Cisco routers beginning with the 2600 series. Before you can configure ISL between two devices, however, some specific rules must be followed:

Note: Gigabit Ethernet trunk links default to IEEE 802.1Q encapsulation for creating a trunk port. Ethernet has the ability to negotiate whether ISL or 802.1Q encapsulation methods are being used. Fast Ethernet defaults to ISL as the trunking encapsulation method.

➤ Use ISL only on 100 Mbps or higher speed links. (A 10-Mbps link can be used, but this choice is not recommended.)

➤ Verify that you have sufficient memory on the switch or router, because ISL encapsulates and de-encapsulates the frame needing higher processing overhead.

➤ Use ISL+ to encapsulate Token Ring.

➤ Configure ISL links as point-to-point links.

802.1Q Standard

The IEEE 802.1Q standard is an industry standard for trunking and can be used when a Cisco device needs to have a trunked link to a non–Cisco device. On the Cisco router, you can use the **encapsulation dot1q** command on Cisco IOS version 12.0.1(t) or higher.

On the Catalyst 5000 series software version 4.1 or later, use the **set trunk** command:

```
catalyst5000> (enable) set trunk 2/1 ?
  <mode>                  Trunk mode
                            (on,off,desirable,auto,nonegotiate)
  <type>                  Trunk type
                            (isl,dot1q,dot10,lane,negotiate)
  <vlan>                  VLAN number

catalyst5000> (enable) set trunk 2/1 on dot1q
Port(s)  2/1 trunk mode set to on.
Port(s)  2/1 trunk type set to dot1q.

catalyst5000> (enable)
```

The 802.1Q header is somewhat different than that of the ISL header. Only 4 bytes are added to the frame. ISL adds 30 bytes to an ISL header and trailer. Instead of encapsulating the frame, as ISL does, 802.1Q adds the VLAN number inside the frame.

Most trunking issues result from a misconfiguration of the VLANs or the interfaces on each side of a trunk link. ISL and 802.1Q cannot be used on the same trunk link.

Inter-VLAN Routing Troubleshooting

The Route Switch Module (RSM) is one of many external modules and cards called *internal route processors* that are available for the 5000 and 6000 families of switches. These cards and modules give the switch a local resource to resolve Layer 3 addresses and perform inter-VLAN routing. Although the RSM is the focus for troubleshooting in this course and uses an IOS similar to that used on a router, you need to learn about other cards as well, which include the Multilayer Switch Module (MSM), Multilayer Switch Feature Card (MSFC), Route Switch Feature Card (RSFC), FlexWAN module, NetFlow Feature Card (NFFC), and NetFlow Feature Card II (NFFCII).

The internal route processor can be used to provide routing between VLANs. Using an external router to route between VLANs adds additional overhead and complexity that an internal route processor can relieve. An internal route processor on the switch uses an internal connection to the switch and does not need to use up an interface on the switch to create a trunk port from the switch to the internal route processor.

An external router should be used when you need a higher performance level, such as that provided by the 7000 series routers or the 12000 Gigabit Switch Router (GSR). You can also combine the RSM with a NetFlow Feature Card (NFFC or NFFC II), which is a daughter card that can provide multilayer switching (MLS).

The internal route processor uses an IOS that is similar to that used on a router. To access an internal route processor on the Cisco Catalyst 5000 family of switches, use the **session** command followed by the slot number:

```
catalyst5000>(enable) session 3

Building configuration...

Current configuration:
!

version 11.3
service timestamps debug uptime
service timestamps log uptime
no service password-encryption
!
```

10

```
hostname RSM1
!

interface Vlan1
 description VLAN1
 ip address 38.187.128.10 255.255.255.0
 no ip redirects
 standby 1 timers 5 15
 standby 1 priority 10
 standby 1 preempt
 standby 1 ip 38.187.128.11
```

To configure an external router for each type of connection, each VLAN must be defined on a subinterface, and the main interface must be left without a configuration. To keep track of the VLANs on an interface, it's good practice to make the subinterface number the same as the VLAN number. The following code displays the commands involved in configuring FastEthernet port 2, subinterface 1 for VLAN 1, and setting the encapsulation method on the link for ISL trunking:

```
interface fastethernet 0/2
no ip address
no shutdown
full-duplex
interface fastethernet 0/2.1
description vlan1
ip address 10.1.1.1 255.255.255.0
encapsulation isl 1
```

Incorrect VTP Revision Numbers

What happens when a new switch is configured as a server and the revision number is higher than the current revision number used in the domain? Oops! If the rest of the domain gets that information, it will reconfigure every single member with the configuration on that new switch. This event could mount to become a disaster on your network. Unfortunately, any time a switch sees a higher revision number, it takes the information it just received, considers it more current, and overwrites the existing database with the new configuration information.

Many network administrators make the bad mistake of using the **clear config all** command, believing that it will erase the current revision number. This command doesn't do what it says it does—it doesn't really "clear all." VTP has its own non-volatile random access memory (NVRAM), so the VTP information, as well as the revision number, will still be present if you execute the **clear config all** command. You can overcome the problem of not clearing the VTP configration in either of

Troubleshooting VLANs on Routers

The following are some commands that can be used to troubleshoot VLAN-related issues on Cisco routers. Some of the commands are similar to the IOS commands found on Cisco Catalyst switches.

- ➤ **debug spantree**
- ➤ **debug span**
- ➤ **debug vlan packet**
- ➤ **show arp**
- ➤ **show bridge**
- ➤ **show arp**
- ➤ **show cache**
- ➤ **show cdp neighbor**
- ➤ **show config**
- ➤ **show interface**
- ➤ **show span**
- ➤ **show spanning-tree**
- ➤ **show vlan**

10

two ways, the easiest of which is to cycle the power on the switch after placing the switch in client mode. The switch must be in client mode because the switch will store VTP information in the special NVRAM when the server is in server mode. As a result, merely powering down the switch will not reset the revision number or cause the switch to lose its VTP database.

The other way to address this problem is to make the switch a client. Connect it to the network to get new revisions and then configure the switch as a VTP server.

*Note: you can also reset the revision number with the **set vtp domain name** command but this command will not appear on the exam.*

Lost Password

A lost password on the Cisco Catalyst 5000 switch can be recovered using the following steps:

1. Attach a workstation to the console port.

2. Recycle the power on the switch.

3. Press the Enter key at the prompt. There is a null password for the first 30 seconds. This means that you can press the Enter key from the console because the password is blank.

4. Use the **enable** command and press Enter again for the password. Again there is a null password, meaning no password for the first 30 seconds.

5. Use the **set password** and **set enablepass** commands to set the password.

Troubleshooting Commands

Some command-line interface commands are available that can aid you in troubleshooting a switch. Likewise, a few GUI applications are available that you can use to simplify some of the functions of maintaining and configuring the Cisco IOS. These helpful applications are discussed later in this chapter.

This section looks at some of the commands that you can use to view the switch configuration and perform diagnostics to troubleshoot switch problems and configuration issues.

The following is a list of commands and an example of the output you should see when using these commands:

➤ **show cam**

➤ **show cdp**

➤ **show config**

➤ **show flash**

➤ **show interface**

➤ **show log**

➤ **show mac**

➤ **show module**

➤ **show port**

➤ **show spantree**

➤ **show system**

➤ **show test**

➤ **show version**

➤ **show vtp domain**

show cam Command

Problems occur when network devices are configured with identical MAC addresses on more than one interface of a switch. When this happens, particularly in the same broadcast domain, it can become a major problem in your network. Imagine ARP trying to resolve an IP address to a MAC address and getting more than one response.

Using the **show cam** command, you can view the list of known MAC addresses for interfaces attached to each switch port. Many dual-homed Unix workstations, such as those from Sun Microsystems, come with the same MAC address manually assigned on all the installed interfaces. This leaves the door wide open for a duplicate MAC address in the local network, preventing communication. If you are part of a network that divides the administration of network devices within the organization, it is recommended that a central process be created to review and document assigned MAC addresses, to avoid the problem of the same MAC address being assigned to more than one device in your network.

The following is an example of the output resulting from using the **show cam** command:

```
Catalyst5002> (enable) show cam ?

Usage: show cam [count] <dynamic|static|permanent|system>    [vlan]
       show cam <dynamic|static|permanent> <mod_num/port_num>
       show cam <mac_addr> [vlan]
       show cam agingtime

Catalyst5002> (enable) show cam dynamic 2

VLAN  Dest MAC/Route Des  Destination Ports or VCs
2     00-30-19-4C-80-A6   2/4
2     00-30-19-4C-80-A8   2/18
2     00-30-19-4C-80-A6   2/15
2     00-30-19-4C-80-A6   2/12
2     00-30-19-4C-80-BC   2/9
2     00-30-19-4C-80-3F   2/10
2     00-30-19-4C-80-D4   2/6
2     00-30-19-4C-80-B3   2/7
2     00-30-19-4C-80-A2   2/2
2     00-80-00-00-12-D0   2/22
2     00-30-19-4C-80-C4   2/1
2     00-30-19-4C-80-3B   2/23

Total Matching CAM Entries Displayed = 12
```

10

show cdp Command

Cisco Discovery Protocol is a Cisco proprietary protocol used to discover neighboring Cisco devices. The **show cdp** command displays the hardware, IOS version, active interfaces, and much more. This information is passed between Cisco devices through CDP packets sent between Cisco devices on physical media that supports SNAP.

CDP packets are multicast packets that are advertised by the Cisco router or switches but not forwarded. This protocol is available on Cisco IOS version IOS 10.3 and later. The **show cdp** command has two syntaxes. The following code shows the command and the output from the two available syntaxes:

```
catalyst5000> (enable) show cdp ?
  neighbors              Show CDP neighbors info
  port                   Show CDP port info
  <cr>

catalyst5000> (enable) show cdp
CDP              : enabled
Message Interval : 60
Hold Time        : 180
Version          : V2
catalyst5000> (enable)

catalyst5000> (enable) show cdp neighbors
* - indicates vlan mismatch.
# - indicates duplex mismatch.
Port     Device-ID                       Port-ID             Platform
----     ---------                       -------             --------
2/24     Router                          FastEthernet0#      cisco 1750
catalyst5000> (enable) show cdp port 2/24
CDP              : enabled
Message Interval : 60
Hold Time        : 180
Version          : V2

Port     CDP Status
----     ----------
2/24     enabled

catalyst5000> (enable)
```

show config Command

The **show config** command displays the entire configuration of the switch and its modules except for the installed ATM modules. Of course, the internal route processors are separate entities and store their own configurations, so those modules are not included in the output. The accumulation of all the information from these components provides a large amount of troubleshooting information. The output from this includes the configured passwords, system information, protocol settings, interface configurations, and system log settings.

The following is an example of the **show config** command and its output:

```
Catalyst5002> (enable) show config

.....

begin

!
set password $22$hgjhru^jf#sdc
set enablepass $22$hgjhru$fhkn
set prompt Catlayst5002
set length 24 default
set logout 0
set banner motd 'Unauthorized Use Prohibited!'

!
#system
set system baud  9600
set system modem disable
set system name  Catalyst5002
set system location Sacramento, CA
set system contact Sean Odom/Gina Galbraith
!
#snmp
set snmp community read-only       public
set snmp community read-write      private
set snmp community read-write-all all
set snmp rmon disable
set snmp trap enable  module
set snmp trap enable  chassis
set snmp trap enable  bridge
set snmp trap enable  repeater
set snmp trap enable  vtp
set snmp trap enable  auth
set snmp trap enable  ippermit
set snmp trap enable  vmps
```

10

```
!
#ip
set interface sc0 2 68.127.186.100 255.255.255.0 68.127.186.255
set interface sl0 0.0.0.0 0.0.0.0
set arp agingtime 1200
set ip redirect    enable
set ip unreachable    enable
set ip fragmentation enable
set ip route 0.0.0.0 68.127.186.254 0
set ip alias default 0.0.0.0

!
#Command alias

!
#vmps
set vmps server retry 3
set vmps server reconfirminterval 60
set vmps tftpserver 0.0.0.0 vmps-config-database.1
set vmps state disable

!
#dns
set ip dns disable
!
#tacacs+
set tacacs attempts 3
set tacacs directedrequest disable
set tacacs timeout 5
set authentication login tacacs disable
set authentication login local enable
set authentication enable tacacs disable
set authentication enable local enable
!
#bridge
set bridge ipx snaptoether 8023raw
set bridge ipx 8022toether 8023
set bridge ipx 8023rawtofddi snap
!
#vtp
set vtp domain Coriolis
set vtp mode server
set vtp v2 enable
set vtp pruneeligible 9-1005
clear vtp pruneeligible 1001-1005
set vlan 1 name default type ethernet mtu 1500 said 100001  state
 active
```

```
set vlan 1002 name fddi-default type fddi mtu 1500 said  101002 state
 active
set vlan 1004 name fddinet-default type fddinet mtu 1500  said 101004
 state active bridge 0x0 stp ieee
set vlan 1005 name trnet-default type trbrf mtu 1500 said  101005 state
 active bridge 0x0 stp ieee
set vlan 1003 name Token-Ring-default type trcrf mtu 1500  said 101003
 state active parent 0 ring 0x0 mode srb  aremaxhop 7 stemaxhop 7
!
#spantree

!
#uplinkfast groups
set spantree uplinkfast disable

!
#vlan 1
set spantree enable 1
set spantree fwddelay 15 1
set spantree hello 2 1
set spantree maxage 20 1
set spantree priority 32768 1

!
#vlan 2
set spantree enable 1
set spantree fwddelay 15 1
set spantree hello 2 1
set spantree maxage 20 1
set spantree priority 32768 1

!
#vlan 10
set spantree enable 1
set spantree fwddelay 15 1
set spantree hello 2 1
set spantree maxage 20 1
set spantree priority 32768 1

#vlan 1003
set spantree enable 1003
set spantree fwddelay 4 1003
set spantree hello 2 1003
set spantree maxage 10 1003
set spantree priority 32768 1003
set spantree portstate 1003 auto 0
```

10

```
set spantree portcost 1003 80
set spantree portpri 1003 4
set spantree portfast 1003 disable

#vlan 1005
set spantree enable 1005
set spantree fwddelay 15  1005
set spantree hello 2 1005
set spantree maxage 20 1005
set spantree priority 32768 1005
set spantree multicast-address 1005 ieee

!
#cgmp
set cgmp disable
set cgmp leave disable
!
#syslog
set logging console enable
set logging server disable
set logging level cdp 2 default
set logging level cgmp 2 default
set logging level disl 5 default
set logging level dvlan 2 default
set logging level earl 2 default
set logging level fddi 2 default
set logging level ip 2 default
set logging level pruning 2 default
set logging level snmp 2 default
set logging level spantree 2 default
set logging level sys 5 default
set logging level tac 2 default
set logging level tcp 2 default
set logging level telnet 2 default
set logging level tftp 2 default
set logging level vtp 2 default
set logging level vmps 2 default
set logging level kernel 2 default
set logging level filesys 2 default
set logging level drip 2 default
set logging level pagp 5 default

!
#ntp
set ntp broadcastclient disable
set ntp broadcastdelay 3000
```

```
set ntp client disable
set timezone PST 0 0
set summertime disable


!
#permit list
set ip permit disable
!
#drip
set tokenring reduction enable
set tokenring distrib-crf disable


!
#module 1 : 2-port 100BaseFX MM Supervisor
set module name 1
set vlan 1 1/1-2
set port channel 1/1-2 off
set port channel 1/1-2 auto
set port enable 1/1-2
set port level 1/1-2 normal
set port duplex 1/1-2 half
set port trap 1/1-2 enable
set port name 1/1-2
set port security 1/1-2 disable
set port broadcast 1/1-2 100%
set port membership 1/1-2 static
set cdp enable 1/1-2
set cdp interval 1/1-2 60
set trunk 1/1 auto 1-1005
set trunk 1/2 auto 1-1005
set spantree portfast 1/1-2 disable
set spantree portcost 1/1-2 19
set spantree portpri 1/1-2 32
set spantree portvlanpri 1/1 10
set spantree portvlanpri 1/2 10
set spantree portvlancost 1/1 cost 18
set spantree portvlancost 1/2 cost 18
!
#module 2 : 24-port 10/100BaseTX Ethernet
set module name    2
set module enable  2
set vlan 1 2/1-24
set port enable 2/1-24
set port level 2/1-24 normal
set port speed 2/11-24 auto
set port speed 2/19 10
set port duplex 2/1-2 full
```

10

```
set port trap 2/1-24  enable
set port name 2/1-24
set port security 2/1-24  disable
set port broadcast 2/1-24  0
set port membership 2/1-24  static
set cdp enable 2/1-24
set cdp interval 2/1-24 60
set spantree portfast    2/1-24 disable
set spantree portcost    2/11 10
set spantree portcost    2/12 10
set spantree portcost    2/17 10
set spantree portcost    2/18 10
set spantree portcost    2/19 100
set spantree portcost    2/21 10
set spantree portcost    2/1-10,2/13-16,2/20,2/22-24 19
set spantree portpri     2/1-24 32

!
#switch port analyzer
set span enable
!
#cam
set cam agingtime 1-2,10,1003,1005 300

end
```

show flash Command

The Cisco 5000 IOS uses a Set/Clear–based command set that is different from the IOS found on Cisco routers. The IOS is stored in the flash memory stored on the Supervisor Engine module. The **show flash** command reports the space required for the installed software and the version of code. This includes the file names, date installed, time installed, and file sizes.

The following is example output from installing a brand-new Supervisor Engine 3 module and software in a switch:

```
catalyst5000> (enable) show flash

-#- ED --type-- --crc---  -seek- nlen -length- ------date/time----- name
  1 .. ffffffff d45a43c9  4eae44  22  4894147 Aug 09 2000 14:09:25
    cat5000-sup3.5-5-2.bin

2707900 bytes available (4894276 bytes used)

catalyst5000> (enable)
```

show interface Command

The **show interface** command can be used to get the IP configuration of the Supervisor Engine module. The VLAN information shown is for the management VLAN for the SC0 interface. This is the interface assigned to the default Supervisor Engine used for configuring the IP information for the switch as well as the broadcast address. The following is the output:

```
Catalyst5002> (enable) show interface
sl0: flags=51<UP,POINTOPOINT,RUNNING>
        slip 0.0.0.0 dest 0.0.0.0
sc0: flags=63<UP,BROADCAST,RUNNING>
        vlan 1 inet 68.127.187.1 netmask 255.255.255.0 broadcast
    68.127.187.255
```

show log Command

Using the **show log** command, you can look at the significant events, including reboots of all the modules, traps, logged events, and power-supply failures. An example of the output for this command follows:

```
catalyst5000> (enable) show log

Network Management Processor (ACTIVE NMP) Log:
  Reset count:    30
  Re-boot History:    Aug 09 2000 14:26:18 0, Aug 09 2000 14:18:51 0
                      Aug 09 2000 13:44:30 0, Aug 09 2000 12:12: 8 0
                      Jul 07 2000 13: 5:32 0, Jul 07 2000 12:22:38 0
                      Jun 16 2000 16:53:25 0, Jun 16 2000 16: 7:48 0
                      Jun 16 2000 15:19:11 0, Jun 16 2000 12:17:32 0
  Bootrom Checksum Failures:       0   UART Failures:                  0
  Flash Checksum Failures:         0   Flash Program Failures:         0
  Power Supply 1 Failures:        23   Power Supply 2 Failures:       17
  DRAM Failures:                   0

  Exceptions:                      0

  Loaded NMP version:          5.5(2)
  Reload same NMP version count: 1

  Last software reset by user: 8/9/2000,14:25:15

  MCP Exceptions/Hang:             0

Heap Memory Log:
```

10

```
    Corrupted Block = none

    NVRAM log:

    01. 2/27/2000,15:28:39: updateRuntimeWithNVRAM:Redundancy switch over: 2
    02. 1/14/1999,15:36:45: updateRuntimeWithNVRAM:Redundancy switch over: 2
    03. 6/16/2000,12:18:16: updateRuntimeWithNVRAM:Redundancy switch over: 2
    04. 6/16/2000,16:57:26: updateRuntimeWithNVRAM:Redundancy switch over: 2
    05. 8/9/2000,14:21:41: convert_post_SAC_CiscoMIB:Block 0 converted from
        version 6 to 11
    06. 8/9/2000,14:22:17: supVersion:Nmp version 5.5(2.0)

    Module 2 Log:
      Reset Count:    2
      Reset History: Wed Aug 9 2000, 14:26:58
                     Wed Aug 9 2000, 14:22:40

    Module 3 Log:
      Reset Count:    2
      Reset History: Wed Aug 9 2000, 14:26:50
                     Wed Aug 9 2000, 14:22:32

    02. 1/14/1999,15:36:45: updateRuntimeWithNVRAM:Redundancy switch over: 2
    03. 6/16/2000,12:18:16: updateRuntimeWithNVRAM:Redundancy switch over: 2
    04. 6/16/2000,16:57:26: updateRuntimeWithNVRAM:Redundancy switch over: 2
    05. 8/9/2000,14:21:41: convert_post_SAC_CiscoMIB:Block 0 converted from
        version 6 to 11
    06. 8/9/2000,14:22:17: supVersion:Nmp version 5.5(2.0)

    Module 2 Log:
      Reset Count:    2
      Reset History: Wed Aug 9 2000, 14:26:58
                     Wed Aug 9 2000, 14:22:40

    Module 3 Log:
      Reset Count:    2
      Reset History: Wed Aug 9 2000, 14:26:50
                     Wed Aug 9 2000, 14:22:32

    Module 5 Log:
      Reset Count:    2
      Reset History: Wed Aug 9 2000, 14:27:13
                     Wed Aug 9 2000, 14:23:17

catalyst5000> (enable)
```

show mac Command

The output for this command is quite long, but it's very informative of the state of the switch ports. By using this command, you can display numerous counters that are maintained during normal operation on all the switch ports. These counters include information on the traffic for each port, the number of incoming frames, the number of frame discards, the total number of frames sent, and the maximum transmission unit (MTU) violations.

```
catalyst5000> (enable) show mac ?
  <mod>                        Module number
  <mod/port>                   Module number and Port number(s)
  <cr>

catalyst5000> (enable) show mac
```

MAC	Rcv-Frms	Xmit-Frms	Rcv-M	Xmit-M	Rcv-Broad	Xmit-Broad
1/1	0	0	0	0	0	0
1/2	0	0	0	0	0	0
2/1	33840	22431	53	323	2342	887
2/2	20941	21026	132	432	1284	95
2/3	7892	6489	134	445	1345	178
2/4	57376	33179	674	344	234	2548
2/5	34951	26135	138	142	12412	23134
2/6	0	0	0	0	0	0
2/7	0	0	0	0	0	0
2/8	0	0	0	0	0	0
2/9	0	0	0	0	0	0
2/10	0	0	0	0	0	0
2/11	0	0	0	0	0	0
2/12	0	0	0	0	0	0
2/13	0	0	0	0	0	0
2/14	0	0	0	0	0	0
2/15	0	0	0	0	0	0
2/16	0	0	0	0	0	0
2/17	0	0	0	0	0	0
2/18	0	0	0	0	0	0
2/19	0	0	0	0	0	0
2/20	0	0	0	0	0	0
2/21	0	0	0	0	0	0
2/22	0	0	0	0	0	0
2/23	0	0	0	0	0	0
2/24	0	0	0	0	0	0

MAC	Dely-Exced	MTU-Exced	In-Dcrd	Lrn-Dcrd	In-Lost	Out-Lost
1/1	0	0	0	0	0	0
1/2	0	0	0	0	0	0

10

Port						
2/1	0	0	0	0	0	0
2/2	0	0	0	0	0	0
2/3	0	0	0	0	0	0
2/4	0	0	0	0	0	0
2/5	0	0	0	0	0	0
2/6	0	0	0	0	0	0
2/7	0	0	0	0	0	0
2/8	0	0	0	0	0	0
2/9	0	0	0	0	0	0
2/10	0	0	0	0	0	0
2/11	0	0	0	0	0	0
2/12	0	0	0	0	0	0
2/13	0	0	0	0	0	0
2/14	0	0	0	0	0	0
2/15	0	0	0	0	0	0
2/16	0	0	0	0	0	0
2/17	0	0	0	0	0	0
2/18	0	0	0	0	0	0
2/19	0	0	0	0	0	0
2/20	0	0	0	0	0	0
2/21	0	0	0	0	0	0
2/22	0	0	0	0	0	0
2/23	0	0	0	0	0	0
2/24	0	0	0	0	0	0

Port	Rcv-Unicast	Rcv-Multicast	Rcv-Broadcast
1/1	0	0	0
1/2	0	0	0
2/1	324453	245	56778
2/2	1443834	735	566432
2/3	99675	3467	66432
2/4	345562	453	77645
2/5	0	0	0
2/6	0	0	0
2/7	0	0	0
2/8	0	0	0
2/9	0	0	0
2/10	0	0	0
2/11	0	0	0
2/12	0	0	0
2/13	0	0	0
2/14	0	0	0
2/15	0	0	0
2/16	0	0	0
2/17	0	0	0
2/18	0	0	0

Port		
2/19	0	0	0
2/20	0	0	0
2/21	0	0	0
2/22	0	0	0
2/23	0	0	0
2/24	0	0	0

Port	Xmit-Unicast	Xmit-Multicast	Xmit-Broadcast
1/1	0	0	0
1/2	0	0	0
2/1	1819	141	97
2/2	798	140	101
2/3	6260	195	83
2/4	921	195	107
2/5	0	0	0
2/6	0	0	0
2/7	0	0	0
2/8	0	0	0
2/9	0	0	0
2/8	0	0	0
2/9	0	0	0
2/10	0	0	0
2/11	0	0	0
2/12	0	0	0
2/13	0	0	0
2/14	0	0	0
2/15	0	0	0
2/16	0	0	0
2/17	0	0	0
2/18	0	0	0
2/19	0	0	0
2/20	0	0	0
2/21	0	0	0
2/22	0	0	0
2/23	0	0	0
2/24	0	0	0

Port	Rcv-Octet	Xmit-Octet
1/1	0	0
1/2	0	0
2/1	2345671	436529
2/2	3442473	465641
2/3	6734553	6345366
2/4	234434	563892
2/5	3265	3545

10

```
 2/6                            0                    0
 2/7                            0                    0
 2/8                            0                    0
 2/9                            0                    0
 2/10                           0                    0
 2/11                           0                    0
 2/12                           0                    0
 2/13                           0                    0
 2/14                           0                    0
 2/15                           0                    0
 2/16                           0                    0
 2/17                           0                    0
 2/18                           0                    0
 2/19                           0                    0
 2/20                           0                    0
 2/21                           0                    0
 2/22                           0                    0
 2/23                           0                    0
 2/24                           0                    0


Last-Time-Cleared
-----------------
Sat Aug 12 2000, 12:24:19


catalyst5000> (enable) show mac 2/24

Port     Rcv-Unicast         Rcv-Multicast        Rcv-Broadcast
----     -----------         -------------        -------------
2/24     71050               6221                 166

Port     Xmit-Unicast        Xmit-Multicast       Xmit-Broadcast
----     -----------         -------------        -------------
2/24     69874               213965               1

Port     Rcv-Octet           Xmit-Octet
----     -----------         ----------
2/24     7245197             20334845

MAC      Dely-Exced  MTU-Exced   In-Discard  Lrn-Discrd  In-Lost   Out-Lost
---      ----------  ---------   ----------  ----------  -------   --------
2/24     0           0           0           0           0         0


Last-Time-Cleared
-----------------
Wed Aug 9 2000, 14:26:21
catalyst5000> (enable)
```

show module Command

This command displays the modules located inside the switch chassis, or each individual module, by identifying a module number. The following is example output from using the **show module** command on a Cisco Catalyst 5000 switch:

```
catalyst5000> (enable) show module

Mod Slot Ports Module-Type          Model       Sub Status
--- ---- ----- -----------          -----       --- ------
1   1    0     Supervisor III       WS-X5530    yes ok
2   2    24    10/100BaseTX Ethernet WS-X5225R  no  ok
3   3    12    100BaseFX MM Ethernet WS-X5111   no  ok
5   5    1     Network Analysis/RMON WS-X5380   no  ok

Mod Module-Name        Serial-Num
--- -----------        ----------
1                      00011454261
2                      00013426578
3                      00003975931
5                      00012148595

Mod MAC-Address(es)                        Hw   Fw    Sw
--- ---------------                        --   --    --
1   00-50-bd-a0-b0-00 to 00-50-bd-a0-b3-ff 2.0  3.1.2 5.5(2)
2   00-d0-06-a1-de-a8 to 00-d0-06-a1-de-bf 3.3  4.3(1) 5.5(2)
3   00-60-5c-21-b5-24 to 00-60-5c-21-b5-2f 1.0  1.3   5.5(2)
5   00-60-09-ff-77-5c                      1.1  4.3.2 4.3(1a)

Mod Sub-Type Sub-Model Sub-Serial Sub-Hw
--- -------- --------- ---------- ------

Mod Slot Ports Module-Type          Model       Sub Status
--- ---- ----- -----------          -----       --- ------
1   1    0     Supervisor III       WS-X5530    yes ok
2   2    24    10/100BaseTX Ethernet WS-X5225R  no  ok
3   3    12    100BaseFX MM Ethernet WS-X5111   no  ok
5   5    1     Network Analysis/RMON WS-X5380   no  ok

Mod Module-Name        Serial-Num
--- -----------        ----------
1                      00011454261
2                      00013426578
3                      00003975931
5                      00012148595
```

```
Mod MAC-Address(es)                             Hw    Fw      Sw
--- ---------------                             --    --      --
1   00-50-bd-a0-b0-00 to 00-50-bd-a0-b3-ff 2.0  3.1.2   5.5(2)
2   00-d0-06-a1-de-a8 to 00-d0-06-a1-de-bf 3.3  4.3(1)  5.5(2)
3   00-60-5c-21-b5-24 to 00-60-5c-21-b5-2f 1.0  1.3     5.5(2)
5   00-60-09-ff-77-5c                       1.1  4.3.2   4.3(1a)


Mod Sub-Type Sub-Model Sub-Serial Sub-Hw
--- -------- --------- ---------- ------
1   NFFC     WS-F5521  0011455134 1.1


catalyst5000> (enable)
```

Now, look at the module in slot 3 using the **show module** command followed by the slot number:

```
catalyst5000> (enable) show module 3


Mod Slot Ports Module-Type           Model         Sub Status
--- ---- ----- -----------           -----         --- ------
3   3    12    100BaseFX MM Ethernet  WS-X5111      no  ok


Mod Module-Name       Serial-Num
--- -----------       ----------
3                     00003975931


Mod MAC-Address(es)                             Hw    Fw      Sw
--- ---------------                             --    --      --
3   00-60-5c-21-b5-24 to 00-60-5c-21-b5-2f 1.0  1.3     5.5(2)


catalyst5000> (enable)
```

show port Command

With the **show port** command, you can obtain specific information about a single port or all the ports on a specified module. The **show port** command output for module 2, port 1 follows:

```
catalyst5000> (enable) show port 2/1


Port  Name   Status    Vlan Level  Duplex Speed  Type
----  ----   ------    ---- -----  ------ -----  ----
2/1   Port1  normal    2    normal full   100    10/100BaseTX
```

```
Port Security Secure-Src-Addr Last-Src-Addr  Shutdown Trap
---- -------- --------------- -------------- -------- ----
2/1  enabled  0090.80a3.32a0  0090.80a3.32a0 No       disabled


Port    Broadcast-Limit Broadcast-Drop
----    --------------- --------------
2/1                   -              -


Port   Status      Channel  Channel  Neighbor     Neighbor
                   Mode     status   device       port
----   ------      -------  -------  --------     --------
2/1    connected   on       not channel


Port  Align-Err FCS-Err  Xmit-Err  Rcv-Err  UnderSize
----  --------- -------  --------  -------  ---------
2/1   0         0        6         0        0


Port  Single-Col Multi-Coll Late-Coll Excess-Col Carri-Sen Runts Giants
----  ---------- ---------- --------- ---------- --------- ----- ------
2/1   3442       603        0         0          0         1     0


Last-Time-Cleared
-----------------
Wed Aug 9 2000, 14:26:21


catalyst5000> (enable)
```

Other **show port** command syntaxes can be used to troubleshoot port and port-related protocol issues. The following is output of the available syntaxes for the **show port** command:

```
catalyst5000> (enable) show port ?
  auxiliaryvlan             Show port auxiliary vlan information
  broadcast                 Show port broadcast information
  cdp                       Show port CDP information
  capabilities              Show port capabilities
  channel                   Show port channel information
  counters                  Show port counters
  fddi                      Show port FDDI information
  flowcontrol               Show port traffic flowcontrol
  filter                    Show Token Ring port filtering information
  ifindex                   Show port IfIndex information
  mac                       Show port MAC counters
  negotiation               Show port flowcontrol negotiation
  protocol                  Show port protocol membership
  qos                       Show port QoS information
```

10

```
        security                    Show port security information
        spantree                    Show port spantree information
        status                      Show port status
        trap                        Show port trap information
        trunk                       Show port trunk information
        <mod>                       Module number
        <mod/port>                  Module number and Port number(s)
        <cr>
catalyst5000> (enable) show port
```

show spantree Command

This command can be used to display the Spanning Tree Protocol configuration, which is a significant protocol in today's redundant-link networks. The output from this command can provide information about whether STP is enabled or disabled; the bridge or port priorities; the root bridge priorities; the path cost to the root; the BPDU; the bridge MAC address; the timer; the port states; and the fast-start configuration of each port. This command is similar on the Set/Clear IOS and the CLI-based IOS. Let's look at an example of the output:

```
catalyst5000> (enable) show spantree


VLAN 1
Spanning tree enabled
Spanning tree type          ieee

Designated Root             00-50-bd-a0-b0-00
Designated Root Priority    32768
Designated Root Cost        0
Designated Root Port        1/0
Root Max Age    12 sec   Hello Time 2  sec   Forward Delay 9  sec

Bridge ID MAC ADDR          00-50-bd-a0-b0-00
Bridge ID Priority          32768
Bridge Max Age 12 sec   Hello Time 2  sec   Forward Delay 9  sec

Port            Vlan Port-State    Cost  Priority Portfast  Channel_id
----            ---- ----------    ----  -------- --------  ----------
    2/1          1   not-connected  19        32 enabled   0
    2/2          1   not-connected  19        32 enabled   0
    2/3          1   not-connected  19        32 enabled   0
    2/4          1   not-connected  19        32 enabled   0
    2/5          1   not-connected  19        32 enabled   0
    2/6          1   not-connected  19        32 disabled  0
    2/7          1   not-connected  19        32 disabled  0
    2/7          1   not-connected  19        32 disabled  0
```

```
2/8       1    not-connected   19    32 disabled   0
2/9       1    not-connected   100   32 disabled   0
2/10      1    not-connected   100   32 disabled   0
2/11      1    not-connected   100   32 disabled   0
2/12      1    not-connected   100   32 disabled   0
2/13      1    not-connected   100   32 disabled   0
2/14      1    not-connected   100   32 disabled   0
2/15      1    not-connected   100   32 disabled   0
2/16      1    not-connected   100   32 disabled   0
2/17      1    not-connected   100   32 disabled   0
2/18      1    not-connected   100   32 disabled   0
2/19      1    not-connected   100   32 disabled   0
2/20      1    not-connected   100   32 disabled   0
2/21      1    not-connected   100   32 disabled   0
2/22      1    not-connected   100   32 disabled   0
2/23      1    not-connected   100   32 disabled   0
2/24      1    forwarding      19    32 disabled   0
```

show system Command

The **show system** command enables you to obtain the component status of the switch components. These components include information on the status of the fans, power supplies, modem, uptime, and system identification configuration.

The output on a Cisco Catalyst 5002 follows:

```
catalyst5000> show system

PS1-Status PS2-Status
---------- ----------
ok         none


Fan-Status Temp-Alarm Sys-Status Uptime d,h:m:s Logout
---------- ---------- ---------- -------------- ------
ok         off        ok          5,05:45:19     20 min


PS1-Type    PS2-Type
--------    --------
WS-C5008A   none


Modem    Baud  Traffic Peak Peak-Time
-----    ----  ------- ---- ---------
disable  9600  0%      0% Wed Aug 9 2000, 14:26:21


System Name  System Location    System Contact
-----------  ---------------    --------------
             Sacramento, CA     Sean Odom/Gina Galbraith
```

show test Command

The **show test** command is used to display the status of the switch chassis, interface cards, power supplies, Encoded Address and Recognition Logic (EARL) ASIC
status tests, and whether an active loopback exists. It also displays the memory status
of the read-only memory (ROM), flash EEPROM, serial EEPROM, and the
nonvolatile RAM.

An example of the **show test** command output follows:

```
catalyst5000> (enable) show test

Diagnostic mode: complete    (mode at next reset: complete)

Environmental Status (. = Pass, F = Fail, U = Unknown, N = Not Present)
   PS (3.3V):    .   PS (12V): .   PS (24V):    .   PS1: .      PS2: N
   Temperature: .   Fan:       .

Module 1 : 0-port Supervisor III
Network Management Processor (NMP) Status: (. = Pass, F = Fail, U =
   Unknown)
   ROM:   .   Flash-EEPROM: .   Ser-EEPROM: .   NVRAM: .   MCP Comm: .

   EARL II Status :
         DisableIndexLearnTest:          U
         DontLearnTest:                  U
         DisableNewLearnTest:            U
         ConditionalLearnTest:           U
         MonitorColorFloodTest:          U
         EarlTrapTest:                   U
         StaticMacAndTypeTest:           U
         BadDvlanTest:                   U
         BadBpduTest:                    U
         IndexMatchTest:                 U
         ProtocolTypeTest:               U
         ProtocolTypeTest:               U
         IgmpTest:                       U
         SourceMissTest:                 U
         SourceModifiedTest:             U
         ArpaToArpaShortcutTest:         U
         ArpaToSnapShortcutTest:         U
         SnapToArpaShortcutTest:         U
         SnapToSnapShortcutTest:         U
         SoftwareShortcutTest:           U
         MulticastExpansionTest:         U
         DontShortcutTest:               U
         ShortcutTableFullTest:          U
```

```
Line Card Diag Status for Module 1  (. = Pass, F = Fail, N = N/A)
 CPU         : .    Sprom    : .    Bootcsum : .    Archsum  : .
 RAM         : .    LTL      : .    CBL      : N    DPRAM     : . SAMBA : N
 Saints      : .    Pkt Bufs : .    Repeater : N    FLASH     : .
 Phoenix     : . TrafficMeter: . UplinkSprom : .  PhoenixSprom: .


 SAINT/SAGE Status :


 PHOENIX Port Status :
SAINT/SAGE Status :


 PHOENIX Port Status :
  Ports 9    17    18    19    20    21    22
      INBAND A->B  B->A  B->C  C->B  A->C  C->A
      ------------------------------------------
            .     .     .     .     .     .     .


 Packet Buffer Status :


 PHOENIX Packet Buffer Status :
  Ports INBAND A<->B B<->C A<->C
  ------------------------------
          .     .     .     .


 Loopback Status [Reported by Module 1] :
  Ports  1  2  9
  --------------
         U  U  .


catalyst5000> (enable)
```

To display a test on a specific module, use the module number after the command. In this case I have a 24-port 10/100BaseTX module in slot 2:

```
catalyst5000> (enable) show test 2

Diagnostic mode: complete   (mode at next reset: complete)


Module 2 : 24-port 10/100BaseTX Ethernet

Line Card Diag Status for Module 2  (. = Pass, F = Fail, N = N/A)
  CPU        : .    Sprom    : .    Bootcsum : .    Archsum   : N
  RAM        : .    LTL      : .    CBL      : .    DPRAM     : N SAMBA : .
  Saints     : .    Pkt Bufs : .    Repeater : N    FLASH     : N
```

10

```
    SAINT/SAGE Status :
    Ports 1 2 3 4 5 6 7 8 9 10 11 12 13 14 15 16 17 18 19 20 21 22 23 24
    -----------------------------------------------------------------
            . . . . . . . . . . . . . . . . . . . . . . . .


    Packet Buffer Status :
    Ports 1 2 3 4 5 6 7 8 9 10 11 12 13 14 15 16 17 18 19 20 21 22 23 24
    -----------------------------------------------------------------
            . . . . . . . . . . . . . . . . . . . . . . . .


    Loopback Status [Reported by Module 1] :
    Ports 1 2 3 4 5 6 7 8 9 10 11 12 13 14 15 16 17 18 19 20 21 22 23 24
    -----------------------------------------------------------------
            . . . . . . . . . . . . . . . . . . . . . . . .


    Packet Buffer Status :
    Ports 1 2 3 4 5 6 7 8 9 10 11 12 13 14 15 16 17 18 19 20 21 22 23 24
    -----------------------------------------------------------------
            . . . . . . . . . . . . . . . . . . . . . . . .


    Loopback Status [Reported by Module 1] :
    Ports 1 2 3 4 5 6 7 8 9 10 11 12 13 14 15 16 17 18 19 20 21 22 23 24
    -----------------------------------------------------------------
            . . . . . . . . . . . . . . . . . . . . . . . .


    Channel Status :
    Ports 1 2 3 4 5 6 7 8 9 10 11 12 13 14 15 16 17 18 19 20 21 22 23 24
    -----------------------------------------------------------------
            . . . . . . . . . . . . . . . . . . . . . . . .


    InlineRewrite Status :
    Ports 1 2 3 4 5 6 7 8 9 10 11 12 13 14 15 16 17 18 19 20 21 22 23 24
    -----------------------------------------------------------------
            . . . . . . . . . . . . . . . . . . . . . . . .
```

show version Command

The **show version** command is used to provide hardware and software version numbers in addition to the switch memory and the system uptime information. An example of this command follows:

```
catalyst5000> (enable) show version

WS-C5000 Software, Version McpSW: 5.5(2) NmpSW: 5.5(2)
Copyright (c) 1995-2000 by Cisco Systems
```

```
NMP S/W compiled on Jul 28 2000, 16:43:52
MCP S/W compiled on Jul 28 2000, 16:38:40

System Bootstrap Version: 3.1.2

Hardware Version: 2.0  Model: WS-C5000  Serial #: 011454261

Mod Port Model      Serial #  Versions
--- ---- -----      --------  --------
1   0    WS-X5530   011454261 Hw : 2.0
                              Fw : 3.1.2
                              Fw1: 4.2(1)
                              Sw : 5.5(2)
         WS-F5521   011455134 Hw : 1.1
2   24   WS-X5225R  013426578 Hw : 3.3
                              Fw : 4.3(1)
                              Sw : 5.5(2)
3   12   WS-X5111   003975931 Hw : 1.0
                              Fw : 1.3
                              Sw : 5.5(2)
5   1    WS-X5380   012148595 Hw : 1.1
Mod Port Model      Serial #  Versions
--- ---- -----      --------  --------
1   0    WS-X5530   011454261 Hw : 2.0
                              Fw : 3.1.2
                              Fw1: 4.2(1)
                              Sw : 5.5(2)
         WS-F5521   011455134 Hw : 1.1
2   24   WS-X5225R  013426578 Hw : 3.3
                              Fw : 4.3(1)
                              Sw : 5.5(2)
3   12   WS-X5111   003975931 Hw : 1.0
                              Fw : 1.3
                              Sw : 5.5(2)
5   1    WS-X5380   012148595 Hw : 1.1
                              Fw : 4.3.2
                              Sw : 4.3(1a)

        DRAM                   FLASH                  NVRAM
Module Total   Used    Free   Total   Used   Free   Total Used Free
------ -----   ----    ----   -----   ----   ----   ----- ---- ----
1      32640K  20434K  12206K 8192K   5548K  2644K  512K  185K 327K

Uptime is 4 days, 4 hours, 13 minutes

catalyst5000> (enable)
```

10

show vtp domain Command

The VLAN Trunk Protocol (VTP) is used to maintain a consistent VLAN configuration throughout the switches in the network. In a VTP management domain, a configuration change is done only once on a VTP server–configured switch. The new configuration is propagated throughout the network. The **show vtp domain** command provides the status and configuration information for VTP.

An example of using the **show vtp domain** command follows:

```
catalyst5000> (enable) show vtp ?
  domain                        Show VTP domain information
  statistics                    Show VTP statistic information

catalyst5000> (enable) show vtp domain

Domain Name  Domain Index  VTP Version  Local Mode  Password
-----------  ------------  -----------  ----------  --------
Coriolis     1             2            server      sean1

Vlan-count Max-vlan-storage Config Revision Notifications
---------- ---------------- ---------------- -------------
5          1023             355              enabled

Last Updater   V2 Mode  Pruning  PruneEligible on Vlans
------------   -------  -------  ----------------------
68.38.127.5    enabled  enabled  2-1000

catalyst5000> (enable)
```

Hardware Troubleshooting

Before you can understand troubleshooting of the switch, you need to understand the switch architecture and the internal components of a switch. This section first looks at the internal architecture of the switch and then moves on to hardware troubleshooting and problem-resolution steps.

The Catalyst 5000 Architecture

The switch's architecture consists of several components, such as the following ASICs (the first three are subcategorized as logic units):

➤ CBL ASIC

➤ EARL ASIC

➤ LTL ASIC

➤ Phoenix ASIC

➤ SAINT ASIC

➤ SAGE ASIC

➤ SAMBA ASIC

There are many ASICs which switches use to provide only one or two specific tasks faster than using a CPU can perform these tasks. ASICs are much faster and allow fast data transfers without introducing the latency associated with bridging and routing performed by the CPU in routers. Figure 10.3 shows a diagram of the Cisco switch architecture of the Cisco Catalyst 5000.

The Catalyst 5000 family of switches uses a 761-Kbps management bus to control the switching process for the Ethernet, Token Ring, Fiber Distributed Data Interface (FDDI), and ATM line modules. This allows the incoming and outgoing frames to use a separate 1.2 or 3.6 Gbps backplane, depending on the model of switch being used. These buses interconnect various cards within the chassis for Ethernet, Token Ring, FDDI, and, in some cases, ATM.

Table 10.1 shows the 5000 family of switch models, the available slots, and the forwarding rate for each switch.

10

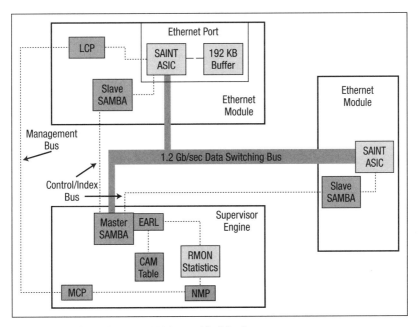

Figure 10.3   Cisco Catalyst 5000 Internal Architecture.

Table 10.1 The key features of the Catalyst 5000 family of switches.

Feature	5000	5002	5500	5505	5509
Modular slots	5	2	13	5	9
Backplane	1.2 Gbps	1.2 Gbps	3.6 Gbps	3.6 Gbps	3.6 Gbps
Forwarding rate	1,000,000 pps	3,000,000 pps	25,000,000 pps	25,000,000 pps	25,000,000 pps

Color Blocking Logic ASIC

The Color Blocking Logic (CBL) ASIC helps the EARL ASIC in making the switch port's forwarding decisions. This ASIC is also used to verify that each frame that comes from a particular VLAN does not leave through a port assigned to another VLAN. One of ASIC's most notable functions is to place ports in the blocking, learning, listening, or forwarding mode for Spanning Tree Protocol.

Encoded Address and Recognition Logic ASIC

The EARL ASIC performs functions that are similar in purpose to the Content Addressable Memory (CAM) and creates a table of known MAC addresses matched to a port number. Bridges use the CAM table to make filtering and forwarding decisions for incoming frames. The EARL ASIC works in a similar fashion and connects to the data-switching bus, enabling it to see every frame that crosses the switching fabric and make a switching decision based on the destination MAC address.

The EARL ASIC has a second responsibility to help in building the address-switching table that is stored in the switch's memory. The address-switching table is a dynamic table that holds up to 128,000 learned MAC addresses, port numbers, and the VLAN number associated with each MAC address.

Note: Entries in the address-switching table are removed after the time-to-live (TTL) has expired. The default TTL at which entries are removed is set to 300 seconds by default. This time can be set from 1 to 20 minutes.

Local Target Logic ASIC

The Local Target Logic (LTL) ASIC is located on each of the Catalyst 5000 switch's line modules. The LTL aids the EARL ASIC in making forwarding decisions for received frames that need to be switched to another interface in the same VLAN as the port of arrival.

Phoenix ASIC

The Phoenix ASIC is used to handle high-speed data traffic for the Supervisor Engine III. The Supervisor Engine is located in slot 1 of the Catalyst 5000 series switch and is the brains of the switch, similar to the motherboard in a PC. This ASIC provides a gigabit bridge between each of the buses located on the Supervisor Engine III module and contains a 384K buffer used to handle traffic between buses located on the engine.

Synergy Advanced Gate-Array Engine ASIC

The Synergy Advanced Gate-Array Engine (SAGE) ASIC performs the same functions as the SAINT (described next) and provides support for non–Ethernet physical media such as FDDI, ATM, LANE, or Token Ring, as well as the Network Management Processor (NMP). As in the SAINT ASIC, the processing performed by the SAGE ASIC takes place in the hardware ASICs, requiring no CPU cycles and adding no additional latency to the switch.

Note: The **show test** *command can be used to test the ASIC's status, including physical media errors.*

Synergy Advanced Interface and Network Termination ASIC

The Synergy Advanced Interface and Network Termination (SAINT) ASIC allows switch interfaces to support both half-duplex and full-duplex Ethernet. This ASIC is also responsible for Ethernet encapsulation, de-encapsulation, and gathering statistics for Ethernet trunk ports, including ISL encapsulation and de-encapsulation.

Every Ethernet port on an Ethernet module in the switch contains its own independent 192K buffer for inbound and outbound packet buffering. The buffer is divided to provide 168K to outbound traffic and 24K for inbound frames. This buffering for each port is controlled by the SAINT ASIC. When troubleshooting Ethernet port problems, administrators must consider that buffer overflows or underruns may be a factor in their problems.

Synergy Advanced Multipurpose Bus Arbiter ASIC

The Synergy Advanced Multipurpose Bus Arbiter (SAMBA) and the EARL work together to allow port access to the bus to suppress broadcasts, thereby letting frames be forwarded correctly. SAMBA is responsible for access to the bus. Both the Supervisor Engine and the line modules in the Cisco Catalyst 5000 utilize this ASIC.

Warning! A SAMBA utility exists for NetBIOS Server Message Block (SMB) and for Unix platforms that should not be confused with the SAMBA ASIC.

The SAMBA ASIC is connected to the switch bus in one of two modes: master or slave. Access to a port's bus is based on its priority of normal, high, or critical. The master mode is used to make decisions regarding the interval in which the switch interfaces have access to the switch bus.

Power Failure

A power failure is a very apparent sign of trouble. If no power to the switch exists, the fans fail to turn on, no indicator lights appear lit on the front or back of the switch, and no prompt appears on the console port.

10

Warning! Make sure you use proper grounding techniques before removing or touching any components, and make sure that the switch is unplugged from all power sources.

Follow these steps in troubleshooting a power failure:

1. Check the physical cable for breaks.

2. Check that all cables are securely installed.

3. Check the outlet with a multimeter for proper throughput.

4. Reseat the RAM in the chassis.

5. Check the connection and verify that all interfaces, cards, and modules are securely fastened in the chassis.

6. Make sure all gold-plated connections for the cards, modules, and RAM are not corroded and can make a good connection. To clean the gold-plated connections, use an eraser from a pencil.

7. Contact Cisco TAC or an authorized Cisco repair vendor for further troubleshooting and replacement parts.

POST

The power-on self test (POST) can be a powerful tool in solving hardware issues. The POST is displayed on the screen when the switch powers. Each LED on the switch becomes lit one at a time indicating that a different test is being performed.

The POST tests the following components:

➤ Ports (loopback)

➤ Ethernet address PROM

➤ CAM (MAC Address) Table

➤ RS-232 Console Port

➤ Realtime Clock

➤ CAM memory (SRAM)

➤ Timer interrupt

➤ Port control status

➤ Flag Memory (DRAM)

➤ Buffer Memory (DRAM)

➤ Forwarding Engine Memory (SRAM)

Isolating Catalyst 5000 Problems

To isolate a software or hardware problem on the Catalyst 5000, follow these steps:

1. Check the switch indicator lights.
2. Check the switch configuration.
3. Check the physical links.
4. Check the connection between switches.
5. Check the VLAN configuration.

➤ Forwarding Engine CPU

➤ ECU memory (DRAM)

Switch Indicator Lights

The Catalyst 5000 family uses quite a few LEDs that can indicate a problem or what the current utilization is of the switch. The Supervisor Engine has five different LEDs that indicate the system, fan, power supplies, load utilization, and whether or not the Supervisor Engine is active, as shown in Figure 10.4.

Note: The load bar indicates the current load on the switch. If the local bar is over 80 percent, either a network problem exists, such as a broadcast storm, or an upgrade in the switching devices is needed.

10

The system status light indicates the following, depending on the color:

➤ *Green*—All diagnostics passed.

➤ *Orange*—The second power supply failed.

➤ *Red*—A diagnostic test on the switch failed.

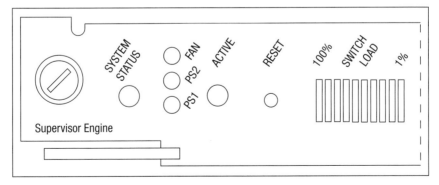

Figure 10.4 The Supervisor Engine LEDs.

The fan LED indicates the following:

➤ *Red*—The fan has failed to power up.

➤ *Green*—The fan is operating correctly.

Power supply 1 (PS1) and power supply (PS2) LEDs indicate the following:

➤ *Red*—Power supply failure.

➤ *Green*—Power supply operating normally.

➤ *Off*—The power supply bay is empty or off.

The active LED indicates the following:

➤ *Orange*—The Supervisor Engine is in standby mode.

➤ *Green*—The Supervisor Engine is operating correctly.

LEDs also exist on each individual line module, as shown in Figure 10.5. These LEDs indicate the status of each module. A green light indicates that a good established link exists. An orange or amber light indicates that a problem exists with the link. A red light indicates a nonport test has failed. A green switch port (SP) light indicates the port is operating at 100BaseT. When the SP light is off, it is operating in 10BaseT.

Troubleshooting Cables

With the introduction of 1- and 10-Gbps links, as well as Fast and Gigabit EtherChannel, data can move around today's networks at greater speeds than ever. These higher speeds add never-before-encountered complexities. Earlier implementations allowed cable plants greater distances and flexibility. In today's high-speed networks, the distance limitations should be strictly adhered to. Many times, administrators will upgrade the network interface cards on both ends of a former

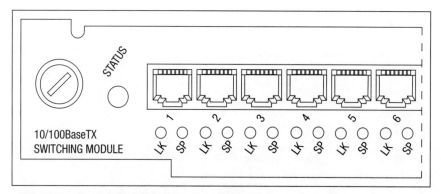

Figure 10.5   The 10/100 Ethernet switching module.

10-Mbps link and find that the 100-Mbps link fails to work or has an excessive number of errors, forcing the link to become unusable. Going over on the 10BaseT cable distance limits didn't have the detrimental effects as they do with 100BaseT.

You may also have a noncompatible cable type. For instance, 10BaseT will work over Category 3, 4, 5, or 6 twisted-pair cable, whereas 100BaseT requires Category 5 or 6. Table 10.2 examines the common cable limits for cabling in today's networks.

Cable problems can appear suddenly or as an intermittent problem. Intermittent errors are sometimes hard to troubleshoot and can appear as problems unrelated to cabling. As an administrator, you have to be aware that almost any connectivity issue can be cable-related, and to resolve connectivity issues, you must replace a cable with a cable that you know works.

You can also use multimeters, time domain reflectometers (TDRs), cable analyzers, or breakout boxes to test for cable connectivity errors. Never conclude that just because a cable is installed or tested by a certified cable installer that it can't be improperly made, have a break, or have a failure in its connectors. Cables are moving parts and, as with any moving parts, are subject to wear and tear.

A connection to a network node from a switch or hub uses a straight-through cable. A crossover cable is used to connect two network devices, such as a hub to a hub, a switch to a switch, a switch to a router, and so on. When trying to configure switches or routers, you will fail to get a connection between the devices if you use a straight-through cable when you should be using a crossover cable.

10

Chapter Summary

This chapter went beyond the subject matter discussed for switches in the chapters on VLAN and Spanning Tree Protocol. This chapter covered many aspects of switching, including parts of the switching architecture, the switch functions, and commands available to monitor. It also covered Cisco Catalyst hardware and software problems.

Table 10.2 Common cabling distance limitations.

Cable	Distance	Limit Cable Speed (Mbps)
Category 3	100 meters	10
Category 4	100 meters	16
Category 5	100 meters	10/100/1000
Category 6	100 meters	10/100/1000
Multimode fiber (half)	2,000 meters	10/100
Single/Multimode fiber ((full)	400 meters	10/100
Single-mode fiber	10,000 meters	10/100

Some of the problems areas covered in this chapter include:

➤ Locating duplicate MAC addresses

➤ Checking cable requirements

➤ Checking the ASICs

➤ Configuring route processors for inter-VLAN routing and trunking

➤ Looking at Spanning Tree Protocol statistics

➤ Analyzing VTP revision number problems

➤ Verifying configuration entries and statistics on both sides of a link between the router and the switches, or between switches

➤ Using CDP, **show**, and **debug** commands

This chapter should be studied carefully, because many of the exam topics relating to switching are covered in this chapter. It attempts to include the output from each device so that you understand what the output looks like without having to use the command on an actual Cisco Catalyst 5000 device.

Review Questions

1. Which ASIC is responsible for Ethernet frame encapsulation and de-encapsulation.

   a. Phoenix

   b. SAGE

   c. CAM

   d. SAINT

   e. CEF

2. Which of the following commands provides information such as the status and errors on an Ethernet Module port?

   a. **show all**

   b. **show port**

   c. **show port config**

   d. **show port all**

3. Which of the following are VLAN encapsulation types supported on Cisco switches? [Choose the two best answers]

   a. Inter-Switch Link (ISL)

   b. IEEE 802.5

   c. STP

   d. IEEE 802.1Q

4. An ISL trunked port can handle how many of the switch's active VLANs?

   a. 1

   b. 6

   c. 64

   d. All Active VLANs up to 1000.

5. If you are receiving a duplicate MAC address error, which of the following commands will show the MAC address of all nodes attached to the switch?

   a. **show port all**

   b. **debug mac**

   c. **show mac cache**

   d. **show cam dynamic**

6. Which of the following cable types cannot support Ethernet 100BaseTX traffic?

   a. Category 5

   b. Category 3

   c. Category 6

   d. All of the above

7. The Catalyst 5000 switch's utilization statistics can be viewed which of the following commands? [Choose the two best answers]

   a. Viewing LEDs on the Ethernet Module

   b. Using the **show test** command

   c. Using Cisco software such as CWSI

   d. Using the **show all** command

   e. Viewing the Load LED on the Supervisor Engine module

   f. All of the above

8. Although the management VLAN can be changed, what VLAN is the management VLAN by default.

   a. VLAN 1

   b. The VLAN assigned to an ISL trunked port

   c. VLAN 1005

   d. VLAN 64

10

9. Which of the following Catalyst switch commands enable you to gather statistics regarding the Spanning Tree Protocol? [Choose the two best answers]

   a. **show span**

   b. **show vlan**

   c. **show spantree**

   d. **show port spantree**

10. Which of the following port types allows more than one VLAN to traverse its links?

    a. Any switched port

    b. Any port that uses 10BaseT

    c. An EtherChannel port

    d. A switched port with ISL encapsulation configured

11. Which of the following trunking types would be used on a switch port if the port were connecting to a non-Cisco router or switch?

    a. IEEE 802.5

    b. IEEE 802.3

    c. ISL

    d. IEEE 802.1Q

12. Which of the following provides a GUI to view the VLAN configuration on a switch?

    a. VLANDesigner

    b. TrafficDirector

    c. VLANDirector

    d. VLANScope

13. What is the result if you take a VTP-configured switch from one domain, where it was configured as a server, and add it to a different VTP domain name, and the switch contains a higher revision number from the old domain than the new domain?

    a. The switch will assume the configuration from the new domain.

    b. The new domain VTP configuration is overwritten with the configuration from the old domain.

    c. Nothing, because you must reboot first.

    d. None of the above.

14. Cisco Discovery Protocol is used for which of the following?

    a. Looking at the VLAN configuration for VTP

    b. Checking the Cisco switch and router logs

    c. Learning what Cisco devices reside in the network

    d. All of the above

15. Spanning Tree Protocol stops data loops by placing redundant ports in which of the following states?

    a. Stopped

    b. Disabled

    c. Closed

    d. Blocked

16. To learn about neighboring Cisco devices, which of the following commands would be used?

    a. **show neighbors all**

    b. **show cdp neighbors**

    c. **show cdp neighbors all**

    d. **show cdp**

17. Which of the following commands can be used on a router's subinterface to assign an encapsulation type?

    a. **set encapsulation isl 1**

    b. **encapsulation isl 1**

    c. **interface encasulation isl 1**

    d. **isl encapsulation 1**

18. For one VLAN to speak to another, a device must be used to resolve what layer addresses?

    a. Layer 1

    b. Layer 2

    c. Layer 3

    d. Physical layer

19. To determine the amount of time the switch has been up since the power was last recycled, which of the following commands would be used?

    a. **show all**

    b. **show uptime**

    c. **show config**

    d. **show version**

10

20. Which command will enables you to display the following output?

Domain Name	Domain	Index VTP	Version	Local Mode	Password
Coriolis		1	2	server	sean1

Vlan-count	Max-vlan-storage	Config Revision	Notifications
5	1023	355	enabled

Last Updater	V2 Mode	Pruning	PruneEligible on Vlans
68.38.127.5	enabled	enabled	2-1000

   a. **show vtp**

   b. **show vlan**

   c. **show vtp all**

   d. **show vtp domain**

Real-World Project

Joe Snow has been hired to answer the help desk phones for his company. Being at the main office for his company, the help desk assists field technicians who work for the company in the capacity of assisting their clients. Just before lunch, Joe receives a call from Gina, a fellow employee who is stationed at The Coriolis Group, working with its IT department. Gina is calling to resolve a problem on a Catalyst 5000. The Coriolis Group has a switch that, when rebooted, has its Load Bar LED jump to 100 percent utilization about a minute after the switch is powered up.

When Gina arrived, she tried to enter the switch from the console port with her laptop, but none of the passwords that the local IT administrator is giving her enables her to access the switch. She needs to recover the password and can't remember how it is done, so she is calling Joe for assistance.

Project 10.1

To recover a password, perform the following steps:

Gina is already connected to the console port, so she needs to follow these steps:

1. Recycle the power on the switch.

2. Press the Enter key at the prompt. There is a null password meaning, no password for the first 30 seconds, this means that for 30 seconds you can use the Enter key as the password as shown here:

```
Password: <enter>
```

3. Use the **enable** command and press Enter again for the Enable password. Again, there is a null password meaning, no password for the first 30 seconds:

```
Catalyst5002> enable

Enter password: <enter>
```

4. Use the **set password** and **set enablepass** commands to set the password:

```
Catalyst5002> (enable) set password [press enter]
Enter old password:
Enter new password: coriolis1
Retype new password: coriolis1
Password changed.

Catalyst5002> (enable) set enablepass
Enter old password: <enter>
Enter new password: coriolis2
Retype new password: corilis2
Password changed.
Catalyst5002(enable)
```

10

CHAPTER ELEVEN

Policy-Based Networking

After completing this chapter, you will be able to:

✓ Recognize the need for policy-based networking

✓ Know how to allocate resources using QoS

✓ Configure queuing on an interface

✓ Understand how weighted random early detection works on an interface

✓ Configure extended access lists to allow certain types of traffic

✓ Identify security policies and how to use them on a network

Although this chapter gives you the basis for policy-based networking, it does not cover every aspect of it, because this subject is very extensive. This chapter provides an insight into Quality of Service (QoS) and how to configure queuing on router interfaces. After reading this chapter, you will be able to identify how you can allocate bandwidth by using queuing techniques, and how you can allow certain types of traffic by using access lists. Although access lists are described in this chapter, as well as how to apply them on an interface, the coverage provided is basically an overview.

Policy-based networking is established by implementing network support that gives you the ability to control the bandwidth on your network. There are several different services of support that include identifying and using network resources, QoS, access lists, and network security.

Quality of Service

QoS is designed to provide a quality level of network performance by utilizing the bandwidth and reducing latency, jitters, and packet loss, all of which can result in poor application response time. Due to diverse applications such as video conferencing, video-based seminars, and voice-over-IP (VoIP) demanding more of the network's bandwidth, the need has arisen for QoS. The goal of QoS is to maintain a high level of service over various technologies, such as Frame Relay, IP-routed networks, Ethernet, and 802.1 networks, and ATM, just to name a few. QoS is established when you have the ability to control your network bandwidth through various different queuing techniques to prioritize the traffic on your network.

QoS is based on the following types of building blocks to maintain a high quality of service:

➤ *Smart queuing*—Includes weighted fair queuing (WFQ), priority queuing, and custom queuing.

➤ *Congestion avoidance*—Includes weighted random early detection (WRED) and random early detection (RED).

➤ *Traffic filtering*—Includes generic traffic shaping (GTS) and Frame-Relay traffic shaping (FRTS).

Queuing

Prioritization is most effective on WAN links where the combination of bursty traffic and lower data rates can cause a temporary congestion. Some applications, such as video applications, will not be able to operate efficiently if these bursts occur. Video conferencing requires a specified amount of bandwidth, without interruption, for the video to have an acceptable view.

To determine whether policy-based networking will help your network, ask yourself the following questions:

➤ Is your network, especially your WAN, congested? Look at your network's utilization of this link by using a Network Advisor by HP or a Sniffer by Network Associates on your WAN or link. If your link is not congested after running your applications, you may not need to use the various queuing options.

➤ Is your network link, especially your WAN link, congested? If so, determine whether the queuing techniques will help you, by determining the type of traffic on the link. Identifying what the pattern of traffic is on your link may take some time. If certain applications are failing over the link, establish the best queuing mechanism that will help your traffic flow.

➤ After determining the types of traffic and making changes, is the link still congested at times? After isolating the traffic to your link, determine whether the applications that may not be included in your queuing techniques will be able to handle the delay of traffic with the queuing techniques implemented.

When a router receives a packet through an interface, a protocol-dependent switching process handles it and the router delivers the packet out another interface. This sounds simple enough, but the process of packet delivery is much more complicated when the packets are far larger than the bandwidth they have to travel to reach the destination address. When a router receives data that exceeds the bandwidth, the excess data is placed in the routers' buffers until the router is able to send it across the wire. An algorithm commonly referred to as FIFO (first in, first out) handles the process of buffering for packet transmission. This algorithm delivers the packet from the buffers in the order it was received. Until recently, the FIFO algorithm was the default for all router interfaces. However, with the dramatic increase in the demand on network bandwidth, queuing technology is becoming much more popular than FIFO.

Queuing enables you to prioritize the traffic that flows on your network. With policy-based networking, you can allocate your network bandwidth relative to your network needs. Due to the demands of some applications, you must utilize your bandwidth for them to run properly. Cisco IOS software can utilize any of three queuing options as an alternative to the basic FIFO queuing:

➤ *Weighted fair queuing (WFQ)*—Prioritizes traffic to ensure a fair response for most common user applications.

➤ *Custom queuing*—Establishes different amounts of bandwidth allocation for different applications.

➤ *Priority queuing*—Prioritizes the order of transmission for different traffic or protocols depending on their priority level.

Weighted Fair Queuing

As an administrator, you probably have received a few calls stating that the network has come to a slow crawl or a screeching halt. Of course, by the time you get to look at the problem, the network usually is working wonderfully, with very low bandwidth utilization and fast packet response times. What you may not know is that moments earlier, someone tried to send across the wire a huge file that exceeds the bandwidth. The packets of the huge file are waiting in the buffer to be sent, along with the rest of the other users' files that are being stored in the buffers. At this point, the packets are waiting in the router's buffer like a large group of first-graders waiting to go out to recess. In this case, you may have one user that bogs down the network and slows down the other users' files in order for his or her file to reach its destination first.

WFQ shares the bandwidth equally with all traffic by taking the files or packets and making them into conversations. Each file transfer is converted into a conversation and typically is identified by the source/destination address and MAC addresses, along with port or socket numbers. After the conversation is created, it is given an opportunity to share the bandwidth without monopolizing it. This means Telnet sessions and other low-volume traffic can be sent without having to wait for large-volume traffic to be sent, such as an FTP transfer. WFQ can break conversations into groups and send just a portion of the conversation across the wire, while also sending smaller conversations. The larger conversations can then send another group of the conversation until all of the combined groups complete the conversation. Figure 11.1 shows how WFQ works.

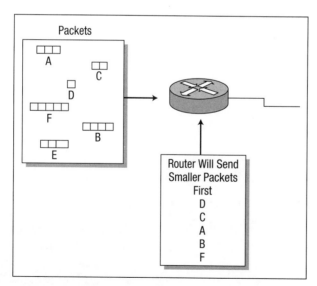

Figure 11.1   Weighted fair queuing.

Note: WFQ is enabled by default on all interfaces that have a bandwidth less than or equal to 2.048Mbps and that do not use balanced *Link Access Procedure on the D channel (LAPD), X.25, compressed Point-To-Point Protocol (PPP), or Synchronous Data Link Control (SDLC). The protocols do not have the capability of WFQ.*

WFQ also allows for an assigned threshold to be specified on an interface to eliminate the monopoly of the bandwidth, because the whole premise of this queuing is to send traffic in a fair manner. Cisco IOS enables you to set a discard-threshold value of 1 to 512 messages, which creates a threshold for the maximum number of messages allowed in queue. This applies only to high-volume traffic, to avoid such traffic monopolizing the bandwidth. If the number of messages of high-volume conversations exceeds the threshold, the packets will be discarded. After the conversations of high-volume traffic have decreased by one fourth, new conversations of high-volume traffic are placed in the queue.

Note: The default discard-threshold value is set to 64 messages.

Configuring Weighted Fair Queuing

In Global Configuration Mode, you must execute the following fair-queuing commands (as seen in italic) for a WAN interface:

```
Support#config t
Support(config)#int serial 1
Support(config-if)#encapsulation frame-relay
Support(config-if)#fair-queue 128
```

The **fair-queue** command of 128 will set a threshold for a frame relay link of 56Kbps:

```
Support(config-if)#bandwidth 56
```

The **bandwidth** command specifies 56Kbps:

```
Support(config-if)#^z
```
To verify weighted fair queuing, use the following:

```
Support#show queueing
Interface   Discard    Dynamic        Reserved
            threshold  queue count    queue count
Serial 1    128        256            0
```

Priority Queuing

Certain types of traffic may require a guaranteed amount of bandwidth for an application to run properly. If such cases, priority queuing enables you to guarantee a certain amount of bandwidth. Priority queuing is much less equitable than WFQ with bandwidth. WFQ gives fair access to the bandwidth available. With priority queuing, you can identify a specific type of traffic on your network and give it priority over the rest of the traffic. The priority levels you can assign are high, medium, normal, and low. The high-priority traffic is sent first, followed by medium, normal, and then low-priority traffic. This type of queuing is designed for low-bandwidth links up to 64Kbps that can focus on mission-critical traffic having guaranteed bandwidth without congestion interference. Figure 11.2 shows a diagram of the priority-queuing process.

The four priority queues of high, medium, normal, and low can be assigned by protocol, Transmission Control Protocol (TCP) port number, or a specific interface. When a packet is received on the router interface, the packet is compared to the list of priority queues and is placed accordingly. If it is high-priority traffic, it is placed in the high-priority buffer and sent or waits to be sent (if other high-priority traffic is buffered before it). When assigning priorities for traffic, it is a good idea to place only critical/sensitive traffic in the high-priority queue, and assign the rest of the traffic accordingly. If the majority of the traffic is assigned a high priority, the purpose of the priority levels is defeated, because new high-priority traffic still has to wait for any existing high-priority traffic in the buffer to be sent. When assigning priority queues, it is a good idea to specify a default queue for the traffic you have not specified on the priority list.

Note: If you do not specify a default queue, all traffic not specified on the priority list will be placed in the normal queue.

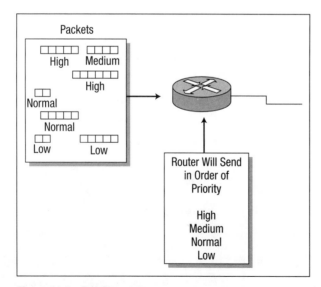

Figure 11.2 Priority queuing.

Table 11.1   Priority queue defaults.

Queue	Default Value
High	20 datagrams
Medium	40 datagrams
Normal	60 datagrams
Low	80 datagrams

After you assign a default queue, you can specify a maximum number of packets allowed in the queue at one time. Changing the queue defaults is not recommended, but it can be done. Table 11.1 lists the default value for each queue.

Configuring Priority Queuing

In global configuration mode, assign a priority level to the desired traffic:

```
Support(config)#priority-list 1 protocol ipx high
```

The priority list is specified by the user and can be numbered from 1 to 16:

```
Support(config)#priority-list 1 interface ethernet 0 medium
```

A specific interface can be set for a specific priority:

```
Support(config)#priority-list 1 protocol appletalk medium
Support(config)#priority-list 1 default low
```

This sets the default traffic to a default priority. Remember that if you do not set a specific default for all other traffic not specified on your list, the default is to set the traffic at normal priority.

To change the default values of the queues, you must use the following command:

```
Support(config)#priority-list 1 queue-limit 10 20 30 40
```

The preceding command assigns a limit to (in this order) high, medium, normal, and low.

Custom Queuing

Custom queuing is similar to priority queuing, except that it enables you to allocate bandwidth for your network traffic. When using priority queuing, the majority of the traffic may be assigned a high priority and lower priority levels conversations may be extremely slow or never get sent at all. With custom queuing, you can allocate a certain percentage of your bandwidth to a particular traffic type. Custom queuing uses filters to assign specific types of traffic to a numbered queue from 1 to 16.

Note: *Technically, custom queuing allows 0 to 16 filters, but the 0 queue is reserved for the system packets, such as keepalives.*

You can control the amount of data being sent each time a queue is processed. The amount of data sent depends on the set amount of bytes that is specified by the administrator. By default, each queue can send up to 1,500 bytes each time. When a numbered queue is called upon, it will transmit packets until the maximum number of bytes is reached. It will then move to the next queue.

Configuring Custom Queuing

In global configuration mode, use the following steps to define a queue list for specific traffic:

1. Assign interface E1 to queue 1:

   ```
   Support#config t
   Support(config)#queue-list 2 protocol interface E1 1
   ```

2. Assign IP traffic to queue 2:

   ```
   Support(config)#queue-list 2 protocol ip 2
   ```

3. Assign the protocol AppleTalk to queue 3:

   ```
   Support(config)#queue-list 2 protocol appletalk 3
   ```

4. Assign IP traffic specific to TCP port 20, which is FTP to queue 4:

   ```
   Support(config)#queue-list 2 protocol ip 4 tcp 20
   ```

5. Assign all other traffic to queue 5:

   ```
   Support(config)#queue-list 2 default 5
   ```

6. Assign a packet limit of 45 to queue 1, which is the E1 interface:

   ```
   Support(config)#queue-list 2 queue 1 limit 45
   ```

7. Assign a maximum byte command of 4,000 to queue 2:

   ```
   Support(config)#queue-list 2 queue 5 byte-count 4000
   ```

8. Assign the configured queue list to the interface:

```
Support(config)#interface serial 1
Support(config-if)#custom-queue-list 2
```

The command above assigns the configured queue list to the interface.

```
Support(config-if)#^z
Support#
```

Figure 11.3 shows how the custom queuing process is managed.

Verifying Custom Queuing

After configuring custom queuing on your interface, you will want to verify your configurations, as follows:

```
Support#show queueing custom
Current custom queue configuration:

List    Queue Args
2   5   default
2   1   interface Ethernet1
2   2   protocol ip
2   3   protocol appletalk
2   4   protocol ip    tcp port ftp
2   1   limit 45
2   5   byte-count 4000
```

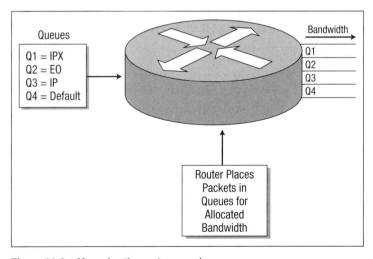

Figure 11.3 Managing the custom queuing process.

The output from the preceding results in the following:

➤ *Queue argument 5*—assigned to all traffic other than specified.

➤ *Queue argument 1*—defines the incoming traffic on E1 and places it in queue 1.

➤ *Queue argument 2*—sends IP traffic to queue 2.

➤ *Queue argument 3*—places all AppleTalk traffic in queue 3.

➤ *Queue argument 4*—sends specified TCP port traffic, which is FTP, to queue 4.

➤ *Queue 1*—deals with incoming Ethernet traffic and has a maximum setting of 45 packets in the queue.

➤ *Queue 5*—has a specified byte amount of 4,000 bytes for all other traffic not specified. The default is 1,500 bytes for the maximum queue amount.

Congestion Avoidance

It is commonplace in all networks to have some slowness and errors at one time or another. Of course, the hard part is to isolate the problems causing the congestion or bottlenecks, to alleviate the problems. Waiting until the network has faults to try to solve some of these common headaches is not recommended. The IOS uses a collision-avoidance technique to try to identify these problems and fix them before they actually occur. The tool used in the IOS is *weighted random early detection (WRED)*, which can be used on an interface to manage how the packets are handled on outbound traffic. An earlier version of this tool, *random early detection (RED)*, mainly worked with TCP and IP networks.

Although some interfaces are busier than others, they are still expected to maintain the same performance as the others. An interface has a maximum threshold that must be surpassed before it will start dropping packets. The more congested or flooded an interface becomes, the more packets it will drop to try to maintain a certain level of performance. WRED is a congestion-avoidance technique that identifies TCP packets being dropped, and can signal the inter-face to lower its transmission rate. Doing this reduces the transmission rate, allowing for traffic to flow at a slower rate and thus avoiding huge congestion. As with freeways, if the traffic is flowing it can reach its destination faster and smoother than if it has to come to a halt. Because the traffic being dropped consists of TCP packets, those packets will try to retransmit, resulting in no data being lost when the packets are dropped.

Because WRED is basically a queuing technique, it is selective before it drops packets. WRED takes certain factors into consideration before packets are dropped:

➤ *Bandwidth*—WRED looks at the flow of traffic and decides the amount of bandwidth taken by each flow. The larger traffic flows are most likely to get packets dropped.

➤ *Resource Reservation Protocol (RSVP) flows*—Precedence is given to these flows.

➤ *IP precedence*—Lower-priority packets are more likely to be dropped.

➤ *Interface configuration for packet dropping*—An interface can be configured to determine the priority of packets being dropped.

After weighing all of these factors, WRED decides which packets to drop, resulting in high-priority traffic being sent and low-bandwidth traffic being saved. When WRED is implemented on an interface, it saves the interface from severe packet loss and works to preserve the bandwidth available. WRED works best with TCP/IP networks, but does not work well with other protocols, such as the User Datagram Protocol (UDP) or Novell's NetWare (IPX).

Traffic Filtering

Wouldn't it be nice if all networks could have a magic ball telling the network administrator when and where the traffic will be sent, and how it will affect the network at any given time? If that were possible, networks wouldn't need queuing and WRED. Congestion avoidance and queuing were created to react when an interface is congested or exceeds a maximum threshold. Traffic filtering is a little more proactive on the network than congestion avoidance and queuing, which only come into play after an interface is being slammed. Traffic filtering can be used at all times to shape the traffic flows even when very little congestion exists. Traffic filtering is based on setting policies on the interface to a desired traffic flow. Traffic filtering consists of traffic shaping (molding the traffic to meet rate requirements), and traffic limiting, sometimes called traffic policing (does not mold the traffic flow but prevents the flow from exceeding the rate). A few types of policies can be used in traffic filtering, including generic traffic shaping (GTS), Frame-Relay traffic shaping (FRTS), and limits on routers and switches traffic.

11

Generic Traffic Shaping

GTS is a basic traffic rate control that enables you to target a rate that relates to a specific type of traffic, and define a burst size and an exceed burst size. After defining these values, GTS uses the buffer to hold packets to allow for a constant flow at the target rate and the burst size. Depending on the values set, GTS sends a specific amount of traffic to maintain the value. GTS policies can be set on all interfaces except for those that use FRTS.

GTS enables you to create a policy that limits a certain type of traffic to bits per second. As an administrator, you can limit the amount of WWW traffic by restricting the traffic to 100Kbps. After you define the policy, GTS will shape the traffic to not exceed the value of 100Kbps. By defining this amount, the remainder of the bandwidth can be allocated to all other types of traffic. If the interface has a lower volume than 100Kbps, GTS will allow other traffic to use the WWW traffic bandwidth.

Frame-Relay Traffic Shaping

Frame Relay is a WAN protocol that uses virtual circuits (VCs). FRTS enables you to define an average bandwidth size for VCs. FRTS is utilized best where the destination interface is slower than the transmission interface. In this situation, FRTS allows you to define a FRTS rate on the transmission interface, which will enable the destination to keep up with the traffic flow.

FRTS uses a buffer to hold packets to maintain a specific traffic flow. Like GTS, you can also define a maximum burst size that tells the interface the buffer is full. When the buffer is full, the interface will start to drop packets. You may also combine FRTS with any type of QoS property.

Router Limiting

Using the committed access rate (CAR), a router can set a bandwidth limit for specific types of traffic on an interface. CAR does not attempt to shape or smooth the traffic, like GTS or FRTS, because CAR does not buffer the traffic. Because CAR does not buffer the traffic, no delay in sending the traffic occurs unless it exceeds the rate policy that has been set.

As with GTS, you can create a policy with CAR. You can set the interface to limit WWW traffic to 100Kbps, and this will allow only that amount of the bandwidth to be used.

Switch Limiting

Traffic shaping can be set all the way to the closet level of a network. This means traffic straight from the desktop can be filtered. Traffic policing enables you to set a bandwidth limit for specific types of traffic on Catalyst switch ports. Creating a limit of WWW traffic to an average rate of 100Kbps with a maximum burst of 200Kbps will put a cap on the WWW traffic coming from that port. If the WWW traffic is not utilizing the allocated bandwidth, the excess bandwidth will be used for other traffic. As with other traffic filtering, if the traffic exceeds the burst limits, it will start to drop packets.

Access Lists

An access list is a set of commands that permits or denies packets based on their IP addresses or upper-layer IP protocols on router interfaces. Access lists are configured on a router to be selective in the traffic the router forwards. Access lists are based on particular protocols, including TCP/IP, IPX/SPX, AppleTalk, DECnet, and Banyan VINES. Access lists can be used for the following:

➤ Controlling bandwidth on your network and identifying traffic to trigger dialing in dial-on-demand routing (DDR).

➤ Restricting unauthorized users, reducing unwanted traffic, and still allowing broadcasts to be forwarded beyond the local router to the designated server.

➤ Permitting or denying traffic through the network based on the type of access list configured on the router.

When a router interface receives a packet, it compares the packet to the access list on the interface and allows the packet through or drops the packet based on access list statements. For example, when using standard access lists, the router only examines the source address and then compares it to the list. When using specialized access lists, the router can alter fields, such as the IP precedence field used for QoS signaling.

Routers read an access list with the top-down approach, trying to find a specified command pertaining to the packet the router is processing. If the router does not find a match throughout the list, the packet is dropped with the implicit "deny all," which is the default on the router. If the access list denies the packet, it returns an Internet Control Message Protocol (ICMP) Destination Unreachable message with a cause code of "Communication Administratively Prohibited," and then drops the packet. If the router does find a match, it processes it as the statement reads, to permit or deny.

In configuring your access list, it is a good idea to design an access list to match the largest amount of traffic toward the top of the list, so as to not make the router look at every statement. After you create an access list, you need to apply it to an interface to determine whether it will scrutinize inbound traffic or outbound traffic. Multiple access lists can be applied to the same router, but only one access list can be applied to an inbound or outbound interface. Access lists are identified by an access group number that are assigned to an interface. Table 11.2 provides a list of access list numbers.

11

Table 11.2   Access list numbers.

Type of Access List	Range
IP standard	1-99
IP extended	100-199
Protocol/Bridge type-code	200-299
DECnet standard and extended	300-399
XNS standard	400-499
NS extended	500-599
X AppleTalk	600-699
48-bit MAC address	700-799
IPX standard	800-899
IPX extended	900-999
IPX SAP	1000-1099
48-bit MAC address extended	1100-1199
IPX summary address	1200-1299

Extended Access Lists

An extended access list can be used to provide more control of traffic in your network, because you can scrutinize traffic on your routers. With an extended access list, you can look at source address, destination addresses, and ports of TCP and UDP, and have the router forward or drop packets based on the access lists applied on the router interface.

Well-known ports assigned by the Internet Assigned Numbers Authority (IANA) can be used to create an extended access list. The port number uniquely identifies the upper-layer process that it is the source or destination of any data. Table 11.3 provides a list of common port numbers.

Configuring an Extended Access List

In configuring extended access lists, the command line can include the access list number, protocol, source, destination, and port number. The code and descriptions that follow provide an example of how to configure an extended access list.

The following line permits TCP traffic from host 116.23.1.1 to host 116.23.5.1, provided that the port number is 8080:

```
Support#config t
Support(config)#access-list 101 permit tcp host 116.23.1.1
host 116.23.5.1 eq 8080
```

The next line permits TCP packets from any source address to any destination address on the network and will allow Web access:

```
Support(config)#access-list 101 permit tcp any 116.23.0.0 0.0.255.255
    eq www
```

The following command permits ICMP traffic from any source address to any destination address:

```
Support(config)#access-list 101 permit icmp any 116.23.0.0 0.0.255.255
```

Table 11.3   Known port numbers.

Port Number	Type of Traffic
6	TCP
20	FTP data
21	FTP
23	Telnet
25	SMTP
53	DNS
80	WWW

The following command permits TCP traffic from any source address to the destination address of 116.23.1.1 and allows SMTP traffic:

```
Support(config)#access-list 101 permit tcp any 116.23.1.1 0.0.0.0 eq 25
```

After configuring an access list, you must specify which interface it will be on:

```
Support(config)#int e0
```

The following command applies the access list of 101 and specifies to apply it to outbound traffic:

```
Support(config-if)#ip access-group 101 out
```

```
Support(config-if)#^Z
```

All other traffic on this interface will not be forwarded. If it does not match any of the preceding commands, it will fall into the implicit "deny all" category and be dropped, sending an ICMP Destination Unreachable message.

Security

Security is a large issue in networking, and rightfully so. Hackers are always searching for ways to break into networks to access secured information or utilize the bandwidth to create a dedicated denial of service (DDOS) attack. Similarly, curious employees sometimes try to explore areas they are not authorized to access. Realistically, the network is the key to most companies. Your company can be compromised if someone breaks into the network. If a company has a solid, secure network, customers will trust the company with their business. An adequate security solution must be implemented on all devices throughout the network for it to be secured.

Knowing that security must be implemented throughout the network, even down to the desktop for it truly to be secure, centrally managing security policy is more efficient and reliable than relying on users in your network to follow security protocols. Complex security technologies are necessary to protect mission-critical networks from corruption and intrusion. In most networks today, the combination of private LANs and public WANs connected to remote sites is especially vulnerable, with mission-critical information being passed around. Security technologies allow critical information to be freely passed around in a secure environment with a centralized security system.

A centralized security system is based on three principles:

11

➤ *Identity*—Concerns authentication, authorization, and accounting (AAA), and digital certifications.

➤ *Network integrity*—Concerns firewalls, access lists, and encryption.

➤ *Network monitoring*—Concerns monitoring the network at all times to identify intrusions, security risks, and unauthorized use.

Identity

Knowing the identity of every user on the network is a must. Being able to identify and track any activities to a particular user gives the network administrator more network security. *Access control* is one way you can control who is allowed access to the network server and what services they are allowed to use after they have access. Access control consists of three areas:

➤ *Authentication*—Authenticates the user's identity and determines access permissions for each user.

➤ *Authorization*—Defines which access (by working with authentication) the user will be provided.

➤ *Accounting*—Deals with auditing of the user. It can monitor the user's activities and is a large insurance in network security.

Access control provides the mechanisms to implement network security on your router or access server.

Terminal Access-Controller Access System (TACACS+) takes security another step further for your network. TACACS+ was designed to enhance an older version of the security product, XTACACS. TACACS+ encrypts the entire body of the packet but leaves a standard TACACS+ header. Within the header is a field that indicates whether or not the body is encrypted. For debugging purposes, it is useful to have the body of the packets intact. TACACS+ uses the AAA architecture, which separates authentication, authorization, and accounting. This allows separate authentication solutions that can still use TACACS+ for authorization and accounting without having to reauthenticate.

TACACS+ provides two ways to control the authorization of router commands on a per-user or per-group basis. The first way is to assign privilege levels to commands and have the router verify with the TACACS+ server whether or not the user is authorized at the specified privilege level. The second way is to explicitly specify in the TACACS+ server, on a per-user or per-group basis, the commands that are allowed.

A new level of security that was devised mainly because of the lack of WWW security is the use of digital certificates. A *digital certificate* is certified authority process by a third party company providing identity information based on a device, name, serial number, company, or IP address. The digital certificate also places a copy of the public key of the entity. For the destination to receive the information sent by the source, it must both receive the certificate and have the public key to identify that it is the correct destination at which the file is to be received. The certificate is signed by a *certification authority (CA)*, a third party such as Verisign or Entrust that is explicitly trusted by the receiver to validate identities and to create digital certificates.

Network Integrity

Network integrity deals with protecting information and your resources, such as bandwidth, from unauthorized users. A few ways exist to provide network integrity, such as a firewall, access control lists (ACLs), and encryption. A *firewall* is a structure that exists between your network and the outside world to protect your network from unauthorized users. Figure 11.4 depicts a firewall in a network. In most cases, the unauthorized users are hackers on the Web, represented by the global Internet and the thousands of remote networks it interconnects. Typically, a network firewall consists of several different machines. A firewall can be a simple router, or an actual device, such as the PIX Firewall, that is connected to the Internet (exterior) and forces all incoming traffic to go through a gateway. The router that is connected to the internal (interior) network accepts packets from the gateway only after they have been scrutinized.

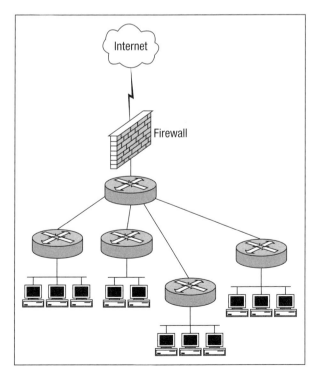

11

Figure 11.4 Firewall in a network.

The gateway can provide per-application and per-user policies that can be set up by the network administrator. The gateway controls the delivery of network-based services both to and from the internal network, providing security in both directions. As a network administrator, you can restrict communication with the Internet to certain people and deny all others. The gateway also enables you to restrict communication with the Internet to only certain applications, denying access to general use other than with the specified applications. If users need access only to a mail application, the application can establish a connection between an exterior and an interior host. The route and packet filters should be set up to reflect the same policies. By doing this, the gateway will be protected from receiving unwanted packets that may overwhelm it while it attempts to discard them.

In using encryption software and hardware in your network, you are providing another building block to enhance your network security. Encryption enables you to secure transmission of sensitive information without it being reviewed or revised. Cisco IOS provides 56-bit and 40-bit Digital Encryption Standard (DES). This type of encryption is enabling Virtual Private Networks (VPNs) and Virtual Private Dial Networks (VPDNs) to become more secure, thus increasing the popularity of this technology.

Network Monitoring

Network monitoring enhances security in networks by identifying security risks and eliminating unauthorized use. Cisco IOS has an option to enable a Cisco IOS Firewall Intrusion Detection System (IDS) on your router. This system monitors packets for a defined set of values, such as its source, destination, and so forth. After your router is running the IDS, it will monitor the interfaces for defined packets and drop them. It may also trigger an alarm to a central point to let the network administrator know of the activities. A monitoring system must be purchased in addition to using the IOS IDS on your routers.

Several different monitoring systems are available on the market to enable network administrators to watch the network from a server or Web page.

Access Control Lists

Access control lists are very similar to access lists and are used for security to prevent unauthorized traffic from entering the network. ACLs use permit and deny statements to prevent unwanted traffic and are usually applied to firewalls or routers that are placed near sensitive traffic. When using access control lists, it is a good idea to log to the network the traffic that is being denied. By logging the traffic, the system administrator can get an idea of the types of traffic trying to enter the network, and the type of traffic that is mainly being forwarded on the network.

Chapter Summary

Policy-based networking was implemented as the need for managing band-width and traffic became a large issue for some networks. Policy-based networking is basically made up of Quality of Service (QoS), access lists, and security on networks.

QoS is made up of three main areas: queuing, congestion avoidance, and traffic filtering. Queuing is most effective on WAN links, because it enables the network administrator to decide how the traffic is forwarded. WFQ can provide a fair bandwidth allocation to all traffic. Custom queuing can establish certain amounts of bandwidth for applications that are mainly used more often on a particular network. Priority queuing can prioritize certain traffic to get forwarded prior to other types of traffic.

Congestion avoidance uses WRED on interfaces and monitors the traffic on the interface. When an interface exceeds a certain threshold (which can be a configured threshold), WRED reacts to lower the transmission rate of the flow of traffic. WRED will drop packets to avoid a huge congestion based on assigned or configured bandwidth, RSVP, IP precedence, or how the interface is configured to drop certain packets. WRED saves the interface from severe packet loss and works to preserve the bandwidth.

Traffic filtering is unlike queuing and congestion avoidance insofar as it's a proactive measure to monitor the traffic and maintain a certain flow. Queuing and congestion avoidance react to traffic only after it exceeds a set amount. FRTS and GTS are a few types of policies used in traffic filtering. GTS enables you to target a rate that relates to a specific type of traffic and allows for a constant flow. GTS can be configured to a set amount of bits per second for traffic and will not exceed that amount. FRTS is used for Frame-Relay's virtual circuits and enables you to allocate a certain amount of bandwidth to a virtual circuit. GTS and FRTS are best used where the destination interface is slower than the transmission interface and allows for a constant traffic flow.

Access lists are configured on a router to decide which traffic is forwarded and which packets are dropped. Access lists restrict unauthorized users and unwanted traffic. An access list consists of a set of commands that permit or deny traffic based on the statements in the access list. If the packets match any commands on the access list, the router does as the command instructs, to permit or deny. If the packets do not match any of the commands, the router will drop the packets due to the implicit "deny all" on the router IOS.

Network security should be a major issue to any network administrator. As companies continue to use more and more combinations of public and private networks, corresponding security measures need to be taken. Having security on your

11

network requires being able to determine the identity of users, having network integrity of firewalls, and monitoring the network. Using authentication, authorization, and accounting (AAA), as well as TACACS+, will give a network an added level of security. TACACS+ encrypts the entire body of the packet, but leaves a standard TACACS+ header to be forwarded over the network. This encryption reduces the chance of the packet being intercepted and changed before it reaches its destination.

Network security refers to the use of a firewall and t encryption. A firewall is usually placed near the Internet traffic and forces all incoming traffic to a particular gateway, so that packets can be scrutinized. The gateway controls delivery of network-based services both to and from the internal network providing security in both directions. Encryption is used in the hardware and software on the network. Encryption enables you to secure sensitive information without it being reviewed or revised. The Cisco IOS provides 56-bit and 40-bit DES. Network monitoring can be accomplished by running a Cisco IOS Firewall Intrusion Detection System on your router. This will monitor the interfaces for certain packets and drop them, and then trigger an alarm to a central point to let the network administrator know of the activities.

Review Questions

1. Weighted fair queuing (WFQ) is on by default on links below or equal to _____ that do not use LAPB, X.25, compressed PPP, or SDLC.

   a. 2.048Mbps

   b. 1.544Mbps

   c. 56Kbps

   d. 1.048Mbps

   e. 512Mbps

2. What is the command to enable WFQ on an interface?

   a. **weighted-fair queueing**

   b. **fair queue**

   c. **fair-queue**

   d. **enable fair-queue**

   e. **enable queueing**

3. What are the four priorities that can be used with priority queuing? [Choose the four best answers]

   a. High

   b. Low

    c. Average

    d. Medium

    e. Large

    f. Normal

4. If you do not specify a priority, it will default to the ___ priority queue?

    a. Normal

    b. Average

    c. Medium

    d. Low

    e. Large

5. How many queues can be configured for custom queuing?

    a. 10

    b. 15

    c. 16

    d. 12

    e. 4

6. What is the default number of bytes of each queue for custom queuing?

    a. 1,200

    b. 2,000

    c. 4,000

    d. 1,000

    e. 1,500

11

7. What is the command to show custom queuing configurations?

    a. **show custom queuing**

    b. **show custom queueing**

    c. **show queueing custom**

    d. **custom queueing**

    e. **custom queuing**

8. What are the tools used with congestion avoidance?

    a. QoS

    b. Random early detection (RED)

    c. Queuing

    d. General traffic shaping (GTS)

    e. Weighted random early detection (WRED)

9. What are two policies that can be used in traffic filtering?

   a. GTS

   b. WRED

   c. FRTS

   d. Queuing

   e. RSVP

10. A(n) _____ can be set on a router to set a bandwidth limit for specific types of traffic on an interface to aid in traffic filtering?

    a. WRED

    b. FRTS

    c. CAR

    d. RSVP

    e. RED

11. When using an access list, if the packet is dropped, what message will the router send to the source address?

    a. Time-out message

    b. Packet dropped by router

    c. ICMP message

    d. ICMP Destination Unreachable

    e. Reply

12. In defining an access list, what range will be used in creating an IP extended access list?

    a. 1-99

    b. 400-499

    c. 900-999

    d. 1100-1199

    e. 100-199

13. Which port identifies Web traffic for an access list?

    a. 6

    b. 23

    c. 25

    d. 80

    e. 53

14. In an access list, what is the sequence of commands configured for an extended access list?

    a. Access list number, destination, source, protocol, and the port

    b. Access list number, source, destination, protocol, and the port

    c. Access list number, protocol, source, destination, and the port

    d. Access list number, protocol, port, source, and the destination

    e. Access list number, protocol, source, port, and the destination

15. AAA, which is used in security of networks, stands for what?

    a. Amending, authentication, and authorization

    b. Authentication, authorization, and accounting

    c. Accounting, authentication, and amending

    d. Access, accounting, and auditing

    e. Auditing, authentication, and accounting

Real-World Projects

Joe Snow works for a statewide flooring company and just got a promotion to control and maintain the remote sites of the company. One of his new job assignments is to provide better management of bandwidth at the Fresno remote site, which has been experiencing a lot of network slowness due to a high utilization of the bandwidth. The boss tells Joe to set up the router to allow for the best utilization for the site, depending on the needs of the users.

Project 11.1

To establish whether the WAN link is congested and to determine the best method of queuing, if needed, perform the following steps:

1. Look at your network's utilization by using a Network Advisor by HP or a Sniffer by Network Associates, and determine the type of traffic on the link.

2. Determine the type of traffic that is needed and whether any precedence is needed for certain types of traffic.

3. After speaking to the managers of the remote site, Joe has determined that the users are on a Novell network using IP. The managers also stated that the users use Telnet sessions to complete most of the job duties. Joe has decided to define a priority queuing policy on the router to ensure that the most important traffic is sent first.

11

Project 11.2

To configure the interface for priority queuing, perform the following steps:

1. At the Privileged EXEC Mode prompt, type the enable secret password, if one exists.

2. Type the command "config t" to enter global configuration mode.

3. At the Global Configuration Mode prompt, type "priority-list 1 protocol ipx medium" to set the medium queue for IPX traffic.

4. At the Global Configuration Mode, type "priority-list 1 protocol ip normal" to set the IP traffic in the normal queue.

5. At the Global Configuration Mode, type "priority-list 1 default low" to allow all other types of traffic to be sent as low priority.

6. At the Global Configuration Mode type "interface serial 1" to be able to configure the serial 1 interface.

7. At the Interface Configuration Mode, type "priority-group 1" to apply the priority list to the interface.

8. At the Interface Configuration Mode, type "^Z" to exit the interface, and then type "copy run start" to save the configurations.

After Joe had the interface configured, he checked to make sure the interface was working.

Project 11.3

To check the interface status, perform the following steps:

1. At the exec mode, type "show queueing priority" to verify the configurations on the interface.

2. The interface status should be displayed with a list of queuing arguments and their priorities.

CHAPTER TWELVE

Advanced Troubleshooting Tools

After completing this chapter, you will be able to:

✓ Contact the Cisco Technical Assistance Center

✓ Use the fault-tracking commands

✓ Perform a core dump

✓ Employ third-party troubleshooting tools

✓ Troubleshoot and understand Ethernet problems

In this chapter, you will learn about the different resources you have available to help you troubleshoot problems on your network. You have already learned (in Chapter 3) the basic troubleshooting tools, including the **show** and **debug** commands. In using the advanced troubleshooting tools, you can build upon the information and experience you obtained using the basic tools. This chapter does not provide an in-depth discussion of how to analyze packets by using an analyzer.

Cisco Technical Assistance Center

With every network problem, documentation is essential. Most problems are easy to fix, but the difficult problems require documentation of all the steps that are taken to solve the problem. Most administrators will experience more than one problem for which outside assistance is necessary. Cisco has created a resource for these occasions, called the Technical Assistance Center (TAC).

When you are troubleshooting difficult problems, you may contact the TAC. (If you don't have an existing maintenance contract, warranty, or service contract, you will be billed for TAC's services.) TAC has information about certain codes that isn't available to the general public, and can access a lot of information quickly, as opposed to you trying to find it. TAC is available to you via email, fax, phone, and the Cisco Web site, Cisco Connection Online (CCO).

Before you call TAC, you should execute the **show tech-support** command from the problem equipment. The output of this command will provide TAC with additional information to help solve the problem. It is also a good idea to keep records of configuration changes, **show** or **debug** command output, and any other information relevant to the problem. TAC may request any of this information.

In contacting TAC, you must follow a standard process that Cisco has created, to receive the best possible service. The following are the steps you must follow to get assistance from TAC personnel:

1. When you first call TAC, the Customer Response Center will ask for particular information, including the following: name, company name, address, email address, contact name, telephone number, equipment type, equipment serial number, and a contract number, if any. At this point, the operator will assign a ticket number. It is a good idea to write down the ticket number, because it will be your reference for future contact.

2. The operator will ask for a brief description of the problem and for any additional information regarding the steps that you have taken to resolve the problem. This is the time to describe all documentation that you have gathered. The operator will then assign a priority for your case and send it to the proper engineers. When assigning a priority, the operator uses these guidelines:

➤ *Priority 1*—Your production network is down or a portion of your production network is down. This priority requires a TAC engineer to stay on the phone during the entire outage or until the priority is downgraded.

➤ *Priority 2*—You have noticed a significant change in your network performance that is almost crippling your network.

➤ *Priority 3*—You have noticed that your network performance has been depleting over time and not rebounding.

➤ *Priority 4*—You need additional information from TAC, including answers to questions about code versions, configuration issues, and additional product information.

3. After your ticket has been routed to an engineering group, you will be able to receive automated updates on the status of the ticket. At this point, you will also be able to add any information and questions you may have regarding your problem via email or telephone.

Knowing how and when to utilize TAC is a great resource to you. TAC engineers see a lot of the same problems on a daily basis and keep a detailed database to help customers. Any and all information will be helpful to TAC. Another great source for information is Cisco's Web site, described next.

Cisco Connection Online

Cisco's Web site provides a wealth of information regarding everything from new technology developments to code upgrades. For some people, it is almost too much information to gather, so carefully defining your search on the site is helpful.

The CCO provides a general product overview and a list of services Cisco offers. The CCO is designed for you to see any information regarding your equipment and any changes or "bugs" that have been found. The information pages enable you to see IOS configurations for routers and switches, along with troubleshooting tools. The CCO does provide more extensive information if you have a login account, in which case you are provided with extensive technical documents, Cisco code upgrades, detailed product information, and access to TAC.

To obtain a login account for CCO, you must be registered as a Cisco user who has purchased a service contract from Cisco or an authorized Cisco partner.

Core Dumps

When contacting CCO, one of the troubleshooting methods they may ask you to perform is a core dump. If a router crashes, it may be useful to obtain a copy of the memory to see whether it indicates a cause for the crash. A core dump contains a picture of the information that is currently in the system memory. If your system memory (RAM) is very large, the core dump file also will be very large.

12

When you create a core dump, you must understand the potential impact it can have on your network if it is a production network. Using core dump commands most likely will disrupt a production network while they are being performed. Use caution when using the commands.

The exception Command

When you retrieve a core dump from your router, the core dump will be in the form of a binary file. The binary file length will depend on the size of the memory in your router. After you retrieve the core dump, you must transfer the binary file to a server such as Trivial File Transfer Protocol (TFTP), File Transfer Protocol (FTP), or Remote Copy Protocol (RCP) server. At this point, you can send the file to Cisco personnel where it is then interpreted. Technical support representatives have access to the source code and memory maps to help identify the problem of the router before it crashed.

You use the **exception** command to create a core dump. This command is used only after the router has crashed. Using the **exception** command enables you to configure a router to execute a core dump if a router has crashed. Before you use the **exception** command, you must know the IP address of a server, such as a TFTP, FTP, or RCP server. The following is an example of configuring an **exception** command to a TFTP server:

```
Support#
Support#config t
Enter configuration commands, one per line. End with
    CNTL/Z.
Support(config)#exception dump 131.52.61.2
Support(config)#^Z
Support#
```

A TFTP server doesn't require any additional commands, whereas sending a core dump to an FTP or an RCP server requires a few additional commands to allow the transfer. The following is an example of configuring a core dump to an FTP server:

```
Support#
Support#config t
Enter configuration commands, one per line. End with
    CNTL/Z.
Support(config)#exception protocol ftp
Support(config)#ip ftp username support
Support(config)#ip ftp password ccnp
Support(config)#ip ftp source-interface s1
Support(config)#exception dump 131.52.61.2
Support(config)#^Z
```

```
Support#
```

Sending a core dump to an RCP server also requires additional commands. The following is an example of configuring a core dump to an RCP server:

```
Support#
Support#config t
Enter configuration commands, one per line. End with
   CNTL/Z.
Support(config)#exception protocol rcp
Support(config)#exception dump 131.52.61.2
Support(config)#ip rcmd remote-username support
Support(config)#ip rcmd rcp-enable
Support(config)#ip rcmd rsh-enable
Support(config)#ip rcmd remote-host support 131.52.61.2 support
Support(config)#^Z
Support#
```

The write core Command

When a router is still on a network, you may also create a core dump from the command line. As previously mentioned, when you create a core dump you must understand the impact it can have on a production network. Use caution when using the commands, and use them only upon request by Cisco TAC personnel.

The **write core** command enables the user to execute a core dump from a router that hasn't crashed. Using this command enables the router to generate a core dump without reloading, and is useful if the router is malfunctioning. Theoretically, the router is dumping its memory to a file, and this action may have an adverse effect on the router. Be prepared for this situation, which is the reason you should perform this command only with TAC personnel available.

The following is an example of configuring a **write core** command:

```
Support#
Support#write core
Remote host? 131.52.61.2
Name of core file to wite [Router_A-core]?
Write file Router_A-core on host 131.52.61.2? [confirm]
Writing Router_A-core !!!!!!!!!!!!!!!!!!!!!!!!!!!!!!!!!!!!!!!!!! [OK]
Support#
```

After you execute this command, the Cisco TAC personnel will be able to look at the dump and try to determine the problem the router is having. The core dump file will not be useful without the Cisco TAC personnel to interpret the source code.

12

The **show stacks** and **version** Commands

Along with creating a core dump file, you may also want to include a few other files for the Cisco TAC. In the Privilege Exec Mode, you can perform a **show stacks** command, which will display data saved by the ROM monitor, including a failure type, an operand address, and a failure counter. It is a good idea to do this before the router is reset, because the information will change with a reload.

In using the **show version** command, a display of the image, version number, and function enables the Cisco TAC personnel to make a more informed decision about how to handle the problem. Some versions of code may have various "bugs" that may contribute to the problem you are experiencing. For example, if you have just configured your router to redistribute Open Shortest Path First (OSPF) with Routing Information Protocol (RIP) and the routing seems to have a problem, call TAC. TAC is privy to information about problems with different code versions that may not yet be published on the web site, and may offer another version of code that will fix the "bug".

Troubleshooting Ethernet

Ethernet problems are commonplace, because Ethernet is widely used in networks. Most Ethernet problems occur at the Physical layer, and looking for certain errors will indicate the problem in most cases. For example, collisions normally occur as a result of a duplexing problem.

When you're troubleshooting Ethernet, it is vital that you understand what the errors are. When you're looking at Ethernet interfaces, you should be able to recognize an error and understand what is causing the error. In looking at the following output, notice the packets received and sent on the interface, and the errors the interface may have incurred.

```
Support#
Support#show interfaces ethernet0
Ethernet0 is up, line protocol is up
  Hardware is Lance, address is 0060.6115.a449 (bia 0060.6115.a449)
  Internet address is 131.52.169.126/25
  MTU 1500 bytes, BW 10000 Kbit, DLY 1000 usec, rely 255/255, load 1/255
  Encapsulation ARPA, loopback not set, keepalive set (10 sec)
  ARP type: ARPA, ARP Timeout 04:00:00
  Last input 00:00:00, output 00:00:00, output hang never
  Last clearing of "show interface" counters never
  Queueing strategy: fifo
  Output queue 0/40, 154 drops; input queue 0/75, 278 drops
  5 minute input rate 1000 bits/sec, 1 packets/sec
  5 minute output rate 1000 bits/sec, 1 packets/sec
     147416665 packets input, 316504203 bytes, 111 no buffer
```

```
     Received 55676605 broadcasts, 0 runts, 0 giants, 278 throttles
     9111 input errors, 0 CRC, 0 frame, 0 overrun, 9111 ignored, 0 abort
     0 input packets with dribble condition detected
     124613539 packets output, 2814229872 bytes, 0 underruns
     7 output errors, 327951 collisions, 1 interface resets
     0 babbles, 0 late collision, 180881 deferred
     7 lost carrier, 0 no carrier
     0 output buffer failures, 0 output buffers swapped out
Support#
```

The following list describes a few of the errors reported for the interface in the preceding output:

➤ *Input rate*—The time the last packet was successfully received on the interface.

➤ *Output rate*—The time the last packet was successfully transmitted on the interface.

➤ *Packets input*—The total number of error-free packets received.

➤ *Runts*—The number of packets discarded because they were too small. In Ethernet, a packet less than 64 bytes is considered a runt.

➤ *Giants*—The number of packets discarded because they were too large. In Ethernet, a packet greater than 1,518 bytes is considered a giant.

➤ *Input error*—This error amount includes runts, giants, no buffer, CRC, frame, overrun, and ignored counts.

➤ *CRC*—Cyclic redundancy checksum (CRC) calculates the checksum to see whether the amount of data sent is the same amount received.

➤ *Frame*—Number of packets received with a CRC error or a noninteger number of octets.

➤ *Overrun*—The number of times the hardware receiver (system buffer) was unable to process data because the receiver buffer was exceeded.

➤ *Ignored*—Number of packets the interface dropped because the interface buffer was exceeded.

➤ *Input packets with dribble condition detected*—A frame error counter that indicates frames that are too long. This is for informational purposes only; the router will still process the frame.

➤ *Output errors*—Total of all errors being reported for that interface.

➤ *Collisions*—Report of Ethernet collisions that required the retransmission of packets.

➤ *Interface resets*—Number of times the interface has been reset.

12

You must be able to understand and identify errors quickly. In most cases, some of the best indicators are the collision rate and frame errors. Looking at the collisions and frame errors will isolate the problem to a physical connection or a bad piece of equipment.

Collisions

In an Ethernet and IEEE 802.3 environment, both employ the carrier sense multiple access collision detect (CSMA/CD) to ensure fewer packet collisions on the network. Before sending data, CSMA/CD stations listen to the network and see if anyone else on the network is sending data. If the station hears nothing on the wire, the station will send its data. A collision occurs when two stations listen for the network traffic, and hear nothing, and the stations transmit simultaneously. In this case, both data transmissions must be retransmitted at a later time.

In the following output example, notice toward the bottom the number of collisions that have occurred on the interface. Ethernet employs the CSMA/CD protocols and collisions are a normal occurrence for Ethernet, except when both joining devices are running full duplex. Only after the collisions exceed 5 to 8 percent of the output packets should you be concerned.

Notice the packet output is 1,246,135 and the collisions total 327,956. Dividing the number of collisions by the number of packets output indicates a collision rate of 26 percent. Because this is much higher than 5 to 8 percent, it is cause for concern. The higher the collision rate, the more packets that need to be retransmitted, thus causing more congestion. Numerous collisions are caused by duplexing problems. Checking to see whether the duplex is set at half or full is the solution to most collision errors. Ethernet needs to have the duplexing set either at half or full on joining devices. In looking at the following output, notice the excessive collisions and runt frames.

```
Support#
Support#show interfaces ethernet0
Ethernet0 is up, line protocol is up
  Hardware is Lance, address is 0060.6115.a449 (bia 0060.6115.a449)
  Internet address is 131.52.169.126/25
  MTU 1500 bytes, BW 10000 Kbit, DLY 1000 usec, rely 255/255, load 1/255
  Encapsulation ARPA, loopback not set, keepalive set (10 sec)
  ARP type: ARPA, ARP Timeout 04:00:00
  Last input 00:00:00, output 00:00:00, output hang never
  Last clearing of "show interface" counters never
  Queueing strategy: fifo
  Output queue 0/40, 154 drops; input queue 0/75, 278 drops
  5 minute input rate 1000 bits/sec, 1 packets/sec
  5 minute output rate 1000 bits/sec, 1 packets/sec
```

```
     1474166 packets input, 3165042 bytes, 111 no buffer
     Received 556 broadcasts, 1222 runts, 0 giants, 278 throttles
     0 input errors, 0 CRC, 0 frame,  overrun, 0 ignored, 0 abort
     0 input packets with dribble condition detected
     1246135 packets output, 28142298 bytes, 0 underruns
     7 output errors, 327956 collisions, 0 interface resets
     0 babbles, 0 late collision, 180881 deferred
     7 lost carrier, 0 no carrier
     0 output buffer failures, 0 output buffers swapped out
Support#
```

The following are a few clues to finding what the possible problem may be:

➤ *An excessive collision rate*—Determined by dividing the number of collisions by the number of packets output. If this exceeds 5 to 8 percent, then a problem exists.

➤ *Excessive runt frames*—Almost always a cause of excessive collisions. If you suspect a high collision rate, always look at the number of runt frames, because this may save you the time of calculating the rate. If the runt frames occur when collisions are not excessive or in a switched environment, this may be the result of underruns or bad software on a network interface card.

Here are a few possible solutions to a collision problem:

➤ Many collisions are caused by duplexing problems. Checking whether the duplex is set at half or full is the solution. Ethernet needs to have the duplexing set either at half or full on both sides.

➤ Faulty cabling is a likely problem with collisions. Test your Category 5 cabling to make sure it is good. You will see interface resets or carrier transitions if the cabling is faulty.

➤ A bad transceiver will cause collisions and that would be the next thing to check.

➤ If none of the preceding solutions has fixed your problem, you may have a bad interface on the router.

Ethernet Noise

As previously stated, most Ethernet problems can be traced to the Physical layer. One of the many things that can affect an Ethernet network is noise. Noise can be caused by various conditions, including misplacement of Category 5 cables or bad cables. A quick way to isolate an Ethernet problem pertaining to noise is to look at the CRC errors and the collision errors. The following output is an example of a problem Ethernet interface:

12

```
Support#
Support#show interfaces ethernet0
Ethernet0 is up, line protocol is up
  Hardware is Lance, address is 0060.6115.a449 (bia 0060.6115.a449)
  Internet address is 131.52.169.126/25
  MTU 1500 bytes, BW 10000 Kbit, DLY 1000 usec, rely 255/255, load 1/255
  Encapsulation ARPA, loopback not set, keepalive set (10 sec)
  ARP type: ARPA, ARP Timeout 04:00:00
  Last input 00:00:00, output 00:00:00, output hang never
  Last clearing of "show interface" counters never
  Queueing strategy: fifo
Output queue 0/40, 154 drops; input queue 0/75, 278 drops
  5 minute input rate 1000 bits/sec, 1 packets/sec
  5 minute output rate 1000 bits/sec, 1 packets/sec
     1474166 packets input, 3165042 bytes, 111 no buffer
     Received 556 broadcasts, 1222 runts, 0 giants, 278 throttles
     0 input errors, 5255 CRC, 0 frame,  overrun, 0 ignored, 0 abort
     0 input packets with dribble condition detected
     1246135 packets output, 28142298 bytes, 0 underruns
     7 output errors, 7 collisions, 0 interface resets
     0 babbles, 0 late collision, 180881 deferred
     7 lost carrier, 0 no carrier
0 output buffer failures, 0 output buffers swapped out
Support#
```

The preceding output shows 5,255 CRC errors and 7 collisions. When you see a high rate of CRC errors and very few collisions, it is usually an indicator of excessive noise. Here are a few possible solutions to the errors reported:

➤ Test the Category 5 cable plugged into the Ethernet interface, if it is a bad cable, replace the cable.

➤ Make sure the cable is Category 5 if you are using a network of 100 Mbps or greater. Replace the cable with Category 5 if not.

➤ Look at the conditions the Ethernet cable is residing on or near. A hot surface, or a vibrating surface, may cause noise to the cable. Place the cable so it is not touching or around anything that can cause noise.

➤ Look at the piece of equipment the Category 5 cable is plugged into, and make sure it is not the cause of the errors. Sometimes the interface or NIC is bad and can be emitting the errors. If it is bad equipment, replace the equipment.

Going through the preceding steps usually solves the problems reported in the example output.

Router Boot Fault-Tolerance

Cisco routers have the capabilities to allow for fault tolerance of the boot process. A router boot process usually is thought of in just one way—booting from flash memory. Cisco routers can actually boot in three ways:

➤ *Flash*—Boot from a removable flash memory card.

➤ *Netboot*—Boot from a server across an Ethernet, token ring, or FDDI network using TFTP, the DEC Maintenance Operation Protocol (MOP), or RCP.

➤ *ROM*—Boot from built-in read-only memory (ROM).

Fault-tolerance booting enables you to configure the router to boot in a particular order. Cisco recommends configuring the boot process in the following order: flash memory, netboot, and then ROM.

The following is an example of a fault-tolerant boot sequence configuration:

```
Support#
Support#config t
Enter configuration commands, one per line. End with
 CNTL/Z.
Support(config)#boot system flash gsxx
Support(config)#boot system gsxx 131.52.169.126
Support(config)#boot system rom
Support(config)#^Z
Support#
Support#copy running-config startup-config
[ok]
Support#
```

Configuring your routers by using the fault-tolerant method enables your routers to boot from three sources. This process alleviates any problems that may be associated with a network outage.

Network Analyzers

A valuable tool in a network is a network analyzer, also referred to as a protocol analyzer. Network analyzers offer real-time statistics of your network. A few of the network analyzers available include Agilent's (formerly HP's) Internet Advisor, Network Associates' Sniffer, and Cisco's EtherPeek. A network analyzer can be extremely helpful if you are receiving complaints of the network running slowly and you can't detect any problems using router tools. The network analyzer can see packets that are traversing the network, and offers a real-time picture of the network performance, protocols, statistics, and network traffic. Network analyzers can not only monitor network traffic and collect key network statistics, but can also enable administrators to extract and review vital information to effectively trouble-shoot and manage a network.

Before you hook up an analyzer to your network, you must decide what part of your network you want to monitor. The analyzer must be connected to the network or broadcast domain that you want to monitor. When used on the network, analyzers are non intrusive because they actually copy packets into memory to analyze them without affecting the communication on the network. After a specified packet is in the analyzer memory, the analyzer software decodes the packet and presents the packet in a readable fashion for the administrator.

Most analyzers are easy to use because they usually have a GUI interface that is easy to program. Several help programs are available to interpret the information the analyzer captures. When you use an analyzer for troubleshooting, it may be helpful to isolate the traffic you are interested in, because the analyzer will provide information pertaining to all network traffic.

Network analyzers can also be used on workstations for which performance is an issue, to see whether the problem is network-related or PC-related. Network analyzers can monitor most types of media, but require additional purchases for each media module the analyzer uses such as Gigabit fiber or 100Base-T Ethernet, just to name two. Network analyzers are pricey, and some companies can't afford such a tool. In large campus networks where several types of applications are running, a network analyzer is a troubleshooting must.

Chapter Summary

When you use basic troubleshooting tools, you should always utilize the **show** and **debug** commands for an initial picture of the problem. Several resources are available to network administrators for cases in which a problem can't be solved by using **show** and **debug**. Cisco offers the Technical Assistance Center (TAC) to answer and aid you in network problems. If you do not have a contract or warranty for the equipment you are having problems with, Cisco can bill you directly. TAC is accessible from the phone, email, fax, and the Cisco Web site (CCO).

One of the procedures TAC may ask you to perform is a core dump, which can give information about the system memory (RAM) if the router crashes or is operating improperly. Because performing a core dump may impact a network, it is advised that you perform it only on the instruction of TAC. The core dump will be in the form of a binary file. After you have retrieved the core dump, the binary file must be transferred to a server and interpreted by technical personnel for Cisco.

Technical support representatives have access to the source code and memory maps to help identify the problem of the router.

To troubleshoot Ethernet, you need to learn what the errors indicate. When looking at an Ethernet interface, you should be able to recognize an error and understand what is causing it. For example, if an Ethernet interface is reporting a large number of CRC errors and very few collisions, it usually is an indicator of excessive noise. If an Ethernet interface is receiving a large number of collisions in comparison to the output packets, you might want to calculate the collision rate. If the collision rate exceeds the healthy performance of 5 to 8 percent, you may want to start your troubleshooting by looking at the duplexing.

Configuring your routers to boot a few different ways adds fault tolerance to the boot process. Normally, the router boots only from the flash memory or possibly a network. Configuring the router to boot a few different ways provides the router more than one opportunity for a successful bootup process.

Using a network analyzer gives you the flexibility to see what is really happening on your network. The network analyzer can see packets that are traversing the network, and offers a real-time picture of the performance, protocols, statistics, and network traffic. Analyzers enable administrators to extract and review a particular piece of information without looking at all the traffic on the network.

Review Questions

1. In using the **core dump** command, the information you are requesting is being copied from _____ memory.

    a. RAM

    b. Flash

    c. Running

    d. ROM

2. The _____ command enables you to create a core dump when the router crashes.

    a. **core dump**

    b. **write memory**

    c. **exception**

    d. **create core**

12

3. The IOS enables you to send a core dump through which types of protocol servers? [Choose the three best answers]

   a. File Transfer Protocol (FTP)

   b. Trivial File Transfer Protocol (TFTP)

   c. Transmission Control Protocol (TCP)

   d. Remote Copy Protocol (RCP)

4. To execute a core dump from a router that hasn't crashed, you must use the _____ command.

   a. **write core dump**

   b. **core dump**

   c. **write core**

   d. **write dump**

5. In troubleshooting Ethernet, what is the recommended acceptance of collision rates for output packets?

   a. 20 to 25 percent

   b. 12 to 18 percent

   c. 1 to 5 percent

   d. 5 to 8 percent

6. Network analyzers can look at real-time network _____, network _____, and network _____. [Choose the three best answers]

   a. Routes

   b. Statistics

   c. Performance

   d. Protocols

7. When troubleshooting an Ethernet interface, if you find excessive CRC errors and very few collisions, what is the first piece of equipment you should look at?

   a. Serial interface

   b. Category 5 cable

   c. NIC card

   d. AUI cable

8. In an Ethernet network, an input error reports errors including _____.
   [Choose the three best answers]

   a. Runts

   b. Giants

   c. CRCs

   d. Interface errors

9. Using the **show stacks** command will display data saved by the ROM monitor, and the output will display _____. [Choose the two best answers]

   a. Failure type

   b. Failure counter

   c. RAM memory

   d. Stack errors

10. Network analyzers are often called or referred to as _____.

    a. Traffic cops

    b. Network devices

    c. TCP/IP analyzers

    d. Protocol analyzers

11. When looking at an Ethernet interface, _____ errors refer to the num-
    ber of packets that had to be re-sent because of collisions.

    a. Reset

    b. Collision

    c. CRC

    d. Runt

12. A packet analyzer looks at each packet and places it in the analyzer's memory.

    a. True

    b. False

13. On an Ethernet interface, the total number of error-free packets received refers
    to the _____ error.

    a. Collision

    b. Reset

    c. CRC

    d. Packets input

12

14. What is the command to use to look at the errors on Ethernet 1 interface?

    a. **interface e0**

    b. **interface e1**

    c. **show interface e0**

    d. **show interfaces e1**

15. In Ethernet, runt errors are the number of packets discarded because the packets were less than _____ bytes.

    a. 98

    b. 60

    c. 64

    d. 84

Real-World Projects

Joe Snow has just received a call notifying him that the users in the Human Resource building are not able to access anything on the network. Joe looks at his topology of the network and realizes the network in question is on router 131.10.1.1.

Project 12.1

To establish connectivity on the router, Joe uses the following steps:

1. He plugs his router cable into the console port of the router.

2. He performs several extended ping tests; the response time is very slow. The network seems to be at a crawl.

3. He performs several **show** and **debug** commands; however, he can't seem to find the problem. He knows that he needs to expedite his fix, because the users are not able to access the network.

Project 12.2

To look at the interface, Joe uses the following steps:

1. He types **config t** to enter Configuration Mode.

2. He types **show interfaces e0** to look at the Ethernet interface, which appears as follows:

```
Ethernet0 is up, line protocol is up
  Hardware is Lance, address is 0060.6115.a449 (bia 0060.6115.a449)
  Internet address is 131.1.1.1./25
```

```
    MTU 1500 bytes, BW 10000 Kbit, DLY 1000 usec, rely 255/255, load 1/255
    Encapsulation ARPA, loopback not set, keepalive set (10 sec)
    ARP type: ARPA, ARP Timeout 04:00:00
    Last input 00:00:00, output 00:00:00, output hang never
    Last clearing of "show interface" counters never
    Queueing strategy: fifo
 Output queue 0/40, 154 drops; input queue 0/75, 278 drops
    5 minute input rate 1000 bits/sec, 1 packets/sec
    5 minute output rate 1000 bits/sec, 1 packets/sec
        1474166 packets input, 3165042 bytes, 111 no buffer
        Received 556 broadcasts, 10runts, 0 giants, 2 throttles
        0 input errors, 0 CRC, 0 frame,  overrun, 0 ignored, 0 abort
        0 input packets with dribble condition detected
        1246135 packets output, 28142298 bytes, 0 underruns
        7 output errors, 2 collisions, 0 interface resets
        0 babbles, 0 late collision, 180881 deferred
        7 lost carrier, 0 no carrier
 0 output buffer failures, 0 output buffers swapped out
```

3. He doesn't see any errors in Ethernet0 and now wants to look at Ethernet1.
   He types **exit** and then **show interfaces e1**, which displays the following:

```
Ethernet1 is up, line protocol is up
   Hardware is Lance, address is 0060.6115.a449 (bia 0060.6115.a449)
   Internet address is 131.1.1.1./25
   MTU 1500 bytes, BW 10000 Kbit, DLY 1000 usec, rely 255/255, load 1/255
   Encapsulation ARPA, loopback not set, keepalive set (10 sec)
   ARP type: ARPA, ARP Timeout 04:00:00
   Last input 00:00:00, output 00:00:00, output hang never
   Last clearing of "show interface" counters never
   Queueing strategy: fifo
 Output queue 0/40, 154 drops; input queue 0/75, 278 drops
   5 minute input rate 1000 bits/sec, 1 packets/sec
 5 minute output rate 1000 bits/sec, 1 packets/sec
        1474166 packets input, 3165042 bytes, 111 no buffer
        Received 556 broadcasts, 10runts, 0 giants, 2 throttles
        0 input errors, 5300CRC, 0 frame,  overrun, 0 ignored, 0 abort
        0 input packets with dribble condition detected
        1246135 packets output, 28142298 bytes, 0 underruns
        7 output errors, 12 collisions, 0 interface resets
        0 babbles, 0 late collision, 180881 deferred
        7 lost carrier, 0 no carrier
 0 output buffer failures, 0 output buffers swapped out
```

12

Project 12.3

To troubleshoot the errors on the interface, Joe uses the following steps:

1. He knows that a high rate of CRC errors and very few collisions usually indicates excessive noise.

2. He begins to swap the Ethernet cable that Ethernet1 was using with a Category 5 cable that he knows is good.

3. He notices the Ethernet cable is actually lodged in between two air conditioning systems that are constantly operating and vibrating. He looks at the Category 5 cable and sees that it is also severely cracked and bent. He can see that it is an older cable.

4. He knows that Ethernet can be affected by certain types of electrical systems and defective cabling, so he swaps the cable with a new Category 5 cable and starts to perform another extended ping by typing the **ping** command.

5. He notices a vast improvement in the network response times.

6. He then looks at the interface again and notices the errors are not incrementing. He calls the users and asks them to try the network again.

7. The users report that they are able to access the network now.

CHAPTER THIRTEEN

Troubleshooting Integrated Services Digital Network

After completing this chapter, you will be able to:

✓ Configure dial-on-demand routing

✓ Identify frequent ISDN problems

✓ Understand and troubleshoot CHAP

✓ Troubleshoot dialer mappings

✓ Troubleshoot PPP

✓ Configure and troubleshoot dialer and access lists

✓ Understand Layer 1 through Layer 3 and the connection process

✓ Understand q.921 and q.931 signaling

✓ Use ISDN troubleshooting **show** and **debug** commands

SDN is one of the more difficult wide area network (WAN) protocols to understand and configure. On top of its complexities, many buyers are not told up front that additional charges sometimes apply for using ISDN during business hours. Regardless, ISDN is an option for administrators to consider when connecting LANs together through a WAN, communicating through multimedia technologies such as video conferencing, or connecting your network or household to the Internet because of its flexibility. Frame Relay and xDSL are other options, but ISDN has wider availability in most areas and occasionally has a definite cost advantage. In addition, the configuration difficulties have been removed to a large degree as the service becomes better known, and service providers are more familiar with the technology.

This chapter is written based on use of a Cisco 804, which is shown in Figure 13.1. This router includes a four-port hub, as well as an ISDN/U (ISDN BRI) interface. Although this book focuses on troubleshooting, this chapter provides a brief overview of ISDN. For a more in-depth discussion on ISDN, the following Certification Insider Press books published by The Coriolis Group are recommended:

➤ *Remote Access Exam Cram*, by Craig Dennis and Eric Quinn (ISBN: 1-57610-437-0), 2000

➤ *Remote Access Exam Prep*, by Barry Meinster (ISBN: 1-57610-692-6), 2001

When computers were first introduced, typical analog phone lines, were the most convenient way of getting data from one point to another without the use of "sneakernet" (placing data on a disk and walking it to its destination). However, phone lines sometimes lacked a clear signal, couldn't compress transmissions, couldn't provide for multiple circuits, couldn't provide much bandwidth, and were really expensive to have running all the time in a network.

In the late 1960s, telephone companies began the long process of upgrading their analog trunks and switches to digital networks that allow for clearer signals, compressible data, better trunk utilization, features such as caller ID and three-way calling, higher bandwidths using a single connection to a service provider, and the elimination of amplifiers in the network.

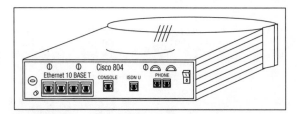

Figure 13.1   A Cisco 804 ISDN router.

ISDN was originally used as a means to move the digital network into the household, to enable a single line to provide two standard phone lines as well as digital services for data. The great thing about this is that ISDN can use the existing copper wire; thus telephone companies were able to add an immediate service that translated into more revenue and improved their existing service.

In the beginning, ISDN was not advertised well and not understood by those who could use it most. Unlike ISDN today, for which a workforce of thousands who understand the technology exists, very few consumers implemented the technology initially, contrary to the expectations of many telephone companies. Additionally, installation issues, availability, and its initial high price all conspired to hinder ISDN's acceptance in the household (or even by businesses). Because of this, X.25 seemed to be the technology of choice in the 1970s.

It took another 15 years before ISDN finally caught on, and in the late part of the 1990s, ISDN suddenly became a popular choice to replace the old X.25 technology because of the use of a D channel (explained later in this chapter). ISDN also became popular for businesses to handle video conferencing, point-of-sale transactions, and data transfers, and to connect small to medium-sized businesses, as well as households, to the Internet.

As with just about any major protocol dealing with the transfer of data from one place to another, certain configuration and troubleshooting issues arise in ISDN. You need to gain a solid knowledge of the types of problems you may encounter not only with ISDN, but also with the way ISDN affects other protocols and networking devices. Most ISDN problems occur in certain areas and can be isolated and resolved easily with a good fundamental knowledge of ISDN. The next section looks at these common issues.

Dial-On-Demand Routing

13

Dial-on-demand routing (DDR) is used to allow more than one Cisco ISDN router to dial an ISDN dialup connection on an as-needed basis. DDR, though, should be used only in low-volume and periodic network connections using either a Public Switched Telephone Network (PSTN) or ISDN line.

If an access list is configured and a packet is received on an interface on the inside network that meets the requirements of interesting (sendable) traffic, the following steps take place:

1. The route to the destination network is determined.

2. A call is initiated to the destination network based on dialer information to that network.

3. The data is transmitted to the destination network.

4. The call is terminated if there is no more data to be transmitted over the link to that network and the configured idle-timeout period has been reached.

To configure DDR, you use the following steps, which are explained in detail next:

1. Define at least one static route, to define the route to the destination network.

2. Use access lists to specify the traffic that is considered interesting or allowed to be sent by the router.

3. Use a route map to configure the dialer information to get to the destination network.

Configuring the Static Routes

To forward traffic across an ISDN link, you should configure static routes on each of the ISDN routers. If you are using a dynamic routing protocol, there will always be data to send and the ISDN link will never drop. A dynamic routing protocol sort of defeats the purpose of dialing the destination network only when data exists to send. Therefore, all participating ISDN routers should have a static route that defines all the known routes to other networks.

You first need to define the destination network, which is 68.78.39.0 (as shown in Figure 13.2), with the following command:

```
Ginas504 (config)#ip route 68.78.39.0 255.255.255.0 172.16.1.1
```

You can also define which interface can be used to get to 63.78.39.0, which is the BRI0 interface, using the following command:

```
Ginas504 (config)#ip route 68.78.39.0 255.255.255.0 bri0
```

Using Dialer Lists to Specify Interesting Traffic

After setting the route tables in each router, you need to configure the router to determine what brings up the ISDN line. An administrator using the **dialer-list** global configuration command defines interesting packets.

The following is the command to turn on all IP traffic:

```
Sean804(config)# dialer-list 1 protocol ip permit
Sean804(config)# int bri0
Sean804(config-if)# dialer-group 1
```

The **dialer-group** command sets the access list on the BRI interface. Extended access lists can be used with the **dialer-list** command to define interesting traffic to include only certain applications. That topic is covered later in the chapter.

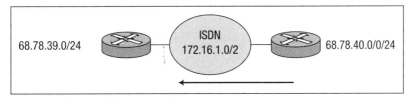

Figure 13.2 The ISDN network with two ISDN routers and their related configuration information.

Other Configuration Commands

The following are three other commands that you should use when configuring your BRI interface:

➤ **dialer load-threshold**

➤ **dialer idle-timeout**

➤ **ppp multilink**

The **dialer load-threshold** command instructs the BRI interface when to bring up the second B channel. You must specify how much of a load must exist on the first B channel before the second is used. This option ranges from 1 to 255, where 255 indicates that the second BRI channel should be brought up when the first is at 100 percent. You must also indicate whether this is based on the load coming in, going out, or both (either) on this interface.

The multilink PPP (MP) allows load balancing between the two B channels in a BRI. It is not vendor-specific and it provides packet fragmentation and reassembly, sequencing, and load calculating. Cisco's MP is based on RFC 1990.

The **dialer idle-timeout** command is used to specify the number of seconds to wait before disconnecting a call if no data is sent. The default is 120 seconds. The following is an example of using the **dialer load-threshold**, **dialer idle-timeout**, and **ppp multilink** commands:

```
Seans804(config-if)# dialer load-threshold 200 either
Seans804(config-if)# dialer idle-timeout 200
Seans804(config-if)# ppp multilink
```

To verify the PPP multilink configuration, use the **show ppp multilink** command.

13

Frequent ISDN Problems

Usually when dealing with ISDN your most frequent problems deal with misconfigured interfaces, the physical cabling, ISDN protocol issues, or misconfigured local service provider switches. In the following sections, let's look at all of these issues and how to resolve them.

Misconfigurations

Configuring ISDN is fairly simple and there are only a few commands needed for the basic configuration. This does take some knowledge, though, on how ISDN works, the different line protocols, and the proper placement of the equipment. In terms of configuring the ISDN router interfaces correctly, let's take a look at the following issues:

➤ The Service Profile Identifier (SPID)

➤ Challenge Handshake Authentication Protocol (CHAP)

➤ Dialer mapping command

➤ Access lists

➤ Point-To-Point Protocol (PPP)

Service Profile Identifier

The SPID is a phone-line identifier used in an analog phone environment. The SPID includes the actual seven-digit telephone number, including the area code and sometimes an extra few digits used by the service provider's switch. A SPID looks similar to this example, 80055510000100, which corresponds to the phone number 800-555-1000. The additional parameters, 0100, serve as an identifier for the local service provider's switch. If you don't have these numbers and you know the service has been connected, you may need to contact the local service provider to receive these numbers.

The SPID occasionally causes confusion because it isn't always necessary. When you configure the switch type, if you use Nortel DMS100 or Nation ISDN (basic-ni), the SPID is required. If you are using Basic-5ess, the SPID may be optional. Your local service provider is the authority on this matter.

The ISDN SPID is a unique number that the local ISDN router must learn in order to successfully identify itself, but only in North America, and the integration of the phone number into the SPID is usually only applicable in public telephone company ISDN installations. In a private ISDN network, the SPID can usually be any 10-digit or longer number.

One item that you must verify is that the IP addresses assigned to the interfaces connecting the two ISDN devices together are in their own network and subnet, just as any other point-to-point WAN connection must be.

Challenge Handshake Authentication Protocol

CHAP provides ISDN with the capability to control access to each router by forcing the ISDN routers to use an authentication technique. This provides confidence to a business that implementing ISDN is a low security risk.

CHAP is used to require a username and encrypted password on all inbound connections. One of the most important items in troubleshooting CHAP is to verify that the CHAP-configured username and passwords match on both interfaces connecting the ISDN routers. One advantage Cisco has over other ISDN routers is the ability to support Microsoft CHAP (MS-CHAP), which was implemented in version 12 of the Cisco IOS, and the Password Authentication Protocol (PAP), which is an earlier version of CHAP.

To use CHAP authentication, you must enable PPP by using the **encapsulation ppp** command and assigning an authentication method, as follows:

```
Seans804(config-if)#ppp auth ?
chap     Challenge Handshake Authentication Protocol(CHAP)
ms-chap Microsoft Challenge Handshake Authentication Protocol(MS-CHAP)
pap      Password Authentication Protocol (PAP)
```

If you suspect a password might be the problem in authenticating, the best way to confirm this is by using the **debug ppp** authentication command. The following output shows the error you will receive when the authentication fails due to an incorrect password configuration:

```
Seans804#debug ppp authentication
PPP authentication debugging is on

Seans804#ping 172.16.1.1
Type escape sequence to abort.
02:18:36: BR0:1 PPP: Phase is AUTHENTICATING, by both
02:18:36: BR0:1 CHAP: O CHALLENGE id 7 len 27 from "Seans804"
02:18:36: BR0:1 CHAP: I CHALLENGE id 7 len 24 from "Ginas804"
02:18:36: BR0:1 CHAP: O RESPONSE id 7 len 27 from "Seans804"
02:18:36: BR0:1 CHAP: I FAILURE id 7 len 25 msg is "MD/DES compare failed"
02:18:36: %ISDN-6-DISCONNECT: Interface BRIO:1 disconnected from
18005551002, call lasted 1 seconds
02:18:38: %LINK-3-UPDOWN: Interface BRIO:1, changed state to down.
02:18:38: %LINK-3-UPDOWN: Interface BRIO:1, changed state to up.
02:18:38: BR0:1 PPP: Treating connection as a callout
02:18:38: BR0:1 PPP: Phase is AUTHENTICATING, by both
02:18:38: BR0:1 CHAP: O CHALLENGE id 8 len 27 from "Seans804"
02:18:38: BR0:1 CHAP: I CHALLENGE id 8 len 24 from "Ginas804"
02:18:38: BR0:1 CHAP: O RESPONSE id 8 len 27 from "Seans804"
02:18:38: BR0:1 CHAP: I FAILURE id 8 len 25 msg is "MD/DES compare failed"
```

As this output demonstrates, CHAP performs authentication by sending authentication packets that consist of an 8-bit Code field, an 8-bit Identifier field, a 16-bit Length field, and a Data field, which can vary in length. The Code field identifies

13

the type of CHAP packet, which varies based on the type of packet being sent, and which may be any of the following four types:

➤ Challenge (Type 1)

➤ Response (Type 2)

➤ Success (Type 3)

➤ Failure (Type 4)

The following is the CHAP authentication process between the Seans804 router and the Ginas804 router:

1. Seans804(Challenge) sends a Challenge packet to the Ginas804 (remote ISDN router).

2. The Ginas804 copies the identifier information into a new packet. It then sends a Response packet along with the *hashed value*, a value calculated from the encrypted password.

3. The Seans804 receives the Response packet and checks the hashed value against its own hashed value. If both hashed values match, Seans804 sends a Success packet back. Otherwise, it sends a Failure packet back to Ginas804.

Configure CHAP authentication is a straightforward process. Here is an example of configuring an ISDN router with a username, password, and PPP CHAP authentication:

```
Seans804# config t
Seans804(config)# username Sean password cisco
Seans804(config)# interface bri0
Seans804(config-if)# encapsualtion ppp
Seans804(config-if)# ppp authentication chap
```

The dialer map Command

The dialer mapping command, **dialer map**, permits the ISDN router to dial an associated number when data that is destined for the next-hop interface is received. When data is received for the identified protocol of the other side of the ISDN line, this command instructs the ISDN router which number to call.

When using this command, you must make sure that the dialer map entries contain valid IP addresses and phone numbers, and that a **dialer map** statement exists for each protocol in the network. The following output walks you through using the **dialer map** command for the IP protocol:

```
Seans804(config)#int bri0
Seans804(config-if)#dialer map ?
```

```
   bridge    Bridging
   clns      ISO CLNS
   ip        IP
   ip        IP
   ipx       Novell IPX
   llc2      LLC2
   netbios   NETBIOS
   snapshot  Snapshot routing support

Seans804(config-if)#dialer map ip ?
  A.B.C.D  Protocol specific address

Seans804(config-if)#dialer map ip 172.16.1.1 ?
  WORD           Dialer string
  broadcast      Broadcasts should be forwarded to this address
  class          dialer map class
  modem-script   Specify regular expression to select modem dialing script
  name           Map to a host
  spc            Semi Permanent Connections
  speed          Set dialer speed
  system-script  Specify regular expression to select system dialing script

Sean804(config-if)#dialer map ip 172.16.1.1 18005551001
Sean804(config-if)#
```

The following example demonstrates the BRI0 interface using the **show running-config** command:

```
!
interface BRI0
 ip address 172.16.1.2 255.255.255.0
 no ip directed-broadcast
 no ip route-cache
 no ip mroute-cache
 dialer idle-timeout 100000
 dialer wait-for-carrier-time 120
 dialer map ip 172.16.1.1 18005551001
 dialer load-threshold 128 either
 dialer-group 1
 isdn switch-type basic-ni
 isdn spid1 5551001401
!
```

Access Lists

Access lists are used with ISDN connections to keep certain types of traffic from being sent across the ISDN link and causing the ISDN router to make an unnecessary connection. Using the rule that the more calls you make, the more you pay, access lists save money. Some services offer Centrix ISDN and other options that circumvent higher costs. Still, if you need a constant connection (more than 40 hours per month), Frame Relay, DSL, and many other permanent virtual connection (PVC) technologies are available with the same or greater bandwidth at a much lower cost.

The following example demonstrates a configured access list and using the **dialer-group** command to apply it to an interface. This access list, shown here in the **show running-config** command, is configured to allow only IP protocols, with the exception to HTTP access, which uses port 80.

```
!
interface BRI0
 ip address 172.16.1.2 255.255.255.0
 no ip directed-broadcast
 no ip route-cache
 no ip mroute-cache
 dialer idle-timeout 100000
 dialer wait-for-carrier-time 120
 dialer map ip 172.16.1.1 18008358664
 dialer map ip 172.16.1.1 18005551002
 dialer load-threshold 128 either
 dialer-group 1
 isdn switch-type basic-ni
 isdn switch-type basic-ni
!
router rip
 redistribute static
 network 63.0.0.0
 network 172.16.0.0
!
ip classless
ip route 0.0.0.0 0.0.0.0 172.16.1.1
ip route 63.78.39.0 255.255.255.0 172.16.1.1
!
access-list 155 deny tcp any any eq 80
access-list 155 permit ip any any
dialer-list 1 protocol ip list 155
!
line con 0
 transport input none
 stopbits 1
line vty 0 4
 password sean
login
!
```

Point-To-Point Protocol

The recommended choice for a secure connection with ISDN routers is PPP. Several other options are available that include a simulated serial connection using HDLC. When troubleshooting, PPP provides additional information regarding the connection, including the protocol type. This rarely presents itself in a manner that is useable to administrators, however; rather, an understanding of the protocol and its capability to provide useful functions, including CHAP, is more often helpful to administrators. Note that the PPP protocol is the same for analog or ISDN connections, so the configuration of PPP on a workstation using an analog modem requires PPP encapsulation on the ISDN host router. PPP also supports compression.

When using the **debug ppp** command, the output provides information about PPP. PPP contains a Protocol field in the output, which can be used to identify the upper-layer information included in the datagram. Table 13.1 lists the protocol values.

Connecting at the Physical Layer

One of the first areas to consider when troubleshooting ISDN is the Physical layer, particularly with new installations. The wiring is one of the most important aspects to consider when no connection can be made. When using ISDN for videoconferencing equipment or connecting to PBX equipment in the local network, you can use Category 3, 4, 5, or even 6 cabling. This chapter, however, will focus on asynchronous Basic Rate Interface (BRI) connections, which use standard copper-pair wiring.

ISDN BRI was originally designed to provide digital services over existing pairs of copper so that the already existing analog phone lines wouldn't need to be replaced. A BRI can be used for videoconferencing, voice services, or data. An additional control channel called the *D channel*, is used by BRI as a replacement for legacy X.25 networks.

13

Table 13.1   PPP field values.

Hex Value	Protocol
0021	IP
0029	AppleTalk
002B	IPX
003D	Multilink
0201	802.1d Hellos
0203	Source Route Bridging Protocol Data Units
8021	IPCP
8029	ATCP
802B	IPXCP
C223	CHAP
C023	PAP

BRI interface connections are different from primary rate interface (PRI) connections. PRI uses a T-1 or DS-1, which is the equivalent of 24 individual 64K channels. A voice connection basic rate is referred to as a DS-0, or a single 64 Kbps B channel of the T-1 connection.

Each ISDN BRI is a 192Kbps circuit that is divided into three individual channels in a connection. The B channels are used as the primary data channels, providing 64Kbps of bandwidth in each direction. The D channel provides 16Kbps of bandwidth for control signaling. The remaining bandwidth of 48Kbps is used for overhead.

A frame that traverses the BRI interfaces is 48 bits, and each BRI circuit can send 4,000 frames per second. A service called *Always on* can use the D channel to send data, which reflects a nondemand mode for the channel. The Always on service is usually used to replace X.25 in point-of-sale (POS) circuits that use 9.6Kbps of bandwidth for the application.

Many administrators troubleshoot only the local side of an ISDN circuit, but it is good to keep in mind that a *local loop* exists on the remote side that must be functioning properly as well. The local loop is the circuit between your side of the demarcation point and the central office (CO), also known as the *carrier operations*. The *demarcation point* is the point at which your ISDN connection connects to the wall in your facility. This is also the point at which the telephone company begins and ends its responsibility for the connection. The local service provider's responsibility is to verify that a connection exists at the wall, and from there it is the local administration's responsibility to get the connection functioning. Of course, it is also the responsibility of the local service provider to provide you with the proper SPIDs and connection type information.

The local loop at this point in the network is referred to as the RT. The RT allows the connection to overcome distance limitations so that a clear signal can reach the CO. The local loop connects your local ISDN router and ISDN switch belonging to the local service provider. The local loop is necessary because all digital signals have distance limitations between two devices.

Now that you know about the local loop and the connections, the next section discusses how to troubleshoot Physical layer connectivity and provides the terminology that you should have a good grasp of.

Troubleshooting the Physical Layer

This section focuses on troubleshooting, but a quick terminology lesson is necessary for the following components, which are shown in Figure 13.3. An explanation of the physical architecture and its proper functionality follows this list.

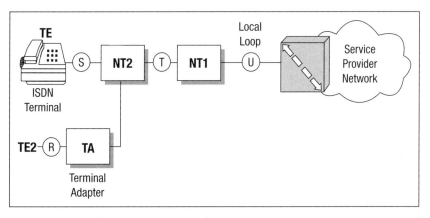

Figure 13.3   The ISDN components and reference points found in the network.

➤ *Line termination (LT) point*—Handles line termination of the local loop and switching functions. An NT1 device is located at the local service provider's site.

➤ *Exchange termination (ET) point*—Handles line termination of the local loop and switching functions.

➤ *Network termination (NT1)*—The network termination point. This is often the demarcation point.

➤ *Terminal equipment type 1 (TE1)*—This is a device that uses a four-wire, twisted-pair digital interface. Most ISDN devices found in today's networks are this type.

➤ *Terminal equipment type 2 (TE2)*—This is a device that does not contain an ISDN interface and that requires a terminal adapter (TA).

➤ *R reference point*—Identifies the reference point between non-ISDN equipment and a TA. This point in the network allows a non-ISDN device to appear to the network as an ISDN device.

➤ *S reference point*—The connection point between the user-end equipment and an NT1 or an NT2. The user-end equipment can be the ISDN router, a TE1, or a TA.

➤ *T reference point*—Defines the reference point between an NT1 device and an NT2 device.

➤ *S/T interface*—A combination of both the S and T interfaces. This interface is governed by the ITU I.430 standard, which defines the connection as a four-wire connection and the ISO 8877 physical connector. The S/T interface is an RJ 45, 8-pin cable using pins 3 and 6 to receive data, and pins 4 and 5 to transmit data. A straight-through pin configuration connects the terminal end point (TE) to the NT, as shown in Table 13.2.

13

Table 13.2 The RJ-45 ISDN S/T interface.

Pin	Terminal End Point	Network Termination
1	Power +	Power
2	Power-	Power
3	Transmit +	Receive +
4	Receive +	Transmit +
5	Receive -	Transmit -
6	Transmit -	Receive -
7	Power-	Power
8	Power +	Power +

> ➤ *U reference point*—The connection point between an NT1 and the LE. It is normally serviced on a single twisted-pair cable to reduce data delivery costs and simplify installations.

Note: *Both the LT and the ET typically are just referred to as the local exchange (LE). Although an RJ-45, RJ-11, or RJ-14 can be used for ISDN terminations, it is recommended that you use an RJ-45.*

Misconfigured Provider Switches

Unfortunately, when a problem exists with ISDN, your own site and the remote site are not the only areas you have to consider. Because this is a WAN-type issue, an administrator must consider the possibility that the service provider failed to configure the ISDN switch properly, particularly when this is a new installation.

To know when the local service provider's equipment may be the reason for a problem in the network, you should have a clear understanding of all the layers in which ISDN may be a problem. Those are in Layers 1 through 3 of the OSI Reference Model.

Troubleshooting the Data Link Layer

Layer 2 of the OSI Reference Model has two protocols that need to be working properly, if they are configured: q.921 and PPP. There is also a service access point identifier associated with q.921.

The q.921 Protocol

The q.921 protocol defines the signaling method used by ISDN at Layer 2 of the OSI Reference Model. The q.921 protocol uses the D channel by using the Link Access Procedure on D channel (LAPD) protocol, which is used by X.25. If the q.921 connection between the CO switch and the local ISDN router does not occur and complete, there can be no network (Layer 3) connectivity.

If you use the **show isdn status** command and find that a Layer 2 problem exists, the best way to troubleshoot q.921 protocol problems is to use the **debug isdn q921** command. Usually, a problem with q.921 relates to the terminal end point identifier (TEI). The TEI value uniquely identifies every terminal in the network. A value of 127 represents the broadcast address to all the terminals. TEIs 64 through 126 are reserved for use after the completion of a Layer 2 ISDN connection. You cannot assign this value, because it is a dynamic assignment.

The following output is from the **show isdn status** command on an incorrectly configured interface:

```
Seans804# show isdn status
Global ISDN Switchtype = basic-ni
ISDN BRIO interface
dsl 0, interface ISDN Switchtype = basic-ni
    Layer 1 Status:
ACTIVE
    Layer 2 Status:
TEI = 79, Ces = 1, SAPI = 0, State = MULTIPLE_FRAME_   ESTABLISHED
    Spid Status:
TEI 79, ces = 1, state = 8(established)
    spid1 configured, no LDN, spid1 NOT sent, spid1 NOT valid
TEI Not Assigned, ces = 2, state = 1(terminal down)
    spid2 configured, no LDN, spid2 NOT sent, spid2 NOT valid
    Layer 3 Status:
0 Active Layer 3 Call(s)
    Activated dsl 0 CCBs = 1
CCB:callid=0x0, sapi=0x0, ces=0x1, B-chan=0 calltype = INTERNAL
Total Allocated ISDN CCBs = 1
```

The following output is correctly configured and shows that all the layers are active and configured correctly:

```
Seans804#show isdn status
Global ISDN Switchtype = basic-ni
ISDN BRIO interface
        dsl 0, interface ISDN Switchtype = basic-ni
    Layer 1 Status:
        ACTIVE
    Layer 2 Status:
        TEI = 105, Ces = 1, SAPI = 0, State = MULTIPLE_FRAME_ESTABLISHED
    Spid Status:
        TEI 105, ces = 1, state = 5(init)
            spid1 configured, no LDN, spid1 sent, spid1 valid
            Endpoint ID Info: epsf = 0, usid = 3, tid = 1
    Layer 3 Status:
        2 Active Layer 3 Call(s)
    Activated dsl 0 CCBs = 0
```

13

Table 13.3   Terminal end point message indicator types.

Indicator Type	Description
1	Requesting ID
2	Assigned ID
3	Denied ID
4	ID Check Request
5	ID Check Response
6	Remove ID
7	ID Verify

When using the **debug isdn q921** command, message types are used to help identify what type of information is being passed. This helps to identify the process that is running when a failure occurs. Table 13.3 shows the message types.

The following is an example of using the **debug isdn q921** command:

```
Seans804# debug isdn q921
ISDN Q921 packets debugging is on
01:11:15: ISDN BR0: TX -> RRp sapi = 0 tei = 92 nr = 12
01:11:14252354: ISDN BR0: RX <- RRf sapi = 0 tei = 92 nr = 12

Sean804#ping 172.16.1.2
Type escape sequence to abort.
Sending 5, 100-byte ICMP Echos to 172.16.1.2, timeout is 2 seconds:
..
01:11:28: ISDN BR0: TX ->
INFOc sapi = 0 tei = 92  ns = 12 nr = 12 i = 0x080
10305040288901801832C0B3138303038333538363631
00:19:98789554100: ISDN BR0: RX <-
INFOc sapi = 0  tei = 92 ns = 12 nr = 13
i =
0x08018302180189952A1B809402603D83073833353836 36318E0B2054454C544F4E45203120
01:11:28: ISDN BR0: TX ->  RRr sapi = 0  tei = 92  nr = 13
01:11:103079256064: ISDN BR0: RX <- INFOc sapi = 0 tei = 9 ns = 13  nr = 13
 i = 0x08018307
01:11:29: ISDN BR0: TX ->
RRr sapi = 0 tei = 92 nr = 14
01:11:29: %LINK-3-UPDOWN: Interface BRIO:1, changed state to up
01:11:29: ISDN BR0: TX ->
INFOc sapi = 0  tei = 92  ns = 13 nr = 14 i = 0x080 1030F
01:12:103079215104: ISDN BR0: RX <- RRr sapi = 0  tei = 92 nr = 14
01:12:25: %LINEPROTO-5-UPDOWN: Line protocol on Interface BRIO:1,
changed state to up
01:12:107379488692: ISDN BR0: RX <- UI sapi = 0 tei = 127 i =
0x08010A05040288
```

```
9018018A3401403B0282816C0941813833353836363337008C13833353836    3632
01:12:25: %LINK-3-UPDOWN: Interface BRIO:2, changed state t.!!!
Success rate is 60 percent (3/5), round-trip min/avg/max = 32/38/48 ms

Seans804#
01:12:26: ISDN BRO: TX ->
 INFOc sapi = 0  tei = 92  ns = 14 nr = 14 i = 0x080
18A0718018A
01:12:267374223360: ISDN BRO: RX <- INFOc sapi = 0  tei = 92 ns = 14 nr =
15
 i = 0x08010A0F
01:12:27: ISDN BRO: TX ->
 RRr sapi = 0 tei = 92  nr = 15
01:12:27: %LINEPROTO-5-UPDOWN: Line protocol on Interface
 BRIO:2, changed state to up
01:12:27: ISDN BRO: TX ->
 RRp sapi = 0  tei = 93 nr = 0
01:12:154618822656: ISDN BRO: RX <- RRf sapi = 0 tei = 93 nr = 0
```

Service Access Point Identifier Field

One thing to watch for in the output of the **debug isdn q921** command is the SAPI, or *service access point identifier*, field. If this field lists a SAPI of 0, then Layer 3 signaling is present. This signaling is provided by q.931, which is covered later in this chapter, under the section "Troubleshooting the Network Layer." The value of 63 indicates a management SAPI for the assignment of the TEI values. A value of 64 indicates that q921 is using call control.

Set Asynchronous Balanced Mode Extended Field

Another field to look at when using the **debug isdn q921** command is the set asynchronous balanced mode extended (SABME) messages. SABME messages are exchanged with TEI message type 7. Should the SABME fail, a disconnect response message is sent and the link establishment is terminated. In this situation, you must determine the reason for the SABME failure.

When the SABME succeeds, an acknowledgment is sent that a Layer 2 connection is established. When this occurs, you should see the TE begin to send INFO-type frames.

Point-To-Point Protocol Troubleshooting

To troubleshoot the PPP protocol and isolate CHAP problems, you should first check both sides of the ISDN link to verify that the usernames and passwords are configured correctly. Knowing the steps that PPP and CHAP use in negotiating a connection can also aid in determining the problem. The following are the steps taken by PPP and CHAP to establish a link. These steps are sometimes referred to as *targets*.

1. The TE sends a CONFREQ, which is a configuration request specifying certain router options.

2. If the request is accepted, a CONFACK is sent back to the TE, which is an acknowledgment. If the request is denied, a CONFREJ is sent to the requesting TE.

3. If CHAP is used for authentication, it continues to steps 4 through 6, which are the three-way handshake process.

4. A challenge message is sent to the remote TE.

5. The remote TE sends a response message.

6. If the response values match, authentication is given.

The following is an example of using the **debug ppp negotiation** command, which is extremely helpful in researching PPP problems and resolving them:

```
Seans804#debug ppp negotiation
PPP protocol negotiation debugging is on

Seans804# ping 172.16.1.1
Type escape sequence to abort.
Sending 5, 100-byte ICMP Echos to 172.16.1.1, timeout is 2     seconds:
02:26:33: %LINK-3-UPDOWN: Interface BRI0:1, changed state to     up
02:26:33: BR0:1 PPP: Treating connection as a callout
02:26:33: BR0:1 PPP: Phase is ESTABLISHING, Active Open
02:26:33: BR0:1 LCP: O CONFREQ [Closed] id 3 len 10
02:26:33: BR0:1 LCP:    MagicNumber 0x50239604    (0x050650239604)
02:26:33: BR0:1 LCP: I CONFREQ [REQsent] id 13 len 10
02:26:33: BR0:1 LCP:    MagicNumber 0x5023961F    (0x05065023961F)
02:26:33: BR0:1 LCP: O CONFACK [REQsent] id 13 len 10
02:26:33: BR0:1 LCP:    MagicNumber 0x5.023961F    (0x05065023961F)
02:26:33: BR0:1 LCP: I CONFACK [ACKsent] id 3 len 10
02:26:33: BR0:1 LCP:    MagicNumber 0x50239604    (0x050650239604)
02:26:33: BR0:1 LCP: State is Open
02:26:33: BR0:1 PPP: Phase is UP
02:26:33: BR0:1 CDPCP: O CONFREQ [Closed] id 3 len 4
02:26:33: BR0:1 IPCP: O CONFREQ [Closed] id 3 len 10
02:26:33: BR0:1 IPCP:    Address 10.1.1.2 (0x03060A010102)
02:26:33: BR0:1 CDPCP: I CONFREQ [REQsent] id 3 len 4
02:26:33: BR0:1 CDPCP: O CONFACK [REQsent] id 3 len 4
02:26:33: BR0:1 IPCP: I CONFREQ [REQsent] id 3 len 10
02:26:33: BR0:1 IPCP:    Address 172.16.1.1 (0x03060A010101)
02:26:33: BR0:1 IPCP: O CONFACK [REQsent] id 3 len 10
02:26:33: BR0:1 IPCP:    Address 10.1.1.1 (0x03060A010101)
```

```
02:26:33: BR0:1 CDPCP: I CONFACK [ACKsent] id 3 len 4
02:26:33: BR0:1 CDPCP: State is Open
02:26:33: BR0:1 IPCP: I CONFACK [ACKsent] id 3 len 10
02:26:33: BR0:1 IPCP:    Address 172.16.1.2 (0x03060A010102)
02:26:33: BR0:1 IPCP: State is Open
02:26:33: BR0 IPCP: Install route to 172.16.1.1
!!!!!
Success rate is 100 percent (5/5), round-trip min/avg/max = 32/38/48 ms
%LINEPROTO-5-UPDOWN: Line protocol on Interface
BRIO:1, changed state to up
02:26:33: %LINK-3-UPDOWN: Interface
BRIO:2, changed state to up
02:26:36: BR0:2 PPP: Treating connection as a callin
02:26:36: BR0:2 PPP: Phase is ESTABLISHING, Passive Open
02:26:36: BR0:2 LCP: State is Listen
02:26:36: BR0:2 LCP: I CONFREQ [Listen] id 3 len 10
02:26:36: BR0:2 LCP:    MagicNumber 0x50239CC8   (0x050650239CC8)
02:26:36: BR0:2 LCP: O CONFREQ [Listen] id 3 len 10
02:26:36: BR0:2 LCP:    MagicNumber 0x50239CDA   (0x050650239CDA)
02:26:36: BR0:2 LCP: O CONFACK [Listen] id 3 len 10
02:26:36: BR0:2 LCP:    MagicNumber 0x50239CC8   (0x050650239CC8)
02:26:36: BR0:2 LCP: I CONFACK [ACKsent] id 3 len 10
02:26:36: BR0:2 LCP:    MagicNumber 0x50239CDA   (0x050650239CDA)
02:26:36: BR0:2 LCP: State is Open
02:26:36: BR0:2 PPP: Phase is UP
02:26:36: BR0:2 CDPCP: O CONFREQ [Closed] id 3 len 4
02:26:36: BR0:2 IPCP: O CONFREQ [Closed] id 3 len 10
02:26:36: BR0:2 IPCP:    Address 172.16.1.2 (0x03060A010102)
02:26:36: BR0:2 CDPCP: I CONFREQ [REQsent] id 3 len 4
02:26:36: BR0:2 CDPCP: O CONFACK [REQsent] id 3 len 4
02:26:36: BR0:2 IPCP: I CONFREQ [REQsent] id 3 len 10
02:26:36: BR0:2 IPCP:    Address 172.16.1.1 (0x03060A010101)
02:26:36: BR0:2 IPCP: O CONFACK [REQsent] id 3 len 10
02:26:36: BR0:2 IPCP:    Address 172.16.1.1 (0x03060A010101)
02:26:36: BR0:2 CDPCP: I CONFACK [ACKsent] id 3 len 4
02:26:36: BR0:2 CDPCP: State is Open
02:26:36: BR0:2 IPCP: I CONFACK [ACKsent] id 3 len 10
02:26:36: BR0:2 IPCP:    Address 172.16.1.2 (0x03060A010102)
02:26:36: BR0:2 IPCP: State is Open
02:26:42: %LINEPROTO-5-UPDOWN: Line protocol on Interface
BRIO:2, changed state to up
02:26:42: BR0:1 LCP: O ECHOREQ [Open] id 12 len 12 magic 0x5020C645
02:26:42: BR0:1 LCP: echo_cnt 1, sent id 12, line up
02:26:42: BR0:1 PPP: I pkt type 0xC021, datagramsize 16
02:26:42: BR0:1 LCP: I ECHOREP [Open] id 12 len 12 magic 0x5020C654
02:26:42: BR0:1 LCP: Received id 12, sent id 12, line up
```

13

```
02:26:42: BRO:2 LCP: O ECHOREQ [Open] id 12 len 12 magic 0x5020CD1B
02:26:42: BRO:2 LCP: echo_cnt 1, sent id 12, line up
02:26:42: BRO:2 PPP: I pkt type 0xC021, datagramsize 16
02:26:42: BRO:2 LCP: I ECHOREP [Open] id 12 len 12 magic 0x5020CD0D
02:26:42: BRO:2 LCP: Received id 12, sent id 12, line up
02:26:42: BRO:1 PPP: I pkt type 0xC021, datagramsize 16
02:26:42: BRO:1 LCP: I ECHOREQ [Open] id 12 len 12 magic 0x5020C654
02:26:42: BRO:1 LCP: O ECHOREP [Open] id 12 len 12 magic 0x5020C645
02:26:42: BRO:2 PPP: I pkt type 0xC021, datagramsize 16
02:26:42: BRO:2 LCP: I ECHOREQ [Open] id 12 len 12 magic 0x5020CD0D
02:26:42: BRO:2 LCP: O ECHOREP [Open] id 12 len 12 magic 0x5020CD1B
02:26:48: BRO:2 PPP: I pkt type 0x0207, datagramsize 15
02:26:48: BRO:2 PPP: I pkt type 0x0207, datagramsize 312
02:26:48: %ISDN-6-DISCONNECT: Interface
BRIO:1 disconnected from 18005551002 To p, call lasted 120 seconds
02:26:48: %LINK-3-UPDOWN: Interface BRIO:1, changed state to down
02:26:107379488949: %ISDN-6-DISCONNECT: Interface
BRIO:2, disconnected from 5551002, call lasted 120 seconds
02:26:48: %LINK-3-UPDOWN: Interface BRIO:2, changed state to down
02:26:48: %LINEPROTO-5-UPDOWN: Line protocol on Interface
BRIO:1, changed state to down
02:26:48: %LINEPROTO-5-UPDOWN: Line protocol on Interface
BRIO:2, changed state to down
```

The **debug ppp packet** command reports the real-time PPP packet flow, including the type of packet and the B channel that is being used. As with other **debug packet** commands, the **debug ppp packet** command records each packet and can be used to monitor traffic flows. The following is the output generated from a successful ping:

```
Sean804# debug ppp packet
PPP packet display debugging is on
Seans804#ping 172.16.1.1
Type escape sequence to abort.
Sending 5, 100-byte ICMP Echos to 172.16.1.1, timeout is 2 seconds:
01:11:19: %LINK-3-UPDOWN: Interface BRIO:1, changed state to up.
01:11:19: BRO:1 LCP: O CONFREQ [Closed] id 4 len 10
01:11:19: BRO:1 LCP:    MagicNumber 0x5025BF23 (0x05065025BF23)
01:11:19: BRO:1 PPP: I pkt type 0xC021, datagramsize 14
01:11:19: BRO:1 PPP: I pkt type 0xC021, datagramsize 14
01:11:19: BRO:1 LCP: I CONFREQ [REQsent] id 14 len 10
01:11:19: BRO:1 LCP:    MagicNumber 0x5025BF46    (0x05065025BF46)
01:11:19: BRO:1 LCP: O CONFACK [REQsent] id 14 len 10
01:11:19: BRO:1 LCP:    MagicNumber 0x5025BF46    (0x05065025BF46)
01:11:19: BRO:1 LCP: I CONFACK [ACKsent] id 4 len 10
01:11:19: BRO:1 LCP:    MagicNumber 0x5025BF23    (0x05065025BF23)
```

```
01:11:20: BR0:1 PPP: I pkt type 0x8207, datagramsize 8
01:11:20: BR0:1 PPP: I pkt type 0x8021, datagramsize 14
01:11:20: BR0:1 CDPCP: O CONFREQ [Closed] id 4 len 4
01:11:20: BR0:1 PPP: I pkt type 0x8207, datagramsize 8
01:11:20: BR0:1 IPCP: O CONFREQ [Closed] id 4 len 10
01:11:20: BR0:1 IPCP:    Address 10.1.1.2 (0x03060A010102)
01:11:20: BR0:1 CDPCP: I CONFREQ [REQsent] id 4 len 4
```

Troubleshooting the Network Layer

ISDN uses the q.931 signaling that is defined in the ITU-T I.451 to connect at Layer 3 of the OSI model. This signaling is responsible for a call's setup and disconnection using the D channel of an ISDN connection. Quite a few message commands exist, which can be viewed by using the **debug isdn q931** command. These messages include the following:

➤ Call setup

➤ Connect

➤ Release

➤ Cancel

➤ Status

➤ Disconnect

➤ User information

The q.931 signaling operates on the D channel, and the **debug isdn q931** command includes information on the reference flag, message types, and information elements.

Call Reference Flag Definitions

The two reference flag values are 0, which indicates that this is a call from another originator, and 1, which indicates that this is a call to an originator.

Message Types

The following are the three different message type values associated with the q.931 protocol:

➤ *0x05*—Setup message type

➤ *0x45*—Disconnect message type

➤ *0x7d*—Status message type

Information Elements

When troubleshooting q.931 signaling at Layer 3, information elements are included in the output that can help identify problems. The following are some information elements and what they mean:

➤ *0x04*—Bearer capability

➤ *0x2c*—Keypad facility

➤ *0x6c*—Calling party number

➤ *0x70*—Called party number

➤ *0x3a*—SPID

Call Setup Steps for q.931 Signaling

ISDN establishes a Layer 3 connection between the local ISDN router and the local service provider's switch over the D channel. The local service provider's switch establishes another connection to the remote switch, which in turn is responsible for setting up a call to the remote ISDN router.

Before you look at the output from **debug isdn q931** command, review the following to get an understanding of some of the pieces of the output and what they mean:

➤ *ALERT*—An alert from the remote TE to the local TE with a ring-back signal.

➤ *SETUP*—The SETUP process sends information for the connection between the local TE and the remote TE.

➤ *Call Proceeding (CALL_PROC)*—A call-proceeding signal between the ET and the TE.

➤ *CONNECT*—The remote TE acknowledges a call and stops the local ring-back process.

➤ *Connect Acknowledgment (CONNECT_ACK)*—An acknowledgment of the remote exchange termination point to the remote Terminal Equipment indicating the setup is complete.

The following is the output of the **debug isdn q931** command:

```
Seans804# debug isdn q931
ISDN Q931 packets debugging is on
12:13:324523: ISDN BR0: RX <- STATUS_ENQ pd = 8 callref = 0x82
12:13:47: ISDN BR0: TX -> STATUS pd = 8  callref = 0x02
12:13:47: Cause i = 0x809E - Response to STATUS
 ENQUIRY or number unassigned
12:13:47: Call State i = 0x0A
```

```
12:13:3246744: ISDN BRO: RX <- STATUS_ENQ pd = 8 callref = 0x06
12:13:47: ISDN BRO: TX -> STATUS pd = 8  callref = 0x86
12:13:47: Cause i = 0x809E - Response to STATUS
 ENQUIRY or number unassigned
12:13:47: Call State i = 0x0A
12:13:3246951: ISDN BRO: RX <- STATUS_ENQ pd = 8 callref = 0x82
12:13:47: ISDN BRO: TX -> STATUS pd = 8  callref = 0x02
12:13:47: Cause i = 0x809E - Response to STATUS
 ENQUIRY or number unassigned
12:13:49: Call State i = 0x0A
12:13:3247341: ISDN BRO: RX <- STATUS_ENQ pd = 8 callref = 0x06
12:13:49: ISDN BRO: TX -> STATUS pd = 8  callref = 0x86
12:13:49: Cause i = 0x809E - Response to STATUS
ENQUIRY or number unassigned
12:13:49: Call State i = 0x0A
12:13:3248465: ISDN BRO: RX <- DISCONNECT pd = 8 callref = 0x82
12:13:3248465: Cause i = 0x8290 - Normal call    clearing
12:13:3248465: Signal i = 0x3F - Tones off
12:13:49: %ISDN-6-DISCONNECT:
Interface BRIO:1 disconnected from 18005551001
To p, call lasted 120 seconds
12:13:49: %LINK-3-UPDOWN: Interface BRIO:1, changed state to down
12:13:49: ISDN BRO: TX -> RELEASE pd = 8  callref = 0x02
12:13:3248465: ISDN BRO: RX <- RELEASE_COMP pd = 8 callref = 0x82
12:13:3248465: %ISDN-6-DISCONNECT:
Interface BRIO:2 disconnected from 8358 663, call lasted 120 seconds
12:13:49: ISDN BRO: TX -> DISCONNECT pd = 8  callref = 0x86
12:13:49: Cause i = 0x8090 - Normal call clearing
12:13:3248465: ISDN BRO: RX <- RELEASE pd = 8 callref = 0x06
12:13:49: %LINK-3-UPDOWN: Interface BRIO:2, changed state to down
12:13:49: ISDN BRO: TX ->
RELEASE_COMP pd = 8  callref =    0x86
12:13:50: %LINEPROTO-5-UPDOWN: Line protocol on Interface
BRIO:1, changed state to down
12:13:50: %LINEPROTO-5-UPDOWN: Line protocol on Interface
BRIO:2, changed state to down
```

Correct Switch Types

ISDN uses a connection between the ISDN router and the phone company's central office switch. Both sides of the connection must be configured with the same switch type. If the switch types are different, it is like putting two people in the same room who speak different languages. The **isdn switch-type** command can be used in both the global and interface configuration modes. The following output from the **help** command lists the different switch types that are supported on the Cisco 804 ISDN router:

13

```
Seans804(config)# isdn switch-type ?
  basic-1tr6      1TR6 switch type for Germany
  basic-5ess      AT&T 5ESS switch type for the U.S.
  basic-dms100    Northern DMS-100 switch type
  basic-nct3      NET3 switch type for UK and Europe
  basic-ni        National ISDN switch type
  basic-ts013     TS013 switch type for Australia
  ntt             NTT switch type for Japan
  vn3             VN3 and VN4 switch types for France
```

You can use the **isdn autodetect** command to automatically detect the switch type if you do not know the correct switching type. Many routers don't support the auto-detect feature, but it is supported on the Cisco 804 router. The switch type is only specific to the local loop switch, and not on the remote side of the connection, which can use a completely different switch type.

Other ISDN Troubleshooting Commands

Many other troubleshooting commands are available to help administrators. The **debug** commands in ISDN are extremely helpful for resolving problems. You need to remember though, that the **debug** commands can actually bring on a latency problem because all **debug** commands are assigned a high priority and can generate a high processor load. The following commands are described in this section:

➤ **clear interface bri**

➤ **debug bri**

➤ **debug dialer**

➤ **show controller bri**

➤ **show dialer**

Tip: Cisco recommends that routers be configured with timestamps when using the **debug** or **log output** commands.

The clear interface bri Command

The **clear interface bri** command followed by the BRI interface number resets the ISDN counters that are available on an ISDN interface. This will also terminate any active connection on an ISDN interface. As the following example indicates, the command has no output:

```
Ginas504# clear int bri0
Ginas504#
```

The **debug bri** Command

The **debug bri** command provides information such as bandwidth about the B channels used in a BRI interface. A B channel is used to carry the data across the active link. Any error on an activate B channel will prevent the flow of data.

Note: A router can still connect if only one B channel fails. If this occurs, check for a misconfigured SPID or other interface configuration issue.

The following output demonstrates the command in action:

```
Seans804# debug bri
Basic Rate network interface debugging is on

Seans804# ping 172.16.1.2
Type escape sequence to abort.
Sending 5, 100-byte ICMP Echos to 172.16.1.2, timeout is 2 seconds:
00:29:48: BRI: enable channel B1
00:29:48: BRI0:MC145572 state handler current state 3 actions 1 next state
3
00:29:48: BRI0:Starting activation
00:29:48: %LINK-3-UPDOWN: Interface BRI0:1, changed state to up.
00:29:49: BRI 0 B1: Set bandwidth to 64Kb
00:29:50: %LINEPROTO-5-UPDOWN: Line protocol on Interface
BRI0:1, changed state to up
00:29:50: BRI 0 B2: Set bandwidth to 64Kb
00:29:50: BRI: enable channel B2
00:29:50: BRI0:MC145572 state handler current state 3 actions 1 next state
3
00:29:50: BRI0:Starting activation
00:29:50: %LINK-3-UPDOWN: Interface BRI0:2, changed state to up.!!!
Success rate is 60 percent (3/5), round-trip min/avg/max = 36/41/52 ms
00:29:50: BRI: enable channel B2
00:29:50: BRI0:MC145572 state handler current state 3 actions 1 next state
3
00:29:50: BRI0:Starting activation
00:29:50: BRI 0 B2: Set bandwidth to 64Kb
00:29:51: %LINEPROTO-5-UPDOWN: Line protocol on Interface
BRI0:2, changed state to up
```

The **debug dialer** Command

The **debug dialer** command can be used to show information regarding the cause of a dialing connection problem. The following is an example of using the command:

```
Seans804# debug dialer
Dial on demand events debugging is on
```

```
Seans804#ping 172.16.1.1
Type escape sequence to abort.
Sending 5, 100-byte ICMP Echos to 172.16.1.1, timeout is 2 seconds:
00:36:15: BRIO: Dialing cause ip (s=172.16.1.2, d=172.16.1.1)
00:36:15: BRIO: Attempting to dial 18005551001
00:36:15: %LINK-3-UPDOWN: Interface BRIO:1, changed state to up.
00:36:15: dialer Protocol up for BRO:1
00:36:15: %LINEPROTO-5-UPDOWN: Line protocol on Interface
BRIO:1, changed state to up
00:36:15: %LINK-3-UPDOWN: Interface BRIO:2, changed state to up.
!!!!!
Success rate is 100 percent (5/5), round-trip min/avg/max = 32/37/48/23/33
ms
00:36:15: dialer Protocol up for BRO:2
00:36:15: %LINEPROTO-5-UPDOWN: Line protocol on Interface
BRIO:2, changed state to up
```

The **show controller bri** Command

The **show controller bri** command displays the interface hardware controller information. This command is most useful when troubleshooting with Cisco's TAC, obtaining the status of an interface, and obtaining the superframe error counter information. The following is the output from this command:

```
Sean804# show controller bri
BRI unit 0:BRI unit 0 with U interface and POTS:
Layer 1 internal state is ACTIVATED
Layer 1 U interface is ACTIVATED.
ISDN Line Information:
    Current EOC commands:
        RTN - Return to normal
    Received overhead bits:
        AIB=1, UOA=1, SCO=1, DEA=1, ACT=1, M50=1, M51=1, M60=1, FEBE=1
    Errors: [FEBE]=0, [NEBE]=0
    Errors: [Superframe Sync Loss]=0, [IDL2 Data    Transparency Loss]=0
            [M4 ACT 1 -> 0]=0
BRI U MLT Timers:  [TPULSE]=0, [T75S]=0
BRI U MLT Timers:  [TPULSE]=0, [T75S]=0

Motorola MC145572 registers:
NR0  = 0      NR1  = 4      NR2  = 0      NR3  = 0      NR4  = E      NR5  = 6
BR0  = F7     BR1  = 7F     BR2  = F0     BR3  = 40     BR4  = 0      BR5  = 0
BR6  = 0      BR7  = 1      BR8  = 1      BR9  = C      BR10 = 0      BR11 = C
BR12 = 0      BR13 = 0      BR14 = 0      BR15 = 46
OR0  = 0      OR1  = 4      OR2  = 8      OR3  = 0      OR4  = 4      OR5  = 8
OR6  = E0     OR7  = 11     OR8  = 0      OR9  = 0
```

```
D Channel Information:
Using SCC3, Microcode ver 101
idb at 0x272BF38, driver data structure at 0x273FB90
SCC Registers:
General [GSMR]=0x780:0x0000003A, Protocol-specific [PSMR]=0x0
Events [SCCE]=0x0000, Mask [SCCM]=0x001F, Status [SCCS]=0x0002
Transmit on Demand [TODR]=0x0, Data Sync [DSR]=0x7E7E
Interrupt Registers:
Config [CICR]=0x00368481, Pending [CIPR]=0x00000640
Mask   [CIMR]=0x30061090, In-srv  [CISR]=0x00000000
Command register [CR]=0xE84
Port A [PADIR]=0x08C3, [PAPAR]=0x07CC
       [PAODR]=0x0040, [PADAT]=0x0FCF
Port B [PBDIR]=0x00E02E, [PBPAR]=0x0020DE
       [PBODR]=0x000000, [PBDAT]=0x0053CF
Port C [PCDIR]=0x000C, [PCPAR]=0x0800
       [PCSO]=0x00C0,  [PCDAT]=0x0433, [PCINT]=0x0000
Port D [PDDIR]=0x001FFF, [PDPAR]=0x000000
       [PDDAT]=0x001FFB
SI     [SIMODE]=0x00001141,  [SIGMR]=0x04, [SISTR]=0x00
       [SICR]=0x00403500
BRGC   [BRGC2]=0x000101A8,  [BRGC3]=0x00000000
SPI Mode [SPMODE]=0x3771, Events [SPIE]=0x0
    Mask [SPIM]=0x0, Command [SPCOM]=0x0
SI Mode [SIMODE]=0x1141, Global [SIGMR]=0x4
   Cmnd [SICMR]=0x0, Stat [SISTR]=0x0
SI Clock Route [SICR]=0x00403500


QMC GLOBAL PARAMETER RAM (at 0x2203E00)
MCBASE=0x022029A8 INTBASE=0x02202B18 INTPTR=0x02202B18
QMC_STATE=0x0000 C_MASK16=0xF0B8 TXPTR=0x1E24 RXPTR=0x1E24


QMC CHANNEL PARAMETER RAM (at 0x2202880)
Rx BD Base [RBASE]=0xC0,
Tx BD Base [TBASE]=0xE0,
Max Rx Buff Len [MRBLR]=1524
Rx State [RSTATE]=0x31000000, BD Ptr [RBPTR]=0xC0
Tx State [TSTATE]=0x300C0FDE, BD Ptr [TBPTR]=0xE0


CHAMR =B000
RX ring with 4 entries at 0x2202A68, Buffer size 1524
Rxhead = 0x2202A68 (0), Rxp = 0x273FBAC (0)
00 pak=0x2884AC8 buf=0x0094260 status=9000 pak_size=0
01 pak=0x28848B4 buf=0x0093BA0 status=9000 pak_size=0
02 pak=0x28DBC5C buf=0x00934E0 status=9000 pak_size=0
03 pak=0x287EDD8 buf=0x0092E20 status=B000 pak_size=0
```

13

```
TX ring with 2 entries at 0x2202A88, tx_count = 0
tx_head = 0x2202A88 (0), head_txp = 0x273FC48 (0)
tx_tail = 0x2202A88 (0), tail_txp = 0x273FC48 (0)
00 pak=0x0000000 buf=0x0000000 status=0000 pak_size=0
01 pak=0x0000000 buf=0x0000000 status=2000 pak_size=0
   0 missed datagrams, 0 overruns
   0 bad datagram encapsulations, 0 memory errors
   0 transmitter underruns

B1 Channel Information:
Using SCC3, Microcode ver 101
idb at 0x2730758, driver data structure at 0x273FE80
SCC Registers:
General [GSMR]=0x780:0x0000003A, Protocol-specific [PSMR]=0x0
Events [SCCE]=0x0000, Mask [SCCM]=0x001F, Status [SCCS]=0x0002
Transmit on Demand [TODR]=0x0, Data Sync [DSR]=0x7E7E

QMC GLOBAL PARAMETER RAM (at 0x2203E00)
MCBASE=0x022029A8 INTBASE=0x02202B18 INTPTR=0x02202B18
QMC_STATE=0x0000 C_MASK16=0xF0B8 TXPTR=0x1E20 RXPTR=0x1E20
CHAMR =8007
RX ring with 8 entries at 0x22029A8, Buffer size 1524
Rxhead = 0x22029A8 (0), Rxp = 0x273FE9C (0)
00 pak=0x2867550 buf=0x00899A0 status=9000 pak_size=0
01 pak=0x286733C buf=0x00892E0 status=9000 pak_size=0
02 pak=0x2878AE0 buf=0x0088C20 status=9000 pak_size=0
03 pak=0x28788CC buf=0x0088560 status=9000 pak_size=0
04 pak=0x28786B8 buf=0x0087EA0 status=9000 pak_size=0
05 pak=0x28784A4 buf=0x00877E0 status=9000 pak_size=0
06 pak=0x288E02C buf=0x0087120 status=9000 pak_size=0
07 pak=0x28CA02C buf=0x0086A60 status=B000 pak_size=0

TX ring with 4 entries at 0x22029E8, tx_count = 0
tx_head = 0x22029E8 (0), head_txp = 0x273FF38 (0)
tx_tail = 0x22029E8 (0), tail_txp = 0x273FF38 (0)
00 pak=0x0000000 buf=0x0000000 status=0000 pak_size=0
01 pak=0x0000000 buf=0x0000000 status=0000 pak_size=0
02 pak=0x0000000 buf=0x0000000 status=0000 pak_size=0
03 pak=0x0000000 buf=0x0000000 status=2000 pak_size=0
   0 missed datagrams, 0 overruns
   0 bad datagram encapsulations, 0 memory errors
   0 transmitter underruns

B2 Channel Information:
Using SCC3, Microcode ver 101
idb at 0x2736A4C, driver data structure at 0x2740170
```

```
SCC Registers:
General [GSMR]=0x780:0x0000003A, Protocol-specific [PSMR]=0x0
Events [SCCE]=0x0000, Mask [SCCM]=0x001F, Status [SCCS]=0x0002
Transmit on Demand [TODR]=0x0, Data Sync [DSR]=0x7E7E

QMC GLOBAL PARAMETER RAM (at 0x2203E00)
MCBASE=0x022029A8 INTBASE=0x02202B18 INTPTR=0x02202B18
QMC_STATE=0x0000 C_MASK16=0xF0B8 TXPTR=0x1E28 RXPTR=0x1E28

QMC CHANNEL PARAMETER RAM (at 0x2202840)
Rx BD Base [RBASE]=0x60,
Tx BD Base [TBASE]=0xA0,
Max Rx Buff Len [MRBLR]=1524
Rx State [RSTATE]=0x0, BD Ptr [RBPTR]=0x60
Tx State [TSTATE]=0x30000000, BD Ptr [TBPTR]=0xA0

CHAMR =8007
RX ring with 8 entries at 0x2202A08, Buffer size 1524
Rxhead = 0x2202A08 (0), Rxp = 0x274018C (0)
00 pak=0x285D8F0 buf=0x008F820 status=9000 pak_size=0
01 pak=0x285D6DC buf=0x008F160 status=9000 pak_size=0
02 pak=0x285D4C8 buf=0x008EAA0 status=9000 pak_size=0
03 pak=0x285D2B4 buf=0x008E3E0 status=9000 pak_size=0
04 pak=0x28B907C buf=0x008DD20 status=9000 pak_size=0
05 pak=0x28B307C buf=0x008D660 status=9000 pak_size=0
06 pak=0x28AE07C buf=0x008CFA0 status=9000 pak_size=0
07 pak=0x28CA87C buf=0x008C8E0 status=B000 pak_size=0

TX ring with 4 entries at 0x2202A48, tx_count = 0
tx_head = 0x2202A48 (0), head_txp = 0x2740228 (0)
tx_tail = 0x2202A48 (0), tail_txp = 0x2740228 (0)
00 pak=0x0000000 buf=0x0000000 status=0000 pak_size=0
01 pak=0x0000000 buf=0x0000000 status=0000 pak_size=0
02 pak=0x0000000 buf=0x0000000 status=0000 pak_size=0
03 pak=0x0000000 buf=0x0000000 status=2000 pak_size=0
  0 missed datagrams, 0 overruns
  0 bad datagram encapsulations, 0 memory errors
  0 transmitter underruns
```

The **show dialer** Command

The **show dialer** command displays information about DDR connections. This includes the phone number dialed, connection successes, idle timers, and the number of calls that were accepted or rejected due to an administrative policy configuration. The output from this command follows:

```
Seans804# show dialer
BRI0 - dialer type = ISDN
Dial String       Successes    Failures    Last called      Last status
18005551001              2          6       00:03:36         successful
8 incoming call(s) have been screened.
0 incoming call(s) rejected for callback.
BRI0:1 - dialer type = ISDN
Idle timer (120 secs), Fast idle timer (20 secs)
Wait for carrier (30 secs), Re-enable (15 secs)
Dialer state is idle
BRI0:2 - dialer type = ISDN
Idle timer (120 secs), Fast idle timer (20 secs)
Wait for carrier (30 secs), Re-enable (15 secs)
Dialer state is idle
```

Chapter Summary

This chapter focused on configuration and troubleshooting issues related to ISDN. After reading this chapter, you should understand the common issues confronting administrators in ISDN networks, understand ISDN encapsulation, know how to use SPIDs, know the Layer 1 through 3 connection process and the protocols used, and be familiar with the ISDN troubleshooting commands.

This chapter covered much of what needs to be known to troubleshoot ISDN connections. Pay particular attention to the router configurations that were discussed, considering physical cabling to be faulty, the CO's switch configurations, and protocol issues such as q.921 and q.931 signaling, when trying to diagnose an ISDN problem.

Review Questions

1. Which ISDN command will bring up the second B channel when the first has reached a load of approximately 50 percent?

   a. **isdn load–balance 50**

   b. **isdn dialer load–threshold 50**

   c. **dialer load–threshold 125**

   d. **load 50 start**

2. ISDN Basic Rate Interface (BRI) provides which of the following?

   a. Two 64Kbps B channels and one 16Kbps D channel

   b. Total bit rate of up to 768Kbps

   c. Two 56Kbps B channels for data

   d. 10Mbps on two channels and a third for control using 192Kbps

3. At which OSI layer does q.931 provide signaling?

   a. Layer 1 of the OSI Reference Model

   b. Layer 2 of the OSI Reference Model

   c. Layer 3 of the OSI Reference Model

   d. Layer 4 of the OSI Reference Model

   e. Layers 1 through 4 of the OSI Reference Model

4. If Sean's Cisco 804 router is configured for ISDN BRI and PPP and uses an IP address of 172.16.10.1 and a 30-bit subnet mask, which of the following should be the IP address of Gina's 804 router's BRI at the remote end of the connection?

   a. 172.16.1.254

   b. 172.16.1.5

   c. 172.16.1.2

   d. Any of the above IP addresses

   e. No IP address

5. Which of the following two command prompts can execute the **isdn switch-type** command?

   a. User mode command prompt

   b. Privilege EXEC Mode command prompt

   c. Global configuration mode command prompt

   d. Interface configuration mode command prompt

6. Which of the following ISDN-specific protocols is used to establish a Layer 2 connection?

   a. q.921

   b. PPP

   c. CHAP

   d. q.931

   e. Ethernet

7. What is the TEI value used for broadcasts?

   a. 255

   b. 128

   c. 64

   d. 127

13

8. Which of the following is a valid North American SPID?

   a. 172.16.1.1

   b. 800.555.1.002

   c. 300.106

   d. 5551002

   e. 55510020100

9. The q.931 and q.921 protocols use which of the following BRI channels for communication?

   a. B channel 1

   b. B channel 2

   c. Both B channels

   d. D channel

10. CHAP requires which of the following to be configured? [Choose the two best answers]

    a. Telnet

    b. Virtual Private Networking

    c. Username

    d. The secret password on the router

    e. PPP

11. If you have a newly configured router and an ISDN call succeeds, but pings and other packets fail, what is the likely cause?

    a. CHAP misconfiguration

    b. PPP is not enabled

    c. Incorrect line speeds are configured

    d. Static routes are incorrectly configured

    e. A faulty cable

12. Which protocol defines the signaling method used by ISDN at Layer 2?

    a. q.921

    b. PPP

    c. q.931

    d. CHAP

13. Which of the following commands would you use to troubleshoot connection establishment at the Network layer?

 a. **debug isdn q921**

 b. **debug isdn q911**

 c. **debug interface bri**

 d. **debug isdn q931**

14. If an ISDN router will not dial, which of the following is the likely problem?

 a. Misconfigured SPID

 b. A dialer list filter

 c. Incorrect switch type

 d. Power problem

 e. Misconfigured dialer map

 f. All of the above

15. The default ISDN idle timer is set to which of the following?

 a. 20 seconds

 b. 30 seconds

 c. 90 seconds

 d. One minute

 e. Two minutes

 f. Five minutes

16. Which of the following are advantages of using CHAP authentication? [Choose the two best answers]

 a. Password authentication

 b. Password encryption

 c. Compression and encryption of data packets

 d. Virtual LANs are attached to ISDN switched connections

17. Which of the following devices is a non–ISDN device that connects to a terminal adapter?

 a. NT1

 b. TE2

 c. TA

 d. LT

13

18. To verify all three layers of an ISDN circuit prior to dialing, an administrator should use which of the following commands?

    a. **show ppp multilink**

    b. **debug ppp**

    c. **debug bri**

    d. **show run**

    e. **show isdn status**

19. On certain routers, if the switch type is unknown, which of the following commands should you use?

    a. **isdn switch-type 0**

    b. **isdn auto switch-type**

    c. **config switch-type auto**

    d. **isdn switch-type all**

    e. **isdn autodetect**

20. If you need to troubleshoot a connection between the local TE and a remote TE, which of the following commands do you use?

    a. **debug lapb**

    b. **show run**

    c. **debug isdn q921**

    d. **debug ppp negotiation**

    e. **config check**

Real-World Project

Joe Snow, an expert in configuring and troubleshooting ISDN, has been placed in charge of making sure that several of his coworkers are ready to pass the ISDN portion of their Cisco test. Joe writes down nine steps to configure on a piece of paper (and based on Figure 13.2). You must use his Cisco 804 to demonstrate how to do each one.

The following lists the nine items:

1. Configure the switch type to basic-ni switch.

2. Configure the IP address and SPID for the BRI 0 interface. The IP address of the interface should be 172.16.1.1 with a 24-bit mask. Make SPID 1 55510010101 8005551001.

3. Use a dialer list to specify IP as the only interesting traffic.

4. Add the dialer-list number to the BRI interface.

5. Configure the dialer string to call 800-555-1001.

6. Configure the dialer load-threshold to bring up the second BRI at 100 percent bandwidth usage.

7. Configure the BRI interface to load-balance over both BRI channels.

8. Configure the BRI channel to drop the connection if no interesting traffic is sent for 60 seconds.

9. Show that all ISDN connections at Layers 2 and 3 are configured correctly.

Project 13.1

Jennifer, who is one of Joe's coworkers, takes the challenge. Her screen outputs are listed below each item.

To configure and troubleshoot, perform the following steps:

1. Configure the switch type to basic-ni switch.

```
Joes804#enable
Joes804#config terminal
Joes804(Config)# isdn switch-type basic-ni
```

2. Configure the IP address and SPID for the BRI 0 interface. The IP address of the interface should be 172.16.1.1 with a 24-bit mask. Make SPID 1 55510010101 8005551001.

```
Joes804#enable
Joes804#config terminal
Joes804(Config)# int bri0
Joes804(Config-if)# isdn spid 1 55510010100 18005551001
Joes804(Config-if)# ip address 172.16.1.1 255.255.255.0
Joes804(Config-if)# no shut
```

3. Use a dialer list to specify IP as the only interesting traffic.

```
Joes804#enable
Joes804#config terminal
Joes804(Config)# dialer-list 1 protocol ip permit
```

Note: Jennifer notes that this command can be used in the interface configuration mode as well.

13

4. Add the dialer–list number to the BRI interface.

```
Joes804#enable
Joes804#config terminal
Joes804(Config)# interface bri0
Joes804(Config-if)# dialer-group 1
```

5. Configure the dialer string to call 800–555–1001.

```
Joes804#enable
Joes804#config terminal
Joes804(Config)# interface bri0
Joes804(Config-if)# dialer string 18005551001
```

6. Configure the dialer load–threshold to bring up the second BRI at 100 percent bandwidth usage.

```
Joes804#enable
Joes804#config terminal
Joes804(Config)# interface bri0
Joes804(Config-if)# dialer load-threshold 255 either
```

7. Configure the BRI interface to load-balance over both BRI channels.

```
Joes804# enable
Joes804# config terminal
Joes804(Config)# interface bri0
Joes804(Config-if)# ppp multilink
```

8. Configure the BRI channel to drop the connection if no interesting traffic is sent for 60 seconds.

```
Joes804# enable
Joes804# config terminal
Joes804(Config)# interface bri0
Joes804(Config-if)# dialer idle-timeout 60
```

9. Show that all ISDN connections at Layers 2 and 3 are configured correctly.

```
Joes804# enable
Joes804# show isdn status
Global ISDN Switchtype = basic-ni
ISDN BRIO interface
        dsl 0, interface ISDN Switchtype = basic-ni
    Layer 1 Status:
        ACTIVE
    Layer 2 Status:
        TEI = 105, Ces = 1, SAPI = 0, State =
MULTIPLE_FRAME_ESTABLISHED
    Spid Status:
        TEI 105, ces = 1, state = 5(init)
            spid1 configured, no LDN, spid1 sent, spid1 valid
            Endpoint ID Info: epsf = 0, usid = 3, tid = 1
    Layer 3 Status:
        0 Active Layer 3 Call(s)
Activated dsl 0 CCBs = 0
```

13

CHAPTER FOURTEEN

Troubleshooting Routing Protocols

After completing this chapter, you will be able to:

✓ Know the different types of protocols

✓ Compare distance-vector versus link-state

✓ Use IOS commands to troubleshoot protocol problems

✓ Compare IGRP and EIGRP

Protocols are what the networking world depends on to route traffic. This chapter discusses different protocols used in networking and explains how they work. This chapter also provides an overview of the algorithms the protocol uses to decide the best path. Finally, this chapter describes some commands to help you isolate any problems you may encounter with protocols.

Interior Routing Protocols

Routing protocols are a necessity in the networking world. Learning how they make a routing decision and where to use them are the keys to being a network professional. *Interior routing* is implemented at the Internet layer of the TCP/IP suite of protocols. Interior routing protocols use IP as a routing protocol and use a specific algorithm for different protocols. Each type of interior routing protocol uses different algorithms and mechanisms to accomplish routing.

The following are a few examples of interior routing protocols:

➤ *Routing Information Protocol (RIP)*—RIP is one of the most commonly used routing protocols for the Internet. RIP uses a maximum hop count of 15, to calculate a routing path. RIP is a distance-vector routing protocol, and has a default distance of 120.

➤ *Interior Gateway Routing Protocol (IGRP)*—IGRP is a protocol proprietary to Cisco equipment. It was designed to overcome some of RIP's limitations. IGRP uses a hop count of a maximum of 255 to calculate a routing path. IGRP is a distance-vector routing protocol, and has a default distance of 100.

➤ *Open Shortest Path First (OSPF)*—OSPF is a link-state routing protocol that uses an autonomous system to accomplish routing. It is used for large networks, because its maximum metric limit is 65,535. OSPF has a default distance of 110.

➤ *Enhanced Interior Gateway Routing Protocol (EIGRP)*—EIGRP is a proprietary routing protocol for Cisco. EIGRP combines link-state routing and distance-vector routing to achieve a balanced hybrid routing protocol. EIGRP has a default distance of 90.

In the network environment, two classifications of routing protocols exist: static and dynamic. *Primarily network/system engineers use static routes.* Dynamic routes are created by the routing protocols. Determining which routing protocol to use is usually determined by the size of your network. For example, in a small office environment you may want to use a static route. In a larger environment, using static routes may get complicated and using a dynamic style of routing is usually the best method.

Another way of determining the best routing protocol to use is to look at the routing protocols and what type of measurements they use to reach a destination. Each protocol uses a different way to calculate the best route in reaching a destination. The measurements are referred to as *metrics*. Some of the most common metrics are path length (hop count), reliability, delay, bandwidth, load, and link cost. These metrics are used to calculate the overall quality of the route and the distance. The routing protocols also use different methods to exchange information with other routers on the network.

Dynamic Routing

Routing protocols use their own variables in selecting routes, and understanding how the protocol is designed will help you identify how traffic is being routed on your network. Depending on your network devices (some protocols are proprietary) and bandwidth needs will help you decide on a routing protocol that fits your network. Dynamic routing uses two types of routing protocols: link-state and dynamic distance-vector.

Link-State

Protocols using the link-state routing algorithm possess a complex table of network topology information for routing. The link-state routing process uses link-state packets (LSPs) to inform other routers of distant links. The routers all use the "hello packets" to inform the other routers on the network where they are and their proximity. After the routers have all updated their fellow routers, each router possesses a routing table to refer to when they need to make routing decisions and determine the best path.

One of the benefits of using a link-state routing algorithm is how it reports the best path. The best path may not be the shortest distance, but a faster way. Link-state uses many factors when declaring the best path, such as hop count, bandwidth, congestion, and link speed.

Convergence

Convergence is the time required for all the routers to update their routing tables after a change to the network. When one router is informed of a change on the network, it reports the change to its neighbors, and its neighbors report to their neighbors, and so on. Convergence time is not a definite time, but depends on the number of routers and the size of the network.

For a router to converge with its neighbors, it must remember its name and the cost of the path to the neighboring router. Then it must send an LSP with the information to a neighboring router. Routers must also receive LSPs so that they can update their own routing tables. After they have exchanged the information, the routers will have a topology of the existing network and the best paths.

14

Distance-Vector

The distance-vector routing protocol is designed to send a copy of its entire routing table to all of its neighbors. This enables all the routers to know the routing paths and determine the lowest cost (shortest distance) for the traffic before forwarding the packets. This information comprises the local routing table and is re-advertised to its neighbors for an optimal route on the network. When operating a large campus environment, finding the best path for traffic will make better use of the network.

Using distance-vector routing does have a drawback: it does not update the routers at the same time. Distance-vector routing protocols update the routers on the network every 30 to 90 seconds, so when a router fails, the other routers on the network may not receive the information that it has failed. Because of the time difference in route updates, there may be a router or routers that don't realize a path isn't working. It is very important for your network to learn and update its neighboring routers on the best path for traffic in order to prevent problems of a *routing loop*. Routing loops can destroy an internetwork and can multiply for a long time trying to find the packet destination. The distance-vector protocol uses a few different methods to prevent routing loops. These include split horizon, poison reverse, triggered updates, and hold-down timers.

Split Horizon

Split horizon can reduce incorrect routing information and excessive routing with a simple rule. The split-horizon rule uses the premise of not sending information back the same way that it came. In the split-horizon rule, if a router receives an update from network A through interface B, the router will not update that route to network A through interface B.

Split Horizon-Poison Reverse

Split horizon is designed to stop routing loops between routers that have formed nearby relationships with other routers. The poison-reverse technique allows networks to be advertised with a hop count set to infinity, thus causing all routes to be flushed from the routing tables. In this type of environment, it will stop a two-node routing loop and reduce the possibility of large routing loops.

Hold-Down Timers

Hold-down timers are in use to prevent known routing updates to be sent that might inaccurately update a route that was invalid. It is common in networking for a router or interface to go down for various reasons such as loss of power, cable is loose, or someone accidentally hits the power switch. When a router or interface goes down, the down router will trigger the other routers to update their routing tables. If the down router or interface suddenly comes back online, the rest of the network is still trying to update their tables. This is where hold-down timers come into play. You can set the hold-down timers for a period of time to allow for network glitches without all the routers on the network trying to update. With the hold-down timer, if a router or interface goes down, the router's hold-down timer will wait a specified amount of time before it tries to update the routing table. In most cases, if the down router is caused by a minor glitch, the router will come back online and the network will not be affected.

Triggered Updates

Triggered updates are used to allow routers to inform their neighbors immediately of the routing changes so they don't have to wait for the regular timed updates. Some protocols, such as EIGRP, use only triggered updates to let the network know of a change.

Routing Information Protocol

RIP is a distance-vector protocol that uses hop-count metrics to get from one router to the next. RIP is limited to 15 hop counts. RIP is mostly used in the routing of global Internet and is an Interior Gateway Protocol (IGP). What this means is that RIP performs routing in a single autonomous system. On the other side is the Exterior Gateway Protocol (EGP), which is used to perform routing updates on different autonomous systems.

RIPv2 is another version of RIP. The main difference between the two is that RIP is used only for classful routing and RIPv2 is used for classless routing. RIP sends routing updates at regular intervals and when a routing table has changed. Routers running the RIP protocol maintain the best route because it is the shortest or the one with fewest hops. After the router updates its routing table, it sends it out to all of its neighboring routers, which is done independently of the other updates.

RIP uses a single routing metric. RIP measures the distance between the source and destination network. When a router receives an update that has new or changed information in it, the router will add a metric to that source address, which is the IP address of the sender. In the path from source to destination, it would be defined as one hop count until it has reached 15. The next hop would be 16, and then it would be sent back as an unreachable network or destination address.

By implementing the limit of hop counts, the RIP protocol prevents routing loops from an infinite cycle. In order for RIP to adjust for rapid changes in the network, it implements the split horizon and hold-down timers to prevent incorrect routing information from being propagated. The RIP hop count also helps prevent routing loops in an infinite circle. RIP also uses timers to help regulate its performance.

The timers are the routing-update timer, route-timeout timer, and route-flush timer. The *routing-update timer* is usually set to 30 seconds and clocks the periodic update intervals. To prevent collisions, the router puts in a random number of

14

seconds each time the timer is reset. In the routing table, there is also a process called *route-timeout*. When this timeout expires, the route is determined to be unreachable but is maintained in the routing table until the *route-flush timer* expires. The update timer is 30 seconds, the invalid timer is 90 seconds, the hold–down timer is 100 seconds, and the flush timer is 270 seconds.

Troubleshooting RIP

Two versions of RIP exist, the distinction between which is that RIP1 had limited use and scalability. RIP2 is almost the same, but the new version is able to support Classless Interdomain Routing (CIDR), route summarization, and variable–length subnet masks (VLSMs). The following example shows a few commands used in troubleshooting, as well as the output. The **show ip route** command displays the routing table of the networks and how they are reaching other networks.

```
Support#
Support#show ip route
Codes: C - connected, S - static, I - IGRP, R - RIP, M - mobile,
 B - BGPD - EIGRP, EX - EIGRP external, O - OSPF,
        IA - OSPF inter area
        N1 - OSPF NSSA external type 1,
        N2 - OSPF NSSA external type 2
        E1 - OSPF external type 1, E2 - OSPF external type 2,
        E - EGP
        i - IS-IS, L1 - IS-IS level-1, L2 - IS-IS level-2,
        * - candidate default
        U - per-user static route, o - ODR
Gateway of last resort is not set

     172.16.0.0/24 is subnetted, 6 subnets
R       currentip  [120/2] via 172.16.20.2, 00:00:12, Serial0
R       10.10.20.0 [120/2] via 172.16.20.2, 00:00:12, Serial0
R       10.10.20.0 [120/2] via 172.16.20.2, 00:00:12, Serial0
R       172.16.30.0 [120/2] via 172.16.20.2, 00:00:12, Serial0
C       172.16.30.0 is directly connected, Serial0
C       10.10.20.0 is directly connected, Ethernet0
Support#
```

Using the **show ip interface** command will display the IP interface configuration. The following output shows an example of using the **show ip interface** command:

```
Support#
Support#show ip interface
Ethernet0 is administratively down, line protocol is down
  Internet protocol processing disabled
```

```
Serial0 is up, line protocol is up
  Internet address is 10.10.20.3/24
  Broadcast address is 255.255.255.255
  Address determined by setup command
  Peer address is 10.10.20.1
  MTU is 1500 bytes
  Helper address is not set
  Directed broadcast forwarding is disabled
  Multicast reserved groups joined: 224.0.0.9
  Outgoing access list is not set
  Inbound  access list is not set
  Proxy ARP is enabled
  Security level is default
  Split horizon is enabled
  ICMP redirects are always sent
  ICMP unreachables are always sent
  ICMP mask replies are never sent
  IP fast switching is enabled
  IP fast switching on the same interface is enabled
  IP Fast switching turbo vector
  IP multicast fast switching is enabled
  IP multicast distributed fast switching is disabled
  IP route-cache flags are Fast
  Router Discovery is disabled
  IP output packet accounting is disabled
  IP access violation accounting is disabled
  TCP/IP header compression is disabled
  RTP/IP header compression is disabled
  Probe proxy name replies are disabled
  Policy routing is disabled
  Network address translation is disabled
  Web Cache Redirect is disabled
  BGP Policy Mapping is disabled
Serial1 is up, line protocol is up
  Internet address is 10.10.20.4/24
  Broadcast address is 255.255.255.255
  Address determined by setup command
  Peer address is 10.10.20.2
  MTU is 1500 bytes
  Helper address is not set
  Directed broadcast forwarding is disabled
  Multicast reserved groups joined: 224.0.0.9
  Outgoing access list is not set
  Inbound  access list is not set
  Proxy ARP is enabled
  Security level is default
```

14

```
        Split horizon is enabled
        ICMP redirects are always sent
        ICMP unreachables are always sent
        ICMP mask replies are never sent.
        IP fast switching is enabled
        IP fast switching on the same interface is enabled
        IP Fast switching turbo vector
        IP multicast fast switching is enabled
        IP multicast distributed fast switching is disabled
        IP route-cache flags are Fast
        Router Discovery is disabled
        IP output packet accounting is disabled
        IP access violation accounting is disabled
        TCP/IP header compression is disabled
        RTP/IP header compression is disabled
        Probe proxy name replies are disabled
        Policy routing is disabled
        Network address translation is disabled
        Web Cache Redirect is disabled
        BGP Policy Mapping is disabled
Support#
```

When using the **show protocol** command, you will be able to identify the protocol or protocols running on the router, as the following example demonstrates:

```
Support#
Support#show protocol
Global values:
  Internet Protocol routing is enabled
Ethernet0 is up, line protocol is up
  Internet address is 10.10.20.1/24
Serial0 is up, line protocol is up
  Internet address is 172.16.30.1/24
Serial1 is administratively down, line protocol is down
TokenRing0 is administratively down, line protocol is down
Support#
```

The debug Commands

The **debug** commands are very useful when used correctly, but they can do more harm than good if not used properly. It takes a lot of resources from the router to perform debugging. In a large environment, using the **debug** commands improperly may cause your network to be very slow or come to a halt. The **debug** commands can be used after using various **show** commands to investigate where the problem exists.

If you need some more general information, use the **debug ip rip** command, which shows all the possibilities with the RIP protocol. Some typical problems that you may encounter with the RIP protocol are *network congestion* and *broadcast storms*. To avoid this, configure RIP to allow unicast updates. You can also use the **passive interface** command on specific interfaces to tell the updates to go elsewhere.

Congestion can also occur from frequent routing updates. To avoid this, you can adjust your timers, which are in the RIP protocol. You may also run into RIP version mismatches. For example, if router1 is running RIP1 and router2 is running RIP2, they will both utilize the same command line but will not be able to talk to one another on the network. To remedy this, use the **show** commands and make sure both of the RIP protocols match up.

IPX RIP

IPX RIP is used on Novell networks using the RIP protocol. IPX RIP uses the lowest delay metric, called *tick-based routing*, and then uses the hop count to determine the best path over the network. A tick is measured in 1/18 of a second increments. When multiple tick-based routing equals least cost, the lowest hop count is chosen. If both hop counts are still equal, then RIP chooses the best path.

Internet Gateway Routing Protocol

IGRP is a Cisco proprietary routing protocol that was designed as a new version or upgrade from RIP, the only existing protocol at the time. IGRP does not use RIP's hop count of 15 method; the IGRP routing protocol uses up to 255 hops. IGRP is a *classful* routing protocol, meaning it does not include any subnet information about the network.

With route information, three types of routes are recognized by IGRP:

➤ *Interior*—A network directly connected to a router interface.

➤ *System*—Advertised routes by other IGRP neighbors within the same AS (autonomous system) number. The AS is the number that identifies the IGRP individual session.

➤ *Exterior*—Routes learned from other IGRP sessions with different AS numbers. This information is used by the router to set the *gateway of last resort*. This is a route a packet takes if it is not specified to a certain route.

IGRP also uses more than just hop counts to determine the best path from or to a network. It uses a combination of internetwork delay, bandwidth, link reliability, and load to determine the best path on the network. IGRP also uses split horizon, poison reverse, hold-down timers, and triggered updates, as stated in the beginning of this chapter. In using IGRP, if routing metrics have increased by 1.1 or more,

14

than the poison reverse update is started. The reason for this is if there is an increase in the routing metrics, than there might be a routing loop. Not unlike RIP, the IGRP routing protocol also implements a number of timers.

Troubleshooting IGRP

IGRP uses the distance-vector routing protocol and, because of this, uses a one-dimensional array of information to calculate the best path. The vector consists of four elements, including bandwidth, delay, load, and reliability. The MTU, or maximum transfer unit, is not part of the vector of metrics but is used in the final route information. IGRP is intended to replace RIP in order to create a more stable, quick-converging protocol that can scale up to a growing network. If you implement a large-scale network, you may want to use the link-state protocol, because the distance-vector protocols come with overhead and delay time.

The IGRP protocol has a few items that provide a quick convergence time:

➤ *Configurable metrics*—Metrics involved in the algorithm responsible for calculating route information may be configured by the user.

➤ *Flash updates*—Updates are sent out immediately when the metrics route changes, not waiting for the routine updates.

➤ *Poison reverse*—Used to prevent routing loops.

➤ *Unequal-cost load balancing*—Allows packets to be changed/distributed across multiple paths.

Open Shortest Path First

OSPF uses the link-state technology, as does RIP. The Internet Engineering Task Force (IETF) developed OSPF in 1988. The most recent version is OSPFv2 (more information is available in RFC 1583). OSPF is an Interior Gateway Protocol that was developed to address large, scalable internetworks that RIP was not able to address. OSPF sends its link-state information every 30 minutes (unlike RIP, which sends updates every 30 seconds). OSPF addresses a few issues that were of concern in earlier protocols. These issues include speed convergence, support for variable subnet mask, network reachability, use of bandwidth, and path selection.

Note: Implementing the OSPF protocol requires proper planning and design in a large-scale network environment. OSPF is different from IGRP and EIGRP because it uses pure-link routing. It is also an open standard routing protocol, which means that it was not designed specifically to run on Cisco routers; it was designed to run quickly, to be scalable, and to run efficiently on any routing equipment. Complete details of the OSPF protocol can be found in RFC1131.

Troubleshooting OSPF

Compared to RIP, OSPF fares better in a large network. OSPF does not update every 30 seconds, has a lower cost, and thus preserves the bandwidth. When changes occur on the network, the CPU has to deal with the process and calculation of all the routes on the network. In general, if at all possible, do not add more than 100 routers per area and not more than 700 routers throughout the network. This is not the minimum or the maximum router capacity for OSPF, but a guideline. The more links that exist in a network, the greater the number of routing updates and CPU cycles. Another cause of concern is that the OSPF protocol may have incorrectly configured wildcard masks, which are used to advertise the network.

The **OSPF show** Commands

A few commands are very helpful in troubleshooting OSPF. Knowing when and where to use these commands will help you isolate the problem and fix the problem sooner. The **show** commands are used to provide information on the configuration and function of OSPF on the router.

Using the **show running-config** command displays the running configuration on the router:

```
Support#
Support#show running-configuration
Building configuration...

Current configuration:
!
version 12.0
service timestamps debug uptime
service timestamps log uptime
no service password-encryption
!
hostname Support
!
!
ip subnet-zero
ip host Coriolis 172.68.16.1
ip host ExamPrep 10.10.20.3
!
!
!
interface Loopback0
 ip address 10.0.0.2 255.255.255.255
 no ip directed-broadcast
 ip ospf interface-retry 0
!
```

14

```
interface Ethernet0
 ip address 10.10.20.2 255.255.255.0
 no ip directed-broadcast
 ip ospf interface-retry 0
!
interface Serial0
 ip address 172.68.16.2 255.255.255.0
 no ip directed-broadcast
 encapsulation ppp
 ip ospf interface-retry 0
!
interface Serial1
 ip address 172.68.16.4 255.255.255.0
 no ip directed-broadcast
 encapsulation ppp
 ip ospf interface-retry 0
!
router ospf 100
 network 10.0.0.0 0.255.255.255 area 0
 network 172.68.0.0 0.0.255.255 area 0
!
router rip
 network 10.0.0.0
 network 172.68.0.0
!
ip classless
!
!
line con 0
 transport input none
line aux 0
line vty 0 4
!
end
Support#
```

Using the **show ip route** command displays the IP route information:

```
Support#
Support#show ip route
Codes: C - connected, S - static, I - IGRP, R - RIP, M - mobile, B - BGP
       D - EIGRP, EX - EIGRP external, O - OSPF, IA - OSPF inter area
       N1 - OSPF NSSA external type 1, N2 - OSPF NSSA external type 2
       E1 - OSPF external type 1, E2 - OSPF external type 2, E - EGP
       i - IS-IS, L1 - IS-IS level-1, L2 - IS-IS level-2, * - candidate
          default
       U - per-user static route, o - ODR
```

```
Gateway of last resort is not set

     172.68.0.0/16 is variably subnetted, 3 subnets, 2 masks
C       172.68.16.0/24 is directly connected, Serial0
                     is directly connected, Serial1
C       172.68.16.1/32 is directly connected, Serial0
C       172.68.16.3/32 is directly connected, Serial1
     10.0.0.0/8 is variably subnetted, 4 subnets, 3 masks
O       10.10.0.0/16 [110/74] via 172.68.16.3, 00:03:30, Serial1
                    [110/74] via 172.68.16.1, 00:03:30, Serial0
C       10.0.0.2/32 is directly connected, Loopback0
O       10.0.0.1/32 [110/65] via 172.68.16.3, 00:03:30, Serial1
                    [110/65] via 172.68.16.1, 00:03:30, Serial0
C       10.10.20.0/24 is directly connected, Ethernet0
Support#
```

Using the **show ip route ospf** command shows the OSPF routes only:

```
Support#
Support#show ip route ospf
     10.0.0.0/8 is variably subnetted, 4 subnets, 3 masks
O       10.10.0.0/16 [110/74] via 172.68.16.3, 00:02:57, Serial1
                    [110/74] via 172.68.16.1, 00:02:57, Serial0
O       10.0.0.1/32 [110/65] via 172.68.16.3, 00:02:57, Serial1
                    [110/65] via 172.68.16.1, 00:02:57, Serial0
Support#
```

Using the **show ip ospf <process id>** command shows information related to the process ID:

```
Support#
Support#show ip ospf
 Routing Process "ospf 100" with ID 172.68.16.4
 Supports only single TOS(TOS0) routes
 SPF schedule delay 5 secs, Hold time between two SPFs 10 secs
 Minimum LSA interval 5 secs. Minimum LSA arrival 1 secs
 Number of external LSA 0. Checksum Sum 0x0
 Number of DCbitless external LSA 0
 Number of DoNotAge external LSA 0
 Number of areas in this router is 1. 1 normal 0 stub 0 nssa
    Area BACKBONE(0)
        Number of interfaces in this area is 4
        Area has no authentication
        SPF algorithm executed 4 times
        Area ranges are
        Number of LSA 2. Checksum Sum 0x839B
```

14

```
            Number of DCbitless LSA 0
            Number of indication LSA 0
            Number of DoNotAge LSA 0
Support#
```

Using the **show ip ospf border-routers** command shows the routes that join the network from different paths:

```
Support#
Support#show ip ospf border-routers

OSPF Process 100 internal Routing Table

Codes: i - Intra-area route, I - Inter-area route
Support#
```

Using the **show ip ospf database** command shows the database of the OSPF summaries:

```
Support#
Support#show ip ospf database

        OSPF Router with ID (172.68.16.4) (Process ID 100)


              Router Link States (Area 0)

Link ID        ADV Router      Age      Seq#        Checksum Link count
172.68.16.3    172.68.16.3     379      0x80000008 0xB8F     6
172.68.16.4    172.68.16.4     362      0x80000007 0x780C    6
Support#
```

Using the **show ip ospf interface** command shows the OSPF information on the specified interface:

```
Support#
Support#show ip ospf int
Ethernet0 is up, line protocol is up
  Internet Address 10.10.20.2/24, Area 0
  Process ID 100, Router ID 172.68.16.4, Network Type BROADCAST, Cost: 10
  Transmit Delay is 1 sec, State DR, Priority 1
  Designated Router (ID) 172.68.16.4, Interface address 10.10.20.2
  No backup designated router on this network
  Timer intervals configured, Hello 10, Dead 40, Wait 40, Retransmit 5
    Hello due in 00:00:00
```

```
    Neighbor Count is 0, Adjacent neighbor count is 0
    Suppress hello for 0 neighbor(s)
Loopback0 is up, line protocol is up
  Internet Address 10.0.0.2/32, Area 0
  Process ID 100, Router ID 172.68.16.4, Network Type LOOPBACK, Cost: 1
  Loopback interface is treated as a stub Host
Serial0 is up, line protocol is up
  Internet Address 172.68.16.2/24, Area 0
  Process ID 100, Router ID 172.68.16.4, Network Type POINT_TO_POINT, Cost:
64
  Transmit Delay is 1 sec, State POINT_TO_POINT,
  Timer intervals configured, Hello 10, Dead 40, Wait 40, Retransmit 5
    Hello due in 00:00:04
  Neighbor Count is 1, Adjacent neighbor count is 1
    Adjacent with neighbor 172.68.16.3
  Suppress hello for 0 neighbor(s)
Serial1 is up, line protocol is up
  Internet Address 172.68.16.4/24, Area 0
  Process ID 100, Router ID 172.68.16.4, Network Type POINT_TO_POINT, Cost:
64
  Transmit Delay is 1 sec, State POINT_TO_POINT,
  Timer intervals configured, Hello 10, Dead 40, Wait 40, Retransmit 5
    Hello due in 00:00:03
  Neighbor Count is 1, Adjacent neighbor count is 1
    Adjacent with neighbor 172.68.16.3
  Suppress hello for 0 neighbor(s)
Support#
```

Using the **show ip ospf neighbor** command shows related neighbor information:

```
Support#
Support#show ip ospf neighbor

Neighbor ID    Pri   State        Dead Time   Address        Interface
172.68.16.3     1    FULL/  -     00:00:34    172.68.16.1    Serial0
172.68.16.3     1    FULL/  -     00:00:34    172.68.16.3    Serial1
Support#
```

Using the **show ip ospf summary-address** command shows the summary addresses of the redistribution list:

```
Support#
Support#show ip ospf summary-address

OSPF Process 100, Summary-address
Summary#
```

Debug Commands

When properly used, the **debug** commands in the IOS can show you answers to the most difficult problems. When issuing a **debug** command, you may find that an invalid host assignment exists on the subnetwork or that some incorrect routing information is coming from an upstream router. In looking at the following code, you are able to see many options that are available with OSPF debugging.

```
Support#
Support#debug ip ospf ?
  adj               OSPF adjacency events
  database-timer    OSPF database timer
  events            OSPF events
  flood             OSPF flooding
  lsa-generation    OSPF lsa generation
  packet            OSPF packets
  retransmission    OSPF retransmission events
  spf               OSPF spf
  tree              OSPF database tree
Support#
```

Using the **debug ip ospf events** command shows all the OSPF events:

```
Support#
Support# debug ip ospf events
OSPF:hello with invalid timers on interface Ethernet0
hello interval received 10 configured 10
net mask received 255.255.255.0 configured 255.255.255.0
dead interval received 40 configured 30
Support#
```

Using the **debug ip ospf packet** command enables you to see the OSPF packet:

```
Support#
Support# debug ip ospf packet
OSPF: rcv. v:2 t:1 1:48 rid:200.0.0.117
      aid:0.0.0.0 chk:6AB2 aut:0 auk
Support#
```

IGRP vs. EIGRP

IGRP was developed in the mid 1980s as an improvement for RIP. Although RIP is still a good routing protocol for smaller networks (up to 15 hops), EIGRP may be a more efficient protocol in a large network. IGRP has some improvements, such as hop counts of 1 to 255, and uses an autonomous system (AS). IGRP is a distance-vector protocol that was designed to be more stable than RIP and to be used on larger network environments. IGRP is a classful routing protocol, meaning it does not include subnets in the route field information. Only three types of routes are recognized by IGRP: interior, system, and exterior. IGRP also uses routing stability, which includes hold-down timers, split horizon, and poison-reverse updates. After IGRP was used for a while, Cisco released another proprietary protocol, the Enhanced Interior Gateway Routing Protocol (EIGRP).

One of the problems resolved by EIGRP was that IGRP, when running, would send its whole route table if some change occurred in the network. EIGRP is a hybrid, because it uses both distance-vector and link-state routing algorithms. Enabling EIGRP to support both routing algorithms means less opportunity exists for route failure. EIGRP is much better than IGRP because it uses equal-cost load balancing, formal relationships, and incremental routing updates. EIGRP, like IGRP, is very scalable and stable. EIGRP also uses an autonomous system to distinguish a route. You can even have multiple sessions with EIGRP in order for EIGRP to calculate the best route and load sharing. It uses the route database, the topology database, and a neighbor table. EIGRP converges more quickly than IGRP because it calculates only when a change in the network directly affects the routing table.

Troubleshooting EIGRP

EIGRP was created by Cisco to help make up for IGRP's inherent problems. Being a hybrid protocol enables EIGRP to be a much more efficient routing protocol. EIGRP is also very easy to configure. One of the nicest features about using this protocol is that you are not limited by hop counts, and you also have the use of timing, clocking, and load balancing. The following are some of the prominent features of EIGRP:

➤ *Route tagging*—Makes a distinction between routes learned via a different EIGRP session

➤ *Neighbor relationships*—Uses hello packets to establish peering

➤ *Incremental routing updates*—Only changes are advertised, not the whole routing table

➤ *Classless routing*—Supports VLSM and subnets

➤ *Configurable networks*—Information can be set through configuration commands

➤ *Equal-cost load balancing*—Traffic is sent equally across multiple connections to be able to calculate the best path for load sharing. EIGRP uses a database to store information for the routed information. All the databases are the same for IP-EIGRP, IPX-EIGRP, AT-EIGRP, and Apple-Talk-EIGRP. EIGRP uses hello packets to update its routing table, and then allows the exchange of route information. EIGRP sends hello packets every 5 seconds on a high-bandwidth level, and every 60 seconds on a low-bandwidth level.

14

When EIGRP sends a hello packet, it is called a *hello interval* and can be adjusted using the **ip eigrp hello-interval** command. EIGRP also uses a *hold time*, which is the amount of time used before the router will consider the neighbor alive and start to accept hello packets. The hold time is usually set at three times the hold time value, normally 15 seconds to 180 seconds, but you can change this range by issuing the command **ip eigrp hold-down interface**. If you are going to adjust the hold time values, you must be careful calculating the values.

The show Commands

The **show** commands are helpful in troubleshooting any type of protocol problem. Knowing the commands that will return the information you are looking for is very helpful. The following are a few commonly used commands to aid in trouble-shooting EIGRP.

Using **show ip route eigrp** displays only EIGRP routes:

```
Support#
Support#show ip route eigrp
     172.68.0.0/16 is variably subnetted, 2 subnets, 2 masks
D       172.68.0.0/16 is a summary, 00:07:33, Null0
     10.0.0.0/8 is variably subnetted, 2 subnets, 2 masks
D       10.0.0.0/8 is a summary, 00:07:34, Null0
Support#
```

Using **show ip eigrp neighbors** displays the connected neighbor and the route summary for the neighbor:

```
Support#
Support#show ip eigrp neighbors
IP-EIGRP neighbors for process 100
H    Address              Interface   Hold Uptime    SRTT   RTO  Q  Seq
                                      (sec)          (ms)        Cnt Num
1    10.10.20.1           Et0           11 00:08:10 1576   5000  0  11
3    172.68.16.3          Se1           12 00:08:15    0   4500  0  10
2    172.68.16.1          Se0           12 00:08:15    0   4500  0  9
0    10.10.20.3           Et0           13 00:09:07   13    200  0  8
Support#
```

Using **show ip eigrp topology** displays the topology table for EIGRP:

```
Support#
Support#show ip eigrp topology
IP-EIGRP Topology Table for process 100
```

```
Codes: P - Passive, A - Active, U - Update, Q - Query, R - Reply,
       r - Reply status
P 10.0.0.0/8, 1 successors, FD is 281600
        via Summary (281600/0), Null0
P 10.10.20.0/24, 1 successors, FD is 281600
        via Connected, Ethernet0
P 172.68.0.0/16, 1 successors, FD is 2169856
        via Summary (2169856/0), Null0
P 172.68.16.0/24, 1 successors, FD is 2169856
        via Connected, Serial0
        via Connected, Serial1
Support#
```

Using **show ip eigrp traffic** displays the hello and routing updates:

```
Support#
Support#show ip eigrp traffic
IP-EIGRP Traffic Statistics for process 100
  Hellos sent/received: 434/544
  Updates sent/received: 14/19
  Queries sent/received: 0/2
  Replies sent/received: 2/0
  Acks sent/received: 11/5
  Input queue high water mark 3, 0 drops
Support#
```

Using **show ip eigrp events** displays a log of the most recent EIGRP information pertaining to what is happening on the network:

```
Support#
Support#show ip eigrp events
Event information for AS 100:
1    00:52:19.879 Poison squashed: 172.68.0.0/16 reverse
2    00:52:18.807 Metric set: 172.68.0.0/16 2169856
3    00:52:18.807 Route install: 172.68.0.0/16 0.0.0.0
4    00:52:18.807 FC sat rdbmet/succmet: 2169856 0
5    00:52:18.807 FC sat nh/ndbmet: 0.0.0.0 2169856
6    00:52:18.807 Find FS: 172.68.0.0/16 2169856
7    00:52:18.807 Rcv update met/succmet: 2707456 2195456
8    00:52:18.807 Rcv update dest/nh: 172.68.0.0/16 172.68.16.3
9    00:52:18.799 Metric set: 172.68.0.0/16 2169856
10   00:52:18.799 Route install: 172.68.0.0/16 0.0.0.0
11   00:52:18.799 FC sat rdbmet/succmet: 2169856 0
12   00:52:18.799 FC sat nh/ndbmet: 0.0.0.0 2169856
13   00:52:18.799 Find FS: 172.68.0.0/16 2169856
14   00:52:18.799 Rcv update met/succmet: 2707456 2195456
```

14

```
15    00:52:18.799 Rcv update dest/nh: 172.68.0.0/16 172.68.16.1
16    00:52:18.279 Peer up: 10.10.20.1 Ethernet0
17    00:52:18.079 Metric set: 172.68.16.0/24 2169856
18    00:52:18.079 FC sat rdbmet/succmet: 2169856 0
19    00:52:18.079 FC sat nh/ndbmet: 0.0.0.0 2169856
20    00:52:18.079 Find FS: 172.68.16.0/24 2169856
21    00:52:18.079 Rcv update met/succmet: 2681856 2169856
22    00:52:18.079 Rcv update dest/nh: 172.68.16.0/24 172.68.16.3
Support#
```

Exterior Routing Protocols

The best way to categorize routing protocols is to decide if they are interior or exterior. An **interior routing protocol** such as RIP or IGRP is used to exchange routing information within an autonomous system. An exterior routing protocol such as BGP is used to connect between autonomous systems. BGP is the most widely used exterior routing protocol used by almost anyone who wants to communicate on the Internet.

Border Gateway Protocol (BGP)

Border Gateway Protocol (BGP) version 4 is the latest version of BGP and is defined in RFC 1771. BGP is an exterior routing protocol used to connect between autonomous systems. An autonomous system is defined as a set of routers under a single technical administration, using an interior gateway protocol and common metric to route packets within the autonomous system (AS), and using an exterior gateway protocol to route packets to other autonomous systems (ASs).

The main goal of BGP is to provide an interdomain routing system that will guarantee a loop-free exchange or routing information between autonomous systems. BGP was designed to allow ISPs to communicate and exchange packets.

BGP is not always the best protocol to use in all networks. If any of the following describes your network, you might want to use another protocol:

➤ If your network only has a single connection to the internet or another AS

➤ Limited memory or processor power on BGP routers to handle constant updates

➤ Very limited understanding of route filtering and BGP path selection process

➤ Very little bandwidth between autonomous systems

If your network is limited to the above list, you may want to use static routes to connect to another autonomous system.

Intermediate System-to-Intermediate System (IS-IS)

The International Organization for Standardization (ISO) came up with a routing protocol to use with the Open System Interconnection (OSI) protocol suite. The ISO protocol suite includes the Intermediate System-to-Intermediate System (IS-IS) protocol, End System-to-Intermediate System (ES-IS) protocol, and Interdomain Routing Protocol (IDRP). For the purpose of this book, only IS-IS is covered in depth.

The IS-IS protocol was originally used to route in ISO Connectionless Network Protocol (CLNP) networks. A version of IS-IS has been created to work on both the CLNP and IP networks. This version is referred to as *integrated IS-IS* (also referred to as *dual IS-IS*). You can find more information on the OSI protocol suite in the ISO document that defines IS-IS, which is ISO 10589.

The ISO networking model uses some specific terminology. These terms are the basis for the ES-IS and IS-IS OSI products. The ES-IS protocol enables ES and IS to discover each other. The IS-IS protocol provides routing between ISs. The following are some important terms relating to IS-IS:

➤ *Area*—A group of contiguous networks and an attached host specified to be an area by the network administrator/manager

➤ *Domain*—A collection of connected areas; for example, a routing domain provides full connectivity to all end systems within the domain

➤ *End system (ES)*—Any nonrouting network nodes

➤ *Intermediate system (IS)*—A router

➤ *Level 1 routing*—Routing within a level 1 area

➤ *Level 2 routing*—Routing between two level 1 areas

IS-IS is an OSI link-state hierarchical routing protocol that floods the network with link-state information in order to build a complete picture of the network topology. To simplify the router design and operation, IS-IS distinguishes between two levels of IS. Level 1 IS communicate within a level 1 area, and level 2 IS routes between level 1 areas and creates an interdomain routing backbone. IS-IS uses a default metric with a maximum path value of 1,024. The use of the metric is arbitrary and usually assigned by the network administrator. Any single link can have a maximum value of 64, and path links are calculated by summing the link values.

14

IS-IS also defines three optional metrics (cost):

➤ *Delay*—Deals with the delay on the link

➤ *Expense*—Deals with the communication cost associated with the link

➤ *Error*—Deals with the error rate on the link

IS-IS maintains a mapping of these metrics to the Quality of Service (QoS) option in the CLNP packet header. IS-IS uses the mapping to compute routes through the internetwork.

IS-IS uses three basic packet formats: hello packets, link-state packets, and sequence-numbers packets (SNPs). Each of the packet formats has a complex format with three different logical parts. The first is an 8-byte fixed header shared by all three packet formats. The second is packet type specific (either hello, link state, or sequence-numbers packets) with a fixed format. The third is also packet-type specific (either hello, link state, or sequence-numbers packets), but it is a variable length.

Apple Talk RTMP

Although Macintosh computers are not the most widely used computers in a network, many businesses still use and need them in their network. This means a protocol is needed that the MAC can use to operate on a network.

The *routing table maintenance protocol (RTMP)* is similar to the RIP protocol insofar as it, too, is a distance-vector routing protocol. AppleTalk uses the RTMP protocol to send out information from one router to the rest of the routers on the network. Every ten seconds, RTMP sends broadcast packets that contain every routing table that was sent on the network. Also like RIP, RTMP has a hop count of 15; if the packet does not make it to its destination within 15 hops, the packet is deemed as a failure in AppleTalk routing.

Chapter Summary

This chapter discussed interior routing protocols, such as RIP, OSPF, IGRP, and EIGRP. Interior routing protocols use the IP routing protocols and a specific routing algorithm to accomplish their routing.

RIP is a distance-vector routing protocol that uses hop counts for a measurement. OSPF is a link-state routing protocol that uses an autonomous system to achieve its routing. IGRP is a distance-vector protocol that is proprietary to Cisco. EIGRP combines link-state and distance-vector routing to achieve its routing and is also a Cisco proprietary protocol.

The distance-vector routing protocol is designed to send a copy of its entire routing table to all of its neighbors, allowing all the routers to know the routing paths and determine the lowest cost (shortest distance). The link-state routing process uses link-state packets to inform other routers of distant links and proximity. After the routers have all updated their fellow routers, each router possesses a routing table to refer to when it needs to make routing decisions and choose the best path.

Border Gateway Protocol (BGP) is an exterior gateway protocol. The main goal of BGP is to provide an interdomain routing system that will guarantee a loop-free exchange or routing information between autonomous systems. BGP was designed to allow ISPs to communicate and exchange packets.

AppleTalk RTMP is a protocol that maintains Apple routing tables for networks using Apple or MAC computers.

If you develop a good understanding of how the protocols operate in determining paths, you will be able to troubleshoot a lot easier. Using the **show** and **debug** commands will help you isolate the problems on a network.

Review Questions

1. Which routing methods might cause a routing loop? [Choose the two best answers]

   a. Split horizon has been disabled on an interface

   b. IP multicast routing is not enabled

   c. Hold-down timers are not consistent across the network

   d. Invalid IP addresses exist on the network

2. Which of the following protocols provides routing for Apple Talk?

   a. ATP

   b. ZIP

   c. AARP

   d. RTMP

3. Which of the following protocols is considered an exterior routing protocol?

   a. RIP

   b. EIGRP

   c. BGP

   d. OSPF

14

4. Of the following, which protocol is considered a hybrid (meaning it uses both distance-vector and link-state routing algorithm)?

   a. RIP

   b. EIGRP

   c. IGRP

   d. IS-IS

5. Classless subnet masks can be used by which of the following routing protocols? [Choose the two best answers]

   a. IGRP

   b. EIGRP

   c. OSPF

   d. RIP v1

6. Which of the following routing protocols are categorized as link-state protocols? [Choose the two best answers]

   a. RIP

   b. OSPF

   c. NLSP

   d. EIGRP

7. Pick three valid IP **show** commands from the following:

   a. **show ip route**

   b. **show ip interface**

   c. **show ip protocols**

   d. **show ip-route**

   e. **show protocols**

   f. **show ip-interface**

8. Which **debug** command can be used to provide important information when troubleshooting OSPF?

   a. **debug ospf**

   b. **debug eigrp**

   c. **debug arp**

   d. **debug ip arp**

9. Which commands would you use to see the contents of a route map? [Choose the two best answers]

   a. **show running-config**

   b. **show ip route-map**

   c. **show route-map**

   d. **show ip interface**

10. What are the three types of routes recognized by IGRP? [Choose the three best answers]

    a. Default

    b. Interior

    c. Internal

    d. Redistributed

    e. System

    f. External

    g. Exterior

    h. Static

11. Suppose you are running OSPF in your core backbone routers and running RIP on the edge networks. You notice a few of the networks are not receiving IP packets. After logging in to the router, what command should you use to see who is running OSPF?

    a. **show ip protocols**

    b. **show ip ospf neighbors**

    c. **show ip interface**

    d. **sh ip arp**

12. RIP2, following RIP1, is able to support which of the following? [Choose the three best answers]

    a. Subnetting

    b. Classless routing (CIDR)

    c. Route summarization

    d. Variable length subnet mask (VLSM)

13. What command can be issued to view the contents of an IP access list?

    a. **show access-list**

    b. **show ip access-list**

    c. **sh running-config**

    d. All of the above

14

14. In using a classful routing protocol, the routing updates include subnet information?

    a. True

    b. False

15. Which command enables you to see the routing table?

    a. **show ip route rip**

    b. **show ip route**

    c. **show ip interface**

    d. **show running-configuration**

16. Which of the following problems may be occurring if you have this output?

    ```
    Support#
    Support#show interface s0/0
    Serial 0/0 is down, line protocol is down
    Support#
    ```

    a. Bad cable

    b. Bad MAU port

    c. MAU is not initialized

    d. All of the above

17. ARP cache tables are always permanent until cleared manually.

    a. True

    b. False

18. Which of the following routing protocols is proprietary to Cisco?

    a. RIP

    b. IGRP

    c. BGP

    d. OSPF

19. When a router is informed from its neighbor about routing updates, this is a process done by which of the following?

    a. Split horizon

    b. Poison reverse

    c. Hold-down timers

    d. Triggered updates

20. If CDP is enabled, which command will display all directly connected Cisco devices and information about them?

    a. **show cdp**

    b. **show cdp neighbors**

    c. **show neighbors**

    d. **show cdp-neighbors**

Real-World Project

Joe Snow has been troubleshooting networks for quite some time. Joe has been on vacation for the last two weeks. When he first walks through the door after vacation, his boss calls to alert him that a network is down. Internet access is down, and the users on the network need Internet access to perform their jobs. Joe grabs his tools and Cisco support book and heads out the door.

Assessing the Situation

Joe writes down how the network is designed, starting with the following:

➤ The 3624 channel bank is connected to a CSU/DSU

➤ The CSU/DSU is connected to a 2500 router and T-1 line

Connecting to the Router

Joe wants to look at the router and the interfaces, so he connects to the console port of the router via Hyperterminal. After logging in to the router, Joe uses the **show interfaces** command and notices that the serial port is down. Joe's first thought is that the T-1 line has problems. Joe calls the service provider and has the line tested.

Looking at the Router

The service provider reports that the line is testing fine to the CSU/DSU. Joe then looks at the router configuration by using the command **show running** to see whether a configuration problem exists. Joe notices in the configuration that the router is running a wide variety of protocols, but nothing unusual. He then takes the following steps:

1. He issues a **show interfaces** command, which shows whether interfaces are up/up, up/down, or down/down. He notices that the Ethernet interface is up/up, but the serial interface is up/down. At this point, he uses a **show ip route** command to see all the routes running on the interface.

2. He sees something very unusual on the interface. CRC errors and input errors are shown on the serial interface. Joe knows that these types of errors usually are caused by a connection, hardware, or cable problem.

14

3. Joe starts to look at the cabling connected to the router. He notices that the V.35 cable looks crimped and tied very tight, so he swaps the V.35 cable.

4. After swapping the cable, Joe looks at the interface again by using the **show interfaces** command. The errors are no longer on the interface.

5. Joe tries using the **ping** command to test connectivity. The **ping** test is good as its ping was successful.

6. Joe then tries to access the Internet and is able to.

Joe has learned a great lesson: Whenever any CRC or input errors exist, one of the first places to start troubleshooting is at Layer 1 (Physical).

CHAPTER FIFTEEN

IP/TCP Troubleshooting

After completing this chapter, you will be able to:

✓ Understand the Internet Protocol and how it sends datagrams

✓ Understand how IP uses addressing

✓ Under the Transmission Control Protocol and how it sends segments

✓ Know the troubleshooting commands and when they should be used

✓ Know the troubleshooting steps to help solve common network problems

This chapter covers the most popular protocols in the Protocol Suite, including IP, TCP, UDP, and ICMP, just to name a few. After reading this chapter, you will know how IP and TCP send packets, as well as the pros and cons of both protocols. You will learn the commands that will enable you to troubleshoot TCP/IP networks, as well as some troubleshooting steps to follow after encountering a few common problems. Although this chapter will provide you with an overview of the common protocols in the Protocol Suite, it will not provide you with every detail about the protocols.

The Protocol Suite

The use of Internet protocols began when the need arose for protocols to communicate on any set of interconnected networks. Internet protocols consist of many protocols and collectively are often referred to as the *Internet Protocol Suite*. The Protocol Suite consists of such protocols as FTP, Telnet, SMTP, TCP, IP, ARP, and RARP, among many others. The protocols in the Protocol Suite reside at several layers of the OSI model (but do not reside in the Physical layer), and refer to a four-layer IP model. Figure 15.1 shows how the Protocol Suite measures relate to the OSI model and the IP model.

The Internet Protocol (IP) resides at Layer 3 (Network layer) of the OSI model and contains addressing information and control information that enables packets to be routed. IP is documented in RFC 791 (for a list of all RFCs, visit **www.landfield.com/rfcs/rfc2000.html**) and is the primary Network-layer protocol in the Internet Protocol Suite, along with the Transmission Control Protocol (TCP), which together represent the "meat and potatoes" of the Internet protocols.

Internet Protocol

IP itself has two main responsibilities:

➤ Provide connectionless, best-effort delivery of datagrams

➤ Provide fragmentation and reassembly of datagrams to support data links with different maximum transmission unit (MTU) sizes

Figure 15.2 shows what is contained in an IP packet.

The IP packet contains the following 14 fields:

➤ *Version (4 bits)*—Contains the IP version number

➤ *Length of Header (4 bits)*—Contains the length of the header expressed in 32-bit words

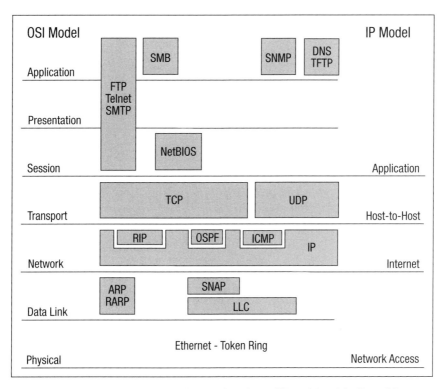

Figure 15.1   The Internet Protocol Suite contained in the OSI model and the IP model.

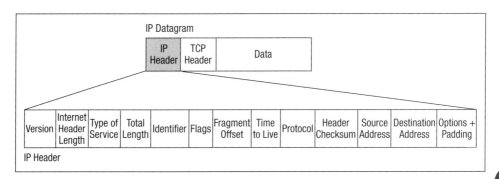

Figure 15.2   The fields that are contained in an IP packet.

15

➤ *Type-of-Service (8 bits)*—Contains information regarding how the datagram is to be handled; the datagram can be assigned different precedence levels at this field

➤ *Total Length (16 bits)*—Contains information regarding the length of the entire packet, including the header and the data

➤ *Identification (16 bits)*—Contains information that helps assemble datagram fragments (usually expressed as an integer)

➤ *Flags (3 bits)*—Contains information controlling fragmentation and whether the packet can be fragmented

➤ *Fragment Offset (13 bits)*—Enables the destination IP to properly reassemble the original datagram

➤ *TTL (8 bits)*—Contains a counter to prevent endless loops; same as time-to-live

➤ *Type or Protocol (8 bits)*—Contains information regarding which upper-level protocol is going to receive the incoming packets after IP processing (in other words, TCP or UDP)

➤ *Header Checksum (16 bits)*—Contains the Frame Check Sequence (FCS)

➤ *Source IP Address (32 bits)*—Contains the address of the sender

➤ *Destination IP Address (32 bits)*—Contains the address of the recipient

➤ *IP Option (variable bit length)*—Enables IP to support network testing, such as debugging and security

After you look at the IP packet, the next thing to know about IP is the addressing scheme. Addressing includes the best and worst aspects of IP. The best aspect of IP is the ability to place millions of nodes on a network such as the Internet. The worst aspect of IP is adopting IP in your network and assigning an IP address to every node in your network. Of course, in today's networks, the use of the Dynamic Host Configuration Protocol (DHCP) has made this a simpler task. DHCP provides automatic TCP/IP configurations for static and dynamic address allocation and management.

IP Addressing

When looking at host addresses in a TCP/IP network, you will find a network number and a host number equaling 32 bits in length. An IP address consists of 4 octets (each octet contains 8 bits) separated by periods, and has a total of 256 combinations representing numbers 0 through 255.

The first octet (or byte) determines the network address; the second octet (or byte) and third octet (or byte, if applicable) designate the subnet address; and the final octet designates the host address. In using IP addressing, your network administrator may use subnets to utilize the address space as subnets allow for your network to be divided into subnetworks. Subnetworks allow for better management of your IP class utilizing address space. The following are the five different classes of IP addressing:

➤ *Class A*—The first 1 byte is assigned to the network and the 3 remaining bytes are used for the node address (network.node.node.node). This class of address is mainly used in large institutions, because of the number of hosts (or nodes), and is represented by the network numbers 1.0.0.0 through 127.0.0.0.

➤ *Class B*—The first 2 bytes are assigned to the network address and the remaining 2 bytes are used for node (or host) addresses (network.network.node.node). This class of address is used for a medium-sized institution, allowing for flexibility with the network and node addressing, (especially using subnetting), and is represented by the network numbers of 128.0.0.0 through 191.0.0.0.

➤ *Class C*—The first 3 bytes are assigned to the network address and the remaining 1 byte is used for the node (or host) addresses (network.network.network. node). This class of address does not allow a large number of hosts to be used for smaller networks, and is represented by the network numbers of 192.0.0.0 through 223.255.255.0.

➤ *Class D*—This class of address is reserved for multicast groups and is represented by the network numbers of 224.0.0.0 through 247.255.255.255.

➤ *Class E*—This class of address is reserved for future use but is represented by the network numbers 248.0.0.0 through 255.255.255.255.

Refer to Table 15.1 for a quick reference of the classes of addresses.

Although the first three classes are mainly for commercial use, a portion is set aside for private address space that is not assigned for commercial use. The portion of address space that is set aside for private use is not routable by the Internet and is considered "illegal." The following ranges have been determined to be private address space: 10.0.0.0 through 10.255.255.255, 172.16.0.0 through 172.31.255. 255, and 192.168.0.0 through 192.168.255.255. You may use private address schemes in your network as long as they do not cross onto the Internet. Most companies, for example, use the 10.0.0.0 to address their network internally, and use a registered address when the network traffic is exiting the internal network to the Internet.

Subnetting

The Internet world is growing in leaps and bounds, and a definite need exists for more addressing space. Most of the classful addresses (Class, A, B, C, D, and E) are

15

Table 15.1   Classful addressing.

Class	Format	Network Numbering
A	network.node.node.node	1.0.0.0 through 127.0.0.0
B	network.network.node.node	128.0.0.0 through 191.255.0.0
C	network.network.network.node	192.0.0.0 through 223.255.255.0
D	Reserved for Multicast	224.0.0.0 through 247.255.255.255
E	Reserved for future use	248.0.0.0 through 255.255.255.255

being used already, and the need for additional space is desired. Classless Interdomain Routing (CIDR) and variable-length subnet masks (VLSMs) have been created as a solution to the addressing problem. With VLSMs, an IP network can be broken into many subnets of various sizes to provide extra network-configuration flexibility.

A subnet is used in conjunction with an IP address to identify the network and the node portion of the address. For example, in a Class B network using 132.79.1.1, the subnet mask would be 255.255.0.0. The 255 indicates the network portion of the address; thus, the use of 255.255.0.0 shows that it is a Class B address. This is an example of classful addressing and the subnet mask.

Of course, when you use the subnet mask with classless addressing, it becomes more complicated (this probably can be considered part of the worst aspect of IP addressing). VLSMs enable you to partition part of the network to better utilize your address space. This is very useful if you have a few sites that don't have many users and you don't want to use a full address space.

Suppose you have a Class C "registered" IP address for your corporation, such as 211.15.1.x with a subnet mask of 255.255.255.0, and you have two locations, each having 70 users. Suppose further that you want to preserve your node space. You could assign both sites 211.15.1.X with a subnet mask of 255.255.255.192 and split the 254 addresses. One location would use the top half of the addressing scheme, while the other location would use the bottom half. This can get a bit confusing and may take some time to get used to. It's basically a game of bit borrowing and utilization of bits.

Internet Control Message Protocol

The Internet Control Message Protocol (ICMP) is a Layer 3 (network) Internet protocol that provides message packets to report errors and other information regarding IP packet processing back to the source. IP does not provide a reporting mechanism for the source address in case of packet failures or other routing issues. This is where ICMP becomes very important to the Internet Protocol, because it does the reporting for it. The messages ICMP generates are helpful in letting the source know what is happening with the packet along its journey to the destination address. The ICMP messages include the following:

➤ *Destination Unreachable*—Includes four different types of messages reported to the source address, including Network Unreachable, Host Unreachable, Protocol Unreachable, and Port Unreachable. Network Unreachable messages usually indicate a problem in routing or addressing of the packet. Host Unreachable usually indicates a delivery failure. Protocol Unreachable usually indicates that the destination address is not supporting the protocol in the packet sent. Port Unreachable usually indicates that a specific port is not available for any of various reasons.

➤ *Echo Request*—Used by the **ping** command to alert the source address that it cannot reach the destination node on the network.

➤ *Redirect*—Sent by the router to notify the source address of a more efficient route. When receiving this message, the packet is delivered safely, but it alerts the source that a better way to the destination exists.

➤ *Time Exceeded*—Sent by the router if the specified time-to-live field in the IP packet is reached without reaching its destination. The time-to-live field is important because it prevents the packet from continuously circulating the network, causing a loop.

Without ICMP reporting back to the source address, the source address would never know why the packet was not delivered. ICMP messages are a big part of troubleshooting and identifying network problems.

ICMP Router Discovery Protocol

The ICMP Router Discovery Protocol (IRDP) specifies how routers communicate with other routers in different domains. IRDP uses Router-Advertisement and Router-Solicitation messages to communicate with the other routers. The messages discover the addresses of routers on attached subnets when each router multicasts it location to the rest of the routers on the network. After the routers have discovered each other, the hosts are then able to listen to the messages from the routers they are attached to.

IRDP employs a method for hosts to discover the existence of neighboring routers and then uses ICMP Redirect messages to identify a better path for the packets for the next time.

Transmission Control Protocol

In the past, IP was not considered a reliable protocol for packet delivery and the need for a more reliable protocol came about. TCP was developed to ensure a more reliable packet delivery, as well as test and report errors, resend data if the delivery was not accomplished, and alerts the upper-layer protocols to the problems in case the TCP can't solve the delivery failure. TCP is a full-duplex, connection-oriented, reliable protocol that is still used in most networks today.

15

TCP allows file transfers to ensure packet delivery and enables Hypertext Transfer Protocol (HTTP), Simple Mail Transport Protocol (SMTP), and File Transfer Protocol (FTP), to name a few, to be more widely used and offer reliability with IP. TCP works by taking large chunks of information from an application and breaking them down into an orderly alignment of segments. It keeps the order of the segments by using a numbering scheme, to enable the segments to be reassembled into the original chunks from the application.

TCP will establish a connection before sending all the segments to the destination. This is part of what makes TCP a reliable delivery protocol. TCP needs an acknowledgment from the recipient that it is ready to make the exchange, creating a virtual circuit between the source and the destination. After making contact and establishing a virtual circuit, TCP establishes the amount of information to be sent and at an agreed-upon rate. After this connection is set up, TCP is ready to make the delivery.

TCP Header

Now that you know about the connection-oriented reliability of TCP, you need to know this will cause more overhead on your network than IP does. That is why using both protocols in different situations is advised. If you are looking for the most reliable protocol for more important applications, you may want to suffer the overhead and use TCP. Figure 15.3 shows the fields that make up a TCP header.

➤ *Source Port (16 bits)*—Contains the port or socket of the upper-layer source that sent the data.

➤ *Destination Port (16 bits)*—Contains the port or socket of the upper-layer destination host.

➤ *Sequence Number (32 bits)*—Contains the assigned number that helps to reassemble data or to resend missing data that was not received.

➤ *Acknowledgment Number (32 bits)*—Contains the sequence number of the following bytes or the data that is to be sent next.

➤ *Offset (4 bits)* —Contains the number of 32-bit words in the header.

➤ *Reserved (6 bits)* —Reserved for future use and is always set to 0.

➤ *Flags (6 bits)* —Contains code bits that carry control information.

➤ *Window (16 bits)*—Contains the amount or size of buffer space the sender is willing to agree upon to send data to the destination.

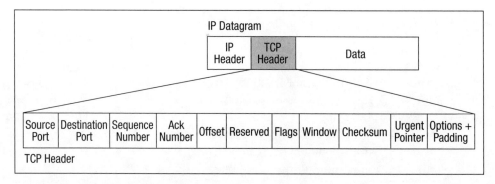

Figure 15.3   The fields of a TCP header.

➤ *Checksum (16 bits)*—Contains the CRC to verify the datagram arrived intact.

➤ *Urgent Pointer (16 bits)*—Contains the indicator to signify the end of urgent data.

➤ *Options and Padding (0 to 32 bits)*—Defines the maximum TCP segment size.

Notice the port number fields in the TCP header. TCP and UDP the port numbers enables different communications to take place in the network simultaneously while ensuring reliability. Port numbers are discussed further in the next section.

User Datagram Protocol

TCP is a reliable Transport-layer protocol, but it still requires some overhead. UDP also operates at the Transport layer, but has less overhead than TCP. However, you have to sacrifice a few things to decrease overhead, such as reliability. Like IP, UDP is a connectionless protocol. However, unlike TCP, UDP doesn't create a virtual circuit, and it doesn't contact the destination host before sending the datagrams. UDP does deliver the information in a timely manner and doesn't require much overhead. It has a good track record of reliable delivery, without the promise of reliability. It is sometimes referred to as the scaled-down, economy Transport-layer protocol.

Figure 15.4 shows an example of a UDP segment. Notice the difference in length of a UDP header compared to a TCP header. The difference in size is what helps UDP use less overhead. The following are the UDP header fields:

➤ *Source Port (16 bits)*—Contains the port or socket of the upper-layer application that is sending the data.

➤ *Destination Port (16 bits)*—Contains the port or socket of the upper-layer application that is receiving the data.

➤ *Length (16 bits)*—Contains the length of the UDP header and data.

➤ *Checksum (16 bits)*—Contains the checksum for packet integrity (optional).

UDP works by receiving upper-layer chunks of information and breaking them into segments. This sounds a lot like what TCP does, but TCP receives the information in streams of data before breaking it into segments. UDP then assigns a number, to help in the reassembly process. The next step is where a large difference lies between TCP and UDP. UDP does not sequence the numbers to ensure reliable delivery—it sends the segments not knowing whether the destination ever receives them or partially receives them.

15

Source Port	Destination Port	Length	Checksum CRC

Figure 15.4   The fields of a UDP header.

Table 15.2   Common port numbers.

Port Number	Protocol	Use
21	TCP	FTP
23	TCP	Telnet
25	TCP	SMTP
53	UDP	DNS
80	TCP	HTTP
161	UDP	SNMP

Port numbers were briefly discussed earlier in the chapter. TCP and UDP use port numbers for communication. A few well-known port numbers exist for TCP and UDP, and a very long list of port numbers is defined in RFC 1700. Port numbers are used in filtering traffic with access lists. RFC 1700 identifies a few basic ranges for port numbers:

➤ *0 to 256*—Reserved for public applications

➤ *256 to 1023*—Reserved for application companies

➤ *1023 and higher*—Assigned by the host applications

Table 15.2 identifies a list of common port numbers.

It is not necessary for both the source and the destination to use the same port for a communication of packet exchange. The source and destination commonly use different ports for communication.

Address Resolution Protocol

The Address Resolution Protocol (ARP) is used to resolve or map an IP address to a MAC address on a network. When IP is trying to send a datagram, the upper-layer protocols need to inform IP of the destination IP address. IP then needs to know the destination's hardware address to be able to send the datagram across the network, in cases like Ethernet. IP will not know the destination address, but can use ARP to resolve the IP address to a MAC sublayer address.

ARP works by having the sending address broadcast an ARP packet containing the IP address of the destination device. ARP then waits for the MAC address to be sent back from a host. Hosts maintain an ARP cache of addresses and can report back to the sender the information requested.

ARP is very helpful if you need to find more information about a particular device on your network. In some cases, you may receive a complaint about a device, and the only piece of information you will receive is the IP address of the device. In such a situation, you can then use ARP to find out the MAC address of the device you are interested in. At this point, depending on your network, you may be able to find everything you want to know about the device with only that information of a MAC address. Or, just having a MAC address may enable you to gather more information and use other tools to find what you are looking for.

Reverse ARP

Just as it sounds, Reverse ARP (RARP) is the reversal of ARP. When using RARP, you can find an IP address simply by knowing the MAC address. This protocol is used by routers to find the IP address of a host when the router knows only the MAC address. RARP works similarly to ARP in that routers send out a packet on the network encompassing the MAC address, and wait for a response referencing the IP address of the device.

Troubleshooting TCP/IP

One of the most useful resources when troubleshooting TCP/IP is the knowledge of which commands will report the information you are looking for. Using the Cisco IOS software tools and commands to manipulate the router to report the information you are looking for will save a lot of time. The following is a list of the commands that you need to know when troubleshooting:

➤ *ping ip*—Used in the privilege mode of the router to verify connections and reachability on a network, using ICMP packets sent to an address or host. The following output shows an example of this command being used:

```
Support#
Support#ping ip
Target IP address: 131.71.148.166
Repeat count [5]:
Datagram size [100]:
Timeout in seconds [2]:
Extended commands [n]:
Sweep range of sizes [n]:
Type escape sequence to abort.
Sending 5, 100-byte ICMP Echos to 131.71.148.166, timeout is 2 seconds:
!!!!!
Success rate is 100 percent (5/5), round-trip min/avg/max = 40/44/60 ms
Support#
```

➤ *show ip interface*—Used to see the IP information that is found on the interface configuration. When using this command, make sure the subnet mask and the subinterface are configured correctly. This command shows whether routes are being learned from the wrong interface or protocol. The following output shows an example of this command in use:

15

```
Support#
Support#show ip interface
Ethernet2/0 is up, line protocol is up
  Internet address is 131.71.111.254/24
  Broadcast address is 255.255.255.255
  Address determined by non-volatile memory
  MTU is 1500 bytes
  Helper address is not set
  Directed broadcast forwarding is disabled
  Multicast reserved groups joined: 10.0.0.9
  Outgoing access list is not set
  Inbound  access list is 101
  Proxy ARP is enabled
  Security level is default
  Split horizon is enabled
  ICMP redirects are always sent
  ICMP unreachables are always sent
  ICMP mask replies are never sent
  IP fast switching is enabled
  IP fast switching on the same interface is disabled
  IP Flow switching is disabled
  IP CEF switching is enabled
  IP Feature Fast switching turbo vector
  IP Feature CEF switching turbo vector
  IP multicast fast switching is enabled
  IP multicast distributed fast switching is disabled
  IP route-cache flags are Fast, CEF
  Router Discovery is disabled
  IP output packet accounting is disabled
  IP access violation accounting is disabled
  TCP/IP header compression is disabled
  RTP/IP header compression is disabled
  Probe proxy name replies are disabled
  Policy routing is disabled
  Network address translation is disabled
  WCCP Redirect outbound is disabled
  WCCP Redirect exclude is disabled
  BGP Policy Mapping is disabled
Ethernet2/1 is up, line protocol is up
  Internet address is 131.71.63.254/24
  Broadcast address is 255.255.255.255
  Address determined by non-volatile memory
  MTU is 1500 bytes
  Helper address is not set
  Directed broadcast forwarding is disabled
  Secondary address 131.71.150.254/24
```

```
            Secondary address 131.71.151.254/24
            Secondary address 131.71.3.254/24
            Secondary address 131.71.5.254/24
            Multicast reserved groups joined: 10.0.0.9
            Outgoing access list is not set
            Inbound  access list is 150
            Proxy ARP is enabled
            Security level is default
            Split horizon is enabled
            ICMP redirects are always sent
            ICMP unreachables are always sent
            ICMP mask replies are never sent
            IP fast switching is enabled
            IP fast switching on the same interface is disabled
            IP Flow switching is disabled
            IP CEF switching is enabled
            IP Feature Fast switching turbo vector
            IP Feature CEF switching turbo vector
            IP multicast fast switching is enabled
            IP multicast distributed fast switching is disabled
            IP route-cache flags are Fast, CEF
            Router Discovery is disabled
            IP output packet accounting is disabled
            IP access violation accounting is disabled
            TCP/IP header compression is disabled
            RTP/IP header compression is disabled
            Probe proxy name replies are disabled
            Policy routing is disabled
            Network address translation is disabled
            WCCP Redirect outbound is disabled
            WCCP Redirect exclude is disabled
            BGP Policy Mapping is disabled
        Support#
```

➤ *show ip protocols*—Used to identify the current routing protocols; can help
you to debug problems, as well as look at administrative distances, routing
redistribution, enabled access lists, and routing information obtained from other
sources. The following output shows an example of this command in practice:

```
Support#
Support#show ip protocols
Routing Protocol is "ospf 1"
  Sending updates every 0 seconds
  Invalid after 0 seconds, hold down 0, flushed after 0
  Outgoing update filter list for all interfaces is
```

15

```
        Incoming update filter list for all interfaces is
        Redistributing: ospf 1
        Routing for Networks:
        Routing Information Sources:
          Gateway         Distance      Last Update
        Distance: (default is 110)

    Routing Protocol is "rip"
      Sending updates every 30 seconds, next due in 13 seconds
      Invalid after 180 seconds, hold down 180, flushed after 240
      Outgoing update filter list for all interfaces is
      Incoming update filter list for all interfaces is
      Redistributing: rip
      Default version control: send version 1, receive any version
        Interface        Send  Recv  Triggered RIP  Key-chain
        Ethernet2/0       1     1 2
        Ethernet2/1       1     1 2
        Interface        Send  Recv  Triggered RIP  Key-chain
      Automatic network summarization is in effect
      Routing for Networks:
        131.71.0.0
      Routing Information Sources:
        Gateway          Distance      Last Update
        131.71.95.200        120        00:02:51
        131.71.110.133       120        00:02:32
        131.71.1.130         120        1d03h
        131.71.1.131         120        4d08h
        131.71.29.188        120        00:02:27
        131.71.81.1          120        00:02:46
        Gateway          Distance      Last Update
        131.71.94.2          120        00:02:31
        131.71.41.115        120        00:02:35
        131.71.106.26        120        00:02:50
        131.71.29.120        120        00:02:37
        131.71.1.23          120        00:00:12
      Distance: (default is 120)
    Support#
```

➤ *show ip route*—Reports information stored in the IP route table. The general command displays all IP routes and corresponding information. The following output shows an example of this command in use:

```
Support#
Support#show ip route
Codes: C - connected, S - static, I - IGRP, R - RIP, M - mobile, B -
```

```
BGP
        D - EIGRP, EX - EIGRP external, O - OSPF, IA - OSPF inter area
        N1 - OSPF NSSA external type 1, N2 - OSPF NSSA external type 2
        E1 - OSPF external type 1, E2 - OSPF external type 2, E - EGP
        i - IS-IS, L1 - IS-IS level-1, L2 - IS-IS level-2, ia - IS-IS
inter area
        * - candidate default, U - per-user static route, o - ODR
        P - periodic downloaded static route

Gateway of last resort is 152.79.1.11 to network 0.0.0.0


     152.79.0.0/16 is variably subnetted, 2 subnets, 2 masks
C       152.79.151.0/24 is directly connected, Ethernet2/1
C       152.79.111.0/24 is directly connected, Ethernet2/0
Support#
```

➤ *show ip traffic*—Displays the statistics about the IP protocol that the router has gathered. Some of the statistics reported are packets being received and sent, error counts, and sometimes broadcasts. The following output shows an example of this command in practice:

```
Support#
Support#show ip traffic
IP statistics:
  Rcvd:  931856425 total, 4287248 local destination
         0 format errors, 0 checksum errors, 18411 bad hop count
         13802 unknown protocol, 0 not a gateway
         0 security failures, 0 bad options, 108 with options
  Opts:  66 end, 0 nop, 0 basic security, 0 loose source route
         0 timestamp, 0 extended security, 66 record route
         0 stream ID, 0 strict source route, 42 alert, 0 cipso
         0 other
  Frags: 0 reassembled, 0 timeouts, 0 couldnət reassemble
         26 fragmented, 0 couldnət fragment
  Bcast: 3995112 received, 2626992 sent
  Mcast: 13844 received, 0 sent
  Sent:  2864509 generated, 926364619 forwarded
  Drop:  2832293 encapsulation failed, 0 unresolved, 0 no adjacency
         2382 no route, 0 unicast RPF, 0 forced drop

ICMP statistics:
  Rcvd: 0 format errors, 0 checksum errors, 0 redirects, 20 unreachable
        18293 echo, 42931 echo reply, 0 mask requests, 0 mask replies,
0 quench
        0 parameter, 0 timestamp, 0 info request, 0 other
```

15

```
                 18 irdp solicitations, 0 irdp advertisements
       Sent: 4 redirects, 5862 unreachable, 42972 echo, 18293 echo reply
             0 mask requests, 0 mask replies, 0 quench, 0 timestamp
             0 info reply, 389 time exceeded, 0 parameter problem
             0 irdp solicitations, 0 irdp advertisements

  UDP statistics:
    Rcvd: 4185105 total, 0 checksum errors, 4000459 no port
    Sent: 2746225 total, 0 forwarded broadcasts

  TCP statistics:
    Rcvd: 27074 total, 0 checksum errors, 133 no port
    Sent: 50792 total

  Probe statistics:
    Rcvd: 0 address requests, 0 address replies
          0 proxy name requests, 0 where-is requests, 0 other
    Sent: 0 address requests, 0 address replies (0 proxy)
          0 proxy name replies, 0 where-is replies

  EGP statistics:
    Rcvd: 0 total, 0 format errors, 0 checksum errors, 0 no listener
    Sent: 0 total

  IGRP statistics:
    Rcvd: 0 total, 0 checksum errors
    Sent: 0 total

  OSPF statistics:
    Rcvd: 0 total, 0 checksum errors
          0 hello, 0 database desc, 0 link state req
          0 link state updates, 0 link state acks

    Sent: 0 total

  IP-IGRP2 statistics:
    Rcvd: 0 total
    Sent: 0 total

  PIMv2 statistics: Sent/Received
    Total: 0/0, 0 checksum errors, 0 format errors
    Registers: 0/0, Register Stops: 0/0,  Hellos: 0/0
    Join/Prunes: 0/0, Asserts: 0/0, grafts: 0/0
    Bootstraps: 0/0, Candidate_RP_Advertisements: 0/0
```

```
 IGMP statistics: Sent/Received
   Total: 0/0, Format errors: 0/0, Checksum errors: 0/0
   Host Queries: 0/0, Host Reports: 0/0, Host Leaves: 0/0
   DVMRP: 0/0, PIM: 0/0

 ARP statistics:
   Rcvd: 1460555 requests, 24281 replies, 3942 reverse, 0 other
   Sent: 816581 requests, 655890 replies (71605 proxy), 0 reverse
 Support#
```

➤ ***show ip arp***—Provides information that is held in the router's ARP cache, such as the IP address, MAC address, encapsulation type, and the interface that it learned the MAC from. The following output shows an example of this command in use:

```
Support#
Support#show ip arp
Protocol  Address         Age (min)   Hardware Addr   Type   Interface
Internet  131.71.44.254         -      0003.fa0b.d461  ARPA   Ethernet2/0
Internet  131.71.150.65        3      0010.5aac.35b0  ARPA   Ethernet2/1
Internet  131.71.29.202        5      0090.27ab.17d0  ARPA   Ethernet2/0
Internet  131.71.55.224        9      0060.a0be.9591  ARPA   Ethernet2/
Internet  131.71.29.203        5      0060.9a76.f0a1  ARPA   Ethernet2/1
Internet  131.71.55.225        9      0060.babe.0685  ARPA   Ethernet2/1
Internet  131.71.111.186       0      0080.5abb.4054  ARPA   Ethernet2/0
Internet  131.71.55.226        9      0060.bac0.0688  ARPA   Ethernet2/0
Internet  131.71.29.200       19      00e0.2aa0.d585  ARPA   Ethernet2/0
Internet  131.71.150.67      132      00a0.24aa.dac8  ARPA   Ethernet2/1
Internet  131.71.150.66        1      0060.8737.95d8  ARPA   Ethernet2/1
Internet  131.71.29.201        7      0020.afb1.cad9  ARPA   Ethernet2/0
Support#
```

➤ ***debug ip icmp***—Displays information about the router sending and receiving ICMP messages. This is one of the best commands to use when you are troubleshooting an end-to-end connection. The following output shows an example of this command in use:

15

Note: Before using **debug** *commands, you have to enable the terminal monitor to see the output. Use the command* **terminal monitor** *before using the* **debug** *commands if you want to see the debugging output on the screen. To disable the terminal monitor, use the* **termnal no monitor** *command.*

```
Support#
Support#terminal monitor
Support#debug ip icmp
```

```
ICMP packet debugging is on
Support#show debugging
Generic IP:
  ICMP packet debugging is on
Support#
*Sep 11 21:38:12: ICMP: echo reply sent, src 131.71.111.254, dst
131.71.109.10
Support#no debug ip icmp
ICMP packet debugging is off
Support#terminal no monitor
```

➤ *debug ip packet*—Performs a utility to check the flow of IP packets being sent between local and remote hosts, and gives general IP debugging information. The following output shows an example of this command in use:

```
Support#
Support#terminal monitor
Support#debug ip packet
IP packet debugging is on
Support#
*Sep 11 21:39:18: IP: s=131.71.5.199 (Ethernet2/1), d=255.255.255.255,
len 108,
rcvd 2
*Sep 11 21:39:18: IP: s=131.71.150.201 (Ethernet2/1),
d=255.255.255.255, len 108
, rcvd 2
*Sep 11 21:39:19: IP: s=131.71.5.199 (Ethernet2/1), d=255.255.255.255,
len 108,
rcvd 2
*Sep 11 21:39:19: IP: s=131.71.150.201 (Ethernet2/1),
d=255.255.255.255, len 108
, rcvd 2
*Sep 11 21:39:19: IP: s=131.71.5.199 (Ethernet2/1), d=255.255.255.255,
len 108,
rcvd 2
*Sep 11 21:39:19: IP: s=131.71.150.201 (Ethernet2/1),
d=255.255.255.255, len 108
, rcvd 2
*Sep 11 21:39:20: IP: s=131.71.5.199 (Ethernet2/1), d=255.255.255.255,
len 108,
rcvd 2
IP packet debugging is off
Support#terminal no monitor
Support#
```

➤ *debug ip rip*—Performs a utility to check the flow of IP RIP packets, RIP routing information, and updates, as shown in the following example output:

```
Support#
Support#terminal monitor
Support#debug ip rip
RIP protocol debugging is on
Support#
*Sep 11 21:40:22: RIP: received v1 update from 131.71.29.120 on
Ethernet2/4
*Sep 11 21:40:22:     131.71.115.6 in 16 hops (inaccessible)
*Sep 11 21:40:24: RIP: received v1 update from 131.71.41.155 on
Ethernet2/0
*Sep 11 21:40:24:     131.71.235.6 in 16 hops (inaccessible)
*Sep 11 21:40:26: RIP: received v1 update from 131.71.4.23 on Fddi8/0
*Sep 11 21:40:26:     131.71.129.0 in 1 hops
*Sep 11 21:40:26: RIP: received v1 update from 131.71.100.133 on
Ethernet4/0
*Sep 11 21:40:26:     131.71.235.6 in 16 hops (inaccessible)
*Sep 11 21:40:28: RIP: received v1 update from 152.79.1.29 on Fddi8/0
*Sep 11 21:40:28:     152.79.135.16 in 1 hops
RIP protocol debugging is on
Support#
Support#debug ip rip
RIP protocol debugging is off
*Sep 11 21:40:36: RIP: sending v1 update to 255.255.255.255 via
Ethernet2/0 (131.71.4.126)
11 21:40:36: RIP: build update entries
*Sep 11 21:40:36:     subnet 0.0.0.0 metric 3
*Sep 11 21:40:36:     subnet 131.71.4.0 metric 1
*Sep 11 21:40:36:     subnet 131.71.3.0 metric 1
*Sep 11 21:40:36:     subnet 131.71.5.0 metric 1
*Sep 11 21:40:36:     subnet 131.71.7.0 metric 1
*Sep 11 21:40:36:     subnet 131.71.8.0 metric 2
*Sep 11 21:40:36:     subnet 131.71.10.0 metric 2
*Sep 11 21:40:36:     subnet 131.71.11.0 metric 2
*Sep 11 21:40:36:     subnet 131.71.12.0 metric 2
*Sep 11 21:40:36:     subnet 131.71.13.0 metric 1
*Sep 11 21:40:36:     subnet 131.71.14.0 metric 2
*Sep 11 21:40:36:     subnet 131.71.15.0 metric 2
*Sep 11 21:40:36:     subnet 131.71.16.0 metric 2
Support#terminal no monitor
Support#
```

15

➤ *debug arp*—Displays information about ARP transactions and whether the router is sending and receiving ARP requests and replies. The following output shows an example of this command in use:

```
Support#
Support#terminal monitor
Support#debug arp
ARP packet debugging is on
Support#
*Sep 11 21:41:11: IP ARP: sent req src 131.71.110.126 0003.f108.d380,
                  dst 131.71.104.90 0000.0000.0000 Ethernet4/0
*Sep 11 21:41:11: IP ARP: sent req src 131.71.12.254 0003.f11b.da44,
                  dst 131.71.30.123 0000.0000.0000 Ethernet2/1
*Sep 11 21:41:12: IP ARP throttled out the ARP Request for
131.71.200.90
*Sep 11 21:41:13: IP ARP: rcvd req src 131.71.117.100 00a0.249e.9aa2,
dst 131.71.106.254 Ethernet4/0
*Sep 11 21:41:13: IP ARP: sent rep src 131.71.126.254 0003.faab.da82,
                  dst 131.71.106.100 00a0.24aa.9d12 Ethernet2/0
*Sep 11 21:41:14: IP ARP: sent req src 131.71.104.1 0003.faab.d180,
                  dst 131.71.100.90 0000.0000.0000 Ethernet2/1
*Sep 11 21:41:15: IP ARP: rcvd req src 152.79.63.226 0010.4b70.9296,
dst 131.71.
63.200 Ethernet2/1
*Sep 11 21:41:15: IP ARP: sent rep src 131.71.43.254 0013.f00b.daa1,
                  dst 131.71.69.226 0110.4b70.9a96 Ethernet2/1
ARP packet debugging is off
Support#terminal no monitor
Support#
```

Troubleshooting Scenarios

When troubleshooting TCP/IP networks, hopefully (and normally) everything won't fail simultaneously so that you will have the opportunity to troubleshoot the problem. One of the best ways to troubleshoot the problem is to look at the path the packet is traveling; start from the inside (source) of the problem and work your way out (destination). You can begin the process by starting at the local router and seeing how far on the network you can get before reaching the problem host. The following are a few different ways to troubleshoot problems:

➤ *Inside-out method*—Starts with the local host and works its way step by step to the problem host.

➤ *Outside-in method*—Starts with the remote host and works its way back to the local host.

➤ *Center-of-path method*—Starts by identifying the center of the path and then troubleshooting in either direction until the problem is found.

The following are a few steps to help you in troubleshooting this process using the inside-out method:

1. Look at any problems with the address, subnet mask, or default gateway.

2. Ping or trace from the local router to see whether and where the path stops. Start with the remote host and work toward the destination host.

3. When using ping, use IP addresses to rule out problems with DNS.

If the router doesn't ping, the problem may be the router. To check the router, follow these steps:

1. Look at the configuration and the up/down state of the router using **show** commands.

2. Use the **show ip route** command to look at the router's routing table to determine whether a path exists to the problem host.

3. Use the **show ip arp** command to look at the ARP tables to make sure that the problem host exists in the table.

4. Use the **show ip cache** command to look at the fast-switching route cache to see whether anomalies exist.

5. Use the **show interfaces** command to look at the interfaces on the router for any errors for LAN or WAN.

After completing the preceding steps, you should have found your problem. Of course, if you were able to ping the local router, you would use the preceding steps to see the problem with the remote host.

If the local router pings and the **traceroute** commands indicate a problem with a router, follow these steps:

1. Look at the configuration and up/down state of the router using **show** commands.

2. Use the **show ip route** command to look at the router's routing table to determine whether a path exists to the problem host.

3. Use the **show ip arp** command to look at the ARP tables to make sure that the problem host exists in the table.

4. Use the **show ip cache** command to look at the fast-switching route cache to see whether anomalies exist.

5. Use the **show interfaces** command to look at the interfaces on the router for any errors for LAN or WAN.

15

TCP/IP Problem Scenarios and Possible Solutions

The following are a few common problems experienced daily with TCP/IP networks.

Scenario 1: Some Hosts Aren't Able to Access Networks through a Router

Here are a few possible solutions to this problem:

➤ Check whether a default gateway is specified on the local host.

➤ Look at the access list and make sure it is written correctly and not denying the host with the implicit "deny all" statement.

➤ Look for a link failure caused by a Physical layer problem or poor network designing.

Scenario 2: Users Are Able to Connect to Some Hosts, but Not Others

Here are a few possible solutions to this problem:

➤ Check whether an incorrect subnet mask or incorrect address is assigned to the host or router that you are having trouble with.

➤ Look at the access list and make sure it is written correctly and not denying the host with the implicit "deny all" statement.

➤ Check whether a default gateway is specified on the local host.

Scenario 3: Users Are Able to Receive Some Services, Such as Telnet, but Not Web Traffic

As a possible solution to this problem, look at the access list, mainly the extended access list, and see whether it is configured correctly. Look at the port numbers to see whether a specific type of traffic is being permitted or denied.

Scenario 4: Some Protocols Are Being Routed and Others Are Not

As a possible solution to this problem, look at the access list, mainly the extended access list, and see whether it is configured correctly. Look at the protocol numbers to see whether a specific type of protocol is being permitted or denied.

Scenario 5: A Host Is Having Problems Reaching Some Areas of Its Own Network

Here are a few possible solutions to this problem:

➤ Look at the access list and make sure certain types of traffic are being denied.

➤ Check whether a default gateway is specified.

➤ Look for a subnet mask configuration mismatch between the router and the host.

Scenario 6: A Router Between Hosts Seems to Be Down

Here are a few possible solutions to this problem:

➤ Ping outward until the problem router is found.

➤ Look at the router configurations and make changes if necessary.

➤ Check for LAN or WAN Physical layer problems.

Scenario 7: Misconfigured Access List or Filter

Here are a few possible solutions to this problem:

➤ Use **ping** and **traceroute** to isolate the problem.

➤ Check the routing table by using the **show ip route** command.

➤ Check for protocols being exchanged at the router level by using **debug ip rip** to see the RIP protocol; other **debug** commands exist for other protocols.

➤ After isolating the problem, try disabling the access list by using the **no ip access group** command. Then, test the routers again by using the **ping** and **traceroute** tools. You may have to try this on more than one router.

Chapter Summary

The Protocol Suite consists of protocols including FTP, Telnet, SMTP, TCP, IP, ARP, and RARP, to name a few. IP is a Network-layer protocol that contains addressing information and some control information that enables packets to be routed. IP has two primary responsibilities: providing connectionless, best-effort delivery of datagrams through an internetwork, and providing fragmentation and reassembly of datagrams to support data links with different MTU sizes. IP utilizes ICMP to provide message packets to report errors and other information regarding IP packet processing back to the source.

An IP address consists of 4 octets. The first octet (or byte) determines the network address; the second octet (or byte) and third octet (or byte, if applicable) designate the subnet address; and the final octet designates the host address. Subnets enable your network to be divided into subnetworks, which allows for better management of your IP class addressing. A subnet is used in conjunction with an IP address to identify the network and the node portion of the address. Because of the demand for IP addressing space, CIDR and VLSMs have been introduced to allow an IP network to be broken into many networks. This allows for a better use of address space.

IP wasn't always sufficiently reliable, which led to the development of TCP. TCP not only ensures a more reliable packet delivery, but also tests and reports errors, resends data, and alerts the upper-layer protocols of any delivery failure problems. TCP resides on the Transport layer and is a full-duplex, connection-oriented, reliable protocol that is still used in most networks.

15

UDP also operates at the Transport layer and has less overhead then other protocols such as TCP, but it does not offer reliability. UDP is a connectionless protocol that delivers information in a timely manner without the overhead. TCP and UDP use port numbers to communicate between source and destination addresses and they do not necessarily need to be using the same port number.

ARP is used to resolve an IP address to a MAC address on a network. ARP works by having the sending address broadcast an ARP packet containing the IP address of the destination device. ARP then waits for the MAC address to be sent back from a host. Hosts on the network maintain an ARP cache of addresses and are able to report back to the sender the information requested.

You need to know a few particular commands when troubleshooting a TCP/IP network. Knowing when and where to use these commands will help the router report the information you are looking for to solve the problem. Various **show** and **debug** commands are found in the Cisco IOS, to help diagnose and fix a problem.

Review Questions

1. Which Internet protocol resides at Layer 3 and provides a best-effort, connectionless delivery of datagrams?

    a. TCP

    b. IP

    c. UDP

    d. RARP

    e. RIP

2. Class A networks are defined by which network numbers?

    a. 1.0.0.0 through 127.0.0.0

    b. 128.0.0.0 through 191.255.0.0

    c. 1.0.0.0 through 125.0.0.0

    d. 248.0.0.0 through 255.255.255.255

3. Class B networks are defined by which network numbers?

    a. 128.0.0.0 through 191.255.0.0

    b. 191.0.0.0 through 223.255.255.0

    c. 248.0.0.0 through 255.255.255.255

    d. 1.0.0.0 through 125.0.0.0

4. Class E networks are defined by which network numbers?

   a. 241.0.0.0 through 255.255.255.255

   b. 1.0.0.0 through 127.0.0.0

   c. 190.0.0.0 through 223.255.255.0

   d. 248.0.0.0 through 255.255.255.255

5. Which protocol resides at Layer 3 (Network) and provides message packets to report errors and other information regarding the IP packet?

   a. TCP

   b. IP

   c. ICMP

   d. RARP

6. Which protocol uses Router-Advertisement and Router-Solicitation messages to communicate with the other routers?

   a. IP

   b. IRDP

   c. ICMP

   d. TCP

7. Which protocol is a connection-oriented, reliable protocol operating at the Transport layer?

   a. IP

   b. UDP

   c. RARP

   d. TCP

8. Which troubleshooting method is based on starting locally and troubleshooting toward the remote problem or host?

   a. Outside-in method

   b. RARP method

   c. Inside-out method

   d. Central method

9. If a router between hosts seems to be down, what are a few steps that you might take to resolve the problem? [Choose the three best answers]

   a. Check for LAN or WAN Network layer problems

   b. Ping outward until the problem router is found

   c. Look at the access list

   d. Check for LAN or WAN Physical layer problems

15

10. If you are having problems with some protocols being routed and others not being routed, what should you check first?

    a. Router interface

    b. Access list

    c. Physical connections

    d. Ping tests

11. To see a routing table of a router to determine whether a path exists, which command should you use?

    a. **show ip**

    b. **show ip route**

    c. **show routing table**

    d. **ip route**

12. To check for anomalies in the fast-switching route cache, which command would you use?

    a. **show fast cache**

    b. **show ip route cache**

    c. **show ip cache**

    d. **show ip fast cache**

13. Which command do you use to look at the ARP tables to make sure that the problem host exists in the table?

    a. **show arp**

    b. **show ip-arp**

    c. **show arp cache**

    d. **show ip arp**

14. If you are experiencing a misconfigured access list or filter, what are some of the steps you might take to solve the problem? [Choose more than one answer]

    a. Check for LAN or WAN Physical layer problems

    b. Use **ping** and **traceroute** to isolate the problem

    c. Check for protocols being exchanged at the router level by using **debug ip rip** command to see RIP; other **debug** commands exist for other protocols

    d. After isolating the problem, try disabling the access list by using the **no ip access group** command, and then test the routers again by using the **ping** and **traceroute** tools

    e. Check whether a default gateway is specified on the local host

15. If a host is having problems reaching some areas of its own network, what are some of the troubleshooting skills can you try? [Choose more than one answer]

    a. Look at the access list and make sure certain types of traffic are being denied

    b. Look to see whether a default gateway is specified

    c. Look for a subnet mask configuration mismatch between the router and the host

    d. Check for protocols being exchanged at the router level by using **debug** commands

    e. Look at the router configurations and make changes if necessary

16. Which application or protocol is used by port 23?

    a. DNS

    b. HTTP

    c. Telnet

    d. SNMP

17. HTTP traffic uses which port?

    a. 80

    b. 23

    c. 53

    d. 161

18. The following output was produced by using the _____ command.

```
Protocol  Address        Age (min)  Hardware Addr   Type   Interface
Internet  131.71.44.254       -     0003.fa0b.d461  ARPA   Ethernet2/0
Internet  131.71.150.65       3     0010.5aac.35b0  ARPA   Ethernet2/1
Internet  131.71.29.202       5     0090.27ab.17d0  ARPA   Ethernet2/0
```

    a. **show arp**

    b. **show ip arp**

    c. **show cache arp**

    d. **show ip**

15

19. The _____ command was used to produce the following output.

```
Codes: C - connected, S - static, I - IGRP, R - RIP, M - mobile, B -
BGP
       D - EIGRP, EX - EIGRP external, O - OSPF, IA - OSPF inter area
       N1 - OSPF NSSA external type 1, N2 - OSPF NSSA external type 2
       E1 - OSPF external type 1, E2 - OSPF external type 2, E - EGP
       i - IS-IS, L1 - IS-IS level-1, L2 - IS-IS level-2, ia - IS-IS
inter area
       * - candidate default, U - per-user static route, o - ODR
       P - periodic downloaded static route

Gateway of last resort is 131.71.21.11 to network 0.0.0.0

     152.79.0.0/16 is variably subnetted, 2 subnets, 2 masks
C        131.71.10.0/24 is directly connected, Ethernet2/1
C        131.71.12.0/24 is directly connected, Ethernet2/0
```

   a. **show ip**

   b. **ip route**

   c. **show ip route**

   d. **debug ip**

20. Which command displays information regarding the router sending and receiving ICMP messages, and is one of the best commands to use when you are troubleshooting an end-to-end connection?

   a. **debug ip-icmp**

   b. **debug-icmp**

   c. **debug icmp**

   d. **debug ip icmp**

Real-World Projects

Joe Snow is walking into his building when his pager rings. He knows that any time the pager alerts him so early, it can never be a good thing. Joe rushes to his desk to answer his page.

It is Rena at the help desk, alerting Joe that the network seems to have a problem. Rena tells Joe that a large group of users from the payroll department called and reported that they weren't getting any access to the network.

Of course, it is a nightmare for everyone when payroll has problems, because they process all checks every week. Joe hangs up with Rena to look at the problem.

Project 15.1

To establish network connectivity, perform the following steps:

1. Joe first looks at is his network topology, which shows that the payroll network is off of the 131.71.1.5 router and is using the Ethernet 2/0 interface. He then logs in to the router to look at the interface the network is using:

```
Ethernet2/0 is up, line protocol is up
  Hardware is cxBus Ethernet, address is 0003.efeb.1c40 (bia
0003.efeb.1c40)
  Description: Subnet 15 for Payroll
  Internet address is 152.79.15.254/24
  MTU 1500 bytes, BW 10000 Kbit, DLY 1000 usec,
     reliability 255/255, txload 1/255, rxload 2/255
  Encapsulation ARPA, loopback not set
  Keepalive set (10 sec)
  ARP type: ARPA, ARP Timeout 04:00:00
  Last input 00:00:04, output 00:00:04, output hang never
  Last clearing of "show interface" counters never
  Queueing strategy: fifo
  Output queue 0/40, 0 drops; input queue 0/75, 0 drops
  5 minute input rate 102000 bits/sec, 28 packets/sec
  5 minute output rate 9000 bits/sec, 23 packets/sec
     106027107 packets input, 4115888129 bytes, 0 no buffer
     Received 20503 broadcasts, 0 runts, 0 giants, 0 throttles
     15 input errors, 6 CRC, 9 frame, 0 overrun, 0 ignored
     0 input packets with dribble condition detected
     85647495 packets output, 4278629414 bytes, 0 underruns
     1 output errors, 224131 collisions, 2 interface resets
     0 babbles, 0 late collision, 0 deferred
     0 lost carrier, 0 no carrier
```

2. Joe notices that both the Ethernet 2/0 interface and the line protocol are up. He also notices the description of "subnet 15 for payroll" with a gateway of 131.71.15.254.

3. Joe performs a **ping** test on the network, to confirm connectivity for the payroll network:

```
SupportCCNP#ping ip
Target IP address: 131.71.15.254
Repeat count [5]:
Datagram size [100]:
Timeout in seconds [2]:
Extended commands [n]:
```

15

```
Sweep range of sizes [n]:
Type escape sequence to abort.
Sending 5, 100-byte ICMP Echos to 131.71.15.254, timeout is 2 seconds:
!!!!!
Success rate is 100 percent (5/5), round-trip min/avg/max = 40/44/60 ms
```

4. At this point, Joe doesn't think it is a connectivity problem.

Project 15.2

To look at the access list, perform the following steps:

5. He wants to look at the access list to make sure it is configured correctly:

```
Support#show access-list
Extended IP access list 101
    permit ip 131.71.138.0 0.0.0.255 any (25852110 matches)
    permit ip 131.71.114.0 0.0.0.255 any (8093745 matches)
    permit ip 131.71.19.0 0.0.0.255 any (3107840 matches)
    permit ip 131.71.69.0 0.0.0.255 any (9490833 matches)
    permit ip 131.71.64.0 0.0.0.255 any (18419018 matches)
    deny ip any any log-input (9559 matches)
```

5. Joe sees the problem. The access list is denying the payroll network with the implicit deny all statement. Joe enters configuration mode to add a line to the access list, which now reads:

```
Support#show access-list
Extended IP access list 101
    permit ip 131.71.138.0 0.0.0.255 any (25852110 matches)
    permit ip 131.71.114.0 0.0.0.255 any (8093745 matches)
    permit ip 131.71.19.0 0.0.0.255 any (3107840 matches)
    permit ip 131.71.69.0 0.0.0.255 any (9490833 matches)
    permit ip 131.71.64.0 0.0.0.255 any (18419018 matches)
    permit ip 131.71.15.0 0.0.0.255 any (2358 matches)
    deny ip any any log-input (9559 matches)
```

Joe calls the users and asks them to try accessing the network again; this time it is successful.

CHAPTER SIXTEEN

Sample Test

Question 1

Both Ethernet and IEEE 802.3 frames begin with a preamble and an SOF field. What do these fields represent? [Choose the two best answers]

❑ a. Identify the actual data in the frame

❑ b. Synchronize the frame reception

❑ c. Tell receiving stations that a frame is coming

❑ d. Identify the source address

❑ e. Calculate the CRC errors

Question 2

A packet is discarded and considered a runt if the Ethernet frame size is _____.

○ a. Greater than 64 bytes

○ b. Smaller than 64 bytes

○ c. Greater than 1,518 bytes

○ d. Smaller than 1,518 bytes

○ e. Smaller than 74 bytes

Question 3

A *giant* is a packet that's discarded because the Ethernet size exceeds how many bytes?

- ○ a. 1,518 bytes
- ○ b. 1,516 bytes
- ○ c. 64 bytes
- ○ d. 68 bytes
- ○ e. 1,200 bytes

Question 4

More than one CRC error per _____ bytes received should be investigated.

- ○ a. Thousand
- ○ b. Hundred
- ○ c. Million
- ○ d. Fifty
- ○ e. Five hundred

Question 5

What is the port number for Telnet?

- ○ a. 21
- ○ b. 5
- ○ c. 1
- ○ d. 53
- ○ e. 23

Question 6

What are the port numbers for FTP? [Choose the two best answers]

☐ a. 21

☐ b. 20

☐ c. 53

☐ d. 1

☐ e. 23

Question 7

Which type of device can locate opens, shorts, and crimps on Category 5 cables?

○ a. Network Monitoring System

○ b. Time domain reflector

○ c. Routing Information Protocol

○ d. Open Shortest Path First

○ e. Border Gateway Protocol

Question 8

What is an optical time domain reflector (OTDR) used for?

○ a. Fiber cable testing

○ b. Copper cable testing

○ c. Watching network performance

○ d. Monitoring network performance

○ e. Watching statistics

16

Question 9

Which command type can provide a snapshot of problems on interfaces, media, or network performance?

○ a. **list** commands

○ b. **ping** commands

○ c. **show** commands

○ d. **trace** commands

○ e. **configuration** commands

Question 10

Which command determines a step-by-step routing path to a destination?

○ a. **ping**

○ b. **trace**

○ c. **telnet**

○ d. **show**

○ e. **debug**

Question 11

A network management system (NMS) uses which protocols to communicate with devices?
[Choose the two best answers]

❑ a. Simple Network Management Protocol (SNMP)

❑ b. Routing Information Protocol (RIP)

❑ c. Cisco Discovery Protocol (CDP)

❑ d. Open Shortest Path First (OSPF)

❑ e. AppleTalk

Question 12

Token Ring can run at what speeds?

○ a. 4 Mbps

○ b. 16 Mbps

○ c. 100 Mbps

○ d. 1,000 Mbps

○ e. All of the above

Question 13

A standard access list can filter only by the _____ address.

○ a. Destination

○ b. Router

○ c. Port

○ d. Protocol

○ e. Source

Question 14

In ISDN, on which OSI layer does q.931 operate and on which channel does it reside?

○ a. Layer 3, B channel

○ b. Layer 2, D channel

○ c. Layer 1, D channel

○ d. Layer 2, B channel

○ e. Layer 3, D channel

16

Question 15

The default idle timer for the B channel of ISDN is?

○ a. 100 seconds

○ b. 90 seconds

○ c. 120 seconds

○ d. 45 seconds

○ e. 10 seconds

Question 16

Call setup and disconnect are determined at which OSI layer for ISDN?

○ a. Layer 3

○ b. Layer 2

○ c. Layer 1

○ d. Layer 4

○ e. Layer 5

Question 17

What is indicated by your interface reporting serial 0 is up and line protocol is up?

○ a. The interface is not working properly

○ b. The interface has been brought down

○ c. The interface may have a cabling issue

○ d. The interface is running properly

○ e. The interface needs to be configured

Question 18

What are the different transfer modes for HDLC? [Choose the three best answers]

❑ a. Normal

❑ b. Asynchronous response

❑ c. Asynchronous balanced

❑ d. Even

❑ e. RIP

Question 19

When troubleshooting serial links, if the interface shows that the serial is down and the line protocol is down, what three steps should you try when troubleshooting? [Choose the three best answers]

❑ a. Check the cabling

❑ b. Use **show** commands

❑ c. Check for a carrier signal from the local provider

❑ d. Look for a hardware failure on the CSU/DSU

❑ e. Use **trace** commands

Question 20

When using a **ping** command, what type of requests are being sent?

○ a. Routing Information Protocol (RIP)

○ b. Open Shortest Path First (OSPF)

○ c. Cisco Discovery Protocol (CDP)

○ d. Internet Control Message Protocol (ICMP)

○ e. Internet Capturing Mechanism (ICM)

16

Question 21

If you suspect that an RIP routing problem may exist, which command do you use to focus the scope of the problem?

○ a. **show ip route**

○ b. **ip route**

○ c. **debug ip rip**

○ d. **router rip**

○ e. **debug rip**

Question 22

In AppleTalk, which protocol is used to enable clients to share files across a network?

○ a. AppleTalk Filing Protocol

○ b. Password Authentication Protocol

○ c. AppleTalk Data Stream Protocol

○ d. Routing Information Protocol

○ e. Cisco Discovery Protocol

Question 23

Which command displays the routing table?

○ a. **traceroute**

○ b. **ping**

○ c. **show ip route**

○ d. **ip route**

○ e. **show ip rip**

Question 24

What are the three LMI types that can be configured on the router? [Choose the three best answers]

❑ a. High-Level Data Link Control

❑ b. Synchronous Data Link Control

❑ c. Cisco

❑ d. ANSI

❑ e. q933a

Question 25

In troubleshooting a serial link, what does the **show controllers serial** command display? [Choose the five best answers]

❑ a. Interface status

❑ b. Cable types

❑ c. Bad encapsulation frames

❑ d. Clock rate

❑ e. Bit errors

❑ f. Router hops

Question 26

In troubleshooting Frame Relay, what command would you use to obtain statistical information about LMI?

○ a. **show frame relay lmi**

○ b. **show frame-relay**

○ c. **debug frame lmi**

○ d. **show frame-relay lmi**

○ e. **debug frame relay**

16

Question 27

When should the **debug lapb** command be used? [Choose the three best answers]

❑ a. When looking at Layer 2 of x.25 circuits

❑ b. When troubleshooting x.25

❑ c. When troubleshooting ISDN

❑ d. When experiencing frequent restarts

❑ e. When looking at Layer 4 of x.25

Question 28

Which four loopback tests can be performed in isolating serial line problems? [Choose the four best answers]

❑ a. Local CSU/DSU loopback to the local router

❑ b. Remote CSU/DSU loopback to the local router

❑ c. Loopback from the local CO switch to the remote CSU/DSU

❑ d. Loopback from the remote CO switch to the local CSU/DSU

❑ e. Local router loopback without a CSU/DSU

❑ f. Remote router loopback without a CSU/DSU

Question 29

Put the following steps in the order they should be performed in an internetworking troubleshooting model: _____.

a. Gather the facts

b. Define a problem in the network

c. Implement the action plan

d. Document the solution

e. Review and evaluate the possibilities

f. Design a plan of action

g. Evaluate and observe the solution

Question 30

To obtain statistics about a PVC (permanent virtual circuit) on all Frame Relay interfaces, which command would you use?

○ a. **show processes**

○ b. **show version**

○ c. **show frame relay**

○ d. **show frame-relay**

○ e. **show controller bri**

Question 31

A fast way to determine connectivity of devices on a network is to use what type of command?

○ a. **traceroute**

○ b. **debug**

○ c. **ping**

○ d. **show**

○ e. **isdn**

Question 32

A Cisco router defaults to using a _____ frame type in a TCP/IP environment.

○ a. Snap

○ b. ARPA

○ c. Novell-ether

○ d. SAP

○ e. SANP

16

Question 33

What are some of the causes for not being able to access certain networks through the router? [Choose the three best answers]

❑ a. The router doesn't have an IP address

❑ b. No default gateway is specified on the local host

❑ c. The configured access list denies traffic

❑ d. The router is missing the specified protocol

❑ e. Link failure

Question 34

Using the _____ command produces the following output.

```
Codes: S - Static, P - Periodic, E - Eigrp, N - NLSP, H- Holdown, + = detail
128 Total IPX Servers
Table ordering is based on routing and server info
Type  Name   Net Address    Port               Route  Hops  Itf
P+    4      SRV-00001      1.0000.0000.0001:0451  4/03   3     Hs3/0
P+    4      SRV-00002      2.0000.0000.0001:0451  4/03   3     Hs3/0
```

○ a. **show ipx server**

○ b. **show server ipx**

○ c. **show ipx route**

○ d. **show servers**

○ e. **show ipx sap**

Question 35

By looking at the following access list, what can you determine from the access list commands? [Choose the three best answers]

```
access-list 101 permit udp any any eq 161
access-list 101 permit udp any any eq 69
access-list 101 permit icmp any any traceroute
access-list 101 deny icmp any any echo-reply
```

○ a. This access list permits UDP traffic on ports 69, 161, and **ping**

○ b. This access list permits UDP traffic on ports 161 and 69

○ c. This access list denies **traceroute**

○ d. This access list denies **ping**

○ e. This access list permits **traceroute**

Question 36

Which commands will show zone information for AppleTalk? [Choose the two best answers]

○ a. **show appletalk**

○ b. **appletalk zone**

○ c. **show appletalk interface**

○ d. **show appletalk zone**

○ e. **show interface**

16

Question 37

Which command was used to produce the following output?

```
Cisco Internetwork Operating System Software
IOS (tm) RSP Software (RSP-IK2SV-M), Version 12.0(7)T, RELEASE SOFTWARE
    (fc2)
Copyright (c) 1986-1999 by cisco Systems, Inc.
Compiled Tue 07-Dec-99 07:50 by phanguye
Image text-base: 0x60010908, data-base: 0x61098000


ROM: System Bootstrap, Version 5.3(16645) [szhang 571], INTERIM SOFTWARE
BOOTFLASH: RSP Software (RSP-BOOT-M), Version 12.0(7), RELEASE SOFTWARE (fc1)


Support uptime is 6 weeks, 5 days, 16 hours, 46 minutes
System returned to ROM by power-on at 06:57:27 UTC Wed Jun 21 2000
System image file is "slot1:hin-mz_120-7_T.bin"


cisco RSP2 (R4600) processor with 131072K/2072K bytes of memory.
R4600 CPU at 100Mhz, Implementation 32, Rev 2.0
Last reset from power-on
G.703/E1 software, Version 1.0.
G.703/JT2 software, Version 1.0.
X.25 software, Version 3.0.0.
Bridging software.
Chassis Interface.
4 EIP controllers (24 Ethernet).
1 FIP controller (1 FDDI).
24 Ethernet/IEEE 802.3 interface(s)
1 FDDI network interface(s)
125K bytes of non-volatile configuration memory.


20480K bytes of Flash PCMCIA card at slot 0 (Sector size 128K).
8192K bytes of Flash internal SIMM (Sector size 256K).
```

(continued)

Question 37 *(continued)*

```
No slave installed in slot 7.
Configuration register is 0x2102
```

○ a. **show version**

○ b. **show running**

○ c. **debug version**

○ d. **debug**

○ e. **show interface**

Question 38

Which command was used to produce the following output?

```
Protocol   Address          Age (min)   Hardware Addr   Type   Interface
Internet   171.64.41.254        -        0003.efeb.1e65  ARPA   Ethernet3/5
Internet   171.64.51.224        3        0060.b0be.95f2  ARPA   Ethernet5/4
Internet   171.64.113.65       63        0010.5acc.0004  ARPA   Ethernet2/1
Internet   171.64.87.134      221        0030.c12d.51g5  ARPA   Ethernet5/3
Internet   171.64.51.225        3        0060.b0be.067a  ARPA   Ethernet5/4
Internet   171.64.113.67       63        00a0.245a.dac6  ARPA   Ethernet2/1
Internet   171.64.113.186      89        0080.5aab.4051  ARPA   Ethernet2/0
Internet   171.64.51.226      146        0060.b0c0.014e  ARPA   Ethernet5/4
Internet   171.64.51.227        3        0800.093c.da12  ARPA   Ethernet5/4
Internet   171.64.113.187      88        0080.5fbb.412f  ARPA   Ethernet2/0
Internet   171.64.51.228        3        0800.091e.1b47  ARPA   Ethernet5/4
```

○ a. **show interfaces**

○ b. **debug interfaces**

○ c. **show arp**

○ d. **arp**

○ e. **debugging arp**

16

Question 39

Which command was used to produce the following output?

```
The current ISDN Switchtype = basic-dms100
ISDN BRI0 interface
    Layer 1 Status:
        ACTIVE
    Layer 2 Status:
        TEI = 75, State = MULTIPLE_FRAME_ESTABLISHED
        TEI = 77, State = MULTIPLE_FRAME_ESTABLISHED
    Spid Status:
        TEI 75, ces = 1, state = 5(init)
            spid1 configured, no LDN, spid1 sent, spid1 valid
            Endpoint ID Info: epsf = 0, usid = 70, tid = 1
        TEI 77, ces = 2, state = 5(init)
            spid2 configured, no LDN, spid2 sent, spid2 valid
            Endpoint ID Info: epsf = 0, usid = 71, tid = 1
    Layer 3 Status:
        1 Active Layer 3 Call(s)
    Activated dsl 0 CCBs = 2
        CCB: callid=0x0, sapi=0, ces=1, B-chan=0
        CCB: callid=0x800A, sapi=0, ces=1, B-chan=1
    Total Allocated ISDN CCBs = 2
```

○ a. **show isdn status**

○ b. **show isdn**

○ c. **show status**

○ d. **show controllers**

○ e. **show interface**

Question 40

Which command was used to produce the following output?

```
    Ethernet/0 is up, line protocol is up
  Hardware is cxBus Ethernet, address is 0001.f11b.d220 (bia 0001.f11b.d220)
  Description: Support subnet 120
  Internet address is 171.64.120.254/24
  MTU 1500 bytes, BW 10000 Kbit, DLY 1000 usec,
      reliability 255/255, txload 1/255, rxload 2/255
  Encapsulation ARPA, loopback not set
  Keepalive set (10 sec)
  ARP type: ARPA, ARP Timeout 04:00:00
  Last input 00:00:01, output 00:00:01, output hang never
  Last clearing of "show interface" counters never
  Queueing strategy: fifo
  Output queue 0/40, 0 drops; input queue 0/75, 0 drops
  5 minute input rate 81000 bits/sec, 17 packets/sec
  5 minute output rate 5000 bits/sec, 16 packets/sec
      3635327 packets input, 1719041457 bytes, 0 no buffer
      Received 3674 broadcasts, 0 runts, 0 giants, 0 throttles
      12 input errors, 8 CRC, 4 frame, 0 overrun, 0 ignored
      0 input packets with dribble condition detected
      3196181 packets output, 159209323 bytes, 0 underruns
      0 output errors, 8984 collisions, 2 interface resets
      0 babbles, 0 late collision, 0 deferred
      0 lost carrier, 0 no carrier
      0 output buffer failures, 0 output buffers swapped out
Ethernet2/1 is up, line protocol is up
  Hardware is cxBus Ethernet, address is 0001.f10b.d541 (bia 0001.f10b.d541)
  Description: CCNP Subnet 13
  Internet address is 171.64.13.254/24
  MTU 1500 bytes, BW 10000 Kbit, DLY 1000 usec,
      reliability 255/255, txload 1/255, rxload 1/255
```

16

(continued)

Question 40 *(continued)*

```
        Encapsulation ARPA, loopback not set

        Keepalive set (10 sec)

        ARP type: ARPA, ARP Timeout 04:00:00

        Last input 00:00:00, output 00:00:02, output hang never

        Last clearing of "show interface" counters never

        Queueing strategy: fifo

        Output queue 0/40, 6040 drops; input queue 0/75, 193 drops

        5 minute input rate 37000 bits/sec, 23 packets/sec

        5 minute output rate 69000 bits/sec, 14 packets/sec

            9617028 packets input, 2152504067 bytes, 0 no buffer

            Received 1764667 broadcasts, 0 runts, 0 giants, 6 throttles

            0 input errors, 0 CRC, 0 frame, 0 overrun, 193 ignored

            0 input packets with dribble condition detected

            10847999 packets output, 2858787678 bytes, 0 underruns

            0 output errors, 777226 collisions, 2 interface resets

            0 babbles, 0 late collision, 0 deferred

            0 lost carrier, 0 no carrier

            0 output buffer failures, 0 output buffers swapped out

Ethernet2/2 is administratively down, line protocol is down

    Hardware is cxBus Ethernet, address is 0008.f10b.a412 (bia 0008.f10b.a412)

    Description: Support Prep subnet 15

    Internet address is 171.64.15.254/24

    MTU 1500 bytes, BW 10000 Kbit, DLY 1000 usec,

        reliability 255/255, txload 1/255, rxload 1/255

    Encapsulation ARPA, loopback not set

    Last input 00:00:00, output 00:00:01, output hang never

    Last clearing of "show interface" counters never

    Queueing strategy: fifo

    Output queue 0/40, 2 drops; input queue 0/75, 84 drops

    5 minute input rate 13000 bits/sec, 10 packets/sec

    5 minute output rate 6000 bits/sec, 6 packets/sec
```

(continued)

Question 40 *(continued)*

```
    4764278 packets input, 1142432574 bytes, 0 no buffer
    Received 659785 broadcasts, 0 runts, 0 giants, 1 throttles
    0 input errors, 0 CRC, 0 frame, 0 overrun, 0 ignored
    0 input packets with dribble condition detected
    4682679 packets output, 1834121390 bytes, 0 underruns
    0 output errors, 190725 collisions, 2 interface resets
    0 babbles, 0 late collision, 0 deferred
    0 lost carrier, 0 no carrier
    0 output buffer failures, 0 output buffers swapped out
```

- ○ a. **show debugging**
- ○ b. **show controllers**
- ○ c. **show interfaces**
- ○ d. **show isdn**
- ○ e. **show frame-relay**

Question 41

Which port states are used in Spanning Tree? [Choose the five best answers]

- ❏ a. Blocking
- ❏ b. Listening
- ❏ c. Disabled
- ❏ d. Forwarding
- ❏ e. Learning
- ❏ f. Switching
- ❏ g. Passing

16

Question 42

In troubleshooting Frame Relay, what are a few possible steps to use if you can't ping a remote host? [Choose the four best answers]

❏ a. Use a breakout box to test the leads

❏ b. Check the cabling for physical breaks

❏ c. Check whether the DLCI is assigned to the wrong interface

❏ d. Check the encapsulation types and make sure they match

❏ e. Check the access list entries

❏ f. Check the interface configuration

Question 43

Using which of the following commands enables you to see the DLCI number assigned? [Choose the two best answers]

❏ a. **show running configuration**

❏ b. **show running-config**

❏ c. **show frame-relay pvc**

❏ d. **show frame relay pvc**

❏ e. **show DLCI**

Question 44

Which command was used to produce the following output?

```
Serial network interface debugging is on

03:52:22: Serial0: HDLC myseq 1390, mineseen 1390*, yourseen 1404, line up
03:52:32: Serial0: HDLC myseq 1391, mineseen 1391*, yourseen 1405, line up
03:52:42: Serial0: HDLC myseq 1392, mineseen 1392*, yourseen 1406, line up
03:52:52: Serial0: HDLC myseq 1393, mineseen 1393*, yourseen 1407, line up
```

- ○ a. **debug serial interface**
- ○ b. **debug interface serial**
- ○ c. **show interface**
- ○ d. **debug serial**
- ○ e. **show debug**

Question 45

Which command was used to produce the following output?

```
07:05:20: Serial0: FR ARP input
07:05:20: datagramstart = 0x628970, datagramsize = 30
07:05:20: FR encap = 0x18E10300
07:05:20: 80 00 00 00 08 06 00 0F 08 00 02 04 00 09 00 00
07:05:20: 3F 4E 26 AE 18 E1 3F 4E 27 AE
07:05:20:
```

- ○ a. **debug frame-relay events**
- ○ b. **frame-relay events**
- ○ c. **debug frame relay events**
- ○ d. **debug events**
- ○ e. **debug frame relay**

16

Question 46

Which command was used to produce the following output?

```
PVC Statistics for interface Serial0 (Frame Relay DTE)
DLCI = 120, DLCI USAGE = LOCAL, PVC STATUS = DELETED, INTERFACE = Serial0

  input pkts 0           output pkts 0           in bytes 0
  out bytes 0            dropped pkts 0          in FECN pkts 0
  in BECN pkts 0         out FECN pkts 0         out BECN pkts 0
  in DE pkts 0           out DE pkts 0
  out bcast pkts 0       out bcast bytes 0
  pvc create time 00:33:13, last time pvc status changed 00:24:49
DLCI = 202, DLCI USAGE = LOCAL, PVC STATUS = DELETED, INTERFACE = Serial0.2

  input pkts 0           output pkts 0           in bytes 0
  out bytes 0            dropped pkts 0          in FECN pkts 0
  in BECN pkts 0         out FECN pkts 0         out BECN pkts 0
  in DE pkts 0           out DE pkts 0
  out bcast pkts 0       out bcast bytes 0
  pvc create time 00:37:35, last time pvc status changed 00:24:20
```

○ a. **debug frame relay**

○ b. **show frame relay**

○ c. **show frame-relay pvc**

○ d. **show frame relay pvc**

○ e. **show pvc**

Question 47

Which command displays FECN and BECN statistics?

- ○ a. **show frame-relay pvc**
- ○ b. **show x25 events**
- ○ c. **show frame relay pvc**
- ○ d. **show running configuration**
- ○ e. **show isdn**

Question 48

When testing a serial link, what type of testing can be used to test end-to-end connectivity?

- ○ a. Cable testing
- ○ b. CSU testing
- ○ c. DSU testing
- ○ d. Loopback testing
- ○ e. LED testing

Question 49

Which Frame Relay encapsulation types are valid? [Choose the two best answers]

- ❑ a. Cisco
- ❑ b. IETF
- ❑ c. Simple Network Management Protocol
- ❑ d. Routing Information Protocol
- ❑ e. American National Standards Institute

16

Question 50

What information does using the **show CDP neighbor detail** command display? [Choose the three best answers]

❑ a. LMI type

❑ b. The neighbor's device ID

❑ c. Local port type and number

❑ d. The neighbor's remote port type and number

❑ e. Router type

Question 51

Which answers are the primary Inter-Switch Link (ISL) field types? [Choose the three best answers]

❑ a. The header

❑ b. The original packet

❑ c. Switching

❑ d. Frame check sequence

❑ e. VLAN

Question 52

In a VLAN, what is the maximum number of switches that should be used for optimal performance?

○ a. 1

○ b. 5

○ c. 7

○ d. 4

○ e. 10

Question 53

Which reference point refers to the interface between non-ISDN Terminal Equipment (TE2) and a terminal adapter (TA)?

○ a. S

○ b. LT

○ c. R

○ d. D

○ e. E

Question 54

When using ISDN, what does "TE1" refer to?

○ a. Line Termination

○ b. T reference point

○ c. Connect to ISDN through terminal adapters, (non-ISDN Terminals)

○ d. Connect to ISDN through terminal adapters, (main-ISDN Terminals)

○ e. U reference point

Question 55

Which command would be used to learn about neighboring devices?

○ a. **show neighbors**

○ b. **show cdp neighbors**

○ c. **show all cdp neighbors**

○ d. **show cdp**

○ e. **show cdp neighbors all**

16

Question 56

For one VLAN to speak to another, a device must be used to resolve what layer addresses?

○ a. Layer 2

○ b. Layer 1

○ c. Layer 3

○ d. Physical layer

○ e. Layer 7

Question 57

Which of the following provides a GUI to view the VLAN configuration on a switch?

○ a. VLANDesigner

○ b. TrafficDirector

○ c. VLANDirector

○ d. VLANScope

○ e. CiscoViewer

Question 58

Which command shows the MAC address of all nodes attached to the switch?

○ a. **show port all**

○ b. **debug mac**

○ c. **show mac cache**

○ d. **show cam dynamic**

○ e. **show mac addresses**

Question 59

When using Spanning Tree Protocol, if the port costs are equal on a switch, STP refers to the _____ to make its forwarding decision.

○ a. Lowest sender bridge ID

○ b. MAC address

○ c. Bridge name

○ d. Hello Timer

○ e. RIP

Question 60

In STP, what is the range of values and the default value for the port priority parameter? [Choose the two best answers]

❏ a. 0–63

❏ b. 0–54

❏ c. 10–63

❏ d. 31

❏ e. 32

❏ f. 6

16

Question 61

The following statement refers to which port state of Spanning Tree Protocol?

The port is not forwarding frames but is learning addresses and putting them in the address table. The learning state is similar to the listening state, except the port can now add information it has learned to the address table. The port is still not allowed to send or receive frames.

○ a. Learning

○ b. Blocking

○ c. Listening

○ d. Forwarding

○ e. Switching

Question 62

The following statement refers to which port state of Spanning Tree Protocol?

The port is forwarding frames, learning addresses, and adding addresses to the routing table. This state means that the port is capable of sending and receiving frames. A port is not placed in a forwarding state until there are no redundant links or the port determines the lowest cost path to the root bridge or switch.

○ a. Switching

○ b. Learning

○ c. Forwarding

○ d. Listening

○ e. Blocking

Question 63

The following statement refers to which port state of Spanning Tree Protocol?

> The port is not forwarding frames or learning new addresses. All ports start in blocking mode to prevent the bridge from creating a bridging loop. The port stays in a blocked state if STP determines that a lower-cost path exists to the root bridge.

- ○ a. Learning
- ○ b. Listening
- ○ c. Blocking
- ○ d. Switching
- ○ e. Forwarding

Question 64

BPDUs are sent out every ___ seconds on every "non-blocking" port to ensure a stable topology without data loops.

- ○ a. 30
- ○ b. 2
- ○ c. 15
- ○ d. 20
- ○ e. 5

Question 65

Which command would you use to display statistics of memory errors, buffer errors, overflow errors, and missed datagrams for the first ethernet interface on a Cisco router?

- ○ a. show errors ethernet 0
- ○ b. show interface ethernet 0
- ○ c. show controllers ethernet 0
- ○ d. show interface 0 errors
- ○ e. show ethernet 0

16

Question 66

For an 802.3 frame, which is best described as the last four bytes?

○ a. Header

○ b. Preamble

○ c. Start of Frame

○ d. End of Frame

○ e. Frame Check Sequence

Question 67

What is one advantage of a connectionless protocol?

○ a. Highly reliable

○ b. Fast error recovery

○ c. Flow control

○ d. Less network traffic

○ e. More network traffic

Question 68

Which command displays hardware type and version information for each module in a Cisco router when troubleshooting a WAN connection?

○ a. **show version**

○ b. **show interfaces serial**

○ c. **show running-config**

○ d. **show controller**

○ e. **show modules**

CHAPTER SEVENTEEN

Answer Key

1. b, c
2. b
3. a
4. c
5. e
6. a, b
7. b
8. a
9. c
10. b
11. a, c
12. e
13. e
14. e
15. c
16. a
17. d
18. a, b, c
19. a, c, d
20. d
21. c
22. a
23. c

24. c, d, e
25. a, b, c, d, e
26. d
27. a, b, d
28. a, b, c, d
29. b, a, e, f, c, g, d
30. d
31. c
32. b
33. b, c, e
34. a
35. b, d, e
36. c, d
37. a
38. c
39. a
40. c
41. a, b, c, d, e
42. c, d, e, f
43. b, c
44. a
45. a
46. c

47. a
48. d
49. a, b
50. b, c, d
51. a, b, d
52. c
53. c
54. c
55. b
56. c
57. c
58. d
59. a
60. a, e
61. a
62. c
63. c
64. b
65. c
66. e
67. d
68. d

Question 1

The correct answers are b and c. The Preamble (an alternating pattern of 1's and 0's) and the Start of Frame (SOF) fields tell the receiving stations that a frame is coming, and synchronize the frame reception. Answer a is incorrect because it relates to the actual data being sent and has a field pertaining to data. Answer d is incorrect because it refers to the Source Address Field and has its own 6-byte field. Answer e is incorrect because it pertains to the CRC which is calculated by the FCS field, not CRC errors.

Question 2

The correct answer is b. A runt is considered below 64 bytes. Answer c is incorrect because a giant is considered over 1,518 bytes.

Question 3

The correct answer is a. A giant exceeds 1,518 bytes.

Question 4

The correct answer is c. More than one CRC error per million bytes received should be investigated.

Question 5

The correct answer is e. The Telnet port number is 23.

Question 6

The correct answers are a and b. FTP can be on port 20 or 21.

Question 7

The correct answer is b. A TDR, or time domain reflector, is a cable tester that's used to isolate problems on the copper cable. Answer a is incorrect because a network monitoring system (NMS) is used only to monitor, not to locate problems. Answers c, d, and e are incorrect because they are not devices, they are protocols.

Question 8

The correct answer is a. An OTDR is a cable tester used to test fiber-optic cabling. Answer b is incorrect because a TDR, not an OTDR, is used to test copper cabling. Answers c, d, and e are incorrect because they refer to a Network Monitoring System, not a testing device.

Question 9

The correct answer is c. Various **show** commands provide a snapshot of interfaces, media, or network performance. Answer b is incorrect because **ping** commands test connectivity. Answer d is incorrect because **trace** commands report a path. Answer e is incorrect because **configuration** commands are used to configure interfaces.

Question 10

The correct answer is b. The **trace** commands are used to trace a route; in other words, using ICMP uses them to report a path to its destination. Answer a is incorrect because **ping** tests for connectivity. Answer c is incorrect because **telnet** is used in connecting to a device and acting as a dumb terminal. Answer d is incorrect because the **show** commands provide a snapshot. Answer e is incorrect because **debug** commands are used for aiding in troubleshooting an interface.

Question 11

The correct answers are a and c. SNMP and CDP are used by an NMS to communicate with devices. Answers b, d, and e are incorrect because they are protocols; they are mainly used for routing.

Question 12

The correct answer is e. Token Ring only ran at speeds of 4 and 16 Mbps, but a high-speed Token Ring was later released that allows speeds of up to 1 gigabit.

Question 13

The correct answer is e. A standard access list can filter only by source address. Answers a, c, and d are incorrect because they can be used to filter by using an extended access list. Answer b is incorrect because an access list can't filter by a router.

17

Question 14

The correct answer is e. Q.931 operates at Layer 3 and resides on the D channel. Answer b is incorrect because Q.921 operates at Layer 2.

Question 15

The correct answer is c. 120 seconds is the default setting.

Question 16

The correct answer is a. Layer 3 (Q.931) is responsible for the call setup and disconnect. Answer b is incorrect because Q.921 operates at Layer 2. Answers c, d, and e are incorrect because they are not responsible for call setup for ISDN.

Question 17

The correct answer is d. When the serial is up and the line is up, the interface is running properly. Answers a and c are incorrect because the interface would not report the serial and interface as being "up." Answer b is incorrect because if the interface has been brought down manually, it would show "administratively down." Answer e is incorrect because if the interface needed to be configured, it would not report the serial or line protocol as being "up."

Question 18

The correct answers are a, b, and c. Normal, asynchronous response, and asynchronous balanced are different modes for HDLC. Answer d is incorrect because "even" isn't an existing mode, and answer e is incorrect because RIP is a routing protocol.

Question 19

The correct answers are a, c, and d. The **trace** commands will fail because the interface is down and you have already used your **show** commands to see the interface. Answer b is incorrect because if the interfaces are showing down, you have already used a command to show how the network looks at the moment. It is now time to try to fix the problem and then use **show** commands.

Question 20

The correct answer is d. ICMP requests are sent to the destination. The destination sends back an echo reply. Answers a and b are incorrect because they are routing protocols that are not used in **ping**. Answer c is incorrect because CDP is not used in **ping**. Answer e is incorrect because ICM is unusable.

Question 21

The correct answer is c. The **debug ip rip** command will give all the RIP information, including whether it is functioning properly. Answer a is incorrect because it will only show IP routes, answer b is incorrect because it is invalid. Answer d is incorrect because it is the command to enable RIP on the router. Answer e is incorrect because it is unusable.

Question 22

The correct answer is a. The AppleTalk Filing Protocol helps enable the clients to share files. Answer b is incorrect because it is a Printer Access Protocol. Answer c is incorrect because it is an AppleTalk Data Stream Protocol. Answer d is incorrect because it is a Routing Information Protocol. Answer e is incorrect because it is a Cisco Discovery Protocol.

Question 23

The correct answer is c. Answer a is incorrect because **traceroute** displays a routing path. Answer b is incorrect because **ping** mainly shows connectivity. Answers d and e are incorrect because they are invalid.

Question 24

The correct answers are c, d, and e. Cisco, ANSI, and Q933a are LMI types that can be configured on the router, but versions later than 11.2 can autosense the LMI type. Answers a and b are incorrect because they are used for encapsulation.

Question 25

The correct answers are a, b, c, d, and e. The **show controllers serial** command is used for serial link troubleshooting and enables you to see information on the interface status, cable types, missed datagrams, overruns, bad encapsulation frames, memory errors, underruns, clock rate, and bit errors. Answer f is incorrect because a **traceroute** can report router hops when performed.

17

Question 26

The correct answer is d. Using **show frame–relay lmi** enables you to see LMI information. The rest of the answers are incorrect because they are unusable.

Question 27

The correct answers are a, b, and d. The **debug lapb** command should be used when troubleshooting x.25 at Layer 2 circuits. This command should also be used if the circuit is experiencing frequent restarts. Answers c and e are incorrect because this command is not used for ISDN or at Layer 4.

Question 28

The correct answers are a, b, c, and d. An administrator can perform two of the loopback tests, but the other two need to be tested by your provider. Answers e and f are incorrect because you need a CSU/DSU to test the links.

Question 29

The correct order is b, a, e, f, c, g, and d.

Question 30

The correct answer is d. The command **show frame relay** obtains the statistical information about PVCs. Answer a is incorrect because it shows the active processes on the router. Answer b is incorrect because it shows the router's firmware version. Answer c is incorrect because it is an invalid command. Answer e is incorrect because it shows the BRI line of the D channel.

Question 31

The correct answer is c. Using a **ping** command is a fast way to determine connectivity. Answer a is incorrect because **traceroute** is best for reporting a path to a device. Answer b is incorrect because it helps to isolate protocol and configuration problems. Answer d is incorrect because the **show** commands are best for monitoring or looking at interfaces. Answer e is incorrect because it is not a command.

Question 32

The correct answer is b. A Cisco router defaults to using an ARPA frame type. Answer a is incorrect because Snap refers to the Ethernet_snap Novell frame type. Answer c is incorrect because Novell-ether refers to the Ethernet_802.3 Novell frame type; Answer d is incorrect because SAP refers to the Ethernet_802.2 Novell frame type. Answer e is incorrect because it is invalid.

Question 33

The correct answers are b, c, and e. No default gateway, access list denials, and link failures can be some of the possible causes for not being able to gain access to certain networks. Answers a and d are incorrect because they are not the best answers.

Question 34

The correct answer is a. Answers b and d are incorrect because they are invalid. Answer c is incorrect because it shows the routes of networks or where networks can be found. Answer e is incorrect because it will not produce the output shown.

Question 35

The correct answers are b, d, and e. This access list shows permission of UDP traffic on ports 161 and 69, as well as **traceroute**. It also shows denial of **ping** traffic. Answer a is incorrect because the access list denies **ping** traffic. Answer c is incorrect because the access list permits **traceroute** commands with a specific **permit** statement.

Question 36

The correct answers are c and d. Answers a and b are incorrect because they are invalid. Answer e is incorrect because it doesn't show any zone information.

Question 37

The correct answer is a. Answer b is incorrect because it show the running configuration. Answer c is incorrect because it is invalid. Answer d is incorrect because the **debug** statements are used in troubleshooting and the **debug** command alone is invalid. Answer e is incorrect because the command shows interface information.

17

Question 38

The correct answer is c. Answers a and b are incorrect because they don't produce or show any information pertaining to ARP. Answers d and e are incorrect because they are invalid commands.

Question 39

The correct answer is a. Using **the show isdn status** command enables you to see the Layer 1–3 status. Answers b and c are incorrect because they are invalid. Answers d and e are incorrect because the commands do not show the status of ISDN layers.

Question 40

The correct answer is c. The **show interfaces** command enables you to see all the interfaces and a basic snapshot of each interface on the router. Answers a and b are incorrect because they do not produce the output showing all the interfaces. Answers d and e are incorrect because they do not pertain to all the interfaces shown by the output.

Question 41

The correct answers are a, b, c, d, and e. Answers f and g are incorrect because they are invalid.

Question 42

The correct answers are c, d, e, and f. Answers a and b are incorrect because they are not likely to be the cause in a Frame Relay issue.

Question 43

The correct answers are b and c. Answer a is incorrect because it will show only the current configuration and not the DLCI number. Answer d is incorrect because the command is invalid (without the hyphen between **frame** and **relay**). Answer e is incorrect because the command is invalid.

Question 44

The correct answer is a. Answers b, d, and e are incorrect because they are invalid commands. Answer c is incorrect because it would not produce the output.

Question 45

The correct answer is a. Using **debug frame-relay events** enables you to see the events of Frame Relay and produce the output shown. Answers b, d, and e are incorrect because they are invalid commands. Answer c is incorrect because the command is missing the hyphen in between **frame** and **relay**.

Question 46

The correct answer is c. Answers a, b, and d are incorrect because they are invalid, because they don't have the hyphen in between **frame** and **relay**. Answer e is incorrect because it is invalid.

Question 47

The correct answer is a. Answers b, c, and e are incorrect because they are invalid commands. Answer d is incorrect because it shows only the running configuration and does not show information of FECN and BECN.

Question 48

The correct answer is d. Answer a is incorrect because a cable tester will test the cables for problems relating to cables, not end-to-end connectivity. Answers b, c, and e are incorrect because they are invalid tests.

Question 49

The correct answers are a and b. Answers c, d, and e are incorrect because they are not encapsulation types.

Question 50

The correct answers are b, c, and d. Answer a is incorrect because LMI type will be shown using Frame Relay commands. Answer e is incorrect because the router type is not shown using the command.

Question 51

The correct answers are a, b, and d. The ISL is a Cisco-proprietary protocol that contains the header, original packet, and FCS as the three primary field types. Answer c is incorrect because it is not a field type. Answer e is incorrect because it pertains to a virtual group of devices or a VLAN, and thus does not pertain to field types.

17

Question 52

The correct answer is c. Seven is the maximum number of switches recommended for optimal performance in a VLAN.

Question 53

The correct answer is c. R refers to the reference point of the interface between non–ISDN Terminal Equipment and a TA. Answer a is incorrect because S refers to the reference point of the interface between ISDN user equipment, either the TE1 or TA and the NT2 or NT1. Answer b is incorrect because LT refers to line termination. Answer d is incorrect because D refers to Data channel, and not a reference point. Answer e is incorrect because it is not a reference point.

Question 54

The correct answer is c. TE1 refers to connecting to ISDN through terminal adapters using non–ISDN Terminal Equipment. Answer a is incorrect because line termination is "LT." Answer b is incorrect because it refers to the interface between the customer site switching equipment and the local loop termination. Answer d is incorrect because it refers to TE2. Answer e is incorrect because it refers to the interface where transmission between the NT1 and the LE occurs.

Question 55

The correct answer is b. The **show cdp neighbors** command allows a Cisco device to learn about its neighbors. Answers a, c, d, and e are invalid commands.

Question 56

The correct answer is c. Layer 3 is used to resolve communication from one VLAN to another. Answer d is incorrect because it refers to Layer 1.

Question 57

The correct answer is c. Answers a, b, d, and e do not enable you to see a GUI interface of the VLAN configuration on a switch.

Question 58

The correct answer is d. Using **show cam dynamic** will show the MAC addresses of all nodes attached. The Cam table is where the MAC addresses are held in the switch of all the workstations connected. Answers a, b, and e do not access the cam where the MAC addresses are held. Answer c is incorrect because it is not the correct command to show the MAC addresses.

Question 59

The correct answer is a. Spanning Tree Protocol refers to the lowest sender bridge ID if the port costs on a switch are equal, to make its forwarding decisions. Answers b, c, and d are incorrect because STP does not refer to these for forwarding decisions in the case mentioned. Answer e is incorrect because it is a routing protocol and it does not refer to the protocol for costs or forwarding decisions.

Question 60

The correct answers are a and e. Answer a refers to 0–63 for the port parameters and answer e refers to the port value of 32, which is the default setting.

Question 61

The correct answer is a. Answers b, c, and d are incorrect because they describe other port states. Answer e is incorrect because it is not a valid port state.

Question 62

The correct answer is c. Answer a is incorrect because it is not a valid port state. Answers b, d, and e. describe other port states.

Question 63

The correct answer is c. Answers a, b, and e are incorrect because they describe other port states. Answer d is incorrect because it is not a valid port state.

Question 64

The correct answer is b. BPDUs are sent out every two seconds on every port to ensure a stable topology without data loops.

17

Question 65

The correct answer is c. Answers a, d, and e are not valid IOS commands. Answer b will give you errors on the Ethernet interface but it will not show errors occurring on the internal hardware. Memory errors indicate you may have a hardware problem with your router.

Question 66

The correct answer is e. A FCS is used in calculating the CRC after the data has been sent or received. Answers a and d do not exist on a 802.3 frame. A Preamble and the Start of Frame are at the beginning of an 802.3 frame.

Question 67

The correct answer is d. A connectionless protocol does not have the overhead of sending back an acknowledgement and thus causing less traffic. Answer a is incorrect, as connectionless protocols are less reliable. Answers b and c are incorrect as connectionless protocols do not have fast error recovery and flow control. A few connectionless protocols are UDP and IPX.

Question 68

The correct answer is d. The **show controller** command will display the current internal status information for the interface controller cards. The **show version** command will only show the version of the IOS. The **show interfaces serial** will only show the interface specified. The **show running-config** will only show the current configuration running on the router. The **show modules** command is an invalid command for the IOS.

Appendix A
Answers to Review Questions

Chapter 1 Solutions

1. **d.** Frame Relay, ISDN, and MAC addresses are all examples of protocols defined at the Data Link layer of the OSI Reference Model.

2. **a.** The Transport layer of the OSI Reference Model is responsible for fragmenting data into usable sizes, uses segments as its protocol data unit (PDU), and is best known for providing TCP and UDP protocols for IP.

3. **c.** The Network Access layer is part of the TCP/IP Internetworking Model. This layer is where logical addressing, routed protocols and routing protocols reside.

4. **f.** FTP and Telnet are examples of applications found at the Application layer of the TCP/IP Internetworking Model (and the OSI Reference Model).

5. **a.** TCP is a connection-oriented protocol where UDP is not. IP is used at the Network layer and is a connectionless protocol and Ethernet is a physical media type.

6. **a.** Gathering facts is the step of the Internetworking Troubleshooting Model used to collect users' information on a given networking issue.

7. **d.** The Core layer of the Cisco Hierarchical Internetworking Model should not have policy networking applied to it. This layer is responsible for getting data from one point in the network to the other as quickly as possible.

8. **e.** Generating usage reports, providing a history of network usage, finding networking bottlenecks, and identifying expansion needs are all benefits of network baselining.

9. **c.** Four layers make up the TCP/IP Internetworking Model; the OSI Reference Model uses seven layers, and the Hierarchical Internetworking Model uses three layers.

10. **b, c.** The Network Access layer of the TCP/IP Internetworking Model maps to the Physical and Data Link layers of the OSI Reference Model.

11. **b.** The last step in the Internetworking Troubleshooting Model is to document the solution; this is one of the most important steps, because documentation enables another administrator to resolve the same problem quickly if it occurs again.

12. **b.** A small network with each node sharing services best represents a peer-to-peer network; no centralization exists in this type of network.

13. **b.** X.25 packet level, IP, and IPX are all examples of protocols defined at the Network layer of the OSI Reference Model.

14. **c.** The IEEE 802.3 specification defines the standards for Ethernet and CSMA/CD; IEEE 802.1 gives an overview of the IEEE 802 specification, IEEE 802.2 defines Logical Link Control, and IEEE 802.5 defines Token Ring networks.

15. **a.** Service Access Points (SAPs) enable connecting layers of the OSI model to communicate with one another since they cannot communicate directly.

16. **c.** The Distribution layer of the Hierarchical Internetworking Model is where most policy networking functions should be applied.

17. **d.** A hierarchical network model provides compatibility between vendors, simplifies the complexities of the network, and is a way to identify placement of devices in the network.

18. **b.** The Access layer of the Hierarchical Internetworking Model is the entry point for network nodes into the network.

19. **e.** A complete network baseline should include CPU utilization statistics, bandwidth utilization statistics, error statistics, and network infrastructure information.

20. **d.** The Presentation layer of the OSI Reference Model defines data formatting, including encryption and decryption. This is the last layer where data is altered before headers and footers are added on its way down the OSI Reference Model.

Chapter 2 Solutions

1. **a, c.** Token Ring and Ethernet are the two most widely used LANs today.

2. **b.** Ethernet technology employs Carrier Sense Multiple Access with Collision Detecton protocol (CSMA/CD known as).

3. **b.** A switch offers the auto-negotiation option of speeds of 10/100Mbps.

4. **c.** Gigabit Ethernet can be written as 1000Mbps (desribing the speed), but is commonly referred to as a "Gig".

5. **c.** UTP is unshielded twisted pair and is used to decribe Category 3, 5, 6, and 7 cabling without shielding.

6. **d.** Token Ring uses a token to circulate the ring and stations wait for the token in order to transmit data. If the token is busy, stations must wait until the token is free.

7. **d.** FDDI consists of two rings, a primary and a secondary.

8. **b, c.** ATM provides very high bandwidth and is best utilized in a network mainly delivering video and sound, which take up a lot of bandwidth.

9. **d.** A router uses DSAPs and SSAPs, and metric paths to make a more informed routing decision. A router can filter by logical address and also determine routes.

10. **b.** A broadcast sends a copy a transmission to all nodes on the network.

11. **c.** Active monitor is the mechanism for detecting and compensating network faults. One station is selected to be active monitor.

12. **a.** 1518 is the maximum Ethernet Frame size.

13. **a.** 802.3 IEEE standard describes Ethernet and CSMA/CD.

14. **d.** The minimum frame size for Ethernet is 64 bytes.

15. **b.** Asynchronous Transfer Mode.

16. **c.** A bridge will decrease the size of the segment and can connect several LANs.

17. **c.** A router can reduce the size of the broadcast domain because routers create a smaller network thus creating a smaller broadcast domain.

18. **c.** A hub can't reduce the size of the collision domain because hubs use a shared environment.

19. **d.** Wireless LANs are capable of transmitting speeds up to 11Mbps but usually operate at 5-6Mbps in normal conditions.

20. **d.** 802.11HR is the IEEE standard for Wireless LANs. The "HR" stands for high rate.

Chapter 3 Solutions

1. **c.** A time domain reflector (TDR) will send an electronic signal and wait for a return.

2. **d.** The **show** command is the best command to use for monitoring activity on a router.

3. **c.** The **debug** command is the best command to use to isolate a problem with the router.

4. **b.** The **ping** commands send an ICMP message and wait for a reply.

5. **a.** The **trace** command will monitor a path from a source to a destination.

6. **c.** The **show interfaces** command will show you all the interfaces on the router.

7. **c.** A **debug** command should only be used when you know there is a problem because of the overhead.

8. **d.** The console port is the default for logging.

9. **d.** The maximum amount of hops is 30.

10. **e. Winipcfg** is the command for Windows 95/98.

11. **c.** Netstat on a Windows machine or a Unix machine will provide protocol statistics.

12. **c.** Network monitors monitor packets and provide a current snapshot.

13. **a.** Simple Network Management Protocol (SNMP) is the most commonly used protocol.

14. **e.** A management information base (MIB) contains the information.

15. **a.** Community string or community names must be set for SNMP.

16. **b.** RMON is one of the most common MIBs used for remote monitoring.

17. **c.** CiscoWorks for Switched Internetworks (CWSI) contains all of the software mentioned.

18. **d.** A protocol analyzer captures, displays, and analyzes how a communication protocol is operating on the network.

19. **c.** Privilege mode allows you to perform extended pings.

20. **a.** The **debug all** command will produce so much output, the router may not be able to handle it.

Chapter 4 Solutions

1. **b.** Internet Protocol uses IP addresses as in all Network layer addresses used on the Internet, part of the a device's address represents the network and the other part identifies the host number that this device is on the network.

2. **b.** A terminal adapter (TA) is used by ISDN to communicate.

3. **d.** Multiprotocol Router (MPR) is used when two NICs are used to segment two networks.

4. **a, b, c, d.** Two-byte frame, Destination Port, preamble and the checksum are part of the frame that is sent across the network to its destination.

5. **b.** ICMP response with a "Time-exceeded" message is sent when the maximum hop count is exceeded and there is no additional routing information available.

6. **b.** FFFFFFFF is equal to the broadcast address of 255.255.255.255, which is the address ARP uses to broadcast over a LAN.

7. **c.** A Domain Name Service (DNS) is used to resolve a hostname to an IP address.

8. **a.** An IP address, subnet mask, and gateway are all required to access the Internet from a LAN using a workstation.

9. **c, d.** FTP uses TCP ports 20 and 21.

10. **b.** Having eight protocols broadcasting on the same segment would be a concern when configuring IP Helper Addressing.

11. **e.** Split Horizon, Route Poisoning, Poison Reverse, and Holddowns are all used to control routing loops in the network.

12. **c.** RIP is a Novell routing protocol that uses ticks and hops.

13. **c.** SAP advertises every 60 seconds.

14. **a, d.** The benefits of using a Packet Burst are that the server or workstation can send a whole set (burst) of packets before it requires an acknowledgement, and it reduces network traffic.

15. **a.** NDS benefits a large network environment with many branch offices within the United States and overseas.

16. **d, e.** DDP and AARP are protocols within AppleTalk stack that provide addressing.

17. **a, d.** You would use a zone in a large organization that has several floors and departments either to organize end users into groups or if you are using AppleTalk.

18. **c.** By implementing Split Horizon, Route Poisoning, and Poison Reverse you can prevent data looping from occurring during an update of the routing table information. Route poisoning is a way of notifying other routers that the link is dead by advertising a maximum hop count or an infinite number.

19. **a.** Global configuration mode in a router allows you to enable AppleTalk routing using the **appletalk routing** command.

20. **a, d.** IP and IPX are both examples of routed protocols.

Chapter 5 Solutions

1. **c.** The 7500 is used as a high-speed backbone router, mainly for large campuses, and replaces the 7000. This series of router is considered a core router and can handle large amounts of data at one time and support many services.

2. **a.** The 1000 router will suffice for a telecommuter who does not require a lot of bandwidth. Small office or home office (SOHO) routers are capable of the amount of traffic a telecommuter needs.

3. **c.** The 12000 router is a GSR that provides high-performance solutions ranging from 5 to 60 Gbps for Internet and large-scale WAN intranet back-bone applications.

4. **c.** The 10000 router is the best core router for the sole purpose of ISPs and supports several thousand T1 ports. This router offers the new forwarding technology called Parallel eXpress Forwarding (PXF) and is designed to support thousands of T1 ports per chassis.

5. **d.** The 7500 core router provides high packet-forwarding performance by distributing the switching operation to the Versatile Interface Processors (VIPs). The Cisco 7500 series is used for high-speed backbone aggregation for high-speed enterprise interconnectivity and integrates Layer 3 services including QoS, security, encryption, and traffic management.

6. **b.** The **show version** command tells you the current version of code running on the router. Knowing the version of code is helpful in troubleshooting as some versions may have a "bug" or offer a particular service you are looking for.

7. **b.** The **show flash** command enables you to see the contents of the flash memory. This is useful for loading new IOS on the router, to make sure sufficient memory is available to support the new version.

8. **d. sh controllers** or **show controllers** will allow you to see if it is a DTE or DCE cable. Looking at which type of cable is attached may help in trouble-shooting or configuring an interface.

9. **b.** The **no login** command enables you to avoid setting a password on the VTY sessions. This is not secure and is not recommended for production routers. This command is good to use in a lab environment.

10. **c.** The **line aux 0** command enables you to set a password on the Aux port.

11. **a.** The keepalives could be set wrong if the serial line (hardware) is up and the line protocol is down.

12. **b.** The clock rate needs to be set on the DCE cable. A good way to remember which cable the clock rate is set, is remembering the "C" in DCE cable for clock.

13. **d.** The **no shut** or **no shutdown** command is used to keep the interface from shutting down. By default, the interface is shut down, so when you are configuring an interface, you must take tell the interface not to shutdown.

14. **d.** MOTD stands for message of the day. The message of the day is very helpful when you want to relay a message to the staff about upcoming network events or outages. The message will be displayed every time an employee logs into the router.

15. **a, d.** The subnet mask and the IP address need to be in the command line when configuring an IP address on an interface. The router will not allow the IP address to be configured if the entire command line does not define the IP address and the subnet mask.

16. **b.** The command for describing an interface when configuring an interface is **description**. The description is very helpful when you are troubleshooting and trying to locate a specific interface.

17. **d.** The command for setting the console port for no timeout is **exec-timeout 0 0**. Setting this command will allow the session to remain open for an unspecified amount of time.

18. **d.** RIP does not need the bandwidth configured.

19. **a.** The **copy flash tftp** command is used to copy a router's IOS to a TFTP server.

20. **b.** The **copy tftp flash** command is used to copy from a TFTP server to the router's flash memory.

21. **a.** Frame Relay is a common configuration using subinterfaces. In Frame Relay, the router sees each subinterface as a separate bridge port and can route incoming frames of a subinterface out another subinterface, all within one physical interface.

22. **a.** The IOS is loaded from flash memory.

23. **a, b. Copy run start** and **copy running-config startup-config** are the two commands that can be used to manually save a configuration from DRAM to NVRAM.

24. **c.** The **hostname** command is used to name your router. After using the command **hostname** (space) and then the name of your router, press Enter and the hostname will appear as the prompt.

25. **e.** Ctrl+P recalls the commands in the buffer, starting with the most recent. You can also use the up arrow to achieve the same results.

Chapter 6 Solutions

1. **a.** The default encapsulation type used on Cisco serial interfaces is HDLC.

2. **b, c.** The **show running-config** and the **show frame-relay map** commands will display the DLCI numbers associated with a serial interface.

3. **a.** The DLCI number has local significance and does not need to be matched on the opposite end of the PVC or SVC.

4. **a, b.** The **show controller serial** command displays the clock rate and cable type. It does not display the LMI type or the error information.

5. **e.** The **debug serial interface** command displays the mineseen, myseq, and your seen fields.

6. **b, c.** If the interface is administratively down, you should check that the interface is not manually shut down or that a duplicate IP address is not configured on another interface.

7. **d.** If the keepalives are not sequencing on a serial interface you should check the local hardware, check for noise on the line, and check for a timing mismatch. Regardless of whether a hostname is configured, it will not affect any functioning component of the router.

8. **a, b.** The **show interface serial** command displays error information as well as the encapsulation type configured on the interface. The AUI interface is not a serial interface and the command does not display the switch model information.

9. **b.** The **show frame-relay pvc** command displays the FECN and BECN statistics.

10. **b, c.** The valid LMI types listed are Cisco and ANSI. ITU-T is the other valid LMI type.

11. **b, c, e.** The LABP-related fields found in the output from the **show interface serial** command are the RNRs, REJs, and SABMs.

12. **c.** To test end-to-end connectivity on a serial link, you would use one of the different loopback tests.

13. **b, c.** The DLCI and IETF are both invalid LMI types.

14. **a.** The output displayed is from the **show frame-relay map** command.

15. **a, d.** The valid Frame Relay encapsulation types are Cisco and IETF. The other answers are invalid.

16. **b.** The output displayed is from the **show interface** command.

17. **e.** To connect a Cisco router to a non-Cisco device, you need to use the IETF encapsulation type.

18. **d.** The output displayed is from the **show frame relay lmi** command.

19. **d.** The LMI stat sent, LMI enq recvd, DTE LMI, and LMI upd recvd fields are Frame Relay or LMI-related fields displayed with the **show interface serial** command. The PVC Status is displayed using the **show frame-relay pvc** command.

20. **c.** Cisco is the default LMI type on a Cisco router. The other answers are all invalid.

Chapter 7 Solutions

1. **a.** The **debug ipx sap activity** command should be used to provide SAP details, including the timestamps.

2. **c.** The **show ipx interface s0** command was used to produce the output.

3. **d.** The output is an example of using the **show ipx server** command and provides information regarding the servers and the network they reside on.

4. **b.** The **show ipx servers** command would show all the known servers in the network.

5. **c.** If no local IPX server is present on the particular segment a GNS request arrived from, the router will respond as the server with the address of the nearest server. If there is a local IPX server, it will respond to the request.

6. **b.** The valid range of numbers for an IPX standard access list is 800–899.

7. **a.** Routing protocols that are compatible with IPX are IPX-EIGRP, NLSP, and IPX RIP. EIGRP's little brother, IGRP, is not IPX-compatible.

8. **c.** The valid number range for an IPX extended access list is 900–999.

9. **c.** The default setting for SAP packet advertisements is 60 seconds.

10. **b.** IPX RIP has the same hop count maximum as IP RIP, which is 15. This means that no more than 15 routers can exist between any two given points in the network.

11. **a.** This output is from the topology table for IPX-EIGRP, as indicated in the first line. The exam will have obvious questions just like this.

12. **e.** IP is the default for Novell clients and servers running NetWare 5.0, so an encapsulation type would not be needed. Options C and D would be correct for the default encapsulation type for Novell clients and servers that are not running NetWare 5.0.

13. **b, c.** A router responds only if no server is present on an IPX network segment. If a NetWare server resides on the network segment, the Cisco router ignores the request and allows the server to respond.

14. **b.** A client uses Get Nearest Server (GNS) requests when it needs to know where the servers are located.

15. **a, b.** This is another trick question. Ethernet II and ARPA are the same thing. You need to remember that Novell calls the encapsulation type Ethernet II and Cisco calls it ARPA, so both answers are correct.

16. **e.** All the items listed are valid criteria for filtering with an extended IPX access list.

17. **a.** An IPX address requires four octets in hexadecimal format that specify both the network and the node.

18. **d.** The **show ipx interface** command can be used to show the interpacket delay.

19. **b.** The **debug ipx ?** command can be used to view the IPX debugging options.

20. **a.** The **show ipx traffic** command provides information on all IPX packets that are received and sent.

Chapter 8 Solutions

1. **b, c.** End-to-end and local VLANs are both basic methods for implementing VLAN boundaries.

2. **d.** Efficient bandwidth utilization, load balancing among multiple paths, and isolation between problem components are all benefits of implementing switches and VLANs.

3. **b.** Server Mode, Client Mode, and Transparent Mode are all valid, making Help Mode an incorrect option.

4. **d.** Transparent Mode is the mode you configure your switch for if you do not want to participate in a VTP management domain but still pass VTP management information to other VTP domain members.

5. **c.** Thirteen slots are available for modules on a Cisco Catalyst 5500 series switch.

6. **b.** Layer 3 route processors, such as an external router or an internal route processor module or card, enable you to communicate between VLANs.

7. **c.** A link that can carry traffic for multiple VLANs best describes a trunk link.

8. **b.** Privilege EXEC Mode would be used to verify your VLAN configuration on your Set/Clear-based command switch, by using the **show vlan** command.

9. **c.** On the Catalyst 5000 series switch, all ports are set to VLAN 1 by default.

10. **d.** An internal or external route processor must be used to route between VLANs at Layer 3.

11. **a.** A switch can belong to only one VTP domain.

12. **d.** A static VLAN port is assigned to a single VLAN where every device that attaches to that port on the switch becomes a member of the configured VLAN.

13. **a.** All ports on a Cisco 1900 series switch are identified by module number 0.

14. **a.** A native VLAN is the VLAN a port would be assigned to if it were not participating in a trunk.

15. **d.** The command **set vlan 10 3/2** enables you to assign port 2 on module 3 to VLAN 10 on a 5500 series switch.

16. **d.** The command **set vtp domain coriolis** enables you to set the switch VTP domain name to **Coriolis**.

17. **a, d.** ISL does not run on an access link to an end user and can be used in conjunction with the Spanning Tree Protocol.

18. **b, c.** VLANs were introduced to address network segmentation and scalability problems of a flat network.

19. **d.** End-user interfaces do not understand VLAN tagging and encapsulation methods used by VLAN trunks.

20. **d.** The purpose of VTP is to keep VLAN information in a VTP domain synchronized between switches.

Chapter 9 Solutions

1. **a.** EtherChannel enables you to bundle up to eight physical links into a single logical link.

2. **a.** Overcoming transparent bridging problems inspired the IEEE 802 Internetworking Committee to create the Spanning Tree Protocol specification.

3. **c, d.** EtherChannel can be used only on 100 and 1,000Mbps links. This means that the only correct options are Fast Ethernet and Gigabit Ethernet.

4. **c.** VLAN 1 carries BPDUs for the spanning tree when CST is implemented. PVST or PVST+ would enable BPDUs to be sent on a separate port for each VLAN.

5. **d.** PVST provides an alternative to CST for use on larger-scale switched networks to allow a separate instance of STP to be used on each individual VLAN.

6. **c.** The correct command to configure a backup root bridge is **set spantree secondary**.

7. **d.** On a Catalyst 1900 or 2820 series switch, STP can be configured on only 64 VLANs. You can have up to 1,005 VLANs, but STP must be disabled on all but 64. By default, STP is enabled on VLANs 1 through 64.

8. **b.** The correct way to change the VLAN port priority to 20 on an IOS-based switch is to use **spantree priority 20**.

9. **b.** The maximum number of physical links that can be used in an EtherChannel bundle is 8.

10. **a, e.** Determining the locations of data loops and notifying other switches of network changes are both responsibilities of BPDUs.

11. **c.** A VLAN port priority can be a numerical value between 0 and 63.

12. **c.** PAgP is used to support EtherChannel in forming logical links.

13. **a.** STP would refer to the Bridge ID, using the lower of the port IDs as the tiebreaker.

14. **b.** The default bridge priority value of a secondary root switch or bridge is a value of 16,384. The value of the root bridge would be 8,192.

15. **b.** The second path between two destinations in a network is called the redundant path.

16. **b.** You cannot use dynamic VLANs with Fast EtherChannel. Dynamic VLANs can change the topology of the network, so they cannot be used.

17. **c.** The Link State Time is not a timer used to influence the convergence time of STP.

18. **a.** Only one root bridge is allowed in each instance of STP.

19. **b.** A broadcast storm, which is a total halt to the network, is the worst-case scenario resulting from data loops in the network.

20. **e.** The default priority on all switches running STP is 32,768.

Chapter 10 Solutions

1. **a.** The SAINT ASIC is used to encapsulate and de-encapsulate Ethernet frames.

2. **b.** The **show port** command, followed by the module number and port number, is used by the switch to display the port status and error counters.

3. **a, d.** A Cisco switch and router support both the IEEE 802.1Q protocol, which allows trunking to a non–Cisco device, and the Inter-Switch Link, which is a Cisco proprietary protocol for trunking.

4. **d.** An ISL trunk port can handle all the Active VLANs that are active on a switch. The maximum is 1000.

5. **d.** The CAM table on the switch is used to keep all the MAC addresses of all the attached nodes on each port. The **show cam dynamic** command is used to view those addresses. The **show cam static** command can be used if port security is in place on the switch.

6. **b.** Category 3 cable can support 10BaseTX but not 100BaseTX. Both Category 5 and 6 can support 100 Mbps data traffic over Ethernet.

7. **c, e.** Some CLI-based commands can aid in getting utilization statistics, but the only two valid answers shown are c. and e.

8. **a.** All ports begin in VLAN 1 by default, which is also the VLAN management VLAN by default.

9. **c, d.** This question is somewhat tricky because of the similarities in the commands. The **show span** command is also a valid answer, but it gives statistics related to the switched port analyzer, so it is wrong.

10. **d.** A switched port with ISL encapsulation configured would be a trunked port. Both ISL and IEEE 802.1Q allow more than one VLAN to traverse the link.

11. **d.** IEEE 802.1Q is an industry-standard protocol supported on Cisco switches and routers to connect a trunked link to a non-Cisco router or switch.

12. **c.** VLANDirector, which is part of the CiscoWorks for Switched Internetworks software, is used to configure and track VLAN configurations.

13. **b.** This scenario happens so often that some of the Cisco Technical Assistance Center employees call VTP "Very Ticked-off Person." The reason? If you have a higher revision number on the new switch configured as a server, the entire domain, even if there are 1,000 VLANs, reconfigures itself for the old domain's configuration. This can create a big mess in a network.

14. **c.** Cisco Discovery Protocol (CDP) is used for discovering the Cisco devices directly connected to the device running CDP. CDP learns the configuration of the directly attached devices network interfaces, and the software information running on each device.

15. **d.** Spanning Tree Protocol places redundant ports in the blocked state using the CBL ASIC. The disabled state is placed on a port by an administrator or the switch, not by STP, if a hardware problem exists.

16. **b.** The **show cdp neighbors** or **show cdp neighbors detail** command can be used to obtain information about neighboring Cisco devices in the network.

17. **b.** The ISL encapsulation type on a router's interface can be assigned using the **encapsulation isl 1** command.

18. **c.** For inter-VLAN routing to take place, a Layer 3 device must be used to resolve the address. A switch cannot communicate between VLANs without some type of route processor intervening.

19. **d.** You can use the **show version** command to determine the amount of time the switch has been up since the switch was last rebooted.

20. **d.** The **show vtp domain** command will enable you to display the output.

Chapter 11 Solutions

1. **a.** Weighted fair queuing (WFQ) is on by default on links below or equal to 2.048Mbs.

2. **c.** The **fair-queue** command is used to enable weighted fair queuing on an interface.

3. **a, b, d, f.** The four priorities used with priority queuing are high, medium, normal, and low.

4. **a.** The default queue of priority queuing is normal if you don't specify where the default traffic goes.

5. **c.** Sixteen queues can be configured for custom queuing.

6. **e.** The default bytes for custom queuing is 1,500.

7. **c.** The command to show custom queuing is **show queueing custom**.

8. **b, e.** The tools used with congestion avoidance are RED and WRED.

9. **a, c.** The two policies used in traffic filtering are GTS and FRTS.

10. **c.** A CAR can be set on a router to set a bandwidth limit for specific types of traffic on an interface to aid in traffic filtering.

11. **d.** The ICMP Destination Unreachable message will be sent by the router if the packet is dropped.

12. **e.** An IP extended access list ranges from 100-199.

13. **d.** Port 80 identifies Web traffic for an access list.

14. **c.** The sequence of commands that is configured for an extended access list is as follows: access list number, protocol, source, destination, and the port.

15. **b.** AAA stands for authentication, authorization, and accounting.

Chapter 12 Solutions

1. **a.** The core dump is taking a picture of the RAM memory.

2. **c.** The **exception** command is used after a router crashes. When using the **exception** command, you must know the IP of a server to send the core dump to.

3. **a, b, d.** The three types of protocol servers are FTP, TFTP, and RCP. The configurations are different for each protocol server in the IOS for core dumps.

4. **c.** The **write core** command is used when a router crashes, and should be used only with Cisco TAC advice.

5. **d.** The recommended acceptable collision rate is 5 to 8 percent. Collision rates are based on the output packets.

6. **b, c, d.** The network analyzer can look at performance, statistics, protocols, and specific traffic. The analyzer can't look at network routes. The analyzer must be attached to the network you want to monitor.

7. **b.** The Category 5 cable is usually the problem with a lot of CRC errors and very few collisions.

8. **a, b, c.** Input errors include runts, giants, no buffer, CRC, frame, overrun, and ignored counts, but not interfaces.

9. **a, b.** The output from the **show stacks** command will show the failure type, an operand address, and a failure counter.

10. **d.** Network analyzers are also called protocol analyzers.

11. **b.** Collision errors report the number of packets that had to be re-sent because of collisions.

12. **a.** After a specified packet is in the analyzer memory, the analyzer software decodes the packet and presents the packet in a readable fashion for the administrator.

13. **d.** The packets input error reports the total number of error-free packets received on the interface.

14. **d.** Using the **show interfaces e1** command provides an in-depth look at the interface and the errors.

15. **c.** Runts are discarded because the packets are too small. Ethernet packets smaller than 64 bytes are discarded.

Chapter 13 Solutions

1. **c.** The **dialer load-threshold 125** command will bring up the second B channel when the first reaches approximately 50 percent load. The command will accept a value of 1 to 255, with 1 being the lowest load and 255 being 100 percent load.

2. **a.** ISDN BRI provides B channels for data (64Kbps each) and one D channel (16Kbps) for clocking and control.

3. **c.** The q.931 signaling standard runs on the D channel and is responsible for Layer 3 call connections and disconnections.

4. **c.** This question requires subnetting knowledge, which you should have at this point in your Cisco studies. A 30-bit subnet mask would allow for only two hosts for each subnet. The only valid answer is 172.16.1.2.

5. **c, d.** You can use the **isdn switch-type** command in the global or interface configuration modes.

6. **a.** The q.921 protocol is used for Layer 2 connections. CHAP and PPP are not specific to ISDN. Ethernet is a Layer 1 topology, and q.931 is used for call connection establishment at Layer 3.

7. **d.** The TEI broadcast value is 127.

8. **e.** The SPID is a 4-digit value added to the 10-digit dialer number.

9. **d.** The q.931 and q.921 protocols use the D channel for signaling.

10. **c, e.** CHAP requires PPP and the username to be configured to allow for authentication.

11. **e.** A faulty cable should be eliminated as the cause of the problem. If the cable is faulty, the call will not succeed. The other causes are all possibilities and should be checked.

12. **a.** The q.921 protocol defines the signaling method used by ISDN at Layer 2. The q.921 protocol uses the D channel by using the Link Access Procedure on D channel (LAPD) protocol, which is used by X.25.

13. **d.** The **debug isdn q931** command displays all connection establishment information and should be used for Layer 3 troubleshooting.

14. **f.** All of these are possible causes of why the router will not dial.

15. **e.** The ISDN idle timer is set for two minutes. This means that a connection will terminate if data is not transmitted for two minutes.

16. **a, b.** CHAP is used for password authentication, and encrypts the password for more secure connections.

17. **b.** A TE2 is a non-ISDN device that requires a TA interface to use the ISDN network.

18. **e.** The **show isdn status** command provides the connection status of all three layers, as well as calls in progress.

19. **e.** The **isdn autodetect** command instructs the router to detect the switch type. The other commands are all invalid commands.

20. **d.** To troubleshoot a connection between two TEs, you need check an end-to-end protocol, of which the only one listed is in the **debug ppp negotiation** command.

Chapter 14 Solutions

1. **a, c.** If split horizon has been disabled on the interface or the hold-down timers are not consistent across the network, a routing loop may be caused.

2. **d.** RTMP (Routing Table Maintenance Protocol) provides distance-vector routing for the Apple Talk phase II protocol.

3. **c.** BGP is considered an exterior routing protocol that connects autonomous systems together. The latest version is BGP v4 and is mainly used by the ISP's.

4. **b.** EIGRP is an enhanced version of IGRP. EIGRP supports both routing algorithms and provides less opportunity for routing failures. EIGRP also converges very fast because it only calculates when a change in the network directly affects the routing table.

5. **b, c.** EIGRP and OSPF support variable-length subnet masks (VLSMs) and classless address spaces. Answers a and d are incorrect because neither RIP v1 nor IGRP supports VLSM or classless addressing.

6. **b, c.** RIP and EIGRP are considered distance-vector routing protocols, whereas OSPF and NLSP are link-state protocols. EIGRP is similar to link-state protocols, such as OSPF, but it also uses the same distance vector found in IGRP.

7. **a, b, c.** The other commands are invalid.

8. **a.** The **debug ospf** command allows for in-depth troubleshooting of OSPF.

9. **a, c.** Using the **show running-config** and **show route-map** commands enables you to see the contents of a route map.

10. **b, e, g.** Interior, system, and exterior are routes recognized by IGRP.

11. **b.** Using the **show ip ospf neighbors** command enables you to see who is running OSPF, and will list all routing information on all of the enabled OSPF interfaces.

12. **b, c, d.** RIP2 is able to support Classless Interdomain Routing (CIDR), route summarization, and variable-length subnet masks (VLSMs).

13. **d.** Any of the commands can be used to view the contents of an IP access list.

14. **b, c, d.** Common methodologies in troubleshooting are inside-out, outside-in, and divide by half.

15. **b.** Using the **show ip route** command enables you to see the routing table.

16. **d.** There could be a bad cable or MAU port, or the MAU port may not be initialized to cause a down/down status.

17. **b.** ARP cache tables are not permanent until cleared manually.

18. **b.** IGRP is Cisco-proprietary.

19. **d.** The process of triggered updates informs the router from its neighbor about routing updates.

20. **b.** Using the **show cdp neighbors** command will display all directly-connected Cisco devices and information about them.

Chapter 15 Solutions

1. **b.** IP provides a best-effort, connectionless delivery of datagrams as opposed to TCP which is considered a connection-oriented protocol.

2. **a.** Class A addressing scheme is 1.0.0.0 through 127.0.0.0 with the exception of 10.0.0.0 which is reserved.

3. **a.** Class B addressing scheme is128.0.0.0 through 191.255.0.0 with the exception of 172.16.0.0 through 172.31.255.255 which is reserved.

4. **d.** Class E addressing scheme is 248.0.0.0 through 255.255.255.255.

5. **c.** ICMP is a Layer 3 (network) Internet protocol that provides message packets to report errors and other information regarding IP packet processing back to the source.

6. **b.** IRDP uses Router-Advertisement and Router-Solicitation messages to communicate with the other routers.

7. **d.** TCP is connection-oriented, reliable protocol that does require a lot of overhead, but using it may be necessary for critical applications if you want reliable delivery.

8. **c.** The inside-out method of troubleshooting starts with the local host (source) and works its way step by step to the problem (destination) host.

9. **a, b, d.** Check for LAN or WAN Physical layer problems and **ping** outward until the problem router is found. Usually if a network is down, the most likely problem is at the Physical layer. Looking at an access list would not explain why a router is down.

10. **b.** Look at the access list first, mainly the extended access list, and check whether any particular protocols are being denied. A router interface is either up or down and physical connections don't care about a protocol if it is passing traffic.

11. **b.** Using the **show ip route** command will allow you to look at the router's routing table and see if the route exists and an address to where it is routing is.

12. **c.** Using the **show ip cache** command will allow you to look at the fast-switching route cache to check for anomalies.

13. **d.** Using the **show ip arp** command will allow you to look at the ARP tables to identify the MAC address of the problem host.

14. **b, c, d.** Use **ping** and **traceroute** to isolate the problem, and check for protocols being exchanged at the router level by using **debug ip rip** command to see RIP, other **debug** commands exist for other protocols. After isolating the problem, try disabling the access list by using the **no ip access group** command. Then, test the routers again by using the **ping** and **traceroute** tools. You may have to try this on more than one router.

15. **a, b, c.** Look at the access list and make sure certain types of traffic are being denied, check whether a default gateway is specified, and look for a subnet mask configuration mismatch between the router and the host.

16. **c.** Port 23 uses TCP and is for Telnet.

17. **a.** HTTP traffic uses port 80 with TCP.

18. **b.** The output was produced by using the **show ip arp** command. The output identifies an IP adress to a MAC address.

19. **c.** The output was produced by using the **show ip route** command which shows the defined path of gateway of last resort and directly connected interfaces. In troubleshooting, often a path is not defined and the router doesn't know where to direct the traffic the router doesn't know about.

20. **d.** The **debug ip icmp** command displays information regarding the router sending and receiving ICMP messages. This is one of the best commands to use when you are troubleshooting an end-to-end connection.

Appendix B
Objectives for Exam 640-506

Debug	Chapter(s)
Use of Cisco IOS Troubleshooting Commands and Debugging Utilities	3, 5, 6, 10, 15

HDLC	Chapter(s)
Troubleshooting Tools, Methods and Targets	5, 6

IOS backups	Chapter(s)
Problem isolation for TCP/IP	15
Troubleshooting Tools, Methods, and Targets	3, 5, 12, 15

Troubleshooting	Chapter(s)
An Efficient Troubleshooting Method	1
Problem Isolation for AppleTalk	4
Problem Isolation for Frame Relay WANs	6
Problem Isolation for ISDN BRI	13
Problem Isolation for Novell IPX	7
Problem Isolation on Catalyst Switches	10
Traffic and Data Links Fundamentals	2, 6
Troubleshooting VLANs on Switches and Routers	8

Appendix C
Study Resources

Books

Luallen, Matthew E. 2000. *Support Exam Cram*. Scottsdale: The Coriolis Group. ISBN:1-57610-681-0. This book is a great study guide for the Support exam.

Dennis, Craig, and Eric Quinn. 2000. *Remote Access Exam Cram*. Scottsdale: The Coriolis Group. ISBN:1-57610-437-0. This is a helpful guide to configuring Frame Relay and X.25.

Meinster, Barry. 2000. *Remote Access Exam Prep*. Scottsdale: The Coriolis Group. ISBN:1-57610-692-6. This is a great in-depth reference to configuring Frame Relay and X.25.

McDysan, David E., and Darren L. Spohn. 1998. *ATM Theory and Applications*. New York: McGraw-Hill. ISBN: 0-0704545-346-2. This book is a great resource on Asynchronous Transfer Mode and LAN Emulation.

Smith, Marina. 1998 *Virtual LANs*. New York: McGraw-Hill. ISBN: 0-07-913623-0. A good resource book on VLANs.

Online Resources

Cisco maintains its own Web site that is a great source for all Cisco documentation. It supplies a huge pool of documentation on all of its products, and also the current documents and updates. You can find the Cisco Web site at **www.cisco.com**.

Troubleshooting

➤ *Troubleshooting Ethernet*—**www.cisco.com/univercd/cc/td/doc/ cisintwk/itg_v1/tr1904.htm**

➤ *Troubleshooting FDDI*—**www.cisco.com/univercd/cc/td/doc/ cisintwk/itg_v1/tr1905.htm**

➤ *Troubleshooting token ring*—**www.cisco.com/univercd/cc/td/doc/ cisintwk/itg_v1/tr1906.htm**

➤ *Troubleshooting TCP/IP*—**www.cisco.com/univercd/cc/td/doc/ cisintwk/itg_v1/tr1907.htm**

➤ *Troubleshooting Frame Relay connections*—**www.cisco.com/univercd/cc/td/ doc/cisintwk/itg_v1/tr1918.htm**

➤ *Troubleshooting ISDN connections*—**www.cisco.com/univercd/cc/td/doc/ cisintwk/itg_v1/tr1917.htm**

➤ *Troubleshooting Access List on Dial Interfaces*—**www.cisco.com/warp/public/ 480/tr_ACL1.html**

Asynchronous Transfer Mode

➤ *Troubleshooting ATM switching environments*—**www.cisco.com/univercd/cc/ td/doc/cisintwk/itg_v1/tr1921.htm**

➤ *Configuring ATM interfaces*—**www.cisco.com/univercd/cc/td/doc/ product/dsl_prod/6260/swcnfg/conatm.htm**

Cisco IOS

➤ *IOS troubleshooting commands*—**www.cisco.com/univercd/cc/td/doc/ product/software/ios113ed/113ed_cr/fun_r/frprt4/frtroubl.htm**

Multilayer Switching

➤ *Troubleshooting IP multilayer switching*—**www.cisco.com/warp/public/ 473/13.html**

➤ *Overview of multilayer switching*—**www.cisco.com/univercd/cc/td/doc/ product/software/ios120/12cgcr/switch_c/xcprt5/xcmls.htm**

Quality of Service

➤ *Troubleshooting QPM*—**www.cisco.com/univercd/cc/td/doc/product/ rtrmgmt/ciscoasu/class/qpm1_1/using_qo/c1trbl.htm#xtocid229500**

➤ *Quality of Service overview*—**www.cisco.com/univercd/cc/td/doc/ product/software/ios121/121cgcr/qos_c/qcdintro.htm**

Spanning Tree Protocol

➤ *Troubleshooting a transparent bridging environment*—**www.cisco.com/univercd/ cc/td/doc/cisintwk/itg_v1/tr1920.htm**

➤ *Configuring STP on a Cisco Catalyst 2900*—**www.cisco.com/univercd/cc/ td/doc/product/lan/c2900xl/29_35sa6/olhelp/stphelp.htm**

Standards Organizations

➤ *American National Standards Institute (ANSI)*—This organization coordinates many specialized standards organizations and technical committees. ANSI's Web site can be found at **www.ansi.org**.

➤ *Electronic Industries Alliance (EIA)*—This is the parent organization for a number of standards groups, including the Telecommunications Industry Association (TIA). TIA/EIA standards relate mostly to cabling. The TIA members are providers of communications and information technology products and services. The TIA/EIA Web site can be found at **www.tiaonline.org**.

➤ *Gigabit Ethernet Alliance*—This group was formed to promote industry cooperation in developing Gigabit Ethernet. You can find this group's Web site at **www.gigabit-ethernet.org**.

➤ *High-Speed Token Ring Alliance*—This group was formed by Token Ring vendors to establish high-speed solutions for token ring. Its Web site can be found at **www.hstra.com**.

➤ *Institute for Electrical and Electronics Engineers (IEEE)*—This standards organization creates and publishes standards related to electronic technologies. It is best known for its 802 committee, which has produced a series of standards documents that describe LAN protocols and physical transmission topology standards. The IEEE's Web site can be found at **www.ieee.org**.

➤ *International Organization for Standardization (ISO)*—This organizations is best known for the Open System Interconnection (OSI) Model. It creates and publishes standards that cover a wide range of topics. The ISO Web site can be found at **www.iso.ch**.

➤ *International Telecommunications Union Telecommunication Standardization Sector (ITU-T)*—This organization is responsible for the networking standards relating to ATM. The ITU-T Web site can be found at **www.itu.int**.

➤ *Internet Engineering Task Force (IETF)*—This organization is responsible for the TCP/IP, Simple Network Management Protocol (SNMP), and Internet standards. A lot of its work relates to upgrading and enlarging the TCP/IP protocol suite and networks utilizing that protocol. The IETF Web site can be found at **www.ietf.org**.

Appendix C

➤ *National Committee for Information Technology Standards (NCITS)*—This organization was formed to produce market condition standards for storage devices, multimedia, programming languages, and security. The T11 committee is responsible for fibre channel standards. You can find the NCITS T11 Web site at **www.t11.org**.

Cisco Group Study and Users Groups

Joining and attending Cisco study and user groups is a great way to gain knowledge of real-world scenarios. At user groups, people can share their experience and expertise to help with questions everyone may experience in day-to-day networking. It is also a great way to keep abreast of the new technologies that are constantly emerging. Lots of user groups exist across this country and into Mexico. The following are some of the best sites we have found for Cisco user groups:

➤ *Capital District Cisco Users Group, Albany, New York*—**www.cdcug.org**

➤ *Cisco Users Group for Central Iowa*—**http://cisco.knis.com**

➤ *Dallas/Ft. Worth Cisco Users Group, Texas*—**http://dfw.cisco-users.org**

➤ *Denver Cisco Users Group, Colorado*—**www.twpm.com/dcug/**

➤ *East Tennessee Cisco Users Group, Tennessee*—**http://www.etcug.org**

➤ *Groupstudy.Com*—**www.groupstudy.com**

➤ *Kansas City Cisco Users Group, Kansas*—**www.cugkansas.com/home.cfm**

➤ *Miami Cisco Users Group, Florida*—**http://miami.ciscousers.org**

➤ *New England Cisco Users Group*—**www.ciscousers.com**

➤ *North Florida/Alabama Region Cisco User Group, Florida & Alabama*—**www.cisco-florabama.com/huntsville.html**

➤ *Northern California Cisco Users Group, Sacramento, California*—**www.csecnet.com/cisco/index.htm**

➤ *Omaha Cisco Users Group, Nebraska*—**http://omaha.cisco-users.org**

➤ *Sacramento Placer County Cisco Study Group, Northern California*—**www.cisco-cert.org**

➤ *South Carolina Cisco Users Group*—**www.angelfire.com/sc/cisco**

➤ *Southern California Cisco Users Group*—**www.sccug.org**

➤ *Tri-State Cisco Users Group, Texas, New Mexico, and Chihuahua, Mexico*—**http://tscug.cisco-users.org**

➤ *The Wichita Cisco Users Group, Kansas*—**http://www.cugkansas.com/new_user.cfm**

Live Cisco Training/Internet-Based Labs

Here are a few places that can aid in your certification and education goals:

➤ *Author Sean Odom's Web site*—Meet Joe Snow! And get valuable updates to this book! **www.thequestforcertification.com**

➤ *GlobalNet Training*—Instructor led Cisco training. **www.globalnettraining.com**

➤ *Knowledgenet*—Cisco e-based training. **www.knowledgenet.com**

➤ *NerdBooks*—The best place to buy computer books just for nerds. **www.nerdbooks.com**

➤ *e-Business Process Solutions*—Cisco Internet Training/VAR. **www.e-bps.com**

➤ *MentorLabs.Com*—online Cisco labs and equipment. **www.mentorlabs.com**

Appendix D
Cisco Quick Subnetting Chart

Class A 255.0.0.0

Bits	/10	/11	/12	/13	/14	/15	/16
Subnet Mask	192	224	240	248	252	254	255
Class A Hosts	4194302	2097150	1048574	524286	262142	131070	65534
Class A Subnets	2	6	14	30	62	126	254

"Host Start Range (256 - subnet number = start range) Whereas 256 - 240 = 16, so network ranges 16, 32, 48, and so on."

Class B 255. 255.0.0

Bits	/18	/19	/20	/21	/22	/23	/24
Subnet Mask	192	224	240	248	252	254	255
Class B Hosts	16382	8190	4094	2046	1022	510	254
Class B Subnets	2	6	14	30	62	126	254
Class A Hosts	16382	8190	4094	2046	1022	510	254
Class A Subnets	1022	2046	4094	8190	16382	32766	65534

"Host Start Range (256 - subnet number = start range) Whereas 256 - 240 = 16, so network ranges 16, 32, 48, and so on."

Class C 255. 255. 255. 0

Bits	/26	/27	/28	/29	/30	/31	/32
Subnet Mask	192	224	240	248	252	254	255
Class C Hosts	62	30	14	6	2	0	0
Class C Subnets	2	6	14	30	62	126	254
Class B Hosts	62	30	14	6	2	0	0
Class B Subnets	1022	2046	4094	8190	16382	32766	65534
Class A Hosts	62	30	14	6	2	0	0
Class A Subnets	262142	524286	1048574	2097150	4194302	8388606	16777214

"Host Start Range (256 - subnet number = start range) Whereas 256 - 240 = 16, so network ranges 16, 32, 48, and so on."

Glossary

10BaseT

The IEEE 802.3 standard for running Ethernet at 10Mbps over shielded or unshielded twisted-pair wiring. The maximum length for a 10BaseT segment is 100 meters, or 328 feet.

10Base2

The IEEE 802.3 standard for running Ethernet at 10Mbps over a thinnet coaxial cable. The maximum length for a 10Base2 segment is 185 meters, or 607 feet.

10Base5

The IEEE 802.3 standard for running Ethernet at 10Mbps over a thicknet coaxial cable. The maximum length for a 10Base5 segment is 500 meters, or 1,640 feet.

10BaseFX

An IEEE standard for running Ethernet over fiber-optic cable.

100BaseFX

An IEEE standard for running Fast Ethernet over fiber-optic cable.

100BaseT

The IEEE 802.3u standard, which is also known as *Fast Ethernet*, for running Ethernet at 100Mbps over a shielded or unshielded twisted-pair cable.

100BaseT4

A technology that allows the use of Fast Ethernet technology over existing Category 3 and Category 4 wiring, utilizing all four pairs of wires.

100BaseVG (Voice Grade)

The IEEE 802.12 standard that allows data transmissions of 100Mbps over Category 3 or data grade wiring, utilizing all sets of wires.

1000BaseX

The IEEE 802.3z standard, also known as *Gigabit Ethernet*, that defines standards for data transmissions of 1000Mbps.

802.10

Used within FDDI backbones. Originally developed by the IEEE as a standard to implement FDDI into metropolitan area networks (MANs), this is a Cisco mechanism that is used to implement VLANs.

AppleTalk Address Resolution Protocol (AARP)

This protocol is used to map the data-link AppleTalk stack to the network address.

Area Border Router (ABR)

The router running an OSPF protocol and placed on the border of one or more OSPF areas. An ABR connects the OSPF areas to the OSPF backbone.

Access layer

In the *Campus Hierarchical Model*, the Access layer is where the workstation connects to the network. Hubs and switches reside here, and it's also where workgroups access the network.

access list

A security feature used with the Cisco IOS to filter traffic types as part of data routing. Access lists are also used to filter traffic between different VLAN numbers.

active monitor

Active monitor is used in Token Ring and refers to the node on a Token Ring network that is responsible for management tasks, such as preventing loops and monitoring the token's activities. A network can have multiple active monitors.

address

A set of numbers, usually expressed in binary format, that are used to identify and locate a resource or device on a network.

address filter

A way of using Layer 2 MAC addresses or switching ports to filter traffic. This process allows you to filter traffic and restrict access without the use of VLANs, and is a feature of the Cisco Catalyst 3000 Series. Although it uses a process similar to access lists on the Cisco IOS, you can apply multiple address filters to the same interface.

address learning

Transparent bridging uses this option to learn the hardware addresses of all of the devices on the internetwork. The switch then filters the network with the known MAC address.

address mapping

This mechanism translates network addresses into different formats so that it can operate interchangeably with different protocols.

Address Resolution Protocol (ARP)

The protocol that is used to map the IP address to the MAC address.

administrative distance

This distance is defined with a number from 0 to 225 that represents the integrity of a routing information source. This term usually refers to a particular protocol. The lower the number, the more trustworthy it is.

administrator

The person who is responsible for the control and security of the user accounts, resources, and data flow on the network.

alignment error

This error occurs in an Ethernet network and identifies that a received frame has extra bits. (An error is detected when the bits received are not divisible by eight.) This error is usually the result of frames being damaged by collisions.

All Routes Explorer (ARE)

On a Token Ring network, if the node of destination is not found on the local network segment, an ARE frame is sent to all the bridges. Each bridge receiving an ARE updates the frame with a RIF and then forwards the frame out all the ports.

American National Standards Institute (ANSI)

The organization that publishes standards for communications, programming languages, and networking.

ANDing

The process of comparing the bits of an IP address with the bits in a subnet mask to determine how a packet will be handled.

anycast address

An address used in ATM for shared multiple-end systems. An anycast address allows a frame to be sent to specific groups of hosts.

AppleTalk

A group of protocols used in Macintosh computer environments. These protocols allow a network—or more than one network—to operate in more than one zone.

AppleTalk Filing Protocol (AFP)

This protocol operates at the Presentation layer that supports the Mac OS file sharing and AppleShare to permit file and application exchanges on a server.

AppleTalk Echo Protocol (AEP)

Similar to PING, this protocol tests for connectivity on a network. It sends a packet request from a source in anticipation of an echo or a response from the destination node.

AppleTalk Session Protocol (ASP)

This protocol creates and synchronizes a communication session between programs.

AppleTalk Update-Based Routing Protocol (AURP)

An AppleTalk routing protocol used in the Macintosh environment.

Application layer

The layer of the OSI model that provides support for end users and for application programs using network resources.

Application Specific Integrated Circuit (ASIC)

ASICs are a feature of many LAN controllers. They are internal to the switch, and they work in conjunction with the internal processor to make Layer 2 forwarding decisions. However, they lack the ability to make flexible software-implemented forwarding decisions. Their ability to perform small tasks quickly and inexpensively makes them key to the switching process. ASICs used in Cisco switches and routers are the Phoenix, FE, LMA, PFPA, SAMBA, SAGE, SAINT, and CEF.

AppleTalk Remote Access (ARA)

This protocol is used in Macintosh environments to retrieve data from a remote location. Both locations must be using Macintosh AppleTalk to utilize this protocol.

AppleTalk Transaction Protocol (ATP)

This protocol operates on the Transport layer for Macintosh environments and ties the request and response together to ensure a reliable exchange of requests and responses.

AppleTalk Update-based Routing Protocol (AURP)

This protocol is responsible for encapsulating AppleTalk traffic in the header of another type of protocol. This encapsulation process allows a connection of AppleTalk internetworks through foreign networks, such as TCP/IP, to create an AppleTalk WAN.

area

Usually used in CLNS, DECnet, or OSPF networks, an area is a logical set of segments and devices that are defined as a particular group. Routers use areas to distinguish a defined group to create a single autonomous system (AS).

Asymmetric Digital Subscriber Line (ADSL)

A service that transmits digital voice and data over existing analog phone lines.

Asynchronous Transfer Mode (ATM)

Originally developed by the ITU-T, ATM is an international standard used in high-speed transmission media such as E3, SONET, and T3 for cell relay. It can be used in multiple service types such as voice, video, or data and sent in fixed-length, 53-byte cells. ATM has become common in today's corporate networks. It guarantees

Glossary

throughput and minimizes delay, and can provide scalability at speeds up to many gigabits per second.

Asynchronous Transmission Synchronization (ATS)

A process used in serial data transfer in which a start bit and a stop bit are added so that the receiving station can know when a particular bit has been transferred. Also known as *bit synchronization*.

ATM Adaptation Layer (AAL)

The ATM layer that adapts data to the ATM 48-byte payload. This layer has a number of adaptations, such as AAL1, AAL2, AAL3/4, and AAL5. AAL5 is by far the most common in today's networks. AAL5 defines how data from a node on the network (such as a PC or server) handles ATM cells. AAL5 is also used by Cisco Catalyst switches with LANE to perform segmentation and reassembly of ATM frames into cells and cells into frames.

ATM System Processor (ASP)

A Cisco ATM cell-switching processing card, located on the Cisco Catalyst 5500 chassis or slot 2 on the LS1010 chassis.

attachment unit interface (AUI)

IEEE 802.3 specification used between a multistation access unit (MAU) and an Ethernet network interface card (NIC). MAUs are typically associated with Token Ring networks, and AUI ports are specific to Ethernet. This cable connects an AUI port on the Ethernet access card to an Ethernet 10Base2, 10Base5, or 10BaseFx transceiver.

attachment unit interface (AUI) connector

A 15-pin, D-type connector that is sometimes used with Ethernet connections.

attenuation

The loss of signal that is experienced as data is transmitted across network media.

Automated Packet Recognition and Translation (APaRT)

A FDDI line module feature found on Cisco Catalyst 2820 and 5000 Series switches that allows for the automatic detection of frame types with translational bridging. It uses the CAM table to get the frame-type information for all end nodes.

autonomous switching

A switching mechanism that allows Cisco routers to process packets faster by using the Ciscobus—and not the system processor—to switch packets.

autonomous system (AS)

A group of networks (defined by routers) that are running the same routing protocol. Autonomous systems are subdivided by areas and must be assigned a 16-bit number to identify the area.

backbone

A high-capacity infrastructure system that provides optimal transport on a LAN. In a LAN, the data running from router to router, switch to switch, or switch to router is typically transported through a faster physical topology than the rest of the local area or virtual LAN devices. The backbone is the physical cable.

BackboneFast

Initiated when a root port or blocked port receives an inferior BPDU from its designated bridge. It allows the secondary or backup port to immediately begin forwarding after a link fault with the root link. It bypasses the MaxAge timer.

backplane

The primary data/control bus located on a Cisco Catalyst switch, and similar to the motherboard in a PC. It interconnects all the modules inside the switch chassis.

bandwidth
The rated throughput capacity of a given network protocol or medium.

base bandwidth
The difference between the lowest and highest frequencies that are available for network signals. The term is also used to describe the rated throughput capacity of a given network protocol or medium.

Basic Rate Interface (BRI)
An ISDN digital communications line that consists of three independent channels: two bearer (or B) channels, each at 64Kbps; and one data (or D) channel at 16Kbps. ISDN BRI is often referred to as *2B+D*.

baseline
Refers to a base level, established using network historical data and routine network utilizations. A network baseline allows for accurate monitoring and measurement, and serves as an effective guide to determine network changes or faults.

baud rate
Named after the French telegraphy expert J. M. Baudot, this term is used to define the speed or rate of signal transfer.

binary
Characterized by its use of ones and zeros, this base 2 numbering system is used in digital signaling.

binding
The process of associating a protocol and a network interface card (NIC).

bit
An electronic digit used in the binary numbering system.

blocking architecture
A condition in which the total bandwidth of the ports is greater than the capacity of the switching fabric.

bridge
A device that connects and passes packets between two network segments that use the same communications protocol. Bridges operate at the Data Link layer of the OSI reference model. A bridge filters, forwards, or floods an incoming frame based on the MAC address of that frame.

bridge ID MAC address
The bridge's ID.

Bridge ID Priority
This is the priority set, and the bridge above is using the default.

Bridge Protocol Data Unit (BPDU)
A multicast frame that is generated by the switch and carries information about itself and changes in the network topology.

bridging address table
A list of MAC addresses. Bridges keep this list and use it when packets are received to determine which segment the destination address is on before sending the packet to the next interface or dropping the packet if it is on the same segment as the sending node.

broadband
A communications strategy that uses analog signaling over multiple communications channels.

Broadband Interexchange Carrier Interconnect (B-ICI)
An interface that is used to connect two ATM carriers.

broadcast
A packet delivery system in which a copy of a packet is given to all hosts attached to the network.

Glossary

broadcast domain

In a nonswitched network, a broadcast domain is all the devices that can receive a broadcast sent on the physical wire from one machine in the network. The broadcast domain is a segment that's not separated by a Layer 2 device or Layer 3 device that can filter broadcasts. On a switched network using VLANs, the broadcast domain is all the ports or collision domains that belong to the same VLAN.

broadcast storm

Occurs when broadcasts throughout the LAN become so numerous that they consume all the available bandwidth on a LAN, slowing the network to a halt.

brouter

A device that combines the benefits of both routers and bridges. Its common usage is to route routable protocols at the Network layer and to bridge nonroutable protocols at the Data Link layer.

brownout

A short-term decrease in the voltage level, usually caused by the startup demands of other electrical devices.

buffer

A storage area to receive/store data while it is waiting to be processed. Buffers are mainly used by devices that receive and store data from faster processing devices, and allow the device to process the data as fast as the processing speeds allow.

bus

A path used by electrical signals to travel between the CPU and the attached hardware.

bus mastering

A method of bus access in which the network interface card (NIC) takes control of the bus to send data through it directly to the system memory, thus bypassing the CPU.

bus topology

A linear LAN architecture that uses a common cable with multipoint connections for the flow of data in a serial progression to all nodes on that network segment.

byte

A set of bits (usually eight) that operates as a unit to signify a single character.

cable modem

A modem that provides Internet access over cable television lines.

campus

A group of buildings in a fixed geographical location, owned and controlled by an organization.

carrier access module (CAM)

A module attaching to the ATM cell switching bus. A CAM can support two port-adapter modules to provide physical ATM line ports used by end nodes. A CAM can be placed in the Cisco Catalyst 5500 in slot 9, 10, 11, or 12; it can be placed in the LS1010 in slot 0, 1, 3, or 4.

Carrier Sense Multiple Access with Collision Avoidance (CSMA/CA)

A media-access method comprising collision-avoidance techniques used in Ethernet.

Carrier Sense Multiple Access with Collision Detection (CSMA/CD)

A media-access method involving collision detection that listens to the network to see if it is in use. If the network is clear, data is transmitted. If a collision occurs, both stations retransmit their data.

Challenge Handshake Authentication Protocol (CHAP)

Protocol used with PPP encapsulation as a security feature that identifies the remote end. After performing CHAP, the router determines if the user is permitted access.

change control
A detailed record that documents every change made to the network.

channel
A communications path used for data transmission.

channelized T1
A link that is separated into 23 B channels and one D channel of 64Kbps each, with the link operating at 1.544Mbps. This link can support DDR, frame relay, and X.25.

channel service unit (CSU)
A network communications device used to connect to the digital equipment lines of the common carrier, usually over a dedicated line or Frame Relay. Used in conjunction with a *data service unit (DSU)*.

checksum
A mathematical method that uses a recalculation method to compare the data sent and received to determine if the destination is receiving the correct amount of data from the source.

circuit emulation services (CES)
A PAM module that allows non-ATM devices utilizing either T1 or E1 interfaces to attach to an ATM switch backplane. This module can be used to connect PBX, video conferencing, and non-ATM routers to the network backbone.

Cisco Connection Online (CCO)
Cisco's Web site that offers device documentation and technical support. It also features new technology and the recent upgrades of device codes.

Cisco Discovery Protocol (CDP)
A Cisco protocol that gathers and stores information regarding other neighboring devices on the network. It can be used in Ethernet, Token Ring, Serial, and FDDI media types. All Cisco devices including hubs support CDP.

Cisco Express Forwarding (CEF)
Cisco's newest ASIC which utilizes the Forwarding Information Base and an adjacency table to route Layer 2 and Layer 3 addresses with very high performance.

Cisco Group Management Protocol (CGMP)
A Cisco protocol used by the Catalyst switch to forward multicast frames intelligently. CGMP dynamically discovers user stations participating in multicast applications. When receiving a multicast, it forwards the multicast directly to the users instead of broadcasting the multicast throughout the network.

CiscoView
A GUI-based management software integrated with SNMP for monitoring and configuration of networking devices. Allows management of devices running an SNMP agent on the device itself to compile data on the device for monitoring purposes.

Class A network
A TCP/IP network that uses addresses starting between 1 and 126 and that supports up to 126 subnets with 16,777,214 unique hosts each.

Class B network
A TCP/IP network that uses addresses starting between 128 and 191 and that supports up to 16,384 subnets with 65,534 unique hosts each.

Class C network
A TCP/IP network that uses addresses starting between 192 and 223 and supports up to 2,097,152 subnets with 254 unique hosts each.

Glossary

Class D network

A TCP/IP network that uses addresses starting between 224 and 240. Typically reserved for experimental uses and not found in production networks.

Class E network

A TCP/IP network that uses addresses starting between 240 and 254. Typically reserved for experimental uses and not found in production networks.

classless interdomain routing (CIDR)

A technique that allows multiple addresses to be consolidated into a single entry.

Clear Header

A field (part of the 802.10 header) that copies the encrypted Protected Header for security purposes to help guarantee against tampering with the frame. Also known as the *Secure Data Exchange (SDE) Protocol Data Unit.*

ClearChannel architecture

The switching architecture found in the Cisco Catalyst Series 1900 and 2820 switches. The architecture comprises the 1Gbps Packet Exchange Bus, Forwarding Engine, Embedded Control Unit, a management interface, and a 3MB shared memory buffer.

client

A node that requests a service from another node on a network.

client/server networking

Networking architecture utilizing front-end demand nodes that request and process data stored by the back end or resource node.

coaxial cable

Commonly referred to as *coax*, this is the standard cable used in cable TV and in older bus topology networks. The cable is made of a solid copper core which is insulated and surrounded by a sheath of braided metal strands and then covered with a thick plastic or rubber covering.

collision

The result of two frames transmitting simultaneously. When these two frames collide in an Ethernet network, both frames are destroyed.

collision domain

All the interfaces on a single segment that can send data on the same physical wire. In a hub, all the interfaces that are connected to its ports are in their own collision domain. In the case of a switch, all the nodes connected to each individual port are in their own collision domain.

color blocking logic (CBL)

A feature of the SAMBA ASIC used to enable the EARL to make forwarding decisions. It also ensures that a tagged frame coming from a particular VLAN does not exit through a port that belongs to another VLAN. CBL also assists in placing ports in one of four different modes for the Spanning Tree Protocol: blocking, learning, listening, or forwarding.

Command-Line Interface (CLI)

Software on Cisco devices that allows you to use commands to configure and control the devices.

common carrier

The supplier of communications utilities, such as phone lines, to the general public.

communication

The transfer of information among nodes on a network.

congestion

A large amount of traffic that exceeds the network's capability to process traffic in a timely manner.

connection-oriented communication

Packet transfer in which the delivery is guaranteed.

connectionless-oriented communication

Packet transfer in which the delivery is not guaranteed.

connectivity

The linking of nodes on a network so communication can take place.

Content Addressable Memory (CAM)

A table used by a bridge to make forwarding and filtering decisions. The CAM table contains MAC addresses with port addresses leading to the physical interfaces. The CAM table uses a specialized interface that is faster than RAM to make the forwarding and filtering decisions. The CAM table updates information by examining the frames it receives from a segment and then updating the table with the source MAC address from the frame.

control plane

Functions that dictate how data actually flows through the switch fabric.

convergence

The amount of time it takes for all routers on the network to update their routing tables.

Copper Distributed Data Interface (CDDI)

The implementation of the FDDI standard using electrical cable rather than optical cable.

core block

The end point for networks, requiring fast access and no policy implementation.

Core layer

In the OSI hierarchical model, the backbone of the network, designed for high-speed data transmission.

cost

The number of hop counts it takes a transmission to reach a destination via a certain path. Routing protocols use cost to determine paths, with the premise being that, the lower the cost, the better the path.

crosstalk

Electronic interference caused when two wires are too close to each other.

cut-through packet switching

A switching method that does not copy the entire packet into the switch buffers. Instead, the destination address is placed in buffers, the route to the destination node is determined, and the packet is quickly sent out the corresponding port. The switch begins forwarding the frame as soon as the first 13 bytes and MAC address are received. It relies on the receiving device to discard the frame if there is corruption. Cut-through packet switching maintains a low latency.

cyclic redundancy check (CRC)

A method that is used to check for errors in packets that have been transferred across a network. A computation bit is added to the packet and recalculated at the destination to determine if the entire packet contents have been transferred correctly.

D channel

The D channel is a 16Kbps (BRI) or 64Kbps (PRI) ISDN channel.

D connectors

Connectors shaped like a *D* that use pins and sockets to establish connections between peripheral devices using serial or parallel ports. The number used in the nomenclature is the number of pins that the connector uses for connectivity. For example, a DB-9 connector has nine pins, and a DB-25 has 25.

Glossary

DAC

A device connected to the FDDI counter-rotating rings. The DAC serves as a hub to provide passive connections to the rings for peripheral devices.

data communications equipment (DCE)

The physical connection to the network that provides clicking between a DTE and a DCE device. DCE is also used in a lab environment with DTE to simulate a WAN environment. Also defined as *data circuit-terminating equipment*.

data field

The field or section in a frame that contains the data.

data plane

Functions applied directly against the actual data being directed in and out of the switching fabric.

Data-Link Connection Identifier (DLCI)

The identifier of virtual circuits used in Frame Relay networks.

Data Link layer

This is Layer 2 of the OSI reference model. The Data Link layer is above the Physical layer. Data comes off the cable, through the Physical layer, and into the Data Link layer.

data service unit (DSU)

Formats and controls data for transmission over digital lines. Used in conjunction with a *channel service unit (CSU)*.

data terminal equipment (DTE)

A physical device at the user end of a user-network interface. These devices serve as a data source, a destination, or both, and include computers, protocol translators, and multiplexers. A DTE combined with a DCE also simulates a WAN environment used in a lab.

datagram

Information groupings that are transmitted as a unit at the Network layer.

DB-9

A connector with nine pins that is used for serial-port or parallel-port connection between PCs and peripheral devices.

DB-25

A connector with 25 pins that is used for serial-port or parallel-port connection between PCs and peripheral devices.

debug

A CLI command that allows for detailed information or a snapshot of certain interfaces or links. This command is used in troubleshooting a problem, not for monitoring.

dedicated line

Generally used in WANs to provide a constant connection between two points.

default gateway

Normally, a router or a multihomed computer to which packets are sent when they are destined for a host which is not on their segment of the network.

demand node

Any end user or interface that requests and accesses network resources, such as servers or printers.

demarc

An established point between the carrier equipment and the customer premise equipment (CPE).

designated bridge

A segment forwarding a frame to the route bridge with the lowest cost.

designated root bridge

The MAC address of the root bridge.

designated root cost

The cost of the shortest path to the root bridge.

designated root port

The port that is chosen as the lowest cost to the root bridge.

designated root priority

The priority of the root bridge. All bridges have a default priority of 32,768.

destination address

The network address where the frame is being sent. In a packet, this address is encapsulated in a field of the packet so that all nodes know where the frame is being sent.

Destination Service Access Point (DSAP)

A one-byte field in the frame that combines with the service access point (SAP) to inform the receiving host of the identity of the destination host.

dial-up line

A circuit that is established by a switched-circuit connection from the telephone company network.

dialed number identification service

The method for delivery of automatic number identification using out-of-band signaling.

diameter

A unit of measurement between the root switch and child switches, calculated from the root bridge. The root bridge counts as the first switch, and each subsequent child switch out from the root bridge is added to produce the diameter number.

dial-up networking

The connection of a remote node to a network using *POTS* or *PSTN*.

digital subscriber line (DSL)

A public network technology that delivers high bandwidth over conventional copper wiring at limited distances.

distance-vector algorithm

An algorithm for finding the shortest path to a destination. The algorithm requires each router to update its neighbors of given hop routes.

distributed switching

An implementation in which switching decisions are made at either the local port or the line module.

Distribution layer

In the hierarchical model, this layer functions as the separation point between the core and Access layers of the network. The devices in the Distribution layer implement the policies that define how packets are to be distributed to the groups within the network.

domain

A logical grouping of interfaces in a network or intranet to identify a controlled network of nodes that are grouped as an administrative unit.

domain name system (DNS)

Used to identify host names that correspond to IP addresses.

dual attached stations (DAS)

A connection that allows a device to connect to both FDDI counter-rotating rings.

dual-homed

A FDDI end station attached to two DACs for redundancy.

dumb terminal

A user station that can access another computer or switch but cannot provide any processing at the local level.

Glossary

Dynamic Host Configuration Protocol (DHCP)

A protocol that provides an IP address to requesting nodes on the network.

Dynamic ISL

A protocol that performs trunking negotiation and verifies that the two connected ports can become trunk links. A Dynamic ISL port can be configured in one of four modes: On, Off, Desirable, or Auto.

dynamic VLAN port

A VLAN number assigned to a certain MAC address. The node attaching to any dynamic port on the switch is a member of the VLAN assigned to the MAC address. Dynamically assigned VLANs are configured with CiscoWorks 2000 or CiscoWorks for Switched Internetworks software.

dynamic window

A mechanism that prevents the sender of data from overwhelming the receiver. The amount of data that can be buffered in a dynamic window can vary. See also *flow control*.

electronically erasable programmable read-only memory (EEPROM)

The memory in a router that can be erased and reprogrammed.

electromagnetic interference (EMI)

External interference from electromagnetic signals, causing reduction of data integrity and increased error rates in a transmission medium.

Electronics Industries Association (EIA)

The group that specifies electrical transmission standards. See also *Telecommunications Industry Association*.

embedded control unit (ECU)

A component of the *ClearChannel architecture* that handles frame switching on the Cisco Catalyst Series 1900 and 2820 switches in software. The ECU consists of an Intel 486 processor, flash memory module, and 512K DRAM. It is also used in initializing the switch, using STP on a per-VLAN basis, controlling the LEDs on the chassis, maintaining RMON statistics, and handling in-band and out-of-band management of the switch.

emulated LAN (ELAN)

A feature used by ATM LANE to perform the basic functionality of a VLAN in Token Ring or Ethernet environments. Like VLANs, ELANs require a route processor such as a router to route frames between ELANs.

encapsulation

A technique used by layered protocols in which a layer adds header information to the *protocol data unit (PDU)* from the layer above.

Encoded Address Recognition Logic (EARL) ASIC

An *ASIC* located on the Catalyst 5000 family of switches that sees all the frames that cross the bus and performs a task similar to that of the content addressable memory (CAM). The ASIC is responsible for making switching decisions based on the MAC address and the source VLAN. It's also responsible for updating the address table.

end-to-end VLAN

A *VLAN* in which users (or groups of users) who utilize a common set of security requirements are grouped independently of the physical location. The port becomes a member of the VLAN assigned to the user, or MAC address of the user's machine. This type of VLAN is beneficial for networks whose resource nodes are not centralized in one common area. Users moving around the campus network remain in the same VLAN.

encryption

The modification of data for security purposes prior to transmission so that it is not readable without the proper decoding method.

Enhanced Interior Gateway Routing Protocol (EIGRP)

A Cisco protocol containing link-state and distance-vector protocols to create a more efficient routing protocol.

Enterprise Services

Services that involve crossing the backbone to achieve access. These services are typically located on a subnet that is separate from the rest of the network devices.

EtherChannel

A connection used on the Catalyst 3000 family or Kalpana switches. It allows as many as seven Ethernet links to be bundled and load-balanced frame by frame to provide up to 140Mps of bandwidth. It can utilize half-duplex or full-duplex links.

ethernet interface processor (EIP)

An interface processor card found in the Cisco 7000 supporting Ethernet, via 10Mbps AUI ports, allowing a path to other interfaces.

EtherTalk

The Macintosh environment product that allows Apple Computer networks to be connected via Ethernet.

Extended Industry Standard Architecture (EISA)

The successor to the ISA standard. Provides a 32-bit bus interface used in PCs.

extended IP access list

An access list that allows the extended filtering of packets based on address, protocol, traffic, or port

extended ping

This option is available in the privileged mode of a router, allowing a defined number of ICMP requests sent to a destination.

Fast EtherChannel

A connection used on the Catalyst 5000 family of switches. It allows as many as seven Ethernet links to be bundled and load-balanced frame by frame to provide up to 800Mbps of bandwidth. It can utilize half-duplex or full-duplex links.

Fast Ethernet

The IEEE 802.3 specification allowing for data transfers of up to 100Mbps. See also *100BaseT*.

fast serial interface processor (FSIP)

An interface processor that provides four to eight high-speed serial ports.

fast switching

An option mechanism to use the route cache to speed packet switching based on prior switching decisions.

fault tolerance

A theoretical concept defined as a resistance to failure. It is not an absolute and can be defined only in degrees.

fiber (or fibre) channel

A technology that defines full gigabit-per-second (Gps) data transfer over fiber-optic cable.

Fiber Distributed Data Interface (FDDI)

A high-speed, data-transfer technology that is designed to extend the capabilities of existing LANs using a dual rotating-ring technology similar to Token Ring.

fiber-optic cable

A physical medium capable of conducting modulated light transmissions. Although compared with other transmission media fiber-optic cable is more expensive, it isn't susceptible to electromagnetic interference and is capable of higher data rates. Also known as *fiber optics* or *optical fiber*.

File Transfer Protocol (FTP)

The set of standards or protocols that allows you to transfer complete files between different computer hosts.

firewall

A device or group of devices configured with access lists and other mechanisms to stop unwanted traffic from entering a specific portion of a network.

flash memory

A type of memory that holds its contents (usually the operating system) when the power is cycled off.

flow control

A method used to control the amount of data that is transmitted within a given period of time. There are different types of flow control. See also *dynamic window* and *static window*.

Forwarding Engine (FE)

A major component of ASIC; part of the ClearChannel architecture on the Cisco Catalyst Series 1900 and 2820 switches. It is responsible for learning addresses, allocating buffer space in the shared memory space, frame queuing, forwarding decisions, and maintaining statistics.

Forwarding Information Based Switching (FIB)

Similar to a routing table or information base, FIB is a mirror image of the routing information contained in the IP routing table. It updates this information and recalculates the next-hop information whenever the network's routing or topology changes. FIB maintains a list of all known routes and eliminates the need for the route cache maintenance that is associated with fast switching or optimum switching. FIB is used with the *CEF ASIC*.

fragment-free switching

A fast packet-switching method that reads the first 64 bytes of the frame to determine if the frame is corrupted. If this first part is intact, the frame is forwarded. Also known as *runtless switching*.

frame

The grouping of information that is transmitted as a unit across the network at the Data Link layer.

Frame Check Sequence

This field performs a cyclic redundancy check (CRC) to ensure that all of the frame's data arrives intact.

frame filtering

This process uses a filtering table to drop frames based on a certain value contained in any one of the many fields in the data frame, such as the source or destination address. As part of normal operations, switches share filter tables. The frame's contents are compared to the filter table in the switch, thereby increasing the latency of the switch. Although frame filtering is useful for VLANs, it is not used in the Cisco Catalyst 5000 or 6000 family of switches to implement VLANs.

Frame Length

In a data frame, this field specifies the length of a frame. The maximum length for an 802.3 frame is 1,518 bytes.

Frame Relay

A switching protocol on the Data Link layer, which is used across multiple virtual circuits of a common carrier, giving the user the appearance of a dedicated line.

frame tagging

A VLAN implementation method used to add VLAN information to data frames. A frame is tagged with VLAN information when it enters the switch, and the frame retains this information through the switch fabric. The tagging is removed before the frame exits the switch port with the attached destination interface. The entire process is transparent to the sending and receiving interfaces.

Frame Type

In a data frame, this field names the protocol that is being sent in the frame.

frequency division multiplexing (FDM)

A technology that divides the output channel into multiple, smaller-bandwidth channels, each using a different frequency range.

full backup

A backup method in which every file on the hard drive is copied and saved.

full duplex

Transmission method in which the sending and receiving (Rx and Tx) channels are separate, thus preventing collisions. Data is transmitted in two directions simultaneously on separate physical wires.

gateway

A hardware and software solution that enables communication between two dissimilar networking systems or protocols. Gateways usually operate at the upper layers of the OSI protocol stack, above the Transport layer.

Get Nearest Server (GNS)

Used on an IPX network, NetWare-enabled devices send a request packet to locate the nearest active server of a given type. GNS is part of IPX and SAP.

gigabit (Gb)

One billion bits or one thousand megabits.

Gigabit Ethernet

The IEEE specification for transfer rates up to one gigabit per second. See also *1000BaseX.*

guaranteed flow control

A method of flow control in which the sending and receiving hosts agree upon a rate of data transmission. After a rate is agreed upon, the communication takes place at the guaranteed rate until the sender is finished. No buffering takes place at the receiver.

half duplex

A circuit designed for data transmission in both directions, but not simultaneously.

head-of-line blocking

A situation in which congestion on an outbound port limits throughput to uncongested ports. Head-of-line blocking is completely different from *oversubscription,* in that physical data from another source device blocks the data of the sending device.

high-level data link compression (HDLC)

A Layer 2 serial encapsulation method that is used by PPP to transfer data over serial point-to-point links. HDLC is a bit-oriented protocol that uses frames and checksums to transfer the data.

High-Speed Serial Interface (HSSI)

The network standard for high-speed serial communications over WAN links. It includes Frame Relay, T1, T3, E1, and ISDN.

Glossary

hop

A recorded movement between two network nodes.

host

Any system on a network. In the Unix world, any device that is assigned an IP address.

host ID

A unique identifier for a client or resource on a network.

hostname

The NetBIOS name of the computer or node, given to the first element of the Internet domain name. It must be unique on your network.

Hot Standby Routing Protocol (HSRP)

A Cisco protocol that provides redundancy. Should a link fail, another can be configured to take its place.

hub

A hardware device that connects multiple independent nodes. Also known as a *concentrator* or *multiport repeater*.

Hypertext Transfer Protocol (HTTP)

The protocol used by Web browsers to transfer pages and files from a remote node to your computer.

IEEE

See *Institute of Electrical and Electronics Engineers*.

IEEE 802.1

The standard that defines the OSI model's physical and Data Link layers. This standard allows two IEEE LAN stations to communicate over a LAN or WAN and is often referred to as the *internetworking standard*. It also includes the *Spanning Tree Algorithm* specifications.

IEEE 802.2

The standard that defines the Logical Link Control (LLC) sublayer for the entire series of protocols covered by the 802.x standards. This standard specifies the adding of header fields, which tell the receiving host which upper layer sent the information. It also defines specifications for the implementation of the LLC sublayer of the Data Link layer.

IEEE 802.3

The standard that specifies Physical-layer attributes—such as signaling types, data rates, and topologies—and the media-access method used. It also defines specifications for the implementation of the Physical layer and the MAC sublayer of the Data Link layer, using CSMA/CD. This standard also includes the original specifications for *Fast Ethernet*.

IEEE 802.4

The standard that defines how production machines should communicate and establishes a common protocol for use in connecting these machines. It also defines specifications for the implementation of the Physical layer and the MAC sublayer of the Data Link layer using Token Ring access over a *bus topology*.

IEEE 802.5

Although this standard is often used to define Token Ring, it does not specify a particular topology or transmission medium. It provides specifications for the implementation of the Physical layer and the MAC sublayer of the Data Link Layer using a token-passing media-access method over a *ring topology*.

IEEE 802.6

The standard that defines the distributed queue dual bus (DQDB) technology to transfer high-speed data between nodes. It provides specifications for the implementation of metropolitan area networks (MANs).

IEEE 802.7

The standard that defines the design, installation, and testing of broadband-based communications and related physical media connectivity.

IEEE 802.8

The standard that defines the Fiber Optic Technical Advisory Group, which advises the other 802-standard committees on various fiber-optic technologies and standards.

IEEE 802.9

The standard that defines the integration of voice and data transmissions using isochronous Ethernet (IsoEnet).

IEEE 802.10

Another Cisco-adopted protocol, used primarily to transport VLAN information over Fiber Distributed Data Interface (FDDI). This protocol is primarily used in FDDI backbones to transport VLAN information and data.

IEEE 802.11HR

The standard that defines the implementation of wireless technologies, such as infrared and spread-spectrum radio. The HR defines faster technology up to 11Mbps.

IEEE 802.12

The standard that defines 100BaseVG/ AnyLAN, which uses a 1000Mbps signaling rate and a special media-access method allowing 100Mbps data traffic over voice-grade cable.

IEEE 802.1Q

The IEEE 802.1Q standard protocol for inserting a frame tag VLAN identifier in the frame header. As a frame enters the switch fabric, it is tagged with additional information regarding the VLAN properties. This tag remains in the frame as it is forwarded between switches and is removed prior to exiting the access link to the destination interface. This process is completely transparent to the user.

Industry Standards Architecture (ISA)

The standard of the older, more common 8- and 16-bit bus and card architectures.

input/output (I/O)

Any operation in which data either enters a node or is sent out of a node.

Institute of Electrical and Electronics Engineers (IEEE)

A professional organization that develops standards for networking and communications.

Integrated Local Management Interface (ILMI)

A protocol created by the ATM forum to allow any ATM switch and ATM device to communicate using the Simple Network Management Protocol (SNMP).

Integrated Services Digital Network (ISDN)

An internationally adopted standard for end-to-end digital communications over Public Switched Telephone Network (PSTN) that permits telephone networks to carry data, voice, and other source traffic.

intelligent hubs

Hubs that contain some management or monitoring capability.

Interior Gateway Routing Protocol (IGRP)

A Cisco protocol using a distance-vector algorithm to calculate the best path using the factors of load, bandwidth, delay, and reliability.

interface

A device, such as a card or a plug, that connects pieces of hardware with the computer so that information can be moved from place to place (such as between computers and printers, hard disks, and other devices, or between two or more nodes on a network).

internal IPX address

A unique eight-digit number that is used to identify a server. This address is usually generated at random when the server is installed.

internal loopback address

Used for testing with TCP/IP. This address—127.0.0.1—allows a test packet to reflect back into the sending adapter to determine if it is functioning properly.

International Standards Organization (ISO)

A voluntary organization, founded in 1946, which is responsible for creating international standards in many areas, including communications and computers.

Internet Assigned Numbers Authority (IANA)

The organization which is responsible for Internet protocol addresses, domain names, and protocol parameters.

Internet Control Message Protocol (ICMP)

The Network-layer Internet protocol, documented in RFC 792, that reports errors and provides other information relevant to IP packet processing.

Internet Engineering Task Force (IETF)

A group of research volunteers responsible for specifying the protocols used on the Internet and for specifying the architecture of the Internet.

Internet Group Management Protocol (IGMP)

The protocol responsible for managing and reporting IP multicast group memberships.

Internet layer

In the TCP/IP architectural model, this layer is responsible for the addressing, packaging, and routing functions. Protocols operating at this layer of the model are responsible for encapsulating packets into Internet datagrams. All necessary routing algorithms are run here.

Internet Network Information Center (InterNIC)

The group that provides Internet services such as domain registration and information and directory and database services.

Internet Protocol (IP)

The Network-layer protocol, documented in RFC 791, that offers a connectionless internetwork service. IP provides features for addressing, packet fragmentation and reassembly, type-of-service specification, and security.

Internet Research Task Force (IRTF)

The research arm of the *Internet Architecture Board*. This group performs research in areas of Internet protocols, applications, architecture, and technology.

internetwork

A group of networks that are connected by routers or other connectivity devices so that the networks function as one network.

Internetwork Operating System

Cisco's proprietary operating system used in its routers and switches.

Internetwork Packet Exchange (IPX)

The Network-layer protocol generally used by Novell's NetWare network operating system. IPX provides connectionless communication, supporting packet up to 64K in size.

Internetwork Packet Exchange/Sequenced Packet Exchange (IPX/SPX)

This protocol is the default used in NetWare networks, and it is a combination of the IPX protocol (to provide addressing) and SPX (to provide guaranteed delivery for IPX). It's similar in nature to its counterpart, TCP/IP.

Inter-Switch Link (ISL)

A special Cisco proprietary Ethernet protocol that assigns a 26-byte header to an encapsulated frame and a four-byte checksum, sometimes referred to as the *FCS* or the *CRC*.

IPSec

A protocol designed for virtual private networks (VPNs). Used to provide strong security standards for encryption and authentication.

IPX address

The unique address that identifies a node in the network.

kilobit (Kb)

One thousand bits.

kilobyte (K)

One thousand bytes.

LAN Emulation (LANE)

A standard created by the ATM forum to govern the connections of ATM endstations to either Ethernet or Token Ring devices.

LAN Module ASIC (LMA)

An ASIC part of the Cisco Catalyst 3000 Series switch that provides frame buffering, address learning, bus arbitration, and switching decisions for Ethernet ports.

latency

The time used to forward a packet in and out of a device. Commonly used in reference to routing and switching.

Layer 2 Forwarding Protocol (L2F)

A dial-up VPN protocol designed to work in conjunction with PPP to support authentication standards, such as TACACS+ and RADIUS, for secure transmissions over the Internet.

Layer 2 Tunneling Protocol (L2TP)

A dial-up VPN protocol that defines its own tunneling protocol and works with the advanced security methods of IPSec. L2TP allows PPP sessions to be tunneled across an arbitrary medium to a home gateway at an ISP or corporation.

learning bridge

A bridge that builds its own bridging address table rather than requiring you to enter information manually. Also known as a *smart bridge*.

line module communication processor (LCP)

Located on each line module, the LCP is responsible for providing communications for the MCP located on the supervisor engine.

Link Accessed Procedure Balanced (LAPB)

This is a bit-oriented, Data Link layer protocol for the X.25 protocol stack. It is a derivative of HDLC.

Link Access Procedure on the D Channel (LAPD)

A Data Link layer protocol for ISDN which is used specifically for the D channel on ISDN. LAPD was created from LAPB for signaling requirements of ISDN.

link-state routing algorithm

An algorithm that waits for each router to broadcast its location and the cost of reaching the router and its neighbors.

local-area network (LAN)

A group of connected computers that are located in a geographic area—usually a building or campus—and that share data and services.

Glossary

local broadcast

A broadcast on the local network, looking for the IP address of the destination host.

local services

Local services describes the scenario in which the device that is supplying the services resides on the same subnet as the device that is requesting them.

local target logic (LTL)

A feature of some line modules that assists the EARL in making forwarding decisions.

local VLAN

Beneficial for networks whose resources are centralized and in one geographical location. The VLAN can span one switch or many switches within the same floor or building.

logical addressing scheme

The addressing method used in providing manually assigned node addressing.

Logical Link Control (LLC)

A sublayer of the Data Link layer of the OSI reference model that provides an interface for the Network-layer protocols and the Media Access Control (MAC) sublayer, which is also part of the Data Link layer.

loop

A continuous circle through a series of nodes in a network that a packet travels until it eventually times out. Without a protocol such as STP to detect loops, the data could continuously circle the network if no life cycle is assigned to the packet.

loopback plug

A device used for loopback testing.

loopback testing

A troubleshooting method in which the output and input wires are crossed or shorted in a manner that allows all outgoing data to be routed back into the card.

management

Fault, capacity, accounting, performance, and security control for a network.

Management Information Base (MIB)

A MIB running on a device gathers information from the device and sends it to a central location using SNMP management software.

master communication processor (MCP)

A feature of the supervisor engine that takes commands from the network management processor (NCP) and forwards them to the correct line module communication processor (LCP). MCP is also responsible for testing, configuring, and controlling the local ports using LTL and CBL. It also performs diagnostics on the memory, SAINT ASICs, LTL, and CBL. MCP is also responsible for downloading software to the line modules.

Media Access Control (MAC) address

A six-octet number that uniquely identifies a host on a network. It is a unique number that is burned into the network interface card, so it cannot be changed.

Media Access Control (MAC) layer

In the OSI model, the lower of the two sublayers of the Data Link layer. Defined by the IEEE as responsible for interaction with the Physical layer.

media access unit (MAU)

The IEEE 802.3 specification that refers to a transceiver. Not to be confused with a Token Ring MAU (multistation access unit), which is sometimes abbreviated *MSAU*.

megabit (Mb or Mbit)

One million bits. This term is used to rate transmission transfer speeds (not to be confused with *megabyte*).

megabyte (MB)

One million bytes. This term is usually used to refer to file size.

message

A portion of information that is sent from one node to another. Messages are created at the upper layers of the OSI reference model.

microsegmentation

The process of using switches to divide a network into smaller segments.

microwaves

Very short radio waves used to transmit data over 890MHz.

modem

A device used to modulate and demodulate the signals that pass through it. It converts the direct current pulses of the serial digital code from the controller into the analog signal that is compatible with the telephone network.

multicast

A single-packet transmission from one sender to a specific group of destination nodes.

multilayer switches

A combination of Layer 2, 3, and 4 switches that use the concept of route once, switch many.

multiprocessor

Support for multiple processors in a single machine.

Multiprotocol over ATM (MPOA)

An ATM forum standard that includes enhancements to LANE and adds Layer 3 switching capabilities to ATM switches.

multistation access unit (MAU or MSAU)

A concentrator or hub used in a Token Ring network. It organizes the connected nodes into an internal ring and uses the RI (ring in) and RO (ring out) connectors to expand to other MAUs on the network.

netflow switching

A feature incorporated into the MSM, NFFC, and NFFC II that was originally instituted and developed for Cisco's Enterprise Routers. NetFlow allows for transparent switching in hardware while incorporating Quality of Service (QoS) features including security, multicast forwarding, multilayer switching, NetFlow data exporting, and packet filtering at Layer 3 and Layer 4 application ports.

NetWare Core Protocol (NCP)

The NetWare protocol that provides a method for hosts to make calls to a NetWare server for services and network resources.

netware loadable module (NLM)

A service or process running on a NetWare server.

network address translation (NAT)

An algorithm to allow translation of a network address from one network to a foreign network so it can be used on the foreign network.

network analyzer

A device, also called a *protocol analyzer*, that collects and analyzes data to see a particular protocol or address packet to aid in troubleshooting.

network down

Describes the situation in which the clients are unable to use the network. This can be administrative, scheduled downtime for upgrades or maintenance, or it can be the result of a serious error.

Glossary

Network Driver Interface Specification (NDIS)

A Microsoft-proprietary specification or standard for a protocol-independent device driver. These drivers allow the NIC to bind multiple protocols to the same NIC, allowing the card to be used by multiple operating systems. Similar to *Open Data-Link Interface (ODI)*.

network ID

The part of the TCP/IP address that specifies the network portion of the IP address. It is determined by the class of the address, which is determined by the subnet mask used.

network interface card (NIC)

The hardware component that serves as the interface, or connecting component, between your network and the node. It has a transceiver, a MAC address, and a physical connector for the network cable. Also known as a *network adapter*.

Network Interface layer

The bottom layer of the TCP/IP architectural model, it's responsible for sending and receiving frames.

Network layer

The third layer of the OSI reference model, where routing based on node addresses (IP or IPX addresses) occurs.

network management processor (NMP)

A feature of the Catalyst supervisor engine that is responsible for general control and some management functions of the switch. It is responsible for executing the system's configuration changes, the CLI, and running diagnostics on boot components as well as new additional components.

Network Management Systems (NMS)

A complete package of hardware and software for monitoring a network and gathering information such as performance and security.

network monitor

A software-based tool that monitors a network using SNMP or ICMP to gather statistical data and to determine a baseline.

Network Time Protocol (NTP)

A protocol that allows all network equipment to synchronize the date and time on the private or internetwork environment.

network-to-network interface (NNI)

An interface that provides connectivity between two ATM switches.

nonblocking

A condition in which the fabric contains more bandwidth than the sum total of all the ports' bandwidth combined.

nonvolatile RAM (NVRAM)

Static memory similar to that of the flash. Memory stored in NVRAM does not get lost when the power is turned off. On a switch, the NVRAM stores the VLAN configuration, system configuration, SNMP parameters, STP configuration, and configuration of each port.

Novell Directory Services (NDS)

The user, group, and security information database of network resources that is used in a NetWare 4.x and/or NetWare 5.x internetwork.

Open Shortest Path First (OSPF)

A link-state protocol that uses factors such as load balancing and least-cost routing to determine the shortest path.

Open Systems Interconnection (OSI) Model

A seven-layer model created by the ISO to standardize and explain the interactions of networking protocols.

optical time domain reflector (OTDR)
An advanced cable tester that analyzes fiber by sending pulses.

oversubscription
A condition in which the total bandwidth of the ports is greater than the capacity of the switching fabric. Also referred to as a *blocking architecture*.

Packet Internet Groper (PING)
A TCP/IP protocol-stack utility that works with the Internet Control Message Protocol to test connectivity to other systems by using an echo request and reply.

password
A set of characters that is used with a username to authenticate a user on the network and to provide the user with rights and permissions to files and resources.

patch panel
A device wherein the wiring used in coaxial or twisted-pair networks converges in a central location and is then connected to the back of the panel.

peer-to-peer networking
A network environment without dedicated servers, where communication occurs between similarly capable network nodes that act as both client and server.

permanent virtual circuit (PVC)
A logical path established in packet-switching networks between two locations. Similar to a dedicated leased line. Also known as a *permanent virtual connection* in ATM terminology (but not to be confused with *private virtual circuit*, which is also known as a *PVC*.)

permissions
The authorization that is provided to users, allowing them to access objects on the network. The network administrators generally assign permissions. Slightly different from—but often used interchangeably with—the term *rights*.

physical addressing scheme
Refers to the MAC address on every network card manufactured.

Physical layer
The bottom layer (Layer 1) of the OSI reference model, where all physical connectivity is defined.

plain old telephone system (POTS)
The current analog public telephone system. Also known as the *PSTN*.

plug-and-play
Architecture designed to allow hardware devices to be detected by the operating system and for the driver to be automatically loaded.

Point-To-Point Protocol (PPP)
A common dial-up networking protocol that includes provisions for security and protocol negotiation and provides host-to-network and switch-to-switch connections for one or more user sessions. PPP is the common modem connection used for Internet dial-up.

Point-To-Point Tunneling Protocol (PPTP)
A protocol that encapsulates private network data in IP packets. These packets are transmitted over synchronous and asynchronous circuits to hide the underlying routing and switching infrastructure of the Internet from both senders and receivers.

polling
The media-access method for transmitting data, in which a controlling device is used to contact each node to determine if it has data to send.

Glossary

port adapter modules

Modules attached to the carrier access modules on the LS1010 ATM and Catalyst 5500 Series ATM bus that provide physical ATM line ports for the user stations.

Port Aggregation Protocol (PAgP)

Manages the Fast EtherChannel bundles and aids in the automatic creation of Fast EtherChannel links.

PortFast

A protocol that forces an STP port to enter the forwarding state immediately after startup for a single workstation or server connected to a switch port.

power-on self-test (POST)

A series of tests that automatically run on a Cisco Catalyst switch when the power is turned on. The POST tests the hardware, memory, processors, ports, and ASICs to verify that they are functioning properly.

Presentation layer

Layer 6 of the OSI reference model. Prepares information to be used by the Application layer.

primary rate interface (PRI)

A higher-level network interface standard for use with ISDN. Defined at the rate of 1.544Mbps, it consists of a single 64Kbps D channel plus 23 (T1) or 30 (E1) B channels for voice or data.

priority queuing

A priority-based configuration that allows certain types of traffic to be routed before others based upon the level of priority configured for that type of traffic. You can configure a priority based on the particular traffic type, packet size, protocol, or interface.

private virtual circuit (PVC)

A logical connection between locations through a Frame Relay and ATM cloud.

When a company has three branch offices and each location physically connects through a series of switches to the network cloud of the Frame Relay provider, it appears to the users as if the three branch offices were directly connected to the local network. (Not to be confused with *permanent virtual circuit*, which is also known as *PVC*.)

proprietary

A standard or specification that is created by a manufacturer, vendor, or other private enterprise and is not always a recognized standard.

Proprietary Fat Pipe ASIC (PFPA)

An ASIC utilized on the Catalyst 3000 Series switches that use non–10BaseT ports such as Fast Ethernet, 100VG/AnyLAN, ATM, or the Stackport of the Stack Port Matrix. The PFPA is functionally the same as the LMA.

protocol

A set of rules that govern network communications among networks, computers, peripherals, and operating systems.

protocol analyzer

A device that collects and analyzes data to see a particular protocol or address packet to aid in troubleshooting. Also called a *network analyzer*.

Protocol Identification

In a frame, this five-byte field identifies and communicates to the destination node the protocol that is being used in the data transmission.

protocol stack

Two or more protocols that work together (such as TCP and IP, or IPX and SPX). Also known as a *protocol suite*.

public switched telephone network (PSTN)

All the telephone networks and services in the world. The same as POTS, PSTN refers to the world's collection of interconnected public telephone networks that are either commercial or government owned. PSTN is a digital network, with the exception of the connection between local exchanges and customers, which remains analog.

q.921

Resides on the D channel of ISDN as a Layer 2 protocol to provide protocol connectivity from the central office switch to the router.

q.931

Resides on ISDN as a Layer 3 protocol to provide a snapshot of messages of ISDN connections.

quality of service (QoS)

A guarantee of a particular level of service for a connection. QoS uses queuing and other methods to guarantee that bandwidth is available for a certain protocol, application, or address. QoS is important for implementing applications such as voice and video.

queuing

A method of providing QoS by the use of buffering and priority control mechanisms to control data congestion on the network.

read/writes

The counting of packets on the ingress (read) as well as the egress (write) from the switching fabric.

redistribution

Allowing a protocol to be integrated in a network using a different protocol.

resource node

Any interface on the network that provides a service for a demand node. Resource nodes can be such things as servers and printers. Incorrect placement of your resource nodes can have terrible effects on your network.

Remote Network Monitoring (RMON)

An Internet Engineering Task Force (IETF) standard that defines how devices gather and share the network monitoring information which is sent to an SNMP Management Station. RMON gather Layer 2 information concerning bandwidth use, collisions, and errors. Catalyst switches can gather four of the nine different information types: statistics, history, alarms, and event. The other five groups can be monitored using a SPAN port and an attached protocol analyzer or probe.

remote node

A node or computer that is connected to the network through a dial-up connection. Dialing in to the Internet from home is a perfect and common example of the concept.

remote services

Services in which the device that supplies the services resides on a separate subnet from the device that requests the services.

repeater

A device that regenerates and retransmits the signal on a network. Generally used to strengthen signals going long distances.

Request for Comments (RFC)

The method used to post documents regarding networking or Internet-related standards or ideas. Some RFCs are adopted and accepted by the Internet Architecture Board as standards.

resource node

An interface on the network that provides a service for a demand node. Resource nodes

Glossary

can be items such as servers and printers. The incorrect placement of your resource nodes can also have terrible effects on your network.

Reverse Address Resolution Protocol (RARP)

The protocol that allows a MAC address to be mapped or correlated to identify the IP address of the device. Opposite of ARP.

rights

Authorization provided to users, allowing them to perform certain tasks. The network administrators generally assign rights. Slightly different from—but often used interchangeably with—the term *permissions*.

ring in (RI)

A connector used in an IBM Token Ring network on a multistation access unit (MAU) to expand to other MAUs on the network. Counterpart to the RO (ring out), the RI connector on the MAU connects to the media to accept the token from the ring.

ring topology

A network structure that is physically and logically organized in a ring formation with devices connected to the ring.

ring out (RO)

A connector used in an IBM Token Ring network on a multistation access unit (MAU) to expand to other MAUs on the network. A counterpart to the RI (ring in), the RO connector on the MAU connects to the media to send the token out to the ring.

RJ-11 connector

The typical connector used with telephone systems, having either four or six conductors. A red/green pair of wires is used for voice and data, and a black/white pair is used for low-voltage signals.

RJ-45 connector

An Ethernet cable connector used with twisted-pair cable, which can support eight conductors for four pairs of wires.

root timers

These are the timers received from the root bridge.

Routing Information Field (RIF)

A field on Source Route Bridge Token Ring frames that contains information regarding the rings and bridges that the frame must travel to the destination interface.

Routing Information Protocol (RIP)

Protocol that uses hop counts as a routing metric to control the direction and flow of packets between routers and switches on an internetwork.

runtless switching

A switching method in which the switch reads the first 64 bytes to verify that there is no corruption of the packet. If the packet is corrupted, a preset maximum of errors changes the switching type from cut-through switching to store-and-forward switching. Also known as *fragment-free switching*.

Secure Data Exchange (SDE) Protocol Data Unit

A field (part of the 802.10 header) that copies the encrypted Protected Header for security purposes to help guarantee against tampering with the frame. Also known as the *Clear Header*.

Security Association Identifier (SAID)

One of the three values that make up a Clear Header on the FDDI frame type. It is used for security for the Clear Header, which contains a SAID, LSAP, and the Management Defined Field (MDF).

Sequenced Packet Exchange (SPX)
Protocol used in conjunction with IPX when connection-oriented delivery is required. It is used mainly in NetWare network environments.

server
A resource node that fulfills service requests for demand nodes. Usually referred to by the type of service it performs, such as file server, email server, or print server.

service access point (SAP)
A field in a frame that instructs the receiving host which protocol the frame is intended for.

Service Advertising Protocol (SAP)
NetWare protocol used on an IPX network. SAP maintains server information tables, listing each service that has been advertised to it, and provides this information to any nodes attempting to locate a service.

Service Advertising Protocol agent (SAP agent)
Router or other node on an IPX network that maintains a server information table. Such a table lists each service that has been advertised to it and provides this information to any nodes that are attempting to locate a service.

Service Profile Identifier (SPID)
This number is assigned by the service provider and network administrators and identifies a BRI port and services provided to the number. Although ISDN uses SPIDS in North America to access the service provider, it is optional in other areas.

Session
The dialog that exists between two computers.

Session layer
This fifth layer of the OSI reference model establishes, manages, and terminates sessions between applications on different nodes.

shared systems
The infrastructure component routed directly into the backbone of an internetwork for optimal systems access. Provides connectivity to servers and other shared systems.

shielded twisted pair (STP)
Twisted-pair network cable that uses shielding to insulate the cable from electromagnetic interference.

Simple Network Management Protocol (SNMP)
A protocol used in TCP/IP networks to provide network devices with a method to monitor and control network devices. It is used to manage configurations, statistics collection, performance, and security, and to report network management information to a management console that is a member of the same community.

Simple Network Management Protocol (SNMP) trap
An SNMP protocol utility that sends out an alarm in an identified community, notifying its members that some network activity differs from the established threshold, as defined by the administrator.

Simple Server Redundancy Protocol (SSRP)
A Cisco protocol that provides redundancy for all LANE server components.

single attached station (SAS)
A FDDI device that has a single connection to a single DAC.

smart bridge
A bridge that builds its own bridging address table, thus not requiring any manual configuration or intervention. Also known as a *learning bridge*.

Glossary

socket

A logical interprocess communications mechanism through which a program communicates with another program or with a network.

socket identifier

An eight-bit number that is used to identify the socket. Developers and designers of services and protocols usually assign socket identifiers. Also known as a *socket number*.

source address

The address of the host who sent the frame. The source address is contained in the frame so that the destination node knows who sent the data.

source route bridging (SRB)

A type of bridging that is used to segment Token Ring networks. Requires all rings and bridges to have a unique number.

source route switching (SRS)

A type of bridging that combines SRB and SRT. Developed to allow more physical rings on the network. It allows for increasing bandwidth needs while preserving the benefits of SRB.

source route translational bridging (SR/TLB)

A type of bridging that bridges a Token Ring segment to another physical media type such as Ethernet or FDDI. It is transparent to the source and destination interfaces.

source route transparent bridging (SRT)

A type of bridging that combines SRB and TB. Using SRT, the bridge places a RIF into a frame traveling from the TB to the SRB side. It then strips the RIF when the frame travels from the SRB port to the TB port.

Source Service Access Point (SSAP)

A one-byte field in the frame that combines with the SAP to tell the receiving host the identity of the source or sending host.

Spanning Tree Algorithm (STA)

Defined by IEEE 802.1 as part of the Spanning Tree Protocol to eliminate loops in an internetwork with multiple paths. The Spanning Tree Algorithm is responsible for performing Spanning Tree Protocol topology recalculations when a switch is powered up and when a topology change occurs.

Spanning Tree Protocol (STP)

Defined by IEEE 802.1, STP was developed to eliminate the loops caused by the multiple paths in an internetwork. STP communicates topology changes from switch to switch with the use of bridge protocol data units (BPDUs). See also *color blocking logic*.

split-horizon

Routing mechanism that inquires about routes to prevent information from using the same interface through which the information was received, therefore preventing a loop.

standard IP access list

An access list that only filters based on the source address.

star topology

A logical network topology with end points that join at a common area using point-to-point links.

static IP addresses

IP addresses that are assigned to each network device individually. Often referred to as *hard-coded*.

static VLAN port

A port on a switch manually assigned a VLAN number. Any node or interface connected to the port automatically becomes a member of the assigned VLAN.

static window

A mechanism used in flow control to prevents a data sender from overwhelming the receiver. Only a set amount of data can be buffered in a static window. See also *flow control*.

station IPX address

A 12-digit number that is used to uniquely identify each device on an IPX network.

storage area network

A subnetwork of storage devices, usually found on high-speed networks and shared by all servers on the network.

store-and-forward

A fast packet-switching method that produces a higher latency than other switching methods, because the switch waits for the entire packet to arrive before checking the CRC. It then forwards or discards the packet.

StreetTalk

A global naming service created by Banyan and included with the Banyan VINES network operating system.

subinterface

A virtual interface that can be configured on an interface.

subnet mask

A 32-bit address that is used to mask or screen a portion of the IP address to differentiate the part of the address that designates the network from the part that designates the host.

subnetting

The process of dividing your assigned IP address range into smaller clusters of hosts.

Subnetwork Access Protocol (SNAP)

An Internet protocol that specifies a standard method of encapsulating IP datagrams and ARP messages on a network.

supernetting

Aggregating IP network addresses and advertising them as a single classless network address.

switch

A Layer 2 networking device that forwards frames based on destination addresses.

switch block

Switching devices located in wiring closets, requiring high-speed uplinks and redundancy.

Switched Multimegabit Data Service (SMDS)

Defined by IEEE 802.6, SMDS is the Physical-layer implementation for data transmission over public lines at speeds between 1.544Mbps (T1) and 44.736Mbps (T3) using cell relay and fixed-length cells.

switched port analyzer (SPAN)

A port at which traffic from another port or group of ports is attached to a protocol analyzer or probe device. The SPAN aids in the diagnoses of problems that are related to traffic patterns on the network.

switched virtual circuit

A virtual circuit that is established dynamically on demand to form a dedicated link and is then broken when transmission is complete. Also known as a *switched virtual connection* in ATM terminology.

Glossary

switching fabric

A term used to describe the "highway" that the data travels to get from the input port on a switch to the output port.

Synchronous Data Link Control (SDLC)

A bit-oriented serial protocol for the Data Link layer of SNA. SDLC created the basics for HDLC and LAPB protocols.

synchronous transmission

A digital signal transmission method that uses a precise clocking method and a predefined number of bits sent at a constant rate.

syslog

Messages sent to a remote machine regarding the switch system configuration, such as software and configuration changes.

T1

Digital WAN carrier facility that transmits DS-1-formatted data at 1.544Mbps through the telephone switching network, using AMI or B8ZS coding.

T3

Digital WAN carrier facility that transmits DS-3 formatted data at 44.763Mbps.

TACACS+

A security feature that uses an MD5 encrypted algorithm to enforce strict authentication controls. It requires both a user name and a password, thus allowing administrators to better track network usage and changes based on user accounts.

TCP/IP

See *Transmission Control Protocol/Internet Protocol.*

Telecommunications Industry Association (TIA)

An organization that develops standards with the *EIA (Electronics Industries Association)* for telecommunications technologies.

Telnet

Standard terminal-emulation protocol in the TCP/IP protocol stack. Telnet is used to perform terminal emulation over TCP/IP via remote terminal connections, enabling users to log in to remote systems and use their resources as if the users were locally on that system.

thicknet coax

Thick cable most commonly found in the backbone of a coaxial network. Usually approximately 0.375 inches in diameter.

thinnet coax

Thinner than thicknet. Approximately 0.25 inches in diameter, it is commonly used in older bus topologies to connect the nodes to the network.

time domain reflectors (TDRs)

An advanced cable tester that can isolate a cable fault within a few feet of the actual problem on the wire.

time-to-live (TTL)

Indicator of how long a packet remains alive on the network.

token

A frame that provides controlling information. In a Token Ring network, the node that possesses the token is the one that is allowed to transmit next.

Token Ring

An IBM proprietary, token-passing, LAN topology defined by the IEEE 802.5 standard. Token Ring operates at either at 4Mbps or 16Mbps in a star topology.

Token Ring adapters

Traditional ISA or Microchannel devices with 4Mbps or 16Mbps transfer capability, used to connect nodes to a Token Ring network.

topology

The shape or layout of a physical network and the flow of data through the network.

trace

Also referred to as *traceroute*. A reporting method to track the path of a packet from a source to a destination.

Transmission Control Protocol (TCP)

Part of the TCP/IP protocol stack. A connection-oriented, reliable, data-transmission communication service that operates at the OSI Transport layer.

Transmission Control Protocol/Internet Protocol (TCP/IP)

The suite of protocols combining TCP and IP, developed to support the construction of worldwide internetworks. See also *Transmission Control Protocol* and *Internet Protocol*.

Transmission Control Protocol/Internet Protocol (TCP/IP) socket

A *socket*, or connection to an endpoint, that is used in TCP/IP communication transmissions.

transmit

The process of sending data using light, electronic, or electric signals. In networking, this is usually done in the form of digital signals that are composed of bits.

Transparent Bridging (TB)

A bridging type that uses the MAC address to make forwarding and filtering decisions transparent to the sender and receiver interfaces. Used in Ethernet.

Transport layer

Layer 4 of the OSI reference model. Controls the flow of information.

Trivial File Transfer Protocol (TFTP)

A simplified version of FTP that allows files to be transferred over a network from one computer to another. Also used to install the Cisco IOS on an IOS-based switch, router, or GSR.

troubleshooting model

A series of guidelines to follow to aid in the troubleshooting process to resolve network issues.

trunk link

A special type of VLAN connections. Unlike a user port, trunk links expect the device at the other end of the connection to understand the inserted frame tags. Standard Ethernet and Token Ring cards do not understand frame tags.

twisted pair

A type of cable that uses multiple twisted pairs of copper wire.

unicast

A frame in which the destination MAC address specifies the single computer of destination. Summarized as direct network traffic between two individual nodes.

unshielded twisted pair (UTP)

A type of cable that uses multiple twisted pairs of copper wire in a casing that does not provide much protection from EMI. UTP is rated in five categories and is the most common cable in Ethernet networks.

UplinkFast

Provides fast convergence after a STP topology change and achieves load balancing between redundant links.

User Datagram Protocol (UDP)

Operating at the Transport layer of the OSI model, this communications protocol provides connectionless and unreliable communications services. It requires a transmission protocol such as IP to guide it to the destination host.

Glossary

user-to-network interface (UNI)

An interface that provides a connection between an ATM end-station interface and an ATM switch interface.

virtual interface processor (VIP)

An interface card that allows the use of IOS and multilayer switching.

virtual LAN (VLAN)

Allows a network administrator to divide a bridged network into several broadcast domains. Each VLAN is considered its own separate subnet, and Layer 3 routing is still required to route between VLANs. VLANs can be based on the port identifier of the switch, the MAC address, Layer 3 addressing, directory information, or application information. VLANs can be implemented on different media types such as Ethernet, FDDI, Token Ring, or ATM. The benefits of VLANs are limited broadcast domains, added security, and redundancy.

virtual private network (VPN)

A network that uses a public network (such as the Internet) as a backbone to connect two or more private networks. VPN provides users with the equivalent of a private network in terms of security.

VLAN Trunking Protocol (VTP)

A protocol used to enhance and configure the extension of broadcast domains across multiple switches. VTP dynamically reports the addition of VLANs throughout the switched network, thus creating a consistent switched network.

VLAN Trunking Protocol (VTP) pruning

A protocol used to reduce the number of switches participating in VTP by removing switches from the database that do not have certain VLANs assigned to numbered ports. For example, if switch 1 and switch 2 have ports belonging to VLAN 6 and switch 3 does not, switch 2 won't forward VLAN 6 traffic on the trunk link to switch 3 unless switch 3 is a gateway to another switch that has VLAN 6 member ports. If VTP pruning were not enabled on a trunk port, all VLAN traffic would travel through the trunk links to all the switches whether they had destination ports or not.

wide-area network (WAN)

This data communications network serves users across a broad geographical area. WANs often use transmission devices such as modems and channel service units/data service units (CSU/DSU) to carry signals over leased lines or common carrier lines.

window flow control

A flow-control method in which the receiving host buffers the data it receives and holds it in the buffer until it can be processed. After it is processed, an acknowledgment is sent to the sender.

zone

A logical grouping of network devices in an AppleTalk environment.

Zone Information Protocol (ZIP)

A Session-layer protocol used to map network numbers to a particular zone name of an AppleTalk network.

Index

B

T

W

X

Z

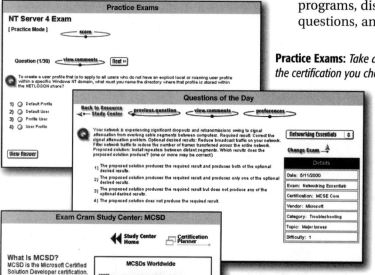

What's on the CD-ROM

The *CCNP Support Exam Prep*'s companion CD-ROM contains elements specifically selected to enhance the usefulness of this book, including:

➤ *One 100-question practice exam*—The practice exam questions simulate the interface and format of the actual certification exams.

➤ *An HTML version of "Appendix B: Other Resources"*—You can view and link directly to the resources listed, using your Web browser.

System Requirements

Software

➤ Your operating system must be Windows 95, 98, NT 4 or higher.

➤ You'll also need a Web browser to view some of the resources on this book's CD-ROM.

Hardware

➤ An Intel (or equivalent) Pentium 100MHz processor is the minimum platform required; an Intel (or equivalent) Pentium 133MHz processor is recommended.

➤ 32MB of RAM is the minimum requirement.

➤ The Java Studio application requires approximately 50MB of disk storage space.

➤ A color monitor (256 colors) is recommended.

Software developed by Dreamtech Software, India